Using Quattro Pro

Patrick J. Burns

que®
CORPORATION
LEADING COMPUTER KNOWLEDGE

Using Quattro Pro

Library of Congress Catalog No.: 90-61524

ISBN 0-88022-562-9

93 92 91 90   4 3 2 1

Interpretation of the printing code: the rightmost double-digit number is the year of the book's printing; the rightmost single-digit number, the number of the book's printing. For example, a printing code of 90-1 shows that the first printing of the book occurred in 1990.

Using Quattro Pro is based on Quattro Pro Version 1.1.

For Big Jack and Nell: Thank you for your good company during our voyage to Ireland. Most of all, thank you for your friendship.

Publishing Director

Lloyd J. Short

Product Director

Shelley O'Hara

Acquisitions Editor

Karen A. Bluestein

Project Manager

Paul Boger

Production Editor

Kelly D. Dobbs

Editors

Sharon Boller
Lori A. Lyons
Greg Robertson
Daniel Schnake

Technical Editor

Michael J. Francis

Indexer

Hilary Adams

Editorial Assistant

Patricia J. Brooks

Book Design and Production

Dan Armstrong
Bill Basham
Claudia Bell
Jill D. Bomaster
Brad Chinn
Don Clemons
Sally Copenhaver
Travia Davis
Tom Emrick
Denny Hager
Corinne Harmon
Tami Hughes
Bill Hurley
Betty Kish
Larry Lynch
Jennifer Matthews
Cindy L. Phipps
Joe Ramon
Dennis Sheehan
Louise Shinault
Bruce Steed
Mary Beth Wakefield
Jenny Watson

*Composed in Garamond and Excellent 47
by Que Corporation.*

ABOUT THE AUTHOR ▼

Patrick J. Burns

Patrick J. Burns has a B.S. in finance and economics. A native of Pennsylvania, he is a world-wide traveller, who has lived in Europe and Asia. He is a founder and principal of BK Global, a Pacific Rim import-export concern.

His work in the computer field includes Beta site testing, confidential review, and program development of software packages for major publishers.

The co-author of *Excel Business Applications: IBM Version*, published by Que Corporation, he has contributed to four other books about using Lotus 1-2-3, Microsoft Excel, and Excel macro programming.

▼ CONTENTS AT A GLANCE

TABLE OF CONTENTS ▼

II   Printing and Graphing

ACKNOWLEDGMENTS

To Shelley O'Hara and Kelly D. Dobbs: My sincere thanks for your patience, considerate guidance, and consistently competent editing throughout the development of the first edition of this book.

To Tony Meadors and John Dunn: Thank you for sharing your unique perspectives and contributing materially to the effort.

TRADEMARK ACKNOWLEDGMENTS

Que Corporation has made every effort to supply trademark information about company names, products, and services mentioned in this book. Trademarks indicated below were derived from various sources. Que Corporation cannot attest to the accuracy of this information.

1-2-3, Freelance, Lotus, Symphony, and VisiCalc are registered trademarks of Lotus Development Corporation.

AT&T is a registered trademark of AT&T.

Bitstream is a registered trademark and Fontware is a trademark of Bitstream, Inc.

dBASE, dBASE II, dBASE III, and dBASE III Plus are registered trademarks and dBASE IV is a trademark of Ashton-Tate Company.

DESQview is a trademark of Quarterdeck Office Systems.

EPSON is a registered trademark of Epson Corporation.

IBM, IBM PC, IBM AT, and OS/2 are registered trademarks and IBM PC XT and PS/2 are trademarks of International Business Machines Corporation.

Intel(r) is a registered trademark and Above Board is a trademark of Intel Corporation.

Microsoft, Microsoft Windows, MS-DOS, and Multiplan are registered trademarks of Microsoft Corporation.

PostScript is a registered trademark of Adobe Systems, Inc.

Rampage is a registered trademark of AST Research, Inc.

Quadram is a registered trademark of Quadram Corporation.

Quattro Pro and Paradox are registered trademarks and Reflex and VROOMM are trademarks of Borland International, Inc.

WordPerfect is a registered trademark of WordPerfect Corporation.

CONVENTIONS USED IN THIS BOOK ▼

The conventions used in this book have been established to help you learn to use the program quickly and easily. As much as possible, the conventions correspond with those used in the Quattro Pro documentation.

In this book, *italic* type is used to emphasize an important point, introduce a new concept, and, in step-by-step instructions, to indicate a word or phrase that you should type.

Boldface type highlights the keyword that appears in a menu or command name. To execute the **/F**ile **S**ave **R**eplace command, for example, you type /FSR.

Tips provide insider clues to many of the Quattro Pro features. The tips offer time-saving advice and suggestions that help you develop power-user skills.

The following Quattro Pro elements always appear in uppercase:

- Range names, such as PROFIT
- @Function commands, such as @SUM
- Mode and status indicators, like POINT and READY
- Cell references, such as A1..D10

The following Quattro Pro conventions regarding macro programs also have been adopted for this book:

- Macro names are formed with a backslash (\) followed by a lowercase letter, such as \a. This naming convention also indicates that you can execute this macro program by pressing Alt-a.

- All /x macro commands, such as /xc or /xl, appear in lowercase, and all other macro commands, such as {QUIT}, appear as uppercase characters embedded in braces.

- Quattro Pro menu keystrokes in a macro program, such as /fsr, are displayed in lowercase.

- Range names in a macro program, such as /ecPROFIT, are displayed in uppercase.

- The action of pressing the Enter key in a macro is represented by the tilde (~).

All screen shots appearing throughout the book are in graphics display mode.

Introduction

Today's electronic spreadsheet programs replace the manual accounting worksheets of yesteryear. The electronic spreadsheet, in fact, combines the best features of the accountant's multicolumn worksheet with the number-crunching power of today's personal computers. Every spreadsheet program performs the same mathematical operations (addition, subtraction, multiplication, and division) easily and efficiently. The best spreadsheet programs, however, offer you much more than that.

Quattro Pro is one of the most powerful electronic spreadsheet programs available for personal computers. Version 1.0 represents a major overhaul of Borland International's first release of the best-selling Quattro program.

Quattro Pro enables you to turn a spreadsheet into an income statement, a monthly calendar, a written paragraph, a database, or a pie graph. You can use Quattro Pro to record your personal financial budget, do regression analysis for economic forecasting, or store an inventory list of your favorite cassettes and CD's. With the release of Quattro Pro, you can attain more ambitious spreadsheet goals faster, more easily, and more simply.

Using Quattro Pro teaches you how to install, operate, and master the operation of Quattro Professional (Pro) Version 1.0. The step-by-step instructions in each chapter clearly show you Version 1.0's potential for building elegant computer solutions to meet specific personal management and business reporting needs.

What's New in Version 1.0

When Borland released Quattro three years ago, they took the software industry by surprise. Quattro was the first functional, affordable, and fully

1-2-3-compatible spreadsheet program. With Quattro on the market, anyone could afford to enter the electronic number-crunching arena.

With the release of Quattro Pro Version 1.0, Borland demonstrates the company's commitment to keeping pace with changing hardware and software technologies. Version 1.0 runs under the DOS 2.0 (or later) operating system and takes full advantage of the new 80386 hardware. Spreadsheet-users who own older, slower systems, however, also can exploit Version 1.0's power.

Whether you are a beginning spreadsheet user or a dedicated "Quattrophile," you will appreciate Quattro Pro's power, professional look, compatibility, and functionality—qualities that propel Quattro Pro past 1-2-3 and Excel as the next premier spreadsheet.

Quattro Pro is powerful. With Version 1.0, you can link data between multiple spreadsheets, open and view up to 32 windows at the same time, transform a spreadsheet into a relational database, and permanently record repetitive spreadsheet formatting steps into macros for future use. Version 1.0 can operate on an IBM XT, a 386-class machine, and everything in between. With Borland's VROOMM memory manager, you also can load and run Quattro Pro with only 640K of RAM.

Quattro Pro is professional. Version 1.0 offers hundreds of fonts and advanced graphics that enable you to create original, professional-looking, presentation-quality reports. With Quattro Pro, you also can add graphs directly onto your spreadsheets.

Quattro Pro is compatible. Quattro Pro automatically translates files created with earlier versions of Quattro. Version 1.0 also enables you to access the data stored in many popular program formats. Quattro Pro uses files created with 1-2-3, Versions 1A, 2.01, and the *educational* version; Symphony, Versions 1.2 and 2.0; Surpass; Paradox; dBASE II, III, III+, and IV; Reflex, Versions 1 and 2; and files created with Visicalc and Multiplan. With complete 1-2-3 (Version 2.01) macro, file, and keystroke compatibility, you know that your 1-2-3 data is preserved when you switch to Quattro Pro.

Quattro Pro is functional. You immediately feel at home with Quattro Pro. Version 1.0 offers pull-down menus and keystroke shortcuts for command execution. Because Quattro Pro can use Logitech, Mouse Systems, PC Mouse, and Microsoft-compatible mice, operating a spreadsheet is easy.

Some of Quattro Pro's less conspicuous—but equally welcomed—enhancements include an installation program that *automatically detects* the hardware on your system, an Undo option, expanded printer controls, and a larger library of @functions and macro keywords. Quattro Pro also includes the capability to create multiple hardware configurations, which can be invoked and canceled directly from the command menu, to hide spreadsheet borders and columns, to present spreadsheets and graphs on-screen, and to print a graph without leaving the program.

Who Should Read This Book

This book is designed for beginning, intermediate, and advanced Quattro Pro users. This book teaches the beginner how to design and build spreadsheets and coaches more experienced users through the process of recording spreadsheet formatting steps and selecting macro language commands for use in macro programs. For the advanced user, the book demonstrates how to handle many computational tasks at one time and how to control every operation to produce logical, well-organized, and up-to-the-minute reports.

Every user learns how to install and configure Quattro Pro so that they can delegate simple tasks (such as data input) to others, without worrying about compromising the integrity of the business, the program, or the spreadsheet application.

How This Book Is Organized

Using Quattro Pro Version 1.0 shows the reader how to create and use spreadsheets from the first step to the last. All of the important rules and programming procedures are emphasized throughout the book, to create an efficient self-paced curriculum leading to the successful creation of Quattro Pro spreadsheets.

The book is divided into three major sections. Novices who selected Quattro Pro as their first spreadsheet program benefit from the quick starts presented at the beginning of each part. Quick starts enables users of all levels to jump in and use Quattro Pro. If you want to quickly create a spreadsheet, print a document, build a graph, design a database, or create a basic macro program, see the quick start chapters.

Part I, "Using Quattro Pro Spreadsheets," includes Chapters 1 through 7 and covers basic Quattro Pro operations. Beginners benefit from the fundamental basics presented in Chapters 1 through 4. Detailed discussions show you how to get Quattro Pro up and running, and supporting examples illustrate the best ways to design, create, edit, and improve your Quattro Pro spreadsheets.

Also presented are suggestions for using @function commands in your spreadsheets, improving the style of your spreadsheets, setting the Version 1.0 options, and managing your spreadsheet files effectively.

Intermediate users quickly can get up to speed by scanning all three quick start sections. These sections give you a feel for what is new and different about Version 1.0 compared to previous versions of Quattro. Because you already know how to use an electronic spreadsheet program, intermediate users can skip the initial chapters. When you have the time for more detailed reading, begin reading Chapter 4 to learn about Quattro-specific ways to enhance your existing library of spreadsheets.

Part II, "Printing and Graphing," includes Chapters 8, 9, and 10, and illustrates the two methods for presenting Quattro Pro spreadsheets: in graph form or on a printed page. Also included are tips for placing live graphs on your spreadsheets, enhancing the look of your graphs, and preparing your printed output for use in other programs.

Part III, "Advanced Spreadsheet Applications," includes Chapters 11 and 12. Advanced Quattro Pro users and experienced programmers benefit from Part III's presentation of spreadsheet concepts used in developing complicated applications. Chapters 11 and 12 address the creation of databases, macro programs, and advanced macro applications.

Appendixes A through E address advanced user issues such as customizing Quattro Pro so that the program uses your hardware in the most efficient manner, how to build custom Bitstream fonts for screen display, and how to use all of the macro language commands. For the advanced user, this material clearly illustrates how to build customized spreadsheet solutions with Quattro Pro Version 1.0.

Part I: Using Quattro Pro Spreadsheets

Quick Start 1, "Using Quattro Pro," presents the basics for building and using Quattro Pro spreadsheets.

Chapter 1, "Getting Started," introduces the Version 1.0 spreadsheet and the proper way to begin and end a Quattro Pro work session. The next section shows how Quattro Pro interacts with a keyboard and mouse. The chapter progresses into specific discussions of the Version 1.0 screen display: the pull-down menu bar, the mouse palette, the input and status lines, and the spreadsheet area. An overview of using the on-line help feature concludes the chapter.

Chapter 2, "Learning Spreadsheet Basics," shows how to enter, edit, move, and view data on the Quattro Pro spreadsheet. The discussion addresses the rules for entering numbers, formulas, and @function commands. The text explains how to correct errors in formulas and how to use the Undo feature. This chapter concludes with a review of the different Quattro Pro display modes. These basics give you the logical and most ideal methods for consistently using Quattro Pro to build useful spreadsheets applications.

Chapter 3, "Learning Fundamental Commands," teaches you the methods for manipulating cell data to create the most logical, organized spreadsheet presentation. The first section shows how to copy, move, and delete cell data in the spreadsheet. The next section demonstrates techniques for extending the power of the menu commands by using blocks of spreadsheet data. The chapter concludes by showing you how to search for and replace data on a spreadsheet. These fundamental Quattro Pro commands are among the most used during every spreadsheet work session.

Chapter 4, "Improving Your Spreadsheet Style," presents a comprehensive review of the Quattro Pro Style menu. Use the commands found on this menu to enhance the look of a spreadsheet. The text demonstrates how to change the way Quattro Pro displays data in a cell. The procedures for setting the numeric format and formatting text labels also are covered. This chapter also demonstrates how to change and reset the width of columns and how to hide a column. The chapter concludes with a demonstration of how to create presentation-quality spreadsheets using fonts, line drawing, and shading.

Chapter 5, "Using @Function Commands," defines and demonstrates how to use Quattro Pro's built-in @function commands in your spreadsheets. From basic mathematical operations to applying logical and string functions, this chapter shows how to turn spreadsheets into statistical, scientific, and financial analysis tools.

Chapter 6, "Setting Options," stresses the importance of mastering the commands found on the Options menu, because these commands determine how Quattro Pro interacts with computer peripherals such as printers, expanded memory, and mice. Chapter 6 addresses how to create customized global spreadsheet settings to meet the unique needs of the user. Topics covered in this chapter include choosing the right printer and using display mode, fonts, colors, the date and time display, mouse palette settings, and initial startup options. With the Option menu commands, you also determine how Quattro recalculates, protects data, and interacts with data files from other programs.

Chapter 7, "Managing Spreadsheet Files and Windows," covers the most significant Version 1.0 enhancement: multiple spreadsheet operations. Quattro

Pro spreadsheets easily can consolidate information from several sources onto one spreadsheet. This chapter explains why, how, and when you should use multiple spreadsheets. Topics covered in this chapter include inserting text, moving between spreadsheets, and viewing multiple spreadsheets. The examples clearly illustrate several techniques for linking files with formulas.

Part II: Printing and Graphing

Quick Start 2, "Printing a Spreadsheet and Creating a Graph," presents the basics for printing and graphing Quattro Pro spreadsheet data.

Chapter 8, "Printing," provides you with the tools, techniques, and instructions that you need to print spreadsheet reports and graphs in Quattro Pro. In this chapter, you generate an unformatted snapshot of data in the current window and examine your output on-screen (prior to printing) using the Screen Preview facility. Also presented are the procedures and rules for creating print files with a PRN extension. You can generate hard-copy output from PRN files by executing the COPY command at DOS command level. You also learn about printing draft-quality copy and final presentation-quality versions of your spreadsheet reports and graphs.

Chapter 9, "Creating, Managing, and Displaying Graphs," introduces you to one of the program's most appealing aspects: envisioning, designing, and displaying graphs. In this chapter, you learn about the utility and anatomy of the Quattro Pro graph, how to quick-create a basic graph, and how to build a custom graph from the ground up. Throughout this chapter, careful attention is paid to illustrate through figures how to enhance the appearance of a basic graph. Finally, you learn how to manage graph files so that you can recall, update, and review these files during other work sessions.

Chapter 10, "Customizing and Annotating Graphs," picks up where the preceding chapter leaves off. Although Chapter 9 offers many good suggestions for improving the appearance of a basic graph, this chapter introduces techniques for creating customized graphs. A customized graph locates important trends and points out problem areas better than a basic graph. A customized graph also leaves a viewer with more than just a general feeling about spreadsheet data. Using the Graph Annotator tool, you learn how to add boxed text, geometric figures, and clip art to your graphs to create presentation-quality visual aids.

Part III: Advanced Spreadsheet Applications

Quick Start 3, "Creating a Database and Database Macro," presents the basics for using a Quattro Pro spreadsheet as a database and demonstrates how to build simple macro programs.

Chapter 11, "Managing Your Data," demonstrates that in addition to being an electronic spreadsheet program, Quattro Pro is a relational database manager. This chapter focuses on how to transform a spreadsheet into a database so that you can sort, extract, and delete records like with other database programs. This chapter also presents instructions for using Quattro Pro's data analysis tools. You learn how to perform regression analysis, do optimization modeling, build sensitivity tables, and conduct frequency distribution analysis.

Chapter 12, "Creating Macro Programs," shows you how to automatically record macro programs to later replicate keystrokes and menu command selections. These macros can assume many of the repetitive formatting steps that you go through each time you load a new, blank spreadsheet into Quattro Pro. Later chapter material familiarizes you with advanced macro topics such as macro program management, macro debugging, and manually writing macros to meet specific needs.

Appendixes

Appendix A, "Installing Quattro Pro," shows you how to build the ideal computer environment for Quattro Pro. A step-by-step review of the installation process and rules for reconfiguring and enhancing an installed copy of the program are presented.

Appendix B, "Customizing Your Font Library," shows you how to use a macro program to add and delete screen fonts from the program's font directory.

Appendix C, "Macro Commands," presents a comprehensive list of the Quattro Pro macro commands. An example of the appropriate syntax for use in written procedures is provided.

Appendix D, "Menu-Equivalent Commands," presents a comprehensive list of the Quattro Pro menu-equivalent commands. This appendix is organized in chronological order by menu and within each menu by command name.

Appendix E, "Using ASCII Characters," contains a table of control characters and printable characters as presented by the American Standard Code for Information Interchange (ASCII). The table lists 255 characters and their decimal and hexadecimal equivalents.

I

Using Quattro Pro Spreadsheets

Includes

Quick Start: Using Quattro Pro

Getting Started

Learning Spreadsheet Basics

Learning Fundamental Commands

Improving Your Spreadsheet Style

Using @Function Commands

Setting Options

Managing Spreadsheet Files and Windows

Quick Start 1: Using Quattro Pro

Quick Start 1 introduces you to the basic methods for using Quattro Pro Version 1.01. The material in Quick Start 1 covers five activities that are fundamental to using Quattro Pro:

- Loading and quitting the program

- Creating and viewing a spreadsheet

- Using @function commands

- Improving spreadsheet style

- Saving a spreadsheet

Each topic corresponds to a chapter in the first part of this book. When you come across a topic that you want to explore, refer to the corresponding chapter for complete coverage.

Quick Start 1 also shows you how to build a sample spreadsheet from the ground up. Along the way, you will come across features that you have encountered in other programs and features that are new to you. In either case, after completing this hands-on exercise, you can create spreadsheets that can be used to meet many personal management and business reporting needs.

Beginning a Quattro Pro Work Session

After you install your copy of Quattro Pro, you are ready to initiate a work session. (For information on installation, see Appendix A.) To begin a work session, log onto the directory in which Quattro Pro is installed and execute the program. Unless you specified otherwise during the installation, the Quattro Pro program files are stored in a directory called QPRO.

Perform the following steps to begin a new work session:

1. Type *CD \QPRO* and press Enter.

2. Type *Q* and press Enter to load Quattro Pro into your computer's memory.

Each time you load the program into your computer's memory, Quattro Pro displays a blank spreadsheet, SHEET1.WQ1, that is ready for input (see fig. QS1.1).

Fig. QS1.1
The Quattro Pro
screen display.

After this spreadsheet is on-screen, you can enter data or execute commands. To execute a Quattro Pro command, you need to activate one of the nine pull-down menus. To activate a menu, press the forward slash (/) key to enter Quattro Pro's Menu mode. Each menu contains a list of commands that perform various spreadsheet and file activities.

To open the File menu, for example, follow these steps:

1. Press the forward slash key.

2. Use the cursor-movement keys to move to the File menu (if this menu is not already highlighted) and press Enter. You also can click on **F**ile in the menu bar. Quattro Pro displays a list of commands that help you manage your spreadsheet files (see fig. QS1.2).

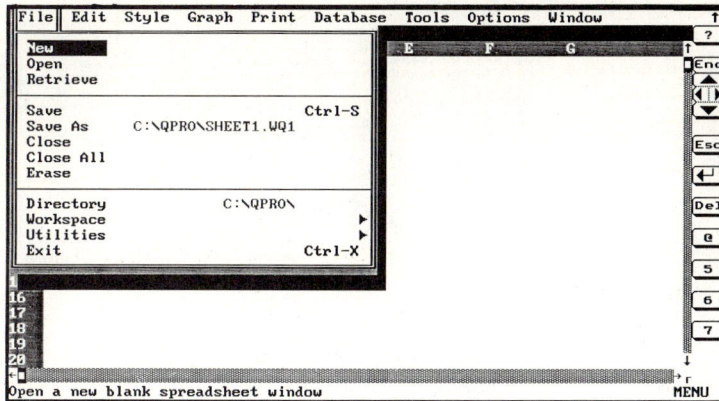

```
File  Edit  Style  Graph  Print  Database  Tools  Options  Window        ↑↓
                                                                          ?
New                               E        F         G              End   ↑
Open                                                                      ▲
Retrieve                                                                 ◄▮►
                                                                         ▼
Save                    Ctrl-S
Save As     C:\QPRO\SHEET1.WQ1                                           Esc
Close
Close All                                                                 ↵
Erase

Directory           C:\QPRO\                                            Del
Workspace                            ▶
Utilities                            ▶                                    @
Exit                    Ctrl-X
                                                                          5

1                                                                         6
16
17                                                                        7
18
19
20

Open a new blank spreadsheet window                            MENU
```

Fig. QS1.2
Pulling down
the File menu.

Each command name appears at the left margin of the menu. Notice that one letter in each name appears in bold. To choose a command when a menu is pulled down, press the boldface letter key.

3. To practice selecting a command, press D to select **D**irectory. You can use this command to change directories. For now, press Esc to cancel the command.

4. Press Esc to close the menu.

Entering and Editing Spreadsheet Data

The remaining material in Quick Start 1 is devoted to building a sample spreadsheet application for J. Dunn & Company, an industrial goods manufacturer. The finished application appears in figure QS1.3.

Entering Data

Version 1.01 of Quattro Pro accepts two types of data as valid entries: labels and values. A *label* is a text entry, and a *value* can be a number, a formula, or a date and time entry.

Fig. QS1.3
The J. Dunn &
Company
purchasing
report.

```
 File  Edit  Style  Graph  Print  Database  Tools  Options  Window        ↑↓
A1: [W4]                                                                    ?
U    A     B     C           D              E          F     G  ↑
1                                                                         End
2                      J. DUNN & COMPANY                                   ▲
3                      PURCHASING REPORT                                  ◄ ►
4                         Vendor #35                                       ▼
5
6          DATE   INVOICE #   LOCATION        PRICE      TOTAL            Esc
7
8          05/19/90  1901    San Francisco     949.99    1,018.86          ↵
9          05/22/90  2171    San Diego       1,879.95    2,016.25
10         05/25/90  2540    Los Angeles     1,250.00    1,340.63         Del
11         05/27/30  2711    San Diego         199.99      214.49
12         05/30/90  2740    San Francisco     250.00      268.13          0
13
14         TOTALS:                          $4,529.93   $4,858.35          5
15                                                                         6
16
17                                                                         7
18
VENDOR35.WQ1 [1]                                                     READY
```

Quattro Pro looks at the first character in an entry to decide whether that entry is a label or a value. When you enter a label into a cell, the mode indicator on the status line displays LABEL; when you enter a value, the mode indicator displays VALUE.

By default, Quattro Pro places an apostrophe in front of every label entry. A value entry must begin with a number (0 through 9) or with one of the following value symbols: + (plus), − (minus), . (period), ((left parenthesis), $ (dollar sign). Quattro Pro assumes that all numbers are positive in value unless you specify otherwise.

Building the basic form of the spreadsheet shown in figure QS1.3 is a three-step process:

1. Enter the report titles.

2. Enter the column and row headings.

3. Enter data into the spreadsheet.

Entering the Report Titles

At the top of your spreadsheet, you want to add a title that explains what the spreadsheet contains. For the example, follow these steps to add a title:

1. Use the cursor-movement keys to move the cell selector to cell A1 or click in cell A1.

2. Type *J. DUNN & COMPANY* and press Enter to record the main report title.

3. Press ↓ to move the cell selector to cell A2, type *PURCHASING REPORT*, and press Enter to record the secondary report title.

4. Press ↓ to move the cell selector to cell A3, type *Vendor #35* and press Enter to record the third and final report title.

Entering the Column and Row Headings

Each column in your spreadsheet contains a certain type of data. For example, the DATE column contains dates. To enter descriptive headings for each of your columns, follow these steps:

1. Move the cell selector to cell A5, type *DATE*, and press Enter to record the column A heading.

2. Move the cell selector to cell B5, type *INVOICE #*, and press Enter to record the column B heading.

3. Move the cell selector to cell C5, type *LOCATION*, and press Enter to record the column C heading.

4. Move the cell selector to cell D5, type *PRICE*, and press Enter to record the column D heading.

5. Move the cell selector to cell E5, type *TOTAL*, and press Enter to record the column E heading.

In addition to the column heading, add a row heading. Follow these steps:

1. Move the cell selector to cell A13.

2. Type *TOTALS:* and press Enter to record the row heading.

Your spreadsheet should look like figure QS1.4.

Entering Data

After you have set up your column and row headings, you can begin to enter data. For the sample spreadsheet, you enter dates, invoice numbers, locations, prices, and totals. Start by entering these dates:

1. Move the cell selector to A7 to begin entering the dates.

2. Press Ctrl-D to enter Date mode. While in Date mode, you can format cells to display numbers as dates.

3. Type *05/19/90* and press Enter to record the first date.

Fig. QS1.4
The spreadsheet report now has titles and column and row headings.

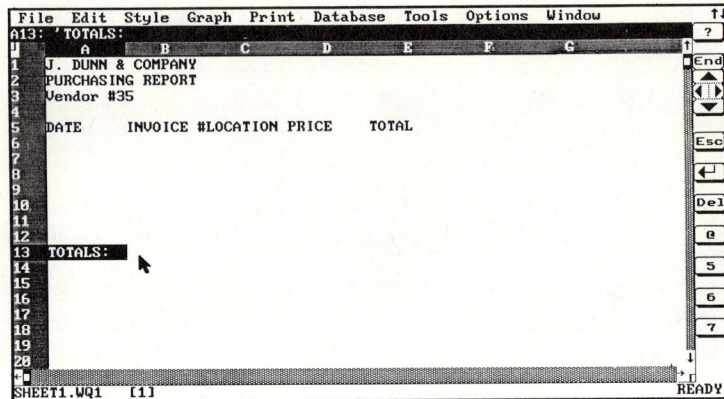

```
 File  Edit  Style  Graph  Print  Database  Tools  Options  Window      ↑↓
A13:  'TOTALS:                                                          ?
      A       B        C         D        E         F        G         ↑
1  J. DUNN & COMPANY                                                   End
2  PURCHASING REPORT                                                    ▲
3  Vendor #35                                                          ◀│▶
4                                                                       ▼
5  DATE      INVOICE #LOCATION PRICE      TOTAL
6                                                                      Esc
7
8                                                                       ↵
9
10                                                                     Del
11
12                                                                      @
13  TOTALS:     ▸
14                                                                      5
15
16                                                                      6
17
18                                                                      7
19
20                                                                      ↓
◀                                                                 ▸□
SHEET1.WQ1   [1]                                                    READY
```

4. Repeat steps 1 through 3 for the remaining four dates. They are as follows: 05/22/90, 05/25/90, 05/27/90, and 05/30/90.

To enter the invoice numbers, follow these steps:

1. Move the cell selector to B7 to begin entering the invoice numbers.

2. Type *1001* and press Enter to record the first invoice number.

3. Repeat steps 1 and 2 for the remaining four invoice numbers. They are as follows: 2171, 2540, 2711, and 2740.

To enter the locations, follow these steps:

1. Move the cell selector to C7 to begin entering the locations.

2. Type *San Francisco* and press Enter to record the purchase location for the first invoice.

3. Repeat steps 1 and 2 for the remaining four location labels. They are as follows: San Diego, Los Angeles, San Diego, and San Francisco.

To enter the prices, follow these steps:

1. Move the cell selector to D7 to begin entering the price data.

2. Type *949.99* and press Enter to record the purchase price for the first invoice.

3. Repeat steps 1 and 2 for the remaining four prices. They are as follows: 1879.95, 1250, 199.99 and 250.

Your spreadsheet should look like figure QS1.5.

Fig. QS1.5
The purchasing report now has dates, invoice numbers, locations, and prices.

Notice that the San Francisco and Los Angeles location labels shown in figure QS1.5 do not display in full. Column C is not wide enough to accommodate them. You fix this display in an upcoming section.

For now, turn your attention to creating formulas that complete the basic form of this spreadsheet report.

Entering Formulas

Quattro Pro evaluates spreadsheet formulas and returns answers in the cells in which the formulas reside. You can create simple arithmetic formulas to add a column of figures, to multiply values, and to return percentages.

To create a formula in cell E7 to add 7.25 percent sales tax to the value appearing in cell D7, do the following:

1. Move the cell selector to cell E7.

2. Type +D7*1.0725.

3. Press Enter to record the formula.

Quattro Pro displays the value 1018.855. Notice that this value is not properly rounded. You learn how to format numbers in an upcoming section. For now, concentrate on copying this formula so that all of the prices in column D display in column E as "tax-included."

Although you can repeat steps 1 through 3 to create the same formulas for cells E8..E11, copy the formula in cell E7 so that it calculates the tax-included total. Follow these steps:

1. Move the cell selector to cell E7.

2. Press / EC to activate the Copy command on the Edit menu.

3. Press Enter to choose cell E7 as the source cell.

4. Move the cell selector to cell E11, which becomes the destination cell on the input line.

5. Press Enter to copy the formula.

Now move the cell selector to cell E8. Look at the input line at the top of the spreadsheet and check to be sure that Quattro Pro has entered the formula +D7*1.0725.

Your spreadsheet should look like figure QS1.6.

Fig. QS1.6
The purchasing report now has tax-included invoice totals.

Quattro Pro's built-in formulas, called @function commands, perform basic and advanced mathematical operations. To display a list of the Quattro Pro @function commands, press Alt-F3 from anywhere on the spreadsheet.

For example, the formula +A1+A2+A3 returns the same answer as the @function formula @SUM(A1..A3). The greatest benefit of @function commands is that when created in Point mode, they greatly simplify the process of adding formulas to a spreadsheet.

To create a formula (while in Point mode) that sums the column D data, do the following:

1. Move the cell selector to cell D13.

2. Type @SUM and press ↑ six times to make cell D7 the active cell.

3. Press the period key (.) to enter Point mode.

4. Press ↓ four times to make cell D11 the active cell.

5. Type) and press Enter to record the formula.

To create a formula that adds the values in the TOTAL column, you can repeat steps 1 through 5 for the values in column E. Instead, copy the formula in cell D13 to cell E13 so that Quattro Pro sums the data appearing in column E. Follow these steps:

1. Move the cell selector to cell D13.

2. Press /EC to activate the Copy command on the Edit menu.

3. Press Enter to choose cell D13 as the source cell.

4. Move the cell selector to cell E13. (This cell becomes the destination cell on the input line.)

5. Press Enter to copy the formula.

Now move the cell selector back to cell E13. Look at the input line at the top of the spreadsheet and check to be sure that Quattro Pro has entered the formula @SUM(E7..E11).

Your spreadsheet should look like figure QS1.7.

Fig. QS1.7 The purchasing report now has formulas that display total purchases data for May, 1990.

Editing Data

Quattro Pro enables you to edit data as you enter the data on the input line or after you press Enter to place the text into a spreadsheet cell. You can reverse the effects of many menu command operations by selecting the /Edit Undo command.

Changing Data in Edit Mode

To edit the contents of a spreadsheet cell, press F2 to enter Edit mode. If you have a mouse, click the cell you want to edit and then click the mouse pointer on the input line just below the pull-down menu bar. Quattro Pro displays the cell data (unformatted) on the input line. When you finish editing, press Enter to record the changes.

To see how easy editing data is, try changing an invoice number appearing on the spreadsheet shown in figure QS1.7. Follow these steps:

1. Place the cell selector in cell B7.

2. Press F2 to enter Edit mode.

3. Press ← three times to place the edit cursor on the first 0.

4. Press Del.

5. Type 9 and press Enter to record the new invoice number.

Using the Alt-F5 Undo Key

The /Edit Undo command enables you to undo the most recent edit or command executed. To use this feature, you first must select /Options Other Undo Enable. After being enabled, store the setting for future work sessions by selecting /Options Update.

To reverse the edit operation you just performed, do the following:

1. Press /EU to activate the Undo command on the Edit menu.

2. Quattro Pro redisplays the original invoice number, 1001, in cell B7.

3. Press /EU again to reinstate the edited invoice number, 1901, in cell B7.

Your spreadsheet should look like figure QS1.8. In this figure, the cell selector is in cell B7, showing that the edited invoice value has been reinstated.

Improving Spreadsheet Style

Another look at figure QS1.8 reveals that although the data is complete, the format leaves much to be desired. For example, the data in certain cells appears crowded, and others have no uniform alignment. The invoice amounts also do not have dollar symbols.

Fig. QS1.8
The purchasing report spreadsheet complete with formulas and cell edits.

Moving Data

When you select /**E**dit **M**ove, you can relocate data from one area on the spreadsheet to another. For example, to move the report titles to a more central location on the J. Dunn & Company spreadsheet, do the following:

1. Press /**EM** to execute the /**E**dit **M**ove command.

2. When prompted, type *A1..A3* and press Enter to choose the source block.

3. When prompted for a destination block, type *C1*.

4. Press Enter to move the report titles to column C.

Your spreadsheet should look like figure QS1.9. In this figure, the titles that were in A1..A3 now appear in C1..C3.

Fig. QS1.9
Moving titles on the purchasing report.

Changing Column Widths

By default, each spreadsheet column is nine characters wide. When you enter data longer than nine characters, use the /**S**tyle **C**olumn Width command to change the width of the column.

For example, to change the widths of the columns C, D, and E on the J. Dunn & Company spreadsheet, try each of the following techniques:

1. Place the cell selector in cell C1.

2. Press /SC to execute the /**S**tyle **C**olumn Width command.

3. Type *17* and press Enter to make column C 17 characters wide.

Now try this method:

1. Place the cell selector in cell D1.

2. Press /SC to execute the /**S**tyle **C**olumn Width command.

3. Press → three times to make column D 12 characters wide.

Now try this method:

1. Place the cell selector in cell E1.

2. Press Ctrl-W, the Ctrl-key shortcut for this command.

3. Type *12* and press Enter to make column D 12 characters wide.

Your spreadsheet should look like figure QS1.10. This figure displays the new width settings for columns C, D, and E.

Fig. QS1.10 Changing column widths on the purchasing report.

Aligning Data in Cells

Uniformly aligned headings make identifying the values that belong to a particular heading easier.

To center align the report title on row 3, do the following:

1. Place the cell selector in cell C3.

2. Press /SAC to execute the /**S**tyle **A**lignment **C**enter command.

3. Press Enter to center align the title label.

To center align each of the column headings on row 5, do the following:

1. Place the cell selector in cell A5.

2. Press Ctrl-A, the Ctrl-key shortcut for this command.

3. Press C, the boldface letter key for the **C**enter option.

4. Press End to enter End mode.

5. Press → to extend the highlighted block to cell E5.

6. Press Enter to center align all of the labels on row 5.

To center align the invoice numbers in column B, do the following:

1. Place the cell selector in cell B7.

2. Press Ctrl-A, the Ctrl-key shortcut for this command.

3. Press C, the boldface letter key for the **C**enter option.

4. Press End to enter End mode.

5. Press ↓ to extend the highlighted block to cell B11.

6. Press Enter to center align all of the values in column B.

Your spreadsheet should look like figure QS1.11. This figure displays the new title, heading, and data alignments.

Formatting Numbers

Properly formatted numbers tell more about the values on a spreadsheet. Format the PRICE and TOTAL column numbers so that they display commas and two decimal paces by performing the following steps:

1. Place the cell selector in cell D7.

2. Press /SN to execute the /**S**tyle **N**umeric Format command.

**Fig. QS1.11
Aligning data
on the
purchasing
report.**

```
  File  Edit  Style  Graph  Print  Database  Tools  Options  Window        ↑↓
B7: 1901                                                                    ?
    ▓   A        B            C            D          E          F    ↑
1                       J. DUNN & COMPANY                          ▓End
2                       PURCHASING REPORT
3                         Vendor #35                                   ▲
4                                                                    ◀▮▶
5     DATE    INVOICE #    LOCATION      PRICE       TOTAL            ▼
6
7    05/19/90   1901     San Francisco    949.99  1018.864275       Esc
8    05/22/90   2171     San Diego       1879.95  2016.246375
9    05/25/90   2540     Los Angeles       1250    1340.625          ↵
10   05/27/30   2711     San Diego        199.99   214.489275
11   05/30/90   2740     San Francisco      250     268.125         Del
12
13   TOTALS:                             4529.93  4858.349925        @
14
15                                                                    5
16                                                                    6
17
18                                                                    7
19
20                                                                   ↓
SHEET1.WQ1    [1]                                              READY
```

3. Press , (comma) to select the comma format.

4. Press Enter to accept the default setting of 2 decimal places.

5. Press →, press End on the numeric keypad, and then press ↓ to highlight cell block D7..E11.

6. Press Enter to format the numbers in the highlighted block.

Now format the numbers on the TOTALS row to display a dollar sign and commas with two decimal places. Follow these steps:

1. Place the cell selector in cell D13.

2. Press Ctrl-F, the Ctrl-key shortcut for this command.

3. Press C to select the currency format.

4. Press Enter to accept the default setting of 2 decimal places.

5. Press → to highlight cell block D13..E13.

6. Press Enter to format the numbers in the highlighted block.

Your spreadsheet should look like figure QS1.12. This figure displays the numeric formats of the values appearing in the report.

Drawing Lines around Data

Adding drawn lines around your spreadsheet data transforms a basic spreadsheet document into a professional-looking report. You can add a few final stylistic touches to the J. Dunn & Company report.

Fig. QS1.12
Formatting numeric data on the purchasing report.

To draw a line around the data area, do the following:

1. Press /SL to execute the /Style Line Drawing command.

2. When prompted, type *A5..E13* and press Enter to choose the source block.

3. When prompted, press O to choose the **O**utside line option.

4. When prompted, press S to choose the **S**ingle line option.

5. Press Q to choose the **Q**uit option and return to the spreadsheet.

Your spreadsheet should look like figure QS1.13. This figure displays the addition of drawn lines around the purchasing report.

Fig. QS1.13
Drawing lines around the purchasing report.

When you draw lines on a spreadsheet, Quattro Pro sometimes displays asterisks in cells in which there once was data. For example, column A now displays asterisks because the drawn line used up a character space, and now the dates are too wide to fit in column A.

To correct this, do the following:

1. Make column A the active column.

2. Press Ctrl-W to execute the /Edit Column Width command.

3. Type *11* and press Enter to make column A 11 characters wide.

Adding the Finishing Touches

To conclude this exercise, add a few finishing touches to the J. Dunn & Company purchasing report. First, insert a column in front of column A to center the report on the spreadsheet by doing the following:

1. Place the cell selector in cell A1.

2. Press Ctrl-I, the Ctrl-key shortcut for the /Edit Insert command.

3. Press C to insert Columns.

4. When Quattro Pro prompts you for a source block, press Enter to accept the single-column default.

By doing this, you lose the line definition at the right edge of the report. This problem is easily corrected by performing the next four steps:

1. Press Ctrl-W, type *4*, and press Enter to make column A four characters wide.

2. Move the cell selector to column G.

3. Press Ctrl-W, type *1*, and press Enter to make column G one character wide.

4. Press Home on the numeric keypad to return the cell selector to cell A1.

To conclude, insert one row on top of the first title line in the report by doing the following:

1. Press Ctrl-I, the Ctrl-key shortcut for the /Edit Insert command.

2. Press R to insert Rows.

3. When Quattro Pro prompts you for a source block, press Enter to accept the single-row default.

Figure QS1.14 shows the finished form of the sample report for J. Dunn & Company.

```
File  Edit  Style  Graph  Print  Database  Tools  Options  Window      ↑↓
A1: [W4]                                                            ?
     A      B        C            D              E          F      G
1
2                         J. DUNN & COMPANY                              End
3                         PURCHASING REPORT                             ▲
4                             Vendor #35                                ◄|►
5                                                                       ▼
6        DATE   INVOICE #    LOCATION         PRICE       TOTAL
7                                                                       Esc
8        05/19/90   1901   San Francisco      949.99    1,018.86
9        05/22/90   2171   San Diego        1,879.95    2,016.25        ↵
10       05/25/90   2540   Los Angeles      1,250.00    1,340.63
11       05/27/30   2711   San Diego          199.99      214.49        Del
12       05/30/90   2740   San Francisco      250.00      268.13
13                                                                       @
14       TOTALS:                            $4,529.93   $4,858.35
                                                                         5
15
16                                                                       6
17
18                                                                       7
                                                                    ↓ r
SHEET1.WQ1    [1]                                                  READY
```

Fig. QS1.14
Presentation-quality version of the J. Dunn & Company purchasing report.

Managing Documents

Managing documents is an important part of each Quattro Pro work session. Without the capabilities to **S**ave, create (**N**ew), **R**etrieve, and **O**pen spreadsheet files—Quattro Pro is useless.

Saving a Spreadsheet

To save the J. Dunn & Company spreadsheet as VENDOR35, do the following:

1. Press /FA to execute the / **F**ile Save **A**s command.

2. When prompted, type *VENDOR35*. Include a drive designator in the file name to save the file to a drive other than the default drive.

3. Press Enter to save the new file name on the current drive.

Ending a Work Session

To end a Quattro Pro work session and save all files open in Quattro Pro's memory, do the following:

1. Press / FX to execute the / **F**ile E**x**it command.

If you have not made any changes to the open spreadsheets since the last
save operation, Quattro Pro clears the screen display and returns you to the
DOS command prompt.

If you have made changes, Quattro Pro displays a prompt box that asks if you
want to Lose Your Changes And Exit? To exit the program without saving
open files, choose **Yes**; to remain on the active spreadsheet, choose **No** (see
fig. QS1.15).

Fig. QS1.15
The File Exit
command
prompt.

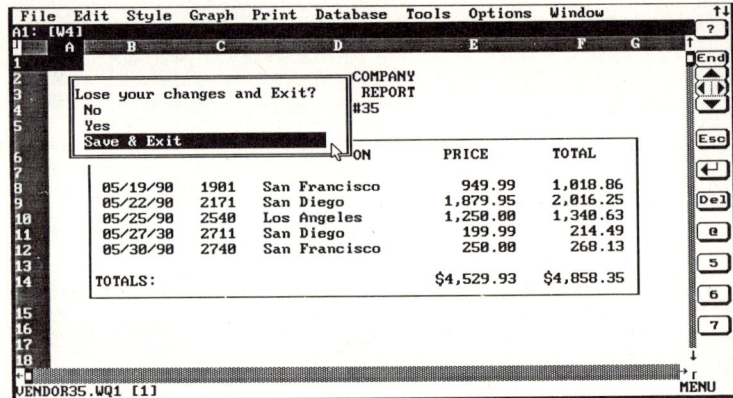

2. When prompted, press S to **S**ave & Exit if you want to save all open
   spreadsheets before returning to DOS.

3. One-by-one, Quattro Pro makes each open spreadsheet active. When
   prompted, press C to **C**ancel, R to **R**eplace, or B to **B**ackup an open
   file prior to exiting the program (see fig. QS1.16).

Fig. QS1.16
The Save & Exit
command
prompt.

If you have a mouse, click on **File** (on the menu bar) to pull down the menu. Then click on the **Exit** command to exit Quattro Pro.

To quickly execute steps 1 through 3, press Ctrl-X, the Quattro Pro shortcut key for terminating a work session.

Summary

After completing this Quick Start, you should be familiar with the following concepts:

- Beginning and ending a work session
- Pulling down a menu and executing a command
- Entering values and labels into spreadsheet cells
- Editing, copying, and moving data on the spreadsheet
- Using the Undo feature to reverse operations
- Creating a basic spreadsheet report that contains a title, column heading, formatted data, and drawn lines
- Saving spreadsheet files

1

Getting Started

The material presented in this chapter helps you envision how to use a spreadsheet for a wide range of simple tasks. Read Chapter 1 carefully because the terminology and ideas in later chapters rely heavily on the concepts presented here.

For first-time spreadsheet users, this chapter talks about the basics of working with Quattro Pro. You see how a spreadsheet is more than just rows and columns of numbers and letters. You also learn how to begin and end a work session and are given a review of using a keyboard and mouse. An in-depth, feature-by-feature review of the new Quattro Pro screen display is presented. Spreadsheet users of every level will find this information useful. The chapter concludes with a discussion of the Quattro Pro built-in help windows. This final section shows you how to get general and context-sensitive help from any location on a spreadsheet.

Chapter 1 is an important stepping stone to later chapters. If you master the basics outlined in this discussion, you will be well prepared to begin tackling the Quattro Pro spreadsheet basics presented in Chapter 2.

Learning about Spreadsheets

On a basic level, Quattro Pro is a large electronic worksheet with millions of cells of storage area. You can enter data into these cells, and you can enter formulas that perform mathematical operations on a group, or block, of cells. Whether you are adding two numbers or two thousand numbers, Quattro Pro calculates an answer in seconds. If you change a number on an accounting worksheet, you have to add the numbers over again. When you change a number in a Quattro Pro formula, the program recalculates the new answer in just a few seconds.

Quattro Pro remembers all of the cell relationships that you define on a spreadsheet. A formula that adds values appearing in two different cells, such as +D8+D9, creates the most common type of cell relationship. If you design a spreadsheet to record your monthly business expenses, for example, you have to do the work only once. For subsequent months, you retrieve and modify the original spreadsheet file by entering new numbers into the cells storing the current month's expenses.

Understanding Columns and Rows

A typical spreadsheet program displays a two-dimensional worksheet made up of columns and rows. You can enter numbers, letters, and formulas into a spreadsheet cell. A *cell* is the intersection of any column and row. The active cell on a Quattro Pro spreadsheet appears as a highlighted rectangle—the *cell selector* (see fig. 1.1). Notice that the row number and column letter at this intersection also are highlighted. Finally, observe the arrow pointer in the middle of the screen. This mouse pointer appears when you attach a mouse to your computer. If you do not use a mouse, Quattro Pro displays a small, highlighted rectangle instead.

Fig. 1.1
The Quattro Pro spreadsheet with the cell selector located in D10.

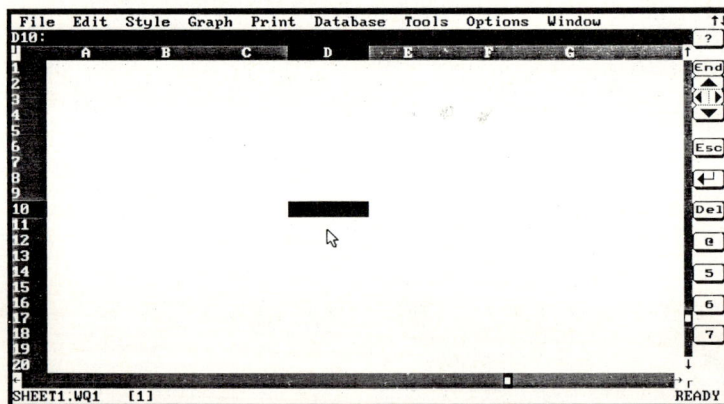

Each cell in a spreadsheet has a unique name. A *cell name* is formed by combining the column and row locations into one description. For example, the cell in figure 1.1 is named D10, which describes the intersection of column D and row 10. Columns always use letter descriptions, and rows always use number descriptions. The name, cell 10D, therefore, has no meaning.

A Quattro Pro spreadsheet contains a total of 256 columns and 8,192 rows. One Quattro Pro spreadsheet, therefore, contains 2,097,152 unique cells.

The rows on a Quattro Pro spreadsheet are numbered from 1 to 8,192, and the columns are labeled from A to IV. The first 26 spreadsheet columns are named by using the alphabet. Columns 27 through 52 are named AA, AB, AC, AD, and so on. Columns 53 through 79 are named BA through BZ. This naming scheme continues through column 256, or column IV. Figure 1.2 shows the last cell on a Quattro Pro spreadsheet, cell IV8192.

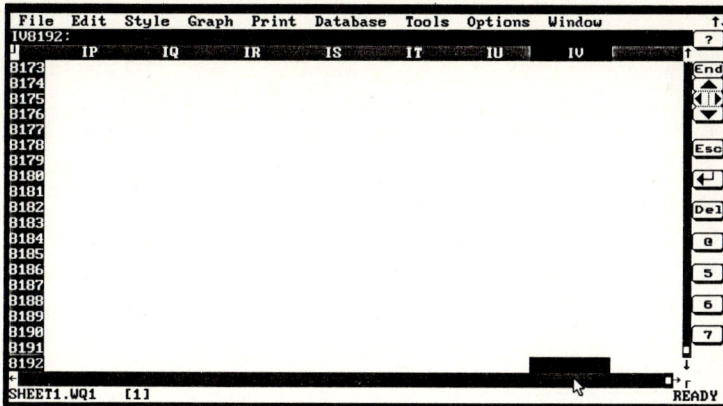

Fig. 1.2
The last cell on a spreadsheet.

Multiple windows is a powerful new feature available in Quattro Pro. This feature enables you to work with up to 32 spreadsheet windows at the same time. The multiple windows feature, therefore, places up to 67,108,864 spreadsheet cells at your disposal. Imagine how many accounting ledger worksheets you need to equal that much calculation space.

The real power of Quattro Pro, however, lies in its capability to remember the relationships that you define when you enter data into the spreadsheet cells. Think back to the formula (+ D8 + D9) defined as an example of a cell relationship. Because Quattro Pro can save a spreadsheet on a disk storage device, you have to type this formula only once. Every time you retrieve a saved spreadsheet from disk into Quattro Pro's memory, the formula and its calculated result reappears.

Organizing Numbers and Letters

When you design a spreadsheet, you need to follow a few basic rules.

First, duplicate the organization and structure of the original document as closely as possible. You typically create spreadsheets to assume the duties of a written document or manually calculated report. Use this document or report as a guide.

To design a three-month income statement report, for example, you can place the ledger account titles in column B, the month descriptions in row 2, and the numbers in cells C3 through F10 (see fig. 1.3).

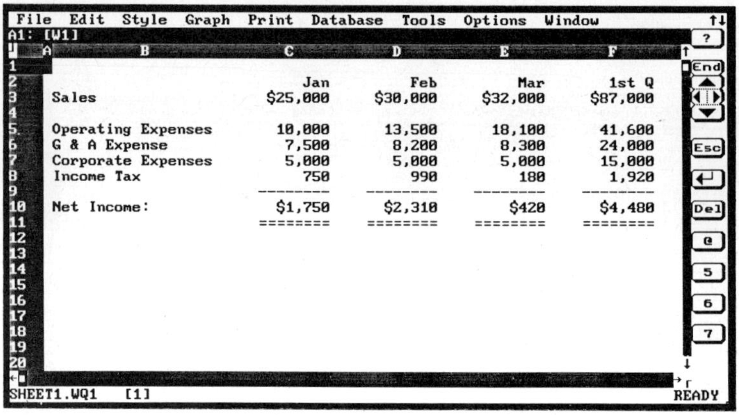

Fig. 1.3
Designing a
logical
spreadsheet.

```
 File  Edit  Style  Graph  Print  Database  Tools  Options  Window        ↑↓
A1: [W1]                                                                     ?
U   A        B            C         D         E         F                  End
1
2                       Jan       Feb       Mar       1st Q                 ▲
3   Sales             $25,000   $30,000   $32,000   $87,000               ◄|▷
4                                                                           ▼
5   Operating Expenses 10,000    13,500    18,100    41,600
6   G & A Expense       7,500     8,200     8,300    24,000               Esc
7   Corporate Expenses  5,000     5,000     5,000    15,000
8   Income Tax            750       990       180     1,920               ◄┘
9                      --------  --------  --------  --------
10  Net Income:         $1,750    $2,310      $420    $4,480              Del
11                     ========  ========  ========  ========
12                                                                         @
13
14                                                                         5
15
16                                                                         6
17
18                                                                         7
19
20
SHEET1.WQ1    [1]                                                        READY
```

Second, avoid mixing numbers and letters in the same cell until you are familiar with the rules for data entry (covered in Chapter 2). For now, remember that when you enter a number into a cell, Quattro Pro stores the number as a value. When you enter a word into a cell, Quattro Pro stores the word as a label by placing an apostrophe (') before the first letter.

Third, as a rule, Quattro Pro can perform mathematical operations on numbers only. If you try to add two text labels, for example, Quattro Pro returns no answer.

In figure 1.3, you can perform mathematical operations on the data in cells C3 through F10. If you try to add or subtract the labels appearing in column B, Quattro Pro displays the value 0 because the program finds no numbers to add or subtract.

Asking What-If Questions

The real purpose of the electronic spreadsheet programs is to ask questions and get acceptable answers. Examples of some typical what-if questions follow:

- What happens to profits if expenses rise by 10 percent?

- What happens to sales if a company loses three salespeople?

- What happens to the average height figure if Mark's height is removed from the sample?

Because Quattro Pro enables you to define numeric relationships, and you can store these relationships, you can play out an infinite number of what-if scenarios by using Quattro Pro spreadsheets. Figure 1.4 shows how easily you can turn the spreadsheet in figure 1.3 into a what-if analysis tool.

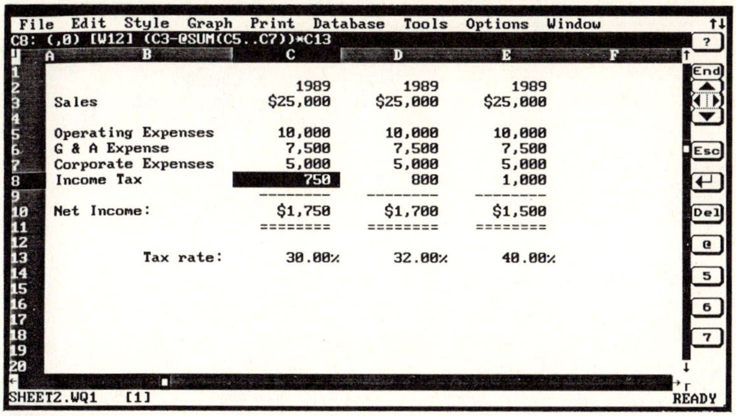

Fig. 1.4 Transforming a report into a financial analysis tool.

The spreadsheet in figure 1.4 uses a yearly format and shows only 1989 data. Except for the Income Tax field, columns D and E contain the same information as column C. The formula in C8 calculates income tax by multiplying pre-tax net income (C3-@SUM(C5 C7)) by the tax rate appearing in C13.

To perform what-if analysis, alter the Tax Rate entry and watch how net income changes. Imagine that you want to see what net income would be under several different tax rate assumptions. By changing the tax rate, you can create different scenarios in which net income rises and falls.

In Version 1.0, Quattro Pro goes one step further by supplying you with a What-If command on the Options menu (see Chapter 6). This powerful menu command enables you to create one-way and two-way sensitivity tables. A *sensitivity table* lists a wide range of possible solutions to a problem that you define. Instead of altering cell values to test the effect on the results displayed in other cells, therefore, you create one table that lists all of the possible results. This approach to asking what-if questions is more flexible, more accurate, and provides you with better information than ever before.

Reviewing the Quattro Pro Spreadsheet

The Quattro Pro spreadsheet is more than a collection of rows, columns, and cells. With a little imagination, you can turn a spreadsheet into a presentation-quality graph, a database application, or a macro program. In fact, the name *Quattro* (the number 4 in Italian) derives from these four main program features.

Constructing a Spreadsheet

The easiest way to design a Quattro Pro spreadsheet is to re-create the appearance of the original document. For example, figure 1.5 illustrates how easily you can duplicate a simple multiplication exercise on a Quattro Pro spreadsheet. The formula in cell C7 multiplies the value in C4 by the value in C5. The formula in cell C7 appears on the input line below the menu bar.

Fig. 1.5
A Quattro Pro spreadsheet.

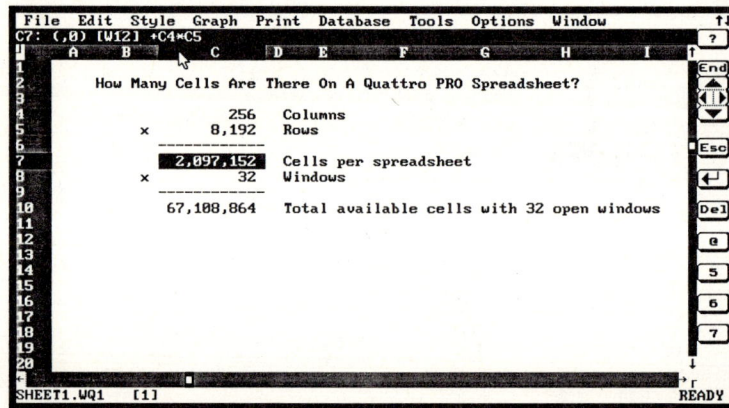

Designing a Graph

With Quattro Pro, you easily can turn your spreadsheet data into an attractive, presentation-quality graph that you can view on-screen or print. Quattro Pro graphs are smart—each time you change numbers on the spreadsheet, the graph adjusts to reflect the new data. Figure 1.6 shows a pie graph representation of crop yields for a California orange grower. See Chapters 9 and 10 for complete coverage of graphs.

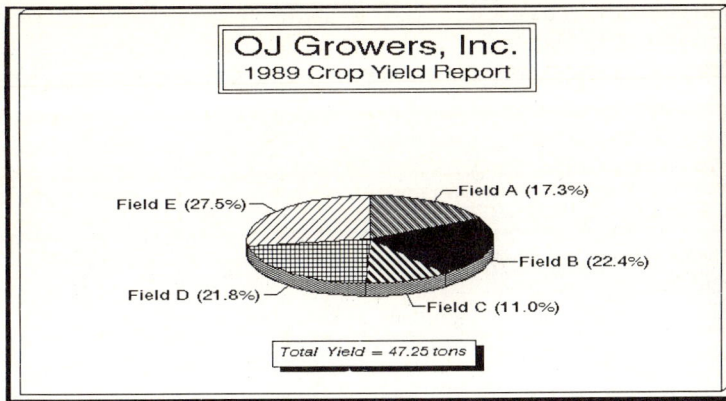

Fig. 1.6
A Quattro Pro
graph.

Building a Database

You also can turn a Quattro Pro spreadsheet into a flat-file database by using the commands found on the Database menu. After you enter your data records, you can sort them, extract records that meet specified criteria, and build new databases with the extracted data. When you set up a database using Quattro Pro, you define rows as records and columns as fields. Figure 1.7 shows a database that inventories CD's and cassette titles. See Chapter 11 for complete coverage of database operations.

Fig. 1.7
A Quattro Pro
database.

Creating a Macro Program

Certain spreadsheet operations are repetitive. Each time you create a spreadsheet, for example, you must format, name, enter data into, save, modify, and print the spreadsheet. A macro program can do many of these operations for you. After you create a macro program, you give the program an Alt-key shortcut. To run the macro program, press the Alt-key shortcut and sit back and watch as Quattro Pro duplicates each of the menu commands that you want executed. Figure 1.8 shows a macro that opens a spreadsheet, changes the column width, and saves the spreadsheet under a new file name. See Chapter 12 for complete coverage of macro programming.

Fig. 1.8
A Quattro Pro
macro.

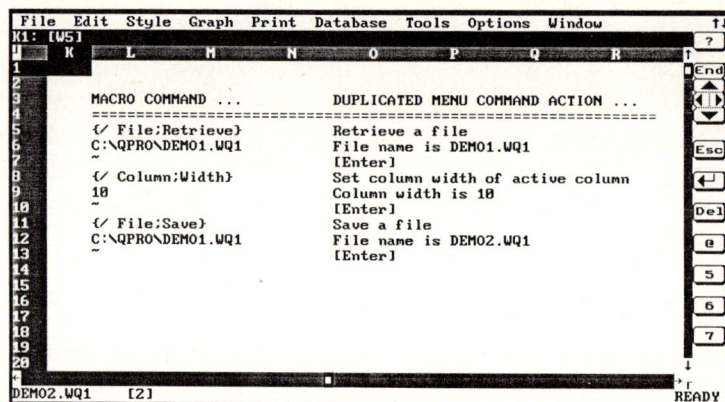

Starting and Ending a Work Session

Q.EXE is the name of the program file that loads Quattro Pro into your computer's RAM memory. The Quattro Pro Installation Utility copies this file into the \QPRO directory on your hard disk drive (see Appendix A for a step-by-step look at the Quattro Pro installation process). To start a new work session, first load Quattro Pro.

Loading the Q.EXE Program

To load the program from the DOS command level, type *CD\QPRO* and press Enter to log into the QPRO directory. Type *Q* and press Enter to load Quattro Pro.

If you are operating the program in a windows environment, such as Microsoft Windows, highlight the filename Q.EXE on-screen and press Enter or double-click your mouse on the file name.

When loaded, Quattro Pro displays a blank spreadsheet with the default filename SHEET1.WQ1. You now can enter data into the spreadsheet, load a different spreadsheet file, or end the current work session. To load an existing spreadsheet into Quattro Pro, choose /**File Retrieve**, type the name of the file you want to edit, and press Enter.

Returning to the Operating System

You can conclude a successful Quattro Pro work session in many ways —some of which may not be desirable. The worst possible outcome of any computer work session is that you quit a program before saving your current work. Quattro Pro helps ensure that you save your work before you exit the program. When you select /**File Exit**, the program displays a dialog box that asks, Lose your changes and Exit?.

Press N to continue with the current work session, choose Y to exit without saving, and press S to save your changes and exit the program.

Get in the habit of saving your spreadsheets several times during each work session. Doing so guards against the possibility of losing all of your work if your system crashes or if the power fails. To save your spreadsheet and continue with your current work session, choose **S**ave from the File menu (press /FS, click Save on the File menu, or press Ctrl-S).

Using Special Startup Parameters

Quattro Pro can be loaded with special startup parameters that further clarify how the program works with your hardware. For example, if you have a limited amount of RAM, use the /x startup parameter to invoke the VROOMM memory manager. Quattro Pro now knows to use your system's existing memory in the most efficient manner.

The VROOMM technology enables much of Quattro Pro's program code to be loaded into memory as needed—instead of the traditional way of all at the same time. VROOMM has enabled Borland to produce this feature-rich product that runs on 512K of system memory. VROOMM also has given Quattro Pro the largest RAM storage capacity of any DOS-based spreadsheet product. VROOMM is always active. VROOMM, by default, reads modules of programming code, *objects*, from disk. When the object is no longer needed, it is discarded. If Quattro Pro needs this object again, the program must read it from disk again.

The /x startup parameter also tells VROOMM the following:

- If extended memory is available, instead of discarding VROOMM objects, store them in extended memory. This memory is *object cache*.

- Before loading an object from disk, first see whether the object resides in the object caches.

- The object cache gives VROOM faster performance because loading from RAM is faster than loading from disk.

Tip | For Microsoft Windows users, you can enter the Quattro Pro startup parameters into the Program Parameters field of your program interchange file (PIF). For example, to load Quattro Pro with a monochrome palette for each new work session, enter */IM* into the Program Parameters field.

For a complete discussion of startup parameters, see Chapter 6.

Working with a Keyboard

You can use one of three accepted keyboard standards with your personal computers, each of which is shown in figures 1.9, 1.10, and 1.11. Each of these keyboards has three sections in common: the function keypad, the alphanumeric keyboard, and the numeric keypad. The extended keyboard pictured in figure 1.11 also has two extra sections: a command keypad and an arrow direction keypad.

**Fig. 1.9
The IBM PC
keyboard.**

**Fig. 1.10
The IBM AT
keyboard.**

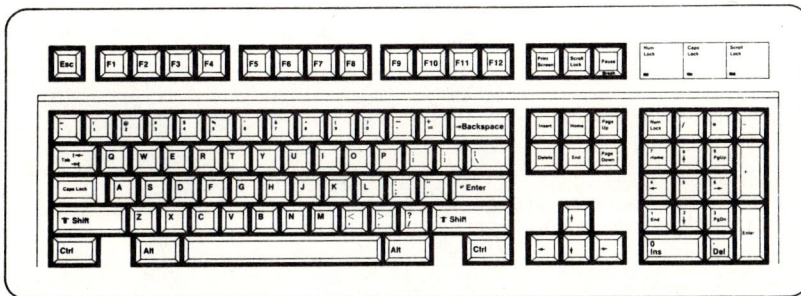

**Fig. 1.11
The IBM AT
Enhanced
keyboard.**

Using the Alphanumeric Keyboard

The alphanumeric keyboard is located in the center of the keyboard. Except for the seven keys appearing in table 1.1, the keys on the alphanumeric keyboard have the same functions as on a typewriter.

Table 1.1
Special Keys on the Alphanumeric Keyboard

Key	Description
Tab	Moves the cell selector one screen to the right; one screen to the left when pressed with the Shift key
Alt	Invokes keyboard macros; when combined with one character, executes macro programs (see Chapter 12)
Shift (⇧)	Changes a lowercase character to uppercase. When pressed, the Shift key also enables the numeric keypad to be used to enter numbers, like a temporary Num Lock.
Backspace (←)	Deletes from right to left, one character at a time, when you are in the EDIT mode
Slash (/)	Use this key to enter MENU mode so that you can choose a menu command. This key also is the divisor bar in a mathematical operation.
Period (.)	Use this key to separate cell addresses like (A1..D10) and to anchor cell addresses when in POINT mode. This key also is the decimal point in mathematical operations.
Tilde (~)	Use this key in macro programs to represent the action of pressing Enter once.

Using the Numeric Keypad

The keys on the numeric keypad are used primarily for cursor movement. Ten keys, however, enable you to perform other actions when using Quattro Pro (see table 1.2).

Table 1.2
Special Action Keys on the Numeric Keypad

Key	Description
Esc	Cancels a menu or command selection. Use this key to interrupt any sequence that ends with Enter by pressing Esc before Enter.

Key	Description
Num Lock	Use this key to dedicate the numeric keypad to numeric entry only. Press the key again to reactivate the special action keys.
Scroll Lock / Break	Use this key to scroll lock (or freeze-frame) the spreadsheet screen. When you move the cursor on a scroll-locked screen, the screen scrolls one row or column in the direction that you move the cursor. On certain keyboards, this key also functions as the Break key. To return to the active spreadsheet from any location in Quattro Pro, press Ctrl-Break.
PrtSc*	Press Shift-PrtSc* to print the contents of the active spreadsheet window on a printer. Enhanced keyboards have a dedicated PrtSc* key that does not require the Shift key.
Home	Use this key to move to the first item on an activated menu. When no menu is activated, use the Home key to relocate the cursor to the home (cell A1) position.
PgUp	Use this key to scroll the spreadsheet up one full screen at a time.
End	Use this key to move to the last item on an activated menu. To enter END mode, make sure that no menus are active and press End. In END mode, press an arrow key to move to the last block of data in that direction, or you can press Home to move the cursor to the lower right corner of the last data block on the spreadsheet.
PgDn	Use this key to scroll the spreadsheet down one full screen at a time.
Ins	Use this key to toggle between the insert and typeover modes. When you are in insert mode, each character you type moves the first character to the right one space.
Del	Use this key to delete the contents of the active cell. In EDIT mode, the Del key deletes the character at the current cursor position.

Using the Cursor-Movement Keys

The four arrow direction keys enable you to move around the active spreadsheet in the direction that they point. You also can use these keys to position the cursor when you are editing the contents of a cell in EDIT mode, to highlight commands on a menu, and to page through the help windows.

The End and Ctrl keys extend the power of the cursor-movement keys by enabling you to take giant steps around the spreadsheet. Table 1.3 explains how to use the cursor-movement keys.

Tip | When you type data into a cell and press Enter to record the data, the cell selector remains in the current cell. To move to another cell, press any cursor-movement key instead of Enter, and Quattro Pro moves you to the next cell in that direction. For example, if you type data into cell A5 and then press ↓, Quattro Pro enters the data into cell A5 and makes A6 the active cell.

Note | If you want to use the cursor-movement keys, the Num Lock key must be in the off position. To dedicate the numerical keypad to numerical entries only, the Num Lock key must be in the on position.

Using the Function Keys

Quattro Pro assigns 10 often-used spreadsheet commands to each of the function keys found at the top or left of your keyboard. For example, to invoke Quattro's GoTo command and move the cell selector to a user-specified address, you press F5.

You can access additional Quattro Pro commands by pressing Ctrl, Shift, or Alt and then pressing the appropriate function key. For example, to display a menu of all of the open windows, you press Shift-F5, the Pick Window key.

When you are using the File Manager or Graph Annotator, certain keys or key combinations have slightly different functions. The use of these special, secondary functions is demonstrated later in the book.

Table 1.4 lists the Quattro Pro function-key assignments available when you are using a spreadsheet.

Table 1.3
Extending the Power of the Cursor-Movement Keys

Key	Description
Left arrow ←	Moves the cell selector one cell to the left
Right arrow →	Moves the cell selector one cell to the right
Up arrow ↑	Moves the cell selector up one cell on the spreadsheet
Down arrow ↓	Moves the cell selector down one cell on the spreadsheet
Ctrl-left arrow	Moves the cell selector one screen to the left
Ctrl-right arrow	Moves the cell selector one screen to the right
End-up arrow	Moves the cell selector up to the next non-blank cell beneath an empty one if the current cell contains an entry. Use this key sequence to move up to the next non-blank cell if the current cell is blank.
End-down arrow	Moves the cell selector down to the next non-blank cell above an empty cell if the current cell contains an entry. Use this key sequence to move down to the next non-blank cell if the current cell is blank.
End-right arrow	Moves the cell selector right to the next non-blank cell followed by an empty cell if the current cell contains an entry. Use this key sequence to move right to the next non-blank cell if the current cell is blank.
End-left arrow	Moves the cell selector left to the next non-blank cell preceded by an empty one if the current cell contains an entry. Use this key sequence to move left to the next non-blank cell if the current cell is blank.

Table 1.4
Quattro Pro Function-Key Assignments

Key	Function Description
F1 Help	Use this key to invoke a help window from anywhere on the spreadsheet or during any spreadsheet operation.
F2 Edit	Use this key to enter EDIT mode so that you can make changes to the contents of a cell.
Shift-F2 Debug	Use this key sequence to enter the DEBUG mode so that you can execute a macro one command at a time.
Alt-F2 Macro Menu	Use this key sequence to display the Macro menu.
F3 Choices	Use this key to display a list of block name choices when Quattro Pro prompts you for a block of cells.
Shift-F3 Macros	Use this key sequence to display a list of the macro commands for a spreadsheet.
Alt-F3 Functions	Use this key sequence to display a list of the @function commands for a spreadsheet.
F4 Abs	Use this key to toggle through the four available cell reference formats. The Abs key changes the format of the cell to the left of the cursor.
F5 GoTo	Use this key to move the cell selector to a specified cell address.
Shift-F5 Pick Windows	Use this key sequence to display a list of the open windows.
Alt-F5 Undo	Use this key sequence to undo spreadsheet cell operations such as erasures, edits, deletions, and file retrievals.
F6 Pane	Use this key to move the cell selector between the active and inactive window panes when a spreadsheet window is split.
Shift-F6 Next Window	Use this key sequence to display the next open window.

Key	Function Description
Alt-F6 Zoom	Use this key sequence to enlarge the active window so that it fills one full screen. When the window is fully enlarged, pressing Alt-F6 shrinks the window back to its original size.
F7 Query	Use this key to repeat the preceding Query command.
Shift-F7 Select	Use this key sequence to enter the EXT mode so that you can select a block of cells by pressing the arrow keys.
Alt-F7 All Select	Use this key sequence to select and deselect active files in the active File Manager list.
F8 Table	Use this key to repeat the last what-if command.
Shift-F8 Move	Use this key sequence to remove files marked in the active File Manager list and store them in temporary memory so that you can paste them in a new location.
F9 Calc	Use this key to calculate formulas on the active spreadsheet when you are in READY mode. When you are in VALUE or EDIT mode, use this key to convert the formula appearing on the input line to the end result.
Shift-F9 Copy	Use this key sequence to copy files marked in the active File Manager list into temporary memory so that you can paste them to a new location.
F10 Graph	Use this key to display a graph of selected data appearing on the current active spreadsheet. Press Esc to return to the active spreadsheet.
Shift-F10 Paste	Use this key sequence to paste files stored in temporary memory into the current directory displayed in the active File Manager file list.

Using the F5 GoTo Key

To relocate the cursor to another cell address, use the F5 key. Pressing F5 invokes Quattro Pro's GoTo function. For example, to go to cell Z100, press F5, type *Z100*, and press Enter.

You also can use the F5 GoTo key to take a quick look at a different part of a spreadsheet and then return to the original cell. For example, to look at cell A75 when A1 is the active cell, press F5, PgDn twice, and Esc. Pressing the Esc key cancels the F5 command, and Quattro Pro returns you to your original cell location: cell A1.

Working with a Mouse

Any command or action that can be executed with a keyboard can be duplicated by using a mouse. A mouse actually simplifies many Quattro Pro spreadsheet operations. With one click of your mouse, you can activate and select a menu; activate and select a menu command; mimic the action of the Esc, Enter, and Del keys; invoke Quattro help windows; select a cell or block of cells; scroll the active spreadsheet vertically or horizontally; resize the active spreadsheet; and so on.

Basic Mouse-Movement Techniques

Many brands of mice are available. Some mouse pointing devices have one or two keys, and others have three or more. To accommodate as many as possible, Quattro Pro uses only the left and rightmost mouse buttons.

Table 1.5 describes the five basic movement techniques that you need to know to use a mouse with Quattro Pro.

Turbo Charging Your Mouse

If your mouse's point and drag action seems sluggish, you need to adjust your mouse's drag sensitivity. The drag sensitivity determines how quickly the mouse pointer responds to your hand movement when you drag the mouse in any direction. A low sensitivity rating causes mouse action to appear sluggish, and a high rating appears to turbo charge your mouse.

Table 1.5
Basic Mouse-Movement Techniques

Technique	Action
Click	Press and release the left or right button once quickly.
Double-click	Press and release the left or right button twice in succession.
Drag	Drag the mouse pointer across the screen display, for example from one cell to another.
Point	Slide the mouse pointing device to relocate the pointer to different parts of the display.
Release	Release a mouse button that you are holding down.

Many mouse manufacturers enable you to increase and decrease drag sensitivity when Quattro Pro is loaded, without requiring you to re-install the driver program.

For example, to invoke the Microsoft Mouse Control Panel, press Ctrl-Alt and either mouse button. The screen shown in figure 1.12 is displayed, and you can click the right or left arrow to increase or decrease your mouse's drag action.

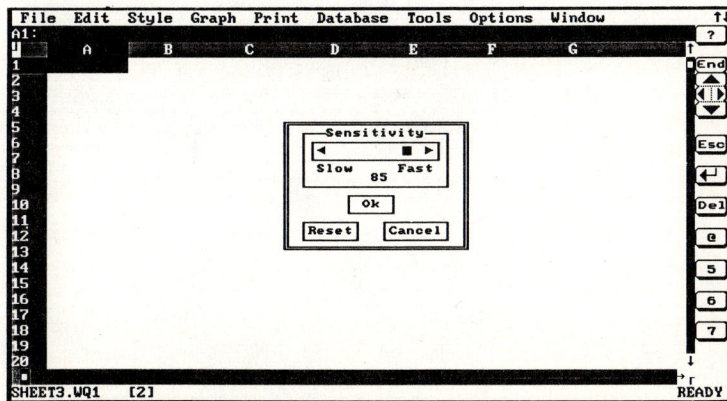

Fig. 1.12
Altering your mouse's drag sensitivity.

The Microsoft mouse drag sensitivity ranges from 0 to 100 (50 is the default setting). Click OK to record a new setting, click Reset to recall the most recent setting, or click Cancel to terminate the operation.

Reviewing the Screen Display

The Quattro Pro screen display has five major areas: the pull-down menu bar, the mouse palette, the input line, the spreadsheet area, and the status line. Figure 1.13 displays the Quattro Pro screen display.

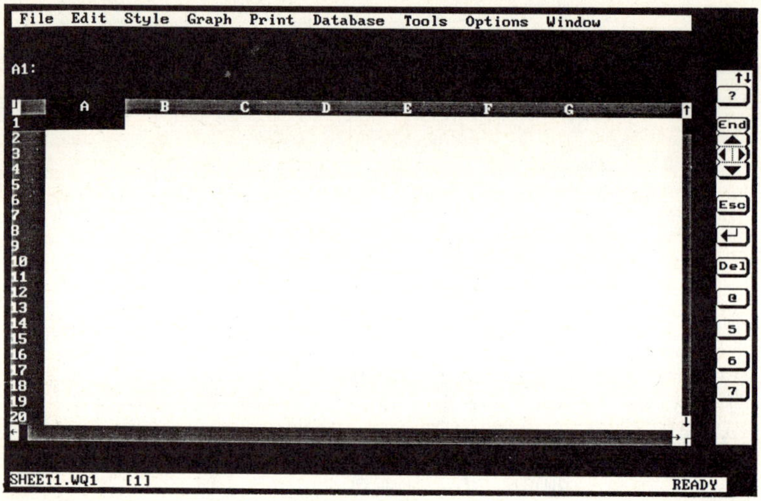

Fig. 1.13
The Quattro Pro screen.

The Pull-Down Menu Bar

Nine options are available on the pull-down menu bar: File, Edit, Style, Graph, Print, Database, Tools, Options, and Windows. Each of these menu options has a different function. The File menu, for example, enables you to perform file operations. To create a file, retrieve an existing file, save and close a file, or do other file activities, you use the commands found on the File menu.

Pulling Down a Menu

To enter Quattro Pro's MENU mode, press the slash (/) key once. This action activates the File menu. To pull down the File menu, press Enter. To activate and pull down another menu, use the cursor-movement keys to highlight the menu name and press Enter.

When you pull down a menu, Quattro Pro displays a list of menu commands. Quattro Pro activates the first command on each menu. To choose that command, press Enter. To activate and choose a different command, use the cursor-movement keys to highlight your choice and press Enter.

Tip | Pressing the bold letter that appears in each command name when a menu already is pulled down executes that command.

If you use a mouse, the process of activating and choosing Quattro Pro menu commands is simplified. Clicking your mouse on a menu name has the dual effect of activating and pulling down that menu. Clicking your mouse on a menu command has the dual effect of activating and choosing that command.

The File menu illustrates the types of data you encounter on a pull-down menu (see fig. 1.14). The menu command names appear at the left margin. Each command has a boldfaced letter. Default settings—such as the startup directory C:\QPRO\—appear in the middle of the menu. The Ctrl-key short-cuts and submenu arrowheads appear on the right margin. A submenu arrowhead resembles a small triangle turned on its right side (▶). When this symbol appears next to a menu command, the command has another sub-menu of commands. When you choose /Edit Insert, Quattro Pro displays a submenu that asks you to specify rows or columns to insert (see fig. 1.15).

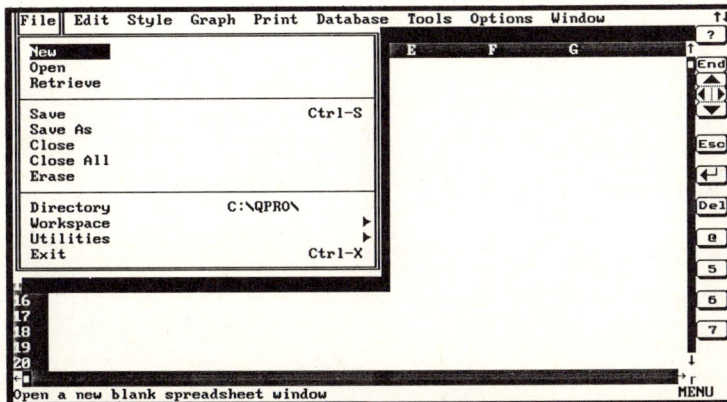

Fig. 1.14
The File menu.

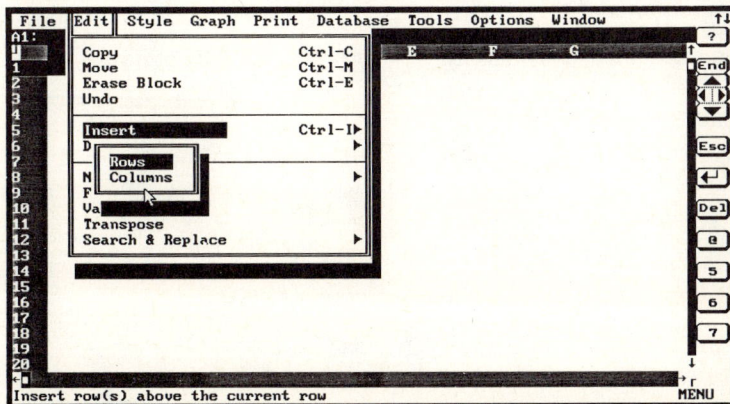

Fig. 1.15
The Insert submenu.

Because neither command on the submenu in figure 1.15 contains an arrow-head, choosing either option executes the Insert command.

Using and Creating Ctrl-Key Shortcuts

You can use Ctrl-key shortcuts instead of the steps required to execute a menu command. For example, to exit Quattro Pro, you activate the File menu, scroll down to Exit, and press Enter. Instead, you can press Ctrl-X from the active spreadsheet and accomplish the same result more quickly. When you don't have a mouse, Ctrl-key shortcuts are the next best thing.

To create your own Ctrl-key shortcuts for frequently used menu commands, follow these steps:

1. Activate a menu and highlight the desired command.

2. Press Ctrl-Enter.

3. Press Ctrl and the letter you want to use as the shortcut key.

If the alphabet key already is in use with another Ctrl-key shortcut, Quattro Pro displays an error message. When you perform this operation successfully, the Ctrl-key shortcut appears next to the command name on the menu.

To delete an existing Ctrl-key shortcut, follow these steps:

1. Activate a menu and highlight the command.

2. Press Ctrl-Enter.

3. Press Del twice.

When you perform this operation successfully, the Ctrl-key combination next to the menu command disappears.

Ctrl-key shortcuts can be invoked only in READY mode when no menu is active. If you create a shortcut for retrieving a file, for example, you cannot execute the Ctrl-key shortcut when the File menu is pulled down. After you create a Ctrl-key shortcut, it is valid for all future work sessions—until you delete the shortcut. Ctrl-key shortcuts also are menu-tree specific. If you switch to a 1-2-3 menu tree, you must re-create Ctrl-key shortcuts.

Table 1.6 displays a list of Quattro Pro's Ctrl-key shortcuts. Except for Ctrl-D, you can re-assign any of the shortcuts to suit your preferences.

Table 1.6
Pre-Assigned Ctrl-Key Shortcuts

Press Ctrl + ...	To execute ...
A	/Style Alignment
C	/ Edit Copy
D	Date Prefix (not re-assignable)
E	/ Edit Erase Block
F	/Style Numeric Format
G	/Graph Fast Graph
I	/ Edit Insert
M	/ Edit Move
N	/ Edit Search & Replace Next
P	/ Edit Search & Replace Previous
R	/ Window Move/Size
S	/ File Save
T	/ Window Tile
W	/Style Column Width
X	/ File Exit

The Mouse Palette

The mouse palette is the rectangular box at the right side of the Quattro Pro screen display. When you load a mouse driver into memory, Quattro Pro detects its presence and displays the mouse palette. If you disconnect the mouse, the palette does not appear the next time you load the program.

You can display your mouse palette in text and graphics modes. To switch between these modes, choose /**O**ptions **D**isplay Mode. When you are in text mode, the mouse pointer appears as a rectangle; when you choose graphics mode, the rectangle becomes an arrow.

The buttons appearing on the palette enable you to reproduce commonly used keyboard keystrokes with one click of your mouse. A brief description of each palette button's function follows.

The Zoom Icon

Click the zoom icon to shrink or enlarge the active window. When you shrink the active window, you reveal other open windows behind the active spreadsheet. When you enlarge the active window, it fills the entire screen.

The Help Icon (?)

Pressing F1 invokes a Quattro Pro help window. On the mouse palette, click the help icon (?) to call up the help window.

The Direction Arrows

Click the direction arrows on the mouse palette to take giant steps around your spreadsheet. When you click the right arrow, for example, your cell selector moves to the right until it locates the first cell containing data. On a blank spreadsheet, for example, the cell selector moves to column IV. This button duplicates the action of pressing the End key plus a cursor-movement key (see table 1.3).

The Esc Key

The Esc key on the palette enables you to mimic the action of pressing Esc from the keyboard. Place the mouse pointer on the Esc button and click once.

The Enter Key

The Enter key icon enables you to mimic the action of pressing Enter. Place the mouse pointer on the icon and click once.

The Del Key

Click the Del button on the mouse palette to mimic the action of pressing the Del key on your keyboard.

The @ Key

Click the @ icon to display a list of Quattro Pro's @functions. This action is equivalent to pressing Alt-F3.

The Macro Buttons (5, 6, and 7)

The macro buttons are labeled 5, 6, and 7. You can assign custom macro operations and text labels to each of these buttons. See Appendix D for a complete list of the valid keyboard macro commands. By default, the buttons execute the {BEEP} macro that causes your computer to sound one beep tone.

Tip | Choose /Options **M**ouse Palette to assign custom macro operations to the mouse palette buttons. Quattro Pro enables you to re-assign the functions of all but the End and ? icon buttons.

The Resize Box

Drag the resize box to change the size of a window. When the window is the correct size, release the mouse button. To reposition a spreadsheet window, drag the horizontal or vertical window border.

The Input Line

The input line on the Quattro Pro screen contains seven data fields and presents two types of information (see fig. 1.16). The type of information displayed depends on whether you are in READY or EDIT mode. You are in READY mode when the active spreadsheet is ready to accept data into any cell. You are in EDIT mode when you press F2 to edit the data in a specific cell. You always can tell what mode you are in by looking at the status line at the bottom of the active spreadsheet. The mode indicator is located in the right corner of the status line. When you are in READY mode, Quattro Pro displays format data for the active cell on the active spreadsheet. For example, if the cell selector is in cell C5 and you are in READY mode, the input line may show the format information displayed in figure 1.16. A brief description of each type of format follows.

The first field displays Label, Date, or Graph. The field displays Graph when the cell selector is on a graph. The field displays Date or Label when you use the /**D**atabase Data Entry command to restrict acceptable cell entries to dates or labels.

The Cell Address field displays the name of the active cell, such as C5.

The third field displays a description of the numeric format and the number of decimal places when applicable. The description (T) indicates that the

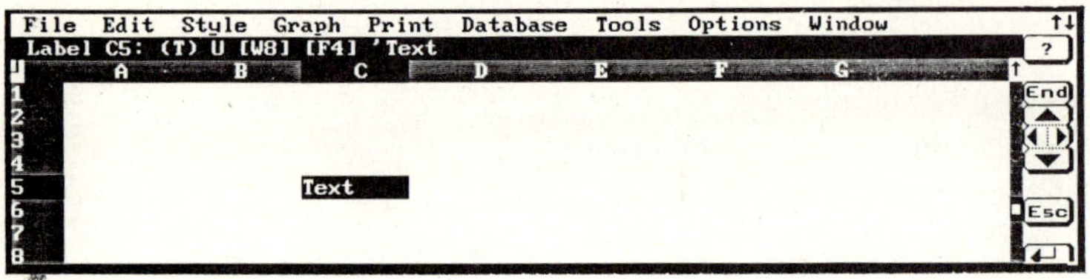

Fig. 1.16
The input line.

cell is formatted to display text. Examples of other numeric formats are: (P2) for percent with 2 decimals, (C4) for currency with 4 decimals, and (,D) for comma delimited with 0 decimals.

The fourth field displays a description of the cell protection status. A U indicates that a cell is unprotected. A P indicates that a cell is protected.

The fifth field displays the width of the active column. Quattro Pro does not display this field when set to the default width. The description (W8) indicates that the active column is eight characters wide.

The sixth field displays a description of the font used in the active cell. The description (F4) indicates that this cell is formatted by using font #4.

The last field displays the unformatted contents of the active cell. For example, this field displays .15 when the formatted cell displays 15.25% on the spreadsheet. In figure 1.16, cell C5 contains a label called 'Text.

Press F2 to place Quattro Pro in EDIT mode when you want to edit the contents of the active cell. Figure 1.17 shows how Quattro Pro displays the contents of cell C5 on the input line when in EDIT mode.

Rules for editing the contents of a cell are covered in Chapter 2.

The Spreadsheet Area

The spreadsheet area is the largest part of the Quattro Pro screen. The spreadsheet area is the part of the spreadsheet that you can see. Remember, a spreadsheet has 256 columns and 8,192 rows, and the part you see on-screen represents just a fraction of the entire spreadsheet. Figure 1.18 high-

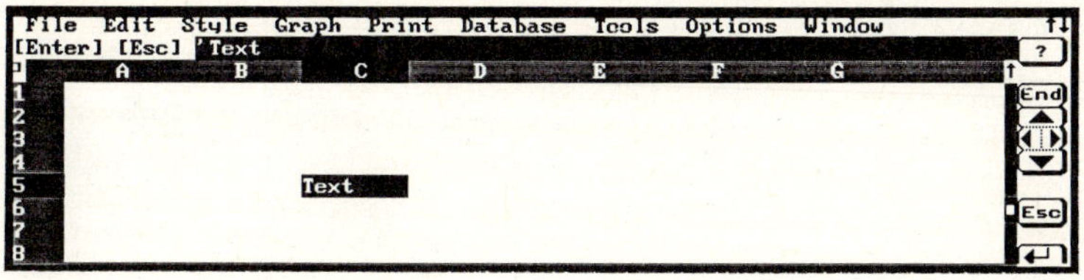

**Fig. 1.17
The input line
in EDIT mode.**

lights the different elements of the spreadsheet window. A brief description of each element follows.

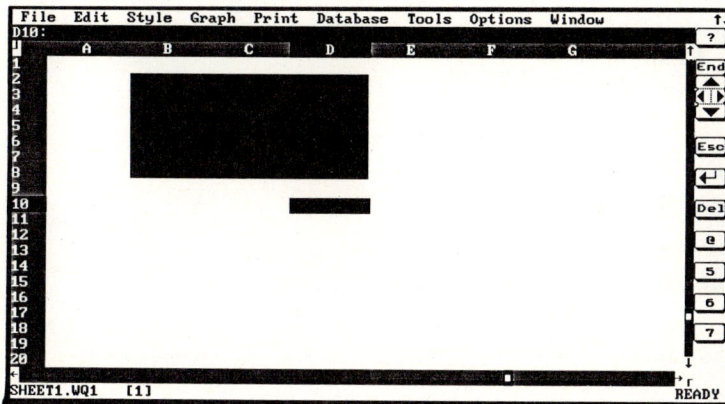

**Fig. 1.18
The spreadsheet
area.**

The Cell Selector

The cell selector is the rectangle that you use to highlight a cell or a block of cells. A block of cells is formed by clicking and holding down the left mouse button while in the active cell and then dragging the cell selector around the spreadsheet area.

Quattro Pro names a block of cells as follows: the first element in the block name is the location of the uppermost left cell in the block range; the second element in the block name is the location of the lowermost right cell in the block range. Quattro Pro separates the two cell locations with two decimal points, as in the cell block name (B2..D8). A *block name* is a set of cell coordinates that describes the far corners of the block.

> **Tip** | Create cell blocks when you want to perform the same operation on multiple columns and rows. For example, you can select the cell block range B2..D8 and change the width of columns B, C, and D.

The Scroll Bars

The horizontal and vertical scroll bars enable you to use your mouse to control the location of the cell selector on the active window. To move the cell selector around the active spreadsheet, point the mouse at a scroll box (see fig. 1.18), click and hold down the left mouse button, and drag the scroll box along the scroll bar.

Horizontal and Vertical Borders

The horizontal border contains the alphabetic name of each column, and the vertical border contains the numeric name of each row in the window. Both borders are highlighted or appear in reverse coloring so that they stand out from the rest of the spreadsheet area.

The Status Line

The status line on the Quattro Pro screen (see fig. 1.19) contains four data fields and presents two types of information. Like the input line, the type of information that the status line displays depends on whether you are in READY or EDIT mode.

When you are in READY mode, Quattro Pro displays information about the active spreadsheet file. For example, if SHEET3.WQ1 is the active spreadsheet and you are in READY mode, the status line may display the information in figure 1.19. A brief description of each part of the status line follows.

File Name

The first field displays the name of the active spreadsheet file. Each time you load Quattro Pro, the default spreadsheet file name on the status line is SHEET1.WQ1. During any work session, however, you may need to close one spreadsheet and create another. Quattro names the files SHEET2.WQ1, SHEET3.WQ1, and so on.

Fig. 1.19
The status line.

Window Number

The second field displays the number of the current window. In figure 1.19, [2] indicates the second window.

Status Indicator

The status indicators to the right of the window number keep you abreast of spreadsheet activity by displaying the current status of certain program features. For example, this field displays NUM when the Num Lock key is on, CAP when the Caps Lock key is on, and so on. The seven Quattro Pro status indicators are defined in table 1.7.

Table 1.7
Status Indicators

Status code	Description
CALC	The current spreadsheet requires recalculation because a value referenced in a formula has been changed.
CAP	The Caps Lock key is on.
CIRC	A formula on the current spreadsheet contains a circular reference. A circular reference occurs when a formulas refers to itself or to cell that refers back to it.
END	The End key is on. This key is inoperative when you are in EXT mode.

Table 1.7—*continued*

Status code	Description
EXT	You have pressed Shift-F7 to extend a block. This status is unavailable when the End key is on.
NUM	The Num Lock key is on.
SCR	The Scroll Lock key is on.

Mode Indicator

The mode indicator is located in the right corner of the status line. The mode indicator tells you in which program execution mode Quattro Pro is. READY, for example, indicates that the current spreadsheet is ready to accept input. The 16 mode indicators are defined in table 1.8.

Table 1.8
Mode Indicators

Status code	Description
DEBUG	Quattro Pro invokes the macro debugger when a macro is started.
EDIT	You are editing a cell on the current spreadsheet.
ERROR	Quattro Pro encountered some type of operation error. Press F1 to learn more about the error or press Esc to cancel the ERROR code and return to the current spreadsheet.
FIND	Quattro Pro is searching for a match to a search string specified in the Query command.
FRMT	You are editing a format line during a Parse operation.
HELP	Quattro Pro is displaying a help window.
LABEL	The entry you are about to make into a spreadsheet cell is a label.
MACRO	Quattro Pro is executing a macro program.
MENU	A menu is activated.

Status code	Description
OVLY	Quattro Pro is loading an overlay file.
POINT	You can select a cell or block with the cell selector. Press F3 to view a list of the block names on the current spreadsheet.
READY	Quattro Pro is ready for you to make an entry or menu selection.
REC	The macro recorder is turned on and is recording your keystrokes and mouse clicks.
REP	The value you enter in a menu command replaces the existing value.
VALUE	The entry you are about to make into a spreadsheet cell is a value.
WAIT	You must wait until Quattro Pro is finished with the current operation.

Getting Help

If you have a question, encounter an error, or forget the purpose of a menu command, Quattro Pro's help window can supply you with the solution quickly. Press F1 to activate the help window from any location on the spreadsheet and during most operations.

When you press F1 while on the active spreadsheet, Quattro Pro displays the help windows shown in figure 1.20.

Boldfaced names appearing in a help window are keywords. When you need additional information about the topics covered in a help window, look for boldfaced keywords. To select a topic, move your cursor to a boldfaced key-word and press Enter (or point and click with a mouse).

Quattro Pro help is context-sensitive; it displays data about the operation currently taking place on your spreadsheet.

Figure 1.21 shows the Graph menu's help window. To display this window, pull down the Graph menu and press F1. The 10 graph types and the three category names appearing at the bottom of the screen (Menu Commands, Commands, Combining Bars and Lines) are the boldfaced keywords.

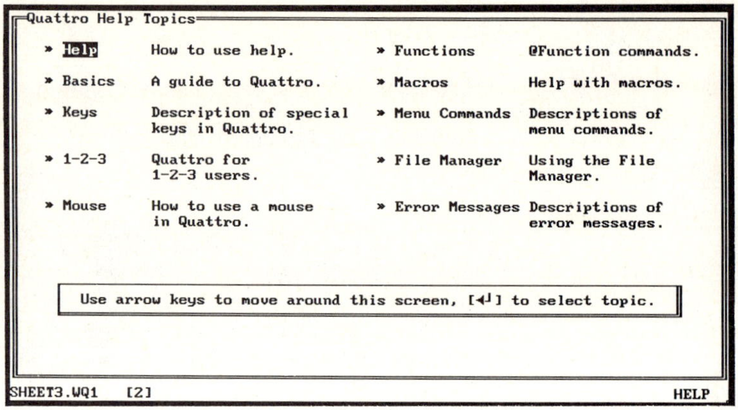

Fig. 1.20
Quattro Pro's
main help
window

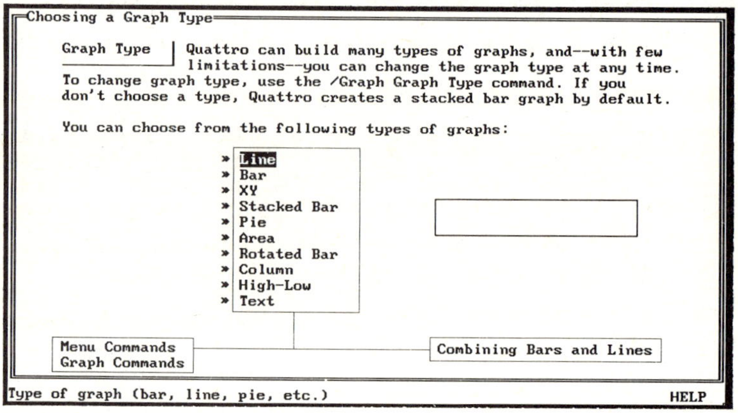

```
┌─Quattro Help Topics─────────────────────────────────────────────────┐
│                                                                       │
│   » Help     How to use help.      » Functions    @Function commands. │
│                                                                       │
│   » Basics   A guide to Quattro.   » Macros       Help with macros.   │
│                                                                       │
│   » Keys     Description of special » Menu Commands Descriptions of   │
│              keys in Quattro.                      menu commands.      │
│                                                                       │
│   » 1-2-3    Quattro for            » File Manager Using the File     │
│              1-2-3 users.                          Manager.            │
│                                                                       │
│   » Mouse    How to use a mouse     » Error Messages Descriptions of  │
│              in Quattro.                           error messages.     │
│                                                                       │
│                                                                       │
│      ┌──────────────────────────────────────────────────────────┐   │
│      │ Use arrow keys to move around this screen, [◄┘] to select topic. │
│      └──────────────────────────────────────────────────────────┘   │
│                                                                       │
│ SHEET3.WQ1   [2]                                              HELP    │
└───────────────────────────────────────────────────────────────────────┘
```

Fig. 1.21
The Graph
menu's help
window.

```
┌─Choosing a Graph Type──────────────────────────────────────────────┐
│                                                                      │
│    Graph Type    │ Quattro can build many types of graphs, and--with few │
│                    limitations--you can change the graph type at any time. │
│                  To change graph type, use the /Graph Graph Type command. If you │
│                  don't choose a type, Quattro creates a stacked bar graph by default. │
│                                                                      │
│    You can choose from the following types of graphs:                │
│                                                                      │
│              ┌──────────────┐                                        │
│           »  │ Line         │                                        │
│           »  │ Bar          │                                        │
│           »  │ XY           │                                        │
│           »  │ Stacked Bar  │          ┌──────────────────┐          │
│           »  │ Pie          │          │                  │          │
│           »  │ Area         │          │                  │          │
│           »  │ Rotated Bar  │          └──────────────────┘          │
│           »  │ Column       │                                        │
│           »  │ High-Low     │                                        │
│           »  │ Text         │                                        │
│              └──────────────┘                                        │
│                                                                      │
│   ┌─────────────────┐                  ┌───────────────────────────┐ │
│   │ Menu Commands   │──────────────────│ Combining Bars and Lines  │ │
│   │ Graph Commands  │                  └───────────────────────────┘ │
│   └─────────────────┘                                                │
│ Type of graph (bar, line, pie, etc.)                         HELP    │
└──────────────────────────────────────────────────────────────────────┘
```

Press Esc to exit a help window and return to the active spreadsheet.

Using the help window liberally saves a lot of time by preventing unnecessary interruptions of work sessions. Using Quattro Pro's help also can save you the time required to flip through reference manuals to find a solution.

Tip | You also can get on-line help by using another method. When you scroll through a menu's commands, a short description of each command's purpose appears on the status line. Use this feature when you need help understanding the purpose of a menu command.

Questions & Answers

This chapter covers most of the basics you need to get started with Quattro Pro. If you have questions about any of the topics covered in this chapter, and you cannot find the right answer using the help windows, scan this section.

Loading Quattro Pro

Q: What do I do if Quattro Pro will not load onto my computer?

A: Check to be sure that you are logged on to the proper directory. In the default condition, this directory is called C:\QPRO.

Quattro Pro may not recognize your display. Try re-installing the program (see Appendix A).

Q: What if the computer displays the message Not enough memory to run Quattro when I try to load the program?

A: Quattro Pro may not load because you have terminate-and-stay-resident (TSR) programs loaded into your computer. Erase all TSR programs from your CONFIG.SYS and AUTOEXEC.BAT files. Re-boot the system and try again (see Appendix A).

Your expanded memory may be incompatible with Quattro Pro. Erase the EMS driver from your CONFIG.SYS file. Re-boot the system and try again (see Appendix A).

Q: What if I loaded Quattro Pro using the \IM monochrome startup parameter, but Quattro Pro did not load the monochrome palette?

A: Precede any special startup parameters with a forward slash (for example, /IM to load Quattro Pro with a monochrome palette.) If you accidentally type \IM, Quattro Pro loads without the proper palette.

Working with a Keyboard and Mouse

Q: When I pressed the forward slash key (/), I could not activate a menu. What happened?

A: The forward slash cannot activate a Quattro Pro menu unless the program is in READY mode. Check the mode indicator on the status line. If it doesn't say READY, press Esc until you are in the correct mode. Try again.

Q: Why does pressing a cursor-movement key cause my spreadsheet screen to shift up and down instead of the cell selector moving from cell to cell?

A: Your Scroll Lock key is on; turn it off.

Q: Why doesn't my mouse work properly with Quattro Pro?

A: When installed, Quattro Pro makes every attempt to recognize and configure itself for use with your mouse. Check Appendix A to be sure that your mouse is compatible with Version 1.0.

Getting Help

Q: I pressed F1 for help, but nothing happened. What is wrong?

A: The program was unable to find the file called QUATTRO.HLP in the Quattro Pro directory (C:\QPRO in the default condition). If this file is not present in this directory, re-install the program (see Appendix A).

Chapter Summary

Chapter 1 introduced you to the electronic spreadsheet program. This chapter showed you how to get started using Quattro Pro. You now should understand the following basic Quattro Pro concepts:

- Using spreadsheet columns and rows

- Knowing how Quattro Pro deals with numbers and letters when you enter them into a spreadsheet cell

- Knowing the difference between spreadsheet, graph, database, and macro programs

- Beginning and ending a work session

- Using a keyboard and mouse

- Interpreting the information that appears on the Version 1.0 screen

- Getting on-line help during program operation

In Chapter 2, you take the next logical step toward learning how to master the operation of Quattro Pro: learning how to enter, edit, move, and view data on the Version 1.0 spreadsheet.

Learning
Spreadsheet Basics

In this chapter, you learn the skills you need to use Quattro Pro on a daily basis. The material presented in this chapter shows you how to enter, edit, and view data on the Quattro Pro spreadsheet. The chapter also defines some important Quattro Pro terminology used throughout the book.

Learning Spreadsheet Terminology

Before you begin creating spreadsheets, you should learn the following Quattro Pro Version 1.0 terms: spreadsheet, cell address, block address, file name, file, window, and workspace.

This book uses spreadsheet to describe the area where data appears.

In Chapter 1, a *cell address* is defined as the basic unit of a spreadsheet. The cell address also is part of a *block address*. For example, D2 is one of two cell addresses appearing in block address D2...D10. A block address contains two coordinates (two cell addresses) that describe the upper and lower parts of a group of cells on a spreadsheet. All Quattro Pro menu commands that require you to enter a cell address also can work on a block address. Working with blocks of spreadsheet data is much more efficient than working with one cell at a time.

When you finish building a spreadsheet, you assign a *file name* to the spreadsheet and save the *file* on a disk drive. To simultaneously accomplish both of these steps, select the /**F**ile **S**ave command. Doing so assigns a unique file name to the spreadsheet so that you easily can locate it the next time you want to review the spreadsheet data. To review the data, select the /**F**ile **R**etrieve command and retrieve the file in which the Quattro Pro spreadsheet is stored.

A new feature of Version 1.0 enables you to open and view up to 32 windows at a time. A *window* is an area on the screen (located in the spreadsheet area) where you view a spreadsheet. When you have only one spreadsheet open during a work session, the spreadsheet window fills the entire screen display. When you open a second spreadsheet, Quattro Pro creates a second window. To display both spreadsheet windows on-screen at the same time, select the /**Window** **Tile** command. Now, each window occupies one half of the entire screen. The more spreadsheet windows you open, the smaller the program must make the windows so that they all fit on the screen at the same time.

Workspace describes all the spreadsheet files that you have loaded into your computer's memory at one time. Workspaces can be extremely useful when you link spreadsheets or when you need to work with several related spreadsheets during one work session.

When you assign a workspace file name, you tell Quattro Pro to remember the names of all of the files currently in memory. The next time you need to work with this group of related spreadsheets, choose /**File** **Workspace** **Restore**, type the name of the workspace file, and press Enter. Quattro Pro loads all of the spreadsheets originally saved as one workspace.

Accessing Quattro Pro Menus

To use Quattro Pro properly, you must familiarize yourself with its menu command language. Fortunately, Quattro Pro uses simple descriptive names for each of the menu commands that you use to enter, edit, manipulate, and view your spreadsheet data. Each of the nine menus has a unique name, offers a unique set of command options, and requires a unique keystroke action to execute commands.

Selecting a Menu

To execute a command, you first need to select one of the nine command menus. To enter Quattro's MENU mode, press the forward slash (/) key once. This action accesses the File menu. If you want to select the File menu, press Enter. If you want to activate and select a different menu, use the cursor-movement keys to highlight the menu name you want and then press Enter.

You can select a menu by using the bold letter key assigned to the menu name. For example, the letter E is the bold letter key for the Edit menu. To select the Edit menu, press /E, and the screen shown in figure 2.1 appears.

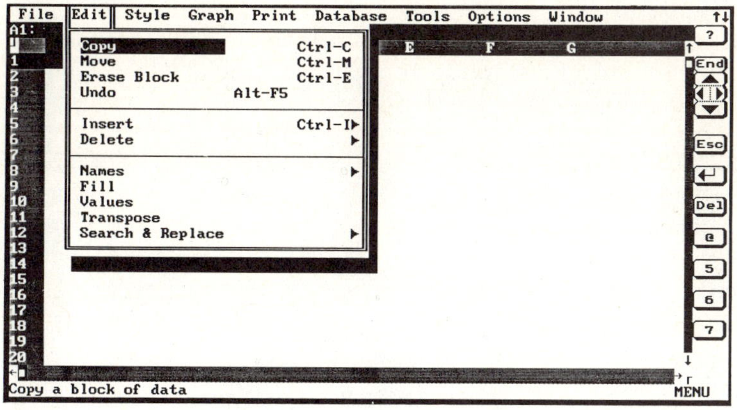

File Edit Style Graph Print Database Tools Options Window

Copy	Ctrl-C
Move	Ctrl-M
Erase Block	Ctrl-E
Undo	Alt-F5
Insert	Ctrl-I▶
Delete	▶
Names	▶
Fill	
Values	
Transpose	
Search & Replace	▶

Copy a block of data   MENU

Fig. 2.1
When you press /E, the Edit menu appears.

If you use a mouse, the process of activating and choosing Quattro Pro menu commands is simplified. When you place the pointer on a menu name and click, you select the menu. When you place the pointer on a menu command and click, you choose the command.

Choosing a Command

When you select (or pull down) a menu, Quattro Pro displays a list of menu commands. By default, Quattro Pro activates the first command on each menu. To choose this command, press Enter. If you want to choose a different command, use the cursor-movement keys to highlight your choice and then press Enter.

Tip | Pressing the / key plus the bold letter key that appears in each menu name selects that menu. Pressing the bold letter key that appears in each command name when a menu already is pulled down executes that command.

Quattro Pro displays a brief description of a command's purpose on the status line when you activate, or highlight, the command name on the menu bar.

Moving through Submenus

When you choose a menu command, Quattro Pro often displays a second submenu, also called a child menu. Quattro Pro uses a hierarchical menu structure, meaning the deeper you go into a given menu branch, the more specific information you get about that command. For example, to set the page length of a report, you must travel through the three child menus pictured in figure 2.2.

Fig. 2.2
To set the page length, you must navigate through three submenus by selecting /Print Layout Margins Page Length.

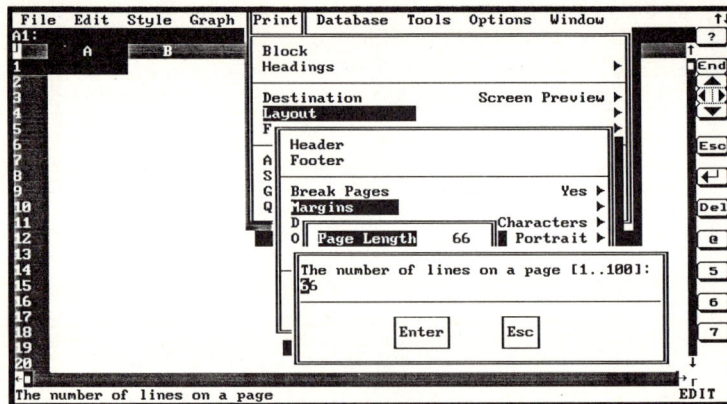

The Quattro Pro menu command structure resembles a tree. If you look at a flowchart that depicts all of the available menu commands, the flowchart looks like a large tree with nine main branches (parent menus), many off-shoot branches (child menus), and hundreds of leaves (commands).

Quitting a Menu Selection or Command Choice

You can cancel a menu selection or command choice in three ways. Most menus have a Quit option. Selecting Quit returns you to the preceding menu. You also can press Esc to back up to the preceding menu. To revert to the active spreadsheet, press Ctrl-Break. This key sequence is like pressing Esc several times to return to the active spreadsheet.

Tip	Although all extended keyboards have a Break key, many of the earlier (PC-XT and some AT) keyboards do not have this key. If your keyboard does not have a Break key, try substituting the Scroll Lock key for the Break key when you use the Ctrl-Break sequence. If this substitution does not work, choose Quit or press the Esc key to return to the active spreadsheet.

Using a Mouse and Menus

- Clicking on a command invokes that command and puts child menus away.

- Clicking on a menu boarder makes that menu active and puts child menus away.

- Clicking on a spreadsheet while the menu is active puts all menus away—like using Ctrl-Break.

Reviewing Data on a Quattro Pro Menu

Figure 2.3 illustrates the types of data you see on a pull-down menu. The menu command names appear at the left margin. Each command has a bold-faced letter key. Certain default settings—such as the default directory C:\QPRO\—appear in the middle of the menu.

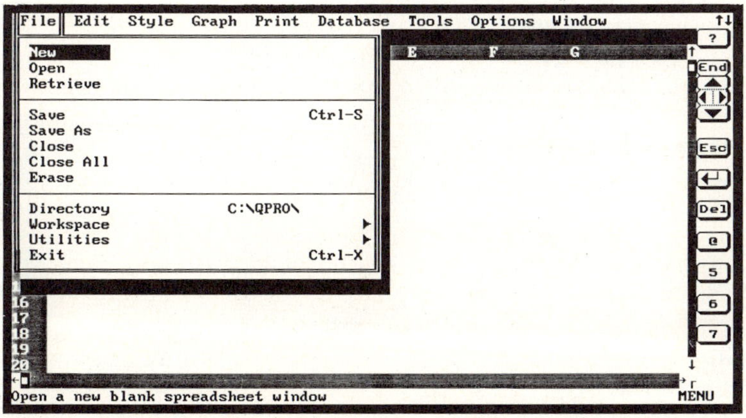

Fig. 2.3
The File menu shows how data in a pull-down menu typically appears.

The Ctrl-key shortcuts and submenu arrowheads appear on the right margin. A submenu arrowhead resembles a small triangle turned on its right side. This symbol appears next to a menu command whenever the command has another submenu of commands. When you choose /Edit Insert, Quattro Pro displays a submenu that asks you to specify what you want to insert, **R**ows or **C**olumns (see fig. 2.4).

Fig. 2.4
When you choose the *I*nsert command from the *E*dit pull-down menu, this submenu appears.

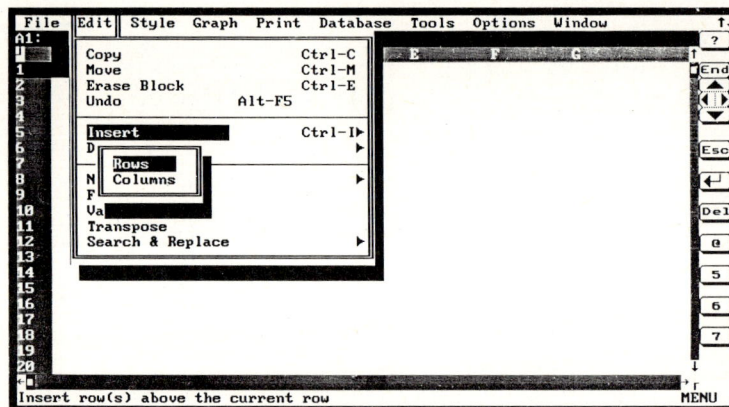

Because neither command on the submenu in figure 2.4 contains an arrowhead, choosing either option executes the Insert command.

Using Ctrl-Key Shortcuts

Most of the Quattro Pro menus offer Ctrl-key shortcuts that enable you to execute a command quickly. Ctrl-key shortcuts replace all of the steps required to execute a menu command. For example, to exit Quattro Pro, you must activate the File menu, scroll down to E**x**it, and press Enter. With the Ctrl-key shortcut, you can press Ctrl-x from the active spreadsheet and accomplish the same result more quickly. Ctrl-key shortcuts are the next best thing to a mouse for saving you time.

Remember three factors when using Ctrl-key shortcuts. First, you must execute Ctrl-key shortcuts from the active spreadsheet. When you create custom Ctrl-key shortcuts (one that loads a file, for example), you can execute the shortcut only when no other menu is active. Second, you may not assign the same Ctrl-key to two different commands. Third, Ctrl-key shortcuts are menu-tree specific. Quattro Pro can display two *menu tree* variations on its default menu structure. One variation displays all menu names and commands as they appear in the original version of Quattro Pro, and the other variation reproduces the look of Lotus 1-2-3. If you switch to the 1-2-3 menu tree, you must create Ctrl-key shortcuts that work with the menu names and command names for the 1-2-3 menu tree.

Creating Custom Ctrl-Key Shortcuts

To create your own Ctrl-key shortcuts for frequently used menu commands, follow these steps:

1. Activate a menu and highlight the desired command.

2. Press Ctrl-Enter.

3. Press Ctrl and the letter you want to use as the shortcut key.

If the letter is already in use with another Ctrl-key shortcut, Quattro Pro displays an error message. When you perform this operation successfully, the Ctrl-key shortcut appears next to the command name on the menu.

Deleting Custom Ctrl-Key Shortcuts

To delete an existing Ctrl-key shortcut, follow these steps:

1. Activate a menu and highlight the desired command.

2. Press Ctrl-Enter.

3. Press Del twice.

When you perform this operation successfully, the Ctrl-key shortcut next to the menu command disappears.

Table 2.1 displays a list of Quattro Pro's Ctrl-key shortcuts. Except for Ctrl-D, you may reassign any of the shortcuts listed to suit your preferences.

Table 2.1
Preassigned Ctrl-Key Shortcuts

Shortcut key	*Equivalent menu command*
A	/**S**tyle **A**lignment
C	/**E**dit **C**opy
D	Date Prefix (cannot be reassigned)
E	/**E**dit **E**rase Block
F	/**S**tyle **N**umeric Format

	Table 2.1—*continued*	
Shortcut key	*Equivalent menu command*
G	/**G**raph **F**ast Graph
I	/**E**dit **I**nsert
M	/**E**dit **M**ove
N	/**E**dit **S**earch & Replace **N**ext
P	/**E**dit **S**earch & Replace **P**revious
R	/**W**indow **M**ove/Size
S	/**F**ile **S**ave
T	/**W**indow **T**ile
W	/**S**tyle **C**olumn **W**idth
X	/**F**ile E**x**it

The Quattro Pro menus place many useful and powerful spreadsheet tools at your fingertips. You use these commands to organize your files, and to format, edit, view, graph, and print the data that you enter into a spreadsheet. Before you use the menu commands, however, you must enter data into a spreadsheet.

Entering Data into the Spreadsheet

Quattro Pro accepts two types of data as valid entries: labels and values. A *label* is defined as a text entry; a *value* can be a number, a formula, or a date and time entry.

To enter data into a spreadsheet cell, do the following:

1. Select a cell using the cursor-movement keys or the mouse to click a cell.

2. Type data using any of the keys on your keyboard.

3. Press Enter to tell Quattro Pro to store the data in the active cell.

4. Press a cursor-movement key to move to a new cell.

After typing data, you can move to a second cell by pressing any cursor-movement key. Pressing a cursor-movement key enables you to store the data you typed and to move to the next cell with one key stroke.

Quattro Pro looks at the first character in an entry to decide whether the character is a label or a value. When you enter a label into a cell, the mode indicator on the status line displays the word **LABEL** (see fig. 2.5). When you enter a value into a spreadsheet cell, the mode indicator displays VALUE (see fig. 2.5).

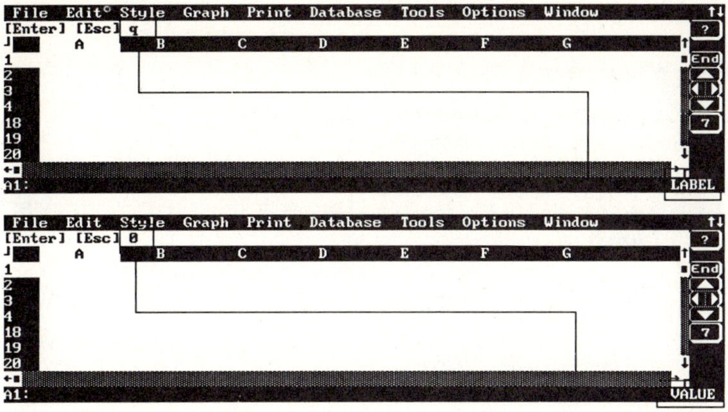

Fig. 2.5
The status line displays LABEL or VALUE, depending on the type of data in your entry.

Always check the mode indicator to make sure that Quattro Pro interprets your data correctly. If you accidentally enter a number as text and the number is used in a spreadsheet formula, the formula cannot calculate an answer correctly.

If you try to enter a table when Quattro Pro is in Value mode, the program sounds an error tone beep. Press Esc, re-enter the data correctly, and press Enter.

Learning about Labels

The word label is just a formal description for text. *Label* also suggests that you can use text as column heading labels and row description labels to describe the data on a spreadsheet. A text entry can be many things. It can be the word **catch** as well as the word **catch22** or **22skidoo**.

Remember, the first character you type tells Quattro Pro how to interpret the rest of the characters in the entry. If the first letter is a number, but the entry is actually a label, you must enter a *label prefix*. A label prefix has two functions. First, the prefix tells Quattro Pro that an entry is text—regardless of its composition of numbers and letters. Second, the prefix tells Quattro Pro how to align the text entry in a spreadsheet cell. Label prefixes are listed in table 2.2.

Table 2.2
Label Prefixes

Label	Description
'	Left justifies text in a cell
"	Right justifies text in a cell
^	Centers text in a cell
\	Repeats a character or group of characters in a cell until the character fills the entire cell.

By default, Quattro Pro places an apostrophe (the left-alignment prefix) in front of every entry initially recognized as text. If you want to change the alignment of text in a cell or if you want to enter a label that begins with a number, type one of the other label prefixes shown in table 2.2 before you type the first character of the entry. Figure 2.6 shows how each of these label prefixes aligns a text entry in a spreadsheet cell.

Fig. 2.6
The four label prefixes change the alignment of your entry on the spreadsheet.

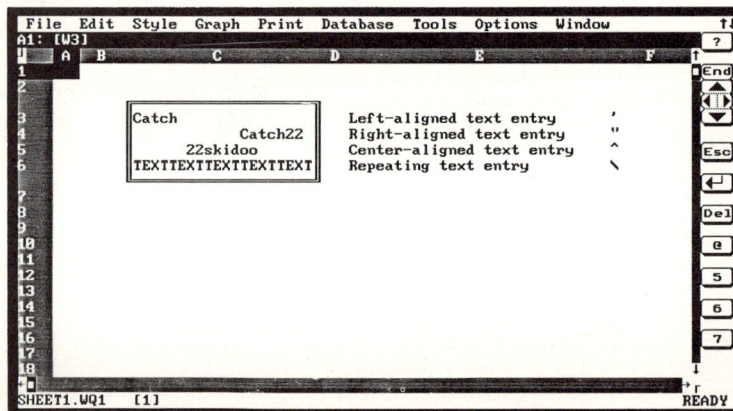

Quattro Pro enables you to enter up to 254 characters per label. When you enter a label longer than the width of the cell's column, Quattro Pro displays the entire label by extending the text into the next cell on the same row (see cell B4 in figure 2.7). If the next cell contains data, Quattro Pro cuts off the initial entry, preventing it from overlapping onto the contents of the next cell.

You can deal with the overlapping cell label shown in cell C6 of figure 2.7 in two ways. First, you can leave the entry as is. Even though you cannot see the entire label entry, it is stored. To check, place the cell selector on the entry and verify that the text displayed on the input line is intact. Second, you can set the column width to equal the width of the entire label entry (as in cell D8). Figure 2.7 illustrates both alternatives.

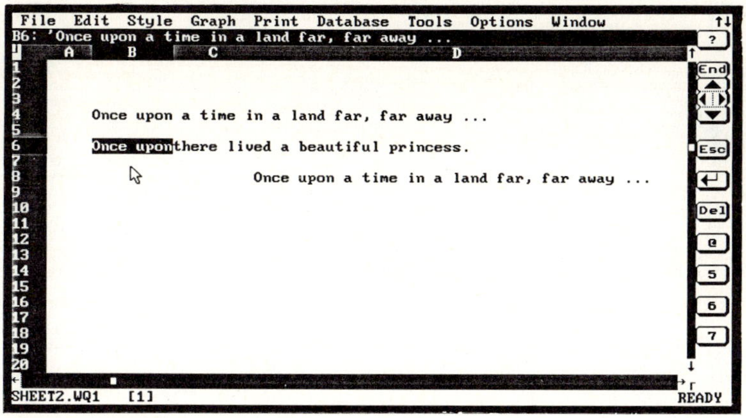

Fig. 2.7
If an entry extends beyond the length of a cell, Quattro Pro cuts off the entry to keep it from extending into the next cell.

Tip | Quattro Pro cuts off an overlapping text entry when you surround the entry with a box graphic using the /Style Line Drawing **O**utside command.

Learning about Values

The term *value* encompasses three types of data: a number, a formula, and a date and time entry (see fig. 2.8). A *number* is any digit or series of digits. A *formula* is an entry that performs a calculation on two or more digits or series of digits. A date and time entry enables you to use a spreadsheet cell to display commonly used date and time formats.

When you enter a value into a spreadsheet, Quattro Pro right aligns the value in the cell. Unlike other spreadsheet programs, Quattro Pro enables you to change the alignment of numbers in a cell with the /Style **A**lignment command (see Chapter 4).

Entering Numbers

Although you can enter numbers and letters as text labels, a value entry must begin with a number (0 through 9) or one of the six value symbols listed in

Fig. 2.8
A value can be a number, a formula, or a date and time entry.

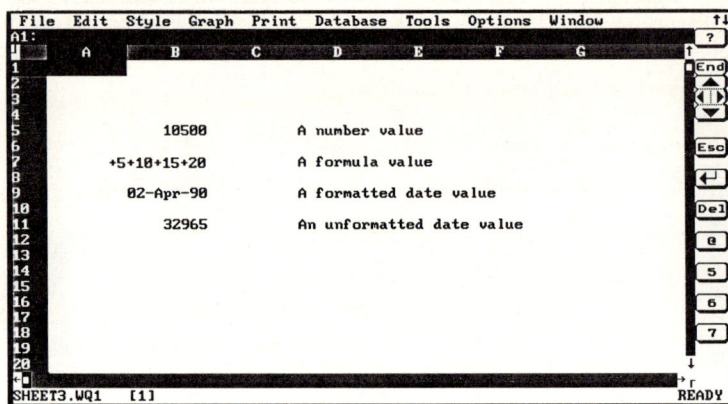

```
 File  Edit  Style  Graph  Print  Database  Tools  Options  Window        ↑↓
A1:                                                                      [ ? ]
   U   A         B         C         D         E         F         G      ▐End
 1                                                                        ▲
 2                                                                        ◄□►
 3                                                                        ▼
 4
 5            10500              A number value
 6                                                                       [Esc]
 7        +5+10+15+20            A formula value
 8                                                                       [ ↵ ]
 9         02-Apr-90            A formatted date value
10                                                                       [Del]
11            32965              An unformatted date value
12                                                                       [ 0 ]
13
14                                                                       [ 5 ]
15
16                                                                       [ 6 ]
17
18                                                                       [ 7 ]
19
20                                                                        ↓
                                                                         →r
SHEET3.WQ1   [1]                                                        READY
```

table 2.3. Quattro Pro also accepts a number entry if you follow the entry with a percent (%) sign, such as 10%.

Table 2.3
Value Symbols

Value symbol	Description
+	Indicates a positive value
−	Indicates a negative value
.	Indicates a decimal point
(	Indicates a parenthetical calculation
$	Indicates a number entered with a currency symbol

Tip | Although Quattro Pro enables you to enter a currency symbol with a number, the program does not display the currency symbol in the cell until you select the /File **N**umeric Format **C**urrency command.

Quattro Pro assumes that all numbers are positive unless you specify otherwise. If you want to change a number's default value, precede the number with any of the value symbols shown in table 2.3.

When you enter a number longer than the width of the active cell's column, Quattro Pro does not overlap the entry into an adjacent blank cell. How Quattro Pro treats these "long" numbers depends on how you format the cell. Figure 2.9 shows how Quattro treats a series of three numbers when the cell's numeric format is changed.

```
 File   Edit   Style  Graph  Print  Database  Tools  Options  Window      ↑↓
A1: [W2]                                                                    ?
  █  A       B            C         D      E        F          G      H    ↑
1                                                                       ■End
2      ┌──────────────────────────────────────────────────────┐        ▲
       │ The number... appears as...    When formatted using ...│        ◀▐▶
3      │                                                        │        ▼
4      │    1250.50       1250.00    Fixed, 2 decimal places    │      Esc
5      │    1250.50       1.25E+03   Scientific, 2 decimal paces│
6      │    1250.50      $1,250.00   Currency, 2 decimal places │       ↵
7      │    1250.50       1,250.00   , (Comma), 2 decimal places│
8      │    1250.50           1250   General                    │      Del
9      │       1.25     +            +, -                        │
10     │       1.25       125.00%    Percent, 2 decimal places   │       @
11     │       1.25    31-Dec-1899   Date 1, (DD-MMM-YY)         │
12     │       1.25           1250   Text                        │       5
13     │       1.25                  Hidden                      │
14     │                                                         │       6
15     │          1    ***************  Fixed, 15 decimal places │
16     │                                                         │       7
17     └─────────────────────────────────────────────────────────┘
18  ■                                                                     ↓
SHEET1.WQ1   [1]                                                     READY
```

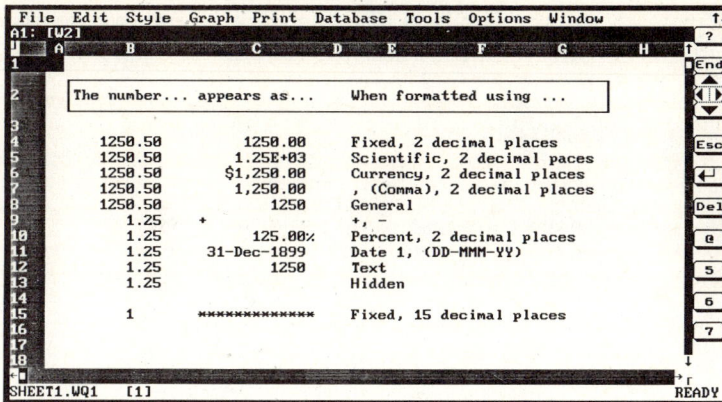

Fig. 2.9
The numeric format that you select can affect the width of a number displayed in a spreadsheet cell.

To reveal the value pictured in cell C15, choose /**S**tyle **C**olumn Width and press the right-arrow key until numbers appear in place of the asterisks.

Although entering numbers into a spreadsheet cell is simple, remember the following rules:

1. Don't use parentheses to enter a negative number. Precede a negative number with a minus sign.

2. Don't enter commas as part of a numerical entry. Format an entry so that it displays commas.

3. Don't add spaces or non-numerical characters between numbers. Mix numbers and characters when you want to make a label entry.

4. Don't substitute a lowercase L for the number 1 or an uppercase O for the number 0.

Use the /**S**tyle **N**umeric Format command to change the displayed and printed format of your spreadsheet numbers (see Chapter 4).

Entering Formulas

A Quattro Pro spreadsheet formula is a powerful tool. In its basic application, the spreadsheet formula adds, subtracts, multiplies, or divides two numbers on a spreadsheet, displaying the answer in a spreadsheet cell that you choose (see fig. 2.10).

Figure 2.10 illustrates how to use basic mathematical formulas in a spreadsheet. The formulas shown in this figure contain four parts: a value symbol, the address of a cell containing a number, a mathematical operator symbol, and another cell address.

The formulas in column F add the numbers in column B to those in column D. For example, to enter the formula appearing in cell F4, you do the following:

1. Place the cell selector in cell F4.

2. Type + to enter Value mode.

3. Type *B4*, the cell address of the first value to add.

4. Type + to choose an addition operation.

5. Type *D4*, the cell address of the second value to add.

6. Press Enter to record the formula in cell F4.

After you store the formula in cell F4, Quattro Pro calculates the answer and displays 25.00.

You can produce this same answer by entering the following formula into cell F4: *+10+15*. This formula, however, does not recalculate an answer if you later change the values appearing in cell B4 or D4.

| Tip | Use cell addresses instead of numbers when you build Quattro Pro formulas. When you change a cell value referenced by a formula, therefore, Quattro Pro recalculates the answer. |

Fig. 2.10
Basic spreadsheet formulas add, subtract, multiply, and divide the data you enter.

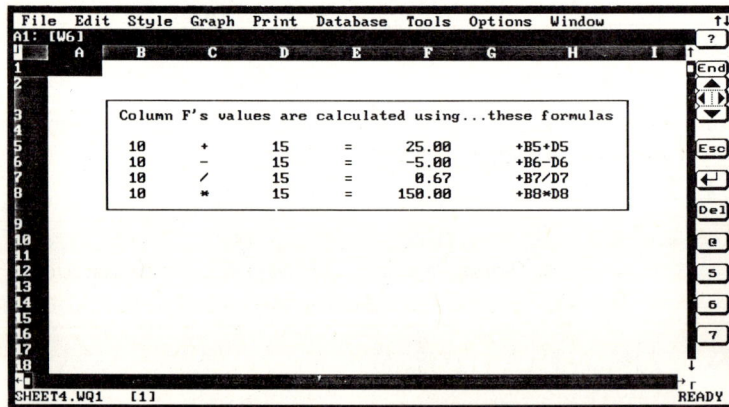

A Quattro Pro formula can be as complex as you need it to be. A more intricate formula may simultaneously perform mathematical operations on multiple sets of numbers and display an answer in a cell of your choosing (see fig. 2.11).

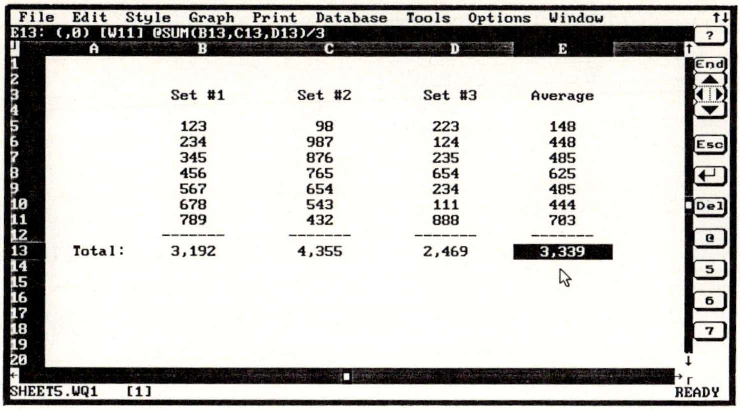

Fig. 2.11
A complex spreadsheet formula adds multiple sets of numbers and gives a total for each set and a total for all the sets combined.

Figure 2.11 illustrates how to use more advanced mathematical formulas in a spreadsheet. The formula shown in this figure contains three parts: the @ symbol, a function command name, and a description of a block of cells.

The formula in cell E13 averages the values appearing in cells B13, C13, and D13. For example, to enter this formula, you do the following:

1. Place the cell selector in cell E13.

2. Type @ to enter Value mode.

3. Type *AVG* to use the built-in average function.

4. Type *(B13..D13)* to specify a block of cells to average.

5. Press Enter to record the formula in cell E13.

After you store the formula in cell E13, Quattro Pro calculates the answer and displays 3339.

Tip | Quattro Pro has an extensive library of built-in @function commands (see Chapter 5). These commands reproduce many types of mathematical operations without requiring you to build long, complex formulas.

You can select any of Quattro Pro's built-in formulas, known as @function commands, to perform specialized calculations for you. Chapter 5 shows you how to use @function commands in your Quattro Pro spreadsheets.

The electronic spreadsheet's capability to create custom formulas makes the program extremely valuable. Quattro Pro manipulates numbers and formulas electronically much more quickly than you can manually.

Valid formula entries can be up to 254 characters long and must begin with a number (0 through 9) or one of the six value symbols listed in table 2.3. A formula also can begin with the at symbol, @, to signify an @function command. Version 1.0 arranges formulas in three groups: arithmetic, text, and logical.

Arithmetic Formulas

Arithmetic formulas perform calculations with numbers, cell addresses, and most of the @function commands using mathematical operators. An operator specifies to Quattro Pro which mathematical operation to do. The formulas pictured in figures 2.10 and 2.11 are examples of arithmetic formulas. Arithmetic formulas can use the operators listed in table 2.4

Table 2.4
Basic Mathematical Operators

Operator	Description
+	Performs addition
−	Performs subtraction
*	Performs multiplication
/	Performs division
^	Raises a number to the power specified by the number following the operator

Quattro Pro makes every attempt to return a value when Quattro Pro encounters an arithmetic formula. Evaluating formulas is usually a simple and straightforward task. Sometimes, however, Quattro Pro returns an unintended or nonsensical answer. For example, when you enter the formula 10/2 into a cell, Quattro Pro returns the value 5. If you want to display a date such as 9/23/62 and you enter this date as 09/23/62, Quattro Pro thinks it is looking at a two-step division formula—9 divided by 23 divided by 62. Quattro Pro returns the value 0.006. This value has no meaning because you are attempting to display a date.

To enter a date directly into a cell so that Quattro Pro displays the value as a date, do the following:

1. Press *Ctrl-D*, and Quattro Pro enters Date mode.

2. Type *9/23/62* on the input line.

3. Press Enter, and Quattro Pro displays a date (see cell B6 in figure 2.12).

> **Tip** | To display a date using another date format, choose the /Edit
> Numeric Format **D**ate command or press Ctrl-F.

The date in cell B8 is the same as the date in cell B6—the entry has been formatted to display in a different date format.

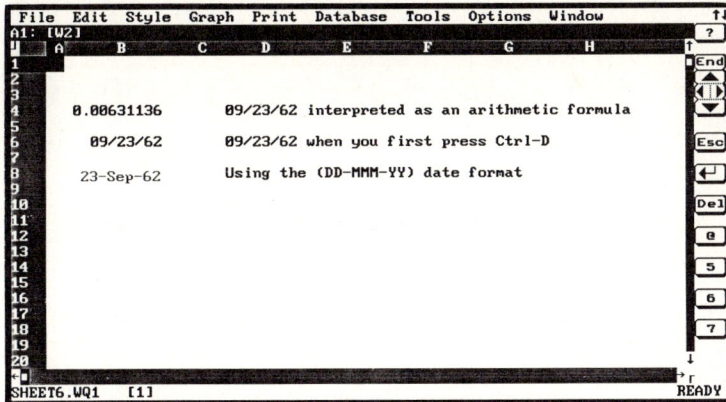

Fig. 2.12 To enter a date on your spreadsheet, you first must press Ctrl-D; otherwise, Quattro Pro displays a numeric value.

Text Formulas

Text formulas enable you to perform specialized tasks that numeric and logical formulas cannot. Text formulas perform operations on strings of text enclosed in quotation marks, labels, and @function commands by using the ampersand sign, &.

Figure 2.13 illustrates a useful application for a text formula. In this figure, labels appear in three cells: B3, B5, and B7. Using the ampersand operator enables you to *concatenate*, or join, these labels in cell B9.

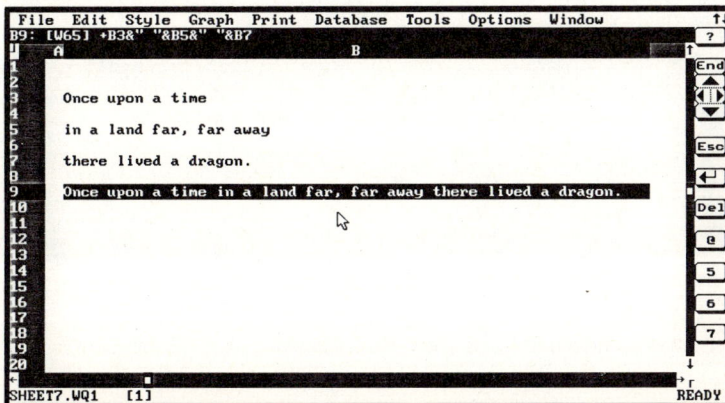

Fig. 2.13 String formulas use the ampersand to join two or more entries.

Briefly, a text formula is made up of three parts: the +, the *constant*, and the *variable*.

The plus symbol tells Quattro Pro to expect a formula.

The constant in a text formula must be surrounded by quotation marks. This formula element does not change. Two constants are in the formula shown in figure 2.13. Each of these constants is one blank space surrounded by quotation marks. This type of constant is used to insert a space between labels when they are joined.

The formula also contains three variables: B3, B5, and B7. Text formula variables are much like the ones used in arithmetic formulas—as the cell values change, so do the displayed results.

Chapter 5 contains examples that illustrate how to use text formulas in spreadsheets to accomplish specific tasks.

Logical Formulas

A logical formula compares two or more pieces of data and gives the result in the form of TRUE or FALSE (see fig. 2.14). If the result of the comparison is true, Quattro Pro returns the value 1; if the result of the comparison is false, Quattro Pro returns the value 0. Logical formulas can use @function commands and the following operators:

$$=, <, >, <=, >=, <>, \#AND\#, \#OR\#, \text{ and } \#NOT\#.$$

Fig. 2.14
Logical
formulas
evaluate TRUE
and FALSE
conditions;
Quattro Pro
returns a value
of 1 if the
condition is
true and a value
of 0 if the
condition is
false.

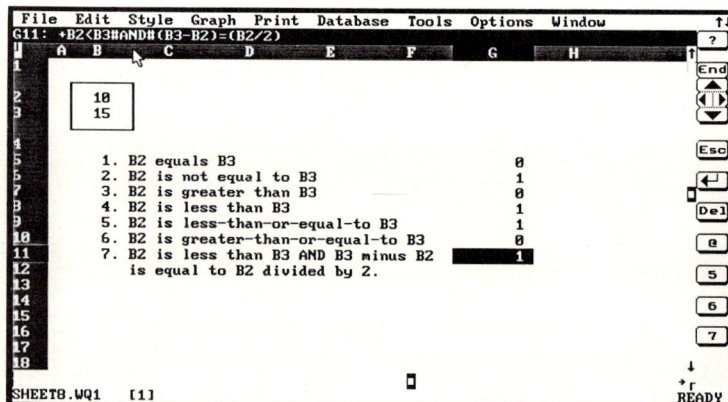

In figure 2.14, cells F5 through F11 contain logical formulas. The logic that each formula tests is expressed verbally in cells C5 through C11. Cells B2 and B3 contain the two variables referenced in each formula.

For example, the logical formula stored in cell F5 is *B2=B3*. This formula determines whether the value in B2 is *equal* to the value in B3. Because this condition is false, Quattro Pro displays a 0.

The logical formula stored in cell F6 is *B2<>B3*. This formula determines whether the value in B2 is *not equal* to the value in B3. Because this condition is true, Quattro Pro displays a 1.

The formula in the highlighted cell in figure 2.14 appears on the input line at the top of the spreadsheet. This logical formula contains the #AND# operator. The #AND#, #OR#, and #NOT# operators have special significance when they appear in logical formulas.

The formula in cell F11 determines the following conditions:

1. Is B2 less than B3?

2. Is the difference between B2 and B3 equal to B2 divided by 2?

3. Are expressions 1 and 2 both true?

Looking at the first logical expression you can see that B2 is less than B3. The difference between B2 and B3 is equal to B2 divided by 2. Individually, both of these expressions are true, and Quattro Pro returns a 1.

Entering Dates and Times

Quattro Pro has several built-in @function commands that enable you to store date and time formats on a spreadsheet by setting the numeric format of a cell to **D**ate or **T**ime. Because date and time formats are considered formulas, you can add and subtract them just like numbers. This feature is helpful in applications that track progress over time.

Figure 2.15 shows a spreadsheet that lists 10 invoices. Using the @NOW function, you can determine the exact age of each invoice for credit collection purposes.

The Quattro Pro shortcut key for entering a date is Ctrl-D. To use this shortcut, do the following:

1. Press Ctrl-D.

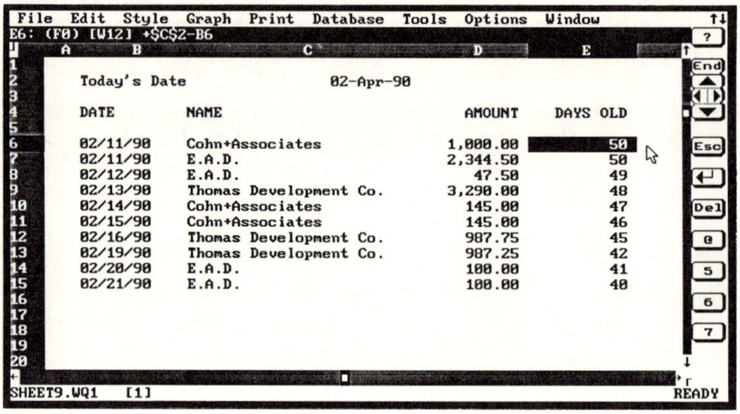

Fig. 2.15
Using date and
time formats,
the @NOW
function
determines the
age of each
invoice.

```
 File   Edit   Style   Graph   Print   Database   Tools   Options   Window        ↑↓
E6: (F0) [W12] +$C$2-B6                                                            ?
   A        B                    C                   D           E
1                                                                              End
2         Today's Date                  02-Apr-90                               ▲
3                                                                             ◄▮►
4         DATE         NAME                        AMOUNT     DAYS OLD           ▼
5
6         02/11/90     Cohn+Associates            1,000.00        50           Esc
7         02/11/90     E.A.D.                     2,344.50        50      ▷
8         02/12/90     E.A.D.                        47.50        49           ↵
9         02/13/90     Thomas Development Co.     3,290.00        48
10        02/14/90     Cohn+Associates              145.00        47          Del
11        02/15/90     Cohn+Associates              145.00        46
12        02/16/90     Thomas Development Co.       987.75        45           @
13        02/19/90     Thomas Development Co.       987.25        42
14        02/20/90     E.A.D.                       100.00        41           5
15        02/21/90     E.A.D.                       100.00        40
16                                                                             6
17
18                                                                             7
19
20                                                                             ↓
SHEET9.WQ1   [1]                                                            READY
```

2. Type a date using one of the following date formats:

   DD-MMM-YY (31-Mar-90)
   DD-MMM (31-Mar, assumes the current year)
   MMM-YY (Mar-90, assumes the first day of the month)

3. Press Enter.

When you choose the appropriate format using the /**Style** **N**umeric Format **D**ate command, Quattro Pro enables you to use short (MM/DD) and long (MM/DD/YY) international dates. The international date format works with numbers, not letters, but you still can enter data as described previously.

Entering @Function Commands

The Quattro Pro @function commands are built in. These commands enable you to perform advanced mathematical operations and return values. You can use @functions by themselves, or you can embed them inside other formulas (see fig. 2.16). Chapter 5 provides complete coverage of the @functions.

In figure 2.16, cells D3, D5, D7, and D9 contain @function commands. Each formula's syntax is listed in column E. The values that the formulas use in their calculations appear in cells B3 through B9.

For example, the formula in cell D3 sums the values appearing in B3 and B9; the formula in D5 averages the values; and the formula in D7 counts the values.

```
 File  Edit  Style  Graph  Print  Database  Tools  Options  Window      ↑↓
A1: [W2]                                                              ?
U    A    B       C       D             E                          ↑
1                                                                 █End
2
3         123            3192.00        @SUM(B3,B4,B5,B6,B7,B8,B9)  ▲
4         234                                                      ◀▣▶
5         345            456.00         @AVG(B3,B4,B5,B6,B7,B8,B9)  ▼
6         456                                                     Esc
7         567            7.00           @COUNT(B3,B4,B5,B6,B7,B8,B9)
8         678                                                      ↵
9         789            2.65   @SQRT(@COUNT(B3,B4,B5,B6,B7,B8,B9))
10                                                                Del
11
12                                                                 @
13
14                                                                 5
15
16                                                                 6
17
18                                                                 7
19
20                                                                 ↓
SHEET10.WQ1  [1]                                                 READY
```

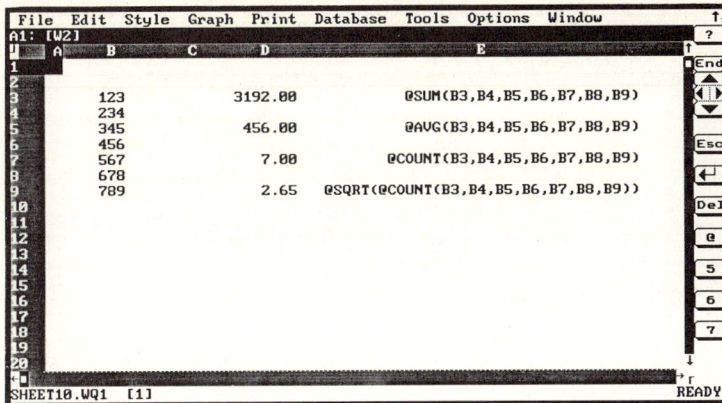

**Fig. 2.16
Using
@functions in a
spreadsheet
enables you to
perform
advanced
mathematical
operations.**

The formula in cell D9 is different than the others because this formula contains two @function commands. This formula counts the number of values in cells B3 through B9 and returns the square root of this number.

You can enter an @function onto a spreadsheet in two ways: manually enter the command or select the command from the @function choice list.

Entering an @Function Manually

To enter an @function manually, press the @ key, type the function name, enter the appropriate arguments, and press Enter. An argument is a cell reference or a number on which Quattro performs the operation. For example, the first three @function commands shown in figure 2.16 use the same arguments: the address of cells B3 through B9. The @AVG command in this figure uses an additional argument: the @SUM command. You can type an @function's name in upper- or lowercase text—Quattro Pro recognizes the @function either way. When you do not remember the name or purpose of a particular @function command, refer to Appendix E.

Using the Choice List To Enter an @Function

When you press Alt-F3, Quattro Pro displays a list of the Version 1.0 @functions. Scroll through the list using the ↑ and the ↓ keys. When you locate the @function you want, press Enter, and Quattro Pro reproduces the @function on the input line, at the cursor position. To complete the @function, type the appropriate cell addresses and mathematical operators called for by the @function and press Enter.

Beyond Basic Data-Entry Techniques

The most common way to enter data is to type the data and press Enter. Quattro Pro, however, has several other data-entry techniques. These techniques help you build formulas that use single cells *and* large blocks of cells. Before you learn these techniques, you need to understand the three types of Quattro Pro cell references and how to enter and modify the references for use in your spreadsheet formulas.

Learning Cell Reference Formats

Quattro Pro has three types of cell reference formats: relative, absolute, and mixed. The cell reference format determines how Quattro Pro reproduces a formula when you copy it from one cell to another.

Defining Relative Reference Format

By default, Quattro Pro records new cell entries using the relative reference format. When you copy a formula from one cell to another, the relative reference format changes the formula to refer to the new cell addresses. If you copy the formula in cell B7 to C7, Quattro Pro adjusts the formula in a relative fashion (see fig. 2.17). Initially, cell B7's formula references data appearing in column B. When you copy this formula to cell C7, Quattro Pro adjusts the cell addresses in the formula, creating a formula that references data in column C.

Fig. 2.17
When you copy the formula used in cell B7 to cell C7, Quattro Pro adjusts the formula.

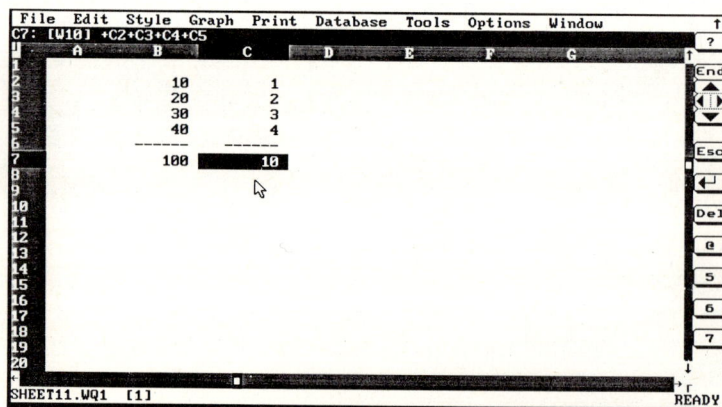

Defining Absolute Reference Format

You use the absolute reference format to anchor a cell address in a formula. When you anchor a cell address, the address does not change when you copy the formula to a different location on the spreadsheet. To format a cell address using an absolute reference format, place the $ symbol in front of the cell address's row number and column letter.

The formula shown in figure 2.17 can be copied using the absolute reference format. If you copy the formula in cell C7 to cell E7, Quattro Pro does not adjust the formula (see fig. 2.18). The formula in cell E7 still sums data appearing in column C and does not sum the data in column E. You can copy this formula to cell IV8192, and the result remains 10. This operation is useful for displaying the result of a calculation in several different locations on the same spreadsheet report.

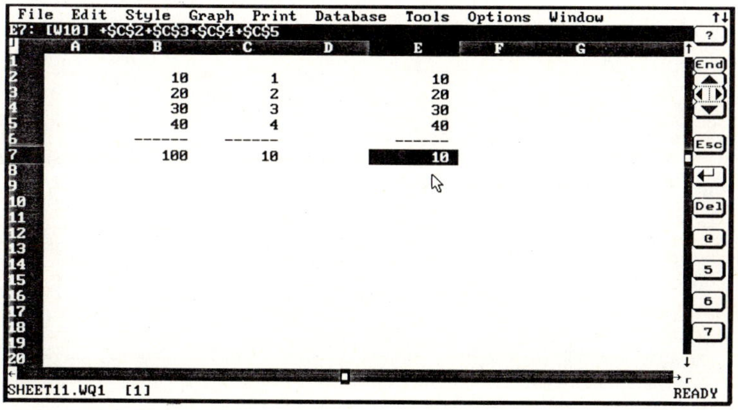

Fig. 2.18
The absolute reference format does not change the cell addresses when you copy a formula to a different cell.

Defining Mixed Reference Format

Formulas that have relative and absolute cell references are called mixed references. A mixed reference indicates that you are anchoring some mix of row numbers and column letters appearing in a formula (see fig. 2.19).

The formula shown in figure 2.19 is a mixed reference formula. The formula in cell C7 adds the value in cell E5 to the summed values in the range C2 through C5. The resulting answer is 20. The last cell address ($E$5) is an absolute reference. The first four cell addresses use the relative reference format. When you copy the formula in cell C7 back to cell B7, Quattro Pro adjusts the formula in a relative and absolute reference fashion. The formula that appears in B7 is as follows:

+B5+B4+B3+B2+$E$5

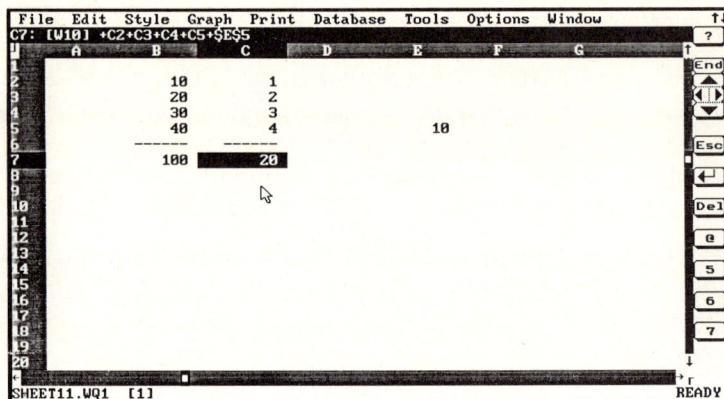

Fig. 2.19
The mixed reference format for both absolute and relative references in a formula.

Changing the Cell Reference Format

Quattro Pro enables you to change the reference format when you edit a formula on the input line. To change the reference format, place the cell selector on the target cell and press F2, the Edit key. Using the cursor-movement keys, place the edit cursor on or next to the cell name that you want to edit. Then, by pressing F4, the Abs key, you can view all of the possible reference formats until you find the format you need.

These formats are as follows:

- $A$1   absolute column and absolute row

- A$1   relative column and absolute row

- $A1   absolute column and relative row

- A1   relative column and relative row

Working with Cell References

Chapter 1 mentions using the Quattro Pro spreadsheet as a *what-if* analysis tool. This type of analysis involves changing the value in one cell and examining its effect on one or more other cells.

The formula in cell C13 in figure 2.20 relies on the cost of goods sold data appearing in cells C10 through C12. When you alter the value of one or more of the cost accounts, the total cost of goods sold and gross margin values change.

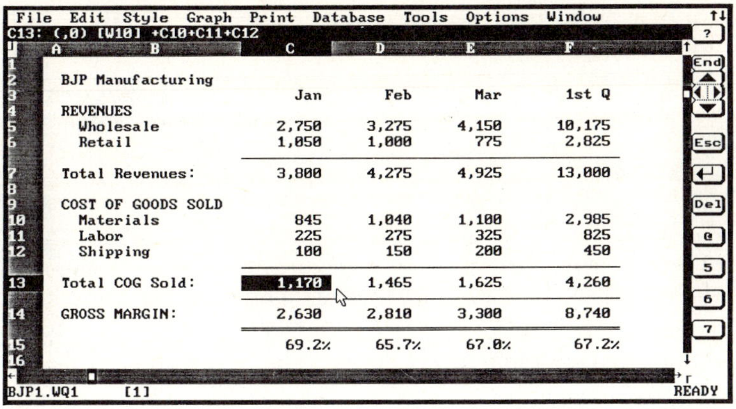

Fig. 2.20
Changes made to the value in C13 affect C10 through C12.

What-if analysis depends on cell referencing. To reference a cell in a formula, you include the cell address (instead of a number) in the formula. For example, January's gross margin equals the difference between total revenues (C7) and total cost of goods sold (the sum of the values in the range C10 through C12). If you replace the formula in cell C14 with the value 2,630, changing the value of any of the revenue or cost accounts has no effect on gross margin because cell C14 no longer relies on these values (see figure 2.21).

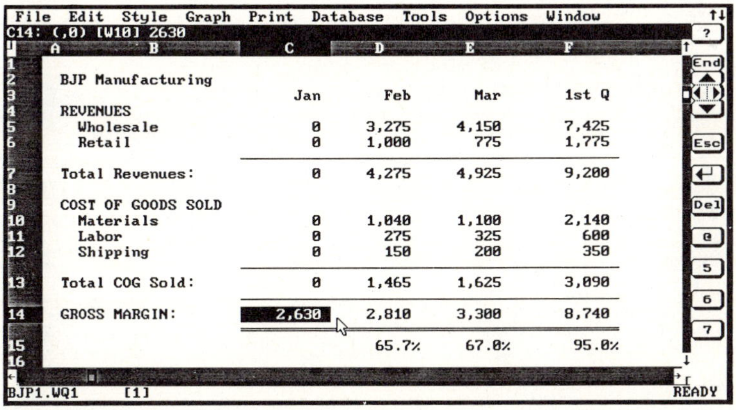

Fig. 2.21
You can streamline formulas by using cell blocks.

What-if analysis requires spreadsheet variables that you can change to test different sets of assumptions.

You can include cell references in your formulas using one of two techniques. The basic method used to add the contents of cells C10, C11, and C12 appears in figure 2.20. Do the following steps:

1. Make cell C13 the active cell by pressing the cursor-movement keys until the cell selector is in C13, or point your mouse arrow at C13 and click.

2. Type + to tell Quattro Pro that you are entering a formula value.

3. Type *C10+C11+C12*.

4. Press Enter to record the formula.

You can accomplish this same result using a technique called *cell selector pointing*. This method enables you to build a formula by pointing to the cell addresses on the spreadsheet that you want in the formula. To point to cell addresses to create a formula, follow these steps:

1. Make cell C13 the active cell.

2. Type + to tell Quattro Pro that you are entering a formula value.

3. Using the cursor-movement keys, make C10 the active cell. The cell address, C10, appears next to the + symbol on the input line.

4. Type + again to tell Quattro Pro that you are continuing to build the formula.

5. Repeat steps 3 and 4 until cell address C11 and C12 are included in the formula.

6. Press Enter to record the formula.

You also can point to the cell references with a mouse:

1. Make cell C13 the active cell.

2. Type + to tell Quattro Pro that you are entering a formula value.

3. Click cell C10.

4. Type + again to tell Quattro Pro that you are continuing to build the formula.

5. Repeat steps 3 and 4 until cell addresses C11 and C12 are included in the formula.

6. Press Enter to record the formula.

Working with Cell Blocks

If you want to sum the contents of the three cells in the cell block range C6 through E6, you can add each cell address by using the formula, C6+D6+E6. Using a cell block range, however, is more efficient. The formula, @SUM(C6..E6), uses an @function to sum the values that appear in the cell block range C6..E6

Using POINT Mode To Build Formulas

You can include a cell block in a formula in two ways. First, you can type the addresses of the first cell in the block, type two periods, and type the last cell address in the block. The second method uses the cell selector and mouse pointing techniques. You can use this method to create a formula that sums the values in the range C6..E6 (see figure 2.21). Follow these steps:

1. Make cell F6 the active cell.

2. Type *@SUM(.*

3. Make cell C6 the active cell. Quattro Pro displays this cell address to the right of the parenthesis in the @SUM command from step 2.

4. Press the period key or the Select key (Shift-F7) to anchor the first cell address and to enter POINT mode. (Check the mode indicator to be sure that you are in POINT mode.)

5. Press the → key twice to include cells D6 and E6 in the cell block range.

6. Type *)*.

7. Press Enter to record the formula.

If you have a mouse, using the pointing technique is easier. To use a mouse to create the formula that sums the values in the range C6..E6, follow these steps:

1. Click cell F6.

2. Type *@SUM(.*

3. Click cell C6.

4. While holding down the left mouse button, drag the mouse to cell E6 and release the button. Quattro Pro highlights each cell that you drag through in the cell block range.

5. Type *)*.

6. Press Enter to record the formula.

Tip You also can use the following alternative mouse technique to highlight any cell block range on a spreadsheet.

1. Click the uppermost left cell in the target cell block range.

2. Point the mouse at the lowermost right cell in the target cell block range.

3. Hold down the right mouse button and click the left button.

Understanding the Order of Precedence

When Quattro Pro first looks at a formula entry, the program determines which parts of the formula must be calculated first, second, third, and so on. The formulas $10 + 10$ and $10 + 5 + 2$ have no order of precedence because they perform only one mathematical operation: addition.

Because the formula $10 + 10/5^{\wedge}2$ contains three mathematical operators, each with a different order of precedence, you may get more than one answer to this problem depending on how you perform the calculation. If you evaluate this formula from left to right, the answer is 16. When you calculate an answer using Quattro Pro's order of precedence, the answer is 10.40. Here, Quattro Pro performs the $(5^{\wedge}2)$ operator first, next divides that answer into 10, and then adds 10 to that result.

Table 2.5 shows the order of precedence that Quattro Pro uses when evaluating mathematical operators in your spreadsheet formulas.

Table 2.5
Quattro Pro's Order of Precedence

Operator	Operation	Order of precedence
^	Exponent	1st
+, −	Positive and negative	2nd
*, /	Multiply and divide	3rd
+, −	Add and subtract	4th
= <>	Tests of equality	5th
<, >	Tests of relative value	5th

Operator	Operation	Order of precedence
<=	Less-than-or-equal test	5th
>=	Greater-than-or-equal test	5th
#NOT#	Logical NOT test	6th
#AND#	Logical AND test	7th
#OR#	Logical OR test	7th
&	String union	7th

Formulas that contain more than one set of parentheses are said to contain nested parentheses. When you enter a formula with nested parentheses, Quattro Pro performs the operations enclosed in the innermost parentheses first. The order of precedence rule holds for multiple operations that appear within one set of parentheses. To show how the order of precedence works, the following example uses nested parentheses to clarify the sample formula:

    (10+(10/(5^2)))
    (1) = 25.0
    (2) = 0.4
    (3) = 10.4

Quattro Pro evaluates this formula as follows: first the program raises 5 to the 2nd power, resulting in 25; then Quattro Pro divides 10 by 25, resulting in 0.4; and finally, the program adds 10 to 0.4 and returns the final result of 10.40.

Nested parentheses clarify the way you want Quattro Pro to evaluate a formula and enable you to create complex formulas using all of the Quattro Pro operators.

Editing Data on the Spreadsheet

Editing cell data is an important function of using a spreadsheet program. Quattro Pro enables you to edit data as you type on the input line or after you press Enter to place data into a spreadsheet cell. Entering new cell data, changing characters or numbers in the active cell, and deleting the contents of a cell are all examples of editing data on the spreadsheet.

To edit the contents of a spreadsheet cell, press F2 to enter EDIT mode. If you have a mouse, click the cell you want to edit and then click the input line directly below the pull-down menu bar. When you click the input line,

Quattro Pro displays the cell data on the input line in the data's unformatted form. You also can toggle between Edit, Value, Point, Date, and Label modes by pressing the Edit key (F2) several times in succession. When you are in EDIT mode, you can use the editing keys listed in table 2.6 to edit the active spreadsheet cell.

When you finish editing the data in a cell, press Enter or click the Enter box on the input line to record the changes.

Table 2.6
Special Keys Available in EDIT Mode

Key	*Description*
Backspace	Deletes from right to left, one character at a time
Ctrl-Backspace	Erases everything on the input line
Ctrl-\	Deletes everything to the right of the cursor on the input line
Del	Deletes the character that the cursor is on
End	Relocates the cursor to the last character on the input line
Enter	Stores data on the input line in the active spreadsheet cell. Press Enter to exit EDIT mode and enter READY mode.
Esc	Erases everything on the input line. Press Esc to cancel EDIT mode and return to READY mode.
Edit (F2)	Enters EDIT mode and displays the contents of the active cell on the input line
Home	Relocates the cursor to the first character on the input line
Ins	Toggles between insert (default) and overwrite (OVR) modes
PgDn	Enters data into the active cell, exits EDIT mode, enters READY mode, and moves the cursor down one screen
PgUp	Enters data into the active cell, exits EDIT mode, enters READY mode, and moves the cursor up one screen

Key	Description
Shift-Tab or Ctrl-←	Moves the cursor five characters to the left on the input line
Tab or Ctrl-→	Moves the cursor five characters to the right on the input line
↑	Enters data into the active cell, exits EDIT mode, enters READY mode, and moves the cursor up one cell
↓	Enters data into the active cell, exits EDIT mode, enters READY mode, and moves the cursor down one cell
→	Enters data into the active cell, exits EDIT mode, enters READY mode, and moves the cursor right one cell
←	Enters data into the active cell, exits EDIT mode, enters READY mode, and moves the cursor left one cell

Tip | Pressing one of the four arrow keys or the PgUp and PgDn keys when in LABEL or VALUE mode enters data into the active cell, moves you to another cell, and enters READY mode. To enter POINT mode (for example, to continue building a formula on the input line), place a mathematical operator after the last character on the input line before you press one of these six keys.

Using the Alt-F5 Undo Key

Everyone has had accidents when working with a spreadsheet—accidentally erasing data, deleting the wrong row or column, or executing a command on the wrong spreadsheet cell. Quattro Pro has a built-in protection mechanism that enables you to reverse the most recent changes made to a cell or the most recent menu command execution. When you need to undo an operation, press Alt-F5, the Quattro Pro Undo key. You activate the Undo key by using the /**O**ptions **O**ther **U**ndo command. To make this setting a default for future work sessions, choose /**O**ptions **U**pdate.

Recalculating Your Spreadsheet Formulas

Quattro Pro recalculates your spreadsheet formulas each time you edit or erase data referenced in a formula. This activity is called *background recalculation* because the operation takes place behind the scenes while you continue to work on your spreadsheet. For small- to medium-sized spreadsheets, background recalculation only takes a second or two. For large spreadsheet applications, background recalculation can take three or more seconds. When you see **BKGD** on the status line at the bottom of the spreadsheet, Quattro Pro is in the background recalculation mode.

You can control how Quattro Pro calculates and recalculates your spreadsheet formulas by choosing /**O**ptions **R**ecalculation Mode. The submenu options for this command are **B**ackground, **A**utomatic, and **M**anual. By default, this command is set to **B**ackground. If you want Quattro Pro to pause and recalculate your spreadsheet formulas, choose **A**utomatic. Choose **M**anual recalculation when you build large spreadsheet applications with formulas that require a great deal of time to recalculate. In this mode, Quattro Pro does nothing until you press F9, the calculation key. When you use cell referencing in a formula, such as @SUM(B1..B5) and then change a value referenced in the range B1..B5, Quattro Pro does not recalculate the formula until you press F9. Quattro Pro displays **CALC** on the status line when your spreadsheet formulas require recalculation.

Tip | Regardless of the way you set the spreadsheet recalculation mode, Quattro Pro always calculates an answer to every new formula that you enter or edit on the spreadsheet.

Viewing the Spreadsheet Data

After you enter and edit data, you view the data. The Window and Options menus contain several commands that enable you to control how Quattro Pro displays your spreadsheets on-screen. Using these commands, you can split a spreadsheet into two vertical panes, two horizontal panes, simultaneously show all open spreadsheets on-screen, or change the Quattro Pro display mode.

The last section in Chapter 2 teaches you the basic ways to create the on-screen look that you need to successfully enter, edit, and view your spreadsheet data. The Options and Windows menus receive full coverage in Chapters 6 and 7.

Viewing the Basic Spreadsheet Window

Quattro Pro's screen display default setting is one full-screen window. One window displays a small spreadsheet with 7 columns and 20 rows. Except for the simplest applications, you want to use the rest of the spreadsheet that exists to the right and below what you can see in one full-screen window.

Splitting the Screen Horizontally or Vertically

As your spreadsheets grow, you may need to simultaneously look at two cells in different parts of the spreadsheet. This feat is possible because Quattro Pro enables you to split your spreadsheet into two vertical or horizontal panes. To create these panes, place the cell selector in a location you want to split and choose /**Window Options Horizontal** (or **Vertical**).

If your application will have more rows than columns, split the spreadsheet horizontally (see fig. 2.22). If your application will have more columns than rows, split the spreadsheet vertically (see fig. 2.23).

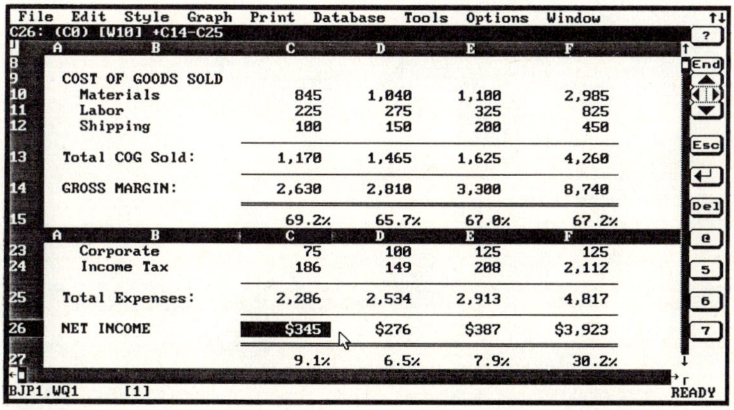

**Fig. 2.22
A window split into two horizontal panes.**

You can arrange your window panes independently, because the cursor movement on one pane does not affect the other pane. If you place your cell selector in the top pane shown in figure 2.22 and press PgDn, only the top pane scrolls down one screen. If you want to synchronize the scroll movement on both window panes, choose /**Window Options Sync**. Press F6, the Window key, to move back and forth between window panes.

Fig. 2.23
A window split into two vertical panes.

Displaying Multiple Windows

As you learn in Chapter 7, Quattro Pro enables you to tile (display side-by-side) all open spreadsheets into one screen display when you select /**Win**dow **Ti**le (see fig. 2.24). This feature is useful when you have a large workspace application and you need to locate a particular spreadsheet in that workspace.

Fig. 2.24
The spreadsheets in this workspace are tiled so that you easily can find the spreadsheet you need.

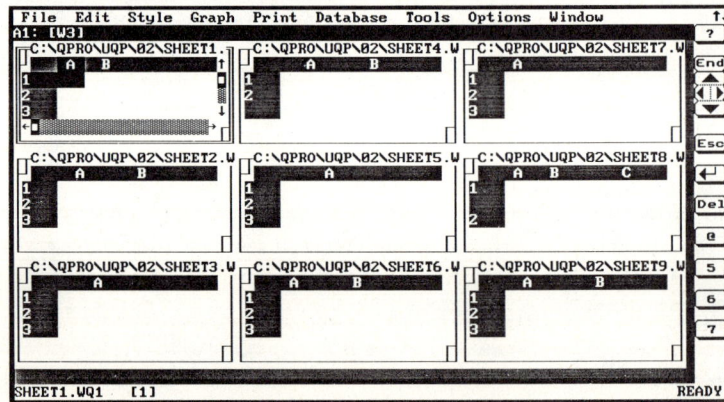

Selecting the Screen Display Mode

Another way to change the basic look of your Quattro Pro screen display is to select a new display mode using the /**Options** **Display Mode** command (see fig. 2.25).

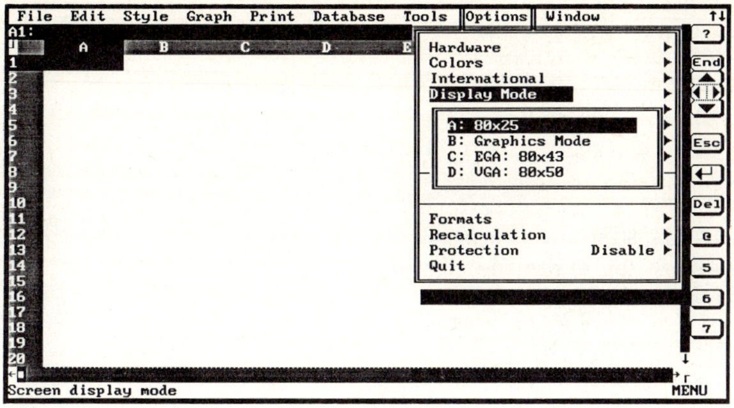

Fig. 2.25
You can select a new screen display by using the /Options *D*isplay Mode command.

For example, if you select the EGA: 80x43 display mode, Quattro Pro can display the entire income statement that appears on the spreadsheets in figures 2.22 and 2.23.

Questions & Answers

This chapter has covered the basic procedures used to enter, edit, and view data on a Quattro Pro spreadsheet. If you have questions about any of the topics covered in this chapter, and you cannot to find the answer using Quattro's help windows, scan this section.

Accessing Quattro Pro Menus

Q: Why did Quattro Pro beep at me when I tried to activate a menu by pressing the forward slash key?

A: One of the common mistakes made when activating a menu is confusing the forward slash with the backslash key. The forward slash key (/) is located at the bottom of your alphanumeric keyboard and always is paired up with the question mark (?) key.

Q: Why did nothing happen when I pressed the first letter in a menu command?

A: Not all Quattro Pro commands use the first letter of the command name as the bold letter key. On the File menu, for example, the Erase and Exit commands both begin with the letter E, but they cannot both use E as a bold letter key.

Creating and Deleting Ctrl-Key Shortcuts

Q: Why did Quattro Pro beep at me when I tried to use a Ctrl-key shortcut to execute a menu command?

A: A Quattro Pro menu is activated. You must be on the active spreadsheet with no activated menus for Ctrl-key shortcuts to work.

Or, the Ctrl-key shortcut you pressed does not exist. Pull down the menu on which the command resides and verify that you pressed the correct shortcut key.

Or, you deleted the shortcut key. If you tried creating and deleting your own shortcut keys, you accidentally may have deleted the one you tried to use.

Entering Labels into the Spreadsheet

Q: Why doesn't Quattro Pro accept a label I am trying to enter?

A: You must adhere to the data-entry rules outlined at the beginning of this chapter. Briefly, labels must be preceded with a label prefix (', ", ^, or \); numbers must be entered without commas; you must press Ctrl-D before typing in dates and times; you must precede formulas with a plus (+) or minus (−) sign; and you must enter an @ function by first typing the @ symbol.

Q: Why did Quattro Pro display the ^ prefix with my label when I tried to center a label that I was entering?

A: When Quattro Pro sees a label character, the program adds the default label prefix (') to the front of the first character. To center a label, type the ^ prefix before you type the first character in the label.

Entering Values into the Spreadsheet

Q: Why doesn't Quattro Pro accept an @function that I am trying to enter?

A: When you enter an @function, do not place a space between the @ symbol and the command name; always follow the command name by parentheses; and be sure to use the correct syntax and all of the appropriate arguments (see Chapter 5). Some @function commands require information in addition to the cell address or cell block range.

Q: Why is Quattro Pro displaying the formula I entered as a label?

A: You initially typed a character or accidentally typed a label prefix before entering the formula. Press F2 to enter EDIT mode, press Home to move to the beginning of the entry, delete the label prefix, and then press Enter to record the formula.

Q: Why didn't Quattro Pro display a new answer when I changed the value of a spreadsheet cell referenced by a formula?

A: Press F9 to recalculate the active spreadsheet. Choose the /**O**ptions **R**ecalculation **M**ode command and set it to **B**ackground or **A**utomatic. In these two modes, Quattro Pro recalculates spreadsheet formulas when you change cell data referenced by the formulas.

Q: Why is Quattro Pro displaying asterisks when I enter values into spreadsheet cells?

A: The values are longer than the width of the cell. To correct this problem, expand the width of the column using the /**S**tyle **C**olumn **W**idth command.

Using Advanced Data-Entry Techniques

Q: Why did Quattro Pro enter a period on the input line when I pressed the period key to extend a cell block while in POINT mode?

A: The only time you can enter POINT mode while entering data is when the cursor is placed after an operator or an open parenthesis.

Editing Data on the Spreadsheet

Q: How come nothing appeared on the input line when I pressed F2 to edit a cell?

A: You may be trying to edit overlapping data that actually is in a different cell. Press the ← a few times until you find the cell containing the label, or press END ←, and the cell selector moves to the first cell to the left that contains data.

Viewing Data on the Spreadsheet

Q: Why can't I split my screen display into two equal panes?

A: Quattro Pro splits a screen at the location of the cell selector. Place the cell selector in the middle of the screen to split it into two equally sized horizontal or vertical panes.

Chapter Summary

Chapter 2 introduced you to the basics of entering, editing, and viewing spreadsheet data. After completing this chapter, you should understand the following Quattro Pro concepts:

- Selecting and choosing menus and menu commands and quitting to the active spreadsheet

- Selecting items found on a Quattro Pro menu

- Using, creating, and deleting custom Ctrl-key shortcuts

- Entering labels and values into a spreadsheet

- Using and changing cell reference formats in formulas

- Using cell blocks and POINT mode to build formulas

- Editing data on the spreadsheet

- Viewing data on the spreadsheet

In Chapter 3, you learn how to build a fully functional spreadsheet application. Chapter 3 provides full coverage of the File and Edit menu commands. Although these commands represent only a small percentage of all Quattro Pro commands, you use these commands each time you create a spreadsheet. Chapter 3 encourages you to follow along in a spreadsheet-building exercise that demonstrates the best methods for using all of the commands on these two menus.

Learning Fundamental Commands

This chapter focuses on the commands found on Quattro Pro's Edit menu. Using the Edit menu commands and your knowledge of entering and editing data, you can manipulate the form and content of your spreadsheet applications.

In a typical spreadsheet-building work session, you load Quattro Pro, and a blank spreadsheet appears. Next, you enter and edit data on the spreadsheet. When you sit back and review the spreadsheet, you realize the data makes much more sense in another arrangement. Maybe you need to switch row and column labels or delete one column of data from the spreadsheet. Each time you need to change data in your spreadsheet, you can do one of two things: erase the spreadsheet and start over or use the Edit menu commands to mold the existing spreadsheet into an organized, logical application.

The Edit menu commands enable you to change the organization, structure, and content of your spreadsheets. You can use these commands to do the following:

- Copy and move cell data
- Perform operations on blocks of cell data
- Insert and delete columns and rows
- Assign unique names to cells and blocks
- Switch or transpose column and row data
- Search for and replace data on the spreadsheet

This chapter introduces the Edit menu commands and single-operation topics such as how to insert a row. Examples of spreadsheet applications built for a fictional company, Speedy Airlines, are used to reinforce your understanding of the purpose and function of each Edit menu command.

Reviewing the Edit Menu

Quattro Pro's Edit menu commands make copying, moving, erasing, and manipulating cell data extremely easy. You use the 11 Edit menu commands to organize and manipulate data on a spreadsheet (see fig. 3.1). Table 3.1 explains the purpose of the Edit menu commands. The name of the command matches the command's function. For example, use **Copy** to copy a value or a label to different parts of the spreadsheet.

Fig. 3.1
Use the Edit menu commands to manipulate data.

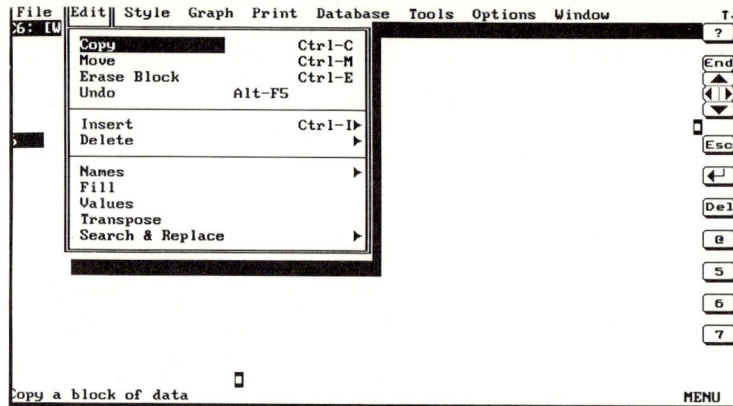

Tip | Four of the commands on this menu have Ctrl-key shortcuts: **Copy**, **Move**, **Erase Block**, and **Insert**. The Ctrl-keys correspond to the boldfaced letters in each command name. When possible, Quattro Pro matches the Ctrl-key and the boldfaced letter key so that you don't have to remember two keys for one command.

Table 3.1
Edit Menu Commands

Command	Description
Copy	Copies the contents of one or more cells into another cell or into a block of cells
Move	Moves the contents of one or more cells to another location on the spreadsheet
Erase Block	Erases the contents of a block of cells

Command	Description
Undo	Reverses the most recent operation you performed using a Quattro Pro menu command
Insert	Inserts a blank row or column on the spreadsheet
Delete	Deletes a row or column from the active spreadsheet
Names	Assigns a unique name to a cell or block of cells. Names can be used in place of cell references in all Quattro Pro operations.
Fill	Enters a sequence of numbers into a user-specified block of cells on the spreadsheet
Values	Replaces all cell formulas on the active spreadsheet with their calculated values
Transpose	Switches the row and column organization of data appearing in a user-specified block of cells
Search & Replace	Searches for a user-specified label or value on the spreadsheet and replaces it with another user-specified label or value.

Preselecting a Cell

The commands on the Edit menu perform operations on single cells and on blocks of cells. This section focuses on single-cell operations.

You can use the commands on the Edit menu in two ways: choose the command and then type the cell address or highlight the cell and then choose the command.

Most Edit menu commands require two pieces of data to work: a source cell address and a destination cell address. By default, Quattro Pro uses the active cell as the source cell address. When you want to use a different source cell, type the new address after you choose the command. When Quattro Pro prompts you, type the destination cell address and press Enter to complete the operation.

You can execute a menu command more quickly if you preselect the source cell and then choose the command. *Preselecting* a cell means making that cell active, or highlighting it, before you execute a menu command. When you preselect a cell before choosing a command, Quattro Pro uses this cell address as the source cell address.

The next section demonstrates how to copy, move, and erase data on a spreadsheet.

Copying, Moving, and Erasing Cell Data

Copy, **M**ove, and **E**rase Block are good examples of intuitive Edit menu commands. You use these three commands more than any other Quattro Pro menu commands because they meet basic and essential spreadsheet-building needs. The Copy command leaves the data in the source cell intact while copying the data to a new cell. This operation is useful for reproducing values and labels in several cells on the same spreadsheet. The **M**ove command deletes the data from the source cell and shifts the data to a new location. This operation is useful because it enables you quickly to shift data around the spreadsheet until you create the design you seek. The **E**rase Block command deletes the contents of one or more cells on the spreadsheet. This command is particularly useful when you need to erase some—but not all—of the data from a spreadsheet.

To see how these commands work, start by reviewing the items shown in figure 3.2. This figure shows the four starting locations of a text label called HERE.

Fig. 3.2
The label HERE starts out in cell C.

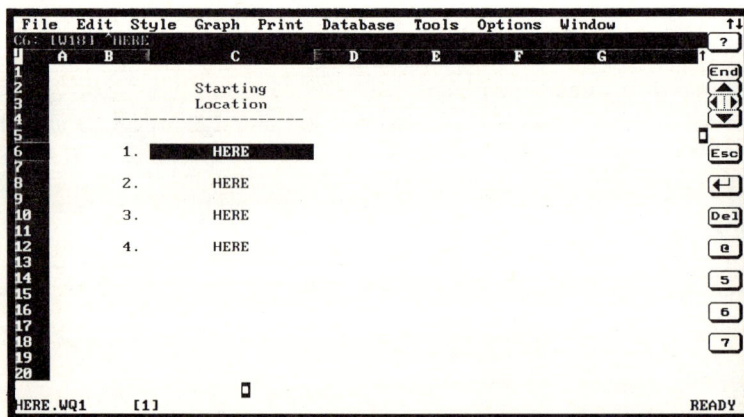

You can copy or move the text label in four ways. You can copy one cell to another cell, copy one cell into a block of cells, move one cell to another cell, or move one cell into a block of cells. Each method gives you a different result (see fig. 3.3).

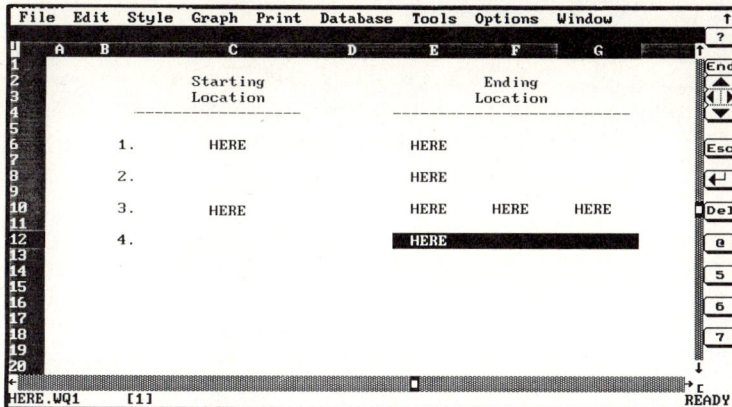

Fig. 3.3
You can copy or move data four different ways.

In example 1, when you copy the contents of cell C6, Quattro Pro duplicates the text label HERE in cell E6. In example 2, when you move the contents of cell C6, Quattro Pro relocates the text label HERE to cell E6.

Examples 3 and 4 use the Copy and Move commands to perform more complex operations. In example 3, Quattro Pro copies the text label in cell C10 into all three cells in the cell block E10..G10. In example 4, Quattro Pro moves the text label from cell C12 into the first address in the cell block E12..G12. Quattro Pro relocates HERE only to the first address in the cell block because Move is a relocating command and not a duplicating command.

Copying the Contents of a Cell

The Copy command saves you time when you build a spreadsheet. If you plan to use a value or a label many times on the same spreadsheet, enter the data once and copy it to other parts of the spreadsheet. You also can copy values and labels to other spreadsheets in Quattro Pro's memory. (Chapter 7 explains how to use multiple spreadsheets.)

You can execute a copy operation more quickly when you preselect the source cell and then choose the command. For example, to copy the contents of cell A5 into cell Z5 follow these steps:

1. Make A5, the cell you want copied, the active cell. To do this, press the cursor-movement keys until the cell selector highlights cell A5 or point at cell A5 with the mouse arrow and click once.

2. Choose Copy from the Edit menu and press Enter when Quattro Pro displays A5 as the source cell address.

3. When Quattro Pro prompts you for a destination, type the new cell location, *Z5*, and press Enter.

Tip | Press Ctrl-C, the Ctrl-key shortcut for the Copy command, to quickly execute a copy operation.

The Copy command is useful for duplicating formulas. When you copy a relative reference formula, Quattro Pro adjusts the cell addresses in the formula in a relative fashion. In figure 3.4, the relative reference formula that sums data in column C is copied into adjacent cells in columns D, E, and F. Quattro Pro adjusts the formula to sum the data in these columns. When you copy an absolute reference formula, Quattro Pro does not adjust the cell addresses, which enables you to display a formula result in a different part of the spreadsheet.

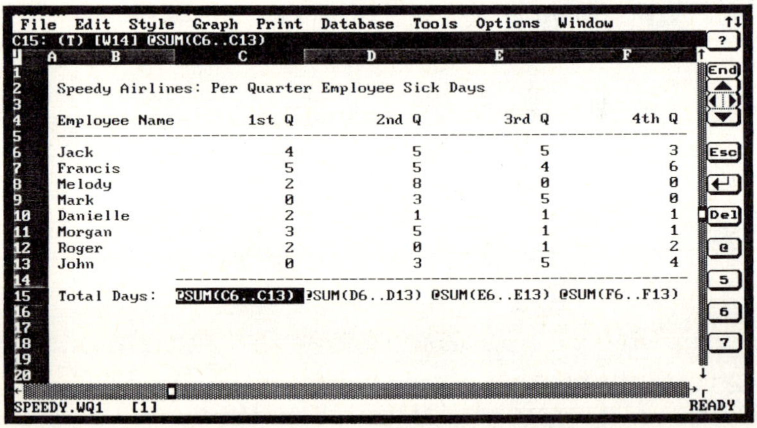

Fig. 3.4
When you copy a relative reference formula, Quattro Pro adjusts the cell addresses.

When you copy a cell, Quattro Pro copies the cell's format— alignment, display format, cell protection, and so on—into the destination cell. For example, cell C15 in figure 3.4 is formatted to display a formula as text. When you copy the cell to the other columns, the formulas still are displayed as text; you don't have to reformat copied cell data. (See Chapter 4 for complete coverage of spreadsheet formatting.)

Moving the Contents of a Cell

Like the Copy command, the Move command also saves you time when building a spreadsheet. You can move a label or a value to a different part of the spreadsheet, and you can move values and labels to other open spreadsheets in Quattro Pro's memory.

You can execute a move operation more quickly when you preselect the source cell and then choose the command. For example, to move the contents of cell D15 to cell D17, follow these steps:

1. Make D15 the active cell. To do this, press the cursor-movement keys until the cell selector highlights cell D15 or point at cell D15 with the mouse arrow and click once.

2. Choose Move from the Edit menu and press Enter when Quattro Pro displays D15 as the source cell address.

3. When Quattro Pro prompts you for a destination, type the new location, *D17*, and press Enter.

Tip | Press Ctrl-M, the Ctrl-key shortcut for the Move command, to quickly execute a move operation.

When you relocate a formula with the Move command, Quattro Pro does not adjust the cell reference formats appearing in the formula (as in a copy operation). This process enables you to display a formula result in a different spreadsheet location. In a move operation, however, Quattro Pro adjusts each formula containing a reference to the moved formula, reflecting the moved formula's new spreadsheet location.

In figure 3.5, the formula in cell D15 is moved into cell D17. The formula's original cell addresses and reference formats do not change.

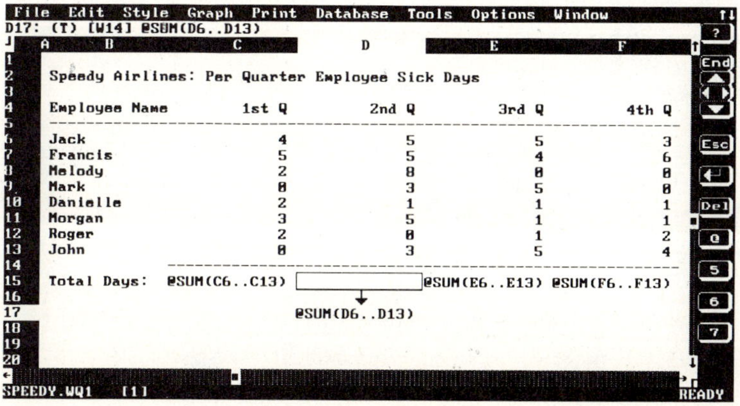

Fig. 3.5 A formula remains unchanged when moved from one cell to another.

When you use the **Move** command to relocate a value whose cell address appears as part of a formula, several things can happen depending upon the formula and where you move the value. The following example illustrates four possible scenarios.

Tip Make sure that the cell you are moving data into is empty because Quattro Pro writes over the data in the destination cell.

Figure 3.6 displays an abbreviated version of the document appearing in figure 3.5. The formulas in cells C10 and D10 are equivalent to the formulas in cells E10 and F10.

Fig. 3.6
The cell address before moving a cell referenced in a formula.

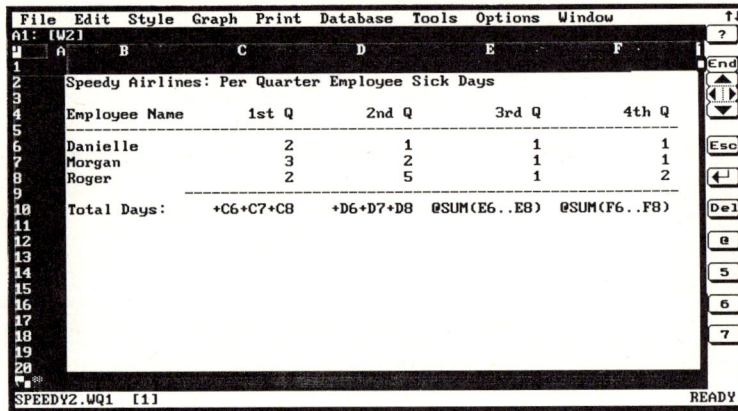

```
  File   Edit   Style   Graph   Print   Database   Tools   Options   Window        ↑↓
A1: [W2]                                                                            ?
   A      B           C             D             E            F                   End
1
2        Speedy Airlines: Per Quarter Employee Sick Days                           ▲
3                                                                                   ▼
4        Employee Name     1st Q         2nd Q         3rd Q        4th Q
5        ------------------------------------------------------------------       Esc
6        Danielle          2             1             1            1
7        Morgan            3             2             1            1              ↵
8        Roger             2             5             1            2
9                          ------------------------------------------------       Del
10       Total Days:    +C6+C7+C8     +D6+D7+D8   @SUM(E6..E8)  @SUM(F6..F8)
11                                                                                  @
12
13
14                                                                                  5
15
16                                                                                  6
17
18                                                                                  7
19
20
SPEEDY2.WQ1   [1]                                                           READY
```

Figure 3.7 shows the results of moving data referenced in spreadsheet formulas. Two types of formulas appear in this figure: individual cell addresses connected by mathematical operators (1st and 2nd Q) and @function commands (3rd and 4th Q). Quattro Pro moves each type of formula differently.

In the 1st Q column, the 3 in cell C7 is moved to cell C12. Quattro Pro adjusts the original cell reference (C7) in the formula to reflect the new location of the data in cell C12.

In the 2nd Q column, the 2 in cell D7 is moved to cell D8. Quattro Pro overwrites the data in cell D8, causing ERR to appear in the formula. In any formula, when you overwrite a cell reference with another cell reference, Quattro Pro displays ERR, indicating an invalid formula. To correct the formula, re-enter a valid address.)

In the 3rd Q column, the 1 in cell E7 is moved to cell E12. Because cell E7 is not specifically referenced in the formula, Quattro Pro does not adjust this cell reference to reflect the data's new location. The program continues to

```
 File   Edit   Style   Graph   Print   Database   Tools   Options   Window      ↑↓
A1: [W2]                                                                       ?
 ▊  A ░░  B         C           D           E           F                   End
1
2      Speedy Airlines: Per Quarter Employee Sick Days                        ▲
3                                                                            ◄│▶
4      Employee Name     1st Q       2nd Q       3rd Q       4th Q            ▼
5      ────────────────────────────────────────────────────────
6      Danielle            2           1           1           1            Esc
7      Morgan                                                  1
8      Roger               2           2           1                        ↵
9      ────────────────────────────────────────────────────────
10     Total Days:     +C6+C12+C8  +D6+D8+ERR  @SUM(E6..E8) @SUM(F6..F12)    Del
11
12                         3                       1           2             @
13
14                                                                          5
15
16                                                                          6
17
18                                                                          7
19
20                                                                           ↓
◄ ▪                                                                     ▶
SPEEDY2.WQ1   [1]                          CIRC                        READY
```

Fig. 3.7
The results of
moving a cell
referenced in a
formula.

add the numbers appearing in cell block E6..E8, but the formula result now equals 2 instead of 3.

In the 4th Q column, the 2 in cell F8 is moved to cell F12. Because F8 is one of the two coordinates in the cell block (F6 is the other coordinate), Quattro Pro adjusts the formula to include cell F12. If you move a cell listed in a formula as a coordinate in a cell block, Quattro Pro changes the formula to reflect the new coordinate location.

Tip	Be careful when using the **Move** command on a cell address that also is a cell block coordinate in a formula. If you move the cell address in such a way that the adjusted cell block now includes the formula's cell address, you create a circular reference. In a circular reference, the result changes each time you press F9 because the formula includes its own result in the calculation. Quattro Pro displays the CIRC indicator on the status line when the program encounters a circular reference in a formula.

Erasing the Contents of a Cell

The **Erase Block** command erases data from one cell, a group of cells, or every cell on the spreadsheet. Erasing data from a cell on a Quattro Pro spreadsheet is like pressing F2 and deleting the characters on the input line. When you erase a value from a formatted cell, Quattro Pro removes only the contents of the cell—not the cell format or alignment settings. If you do not need to save cell formats and you want to erase the entire contents of a spreadsheet, selecting the /**File Erase** command is easier. You cannot erase cell data when spreadsheet protection is activated with the /**Options** **Protec-**tion command (see Chapter 7).

As with the Copy and Move commands, you can erase spreadsheet data more quickly when you preselect the source cell and then choose the command. To erase the contents of a cell, follow these steps:

1. Make the cell you want to delete the active cell.

2. Choose **Erase Block** from the Edit menu.

3. When Quattro Pro displays the source cell address, press Enter.

Tip | Press Ctrl-E, the Ctrl-key shortcut for the /**Edit Erase Block** command to quickly execute an erase block operation. You also can use the Del key to erase data from a cell. Pick a cell to erase, make this cell the active cell, and press Del. Use the Del key to erase one cell and the /**Edit Erase Block** command to erase multiple cells.

Reversing Operations with Undo

When you forget to save a spreadsheet file after a Quattro Pro work session, all of your work goes down the drain. If you have experienced this horror, then you also have probably accidentally erased data on your spreadsheet, deleted the wrong row or column, or executed a command on the wrong spreadsheet cell.

Fortunately, Quattro Pro has a built-in protection mechanism that enables you to recall the most recent changes made to a cell or reverse the most recent menu command execution. When you need to undo an operation, press Alt-F5, the Quattro Pro Undo key.

The Undo facility is activated by choosing /**Options Other Undo Enable**. If you choose /**Options Update**, Quattro Pro enables the Undo key each time you load the program.

Inserting and Deleting
Rows and Columns

Use the /**Edit Insert** and /**Edit Delete** commands to add and remove rows and columns from a spreadsheet. When you delete a row or column, you delete all the data in the row or column. Before you use the /Edit Delete command, scan the target row or column for data you want to keep.

You can use two ways to scan a row or column before executing the Delete command. The most direct way is to use the cursor-movement keys or the Tab and PgDn keys to move around a row or column. This method works well when you don't have much territory to cover but becomes tedious when you need to look at several screens.

The second method enables you to locate data in a row or column quickly in any part of a spreadsheet. To use this method, do the following:

1. Place the cell selector in row 1 of any column or in column A of any row.

2. Press End on your numeric keypad to enter END mode.

3. Press the right-arrow key to search a column or the down-arrow key to search a row. The cell selector moves to the first piece of data Quattro Pro locates. If you find yourself at column IV or in row 8,192, Quattro Pro did not find any data, and you can delete that row or column.

When you choose /Edit Insert, a submenu appears, enabling you to select rows or columns for insertion into the spreadsheet. Quattro Pro inserts a row above the cursor and inserts a column to the left of the cursor.

When you choose /Edit Delete, a submenu also appears, enabling you to specify how many rows or columns to delete from the spreadsheet. Quattro Pro deletes a row or column at the cursor.

Inserting a Row

To insert rows, Quattro Pro needs to know where to begin inserting and how many rows to insert. To insert one row, do the following:

1. Place the cursor in the row below where you want to insert a row.

2. Choose /Edit Insert Rows.

3. Press Enter.

Tip | Press Ctrl-I, the Ctrl-key shortcut for the /Edit Insert command, to quickly execute an insert operation.

To insert multiple rows, do the following:

1. Place the cursor in the row below where you want multiple rows inserted.

2. Choose /**Edit Insert R**ows.

3. Press the down-arrow key until you highlight the number of rows you want inserted or type a valid cell block including all the row numbers.

   For example, type *D6..D8* and press Enter to insert three rows.

4. Press Enter.

Deleting a Row

To delete rows, Quattro Pro needs to know where to begin deleting and how many rows to delete. To delete one row, follow these steps:

1. Place the cursor in the row you want to delete.

2. Choose /**Edit Delete R**ows.

3. Press Enter.

To delete multiple rows, do the following:

1. Place the cursor in the first row you want deleted.

2. Choose /**Edit Delete R**ows.

3. Press the up- or down-arrow key until you highlight the number of rows you want deleted or type a valid cell block including the row numbers.

   For example, type *D6..D8* and press Enter to delete three rows.

4. Press Enter.

Inserting a Column

To insert columns, Quattro Pro needs to know where to begin inserting and how many columns to insert. To insert one column, follow these steps:

1. Place the cursor in the column left of where you want a column inserted.

2. Choose /**E**dit **I**nsert **C**olumns (or press Ctrl-IC).

3. Press Enter.

To insert multiple columns, follow these steps:

1. Place the cursor in the column left of where you want columns inserted.

2. Choose /**E**dit **I**nsert **C**olumns (or press Ctrl-IC).

3. Press the left- or right-arrow key until you highlight the number of columns you want inserted or type a valid cell block including the column letters.

   For example, type *D6..F6* and press Enter to insert three columns.

4. Press Enter.

Deleting a Column

To delete columns, Quattro Pro needs to know where to begin deleting and how many columns to delete. To delete one column, do the following:

1. Place the cursor in the column you want deleted.

2. Choose /**E**dit **D**elete **C**olumns.

3. Press Enter.

To delete multiple columns, do the following:

1. Place the cursor in the first column you want deleted.

2. Choose /**E**dit **D**elete **C**olumns.

3. Press the right-arrow key until you highlight the number of columns you want deleted or type a valid cell block including the column letters.

   For example, type *D6..F6* and press Enter to delete three columns.

4. Press Enter.

Working with Blocks of Cell Data

In addition to working with single cells, the **C**opy, **M**ove, **E**rase Block, **I**nsert, and **D**elete commands also operate on blocks of cells. When you choose one of these five commands, Quattro Pro displays the source cell as a cell block (A1..A1, for example). As you highlight cells, the program changes the display to reflect the new block (A1..D9, for example), giving you the flexibility to work with one, many, or all of the cells on the spreadsheet. You can move large chunks of data, copy an entire document onto a new spreadsheet, or delete large blocks of data from the active spreadsheet.

Quattro Pro's Edit menu has several other commands that operate on cell blocks. These commands, covered at the end of this chapter, enable you to fill, transpose, and search and replace data in cell blocks. Chapter 2 covers the procedure for selecting a block.

Copying a Block

When you copy a block of cells, highlight the cell block before choosing the command. For example, to copy the contents of cell block A1..A5 into cell block D1..D5, you follow these steps:

1. Make cell A1 the active cell and press Shift-F7 to enter the EXT (extend block) mode.

2. Using the cursor-movement keys, highlight cell A5. (Quattro Pro highlights the cell block A1..A5.)

3. Choose Copy from the Edit menu and type *D1..D5* as the destination cell block.

4. Press Enter.

Tip | You can preselect an entire cell block quickly with a mouse. Point at the first cell in the block, click and hold the left mouse button while you drag the mouse through the source range. When you reach the last cell in the block, release the left mouse button. Press /**EC** to begin the copy operation, and Quattro Pro uses the highlighted block as the source cell block. Point the mouse arrow at the first cell in the destination block and press Enter, and Quattro Pro copies the block.

Moving a Block

When you move a block of cells, preselect the cell block before choosing the **Move** command. For example, to move the contents of cell block A1..A5 into cell block D1..D5, follow these steps:

1. Make cell A1 the active cell and press Shift-F7 to enter the EXT (extend block) mode.

2. Using the cursor-movement keys, highlight cell A5. (Quattro Pro highlights the cell block A1..A5.)

3. Choose **M**ove from the Edit menu and type *D1..D5* as the destination cell block.

4. Press Enter.

Tip You can abbreviate the destination cell block used in Quattro Pro menu commands by typing the first coordinate in the cell block. For example, you can type *D1* instead of *D1..D5* in step 3. When you abbreviate the destination cell block, Quattro Pro assumes that you want the destination cell block to have the same block shape as the source cell block.

Erasing a Block

When you erase a block of cells, highlight the cell block before you choose the command. For example, to erase the contents of cell block D1..D5, follow these steps:

1. Make cell D1 the active cell and press Shift-F7 to enter the EXT (extend block) mode or use your mouse to highlight the block.

2. Using the cursor-movement keys, highlight cell D5. (Quattro Pro highlights cell block D1..D5.)

3. Choose **E**rase Block from the Edit menu.

Tip In an **E**rase Block operation, you have no destination cell block. When you choose this command, Quattro Pro erases the source cell block.

Naming a Block

Quattro Pro recognizes different areas of the spreadsheet in three ways. A cell address tells you the exact location of data on a spreadsheet. A cell block displays the first and last cell address in a block of data. These two coordinates enable you to figure out the addresses of all the cells in a block.

The **Names** command assigns text names to cell addresses and cell blocks to create a third type of spreadsheet area: cell block names. You can use cell block names instead of cell addresses in Quattro Pro menu commands and formulas. You can remember a cell block name more easily than you remember a cell block's coordinates. You can create, delete, reset, and make tables of names using the commands found on the **Names** submenu (see fig. 3.8).

Fig. 3.8
The /Edit Names command submenu enables you to create, delete, reset, and make tables of cell block names.

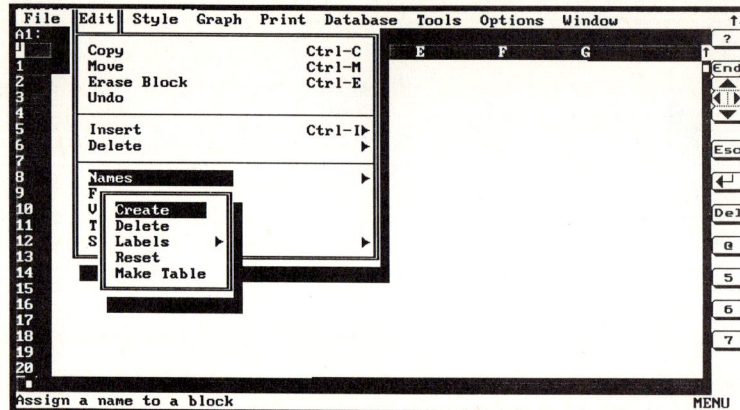

Creating Names

When you create cell block names, you must remember four rules:

1. A valid name can refer to a cell, a cell block, or the entire spreadsheet.

2. Valid names can be up to 15 characters in length.

3. Cell block names can contain any of the characters located on your keyboard. You can use the punctuation characters and the mathematical symbols in a name, but you remember names more easily if you stick to letters.

4. You can combine names, cell addresses, and cell blocks in a formula; create two or more names for the same cell block; and create names for cell blocks with overlapping cell addresses. Figure 3.9 shows examples of valid spreadsheet names.

To create a name for cell block A25..D50, do the following:

1. Make cell A25 the active cell and press Shift-F7 to enter the EXT (extend block) mode (or use your mouse to highlight the block).

2. Using the cursor-movement keys, highlight cell D50. (Quattro Pro highlights cell block A25..D50.)

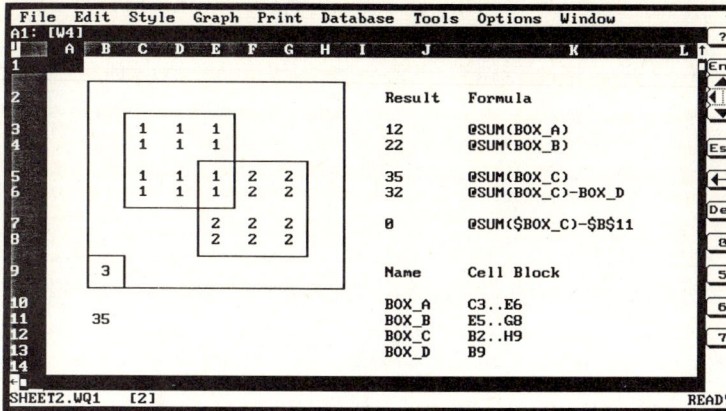

Fig. 3.9
Cell block names can refer to a cell, a cell block, or the whole spreadsheet.

3. Choose /**E**dit **N**ames **C**reate. Quattro Pro prompts you for a block name.

4. Type a valid name and press Enter.

5. Type the coordinates of the cell block you want to name.

6. Press Enter.

Tip Quattro Pro updates a formula when you create a name to replace a cell address or cell block referenced in the formula (see fig. 3.10). For example, if you create the name 1STQ for an existing formula reference such as C6..C8, Quattro Pro substitutes 1STQ for C6..C8 in the formula. If you delete the name 1STQ later, Quattro Pro replaces 1STQ in the formula with the original cell block C6..C8.

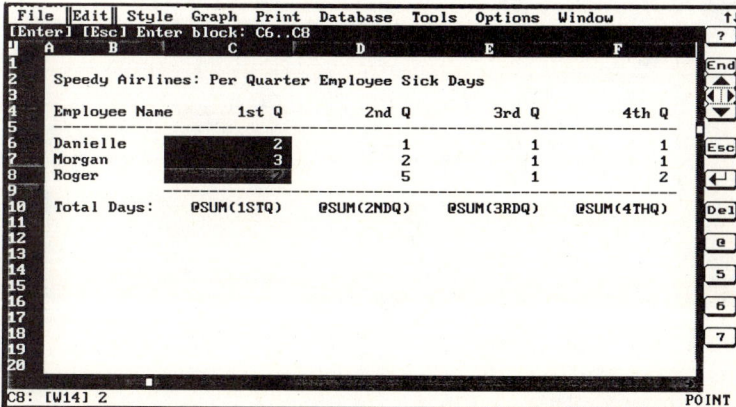

Fig. 3.10
Quattro Pro substitutes a name for a cell block address.

Each time you create a name, Quattro Pro stores the name with the active spreadsheet. After you create the first name on each spreadsheet or each time you modify an existing name, Quattro Pro displays a list of stored names for the active spreadsheet. The number of names you can create for a spreadsheet is limited only by the amount of memory your PC has.

Deleting Names

When you modify and update spreadsheets, you sometimes need to delete names. To remove a stored name from a spreadsheet, use the **Delete** command.

If you delete a named cell block, Quattro Pro keeps the name but removes its cell block assignment when you delete the block. If you delete a name assigned to a cell block, Quattro Pro removes the name from the block names list and redisplays the block address in each formula that originally contained the name.

Tip | When you press F2 to edit a formula containing a name, Quattro Pro displays the cell addresses rather than the stored name on the input line; you immediately know to which cells the name refers. While in EDIT mode, the status line displays the formula with the block name.

The best way to remove a cell block name is to choose the **Delete** command from the Names menu (see fig. 3.11).

Fig. 3.11
You can use the Delete command to remove a cell block name.

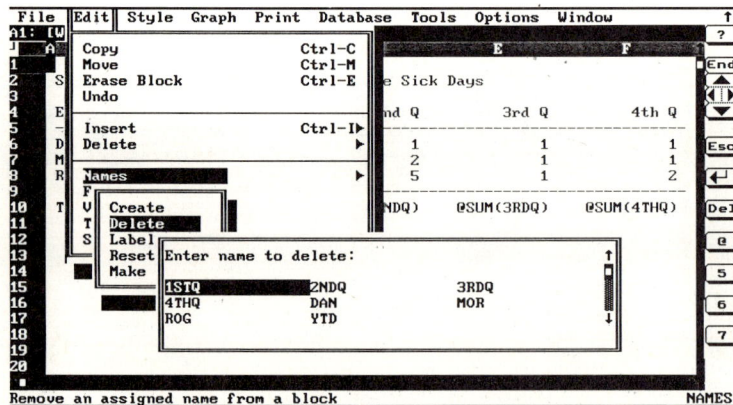

To delete a cell block name, do the following:

1. Choose /**Edit** Names **Delete**. Quattro Pro displays the block names list and prompts you for a block name.

2. Type a valid name or press the cursor-movement keys until you highlight the block you want to delete.

3. Press Enter.

Tip

When you create more block names than Quattro Pro can display on the block names list, you can press F2 and enter a search string. Quattro Pro displays a `Search For *` message on the status line at the bottom of your screen. Press as many letters as are necessary to identify the block name. Press Enter to move the highlight bar to the first name on the list that matches the search string.

Using Labels To Create Names

The **Labels** command quickly creates names for rows and columns of data. This command is useful when you want to use labels on a spreadsheet as the names for a group of values appearing in adjacent cells. For example, the **Labels** command is useful if you want to create names for the values in cell block G5..G9 using the labels appearing in the adjacent cell block F5..F9 (see fig. 3.12). Here, Quattro Pro assigns the name SECTOR 1 to cell G5, SECTOR 2 to cell G6, SECTOR 3 to cell G7, and so on.

The **Labels** command is similar to the **Create** command, except that the **Labels** command operates on only a group of cells appearing in two adjacent columns or rows.

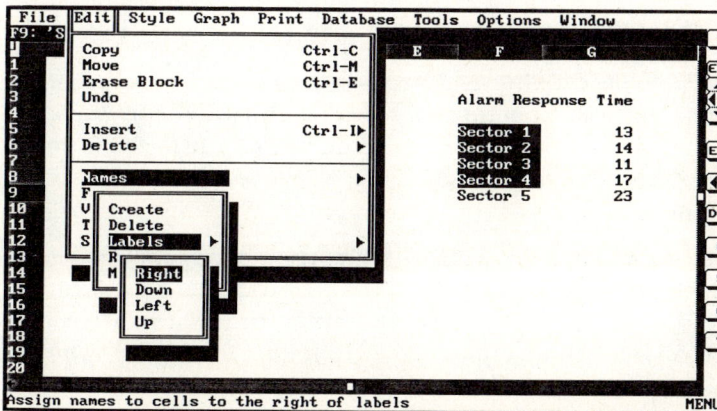

Fig. 3.12
You can create names with the Labels command.

To create names from the labels shown in figure 3.12, do the following:

1. Make cell F5 the active cell and press Shift-F7 to enter the EXT (extend block) mode (or use your mouse to highlight the block).

2. Using the cursor-movement keys, highlight cell F9. (Quattro Pro highlights cell block F5..F9.)

3. Choose /**E**dit **N**ames **L**abels. Quattro Pro displays the Label submenu.

4. Select the **R**ight option. (This choice describes the relative location of the cells to the labels.)

Quattro Pro assigns each label name in column F to the corresponding value in column G.

Resetting Cell Block Names

Sometimes deleting all names from the active spreadsheet is easier than creating names and then deleting the old ones. Suppose that you assign 20 names using the **L**abels command. Later you decide to change the names of the spreadsheet labels. Before you use the **L**abels command to assign new names to the spreadsheet, delete all of the old names and start with a clean slate.

To delete all the names from the spreadsheet, choose the **R**eset command on the /**E**dit **N**ames submenu. The **R**eset command is like the **D**elete command except that the **R**eset command operates on all of the names on the active spreadsheet. When you choose this command, Quattro Pro displays the prompt, `Delete all named blocks?`. Press **N**o to cancel the operation or **Y**es to erase all names from the spreadsheet.

Making a Table of Names

As you build more sophisticated spreadsheets, using names instead of numbers makes creating and remembering formulas much easier. For example, the formula @SUM (EXPENSE) comes to mind more easily than the formula @SUM(F12..F15). If you frequently use names, you need to know how to quickly review all stored names.

The **M**ake **T**able command copies a list of the current spreadsheet's names and their cell block assignments onto the active spreadsheet in a location you specify. Be careful not to overwrite data on the spreadsheet when you execute this command. When determining where to place the table, remember that Quattro Pro requires two columns (one for names and one for cell blocks assignments) and as many rows as names (see fig. 3.13).

```
 File ‖Edit‖ Style  Graph  Print  Database  Tools  Options  Window
[Enter] [Esc] Enter block: G12
   A        B            C              F        G        H
1
2     Speedy Airlines: Per Quarter
3
4     Employee Name       1st Q          4th Q      YTD
5
6     Danielle             2              1          5
7     Morgan               3              1          7
8     Roger                2              2         10
9
10    Total Days:    @SUM(1STQ)   @SUM(4THQ) @SUM(YTD)
11
12                                          1STQ    C6..C8
13                                          2NDQ    D6..D8
14                                          3RDQ    E6..E8
15.                                         4THQ    F6..F8
16                                          DAN     C6..F6
17                                          MOR     C7..F7
18                                          ROG     C8..F8
19                                          YTD     G6..G8
20
G12: [W10] '1STQ                                              POI
```

Fig. 3.13
The Make Table command copies cell block names to a designated location.

To make the table of names shown in this figure, do the following:

1. Make cell G12 the active cell.

2. Choose /Edit Names Make Table.

3. Press Enter to copy the table into the active spreadsheet, beginning in cell G12.

Keep a table of cell block names somewhere on the spreadsheet. When you add or change a name, choose the Make Table command to update your list because Quattro Pro does not perform automatic updates.

Tip | If you copy the names table into a column with a narrow width, Quattro Pro may display asterisks in either table column. In this event, you need to widen the column. Press Ctrl-W (or choose /Edit Column Width) and widen the column until the data reappears.

Quattro Pro also enables you to view stored names on-screen while you are building or editing formulas. To view stored names, do the following:

1. When in EDIT mode, place the edit cursor next to an open parenthesis.

2. Press F3, and Quattro Pro displays the block names list (see figure 3.14).

3. Press the Expand key (+) to see the block coordinates for each cell.

4. Press the Contract key (−) to remove this display from your screen.

5. Press F3 again. Quattro Pro displays a full-screen list of the stored names (see fig. 3.15).

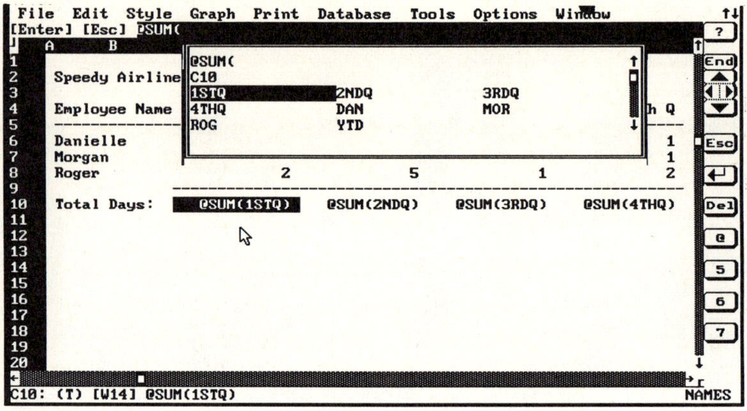

Fig. 3.14
Quattro Pro
displays a block
names list when
you press F3 at
an open
parenthesis.

Fig. 3.15
Press F3 again
to fill the
window with
the block
names list.

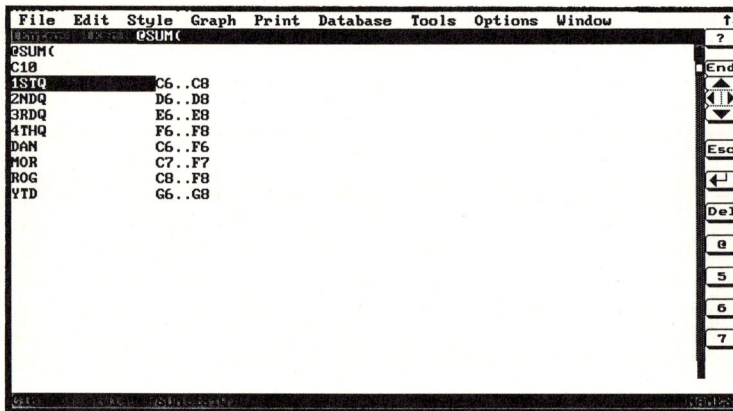

Using Names in Formulas

You know that you can substitute names in place of cell blocks in formulas. Figure 3.13 shows @function commands that contain names instead of cell block coordinates. To create the formula shown in cell C10, do the following:

1. Make cell C10 the active cell.

2. Type *@SUM(* and press F3 to display the block names list.

3. Highlight 1STQ on the list and press Enter to copy the name to the right of the open parenthesis on the input line.

4. Type *)* and press Enter to store the formula in cell C10.

You can build formulas using this method as long as you define the block names first.

Filling a Block with Numbers

When you use a spreadsheet as a reporting tool, it is common practice to order your data according to a date, a transaction number, or an invoice number. For example, to create a check register, use the /**Edit Fill** command to assign a unique number to each transaction. You also can use the **Fill** command to create a series of incremental dates.

The /**Edit Fill** command simplifies the process of entering a large number of sequential values onto a spreadsheet. Using this command, you can enter numbers, formulas, and dates.

To fill numbers into a cell block, do the following:

1. Choose /**Edit Names Fill**. Quattro Pro highlights the active cell as the default destination cell block.

2. Enter a new destination cell block or press the cursor-movement keys to extend the current block. Press Enter.

3. If you are entering sequential dates, press Ctrl-D, enter a start date (in the form, MM/DD/YY), and press Enter; if you are not entering sequential dates, skip to the next step.

4. Enter a step value and press Enter.

5. Enter a stop value and press Enter.

In a fill operation, the *start value* is the value that Quattro Pro places in the first cell of the destination block; the *step value* is the amount by which Quattro Pro increases or decreases the series values; and the *stop value* is the value that Quattro Pro places in the last cell of the destination block.

If you define a destination cell block with two or more columns, Quattro Pro fills in each row in the first column before entering data into the second column, and so on. You also can fill numbers in ascending and descending order by altering the step value (see fig. 3.16).

Changing Formulas to Values

The /**Edit Values** command converts a formula into the result, displays the result as a numerical value, and erases the original formula from the spreadsheet. Although the need for this type of operation may not be obvious, the **Values** command plays an important part in the process of maintaining and modifying your spreadsheet applications.

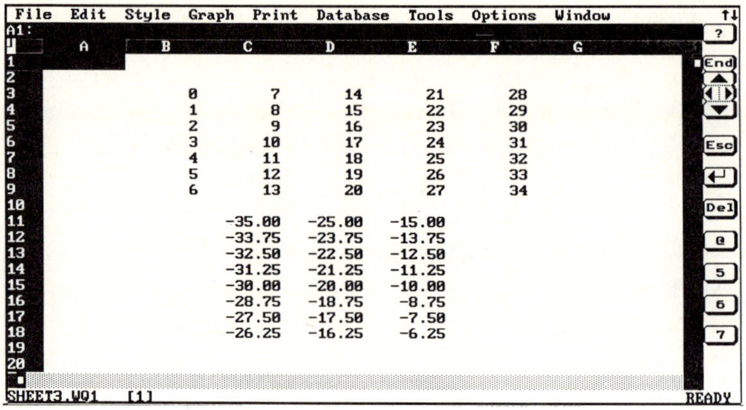

Fig. 3.16
You can fill in cell blocks with ascending and descending numbers.

```
 File   Edit   Style   Graph   Print   Database   Tools   Options   Window        ↑↓
A1:                                                                              ?
      A         B        C         D         E         F         G
1                                                                              End
2
3                 0        7        14        21        28
4                 1        8        15        22        29
5                 2        9        16        23        30
6                 3       10        17        24        31              Esc
7                 4       11        18        25        32
8                 5       12        19        26        33              ↵
9                 6       13        20        27        34
10                                                                     Del
11                     -35.00    -25.00    -15.00
12                     -33.75    -23.75    -13.75                       0
13                     -32.50    -22.50    -12.50
14                     -31.25    -21.25    -11.25                       5
15                     -30.00    -20.00    -10.00
16                     -28.75    -18.75     -8.75                       6
17                     -27.50    -17.50     -7.50
18                     -26.25    -16.25     -6.25                       7
19
20
SHEET3.WQ1    [1]                                                      READY
```

Spreadsheet formulas calculate answers to problems such as, "What is the value of cell C10 plus the value of cell C11?" If you create a formula that produces one answer, and the answer probably will not change, convert the formula to this value. For example, if the value of C10 plus the value of C11 equals 10 and probably always will equal 10, convert the formula C10+C11 to the value 10. This conversion frees memory for Quattro Pro to use for other areas of the spreadsheet in which you have on-going calculations.

Formulas also pinpoint important relationships among two or more variables such as, "What is the ratio of profits to sales for 1989?" You can use one spreadsheet to process your yearly financial data and another to record year-end historical data. The ratio information appears on a second historical report listing key financial ratios. Because last year's financial data is definitely not going to change this year, transfer the ratios as values to the second spreadsheet.

To change formulas to values, follow these steps:

1. Make the first cell in the target block the active cell.

2. Press Shift-F7 to enter the EXT (extend block) mode (or use your mouse to highlight the block.)

3. Using the cursor-movement keys, highlight the last cell in the target block. (Quattro Pro highlights the entire cell block.)

4. Choose /**Edit Values**, and Quattro Pro records the location of the target block.

5. Move the cell selector to the first cell in the destination block.

6. Press Enter to copy the formula results as values into the destination cell block.

Transposing Data in a Cell Block

Another way to manipulate data on a Quattro Pro spreadsheet is by using *transposition*. When you transpose spreadsheet data, you switch the organization of your column and row data. This command is useful after you create a spreadsheet application and decide that the data makes more sense if organized differently.

Use the following guidelines to ensure that your cell block data transposes correctly.

When transposing formatted cell data, you generally should execute this command before formatting your spreadsheet column width. If you already formatted your spreadsheet's column width, your transposed data probably doesn't fit neatly into the current cell widths. Press Ctrl-W to change the column widths until all transposed data appears.

Be sure to transpose a cell block to a different part of the spreadsheet. If you attempt to transpose a cell block onto itself, Quattro Pro loses the column and row organization and shows a block of garbled numbers. After executing the **Edit Transpose** command, you can move or copy the transposed block anywhere on the spreadsheet.

If you try to transpose relative reference formulas, the formulas adjust incorrectly and do not refer to the right cell addresses. You have two options when you want to transpose blocks containing formulas: change all relative references into absolute references and edit them after transposition or use the /**Edit Values** command to convert cell block formulas to computed values.

When you transpose a block of cells, preselect the cell block before choosing the command. Suppose that you want to transpose the contents of cell block A1..D10 into cell A12. To do so, follow these steps:

1. Choose /**Edit Transpose**. (Quattro Pro recognizes A1..D10 as the default cell block.)

2. Type *A12* (or enter another destination cell block at least one column to the right or one row below the source cell block).

3. Press Enter to transpose information into the destination cell block.

Figure 3.17 displays an original and transposed cell block. Notice that the current column width does not accommodate the transposed data.

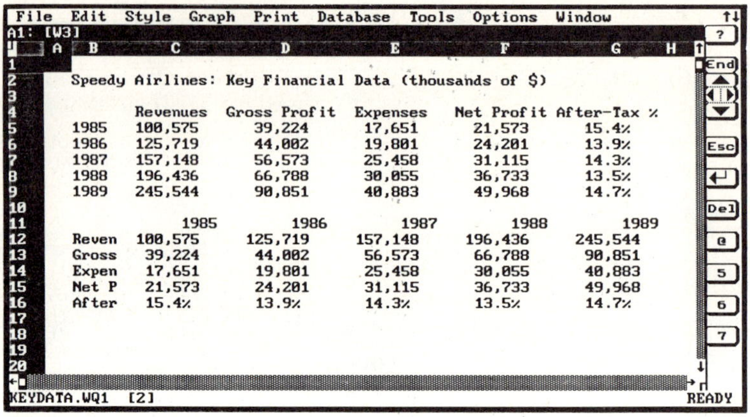

Fig. 3.17
Transposing cell
blocks switches
the column and
row organiza-
tion.

```
 File   Edit   Style   Graph   Print   Database   Tools   Options   Window        ↑↓
A1: [W3]                                                                           ?
 ⊔    A  B      C        D         E           F          G        H    ↑        End
 1
 2      Speedy Airlines: Key Financial Data (thousands of $)                      ▲
 3                                                                                ◀█▶
 4             Revenues  Gross Profit  Expenses   Net Profit After-Tax %          ▼
 5      1985   100,575    39,224       17,651     21,573     15.4%
 6      1986   125,719    44,002       19,801     24,201     13.9%                Esc
 7      1987   157,148    56,573       25,458     31,115     14.3%
 8      1988   196,436    66,788       30,055     36,733     13.5%                ↵
 9      1989   245,544    90,851       40,883     49,968     14.7%
10                                                                               Del
11             1985       1986         1987       1988       1989
12      Reven  100,575    125,719      157,148    196,436    245,544              @
13      Gross  39,224     44,002       56,573     66,788     90,851
14      Expen  17,651     19,801       25,458     30,055     40,883               5
15      Net P  21,573     24,201       31,115     36,733     49,968
16      After  15.4%      13.9%        14.3%      13.5%      14.7%                 6
17
18                                                                                7
19
20
 ⊔█                                                                          →┐
KEYDATA.WQ1  [2]                                                              READY
```

Searching for and Replacing Data

After you enter, edit, display, reorganize, insert, delete, and transpose your spreadsheet data, you may need to search quickly through a large application, replacing letters and numbers with new or updated data. You need Quattro Pro's Search and Replace command.

To use the Search and Replace command, you must tell Quattro Pro what to look for, where to look for the information, and what to replace the searched for item with. If you need to create specialized search conditions, you can further refine the search operation by setting the commands found in the Options section of the Search and Replace submenu.

Figure 3.18 shows the mission statement for Speedy Airlines. A quick review of this document reveals that a few crucial phrases have been omitted. You can use the Search and Replace command to get Speedy back on the right runway.

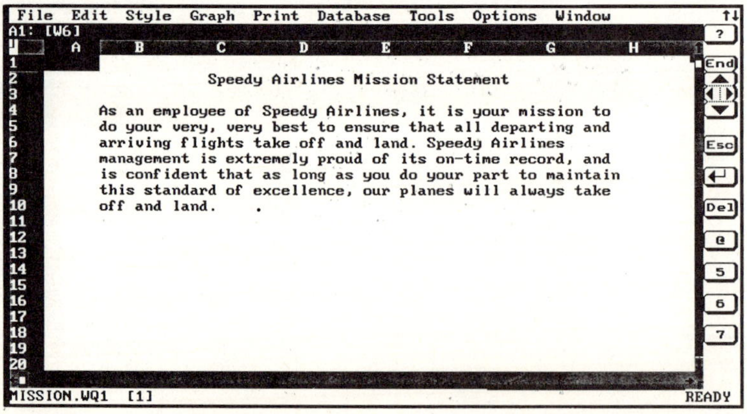

Fig. 3.18
Speedy Airlines'
mission state-
ment.

```
 File   Edit   Style   Graph   Print   Database   Tools   Options   Window        ↑↓
A1: [W6]                                                                           ?
 ⊔    A      B       C        D        E        F        G        H    ↑        End
 1
 2                  Speedy Airlines Mission Statement                             ◀█▶
 3                                                                                ▼
 4           As an employee of Speedy Airlines, it is your mission to
 5           do your very, very best to ensure that all departing and
 6           arriving flights take off and land. Speedy Airlines                  Esc
 7           management is extremely proud of its on-time record, and
 8           is confident that as long as you do your part to maintain            ↵
 9           this standard of excellence, our planes will always take
10           off and land.         .                                             Del
11
12                                                                                @
13
14                                                                                5
15
16                                                                                6
17
18                                                                                7
19
20
 ⊔█                                                                          →┐
MISSION.WQ1  [1]                                                             READY
```

Setting the Search Parameters

With the Search and Replace command, you quickly can update key label descriptions, revise out-of-date numbers, and alter the structure of your spreadsheet formulas. You have complete flexibility to devise the scope of a search-and-replace operation because Quattro Pro enables you to define the parameters on the menu shown in figure 3.19.

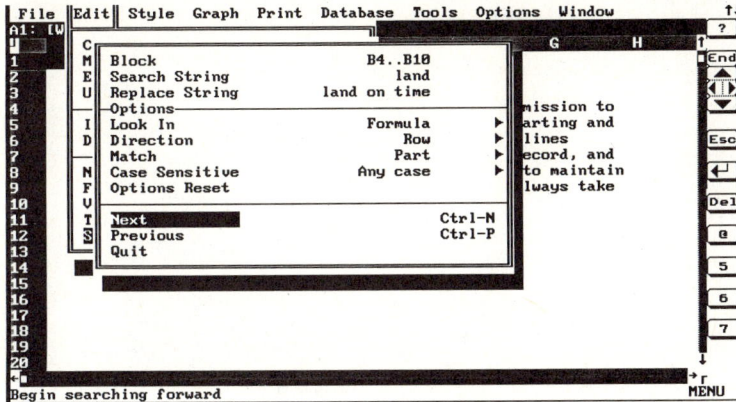

Fig. 3.19 Setting the parameters for Speedy Airlines' search-and-replace operation.

Choosing a Block

By default, Quattro Pro scans the entire spreadsheet for your search data. For large spreadsheet applications, you should restrict the search area to minimize the potential search time.

Suppose that you want to search the text appearing in cell block B4..B10. To do so, follow these steps:

1. Choose /**E**dit **S**earch & Replace **B**lock.

2. Enter *B4..B10*.

3. Press Enter to store the cell block.

Entering a Search String

A crucial phrase, "on time," is missing from two sentences in Speedy's mission statement. In both sentences, "land" is the last word before where "on time" should be added. "Land," therefore, becomes the search string.

To enter *land* as the search string, do the following:

1. Choose **S**earch String.

2. Enter *land*.

3. Press Enter to store the search string.

Entering a Replacement String

To enter *on time* as the replacement string, do the following:

1. Choose **R**eplace String.

2. Enter *on time*.

3. Press Enter to store the replacement string.

Executing the Search Operation

The minimum information needed to execute a search and replace operation is the search and replace string. With this data, Quattro Pro can begin scanning the spreadsheet. Choose **N**ext from the Search and Replace submenu, and Quattro Pro locates the first occurrence of the string. When Quattro Pro locates a valid matching string, the program displays the prompt menu shown in figure 3.20.

Fig. 3.20
Quattro Pro
prompts you to
replace the
string.

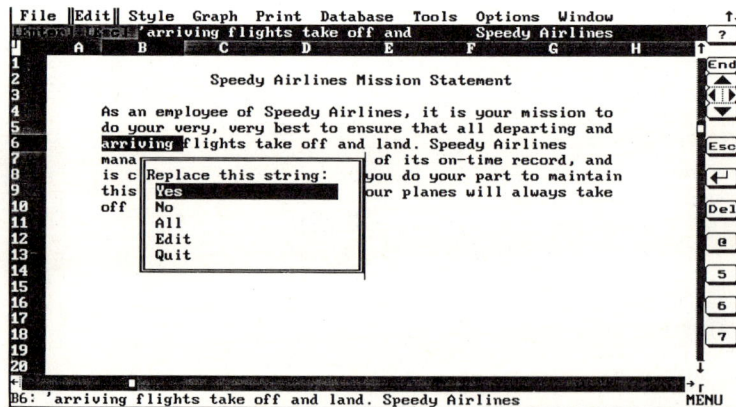

Select **Y**es to replace the string, **N**o to not replace the current string, **A**ll to replace the current string and all other matching strings without further prompting, **E**dit to edit the current string, and **Q**uit to cancel the operation without replacing the current string.

Select **A**ll for the Speedy Airlines example to replace both occurrences of the string without further prompting.

After Quattro Pro concludes the search and replace operation, the program returns you to the active spreadsheet and makes the first cell address in the defined block the active cell, B4 (see fig. 3.21).

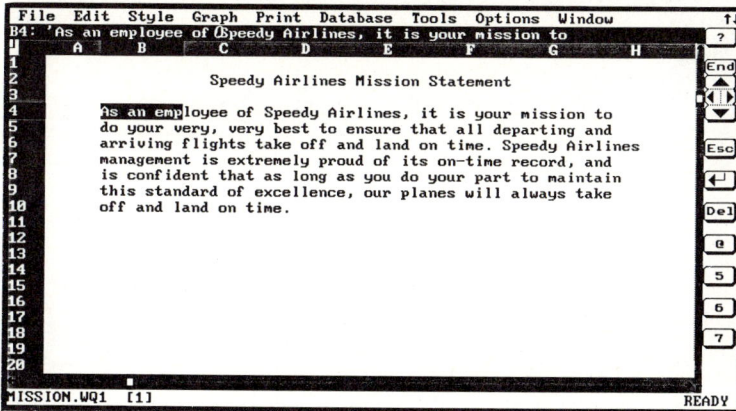

Fig. 3.21 The revised mission statement for Speedy Airlines.

The Options area in the middle of the Search and Replace menu contains five special parameters that you can use to further delineate how Quattro Pro evaluates your spreadsheet data in a search-and-replace operation (see fig. 3.19).

Choose **L**ook In to tell Quattro Pro to review each **F**ormula, each **V**alue, or to set a search string **C**ondition such as all cell values equal to 100 (?=100).

Choose **D**irection to indicate that Quattro Pro should search by **R**ow or by **C**olumn.

Choose **M**atch to tell Quattro Pro whether to locate a search string as part of a **W**hole string or as **P**art of any string containing the search string.

Choose **C**ase Sensitive to tell Quattro Pro whether to look for a string whose capitalization exactly matches the search string or to accept **A**ny Case.

Choose **O**ptions Reset to erase all of the settings that Quattro Pro stores on the right side of the Search and Replace menu. When you choose this command, Quattro Pro returns to the default search-and-replace settings.

Questions & Answers

This chapter introduces you to the fundamental Quattro Pro cell block operations and spreadsheet sculpting techniques. If you have questions about any of the topics covered in this chapter, scan this section.

Copying, Moving, and Erasing Cell Data

Q: When do you preselect a cell block?

A: You may preselect cells prior to choosing any Quattro Pro menu command that performs an operation on a block. If you use a mouse, always preselect cells. If you execute commands from your keyboard, whether or not you preselect depends on how quickly you can extend a block in EXT mode.

Q: Why did a formula's result change when I copied it to a different part of the spreadsheet?

A: You used **Copy** instead of **Move**. When you move a formula, Quattro Pro does not adjust the formula's cell references, and the result does not change. When you copy a formula, Quattro Pro adjusts the cell references in the formula—unless you previously changed the formula to all absolute references.

Press Alt-F5 to undo the operation and choose /**Edit Move**.

Q: Why did my formulas display ERR after I moved a cell on the spreadsheet.

A: You probably wrote over data in a cell referenced by other formulas on the active spreadsheet. If you cause one cell to display ERR and that cell's address appears in other spreadsheet formulas, the other formulas also display ERR.

Press Alt-F5 to undo the operation and choose a new destination cell for the Move operation.

Q: When does it make sense to use the Del key instead of the **Erase Block** command?

A: When you want to remove data from a cell and preserve its format and alignment settings, choose **Erase Block**. When you want to remove data from a cell without preserving the settings, use the Del key. To delete a block of cells, preselect the block and press Del.

Inserting and Deleting Columns and Rows

Q: Why can't I insert a column (or row) on my active spreadsheet?

A: Quattro Pro cannot insert a column or row when data is in the last column or row of the spreadsheet; the program has no room.

Q: What do I do if I deleted a column (or row) containing data I need, and my spreadsheet is displaying ERR everywhere?

A: You deleted a column (or row) containing a cell block coordinate being used in your spreadsheet formulas.

Press Alt-F5 to Undo the operation.

Naming Cell Blocks

Q: Why won't one of my spreadsheet formulas accept a block name that I created?

A: If you create a name for a block of cells and try to use that name in certain mathematical operations, Quattro Pro displays an error message saying that the block is invalid.

If BLOCK is the name for C5..C10 and you attempt to enter the formula +*BLOCK*+*25*, Quattro Pro displays an error message. A cell block name describes an area—it does not compute a value unless you tell it to. For example, the same formula is valid when you include BLOCK in an @function command, such as @SUM(BLOCK)+25.

Q: When I copied a named block on the spreadsheet, Quattro Pro did not copy the block name. Why?

A: Quattro Pro does not enable you to use the same name for two blocks—even if the block is copied. You can create more than one name for the same block. Although when you move a named block, the name moves with it.

Q: I used /**Edit** **Names** **Labels** to create cell block names for a row of data, but when I used the name in a formula, the program did not return the correct answer. Why?

A: The **Labels** command assigns a name only to one, adjacent cell in the direction you specified on the **Labels** submenu. Use the **Create** command to name a cell block.

Q: Why did nothing happen when I pressed F3 to display a list of stored names for the active spreadsheet?

A: Quattro Pro displays a block names list when you are in Edit mode and the cursor is next to an open parenthesis or when Quattro Pro is prompting you for a block name during a menu operation or in POINT <GOTO> mode.

Filling, Transposing, Searching for, and Replacing Data

Q: Why does Quattro Pro display decimal or negative numbers when I try to fill a cell block with dates?

A: Quattro Pro is evaluating your start value (for example, 10/10/89 or 10-10-89) as a formula. To properly use this feature, press Ctrl-D after you enter the destination cell block and before you enter the start value.

Q: When I transposed a cell block on the spreadsheet, why did Quattro Pro display 0's and ERR's.

A: Your original cell block probably contains formulas. Quattro Pro cannot transpose relative reference formulas correctly. Change the references to an absolute format and edit them after the operation. You also can convert the formulas to their calculated values before choosing /**Edit Transpose**.

Q: Why is Quattro Pro not finding a search string that I know exists on my spreadsheet?

A: Review your option settings on the Search and Replace submenu. You may have specified the wrong **Match** or **Case Sensitive** option.

Chapter Summary

Chapter 3 explained how to copy, move, and erase cells and blocks of cells on the Quattro Pro spreadsheet. You also learned how to modify an application's organization by adding and deleting columns and rows. Special cell block operations, such as converting formulas to values, filling in cell blocks with sequential numbers, and searching for and replacing data on the spreadsheet also were discussed. After reading this chapter, you should understand the following Quattro Pro concepts:

- Preselecting cell blocks to perform operations on

- Copying one cell into another or into many cells

- Moving one cell or a block of cells to another part of the spreadsheet

- Erasing cells and cell blocks

- Reversing Quattro Pro operations with the Undo command

- Inserting and deleting multiple rows and columns

- Creating text names for cell blocks

- Using cell block names in formulas

- Converting formulas to their values, filling a cell block with sequential numbers, and transposing column and row data

- Searching for and replacing data on a spreadsheet

In Chapter 4, you learn how to add the finishing touches to your spreadsheet applications by using Quattro Pro's Style menu commands. The commands on this menu help you fine tune your spreadsheet data. When you need to display numbers as dollars or percentages, align data in a cell, draw a line around a cell, change fonts, and add shading so that you can create a final, presentation-quality report for an important meeting, you choose options from Quattro Pro's Style menu.

Improving Your Spreadsheet Style

Although the discussion so far has centered on Quattro Pro's spreadsheet's usefulness as a calculating tool, the inherent power of any electronic spreadsheet lies in its capability to store and remember numerical and formula relationships.

In this chapter, techniques are introduced that enable you to expand the usefulness of a Quattro Pro spreadsheet by turning the spreadsheet into a presentation-quality reporting tool. Although much of the chapter talks about how to create reports that look good, you do not lose sight of the spreadsheet's important role as a mathematical tool.

This chapter introduces you to the 11 commands on the Style menu. These commands are organized into three groups: cell formatting commands, column-adjustment commands, and presentation-quality commands.

The discussion also focuses on how you realign data in a cell; choose the appropriate format for values, labels, dates, and times; and protect important cell data.

The chapter continues by demonstrating how to widen and narrow column widths, how to manage blocks of columns, and how to temporarily hide column data from prying eyes.

The final section in Chapter 4 examines the process of turning a basic spreadsheet application into a presentation-quality report. In this section, you learn how to draw lines and boxes around cells to highlight critical data, add shading to cell blocks, use multiple fonts, and insert page breaks to control report printing.

As you read this chapter, keep in mind that preselecting cells simplifies the use of Quattro Pro menu commands. Preselect cells when you use the Style menu commands because this method is the most efficient for formatting and creating your reports.

Using Style Menu Commands

After you build the basic form of a spreadsheet application, you can use this form or enhance its appearance to point out and clarify important points. Quattro Pro's Style menu enables you to add stylistic effects to your spreadsheet applications. For example, you can draw a box around text and values so that they stand out on-screen, draw double lines under financial statement figures, and shade and protect important cell data.

Quattro Pro enables you to use different typefaces to give your reports and graphs a professional look. For example, you may select a large Courier font for a report title; a medium-sized, boldfaced font for the secondary titles and headings; and a smaller, italicized font for account names or other descriptions. You also can change the width of a column, a block of columns, or hide columns containing private data.

The Style menu commands give you the ability to mold basic spreadsheets into creative and informative reports and graphs. (See Chapter 9 for more information on creating and annotating graphs.)

Reviewing the Style Commands

You can use the 11 Style menu commands shown in figure 4.1 to fine tune and enhance your spreadsheet's data display. Table 4.1 explains the Style menu commands.

Fig. 4.1
The Style menu.

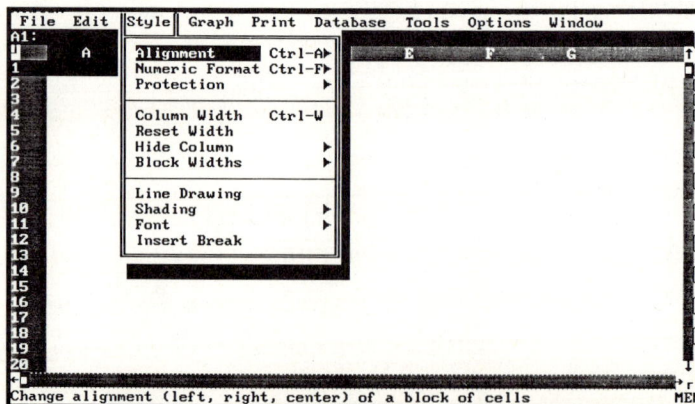

Table 4.1
Style Menu Commands

Command	Description
Alignment	Aligns data at the left edge, right edge, or in the center of a cell
Numeric Format	Formats the spreadsheet display of values and text and hides cell data
Protection	Protects and unprotects cell data on the active spreadsheet
Column Width	Widens and narrows the width of the active column
Reset Width	Resets the width of the active column to the default column width setting
Hide Column	Hides columns on the active spreadsheet
Block Widths	Widens, narrows, varies, and resets the width of multiple columns
Line Drawing	Draws lines and boxes of varying thicknesses around cells
Shading	Adds grey or black shading to spreadsheet cells
Font	Assigns different fonts and font styles to cells to enhance printouts
Insert Break	Inserts a page break at the cursor's location

The Style menu commands are organized roughly in the order they should be used during a work session. When you align and format cell data, you sometimes must alter the column width so that the formatted data fits into a cell. Then you add the final stylistic touches: lines, shading, and custom fonts.

Undoing Style Menu Commands

Pressing Alt-F5 reverses Quattro Pro spreadsheet operations like copying, moving, and erasing blocks of data. This feature, however, cannot undo every Quattro Pro operation.

You cannot undo spreadsheet formats created with the following Style menu commands: **A**lignment, **N**umeric Format, **P**rotection, Column **W**idth, **R**eset Width, and **H**ide Column. You also cannot undo presentation-quality enhancements achieved with the Line Drawing, **F**ont, and **S**hading commands.

You can undo data alignments created manually or alter these alignments when in EDIT mode. You also can undo a page break inserted with the **I**nsert Break command.

Changing the Default Global Settings

Quattro Pro initially uses global format settings to format your data entries. Quattro Pro uses these format settings each time you load a spreadsheet. For example, the program right aligns values and left aligns text in a cell. Consider the income statement spreadsheet shown in figure 4.2. The labels in C3..E7 are aligned per the global default setting. The labels in F3..H7 are right aligned with the /Style **A**lignment command. If you always want labels right aligned in your spreadsheets, select /**O**ptions **F**ormats **A**lign Labels **R**ight, and Quattro Pro changes the global label alignment setting for the current work session.

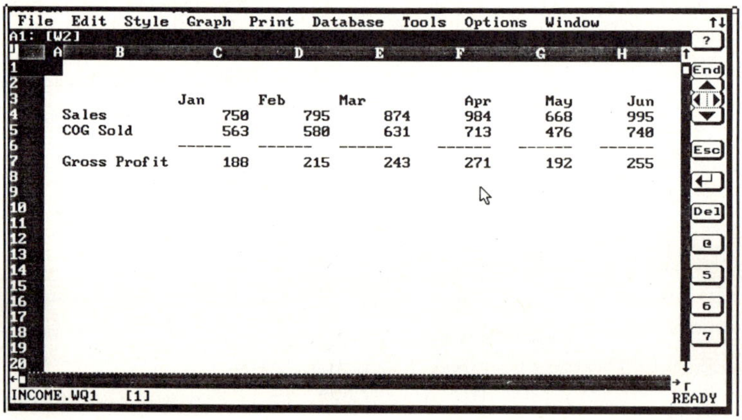

Fig. 4.2
Quattro Pro right aligns values and left aligns text in cells. The labels in C3..E7 are aligned per the global default setting. The labels in F3..H7 are right aligned.

To change one of the global format settings, select /**O**ptions **F**ormats and choose a command from the menu shown in figure 4.3.

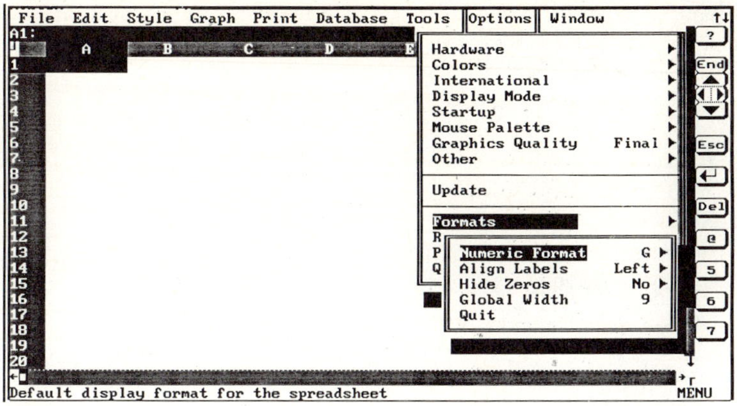

Fig. 4.3
The /Options Formats default settings.

Choose **N**umeric Format to change the global numeric format setting, **A**lign Labels to change the global label alignment setting, **H**ide Zeros to tell Quattro Pro whether or not to display zero values on the spreadsheet, and **G**lobal Width to set the global column width to a new value.

To change the global currency symbol, punctuation method, or date and time settings to conform to international standards, choose /**O**ptions **I**nternational.

Periodically, Quattro Pro pauses to build fonts. For example, when you add a font not built during program installation. When Quattro Pro builds fonts, you must wait for a minute or so until the program is finished before you can continue with the current work session.

If you do not want Quattro Pro to build fonts and interrupt your work sessions, choose /**O**ptions **G**raphics Quality and then **D**raft from the submenu. If, however, you want Quattro Pro to build fonts on an as-needed basis, select the **F**inal option from the submenu.

When you change any of Quattro Pro's global format settings, choose **U**pdate before you end the current work session. The next time you load the program, the new default settings will be in effect. (See Chapter 6 for complete coverage of the **O**ptions menu commands.)

Controlling Data Display

The first three commands on the **S**tyle menu control the display of data within a spreadsheet cell and affect the appearance of data displayed in a printout. These commands enable you to realign data in a cell; format labels, values, dates, and times; and protect and unprotect data in a cell.

Aligning Data

Without the capability to align cell data, your Quattro Pro spreadsheets could look like a jumble of numbers and letters. For example, the data shown in figure 4.4 appears disorganized because it has not been formatted.

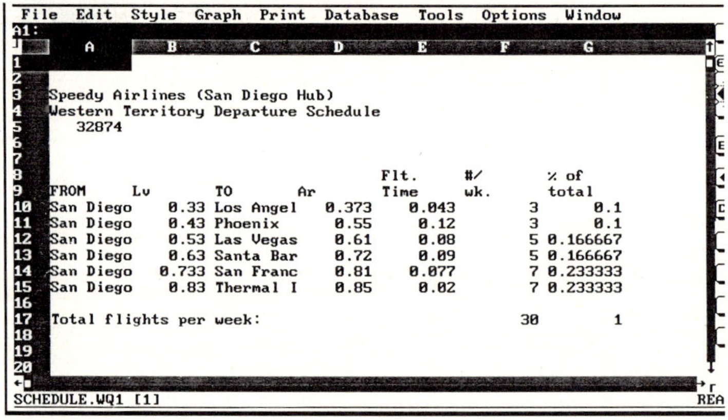

Fig. 4.4
An unformatted
Quattro Pro
spreadsheet.

When you write a report by hand, you intuitively know how to space numbers, letters, words, and paragraphs so that they make sense. When you enter data into a spreadsheet cell, Quattro Pro decides the type of data (value or label) and aligns that data according to predefined default global settings: labels are left aligned in a cell; values, dates, and times are right aligned.

Selecting a New Alignment

Use the /Style Alignment command to alter the alignment of values, labels, dates, and times in a cell block. Quattro Pro displays a submenu with four choices: General, Left, Right, and Center.

The General format is the default alignment setting. This format right aligns values and dates and aligns labels according to the /Options Formats Align Labels Setting.

In a typical spreadsheet, report titles are center aligned, and the column labels and data are right aligned. Row headings usually are left aligned.

To correct the confusing alignment of the data in figure 4.4, follow these steps:

1. Preselect cell block A3..G17.

2. Choose /**Style** **Alignment** and select **Left** from the submenu.

Quattro Pro aligns the data in the cell block. After your column data is aligned under a column heading, reviewing the report becomes easier. This operation is only the first of several others that you perform in this chapter.

Tip   Press Ctrl-A, the alignment shortcut key, to choose the /**Style** **Alignment** command.

Selecting an Alignment Manually

You can change the alignment of a label in two ways without using the **Alignment** command. You can align a label by preceding it with a label prefix character (see table 2.2 in Chapter 2). For example, to center align a label in cell E7, follow these steps:

1. Make cell E7 active.

2. To center a label, type ^ (the carat label prefix).

3. Type the label on the input line.

4. Press Enter to center align the label.

You also can alter an existing label's alignment while in EDIT mode. To realign the label from the preceding example, do the following:

1. Press F2 to edit cell E7.

2. Press Home, and Quattro Pro moves the cursor to the label prefix at the beginning of the entry.

3. Press Del to delete the prefix.

4. Type a new label prefix and press Enter to realign the label.

Tip   Press Alt-F5 to undo either of these manual alignment operations.

You cannot manually adjust the alignment of a value because Quattro Pro does not store an alignment prefix with values. To align or realign a value, choose **Alignment** from the Style menu.

Formatting Values, Labels, Dates, and Times

Without the appropriate numeric format, you may not be able to tell whether a value is a percent, dollar, date, or time. Imagine receiving a bill from your credit card company and not knowing if it's for 1,000 or 10 dollars.

With the /**S**tyle **N**umeric Format command, you can clarify the display of data on a spreadsheet. Using this command, you can create a monetary value by adding a dollar sign and decimal point and automatically add commas to numbers greater than 999. You also can tell Quattro Pro to display a formula instead of a value, add a percent sign to a financial ratio, or display a date and time in several different formats.

The **N**umeric Format command affects the way Quattro Pro displays a value on-screen—not how the program stores the value in a cell. To check this setting, pick any formatted cell and look at its value on the input line. You also can press F2 and look at the value on the status line.

Even if you format the number 25.7565 to display as 26, Quattro Pro uses 25.7565 in all calculations. Quattro Pro performs mathematical operations using entire numbers—not their abbreviated, on-screen equivalents.

Tip	Quattro Pro stores numbers with up to 16 significant digits. A significant digit is any integer except for a leading zero. Quattro Pro does not count decimals, commas, dollar signs, and percent signs as part of the total.

Selecting the Appropriate Numeric Format

To convey a point clearly, you need to choose the most appropriate numeric format for your data. Otherwise, your data can be confusing or completely useless. For example, if you format a percentage as a date, the information is useless. If you format a monetary value with commas and a decimal point but without a dollar sign, the information is incomplete.

When you format a cell, Quattro Pro displays a format code on the input line when the cell is active. This code includes a character that identifies the format and a number that indicates the displayed decimal places. For example, the format code (F2) indicates a fixed format with two decimal places.

Because the date and time formats do not use decimal places, the number in a date or time code reflects the option number on the Date or Time submenu.

Table 4.2 describes each of the format options available on the Numeric Format submenu.

Table 4.2
Numeric Formats

Format	Description
Fixed	Displays values with leading zeros and a user-specified number of decimal places
Scientific	Displays values in scientific notation
Currency	Displays values with a currency symbol and commas to separate thousands; shows negative numbers in parenthesis
,(comma)	Displays values with commas to separate thousands; shows negative numbers in parenthesis
General	Displays numbers as they are entered
+/−	Transforms values into a horizontal bar graph in which + represents a positive integer, − represents a negative integer, and the decimal point (.) represents zero
Percent	Displays values as percentages
Date	Displays values in user-specified date and time formats. You can use five standard date and time formats and several international formats.
Text	Displays formulas as text instead of as results.
Hidden	Conceals the on-screen display of value and label entries. When the cell is selected, entries still appear on the input line.
Reset	Returns the numeric format for this block to the default format (specified with the /Options Formats Numeric Format command); redisplays entries hidden with the Hidden format

Figure 4.5 displays numbers formatted with each of the formats available on the **Numeric Format** submenu. Each cell's format code has been added to the right of the example.

Fig. 4.5
Using numeric
formats in a
spreadsheet.

```
 File  Edit  Style  Graph  Print  Database  Tools  Options  Window      ↑↓
B15: (H) [W15] 12.34                                                     ?
    A         B          C         D          E          F        G   H   
 1   ┌─────────────────────────────────────────────────────────────┐  End
     │ The number 1234     Code      Format         Decimal Places  │   ▲
 2   │                                                              │  ◀▮▶
 3   │         1234.0      (F1)      Fixed          1 decimal       │   ▼
 4   │       1.23E+03      (S2)      Scientific     2 decimals      │  Esc
 5   │     $1,234.000      (C3)      Currency       3 decimals      │
 6   │      1,234.0000     (,4)      Comma          4 decimals      │   ↵
 7   │          1234       (G)       General                        │  Del
 8   ├──────────────────────────────────────────────────────────────┤
     │ The number 12.34    Code      Format         Decimal Places  │   @
 9   │                                                              │
10   │ +++++++++++++       (+)       +/-                            │   5
11   │     1234.00000%     (P5)      Percent        5 decimals      │
12   │      11-Jan-00      (D1)      Date           (Date #1)       │   6
13   │     08:09:36 AM     (D6)      Time           (Date #6)       │
14   │        12.34        (T)       Text                           │   7
15   │ ████████████        (H)       Hidden                         │
16   └──────────────────────────────────────────────────────────────┘
FORMATS.WQ1  [1]                                                     READY
```

Formatting Values

When you enter a number into a cell, Quattro Pro displays the number using the **G**eneral format, which displays most numbers in the form you entered. In some cases—for example, when a value is longer than the width of its cell—Quattro Pro displays a rounded value.

Quattro Pro always rounds a decimal value that has an equal or greater number of digits than the width of the column in which the value is positioned. The program begins rounding with the last digit in the value.

For example, if you enter the decimal value 0.399 into a cell that is five characters wide, Quattro Pro displays 0.4. If you enter 0.309 into a cell of the same width, Quattro Pro displays 0.31 (see fig. 4.6).

Fig. 4.6
How Quattro
Pro treats
unformatted
values.

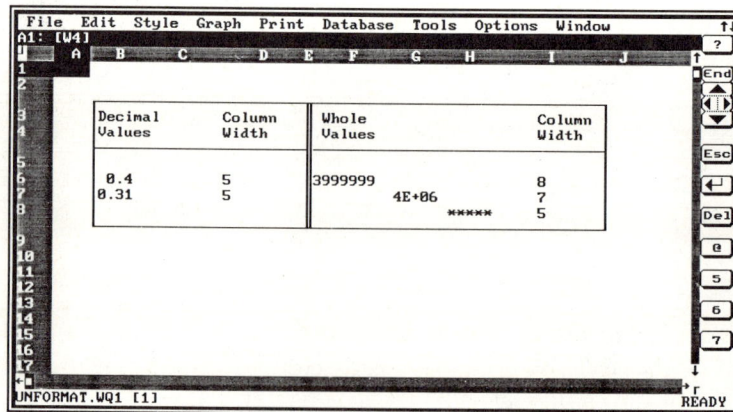

```
 File   Edit  Style  Graph  Print  Database  Tools  Options  Window      ↑↓
A1: [W4]                                                                 ?
   A    B      C       D      E    F      G      H      I      J         ↑
 1   ┌──────────────────────────────────────────────────────────────┐ End
 2   │                                                              │
 3   │ Decimal      Column     │ Whole                Column        │ ◀▮▶
 4   │ Values       Width      │ Values               Width         │  ▼
 5   │                         │                                    │
 6   │  0.4          5         │ 3999999               8            │ Esc
 7   │  0.31         5         │             4E+06     7            │  ↵
 8   │                         │           *****       5            │ Del
 9   └──────────────────────────────────────────────────────────────┘
10                                                                      @
11                                                                      5
12
13                                                                      6
14
15                                                                      7
16
17
UNFORMAT.WQ1 [1]                                                     READY
```

Quattro Pro always displays a whole value in scientific notation when the number of digits in the value is greater than the character width of the active column less one character. For example, if you enter a value that is seven characters long into an eight-character-wide column, the value is displayed as a whole value. If you enter the whole value 3999999 into a cell seven characters wide, Quattro Pro displays 4E+06—the scientific notation form for this value. When you enter this same whole value into a column with a width of five characters or less, Quattro Pro displays asterisks.

Tip | Quattro Pro's rule for displaying whole values versus scientific notation versus asterisks in a cell is slightly different when you draw lines around the cell with the /Style Line Drawing command. A drawn line uses up a space equal to one character width. If you draw a line on the left or right edge of a cell, take this extra space into account when determining an appropriate column width.

To format values on a spreadsheet, do the following.

1. Preselect a cell block to format.

2. Choose /Style Numeric Format.

3. Choose a format option from the submenu.

4. If prompted, select the number of decimal places to appear in numbers (from 0 to 15). (Only the Fixed, Scientific, comma, currency, and Percent options display the decimal prompt.)

5. Press Enter, and Quattro Pro redisplays the numbers in the cell block using the selected format option.

Now that this cell block has a numeric format, you can edit or delete the cell block data without erasing the cell format. When you copy the formatted contents of a cell to another location on the spreadsheet, Quattro Pro reproduces the cell format in the new location. If you move the formatted contents of a cell, Quattro Pro relocates the cell format to the new cell destination.

Tip | Press Ctrl-F, the format shortcut key, to choose the /Style Numeric Format command.

The format option you choose sometimes creates a number longer than the width of the current cell block. When this happens, Quattro Pro fills the cell block with asterisks. To correct this display problem, press Ctrl-W and widen the column until the data reappears.

Formatting Labels

The first nine **Numeric Format** options are intended to enhance the display of values, dates, and times. You can use the **Hidden** and **Reset** options to remove the display of labels, values, dates, and times from your screen.

To hide cell data on a spreadsheet, use the **Hidden** command. When you hide cell data, Quattro Pro removes the data from view; you still can over-write the contents of a hidden cell. To prevent the accidental erasure of a hidden cell, see the "Protecting Important Data" section later in this chapter.

Formatting a label with any other **Numeric Format** command has no effect on the label. For example, if you format a label using **Currency** and two deci-mal places, Quattro Pro continues to display the label in its original form, even though the input line displays (C2). If you replace the label with a value, the currency format takes effect for the value.

When the cell selector is in a hidden cell, Quattro Pro displays the cell con-tents on the input line. To redisplay a hidden label, choose /**Numeric Format** **Reset**.

Formatting Dates

To enter a date value onto a Quattro Pro spreadsheet, do the following:

1. Press Ctrl-D.

2. Enter a date using the exact form of date format 1 or 2 (see table 4.3). You also can enter a date using formats 3 and 6, 4 and 7, or 5 and 8 by using the /**Options International Date** command to choose one pair as the global format.

<table>
<tr><td colspan="2" align="center">**Table 4.3**
Date Command Formats</td></tr>
<tr><td>*Format*</td><td>*Type*</td></tr>
<tr><td>1. DD-MMM-YY</td><td>Day, month, year</td></tr>
<tr><td>2. DD-MMM</td><td>Day, month</td></tr>
<tr><td>3. MM/DD/YY</td><td>Long international #1</td></tr>
<tr><td>4. YY-MM-DD</td><td>Long international #2</td></tr>
<tr><td>5. MM.DD.YY</td><td>Long international #3</td></tr>
<tr><td>6. MM/DD</td><td>Short international #1</td></tr>
<tr><td>7. DD-MM</td><td>Short international #2</td></tr>
<tr><td>8. MM.DD</td><td>Short international #3</td></tr>
</table>

Another way to enter a date is to use a date @function command and then reformat the cell using the **D**ate command. (@DATE, @DATEVALUE, and @NOW are covered in Chapter 5.)

You also can enter a date as a date serial number. Then you can reformat the cell using the **D**ate command. A *date serial number* is an integer that is a unique code assigned by Quattro Pro to historical dates.

You easily can decipher a date serial number when you know how Quattro Pro creates the number. A date serial number equals the number of days between the date you enter and December 30, 1899. For example, the serial number for December 30, 1899 is 0, and the serial number for December 30, 1900 is 365—the number of days between the two dates. Figure 4.7 illustrates the decimal equivalents for several historical dates.

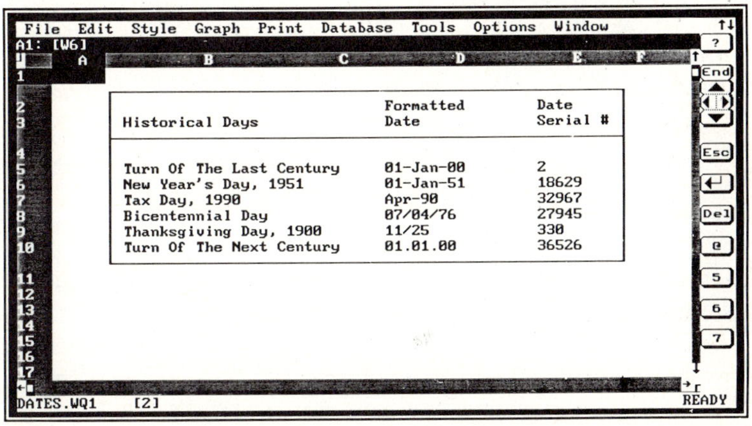

Fig. 4.7
Date serial numbers.

Tip | The date serial numbers for all dates prior to December 30, 1899 are negative. For example, -1 is the date serial number for December 29, 1899.

To enter and format a date serial number, do the following:

1. Enter a valid date serial number in a cell. (Valid serial numbers can be any integer in the range from -36,463 for March 01, 1800 to 73050 for December, 31, 2099.)

2. Choose **D**ate from the **N**umeric Format menu.

3. Select a format option.

Whichever way you enter a date, Quattro Pro always stores a date in its serial number form so that you can use dates in spreadsheet calculations. When you enter a date serial number into a cell, you can edit the date as you can any other number. For example, to add one day to the serial number 500, change the number to 501.

If you press Ctrl-D and then enter a date using an acceptable date format, Quattro Pro temporarily displays the serial number as a date. If you press F2 and edit the serial number, the date reverts back to a serial number display when you press Enter. The only way to affix a date format to a serial number is to format the date with the /**N**umeric Format **D**ate command.

Formatting Times

To enter a value in a time format, do the following:

1. Press Ctrl-D.

2. Enter a time using time format 1 or 2 (see table 4.4). You also can enter a time by using the /**O**ptions **I**nternational **T**ime command to choose format pairs 3 and 6, 4 and 7, 5 and 8, or 9 by itself as the global format.

Table 4.4
Time Command Formats

Format	Type
1. HH:MM:SS AM/PM	Hour, minute, second
2. HH:MM	Hour, minute
3. HH:MM:SS	Long international #1
4. HH.MM.SS	Long international #2
5. HH,MM,SS	Long international #3
6. HH:MM	Short international #1
7. HH.MM	Short international #2
8. HH,MM	Short international #3
9. HHhMMm	Short international #4

Another way to enter a time is to use a time @function command and then reformat the cell by using the **T**ime command. (@HOUR, @MINUTE, and @SECOND are covered in Chapter 5).

You also can enter a time as a *time serial number* and then reformat the cell by using the Time command. The code that Quattro Pro uses to represent a time is different than the code used for a date. Quattro Pro records time as a percentage of the 24-hour day. For example, Quattro Pro assigns the decimal .5 to 12 noon because it occurs 50 percent of the way through a 24-hour day. Figure 4.8 illustrates the Quattro Pro decimal equivalents for each hour.

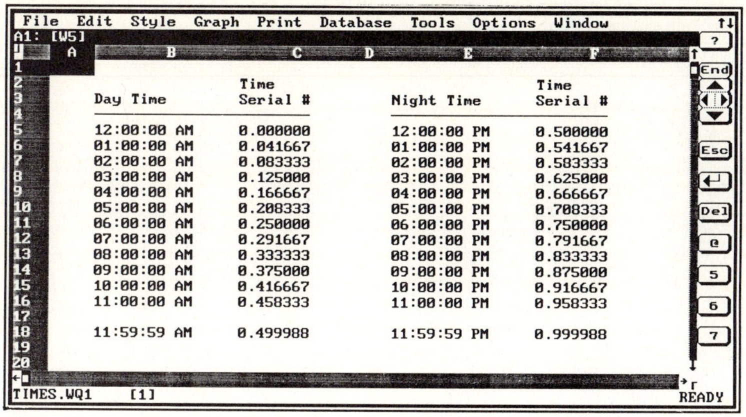

Fig. 4.8
Time serial numbers assigned by Quattro Pro.

To enter and then format a time serial number, do the following:

1. Enter a valid time serial number in a cell.

2. Choose **D**ate and then choose **T**ime from the Numeric Format menu.

3. Select a format option.

Quattro Pro always stores a time in its serial number form so that you can use times in spreadsheet calculations. When you enter a time serial number into a cell, you can edit the time like you can any other number. For example, to add one minute to the serial number .5, add .000694 (the decimal value that equals 1 minute divided by 1440 minutes in a day).

Tip | Quattro Pro accepts 24-hour, or military, clock times. When you use **N**umeric Format, Quattro Pro converts 24-hour times into 12-hour clock time equivalents. For example, 23:00:00 displays as 11:00:00 PM.

If you press Ctrl-D and then enter a time using an acceptable time format, Quattro Pro temporarily displays the serial number as a time. If you press F2 and edit the serial number, the program reverts back to a serial number display when you press Enter to record the editing changes. The only way to affix a time format to a serial number is to format the number with the /**N**umeric Format **D**ate **T**ime command.

Figure 4.9 shows a revised version of the spreadsheet from figure 4.4. This spreadsheet contains all of the appropriate numeric formats. Columns also have been widened where necessary to display all of the detail.

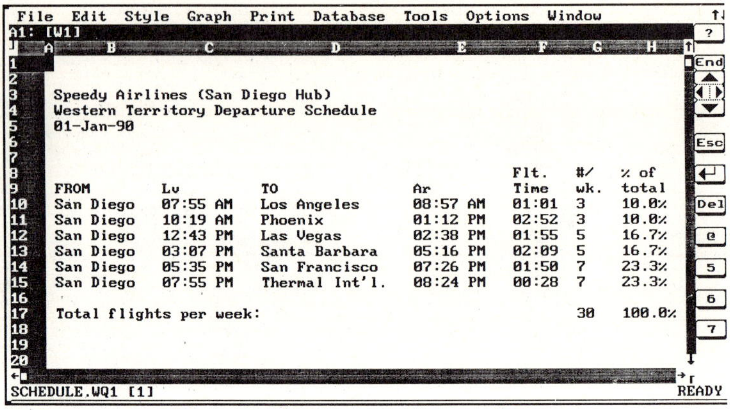

Fig. 4.9
A spreadsheet with numeric formats.

```
 File   Edit   Style   Graph   Print   Database   Tools   Options   Window        ↑↓
A1: [W1]                                                                            ?
  A        B         C           D              E        F      G      H           End
1                                                                                   ▲
2                                                                                  ◀▮▶
3        Speedy Airlines (San Diego Hub)                                            ▼
4        Western Territory Departure Schedule
5        01-Jan-90                                                                 Esc
6
7                                                                                   ↵
8                                                      Flt.   #/    % of
9        FROM      Lv        TO            Ar          Time   wk.   total          Del
10       San Diego 07:55 AM  Los Angeles   08:57 AM   01:01  3     10.0%
11       San Diego 10:19 AM  Phoenix       01:12 PM   02:52  3     10.0%            @
12       San Diego 12:43 PM  Las Vegas     02:38 PM   01:55  5     16.7%
13       San Diego 03:07 PM  Santa Barbara 05:16 PM   02:09  5     16.7%            5
14       San Diego 05:35 PM  San Francisco 07:26 PM   01:50  7     23.3%
15       San Diego 07:55 PM  Thermal Int'l. 08:24 PM  00:28  7     23.3%            6
16
17       Total flights per week:                              30    100.0%          7
18
19
20
←┘                                                                          →r
SCHEDULE.WQ1 [1]                                                            READY
```

Changing Formats

Quattro Pro offers two ways to change cell formats. First, you can choose /**St**yle **N**umeric Format **R**eset and cancel all format settings for a cell block that you define. Second, you can reformat a cell by choosing /**St**yle **N**umeric Format and then selecting a new format option. When you reformat a cell, Quattro Pro overwrites and replaces the original format with the new format.

When you reformat a cell, Quattro Pro sometimes displays a value that doesn't make sense. For example, when you format the value 50 using the **C**urrency option with two decimal places, Quattro Pro displays the value $50.00. If you reformat this value using the **P**ercent option with 2 decimal places, Quattro Pro displays 5000%. You may have to edit the value to create the correct display.

Protecting Important Data

The process of protecting a spreadsheet involves two operations: global spreadsheet protection and individual cell protection. To protect cells from change, the global protection and the individual cell protection settings must be on. By default, all cells on a Quattro Pro spreadsheet are in protected mode, but the setting for spreadsheet protection is disabled. Use the /**O**ptions **P**rotection command to enable or disable global spreadsheet protection.

Unprotecting Spreadsheet Cells

To remove cell protection from a block of cells, do the following:

1. Preselect the block of cells.

2. Choose /**Style P**rotection.

3. Choose **U**nprotect.

Quattro Pro removes protection from the preselected cell block. When you use /**Style P**rotection to unprotect a cell, Quattro Pro displays U on the input line when you make that cell active.

Tip | Quattro Pro makes locating unprotected cells easy because the program always displays unprotected cells in reverse color on a color display and in high intensity on a monochrome display. You may have to adjust the foreground and background intensity knobs on a monochrome display.

Protecting Spreadsheet Cells

Quattro Pro does not enable you to edit, replace, or delete entries from protected cells. You also cannot delete a column or row containing a protected cell. You can erase the entire spreadsheet, however, even if the spreadsheet contains protected cells. To protect a block of cells, do the following:

1. Preselect the block of cells.

2. Choose /**Style P**rotection.

3. Choose **P**rotect.

Quattro Pro protects the preselected cell block. When you use /**O**ptions **P**rotection **E**nable to turn protection on, Quattro Pro displays PR on the input line for every protected cell that you make active.

Remember that when global spreadsheet protection is disabled (using /**O**ptions **P**rotection **D**isable), you can overwrite data on the spreadsheet—regardless of the individual protection status of the spreadsheet cells.

Quattro Pro displays an error message if you attempt to alter the contents of a protected cell. Press Esc to cancel the error message and return to the active spreadsheet.

The next section introduces and demonstrates how to use Quattro Pro's column adjusting commands.

Working with Columns

The middle group of commands on the **Style** menu are column adjustment commands. You can use these commands to change the width of a column or a block of columns and to hide a group of columns on the active spreadsheet.

Four column adjustment commands are on the **Style** menu: **Column Width**, **Reset Width**, **Hide Column**, and **Block Widths**. **Column Width** widens and narrows the current column; **Reset Width** returns the active column back to the default column width; **Hide Column** removes a selected group of columns from display; and **Block Widths** performs operations on a block of columns.

Setting the Width of a Column

Quattro Pro enables you to set the width of an individual column by using the **/Style Column Width** command. Valid column widths range from 1 to 254 characters. To widen or narrow the width of a column, do the following:

1. Place the cell selector in a target column.

2. Choose **/Style Column Width**.

3. Type the number of the desired width (the default is 9) and press Enter.

Quattro Pro adjusts the width of the active column to the number of characters you specify. After you change the width of a column, Quattro Pro displays the new width in brackets on the input line. For example, (W12) indicates a column width of 12.

Tip | Ctrl-W is the default shortcut for the **/Style Column Width** command.

Setting the Width On-Screen

Sometimes estimating the appropriate width for a column is difficult. If you are unsure about which width to use, you can use the following adjustment technique:

1. Place the cell selector in a target column.

2. Choose **/Style Column Width**.

3. Press → to widen or ← to narrow the target column.

4. Press Enter when you create a visually acceptable width.

Setting the Width with a Mouse

If you have a mouse, you easily can change the width of a column by doing the following:

1. Point and click on the target column's letter at the top of the spreadsheet.

2. Drag the column letter right to widen the column or left to narrow the column.

3. Release the mouse button when you attain the ideal width.

Setting the Width in a Window Pane

The capability to split a spreadsheet into two window panes presents an interesting possibility regarding column widths, because with the /Style Column Width command, you can independently change column widths in either window pane.

For example, if you split a window into two vertical or horizontal panes, you can choose different widths for the same column in each pane. When you close a split window, however, Quattro Pro retains only those changes made to columns in the top (horizontal split) or left (vertical split) pane.

Tip | Press F6 to switch between panes in a split window.

Resetting a Column's Width

Use the /Style Reset Width command to reset the width of an adjusted column to its default setting. Follow these steps:

1. Place the cell selector in the target column.

2. Choose /Style Reset Width.

Quattro Pro resets the width of the active column to nine characters (unless you change the default width using /Options Formats Column Width). After you reset the width of a column, Quattro Pro erases from the input line the brackets containing the preceding width.

Tip | You can change the default global column width with the /Options Formats Column Width command.

Working with Multiple Columns

Use the /Style Block Widths command to set the width of multiple columns. When you choose this command, Quattro Pro displays three choices on the submenu. Choose Set Widths to assign a width to multiple columns or Reset Width to reset multiple columns to the default width.

The third command, Auto Width, performs a special block operation. Use this command to adjust the width of a block of columns according to the longest entry in each column.

Setting the Width of a Block of Columns

Use the Block Widths command to set the width of multiple columns in a block. Follow these steps:

1. Preselect the columns in the target block.

2. Choose /Style Block Widths Set Width.

3. Type any number from 1 to 254 or use the ← or → key to indicate the width on-screen.

4. Press Enter.

Quattro Pro adjusts each column included in the block to the specified width.

To reset the width of all columns in a block, follow these steps:

1. Choose /Style Block Width Reset Width. Quattro Pro prompts you for the block to adjust.

2. Specify the block to adjust by highlighting the block or by typing the block address on the input line.

Quattro Pro resets the width of all columns in the block to the default value. Initially, the default column width is nine, but you can change this by using the /Options Formats Global Width command.

Setting the Width of a Block of Columns Automatically

Figure 4.10 shows what the spreadsheet in figure 4.9 looks like before adjusting the column widths. Notice that asterisks appear in cell B5 and in columns C and E. The asterisks appear because the chosen numeric format creates a display wider than the width of the column. Look at the input line at the top of the spreadsheet to see that cell B5's data is intact.

```
 File   Edit   Style   Graph   Print   Database   Tools   Options   Window
B5: (D1) 32874
    A     B        C        D        E        F        G        H
1
2
3        Speedy Airlines (San Diego Hub)
4        Western Territory Departure Schedule
5        *********
6
7
8                                              Flt.     #/      % of
9        FROM     Lv      TO       Ar         Time     wk.     total
10       San Diego*********Los Angel********00:57      3       10.0%
11       San Diego*********Phoenix  ********02:48      3       10.0%
12       San Diego*********Las Vegas********01:50      5       16.7%
13       San Diego*********Santa Bar********02:04      5       16.7%
14       San Diego*********San Franc********01:50      7       23.3%
15       San Diego*********Thermal I********00:24      7       23.3%
16
17       Total flights per week:                       30      100.0%
18
19
20
SCHEDULE.WQ1 [1]                                                        REA
```

Fig. 4.10
A spreadsheet before the column widths are adjusted. Asterisks appear in cell B5 and columns C and E.

The **A**uto Width command provides yet another way to set your spreadsheet column widths. This command is particularly useful when the column data has a similar length—like a date or time serial number—because the command enables you to quickly create a width that accommodates the common length.

To use the **A**uto Width command to adjusts column widths, do the following:

1. Preselect cell block B8..H15.

2. Choose /**S**tyle **B**lock Widths **A**uto Width.

3. When prompted, press Enter to add an extra space to the longest entry in each column (see fig. 4.11).

You may specify from 0 to 40 extra spaces to add to the longest label or value when you choose this command. Normally, 1 to 3 extra spaces creates enough distance between columns for you to see your data.

Figure 4.12 shows the spreadsheet with auto-adjusted columns.

Fig. 4.11
Adding one
space to the
longest entry in
each column to
determine the
column width.

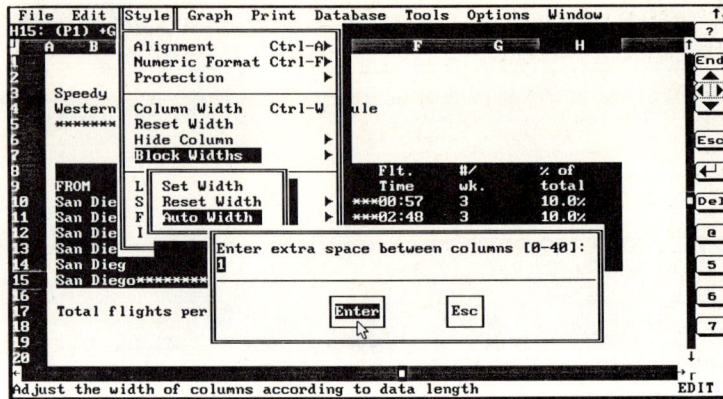

Fig. 4.12
The auto-
adjusted
spreadsheet.

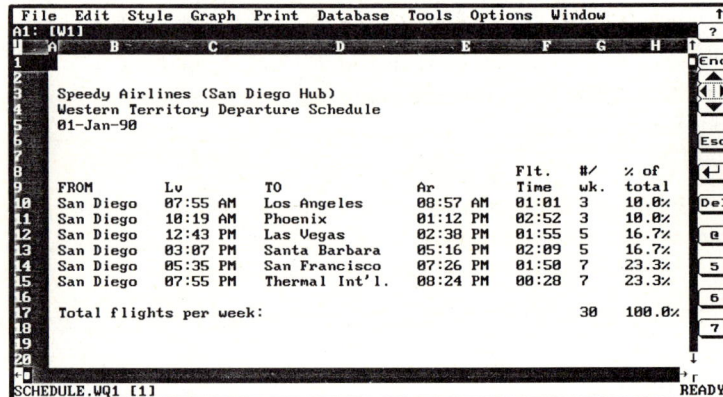

When looking for the longest entry, Quattro Pro examines the first row and all cells following that row. Then the program resets the widths of the columns according to the following formula:

length of longest entry in the block
+ extra characters

For example, if the longest entry is 10 characters long and you specified 2 extra spaces, Quattro Pro sets the width of the column to 12.

If your spreadsheet contains an entry that is substantially longer than any other entry, preselect a cell block that does not include this entry. For example, if you are working with the spreadsheet in figure 4.10, you do not want to include the 37-character label in cell B4 in the cell block.

If the long entry appears in the middle of the spreadsheet, perform two auto-adjustment operations: one on the block above and one on the block below the long entry.

Hiding a Column

Quattro Pro enables you to temporarily hide and unhide columns of data using the /**Style H**idden Column command. This command enables you to prevent unauthorized viewing of proprietary data. When you hide a column, Quattro Pro retains the column data in memory so that you can redisplay the column.

Hiding Data in Columns

To hide columns from view, do the following:

1. Preselect the target column(s).

2. Choose /**Style H**ide Column.

3. Choose **H**ide from the submenu.

4. Press Enter to hide the target column(s).

When Quattro Pro hides columns, your spreadsheet looks as if the target columns were erased and the bordering columns were connected. In other words, Quattro Pro does not re-letter the column names when you execute this command. Instead, the program joins the bordering columns (to the right and left of the hidden columns) so that there are no blank areas on the spreadsheet.

Tip | The **H**idden command creates an interesting screen effect, one that is similar to a vertical window split. Figure 4.13 illustrates how hiding several columns produces a split window effect without the annoying vertical border from the second pane.

Quattro Pro keeps hidden only those columns initially hidden on the top and left panes when you clear the window. Quattro Pro also does not include hidden columns on the printout of a spreadsheet.

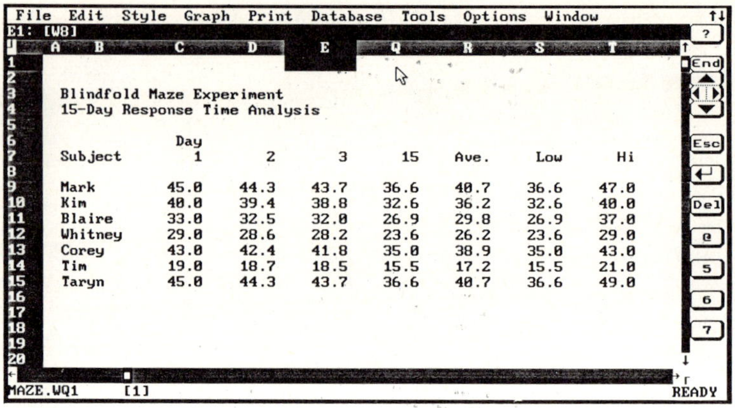

Fig. 4.13
The Hidden command causes a split-window effect.

```
 File   Edit   Style   Graph   Print   Database   Tools   Options   Window       ↑↓
E1: [W8]                                                                          ?
 U    A     B       C       D        E      Q        R       S        T     ↑
 1                                                                          End
 2                                                                          ▲
 3       Blindfold Maze Experiment                        ▷                 ◁│▷
 4       15-Day Response Time Analysis                                      ▼
 5                                                                          Esc
 6                  Day
 7       Subject     1      2        3      15     Ave.     Low      Hi     ↵
 8
 9       Mark       45.0   44.3    43.7    36.6    40.7    36.6    47.0     Del
10       Kim        40.0   39.4    38.8    32.6    36.2    32.6    40.0
11       Blaire     33.0   32.5    32.0    26.9    29.8    26.9    37.0     @
12       Whitney    29.0   28.6    28.2    23.6    26.2    23.6    29.0
13       Corey      43.0   42.4    41.8    35.0    38.9    35.0    43.0     5
14       Tim        19.0   18.7    18.5    15.5    17.2    15.5    21.0
15       Taryn      45.0   44.3    43.7    36.6    40.7    36.6    49.0     6
16
17                                                                          7
18
19
20                                                                          ↓
 ↑         ■                                                    ▶  r
MAZE.WQ1        [1]                                                       READY
```

Unhiding Data in Columns

To display hidden columns, do the following:

1. Choose /**Style H**idden **C**olumn **E**xpose. (Quattro Pro redisplays hidden columns with asterisks (*) next to the column letters.)

2. Type a cell address or cell block address that includes the columns you want to expose.

3. Press Enter to display the hidden columns.

Quattro Pro removes the asterisks and rehides columns that you choose not to expose when you execute this command. The use of certain menu commands (such as /**Edit M**ove and /**Edit C**opy) causes Quattro Pro to temporarily display all hidden columns on the active spreadsheet. When you finish executing the command, Quattro Pro re-hides the columns.

Selecting Presentation-Quality Options

The third and last group of commands on the **Style** menu are the presentation-quality commands. Use these commands to add stylistic enhancements to your spreadsheets. For example, you can draw lines and boxes, add shading to cells, include multiple fonts, add bullets, and insert page breaks to help control spreadsheet printing.

Using Lines and Boxes To Highlight Data

You can add lines to a spreadsheet in the following two ways: enter a repeating hyphen into a cell so that the hyphens fill the cell or use the commands on Quattro Pro's Line Drawing menu.

Quattro Pro uses graphic imaging to form the lines and boxes on a spreadsheet. Instead of drawing lines in cells, therefore, the program actually adds the graphics image between cells on a spreadsheet. When you add lines to a spreadsheet, Quattro Pro expands the area in between rows so that the spreadsheet can accommodate the extra graphic images.

Drawing Lines and Boxes

To use the /Style Line Drawing command to draw single, double, or thick lines and boxes around your spreadsheet cell data, do the following:

1. Preselect a block of cells.

2. Choose /Style Line Drawing.

3. Choose a placement option from the Line Drawing menu (see table 4.5).

4. Choose a line type from the Line Drawing submenu. (Your choices are Single, Double, Thick, and None.)

5. Choose Quit to exit the menus and return to the spreadsheet.

Table 4.5
Line Placement Options

Option	Description
All	Draws a box around the target cell block and adds vertical and horizontal lines between all cells
Outside	Draws a box around the perimeter of the target cell block
Top	Draws a horizontal line on top of the first row in the target cell block
Bottom	Draws a horizontal line underneath the last row in the target cell block

Table 4.5—*continued*

Option	Description
Left	Draws a vertical line along the left edge of the cells in the leftmost column in the target cell block
Right	Draws a vertical line along the right edge of the cells in the rightmost column of the target cell block
Inside	Draws vertical and horizontal lines between all cells in the target cell block
Horizontal	Draws lines between each row in the target cell block. This command does nothing if the target cell block contains only one row
Vertical	Draws lines between each column in the block. This command does nothing if the target cell block contains only one column.
Quit	Returns to the spreadsheet without making any changes

Previewing Enhancements

Most Style menu enhancements are visible on a spreadsheet as soon as you create them. For example, Quattro Pro immediately shows new data alignments, numeric formats, unprotected cells, column widths, hidden columns, drawn lines, and shading effects after you add them to a spreadsheet.

Spreadsheet enhancements such as custom font typefaces and cell bulleting do not immediately display on a spreadsheet. Quattro Pro, therefore, gives you a facility to preview all of your spreadsheet enhancements before you print a spreadsheet.

To use Quattro Pro's Screen Preview facility, do the following:

1. Preselect a cell block on the active spreadsheet that you want to preview.

2. Choose /**Print B**lock, and Quattro Pro displays the cell block address at the right margin of the Print menu, next to the **B**lock command.

3. Choose **D**estination and select the **S**creen Preview option. Quattro Pro returns you to the Print menu.

4. Choose **S**preadsheet Print, and Quattro Pro displays your spreadsheet on-screen, complete with its presentation-quality settings.

If your computer does not have a graphics display system, you can not use the Screen Preview facility. You must print out a spreadsheet to review the look of your presentation-quality settings. (See Chapter 8 for a complete discussion of printing in Quattro Pro.)

Erasing Lines and Boxes

To remove all lines and boxes from a spreadsheet, do the following:

1. Preselect the cell block containing the lines or boxes (the cell block you originally selected as the target cell block).

2. Choose /**S**tyle **L**ine Drawing.

3. Choose the **A**ll placement option.

4. Choose the **N**one type option.

Tip | Quattro Pro enables you to partially remove lines from a spreadsheet. For example, to remove the bottom line from a box, highlight the target cell block and choose /**S**tyle **L**ine Drawing **B**ottom **N**one. To remove the top line, choose /**S**tyle **L**ine Drawing **T**op and **N**one.

Printing Lines and Boxes

You can print a spreadsheet containing lines and boxes in draft mode or in graphics mode. In draft mode, Quattro Pro uses +, −, and the lowercase l to print lines and boxes. In graphics mode, Quattro Pro uses graphics characters to print smooth lines and boxes.

To print in graphics mode, set the /**P**rint **D**estination setting to **G**raphics **P**rinter. (See Chapter 8 for information about printing.)

Figure 4.14 shows how the addition of lines to Speedy Airline's report highlights the arrival and departure data.

Shading Cell Data for Effect

Use the /**S**tyle **S**hading command to shade spreadsheet cells. With this command, you can shade in grey or black. The most common applications for

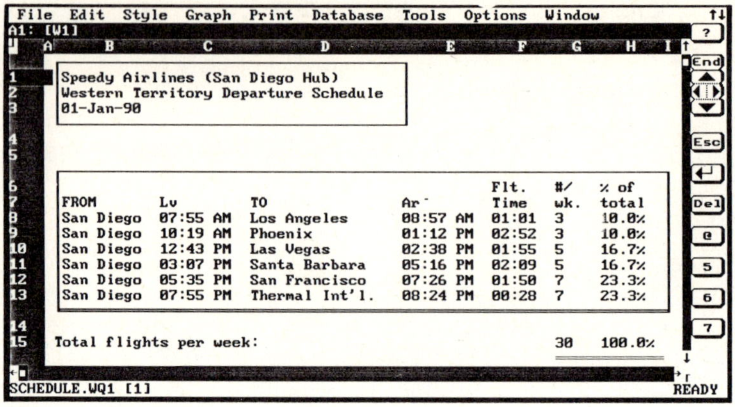

Fig. 4.14
Lines and boxes
added to the
Speedy Airlines
report.

```
 File   Edit   Style   Graph   Print   Database   Tools   Options   Window        ↑↓
A1: [W1]                                                                          ?
┌─ A ──── B ────── C ──────── D ──────── E ───── F ───── G ──── H ─ I            ─
 1                                                                               End
 1    │Speedy Airlines (San Diego Hub)                                     │
 2    │Western Territory Departure Schedule                                │     ↔
 3    │01-Jan-90                                                           │     ▼
 4    └──────────────────────────────────────────────────────────────────┘
 5                                                                               Esc
 6    ┌──────────────────────────────────────────────────────────────────┐     ↵
 7    │                                            Flt.   #/    % of       │
 8    │FROM       Lv         TO            Ar      Time   wk.   total      │     Del
 9    │San Diego  07:55 AM   Los Angeles   08:57 AM  01:01  3     10.0%      │
10    │San Diego  10:19 AM   Phoenix       01:12 PM  02:52  3     10.0%      │     @
11    │San Diego  12:43 PM   Las Vegas     02:38 PM  01:55  5     16.7%      │
12    │San Diego  03:07 PM   Santa Barbara 05:16 PM  02:09  5     16.7%      │     5
13    │San Diego  05:35 PM   San Francisco 07:26 PM  01:50  7     23.3%      │
      │San Diego  07:55 PM   Thermal Int'l.08:24 PM  00:28  7     23.3%      │     6
14    └──────────────────────────────────────────────────────────────────┘
15    Total flights per week:                            30    100.0%             7
                                                          ───────────────
SCHEDULE.WQ1 [1]                                                          READY
```

cell shading are to indicate a data input area and to point out a block of protected cells.

To shade an area of a spreadsheet, follow these steps:

1. Preselect a block of cells to shade.

2. Choose /Style Shading.

3. Choose a shade option from the Shading submenu.

Quattro Pro displays the target cells with shading. When you use the **Grey** shading option, notice that only the part of the cell not occupied by data is colored grey; the shading behind the data is black. On a monochrome screen, black shading appears as bold.

Tip Quattro Pro enables you to change the color of the shading with the /**Options Colors Spreadsheet Shading** command.

To print shaded cells, you first must choose the /**Print Destination Graphics Printer** command to tell Quattro Pro to print in graphics mode. If you don't choose this command, Quattro Pro does not print the shaded cells. When you shade cells bordered by drawn lines, Quattro Pro sometimes overlaps the lines, but this is only an on-screen effect. When you print the spreadsheet, Quattro Pro properly encloses the shading in the lined cells.

Figure 4.15 shows how adding cell shading to cell B3 and cell blocks C7..C12 and E7..E12 makes important data stand out on a report.

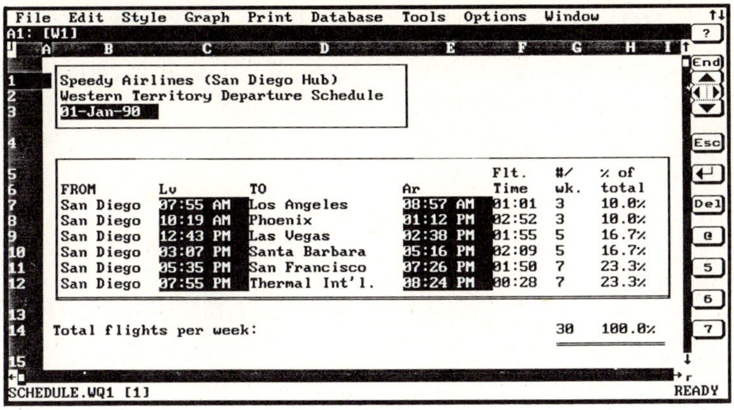

Fig. 4.15 Adding cell shading to the Speedy Airlines report.

Selecting Fonts for Effect

Use the /**Style Font** command to change the typeface, style, color, and point size of the fonts that Quattro Pro uses when printing a spreadsheet. Quattro Pro enables you to use up to eight fonts in one spreadsheet.

The /**Style Font** command affects the fonts that Quattro Pro uses for printing—not for screen display. Quattro Pro, however, displays a spreadsheet's custom font selections when you use the **Screen Preview** command on the **Print** menu (see Chapter 8 for complete coverage of the Print menu.)

Selecting a Font Number

To assign a new font to a cell block on a spreadsheet, do the following:

1. Preselect the target cell block.

2. Choose /**Style Font**.

3. Select a new font from the list by pressing the font number.

When you add, edit, or delete fonts, you do not see any changes in the spreadsheet. To verify the font number selected for a cell, make that cell active and review the font code displayed on the input line. If you see (F2), for example, you have customized this cell using font #2. Quattro Pro does not display a font code on the input line for the default font.

Changing a Font

Quattro Pro uses Bitstream Dutch 12-point Black as the global default font. You can change this global setting by selecting **Edit Fonts** from the **Font** menu. Quattro Pro uses the default font in every cell on a default spreadsheet (SHEET1.WQ1 for example).

When you installed Quattro Pro, you had the option of building none, some, or all of Quattro Pro's fonts. If you selected none, Quattro Pro displays a limited list of fonts to choose from. If you built all of the fonts, you can use any of these fonts with the /Style **Font** **Edit Fonts** command.

Customizing a Font

To edit the typeface, point size, style, or color of any of the fonts shown on the Fonts menu, do the following:

1. Choose /Style **Font**.

2. Choose **Edit Fonts**.

3. Enter the number of the font you want to customize.

4. Choose **Typeface** to change the font's typeface.

5. Choose **Point Size** to change the font's point size.

6. Choose **Style** to change the font's style and then choose **Bold**, **Italic**, **Underlined**, or **Reset** (**Reset** returns the font to the default style.)

7. Choose Color to change the font's printing color.

8. Choose **Quit** when you finish customizing the font.

Quattro Pro displays the new, custom settings for the font in the same slot the original font occupied.

> **Tip** Remember that fonts are used for printing and not on-screen display. Therefore, changing the color of a font produces no visible change on your color display. Use this option only if you own a color printer. The size of the font is not the same as on the spreadsheet. Therefore, changing a column's width may be necessary to accommodate all of the characters you want to print.

Certain Quattro Pro fonts support only some of the features available from the /Style **Font** **Edit** submenu. For example, the Bitstream Courier font does not support the **Bold** option. Although Quattro Pro enables you to specify

Bold on the **E**dit Fonts submenu, the program does not boldface characters on your printouts.

Choose /**S**tyle **F**ont **R**eset to reset all fonts to Quattro Pro's default setting.

Adding Bullets

Quattro Pro has a special stylistic feature called *bulleting* that enables you to add bullets and boxes to your spreadsheets. You cannot find this option anywhere on a Quattro Pro menu—to use this option, you must enter a special code into a spreadsheet cell.

To create a bullet, enter the following code into the cell in which you want the bullet to appear:

\bullet #\ where # = the bullet style number (0-6)

To enter a bullet into a cell by itself, precede the bullet code with a label prefix. If you don't, Quattro Pro interprets the first \ as a repeating label prefix and repeats the entry in the cell. To specify a bullet style, choose one of the numbers that appears in table 4.6.

Table 4.6
Bullet Character Code Designations

Number	Description
0	Box
1	Filled box
2	Checked box
3	Check
4	Shadowed box
5	Shadowed, checked box
6	Filled circle

When you print a spreadsheet containing a bullet code, Quattro Pro prints the bullet character instead of the code. To review how the bullet character looks on-screen, select /**P**rint **B**lock and type the address of a cell block to print. Next set the /**P**rint **D**estination command to **S**creen Preview and choose /**P**rint **S**preadsheet Print.

You also can include bullet characters in a Quattro Pro graph by using the graph annotator (see Chapter 9 for complete coverage of graph annotation.)

| Tip | You may press Alt-F5 to remove a bullet code immediately after you enter the code into a spreadsheet cell. If the bullet code does not appear when you print or preview the spreadsheet, widen that column until the code appears. |

Using Page Breaks To Control Printing

Quattro Pro inserts soft page breaks in a spreadsheet according to the page length specified by the /**Print Layout Margins Page** Length command. If you want to insert hard page breaks to further modify how a spreadsheet is printed, use the /**Style Insert Break** command.

For example, hard page breaks enable you to break up one large print block into many smaller pieces. This technique is useful when you want to print a column of names and addresses on mailing labels or form-fed index cards.

Inserting a Page Break

You use the /**Style Insert Break** command to insert a hard page break on a spreadsheet at the location of the cell selector. To insert a hard page break, do the following:

1. Move the cell selector to the first cell in the row in which you want to begin a new page.

2. Choose /**Style Insert Break**.

Quattro Pro enters the symbol for a hard page break |:: at the specified location. Note that Quattro Pro has no soft page break symbol; the program uses the page length setting to determine normal page breaks.

| Tip | To enter a page break manually, type |:: in the first cell of a blank row. (Quattro Pro does not print data appearing on the same row as a page break.) |

Deleting a Page Break

To delete a page break, do the following:

1. Move the cell selector to the cell in which the page break resides.

2. Press Del on the numeric key pad.

Quattro Pro deletes the hard page break but does not delete the inserted row.

Tip | Press Alt-F5 to remove an inserted hard page break from a spreadsheet.

Questions & Answers

This chapter introduces you to Quattro Pro's cell formatting, column adjusting, and presentation-quality commands. If you have questions about any of the topics covered in this chapter, scan this section for solutions to common problems.

Controlling the Display of Your Data

Q: How do you manually edit the alignment of a number or a formula on a spreadsheet?

A: The only way to align values on a Quattro Pro spreadsheet is by using the /Style Alignment command. Quattro Pro values do not have alignment prefixes; therefore, you cannot edit their alignment while in EDIT mode.

Q: When I enter time serial numbers, why doesn't Quattro Pro display recognizable times?

A: Unless you first press Ctrl-D, Quattro Pro displays date and time serial numbers as integers. To display serial numbers as dates, choose **D**ate or **T**ime from the Numeric Format submenu.

Q: When I enter and then format dates, why does Quattro Pro display the wrong date?

A: If you type a date into a cell (using hyphens or slashes) without first pressing Ctrl-D, Quattro Pro evaluates the entry as a formula. For example, the date entry *10-09* produces the value 1 when treated as a formula (10 minus 9 equals 1). When you format this cell by using the **D**ate command, Quattro Pro sees the date serial number 1 and displays the date December 31, 1899.

Q: How do I perform mathematical operations on dates?

A: You can perform mathematical operations on dates and times just as you do on other numbers. Remember, dates and times are stored in cells as serial numbers—not as date labels.

Q: I protected cells on a spreadsheet, but Quattro Pro still enables me to write over the data in the cells. Why?

A: Turn global spreadsheet protection on with the /**Options P**rotection **E**nable command. With protection enabled, you cannot modify any cells unless they are explicitly unprotected.

Working with Columns

Q: Why does Quattro Pro display an error message when I try to delete columns and rows on my spreadsheets?

A: Turn global spreadsheet protection off with the /**Options P**rotection **D**isable command. Quattro Pro does not delete rows and columns when protected cells are on a spreadsheet and global protection is enabled.

Q: I used the /**Style B**lock Widths **A**uto Width command to auto-set column widths on a spreadsheet, and now all of my columns are too wide. What can I do?

A: Your target cell block probably included a cell with a long label, such as a report title. Choose the same target block and use the **Reset Width** command to return the columns to their default width. Then try the **Auto Width** command again, excluding the cell containing the long label.

Q: I changed the global column width, but my spreadsheet columns are still the same width. Why?

A: Global column widths affect only new default spreadsheets.

Selecting Presentation-Quality Options

Q: Why did nothing happened when I changed several font definitions on my spreadsheet?

A: You can review a spreadsheet cell's font setting in three ways: on-screen using /**P**rint **D**estination **S**creen **P**review, on a printout using /**P**rint **D**estination **G**raphics Printer, or by making a cell active and reviewing the font code on the input line. Although the first two methods enable you to inspect the look of a font, the third method does not. Even so, if you work with a particular font often, reviewing the font code on the input line at least enables you to verify that you used the correct font.

Q: Why don't my custom fonts, shading, and drawn lines look right on my spreadsheet printouts?

A: Choose /**P**rint **D**estination **G**raphics Printer to print custom fonts and shadings. For this option to work, you must have a printer that can print in graphics mode (see your printer manual).

Q: Why don't the font styles on my printouts correspond to the styles I specified in my spreadsheet cells?

A: Make sure that the /**O**ptions **G**raphics **Q**uality command is set to **F**inal. When this command is set to **D**raft, Quattro Pro does not use any Bitstream fonts that haven't been built.

Chapter Summary

This chapter showed you how to align, format, and protect your spreadsheet data. You also learned how to widen and narrow columns and how to perform operations on blocks of columns. The chapter concluded with an in-depth review of drawing lines, shading cells, and using and modifying fonts on a spreadsheet.

After completing this chapter you should understand the following Quattro Pro concepts:

- Aligning values and labels manually with a **S**tyle menu command

- Selecting meaningful and appropriate numeric format values, labels, dates, and times

- Using Ctrl-D to enter dates and times

- Protecting and unprotecting cell data and enabling and disabling global spreadsheet protection

- Setting, resetting, and auto-setting the width of a column or a block of columns

- Setting column widths in a window pane

- Hiding and unhiding column data

- Drawing, erasing, and printing lines and boxes

- Using, modifying, and printing shaded cells on a spreadsheet

- Selecting, changing, and customizing spreadsheet fonts to create presentation-quality reports

- Adding bullets to and inserting hard page breaks in a spreadsheet

- Changing default global format settings on the **O**ptions menu to create your own default spreadsheet formats

In Chapter 5, you learn how to incorporate Quattro Pro's powerful built-in @function commands into your spreadsheet applications. With these special commands, you can do complex mathematical, statistical, and database operations. These commands also enable you to manipulate data strings on a spreadsheet and extend the spreadsheet's capability to do what-if analysis with logical operators.

Using @Function Commands

In the preceding chapters, you learn how to build spreadsheets from the ground up and how to manage the form and content of your reports by using Quattro Pro's menu tree of commands. You also learn how to create basic formula relationships so that you can quickly add, subtract, multiply, and divide data on a spreadsheet.

So far, you have created formulas primarily using mathematical operators. For example, to add cells A5 and C9 and subtract cell D20, you enter +A5+C9-D20 into a third cell. But what if you want to sum the contents of a large block of cells, compute an average, display the total number of values used in the calculations, and then display each piece of information in a separate cell? To do this type of analysis, you must use Quattro Pro's special built-in spreadsheet formulas, called @function commands. @function (pronounced "at function") commands do a wide variety of special calculations and tasks that would be too difficult or too cumbersome for you to accomplish using simple spreadsheet formulas. These commands are the basic building blocks of all advanced spreadsheet applications. You can use them to average a group of numbers, to look up data in a block of cells, to create conditional formulas, and to perform calculations that help you determine the worth of an investment.

Other @function commands do tasks that would be impossible to accomplish with basic mathematical formulas. For example, suppose that you want to generate a random number, convert a value to its hexadecimal equivalent, or determine how much system RAM is available for Quattro Pro. These and many other objectives are easily met by using Quattro Pro's @function commands.

173

In all, Quattro Pro has 114 @function commands, divided into eight categories:

Mathematical
Statistical
String
Miscellaneous
Logical
Financial
Date and Time
Database Statistical

In Chapter 5, you learn how to use @functions in your own spreadsheets to solve unique, specific problems. In the first part of this chapter, you review the structure—or syntax—of the @functions command. When you understand the command syntax, go directly to the @function category that interests you most. The material in these sections reviews each command and often provides examples of how to use the command in a Quattro Pro spreadsheet.

Understanding Command Syntax

Each @function command has a three-part syntax: the @ symbol, the function name, and the argument(s). Table 5.1 describes these three parts.

Table 5.1
Components of the @function Command Syntax

Syntax element	Description
@	Indicates an "at function" command
FunctionName	Describes the type of operation to be performed
Argument$_n$	Denotes the data to use. An argument can be a value or a cell address. The value $_n$ defines the order in which Quattro Pro evaluates an argument in an @function operation.

A typical @function command looks like this:

@AVG(C5..C8)

In this syntax, @ tells Quattro Pro to expect an @function. AVG is the name of the @function that averages numbers, and (C5..C8) is the argument that defines the cell block containing the four numbers to average.

Entering @function Commands

Quattro Pro accepts three types of @function command arguments: numeric values, block values, and string values. A numeric value can be a number, a cell that contains a number, or a reference to another spreadsheet cell that contains a number. Quattro Pro accepts as valid arguments block names and formulas that result in numeric values. You can create many different combinations of arguments, using all these types of numeric numbers.

For example, @AVG(JAN,2500,A25..E30,(@ABS(G50))) is a valid use of the @AVG command as long as the following conditions are true:

- JAN is the name of a block that contains numerical data.

- Block A25..E30 contains numerical data.

- @ABS does not return ERR as its result.

A block value can be a single cell, any two valid cell coordinates, a reference to data on another spreadsheet, a block name, or any combination of these items.

For example, @AVG(JAN,A25..E30,(@ABS(G50))) is a valid use of the @AVG command as long as the following conditions are true:

- JAN is the name of a valid block.

- Block A25..E30 contains data.

- @ABS does not return ERR as its result.

A string value can be a string enclosed in quotes, a cell that contains a label, a reference to a cell on another spreadsheet that contains a label, a block name that contains a label, or another @function command that returns a string value. You can create many different combinations using each type of argument.

For example, @LENGTH(JAN,"Data Set #1",A25..E30,(@PROPER(G50))) is a valid use of the @LENGTH and @PROPER commands as long as the following conditions are true:

- JAN is the name of a block that contains a text string.

- Block A25..E30 contains text string data.

- @PROPER does not return ERR as its result.

When you enter @function commands into a spreadsheet, remember the following simple rules:

1. Do not enter extra spaces between the @ symbol, the function name, and the argument—Quattro Pro cannot properly interpret an @function with extra spaces.

2. You can use upper- or lowercase characters when entering an @function; Quattro Pro always displays the function in uppercase.

3. The arguments in an @function must be enclosed in parentheses.

4. The number and types of arguments used are different for each @function command.

5. You can use one @function command as an argument in another @function command.

Tip Press Alt-F3 to display a list of Quattro Pro's @function commands on-screen. To select a command from the list, highlight the command name and press Enter. Quattro Pro displays the function with a left parenthesis on the input line. To complete the operation, enter the appropriate arguments, a right parenthesis, and then press Enter to calculate a result in the active cell.

The next section introduces Quattro Pro's mathematical @function commands.

Using Mathematical @functions

The mathematical @functions fall into two categories: arithmetic and trigonometric @functions. The mathematical @functions duplicate operations commonly found on scientific and financial calculators.

By using these commands, you can calculate natural and common logarithms; absolute values; cosine, sine, tangent, and their inverses; square roots and random numbers; and many other types of math functions.

Keep these guidelines in mind when using mathematical @functions.

1. Express @SIN, @COS, and @TAN angles in radians, not in degrees.

2. The @ASIN, @ACOS, and @ATAN functions return angles in radian measure.

3. To convert degrees to radians, use the @RADIANS function or multiply the degree value by @PI/180.

4. To convert radians to degrees, use the @DEGREES function, or multiply the radian value by 180/@PI.

5. *e* is the base value of natural logarithms. The value *e*, as stored in Quattro Pro's memory, is 2.718281828459.

Using Arithmetic Commands in a Spreadsheet

Table 5.2 lists the arithmetic @function commands. The following definitions include examples of how you can use these commands in your own spreadsheets.

Table 5.2
Arithmetic Mathematical @function Commands

@function	Description
@ABS(x)	Returns the absolute value of x
@ExP(x)	Returns the constant *e*, raised to the xth power
@INT(x)	Drops the fractional portion of the number x
@LN(x)	Returns the natural logarithm of x
@LOG(x)	Returns the base 10 logarithm of x
@MOD(x,y)	Divides x by y and returns the remainder
@RAND	Supplies a random number between 0 and 1
@ROUND(x,N)	Rounds the value of x to N decimal places
@SQRT(x)	Returns the square root of x

@ABS(x)

@ABS returns the absolute or positive value of x when x is a numerical value.

Examples: @ABS(-20) = 20
@ABS(0) = 0
@ABS(A1) = 0 (if A1 contains a label)

@EXP(x)

The @ExP function gives the mathematical constant *e*, raised to the xth power, where x is a numeric value less than or equal to 709. The @EXP function is the inverse of a natural logarithm function (@LN).

Examples: @EXP(1) = 2.71828
@EXP(0) = 1.00000
@EXP(A1) = 0 (if A1 contains a label)
@EXP(800) = ERR

@INT(x)

The @INT function drops the fractional portion of x when x is a numeric value and returns its integer value.

Examples: @INT(1.9834) = 1
@INT(0.9921) = 0
@INT(A1) = 0 (if A1 contains a label)

@LN(x)

The @LN function returns the natural logarithm of x when x is a numeric value that is greater than 0. In any natural logarithm, the mathematical constant *e* is used as the base. You also can use @LN to return the inverse of @EXP.

Examples: @LN(1.00000) = 0
@LN(2.71828) = 1
@LN(@EXP(10)) = 10
@LN(-1) = ERR
@LN(A1) = ERR (if A1 contains a label)

@LOG(x)

@LOG returns the base 10 logarithm of x when x is a numeric value that is greater than 0.

Examples: @LOG(0) = ERR
@LOG(1) = 0
@LOG(10) = 1
@LOG(A1) = ERR (if A1 contains a label)

@MOD(x,y)

The @MOD function divides the x argument by y and returns any remainder. In this syntax, x must be a numeric value, and y must be a numeric value that is not equal to 0.

    Examples: @MOD(10,10) = 0
              @MOD(10,3.5) = 3
              @MOD(10,0) = ERR
              @MOD(A1,1) = 0 (if A1 contains a label or is blank)
              @MOD(3,A1) = ERR (if A1 contains a label)

@RAND

The @RAND function returns a fractional random number between 0 and 1. @RAND is useful when you need to create a set of random numbers to be used in statistical analysis.

To generate random numbers outside the 0 to 1 range, multiply the @RAND function by the difference between the high and low end of the new range, and then add the new low end number.

This formula is expressed as follows:

    @RAND * (high number − low number) + low number.

    Examples: @RAND*6 + 1 = returns random number between 1 and 5
              @RAND + 7 = returns a random number between 7 and 8

Tip | Quattro Pro generates a new random number for each existing @RAND function on a spreadsheet every time you enter data into the spreadsheet or press F9 to recalculate.

@ROUND(x,Num)

The @ROUND function rounds the value of x to Num decimal places. In this syntax, x must be a numeric value, and Num must be a numeric value that falls in the range −15 to 15.

    Examples: @ROUND(4.53494,3) = 4.535
              @ROUND(4.5,1) = 4.5
              @ROUND(0.5994,16) = ERR
              @ROUND(5.3,A1) = 5 (if A1 contains a label or is blank)
              @ROUND(A1,3) = 0 (if A1 contains a label or is blank)
              @ROUND(13.25,−1) = 10

@SQRT(x)

The @SQRT function supplies the square root of x when x is a numeric value that is greater than or equal to 0. Quattro Pro returns the value 0 when x is a label or a reference to a cell containing a label.

Examples: @SQRT(16) = 4
@SQRT(-25) = ERR
@SQRT(A1) = 0 (if A1 contains a label or is blank)

Using Trigonometric Commands in a Spreadsheet

Table 5.3 lists the trigonometric @function commands. The following definitions include examples how to use these commands in your own spreadsheets.

Table 5.3
Trigonometric @function Commands

@function	Description
@ACOS(x)	Returns the arccosine of radian angle x
@ASIN(x)	Returns the arcsine of radian angle x
@ATAN(x)	Returns the arctangent of radian angle x
@ATAN2(x,y)	Returns the arctangent of radian angle with coordinates x and y
@COS(x)	Returns the cosine of radian angle x
@DEGREES(x)	Converts x radians to degrees
@PI	Returns the value 3.1415926535898
@RADIANS(x)	Converts x degrees to radians
@SIN(x)	Returns the sine of radian angle x
@TAN(x)	Returns the tangent of radian angle x

@ACOS(x)

@ACOS returns the arccosine of angle x when x is a numeric value between
-1 and 1. The result is a radian angle whose cosine is x.

    Examples: @ACOS(-1) = 3.1416
              @ACOS(0) = 1.5708
              @ACOS(1) = 0
              @ACOS(2) = ERR

To convert radians to degrees, use @DEGREES. For example,

    @DEGREES(3.1416) = 180
    @DEGREES(1.5708) = 90
    @DEGREES(@ACOS(1)) = 0

@ASIN(x)

@ASIN returns the arcsine of angle x when x is a numeric value between -1
and 1. The result is a radian angle whose sine is x.

    Examples: @ASIN(-1) = -1.5708
              @ASIN(0) = 0
              @ASIN(1) = 1.5708
              @ASIN(2) = ERR

To convert radians to degrees, use @DEGREES. For example,

    @DEGREES(-1.5708) = -90
    @DEGREES(0) = 0
    @DEGREES(@ASIN(1)) = 90

@ATAN(x)

@ATAN returns the arctangent of angle x when x is a numeric value. The
result is a radian angle whose tangent is x.

    Examples: @ATAN(-1) = -0.7854
              @ATAN(0) = 0
              @ATAN(1) = 0.7854

To convert radians to degrees, use @DEGREES. For example,

    @DEGREES(-0.7854) = -45
    @DEGREES(0) = 0
    @DEGREES(@ATAN(1)) = 45

@ATAN2(x,y)

@ATAN2 returns the arctangent of an angle with coordinates x and y, when both x and y are numeric values. The result is a radian angle whose tangent is x/y.

Examples: @ATAN2(2,3) = 0.9828
@ATAN2(0,3) = 1.5708
@ATAN2(0,0) = ERR

To convert radians to degrees, use @DEGREES. For example,

@DEGREES(ATAN2(0,3)) = 90

@COS(x)

@COS returns the cosine of angle x when x is a numeric value entered in radians.

Examples: @COS(-1) = -0.5403
@COS(0) = 1
@COS(1) = 0.5403

To convert degrees to radians, use @RADIANS. For example,

@COS(@RADIANS(45)) = 0.707107

@DEGREES(x)

@DEGREES converts x radians to degrees when x is a numeric value. To convert x radians to degrees, you also can multiply x by (180/PI).

Examples: @DEGREES(0.5236) = 30
@DEGREES(1.0472) = 60
@DEGREES(1.5708) = 90

@PI

@PI returns the value of pi as 3.1415926535898. Pi is the ratio of a circle's circumference to its diameter.

@RADIANS(x)

@RADIANS converts x degrees to radians when x is a numeric value. To convert x degrees to radians, you also can multiply x by (PI/180).

Examples: @RADIANS(30) = 0.5236
@RADIANS(60) = 1.0472
@RADIANS(90) = 1.5708

@SIN(x)

The @SIN function returns the sine of the radian angle x when x is a numeric value entered in radians.

Examples: @SIN(-1) = -0.8415
@SIN(0) = 0
@SIN(1) = 0.8415

To convert degrees into radians, use @RADIANS. For example,

@SIN(RADIANS(30)) = 0.5

@TAN(x)

The @TAN function returns the tangent of the radian angle x when x is a numeric value entered in radians.

Examples: @TAN(-1) = -1.5574
@TAN(0) = 0
@TAN(1) = 1.5574

To convert degrees into radians, use @RADIANS. For example,

@TAN(@RADIANS(45)) = 1

Using Statistical @functions

The statistical @function commands calculate common statistical measures by using sample and population data sets. Table 5.4 describes the statistical @functions. Most of the statistical @functions use the List argument to define the location of the data set. In this syntax, List can be one or more numeric or block values. When you use more than one cell block in an argument, separate the blocks with commas.

Table 5.4
Statistical @function Commands

@function	Description
@AVG(List)	Calculates the average of the values in List
@COUNT(List)	Counts the number of nonblank cells in List
@MAX(List)	Returns the maximum numeric or date value in List
@MIN(List)	Returns the minimum numeric value in List
@STD(List)	Returns the population standard deviation of List
@STDS(List)	Returns the sample standard deviation of List
@SUM(List)	Sums all the numeric values in List
@SUMPRODUCT(Block1,Block2)	Returns the sum and product of Block1 and Block2
@VAR(List)	Returns the population variance of List
@VARS(List)	Returns the sample variance of List

Figure 5.1 illustrates an application that uses the statistical @function commands to analyze automobile production statistics. In this example, List is the block C5..G8.

As you read through the following command definitions, refer to figure 5.1 to learn more about how to use a particular command in an application.

@AVG(List)

The @AVG function calculates the average of all values in List. Quattro Pro ignores blank cells and treats labels as 0 when it calculates an average.

    Examples: @AVG(C5..C8) = 423.5
                   @AVG(D5..D8) = 396.3

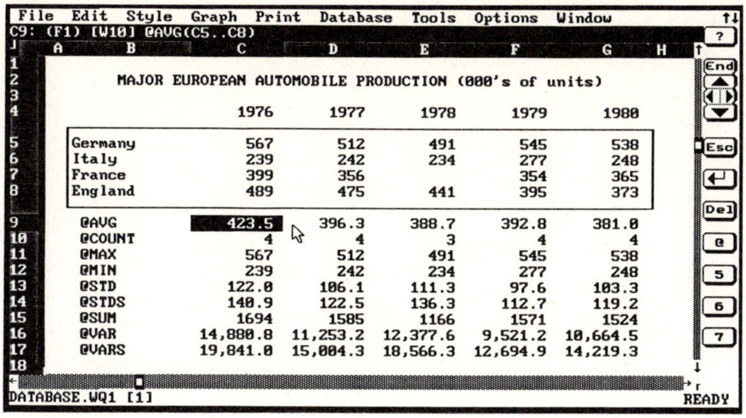

**Fig. 5.1
A statistical
@function
application.**

@COUNT(List)

The @COUNT function counts the number of nonblank cells in List. This function can be used to return the number of cells in List that contain data or to locate the number of missing entries in a range of cells that always contains a fixed number of entries.

> Examples: @COUNT(C5..C8) = 4
> @COUNT(C5..C8,D5..D8) = 8
> @COUNT(E5..E8) = 3

@MAX(List)

The @MAX function returns the maximum numeric or date value in List. This function can be used to select the latest invoice date in a register, to pick the highest production figure from an analysis report, or to locate the final transaction number in an accounting journal.

> Examples: @MAX(D5..D8) = 512
> @MAX(C5..C8,D5..D8) = 567

@MIN(List)

The @MIN function gives the minimum numeric value in List. This function can be used to select the first invoice date in a register, to pick the lowest production figure from an analysis report, or to locate the first transaction number in an accounting journal.

Examples: @MIN(F5..F8) = 277
@MIN(E5..E8,F5..F8) = 234

@STD(List)

The @STD function calculates the standard deviation of the values in List when List is the population data set. The square of this function —@STD(List)^2—returns the population variance.

Standard deviation tells you how much each value in List differs from the average of all the values in List. One use of @STD is to determine the reliability of the average. The lower the standard deviation, the less each value in List varies from the average.

The @STD function ignores blank cells and treats labels as 0. When List contains only blank cells, @STD returns ERR.

Examples: @STD(G5..G8) = 103.3
@STD(B9..G9) = ERR

@STDS(List)

The @STDS function calculates the standard deviation of the values in List when List is a sample drawn from the population data set. The square of this function—@STDS(List)^2—is the sample variance.

The @STDS function ignores any blank cells and treats labels as 0. When List contains only blank cells, @STDS returns ERR.

Example: @STDS(F5..F8) = 112.7

Tip | @STDS is not a 1-2-3 compatible @function command. If you need to calculate standard deviation for data appearing on a 1-2-3 compatible spreadsheet, use the @STD function.

@SUM(List)

The @SUM function returns the sum total of all numeric values in List. This @function is used to add up data in cell blocks.

Examples: @SUM(C5..C8) = 1,694
@SUM(D5..D8) = 1,585
@SUM(C5..C8,D5.4.D8) = 3,279

@SUMPRODUCT(Block1,Block2)

The @SUMPRODUCT function returns the sum and the product of the two block arguments. In this syntax, Quattro Pro multiplies each corresponding cell value in Block1 and Block2 and then adds the results.

To properly use this command, the two blocks must have the same number of rows and columns. The blocks can be a one-dimensional row or column, but they must be equal in length. Quattro Pro returns ERR when the two blocks are unequal in length.

For example, suppose that the following cells contain the data shown:

```
D10 = 1 E10 = 1
D11 = 2 E11 = 2
D12 = 3 E12 = 3
D13 = 4 E13 = 4
```

The data in these cells would yield the following results:

```
@SUMPRODUCT(D10..D11,E10..E11) = 5
@SUMPRODUCT(D12..D13,E12..E13) = 25
@SUMPRODUCT(D10..D13,E10..E13) = 30
```

Tip | @SUMPRODUCT is not a 1-2-3 compatible function—do not use it in a spreadsheet that requires 1-2-3 compatibility.

@VAR(List)

The @VAR function calculates the variance of all nonblank, numeric cells in List when List represents the population data set (the *n-biased* method). In this syntax, Quattro Pro treats text as 0. Take the square root of this function to derive the population standard deviation.

Examples: @VAR(E5..E8) = 12,377.6
@VAR(G5..G8) = 10,664.5

@VARS(List)

The @VARS function supplies the variance of all nonblank, numeric cells in List when List represents a sample drawn from the population data set (the *n-1 biased* method). In this syntax, Quattro Pro treats text as 0. Take the square root of this function to derive the sample standard deviation.

Examples: @VARS(E5..E8) = 12,811.6
@VARS(G5..G8) = 14,219.3

Tip | @VARS is not a 1-2-3 compatible function—do not use it in a spreadsheet that requires 1-2-3 compatibility.

The next section introduces Quattro Pro's string @function commands.

Using String @functions

The string @function commands give you the power to manipulate letters and numbers that appear in a label. These commands work only on labels, although they do treat a number appearing in a label as if it were text.

String manipulation is like doing mathematical operations on letters. Quattro Pro can do this because these @functions use special arguments. Table 5.5 describes these string @functions arguments.

Table 5.5
String @function Command Arguments

Argument	Description
Block	A block value
Code	A numeric value between 1 and 255
DecPlaces	A numeric value between 0 and 15
NewString	A string value that represents the characters to insert at position *Num*
Num	A numeric value >= 0
StartNumber	A numeric value, >= 0, that denotes the character position at which to begin the search
String	A string value; a hexadecimal number in quotes
String1	A valid string value
String2	A valid string value
SubString	A valid string value to search through
x	A numeric value

Among other things, these special functions enable you to add and subtract text strings, alter the upper- and lowercase settings for any character in a string and search through and replace data in labels. Table 5.6 describes the string @functions.

Table 5.6
String @function Commands

@function	Description
@CHAR(Code)	Returns the ASCII character corresponding to Code
@CLEAN(String)	Removes all non-ASCII characters from String
@CODE(String)	Changes the first character in String to ASCII
@EXACT(String1,String2)	Compares the value of String1 to String2
@FIND(SubString, String,StartNumber)	Searches through String for SubString
@HEXTONUM(String)	Converts the hexadecimal number in String to its equivalent decimal value
@LEFT(String,Num)	Displays the far-left Num characters in String
@LENGTH(String)	Returns the number of characters in String
@LOWER(String)	Converts String to lowercase characters
@MID(String,StartNumber,Num)	Returns the first Num characters in String, starting with character number StartNumber
@N(Block)	Returns the numeric value of the upper left cell in Block
@NUMTOHEX(x)	Converts x to its hexadecimal string value
@PROPER(String)	Converts the first letter of every word in String to uppercase

Table 5.6—*continued*

@*function*	*Description*
@REPEAT(String,Num)	Returns Num copies of String as one continuous label
@REPLACE(String, StartNum,Num,NewString)	Replaces characters in String with NewString
@RIGHT(String,Num)	Displays the last Num characters in String
@S(Block)	Returns the string value of the upper left cell in Block
@STRING(x,DecPlaces)	Converts x to a string, rounded to DecPlaces places
@TRIM(String)	Removes extraneous spaces from String
@UPPER(String)	Returns String in uppercase characters
@VALUE(String)	Converts String into a numeric value

@CHAR(Code)

The @CHAR function displays the ASCII character equivalent of Code. The valid code range is 1–255.

    Examples: @CHAR(0) = ERR
               @CHAR(60) = <
               @CHAR(65) = A
               @CHAR(94) = ˆ
               @CHAR(155) = ¢
               @CHAR(256) = ERR

@CLEAN(String)

The @CLEAN function erases all the non-ASCII characters it encounters in String.

@CODE(String)

The @CODE function displays the ASCII code equivalent of the first character it encounters in String. This function is the inverse of the @CHAR function.

Examples: @CODE("<") = 60
@CODE("A") = 65
@CODE("^") = 94

@EXACT(String1,String2)

The @EXACT function compares String1 to String2. When the values are identical, Quattro Pro returns 1; otherwise it returns 0.

Enclose both compare strings in quotes except when the string is a block name. When Quattro Pro compares labels, it ignores numbers and label prefixes.

Examples: @EXACT("trust","Trust") = 0
@EXACT("Trust","Trust") = 1
@EXACT(50,"50") = ERR

@FIND(SubString,String,StartNumber)

@FIND searches through String for SubString. If Quattro Pro finds SubString, it returns the character position of the first occurrence of SubString.

Quattro Pro begins the @FIND operation at position number StartNumber in String. The first character in String is designated as 0, the second as 1, and so on. StartNumber cannot be greater than the number of characters in String, minus 1.

Use the @FIND function with @REPLACE to perform a search and replace operation. When @FIND fails to find at least one occurrence of SubString, Quattro Pro returns ERR.

Examples: @FIND("i","girth",0) = 1
@FIND("h","girth",0) = 4
@FIND("G","girth",0) = ERR

@HEXTONUM(String)

@HEXTONUM converts the hexadecimal number in String to its equivalent decimal value. In this syntax, String must be surrounded by quotes.

    Examples: @HEXTONUM("f") = 15
                @HEXTONUM("35") = 53

@LEFT(String,Num)

The @LEFT function displays the number of characters specified (Num) that it finds in String. This function extracts characters from the left side of String.

Quattro Pro returns ERR when String is a numeric value, a date value, or a blank cell. Quattro Pro returns all of String if Num is longer than the length of String.

    Examples: @LEFT("John",2) = Jo
                @LEFT("John",10) = John
                @LEFT(45,2) = ERR

@LENGTH(String)

@LENGTH returns the character length of String, including spaces. Use the ampersand (&) to combine strings and cell addresses. Place quotes around String when it is a text string. Quattro Pro returns ERR if String references a blank cell or is not surrounded by quotes.

    Examples: @LENGTH("John") = 4
                @LENGTH("Hello"&"Greetings") = 14
                @LENGTH(123456) = ERR

@LOWER(String)

@LOWER converts String to a lowercase character display. Quattro Pro does not alter numbers and symbols appearing in String, but returns ERR when String is a blank cell or is a number or date value.

    Examples: @LOWER("STRING") = string
                @LOWER("Hello, John.") = hello, john.
                @LOWER("94 Carroll Canyon") = 94 carroll canyon
                @LOWER(32876) = ERR

@MID(String,StartNumber,Num)

@MID extracts the first Num characters in String, beginning with character number StartNumber. In this syntax, String must be a text string surrounded by quotes, or a reference to a cell containing a text string surrounded by quotes. Quattro Pro returns a blank cell when StartNumber is greater than the length of String and when Num is 0.

Quattro Pro does not enable you to enter strings without quotes. If you try, the program beeps and displays an error message.

Examples: @MID("John Donavan",5,7) = Donavan
@MID("Tim Atkins",20,5) = ""
@MID("Scott Matthews",6,4) = Matt
@MID(2519,1,2) = ERR

@N(Block)

The @N function returns the numeric value located in the upper left cell of Block. @N returns a 0 if the upper left cell in Block contains a label or is blank.

Examples: @N(A1..A5) = 25 when A1 contains the value 25
@N(A1..A5) = 0 when A1 is blank
@N(A1..A5) = 0 when A1 contains the label "DATA"

Quattro Pro uses the @N function for compatibility with other spreadsheets. This function is used in other spreadsheets to avoid ERR values resulting from attempts to do calculations using labels.

@NUMTOHEX(x)

The @NUMTOHEX function returns the hexadecimal equivalent of x as a string value.

Examples: @NUMTOHEX(106) = 6A
@NUMTOHEX(219) = DB

@PROPER(String)

@PROPER modifies String so that the first letter of each word in String is uppercase and all other letters are lowercase. Blank spaces, punctuation marks, and numbers signify the end of a word.

Examples: @PROPER("JOHN doNAVAN") = John Donavan
@PROPER("JAMES J. PARKER") = James J. Parker
@PROPER("1990's census") = 1990'S Census

@REPEAT(String,Num)

The @REPEAT function returns Num copies of String as a single, continuous label. In this syntax, Num is a numeric value that is greater than or equal to 0. When repeating a text string, enclose String in double quotes.

Examples: @REPEAT("hello!",3) = hello!hello!hello!
@REPEAT("*",20) = ********************

@REPLACE(String,StartNum,Num,NewString)

The @REPLACE function enables you to replace Num characters in String with NewString, beginning at character StartNum in String. In this syntax, Num is a numeric value greater than or equal to 0 that identifies the number of characters to replace.

Examples: @REPLACE("O'Nickels",2,7,"Grady") = O'Grady
@REPLACE("Jenny L. Peters",6,3,"") = Jenny Peters
@REPLACE("Inventory Figures",10,0,"Control ") =
Inventory Control Figures

Tip | When you use this command to insert one string into another, leave a blank space after NewString and before the final quote. This space ensures the proper number of spaces between words.

@RIGHT(String,Num)

The @RIGHT function displays the last Num characters in String. Use this function to extract characters from the right side of a label or string.

@RIGHT returns ERR when String is a not valid string. @RIGHT returns an empty string or "" when Num is 0. Quattro Pro returns the entire string when the character length of Num is greater than the number of characters in String.

Examples: @RIGHT("Jeff Turner",6) = Turner
@RIGHT("Jeff Turner",11) = Jeff Turner
@RIGHT("123",1) = 3
@RIGHT(567,1) = ERR

@S(Block)

@S returns the string value located in the upper left cell of Block. Quattro Pro returns a blank cell if Block contains a numerical value, a date value, or a blank cell.

Examples: @S(A1..A5) = DATA when A1 contains the label "DATA"
@S(A1..A5) = when A1 is blank
@S(A1..A5) = when A1 contains the value 25

@STRING(x,DecPlaces)

The @STRING function converts x to a string rounded to DecPlaces decimal places. In this syntax, x is a numeric value, and DecPlaces must be a numeric value between 0 and 15.

After you convert a number or date to a label with the @STRING function, Quattro Pro does not permit you to format the display of the returned value.

Examples: @STRING(14.88,0) = 15
@STRING(78.7,2) = 78.70
@STRING("John",3) = 0.000

@TRIM(String)

@TRIM removes extraneous spaces from String. This function deletes spaces after the last nonspace character or before the first nonspace character. @TRIM eliminates extra spaces between words. Quattro Pro returns ERR when String is empty or contains a numeric value.

Examples: @TRIM(" extra spaces ") = "extra spaces"
@TRIM("no extra spaces") = "no extra spaces"
@TRIM(456) = ERR

@UPPER(String)

@UPPER returns String in uppercase characters. Quattro Pro does not alter numbers and symbols, but returns ERR when String is a numerical value, a date value, or a blank.

Examples: @UPPER("upper") = UPPER
@UPPER("Hello there") = HELLO THERE
@UPPER(1234) = ERR
@UPPER("94 Carroll Canyon") = 94 CARROLL CANYON

@VALUE(String)

The @VALUE function converts String into a numeric value. String may contain arithmetic operators, but Quattro Pro ignores dollar signs, commas, and leading and trailing spaces. If Quattro Pro encounters an embedded space in String, this function returns ERR.

Examples: @VALUE(" 4.58") = 4.58
@VALUE(" 4.33 ") = 4.33
@VALUE("10. 25") = ERR
@VALUE(12/4) = 3
@VALUE("200,872") = 200872 (comma is omitted)

Using Miscellaneous @functions

The miscellaneous @function commands supply you with information about your spreadsheet and about the current work session. For example, these commands tell you the number of rows or columns in a block, display the format attributes for a cell, and display the amount of extended or expanded memory currently available to Quattro Pro.

When a command's syntax contains Attribute as an argument, you can use any of the attributes listed in table 5.7. Attribute must be enclosed in quotes or must be a reference to a cell that contains a valid attribute. (For a listing of possible formats, see tables 5.8, 5.9, and 5.10.)

Table 5.7
Valid Quattro Pro Attribute Codes

Code	Description
"address"	Specifies the address of the upper left cell in Block
"row"	Specifies the row number of the upper left cell in Block. The "row" code ranges from 1 to 8192.
"col"	Specifies the column number of the upper left cell in Block. The "column" code ranges from 1 to 256.
"contents"	Specifies the contents of the upper left cell in Block
"type"	Specifies the type of data in the upper left cell in Block, as follows: b is a blank cell. 1 is a cell that contains a label. v is a cell that contains a formula or number.
"prefix"	Specifies the label-prefix character of the upper left cell in Block. \ is the repeating label prefix. " is the right-aligned label prefix. ^ is the centered label prefix. ' is the left-aligned label prefix.
"protect"	Specifies the protection status of the upper left cell in Block, as follows: 0 is an unprotected cell 1 is a protected cell
"width"	Specifies the width of the column containing the upper left cell in Block. The "width" code ranges from 1 to 254.
"rwidth"	Specifies the width of Block
"format"	Specifies the current numeric format of the upper left cell in Block. The valid numeric formats are shown in table 5.8.

Table 5.8
Valid Numeric Formats

Code	Description
+	+/− bar graph
,n	Commas, where n = 0 to 15
Cn	Currency, where n = 0 to 15
En	Exponential, where n = 0 to 15
Fn	Fixed, where n = 0 to 15
G	General
H	Hidden
Pn	Percent, where n = 0 to 15
Sn	Scientific, where n = 0 to 15
T	Formulas displayed as text

Table 5.9
Valid Date Formats

Code	Description
D1	DD-MMM-YY
D2	DD-MMM
D3	MMM-YY
D4	MM/DD/YY DD/MM/YY DD.MM.YY YY-MM-DD
D5	MM/DD DD/MM DD.MM MM-DD

You can choose one of four settings for codes D4 and D5 by choosing the /Options International command. When you choose a new default setting, that setting becomes the default long international date format when you choose /Style Numeric Format Date 1 (Long Intl.) or 2 (Short Intl.).

Table 5.10
Valid Time Formats

Code	Description
D6	HH:MM:SS AM/PM
D7	HH:MM AM/PM
D8	HH:MM:SS-24hr HH.MM.SS-24hr HH,MM,SS-24hr HHhMMmSSm
D9	HH:MM-24hr HH.MM-24hr HH,MM, HHhMMm

You can choose one of four settings for codes D8 and D9 by choosing the /Options International command. When you choose a new default setting, that setting becomes the default long international time format when you choose /Style **N**umeric Format **D**ate **T**ime **1** or (Long Intl.) and **2** (Short Intl.).

Miscellaneous @function commands also enable you to look up entries in a data table. A horizontal lookup table is a range containing value information that ascends from left to right in the top row. A vertical lookup table is a range containing value information that ascends from top to bottom in the far left column. Table 5.11 describes the miscellaneous @function commands.

Table 5.11
Miscellaneous @function Commands

@*function*	*Description*
@@(Cell)	Returns the contents of Cell as an address or cell block when Cell is a label
@CELL(Attribute,Block)	Returns attributes for a cell in Block
@CELLINDEX (Attribute,Block,Column,Row)	Returns attributes for a cell offset Column columns and Row rows
@CELLPOINTER (Attribute)	Returns attributes for the active cell
@CHOOSE(Number,List)	Returns the value from List located in the Number position
@COLS(Block)	Returns the number of columns in Block
@CURVALUE(GeneralAction, SpecificAction)	Describes the most recent menu command execution
@ERR	Returns ERR in a cell
@HLOOKUP(x,Block,Row)	Searches for the first value $<=$ to x and returns the value located Row rows below it in Block
@INDEX(Block,Column,Row)	Searches a data table for a value
@MEMAVAIL	Returns the number of available bytes of conventional memory
@MEMEMSAVAIL	Returns the number of available bytes of expanded memory

Table 5.11—*continued*

@*function*	*Description*
@NA	Returns the special value NA (Not Available)
@ROWS(Block)	Returns the number of rows in a given block
@VERSION	Supplies the version number of Quattro Pro
@VLOOKUP(x,Block,Column)	Searches for the first value <= to x, and returns the value located Column columns to the right of it in Block

Figure 5.2 shows how to use a table to analyze every possible attribute for three cells by using the @CELL command. Here, the attributes for the data appearing in D3, E3, and F3 appear in block D4..F13. As you read the next several command definitions, refer to figure 5.2 to learn more about how to use a particular command in an application.

Fig. 5.2
Analyzing attributes in a table.

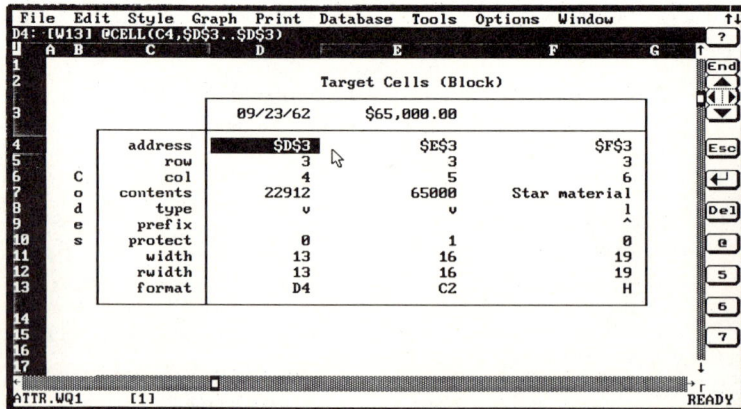

@@(Cell)

The @@(Cell) function converts Cell into a single-cell address. In this syntax, Cell must be a single-cell address or block name in label form. The @@ function translates the label and then returns the contents of that cell.

Examples: @@("B6") = C
@@("E2") = Target Cells (Block)
@@("D4") = $D$3

@CELL(Attribute,Block)

The @CELL function evaluates Block and returns an attribute code specified by Attribute. In this syntax, Attribute must be one of the attribute codes from table 5.7, and Block must be a value or label.

Attribute may be entered in uppercase or lowercase but must be surrounded by quotes. Attribute also can be the address of a cell that contains a value or label.

Examples: @CELL("address",D3) = $D$3 (see fig. 5.2)
@CELL("format",E3) = C2 (see fig. 5.2)
@CELL("protect",F3) = 0 (see fig. 5.2)

@CELLINDEX(Attribute,Block,Column,Row)

The @CELLINDEX function evaluates Block and returns an attribute code specified by Attribute. In this syntax, Attribute must be one of the attribute codes from table 5.7, and Block must be a value or label.

Examples: @CELLINDEX("type",D4..F13,2,4) = 1
@CELLINDEX("width",D4..F13,2,1) = 19

This function works just like @CELL but returns the attribute for a cell offset Column columns and Row rows from the first coordinate in Block (see fig. 5.2.)

@CELLPOINTER(Attribute)

The @CELLPOINTER function evaluates the active cell (where the cell selector is) and returns an attribute code specified by Attribute. In this syntax, Attribute must be one of the attributes codes from table 5.7.

This function works just like @CELL and @CELLINDEX but returns the specified Attribute code for the active cell. If you move the cell selector to a different cell, press F9 to calculate a new result for the @CELLPOINTER function (see fig. 5.2).

Examples: @CELLPOINTER("rwidth") = 19 when F12 is the active cell
@CELLPOINTER("contents") = 65000 when F12 is the active cell

@CHOOSE(Number,List)

The @CHOOSE function returns the value from List located in the Number position. In this syntax, Number is a numeric value that is less than or equal to the number of items in List minus 1, and List is equal to a group of numeric or string values separated by commas.

The value of Number determines which List value is selected. For example, 0 selects the first value in list, 1 the second, 2 the third, and so on. Number may be a cell address, any integer, a string, or a mixture of the three, and List must not exceed 254 characters.

Examples: @CHOOSE(0,"John","Pat","Craig") = John
@CHOOSE(1,"John","Pat","Craig") = Pat
@CHOOSE(2,"John","Pat","Craig") = Craig
@CHOOSE(5,"John","Pat","Craig") = ERR

@COLS(Block)

The @COLS function returns the number of columns in Block. In this syntax, Block may be a cell block or a block name.

Examples: @COLS(A1..IV1) = 256
@COLS(A1..A1) = 1

@CURVALUE(GeneralAction,SpecificAction)

The @CURVALUE function returns a description of a menu command setting specified by GeneralAction and SpecificAction. In this syntax, GeneralAction is a general menu category such as File, and SpecificAction is a specific menu choice such as Save As. Both arguments must be surrounded by quotes.

Examples: @CURVALUE("file","save") = C:\QPRO\SALES.WQ1
(the name of the last file saved with the Save As command on the File menu)

@CURVALUE("file","directory") = C:\QPRO
(the name of the current Directory setting on the File menu)

@CURVALUE("graph","type") = Stacked Bar
(the current **G**raph Type setting on the Graph menu)

@ERR

The @ERR function returns the value ERR. Use this function to return ERR in the active cell, and in any other cells that reference the active cell.

The following @function commands do not return ERR when they reference a cell containing ERR: @COUNT, @DCOUNT, @ISERR, @ISNA, @ISNUMBER, @ISSTRING, and @CELL.

When used in conjunction with the @IF function, @ERR is useful for calling attention to errors on the active spreadsheet. The returned value ERR is not a label—it is a unique number that Quattro Pro reserves to identify error conditions on a spreadsheet.

@HLOOKUP(x,Block,Row)

The @HLOOKUP function moves through Block horizontally, looking for the last value that is less than or equal to x. When the search is successful, Quattro Pro returns the value located Row number of rows below it. This function provides you with an effective way to access information stored in a data table.

In this syntax, x can be a character string, a number, or a cell address (or block name) that references a label or value. When x is a string, Quattro Pro searches for an exact match. @HLOOKUP returns the highest number in the row that is not more than x when Quattro Pro cannot find an equal number.

Block must be a cell block address that describes the location of the data table. Block can describe the whole table or just part of the table to restrict the lookup operation.

Row tells Quattro Pro how many rows to look down through to find the value that it will return. The row argument cannot exceed the number of rows in the data table, or Quattro Pro returns ERR. When Row is 0, @HLOOKUP returns the x value itself.

Quattro Pro searches from left to right through the table rows, looking for a match to x. When it finds an exact match, it stops at that column. When it does not find an exact match, it stops at the column that contains the value closest to but not greater than x.

Figure 5.3 illustrates different ways to look through a data table using the @HLOOKUP command.

In the first example, Quattro Pro searches horizontally through the first row in block C3..G7. When the program locates the last value that is less than or equal to 30 before encountering a value that is greater than 30 (it stops at 22), Quattro Pro displays the cell value three rows down (the value 31).

In the second example, Quattro Pro searches horizontally through the first row in block C3..G7. When the program locates the last value that is less than or equal to 45 before encountering a value that is greater than 45 (it stops at 45), Quattro Pro displays the value in the cell 0 rows down (the value 45).

In the third example, Quattro Pro searches horizontally through the first row in block C3..G7. When the program locates the last value that is less than or equal to 53 before encountering a value that is greater than 53 (it stops at 45), Quattro Pro displays the cell value three rows down (the value 19).

In the fourth example, Quattro Pro searches horizontally through the first row in block C3..G7. When the program locates the last value that is less than or equal to 30 before encountering a value that is greater than 30 (it stops at 22), Quattro Pro attempts to display the value in the cell five rows down. Because this cell falls outside of the defined Block, Quattro Pro displays ERR.

In the fifth example, Quattro Pro searches horizontally through the first row in block C3..G7. When the program encounters the illegal definition for the X argument ("text"), Quattro Pro displays ERR.

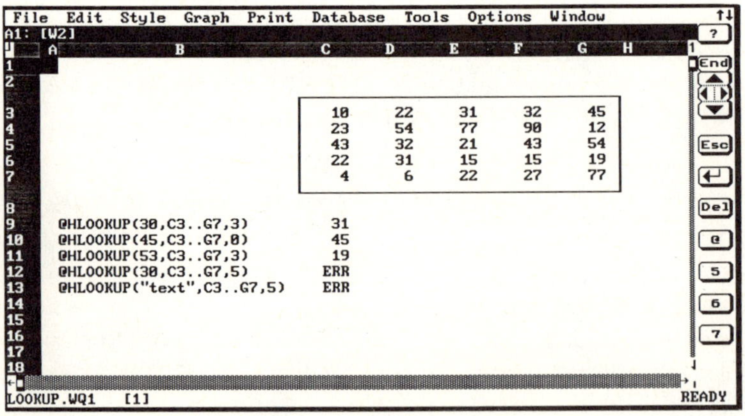

Fig. 5.3
Searching through a data table with @HLOOKUP.

@INDEX(Block,Column,Row)

The @INDEX function uses the data table specified by Block. This function returns a value offset Column number of columns and Row number of rows.

In this syntax, Column and Row are not cell addresses, but offset values. In an @INDEX operation, Quattro Pro starts with the top left cell in Block, moves right Column number of columns, moves down Row number of Rows, and then returns the value located in the active cell.

Column and Row must be values that are less than the number of rows or columns in the block and are greater than or equal to zero. If a decimal is specified, Quattro Pro drops the fractional part of the decimal—it rounds the value.

Figure 5.4 illustrates different ways to look through a data table using the @INDEX command.

In the first example, Quattro Pro begins at the first cell in block C3..G7. The program offsets 3 columns (to the 32 value) and 1 row (to the 90 value) and displays 90.

In the second example, Quattro Pro begins at the first cell in block C3..G7. The program offsets 0 columns (to the 10 value) and 0 rows (to the 10 value) and displays 10.

In the third example, Quattro Pro begins at the first cell in block C3..G7. The program offsets 4 columns (to the 45 value) and 4 rows (to the 77 value) and displays 77.

In the fourth example, Quattro Pro begins at the first cell in block C3..G7. The program offsets 4 columns (to the 45 value) and 5 rows. Because this row offset falls outside the area defined in the Block argument, Quattro Pro displays ERR.

In the fifth example, Quattro Pro begins at the first cell in block C3..G7. The program offsets 7 columns. Because this column offset falls outside the area defined in the Block argument, Quattro Pro displays ERR.

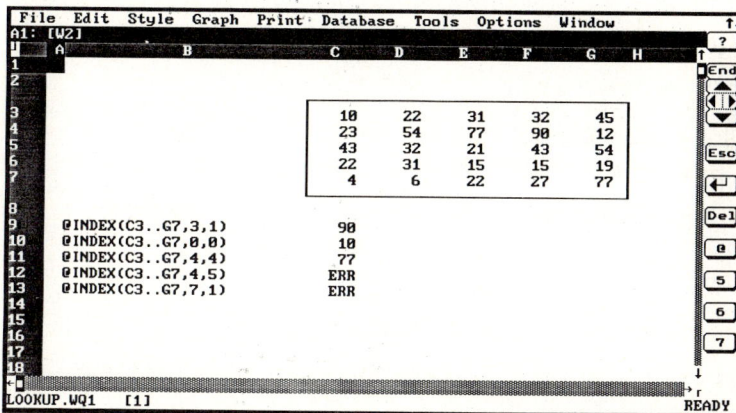

Fig. 5.4 Searching through a data table with @INDEX.

@MEMAVAIL

@MEMAVAIL displays the number of bytes of conventional memory currently available to Quattro Pro.

Example: @MEMAVAIL = 46923 (46,923 bytes of available memory)

@MEMEMSAVAIL

The @MEMEMSAVAIL function displays the number of bytes of expanded memory (EMS) currently available to Quattro Pro. If your system does not contain expanded memory, Quattro Pro returns NA (Not Available).

Example: @MEMEMSAVAIL = 28000 (if your system contains 28K of free EMS)

@NA

The @NA function returns the value NA. Like ERR, NA is a unique number and not a label. When your spreadsheet contains formulas that reference a value entered as @NA, Quattro Pro returns NA.

@NA helps prevent the trickle-down effect of displaying erroneous data in a spreadsheet, because Quattro Pro treats NA as a value and not as an ERR.

Figure 5.5, for example, shows the cell selector in cell H12. The formula in this cell uses data displayed in the range H7..H10. @NA was placed in cell H10 because this expense figure is not available. Quattro Pro displays NA as the result in all cells with formulas that depend upon the data in block H7..H10, whether directly (as the formula in H12) or indirectly (as other formulas that use the H12 result in their own formula).

@ROWS(Block)

The @ROWS function returns the number of rows in Block. In this syntax, Block may be a cell block or a block name.

Examples: @ROWS(A1..IV1) = 1
@ROWS(A1..A10) = 10
@ROWS(ADDRESS) = 50 (if ADDRESS = A1..A50, for example)

```
File  Edit  Style  Graph  Print  Database  Tools  Options  Window        ↑↓
H12: (,0) +H5-@SUM(H7..H10)                                              [?]
  A      B       C        D       E       F       G       H              [End]
1
2                                1987    1988    1989    1990            [▲]
3        Sales                    833     877     912   1,282            [◄│►]
4        Cost of Goods Sold       625     649     670     910            [▼]
5        Gross Margin             208     228     242     372
6                                                                        [Esc]
7        Operating Expenses        42      41      39      56
8        General Expenses          21      23      24      37            [↵]
9        Administrative Expenses   10      11      12      19
10       Corporate Expenses        16      17      18      NA            [Del]
11
12       Net Margin               120     136     149     NA             [@]
13       % margin               14.4%   15.5%   16.3%     NA
14                                                                       [5]
15       Income taxes              60      68      74      NA
16       % taxes                 7.2%    7.7%    8.1%      NA            [6]
17
18       After-tax income          60      68      74      NA            [7]
19       % after-tax             7.2%    7.7%    8.1%      NA
20
NA.WQ1      [1]                                                        READY
```

Fig. 5.5
Use @NA to indicate data not yet available.

@VERSION

The @VERSION function displays Quattro Pro's version number in a user-specified cell.

@VLOOKUP(x,Block,Column)

The @VLOOKUP function works just like @HLOOKUP, except that it searches through Block by columns instead of by rows.

The @VLOOKUP function moves through Block vertically, looking for the last value that is less than or equal to x. When the search is successful, Quattro Pro returns the value located Column number of columns to the right. This function gives you an effective way to access information stored in a data table.

In this syntax, x can be a character string, a number, or a cell address (or block name) that references a label or value. When x is a string, Quattro Pro searches for an exact match. @VLOOKUP returns the highest number in the column not more than x when Quattro Pro cannot find an equal number.

Block must be a cell block address that describes the location of the data table. Block can describe the whole table, or just part of the table, to restrict the lookup operation.

Column tells Quattro Pro how many columns to look through to find the value that it will return. The column argument cannot exceed the number of columns in the data table or Quattro Pro returns ERR. When Column is 0, @VLOOKUP returns the x value itself.

Quattro Pro searches from top to bottom through the table rows, looking for a match to x. When it finds an exact match, it stops at that row. When it does not find an exact match, it stops at the row containing the value closest to but not greater than x.

Figure 5.6 illustrates different ways to look through a data table by using the @VLOOKUP command.

In the first example, Quattro Pro searches vertically through the first column in block C3..G7. When the program locates the last value that is less than or equal to 30 before encountering one that is greater than 30 (it stops at 23), Quattro Pro displays the cell value three columns to the right (the value 31).

In the second example, Quattro Pro searches vertically through the first column in block C3..G7. When the program locates the last value that is less than or equal to 45 before encountering a value that is greater than 45 (it stops at 4), Quattro Pro displays the value in the cell 0 columns to the right (the value 4).

In the third example, Quattro Pro searches vertically through the first column in block C3..G7. When the program locates the last value that is less than or equal to 53 before encountering one that is greater than 53 (it stops at 4), Quattro Pro displays the cell value three columns to the right (the value 27).

In the fourth example, Quattro Pro searches vertically through the first column in block C3..G7. When the program locates the last value that is less than or equal to 30 before encountering a value that is greater than 30 (it stops at 23), Quattro Pro attempts to display the value in the cell five columns to the right. Because this cell falls outside of the defined Block, Quattro Pro displays ERR.

In the fifth example, Quattro Pro searches vertically through the first column in block C3..G7. When the program encounters the illegal definition for the X argument ("text"), Quattro Pro displays ERR.

The next section introduces Quattro Pro's logical @function commands.

Using Logical @functions

The logical @function commands test logical conditions (see table 5.12). Depending on the outcome of the tests, these @functions return different values and perform different actions.

```
File   Edit   Style   Graph   Print   Database   Tools   Options   Window        ↑↓
A1: [W2]                                                                          ?
J    A              B           C      D      E      F      G      H       ↑
1                                                                          End
2                                                                          ▲
3                                 10     22     31     32     45           ◄|►
4                                 23     54     77     90     12           ▼
5                                 43     32     21     43     54           Esc
6                                 22     31     15     15     19           ←┘
7                                  4      6     22     27     77
8                                                                          Del
9    @VLOOKUP(30,C3..G7,3)        90                                       @
10   @VLOOKUP(45,C3..G7,0)         4
11   @VLOOKUP(53,C3..G7,3)        27                                       5
12   @VLOOKUP(30,C3..G7,5)       ERR
13   @VLOOKUP("text",C3..G7,5)   ERR                                       6
14
15                                                                         7
16
17
18
LOOKUP.WQ1   [1]                                                      READY
```

Fig. 5.6
Searching through a data table with @VLOOKUP.

Table 5.12
Logical @function Commands

@function	Description
@FALSE	Returns the logical value 0
@FILEEXISTS(Filename)	Returns the logical value 1 when Filename exists
@IF(Cond, TrueExpr,FalseExpr)	Evaluates a logical condition
@ISERR(x)	Checks the contents of a cell for errors
@ISNA(x)	Tests for the special value NA in a cell
@ISNUMBER(x)	Determines if a cell contains a numeric value
@ISSTRING(x)	Determines if a cell contains a label or text
@TRUE	Returns the logical value 1

Use these functions to control and validate the type of data entered into a cell; for example, you can make sure that cell B3 contains a value and not a label by entering the following function into cell B4:

@IF(@ISNUMBER(B3)=1," ","Needs a number")

This function says that if the value in B3 is a value (1 equals the TRUE condition), display a blank, otherwise display the message Needs a number.

One of the most potent applications for logical @functions is the creation of spreadsheet error-trapping. For example, whenever a formula returns ERR, every other cell that references the original cell also displays ERR. You can prevent this ripple effect by using logical @function commands.

As you read through the following command definitions, refer to the examples to learn more about how to use a particular command in an application.

@FALSE

The @FALSE function displays the logical value 0 when Quattro Pro encounters a false condition. This function commonly is used in @IF formulas to test the validity of numerical calculations and text string comparisons.

> Examples: @FALSE = 0
> @IF(100 = 100,50,@FALSE) = 50
> @IF(10 = 60,"Yes",@FALSE) = 0
> @IF(A1 = "September",@TRUE,@FALSE) = 1 (when A1 = September)

@FILEEXISTS(FileName)

The @FILEEXISTS function returns the value 1 when Quattro Pro finds Filename in the current directory. When Filename does not exist in the current directory, Quattro Pro returns a 0. In this syntax, Filename must include the file name extension and must appear in quotes.

To search for a file in a different directory, include the directory path as part of the FileName argument.

@IF(Cond,TrueExpr,FalseExpr)

The @IF function evaluates Cond and returns TrueExpr when Cond is true, and returns FalseExpr when Cond is false. In this syntax, Cond is a logical expression representing the condition to be tested, and TrueExpr and FalseExpr are numbers or string values surrounded by quotes. Cond must be some logical expression that Quattro Pro can evaluate as true or false.

Typically, Cond is a formula similar to the following function:

> @IF(B5 = 40,@TRUE,@FALSE)

You can create compound conditions by adding #AND#, #OR#, or #NOT# between the logical conditions. When you use #AND#, both expressions must be true for the entire condition to be true. When you use #OR#, at least one of the expressions must be true for the entire condition to be true. When you use #NOT#, the single expression must be false for the entire condition to be true.

Examples: @IF(10>1#AND#25 = 15,"TRUE","FALSE") = FALSE
@IF(10>1#OR#25 = 15,"TRUE","FALSE") = TRUE
@IF(#NOT#10>1,"TRUE","FALSE") = FALSE
@IF(#NOT#10<1,"TRUE","FALSE") = TRUE

The @IF function is most effective when you test multiple conditions from within one @IF function command by nesting other conditions. To nest conditions, include a second @IF function command as one of the expressions.

Example: @IF(A1 = "Larry",1,@IF(A1 = "Curly",2,@IF
(A1 = "Moe",3,"No Stooges")))

This expression tells Quattro Pro to return a 1 if A1 contains the label Larry. If it does not contain the label Larry, Quattro Pro evaluates FalseExpr. This expression tells Quattro Pro to return a 2 if A1 contains the label Curly. If it does not contains the label Curly, Quattro Pro evaluates the FalseExpr. This expression tells Quattro Pro to return a 3 if A1 contains the label Moe. If it does not contain the label Moe, Quattro Pro evaluates the FalseExpr and displays the label No Stooges.

Valid nested @IF expressions cannot exceed 254 characters in length.

@ISERR(x)

The @ISERR function reviews the active cell for errors. When Quattro Pro finds ERR, it returns 1; otherwise it returns 0.

Use the @ISERR function with the @IF function to prevent the ripple effect of formula errors.

Example: @IF(@ISERR(a50),@NA,1.05*SALES)

@ISNA(x)

@ISNA tests to see if x returns the value NA. When x equals NA, Quattro Pro returns a 1; otherwise it returns 0. In this syntax, x can be a cell address or an expression.

Quattro Pro does not interpret a label entered in the form *NA* as the special NA value. To create this value on a spreadsheet, you must use the @NA function.

Examples: @ISNA("NA") = 0
@ISNA(@NA) = 1

@ISNUMBER(x)

@ISNUMBER tests to see if x contains a numeric value. When x contains a numeric value, ERR, NA, or is a blank cell, Quattro Pro returns a 1; otherwise it returns 0. In this syntax, x can be a cell address or an expression.

Examples: @ISNUMBER(100) = 1
@ISNUMBER("100") = 0
@ISNUMBER(4/26/90) = 1
@ISNUMBER(@ERR) = 1
@ISNUMBER("ERR") = 0

@ISSTRING(x)

@ISSTRING tests to see if x contains a label or a text string. When x contains either of these items, Quattro Pro returns 1. Quattro Pro returns 0 when x is a blank cell, a numeric value, or a date value. In this syntax, x can be a cell address or an expression.

Examples: @ISSTRING("STRING") = 1
@ISSTRING(12345) = 0
@ISSTRING(4/26/85) = 0
@ISSTRING("") = 1
@ISSTRING(@ERR) = 0

@TRUE

@TRUE returns the logical value 1 when Quattro Pro encounters a true con-
~n. This function commonly is used in @IF formulas.

°s: @IF(10=10,@TRUE,@FALSE) = 1
@IF(10=9,@TRUE,@FALSE) = 0

Using Financial @functions

Quattro Pro's financial @functions provide you with powerful, real-world tools to help you manage your personal and business finances. You can use Quattro Pro's financial @function commands to aid in capital budgeting, to predict results of various investments, to compute payment schedules, and to evaluate annuities.

For example, @NPV(0.12,B5..B10) tells you the net present value of a series of six future incoming cash flows at a 12 percent interest rate. Such information can help you to determine the desirability of an investment.

You also can calculate depreciation for assets by using a variety of accepted methods; for example, @SLN(20000,3000,10) tells you that the yearly depreciation expense for a 10-year asset that cost $20,000 and has a $3,000 salvage value is $1,700.00.

You must follow these general rules when using financial @function commands:

- Use positive numbers to enter cash inflows and use negative numbers to enter cash outflows (except for the 1-2-3 compatible @functions described later in this section).

- You can enter interest rates as a percent (*8%*) or in decimal form (*0.08*)—Quattro Pro automatically converts percent entries to a decimal format.

- Be sure that the time units within an @function are standard for all arguments, a particularly important concern when using term and interest rate arguments. For example, if you have an annual interest rate of 15%, and a term of 36 months, either convert the annual interest rate to a monthly rate (15%/12) or express the months argument in terms of years (3).

Many of the financial @function commands use the same arguments, but in different order. Table 5.13 defines each of the arguments that Quattro Pro requires for the financial @function commands.

Table 5.13
Financial @function Command Arguments

Argument	Description
Rate	The fixed interest rate per compounding period
Fv	The value an investment will reach in the future
Pv	The present value of an investment
Cost	The cost of an asset

Table 5.13—*continued*

Argument	Description
Salvage	An asset's worth at the end of its useful life
Life	The expected useful life of an asset
Period	The depreciable period of an asset
Pmt	The amount of the period payment
Nper	The number of periods (an integer $>= 2$)
Type	0 denotes end-of-period payments; 1 denotes beginning-of-period payments
Per	The current payment period in Nper
Guess	An estimate of an internal rate of return
Block	A block containing the cash flow values

Five financial @function commands have two syntax forms so that you can save them on a spreadsheet in a Lotus compatible format (see table 5.14). The Quattro Pro syntax is preferable, however, because it is more precise than its 1-2-3 equivalent.

Table 5.14
1-2-3-Compatible Financial @function Commands

Quattro Pro syntax	Lotus 1-2-3 syntax
@FVAL(Rate,Nper,Pmt,<Pv>,<Type>)	@FV
@IRATE(Nper,Pmt,Pv,<Fv>,<Type>)	@RATE
@NPER(Rate,Pmt,Pv,<Fv>,<Type>)	@CTERM @TERM
@PAYMT(Rate,Nper,Pv,<Fv>,<Type>)	@PMT
@PVAL(Rate,Nper,Pmt,<Fv>,<Type>)	@PV

The angle brackets indicate an optional argument. If the closing angle bracket or both brackets are omitted, Quattro Pro assumes that their values are 0.

Table 5.15 lists the financial @function commands.

Table 5.15
Investment Analysis @function Commands

@function	Description
@CTERM(Rate,Fv,Pv)	(1-2-3-compatible form of the @NPER function when the investment is an ordinary annuity)

@function	Description
@DDB(Cost,Salvage,Life,Period)	Calculates accelerated depreciation
@FV(Pmt,Rate,Nper)	(1-2-3-compatible form of the @FVAL function)
@FVAL(Rate,Nper,-Pmt,0)	Returns the future value of an ordinary annuity
@IPAYMT(Rate,Per,Nper, Pv,<Fv>,<Type>)	Returns the interest portion of a loan payment
@IRATE(Nper,Pmt,Pv, <Fv>,<Type>)	Returns the periodic interest rate
@IRR(Guess,Block)	Returns an investment's internal rate of return
@NPER(Rate,Pmt,Pv, <Pv>,<Type>)	Returns the number of periods
@NPV(Rate,Block,<Type>)	Returns the present value of discounted cash flows
@PAYMT(Rate,Nper,Pv, <Fv>,<Type>)	Returns the payment amount for a loan
@PMT(Pv,Rate,Nper)	(1-2-3-compatible form of the @PPAYMT function)
@PPAYMT(Rate,Per,Nper, Pv,<Fv>,<Type>)	Returns the principal portion of a loan payment
@PV(Pmt,Rate,Nper)	(1-2-3-compatible form of the @PVAL function)
@PVAL(Rate,Nper,Pmt, <Fv>,<Type>)	Returns the present value of an annuity
@RATE(Fv,Pv,Nper)	(1-2-3-compatible form of the @IRATE function)
@SLN(Cost,Salvage,Life)	Calculates straight-line depreciation
@SYD(Cost,Salvage,Life,Period)	Calculates sum-of-the-years'-digits' depreciation
@TERM(Pmt,Rate,Fv)	(1-2-3-compatible form of the @NPER function when the investment is an ordinary annuity)

@CTERM(Rate,Fv,Pv)

The @CTERM function returns the number of time periods it would take for an investment of Pv to grow to Fv. In this syntax, the investment earns Rate interest per compounding period.

This function is based on the following formula:

$$\frac{\ln(Fv/Pv)}{\ln(1+Rate)}$$

The @CTERM function assumes that the investment is an ordinary annuity. In an ordinary annuity the cash flows occur at the end of the period.

For example, how long would it take a savings account deposit of $5,000 to grow to $10,000 when the annual interest rate is 8, 9, and 10 percent?

@CTERM(.08,10000,5000) = 9.01 (years)
@CTERM(.09,10000,5000) = 8.04 (years)
@CTERM(.10,10000,5000) = 7.27 (years)

@DDB(Cost,Salvage,Life,Period)

The @DDB function returns the periodic depreciation expense for an asset, using the double-declining balance method. For this function to work properly, the following conditions must be true:

1. Life >= Period >= 1
2. Life and Period must be integers.
3. Cost >= Salvage >= 0

The depreciation value (DDB) and book value are calculated as follows:

1. Book Value = Cost
2. DDB = (2*Book Value)/Life
3. Book Value = Book Value - DDB

For example, what are the first three annual depreciation expenses for an asset that cost $100,000, has a salvage value equal to $17,500, and has a useful life of 10 years?

@DDB(100000,17500,10,1) = 20,000 (see figure 5.7)
@DDB(100000,17500,10,2) = 16,000
@DDB(100000,17500,10,3) = 12,800

```
 File   Edit   Style   Graph   Print   Database   Tools   Options   Window          ↑↓
C6: (,2) [W16] @DDB($C$2,$C$3,$E$2,$B6)                                             ?
 J     A      B          C              D              E          F   ↑
1
2            Cost: 100,000                   Life: 10                          [End]
3            Salvage: 17,500                                                    ▲
                                                                               ◄|►
4                      Double Declining     Straight      Sum-of-the-           ▼
5            Year         Balance           Line         years'-digits        [Esc]
6             1          20,000.00  ◄     8,250.00       15,000.00            [↵]
7             2          16,000.00         8,250.00       13,500.00
8             3          12,800.00         8,250.00       12,000.00            [Del]
9             4          10,240.00         8,250.00       10,500.00
10            5           8,192.00         8,250.00        9,000.00            [ @ ]
11            6           6,553.60         8,250.00        7,500.00
12            7           5,242.88         8,250.00        6,000.00            [ 5 ]
13            8           3,471.52         8,250.00        4,500.00
14            9               0.00         8,250.00        3,000.00            [ 6 ]
15           10               0.00         8,250.00        1,500.00
                                                                               [ 7 ]
16           Total:        82,500           82,500          82,500

ASSETS.WQ1   [1]                                                       READY
```

Fig. 5.7
Cell C6 reveals the formula that calculates the first period depreciation expense under the double-declining balance method.

@FV(Pmt,Rate,Nper)

The @FV function calculates the future value of an investment when Pmt is invested for Nper periods at the rate of Rate per period. This function is based on the following formula:

$$\text{Pmt} \cdot \frac{(1 + \text{Rate})^{\text{Nper}} - 1}{\text{Rate}}$$

For example, what is the future value of making $1,000 deposits into a savings account that earns 8, 9, and 10 percent for periods of 5, 10, and 15 years respectively?

@FV(.08,5,1000) = $5,869.45
@FV(.09,10,1000) = $15,200.30
@FV(.10,15,1000) = $31,787.89

@FVAL(Rate,Nper,Pmt,<Pv>,<Type>)

The @FVAL function is a more precise version of the @FV function. In this syntax, the Pv and Type arguments are optional. Quattro Pro assumes that their values are zero if you omit Type or PV and Type.

Tip | This function is not compatible with Lotus 1-2-3. If you need to save your spreadsheet in a Lotus-compatible format, use the @FV function. Remember, don't precede cash outflows with a negative sign when you use the @FV function.

For example, what are the future values of making five annual end-of-year versus five annual beginning-of-year deposits of $1,000 into a bank account earning 8 percent, whose current balance is $500?

@FVAL(.08,5,-1000,500,1) = $5,604.34
@FVAL(.08,5,-1000,500,0) = $5,134.78

For example, what is the future value of making 15 annual deposits of $1,000 into a money market account that earns 10 percent interest?

@FVAL(.10,15,-1000) = $31,787.89

@IPAYMT(Rate,Per,Nper,Pv,<Fv>,<Type>)

The @IPAYMT function returns the value of the interest portion of a loan payment. In this syntax, Fv and Type are optional arguments. Quattro Pro assumes that their values are zero if you omit Fv or Type.

For example, what is the first year's interest deduction on a 15-year, 9.5 percent mortgage on a $300,000 loan? What is the fifth year's interest deduction?

@IPAYMT(.095/12,1*12,15*12,300000) = -$2,306.34
@IPAYMT(.095/12,5*12,15*12,300000) = -$1,926.15

@IRATE(Nper,Pmt,Pv,<Fv>,<Type>)

@IRATE returns the periodic interest rate earned (paid) on an investment (loan) equal to Pv. Here, Nper is the compounding term of the investment (loan); Pmt represents the per period interest payment earned (paid); and PV is the current value of the investment.

The @IRATE function is a more precise version of the @RATE function. In this syntax, Fv and Type are optional. Quattro Pro assumes that their values are zero if you omit Type or Fv and Type.

For this function to work properly, the first and last cash flows must have opposite signs. If they do not, Quattro Pro assumes that the transaction may not have a meaningful rate, so it returns ERR.

For example, you want to finance the purchase of a $20,000 car and are given the choice of paying $675.81 per month for three years or $538.54 per month for four years. Which is the better deal for you?

@IRATE(36,-675.81,20000) = 1.10% (per month)
@IRATE(48,-538.54,20000) = 1.10% (per month)

For example, what annual interest rate do you need to earn to accumulate $20,000 at the end of three years if you make three annual deposits of $3,000, and your account balance is $5,000 today?

@IRATE(3,-3000,-5000,20000) = 21.37%

Tip | This function is not compatible with Lotus 1-2-3. If you need to save your spreadsheet in a Lotus-compatible format, use the @RATE function. Remember, don't precede cash outflows with a negative sign when you use the @RATE function.

@IRR(Guess,Block)

The @IRR function calculates the internal rate of return on an investment. The @IRR function returns the interest rate that causes the net present value of an investment to be 0. Net present value (NPV) is the net worth today of investing a sum and receiving future cash flows. When the NPV of an investment is 0, it is considered to be a break-even venture.

When you calculate NPV, you discount future cash flows using an interest rate. This rate is equal to your opportunity interest rate—the maximum rate you can earn by investing elsewhere. In other words, if the best you can do is earn 12.5 percent in a bank account, your opportunity interest rate is 12.5 percent.

To evaluate the worth of potential investments, you must design a table that describes how the cash flows in and out of the investment. Figure 5.8 contains a 10-year cash flow table. This table describes the same investment opportunity ($50,000) with differently timed cash flows.

In this syntax, Block contains the cash flows and Guess is a user-supplied estimate of the internal rate of return.

To use this function properly, you must first create a data table that contains each periodic cash flow. Cash outflows must be preceded by a negative sign.

The first cash flow must be negative to indicate that it is the initial investment. The ensuing cash flows can vary from period to period in both size and sign.

For example, what is the internal rate of return of investing $50,000 today, using the cash flow streams shown in figure 5.8?

Option 1 @IRR(.125,C4..C14) = 15.098%
Option 2 @IRR(.125,D4..D14) = 15.386%
Option 3 @IRR(.125,E4..E9) = 14.870%
Option 4 @IRR(.125,F4..F14) = 14.870%

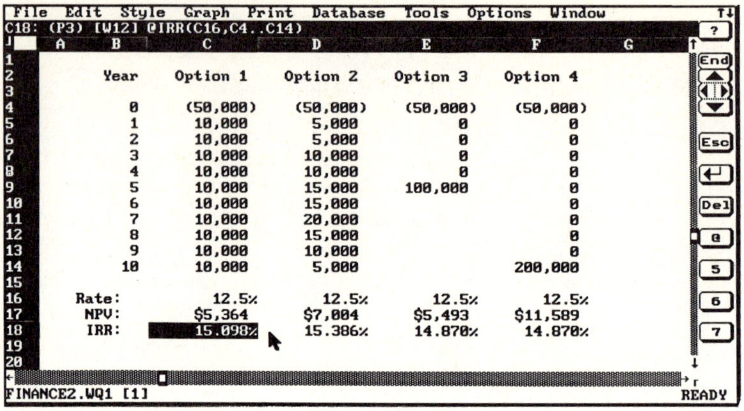

Fig. 5.8
Cell C18 reveals
the formula that
calculates the
internal rate of
return for
investment
option 1.

@NPER(Rate,Pmt,Pv,<Fv>,<Type>)

The @NPER function determines the number of periods it will take for Pv to equal Fv when investing Pmt per period at a rate of Rate.

The @NPER function is a more precise version of the @CTERM and @TERM functions. In this syntax, Fv and Type are optional. Quattro Pro assumes their values are zero if you omit Type or Fv and Type.

Tip | This function is not compatible with Lotus 1-2-3. If you need to save your spreadsheet in a Lotus-compatible format, use @CTERM or @TERM. Remember, don't precede cash outflows with a negative sign when you use the @CTERM or @TERM functions.

For example, how long does it take to accumulate $5,000 if you deposit $1,000 annually into a bank account that pays 10 percent?

@NPER(.10,-1000,0,5000) = 4.25 (years)

For example, how long does it take to accumulate $5,000 if you deposit $250 annually into a bank account that pays 10 percent and has a current balance of $2,500?

@NPER(.10,-250,2500,5000) = 4.25 (years)

For example, how long does it take to accumulate $1,000,000 if you deposit $1,000 annually into a bank account that pays 10 percent?

@NPER(.10,-1000,0,1000000) = 48.42 (years)

@NPV(Rate,Block,<Type>)

The @NPV function calculates the net present value of the cash flows in Block, discounted at a periodic interest rate of Rate.

The @NPV function has one optional argument, Type. If the cash flows occur at the beginning of the period, set Type to 0. If they occur at the end of the period, enter 1.

Tip | The optional argument Type is not 1-2-3 compatible.

For example, what is the net present value of an investment that requires you to invest $50,000 today and pays back dividends per the cash flow streams shown in figure 5.9?

Option 1 @NPV(.125,C4..C14) = $5,364
Option 2 @NPV(.125,D4..D14) = $7,004
Option 3 @NPV(.125,E4..E9) = $5,493
Option 4 @NPV(.125,F4..F14) = $11,589

```
 File  Edit  Style  Graph  Print  Database  Tools  Options  Window        ↑↓
E17: (C0) [W12] @NPV(E16,E4..E9,1)                                         ?
 ┘    A    B        C          D          E          F         G
 1                                                                         End
 2          Year   Option 1   Option 2   Option 3   Option 4
 3
 4          0      (50,000)   (50,000)   (50,000)   (50,000)
 5          1       10,000      5,000          0          0
 6          2       10,000      5,000          0          0               Esc
 7          3       10,000     10,000          0          0
 8          4       10,000     10,000          0          0               ↵
 9          5       10,000     15,000    100,000          0
10          6       10,000     15,000                     0               Del
11          7       10,000     20,000                     0
12          8       10,000     15,000                     0                @
13          9       10,000     10,000                     0
14         10       10,000      5,000               200,000                5
15
16         Rate:     12.5%      12.5%      12.5%      12.5%                 6
17         NPV:     $5,364     $7,004     $5,493    $11,589
18         IRR:     15.098%    15.386%    14.870%    14.870%                7
19
20
 +‖‖‖‖‖‖‖‖‖‖‖‖‖‖‖‖‖‖‖‖‖‖‖‖‖‖‖‖‖□‖‖‖‖‖‖‖‖‖‖‖‖‖‖‖‖‖‖‖‖‖‖‖‖‖►
FINANCE2.WQ1 [1]                                                       READY
```

Fig. 5.9
Cell E17 reveals the formula that calculates the net present value for investment option 3.

@PAYMT(Rate,Nper,Pv,<Fv>,<Type>)

The @PAYMT function returns the value of the principal portion of a loan payment. This function is a more precise version of the @PMT function. In this syntax, Fv and Type are optional arguments. Quattro Pro assumes that their values are zero if you omit Type or Fv and Type.

Tip | This function is not compatible with Lotus 1-2-3. If you need to save your spreadsheet in a Lotus-compatible format, use @PMT. Remember, don't precede cash outflows with a negative sign when you use the @PMT function.

For example, how much do you need to deposit in an account earning 25 percent to accumulate $10,000 in five years?

@PAYMT(.25,5,0,10000) = -$1,218.47

For example, what is the monthly payment for a $225,000, 15-year, 10 percent fixed-interest mortgage? What if the loan term were stretched to 30 years?

@PAYMT(.01,180,225000) = -$2,700.38
@PAYMT(.01,360,225000) = -$2,314.38

@PMT(Pv,Rate,Nper)

@PMT returns the fully amortized payment when borrowing Pv dollars at Rate percent per period over Nper periods. In this syntax, interest is assumed to be paid at the end of each period.

The @PMT function assumes that the investment is an ordinary annuity. In an ordinary annuity, the cash flows occur at the end of the period.

For example, what is the total annual payment on a $100,000, 30-year, 10 percent fixed-interest mortgage?

@PMT(100000,.10,30) = $10,607.92 (per year)

For example, what is the monthly payment for a $225,000, 15-year, 10 percent fixed-interest mortgage? What if the loan term were stretched to 30 years?

@PMT(225000,.01,180) = $2,700.38
@PMT(225000,.01,360) = $2,314.38

@PPAYMT(Rate,Per,Nper,Pv,<Fv>,<Type>)

The @PPAYMT function returns the value of the principal portion of a loan payment. In this syntax, Fv and Type are optional arguments. Quattro Pro assumes their values are zero if you omit Type or Fv and Type.

For example, what is the first year's principal payment on a 15-year, 9.5 percent mortgage on a $300,000 loan? What is the fifth year's principal payment?

@PPAYMT(.095/12,1*12,15*12,300000) = -$826.33
@PPAYMT(.095/12,5*12,15*12,300000) = -$1,206.52

@PV(Pmt,Rate,Nper)

The @PV function calculates the present value of an investment when Pmt is received for Nper periods and is discounted at Rate percent per period.

This function is based on the following formula:

$$\text{Pmt} \cdot \frac{(1-(1\text{Rate})^{-\text{Nper}}}{(\text{Rate})}$$

The @PV function assumes that the investment is an ordinary annuity. In an ordinary annuity, the cash flows occur at the end of the period.

For example, what is the most that you would pay today for an investment that provides you $500 per year for 10 years, if you can earn 7.5 percent on your money elsewhere? What if the investment provides you $750 per year? Or $1,000 per year?

    @PV(500,.075,10) = $3,432.04
    @PV(750,.075,10) = $5,148.06
    @PV(1000,.075,10) = $6,864.08

@PVAL(Rate,Nper,Pmt,<Fv>,<Type>)

The @PVAL function is a more precise version of the @PV function. In this syntax, the Fv and Type arguments are optional. Quattro Pro assumes that they are zero if Type or both arguments are omitted.

Tip | This function is not compatible with Lotus 1-2-3. If you need to save your spreadsheet in a Lotus-compatible format, use @PV. Remember, don't precede cash outflows with a negative sign when you use the @PV function.

For example, the local lottery official offers you three alternative annuities, all of which pay 10 percent. The first pays you $3,850 per year for 10 years, the second pays you $3,350 for 13 years, and the third pays you $100,000 after 15 years. Which annuity is the best alternative?

    @PVAL(.10,10,3850) = $23,656.58
    @PVAL(.10,13,3350) = $23,796.24
    @PVAL(.10,15,0,100000) = $23,939.20

@RATE(Fv,Pv,Nper)

The @RATE function calculates the interest rate needed for an investment of Pv to be worth Fv in Nper compounding periods. If you enter Nper in years, @RATE returns the annual interest rate; if you enter Nper in months, it returns the monthly interest rate.

This function is based on the following formula:

$$\frac{Fv^{1/Nper}}{Pv} - 1$$

The @RATE function assumes that the investment is an ordinary annuity. In an ordinary annuity, the cash flows occur at the end of the period.

For example, what interest rate must you earn for $100,000 to grow to $1,000,000 in 10 years?

@RATE(1000000,100000,10) = 25.89%

For example, what interest rate must you earn for $1,000 to grow to $2,000 in 5 and 10 years?

@RATE(2000,1000,5) = 14.87%
@RATE(2000,1000,10) = 7.18%

@SLN(Cost,Salvage,Life)

The @SLN function returns one year's depreciation expense for an asset, using the straight-line method. This function is based on the following formula:

$$\frac{Cost - Salvage}{Life}$$

For example, what is the annual depreciation expense for an asset that costs $100,000, has a salvage value equal to $17,500, and has a useful life of 10 years?

@SLN(100000,17500,10) = $8,250 (see fig. 5.10)

```
 File  Edit  Style  Graph  Print  Database  Tools  Options  Window        ↑↓
D6: (,2) [W16] @SLN($C$2,$C$3,$E$2)                                       ?
    A        B            C              D             E        F
1
2        Cost: 100,000                     Life: 10
3        Salvage: 17,500
4                 Double Declining      Straight     Sum-of-the-
5         Year      Balance             Line         years'-digits
6          1        20,000.00           8,250.00      15,000.00
7          2        16,000.00           8,250.00      13,500.00
8          3        12,800.00           8,250.00      12,000.00
9          4        10,240.00           8,250.00      10,500.00
10         5         8,192.00           8,250.00       9,000.00
11         6         6,553.60           8,250.00       7,500.00
12         7         5,242.88           8,250.00       6,000.00
13         8         3,471.52           8,250.00       4,500.00
14         9             0.00           8,250.00       3,000.00
15        10             0.00           8,250.00       1,500.00
16       Total:       82,500            82,500         82,500
ASSETS.WQ1   [1]                                              READY
```

Fig. 5.10 Cell D6 reveals the formula that calculates the straight-line depreciation expense for year 1.

@SYD(Cost,Salvage,Life)

The @SYD function returns the periodic depreciation allowance for an asset, using the accelerated depreciation method. This function allows higher depreciation in the earlier years of the asset's life. This function is based on the following formula:

$$\frac{(Cost - Salvage)*(Life - Period + 1)}{Life(Life + 1)/2}$$

For this function to work properly, the following conditions must be true:

1. Cost >= Salvage >= 0

2. Life >= Period >= 1

For example, what are the last three annual depreciation expenses for an asset that cost $100,000, has a salvage value equal to $17,500, and has a useful life of 10 years (see Fig. 5.11)?

@SYD(100000,17500,10,8) = $4,500.00
@SYD(100000,17500,10,9) = $3,000.00
@SYD(100000,17500,10,10) = $1,500.00

@TERM(Pmt,Rate,Fv)

The @TERM function calculates the number of payment periods required to accumulate holdings worth Fv. In this syntax, Pmt represents regular pay-

Fig. 5.11
Cell E15 reveals the formula that calculates the sum of the years' digits depreciation expense for the last year.

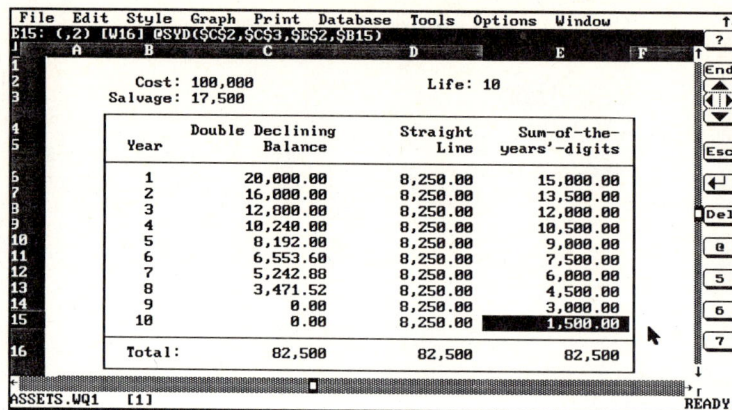

```
 File   Edit   Style   Graph   Print   Database   Tools   Options   Window          ↑↓
E15: (,2) [W16] @SYD($C$2,$C$3,$E$2,$B15)                                           ?
 J      A        B            C                D              E            F    ↑
1                                                                              End
2              Cost: 100,000                      Life: 10                     ▲
3            Salvage: 17,500                                                   ◄│▶
4                                                                              ▼
5                      Double Declining      Straight      Sum-of-the-
        Year              Balance              Line      years'-digits         Esc
6        1              20,000.00            8,250.00       15,000.00          ↵
7        2              16,000.00            8,250.00       13,500.00
8        3              12,800.00            8,250.00       12,000.00          Del
9        4              10,240.00            8,250.00       10,500.00
10       5               8,192.00            8,250.00        9,000.00          0
11       6               6,553.60            8,250.00        7,500.00
12       7               5,242.88            8,250.00        6,000.00          5
13       8               3,471.52            8,250.00        4,500.00
14       9                   0.00            8,250.00        3,000.00          6
15      10                   0.00            8,250.00        1,500.00
                                                                              7
16              Total:        82,500           82,500          82,500
 ←                                    □                              →
ASSETS.WQ1    [1]                                                        READY
```

ments made while accruing interest at the rate of Rate. This function is based on the following formula:

$$\frac{\ln(1 + Fv/Pmt*Rate)}{\ln(1 + Rate)}$$

The @TERM function assumes that the investment is an ordinary annuity. In an ordinary annuity, the cash flows occur at the end of the period.

For example, how long will it take to accumulate $10,000 if you make annual deposits of $1,000 into a bank account that pays 7.5, 8.5, or 9.5 percent?

@TERM(1000,.075,10000) = 7.74 (years)
@TERM(1000,.085,10000) = 7.54 (years)
@TERM(1000,.095,10000) = 7.36 (years)

The next section introduces Quattro Pro's date and time @function commands.

Using Date and Time @function Commands

Quattro Pro's date and time @functions have many uses. One popular use for these @functions is to determine elapsed time between two date or time entries. This type of operation is often a necessary part of business reporting, time management, project scheduling, and so forth.

Date and time @functions also are useful tools when you build spreadsheet applications. For example, place the @TODAY function at the top of your spreadsheet and Quattro Pro will display the current date in that cell each time you load the spreadsheet.

Many of the date and time @function commands use the same arguments. Table 5.16 defines each of the arguments Quattro Pro requires for the date and time @function commands. Table 5.17 lists the commands.

Table 5.16
Date and Time @function Command Arguments

Argument	Description
Yr	A numeric value between 0 and 199
Mo	A numeric value between 1 and 12
Day	A numeric value between 1 and 31
DateString	A numeric or string value in any valid date format surrounded by quotes
DateTimeNumber	Any number under 73050.9999999
Hr	A number between 0 and 23, representing the hour
Min	A number between 0 and 59, representing the minute
Sec	A number between 0 and 59, representing the second
TimeString	A numeric or string value in any valid time format, surrounded by quotes

Table 5.17
Date and Time @function Commands

@function	Description
@DATE(Yr,Mo,Day)	Returns the date serial number of a date
@DATEVALUE(DateString)	Returns the date serial number that corresponds to DateString
@DAY(DateTimeNumber)	Converts a date or time serial number into the number associated with that day (1-31)
@HOUR(DateTimeNumber)	Returns the hour portion of the argument
@MINUTE(DateTimeNumber)	Returns the minute portion of the argument
@MONTH(DateTimeNumber)	Returns the month portion of the argument
@NOW	Returns the serial number for today's time and date
@SECOND(DateTimeNumber)	Returns the second portion of the argument
@TIME(Hr,Min,Sec)	Returns the time serial number portion of the argument
@TIMEVALUE(TimeString)	Returns the time serial number for the argument
@TODAY	Returns the numeric value of the system's date
@YEAR(DateTimeNumber)	Returns the year portion of the argument

As you read through the following command definitions, refer to the examples to learn more about how to use a particular command in an application.

@DATE(Yr,Mo,Day)

The @DATE function displays the date serial number specified by year, month, and day. A valid serial number ranges from 0 to 73,050, which represents the number of days between December 31, 1899 and the date referenced in the formula. December 31, 2099 is the highest date available. Quattro Pro returns ERR when it encounters an illegal date.

Examples: @DATE(87,2,29) = ERR (February 29, 1987 was not a leap year)
@DATE(87,1,1) = 32143 (the serial date for January 1, 1988)

@DATEVALUE(DateString)

The @DATEVALUE function displays the date serial number that corresponds to DateString. Quattro Pro displays ERR when DateString is not in a valid date format, or is not enclosed in quotes.

The five valid DateString formats are the following:

* DD-MMM-YY ("02-Jan-90")

* DD-MMM ("02-Jan")

* MMM-YY ("Jan-90")

* The default Long International date format

* The default Short International date format

Examples: @DATEVALUE("02-Jan-90") = 32875
@DATEVALUE("02-Jan") = 32875 (Quattro Pro assumes the current year)
@DATEVALUE("Jan-90") = 32874 (Quattro Pro assumes the first day of the month)

@DAY(DateTimeNumber)

The @DAY function converts DateTimeNumber into the number associated with that day of the month (1-31). In this syntax, DateTimeNumber can be a day or time serial number.

Examples: @DAY(31779) = 2 (1/2/87)
@DAY(73055) = ERR (the number entered was larger than 73050.9999999)

@HOUR(DateTimeNumber)

The @HOUR function displays the hour portion of DateTimeNumber. In this syntax, DateTimeNumber is a numeric value between 1 and 73050.999999 (the combined date and time serial numbers).

The integer portion of the number is disregarded because only the decimal portion of a serial number pertains to time. The result is between 0 (12:00 midnight) and 23 (11:00 PM).

Examples: @HOUR(.25) = 6
@HOUR(.5) = 12
@HOUR(.75) = 18

@MINUTE(DateTimeNumber)

The @MINUTE function displays the minute portion of DateTimeNumber. The integer portion of the number is disregarded because only the decimal value in a serial number pertains to time. The result is between 0 and 59.

To extract the minute portion of strings in time format rather than serial format, use the @TIME within the @MINUTE function to translate the time into a serial number.

Examples: @MINUTE(.3655) = 46
@MINUTE(@TIME(3,15,22)) = 15

@MONTH(DateTimeNumber)

The @MONTH function displays the month portion of DateTimeNumber. The only portion used is the integer portion, and the result is between 1 (January) and 12 (December).

To extract the month portion of a string in date format rather than serial format, use the @DATEVALUE within the @MONTH function to translate the date into a serial number.

Examples: @MONTH(69858) = 4
@MONTH(@DATEVALUE("3/5/88")) = 3

@NOW

The @NOW function displays the serial number corresponding to the current date time (of your system's clock).

When you perform any function that reevaluates the spreadsheet, the value generated by @NOW is updated to the current date and time each time you press the Calc key (F9).

The decimal portion pertains to time and the integer part of the date or time serial number pertains to the date.

Example: @NOW = 31905.572338 or 5/8/87 or 1:45 PM (The value returned depends upon the cell's format.)

@SECOND(DateTimeNumber)

The @SECOND function displays the second portion of DateTimeNumber. The integer portion of the number is disregarded because only the decimal portion of a serial number pertains to time. The result is between 0 and 59.

Use the @TIMEVALUE within the @SECOND function to translate the time into a serial number to extract the second portion of a string that is in time format instead of serial format.

Examples: @SECOND(.3655445) = 23
@SECOND(@TIMEVALUE("10:08:45 am")) = 45

@TIME(Hr,Min,Sec)

The @TIME function displays the date or time serial number that is represented by Hr:Min:Sec. Each argument must be within the given range, and any fractional portions are omitted.

Examples: @TIME(3,0,0) = 0.125 (3:00 am)
@TIME(18,15,59) = 0.76109953704 (6:15:59 pm)

@TIMEVALUE(TimeString)

The @TIMEVALUE function displays the serial time value that corresponds to the value in TimeString. ERR results if the value in TimeString is not in the correct format or is not enclosed in quotes.

The four valid TimeString formats are

- HH:MM:SS AM/PM (03:45:30 PM)
- HH:MM AM/PM (03:45 PM)
- The default Long International time format

- The default Short International time format

Examples: @TIMEVALUE("03:30:15 AM") = 0.1460069444
@TIMEVALUE("18:15:59") = 0.76109953704

@TODAY

The @TODAY function enters the numeric value of the system's date. This function is equal to the @INT(@NOW) expression.

Examples: @NOW = 33047.8687 (for June 23, 1990 at 08:50:57 p.m.)
@TODAY = 33047 (for June 23, 1990)
@INT(@NOW) = 33047 (for June 23, 1990)

@YEAR(DateTimeNumber)

The @YEAR function gives the year portion of the DateTimeNumber. The result is between 0 (1900) and 199 (2099). The actual year can be displayed by adding 1900 to the result of @YEAR. To extract the year portion of a string in date format, use @DATEVALUE within the @YEAR function to convert the string into a serial number.

Examples: @YEAR(22222) = 60 (1960)
@YEAR(@DATEVALUE("12-Oct-54")) = 54

Using Database Statistical @function Commands

The database statistical @function commands perform the same operations as the statistical @function commands. Here, though, the @functions operate on a specific field entry in the database instead of a block defined as List.

The database statistical @function commands have in common the arguments shown in table 5.18. Table 5.19 lists the functions.

Table 5.18
Database Statistical @function Command Arguments

Argument	Description
Block	The cell block containing the database, including field names
Column	The number of the column containing the field you want to average. The first column in Block is 0, the second is 1, and so on.
Criteria	A cell block containing search criteria

All or part of the database can be specified as Block, but the field names must be included for each field including Block.

Criteria is defined as the coordinates of a block containing a criteria table. A criteria table specifies the search information.

Table 5.19
Database Statistical @function Commands

@function	Description
@DAVdG(Block,Column,Criteria)	Calculates the average of selected field entries in a database
@DCOUNT(Block,Column,Criteria)	Counts the number of selected field entries in a database
@DMAX(Block,Column,Criteria)	Returns the maximum value in a database
@DMIN(Block,Column,Criteria)	Returns the minimum value in a database
@DSTD(Block,Column,Criteria)	Returns the population standard deviation
@DSTDS((Block,Column,Criteria)	Returns the sample standard deviation
@DSUM(Block,Column,Criteria)	Returns the total of selected field entries in a database
@DVAR(Block,Column,Criteria)	Returns the population variance
@DVARS(Block,Column,Criteria)	Returns the sample variance

As you read through the following command definitions, refer to the examples in the statistical @function section to learn more about how to use a particular command in an application.

@DAVG(Block,Column,Criteria)

The @DAVG function averages selected field entries in a database. Only those entries in column number Column whose records meet the criteria specified in Criteria are included.

Criteria is defined as the coordinates of a block containing a criteria table. A criteria table specifies the search information.

The field specified in the criteria and the field being averaged need not be the same. The field averaged is contained within the column you specified as Column.

@DCOUNT(Block,Column,Criteria)

The @DCOUNT function counts selected field entries in a database. Only those entries in column number Column whose records meet the criteria specified in block Criteria are included.

The field specified and the field being counted need not be the same. The field counted is contained within the column you specified as Column.

@DMAX(Block,Column,Criteria)

The @DMAX function finds the maximum value of selected field entries in a database. Only those entries in column number Column whose records meet the criteria specified in block Criteria are included.

The field specified in your criteria and the field whose maximum values you are finding need not be the same. The field you are finding the maximum values for is that contained within the column you specify as Column.

@DMIN(Block,Column,Criteria)

The @DMIN function finds the minimum value of selected field entries in a database. Only those entries in column number Column whose records meet the criteria specified in block Criteria are included.

The field specified in your criteria and the field for which you are finding the minimum value need not be the same. The field for which you are finding the minimum value is that contained within the column specified as Criteria.

@DSTD(Block,Column,Criteria)

The @DSTD function finds the population standard deviation for selected field entries in a database.

Only those entries in column number Column whose records meet the criteria specified in block Criteria are included in @DSTD.

The field specified in your criteria and the field for which the standard deviation which is being found need not be the same. The field for which you are finding the standard deviation is the field contained within the column you specify as Column.

@DSTDS(Block,Column,Criteria)

The @DSTDS function finds the sample standard deviation for the selected field in a database. @DSTDS computes the standard deviation of the population data.

Tip | This function is not compatible with Lotus 1-2-3. Use @DSTD if your spreadsheet requires 1-2-3 compatibility.

@DSUM(Block,Column,Criteria)

The @DSUM function adds up the selected entries in a database. Only those entries whose records meet the criteria specified in block Criteria are included in the column number Column.

The field specified in the criteria and the field whose sum is being found need not be the same. The field that is contained within the column you specified as Column is the field whose sum you are finding.

@DVAR(Block,Column,Criteria)

The @DVAR function calculates the population variance for the selected field in a database. It computes the variance of the sample data.

Only those entries in column number Column whose records meet the criteria specified in block Criteria are included in @DVAR.

The field specified in the criteria and the field for which the variance is being calculated need not be the same. The field counted is contained within the column you specify as Column.

@DVARS(Block,Column,Criteria)

The @DVARS function calculates the sample variance for the selected field entries in a database. It computes the variance of the population data.

Tip | This function is not compatible with 1-2-3. Use @DVAR if your spreadsheet requires 1-2-3 compatibility.

Chapter Summary

Chapter 5 showed you how to use all Quattro Pro @function commands. After completing this chapter, you should understand the following Quattro Pro concepts:

- Creating the correct syntax for an @function command

- Selecting and entering an @function command on a spreadsheet

- Using arithmetic and trigonometric @functions

- Using statistical @functions to return data about sample and population data sets

- Using string @functions to perform "mathematical" operations on text and string labels

- Using miscellaneous @functions to monitor spreadsheet formulas and available system memory

- Using logical @functions to create test conditions that return values

- Using financial @functions to evaluate investments, amortize loans, and depreciate assets

- Using database statistical @functions to perform statistical analyses of data appearing in a database

In Chapter 6, you learn how to customize and streamline your Quattro Pro work sessions by creating default settings that are tailor-made to your specific needs. Chapter 6 will provide comprehensive coverage of Quattro Pro's Options menu. By using the commands on the Options menu, you can modify how Quattro Pro interacts with your system hardware, select complementary screen colors for your display, change the cell format default settings, and configure and then store startup options for the next work session.

6

Setting Options

In Chapter 6, you are introduced to the Options menu commands. The commands on this menu enable you to fine-tune Quattro Pro's system and format settings. These two types of settings are important to your day-to-day work sessions because they control how Quattro Pro interacts with your computer hardware and your active spreadsheet. If you don't change the options, Quattro uses its factory settings for these options.

The Options menu commands are not so much operating commands as they are a set of rules that Quattro Pro follows each time it loads into your computer. Without these settings, Quattro Pro does not know whether to display in text or graphics mode, cannot properly use your computer's expanded memory, has no idea how to color the various parts of its screen display, and cannot send data to the correct printer port.

System options go into effect immediately, but others have an effect only when Quattro Pro loads into your computer. And format options affect only the active spreadsheet. In this chapter you will learn the domain of each type of option as it is discussed.

The first part of Chapter 6 is devoted to reviewing the commands on the Options menu. As in previous chapters, you will come to understand the organization of the commands on this menu. A quick preview of Quattro Pro's coloring palette concludes this section.

The next section shows you how to set and reset options that you use to define Quattro Pro's system settings. These settings remind Quattro Pro about your printer and screen, as well as which colors to use on-screen. You also will learn how to create your own set of "start-up rules" for Quattro Pro to follow the next time it loads.

Next, you review the Update command. Using the Update command saves your current system settings as defaults, which then go into effect the next time you start Quattro Pro.

The last part of the chapter teaches you about defining global format settings, selecting recalculation modes, and invoking global spreadsheet protection. Remember, these final settings affect only individual spreadsheets—Update does not store them for each new spreadsheet you create.

Reviewing the Options Menu

Use the 12 Options menu commands to set, reset, and save the system and format defaults for using Quattro Pro. The Options menu is divided into three sections: system options, Update, and default format options (see fig. 6.1). Quattro Pro displays the current settings for certain commands on this menu at the right margin.

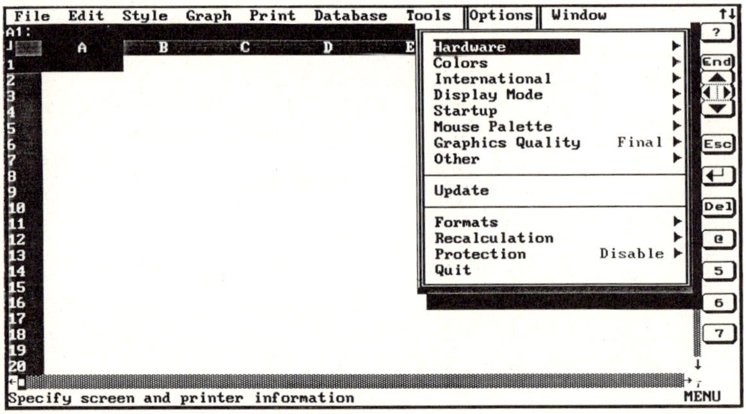

Fig. 6.1
The Options menu commands.

The system options tell Quattro Pro how to interact with your screen display and printer, which colors to display on-screen, and where and how to store files. If Quattro Pro seems to be performing well and you are comfortable with its on-screen appearance, you may not have to change many of the default system settings.

The Update command saves the current Options menu settings. These settings go into effect the next time you start another Quattro Pro work session. Quattro Pro stores the default menu settings in two files on your hard disk drive (RSC.RF and QUATTRO.MU). If you are using the 1-2-3 menu tree, Quattro Pro stores the menu settings in 1-2-3.MU. If you are using the Quattro menu tree, the program uses the 01.MU file.

Tip | Selecting Update saves all updatable system defaults, including those defaults set on other menus.

The lower set of options defines settings that affect only individual spreadsheets. The commands in this section store default numeric formats, enable you to choose the formula recalculation method, and turn global spreadsheet protection on and off.

Table 6.1 explains the purpose of the Options menu commands. As with most other Quattro Pro commands, these commands are intuitive. For example, choose **Colors** to set color options, **Display Mode** to change the display mode, or **Mouse Palette** to reconfigure the mouse palette.

Table 6.1
The Options Menu Commands

Command	Description
Hardware	Shows screen, memory, and printer settings
Colors	Customizes colors for all Quattro Pro screens
International	Displays international standards for currency, date, and time
Display Mode	Sets the display mode
Startup	Displays current startup and default options
Mouse Palette	Changes the macro key button assignments on the mouse palette
Graphics Quality	Toggles between final and draft graphics quality
Other	Sets Undo, Macro, EMS, Clock, and Paradox options
Update	Updates and saves all current default settings
Formats	Sets the global display formats
Recalculation	Sets the recalculation mode
Protection	Enables and disables global spreadsheet protection

Setting Hardware Options

When you select /**Options H**ardware, Quattro Pro displays a submenu with two command options, and three noninteractive fields that display system data only (see table 6.2).

Table 6.2
Choosing Hardware Options

Command	Description
Screen	Sets characteristics for the screen display
Printers	Reconfigures and installs printers
Normal Memory	Displays available conventional memory
EMS	Displays available expanded memory
Coprocessor	Indicates if a coprocessor is installed

The Screen and Printers commands enable you to change the system settings for your screen and printer. The final three commands, distinguished by a line through their names (and no available bold letter shortcut key), display information about how Quattro Pro is using your hardware (see fig. 6.2). You cannot execute these commands. When you add memory or a coprocessor to your system, though, Quattro Pro automatically updates the information in these three fields.

Fig. 6.2
Reviewing the status of your PC's hardware.

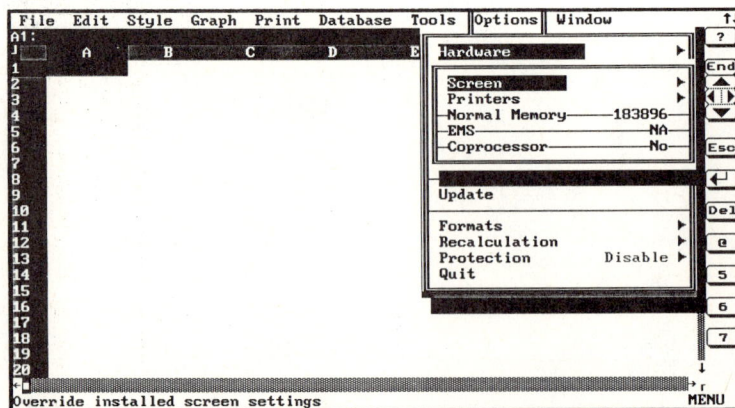

Figure 6.2 illustrates the current hardware status available on the Hardware submenu. Here, Quattro Pro indicates that the computer has 183,896 bytes

of free conventional memory, no expanded memory, and that no coprocessor is available.

Choosing a New Screen

During installation Quattro Pro detects your screen display and installs the proper screen driver file. This file contains special codes that tell Quattro Pro how to display itself. Depending on your display model, and therefore the contents of this file, you may be able to modify certain display characteristics directly from the Options menu.

To change these stored specifications (without reinstalling the program), select /**O**ptions **H**ardware **S**creen. Quattro Pro displays the menu shown in figure 6.3. These commands are described in the next sections.

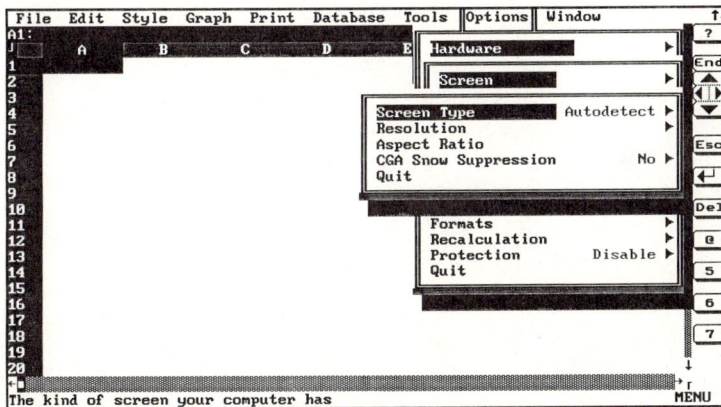

**Fig. 6.3
The Screen submenu commands.**

Screen Type

The Screen Type option enables you to choose a different screen driver for your display. The default setting, Autodetect, causes Quattro Pro to evaluate your screen type on its own. You should let Quattro Pro autodetect your screen type except in special cases, such as when you want to select a special display setting, such as Monochrome EGA. If you select a driver incompatible with your type of screen, Quattro Pro may not display correctly.

To choose a new screen type, select **S**creen Type. Now, select a different driver from the list shown in figure 6.4.

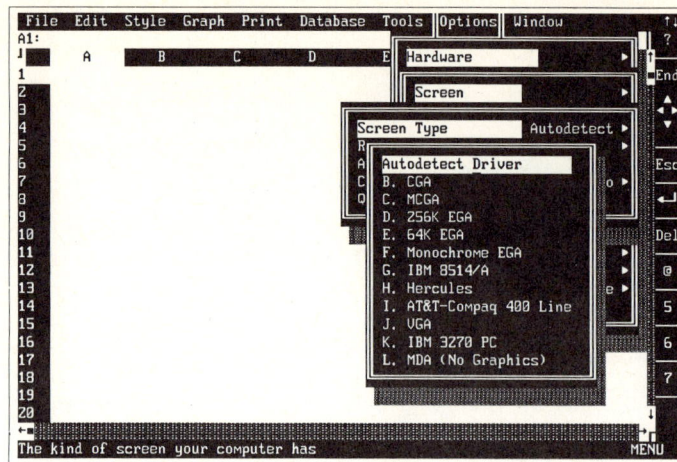

Fig. 6.4
Selecting a new driver from the Screen Type list.

| Tip | Quattro Pro doesn't execute the Screen Type or Resolution command when your display is in graphics display mode. To modify the display mode so that you can change the screen type, select /**Options D**isplay Mode **A:** 80x25 before you execute either of these commands. |

Resolution

The clarity of a graphics image is determined by how many pixels (or dots) your screen is capable of displaying. For example, a resolution of 640 × 480 means that a screen can illuminate 640 dots horizontally and 480 dots vertically. The more dots a screen can display, the crisper the resolution of a graphics image. Some VGA screens are capable of displaying a resolution of 1280 × 1024—an ideal resolution for computer-aided design (CAD) applications.

Many display adapter cards support multiple resolution modes. In this case, you can choose one resolution mode for spreadsheet text and another for spreadsheet graphics. To select a different screen resolution (if this option is available with your screen adapter card), select **R**esolution, and then select a resolution setting from the list Quattro Pro displays.

| Tip | Because Quattro Pro automatically chooses the highest resolution available for your display, you probably will not need to change this value. |

Aspect Ratio

Each screen display has a height-to-width measurement called the *aspect ratio*. A properly adjusted aspect ratio ensures that the shape of a graph is correct, so that a pie graph looks like a pie and not like an egg or a pancake.

To adjust the aspect ratio, select the **A**spect Ratio command from the Screen Type submenu. Quattro Pro displays a circle on your screen. Press the up- and down-arrow keys to mold the figure until it appears as a near-perfect circle on your screen. Press Enter to accept that height-to-width ratio or Esc to cancel the operation.

CGA Snow Suppression

If you have a color graphics adapter (CGA) display, your screen may flicker when you scroll about the spreadsheet window. Use the CGA Snow Suppression command to eliminate this problem. To enable snow suppression, select **Yes** on the submenu that appears when you choose this command.

Choosing Printers

During the initial program installation, you supplied Quattro Pro with your printer's brand name and model number. Quattro Pro used this information to create a driver file containing special codes, codes that tell Quattro Pro how to print spreadsheets and graphs on your particular printer.

To make changes to the printer driver file without reinstalling the program, choose /**O**ptions **H**ardware **P**rinters. Quattro Pro displays the submenu pictured in figure 6.5. This submenu is divided into two sections. The top section contains commands for installing two printers and choosing one of them as the default printer.

The bottom section of this menu contains printer setup commands that enable you to record plotter speed, select printer fonts, adjust line feeds, and toggle between continuous and single-sheet paper feeding.

Notice that the current settings for many of these commands appear in the right margin of the menu.

Fig. 6.5
The Printers
submenu
commands.

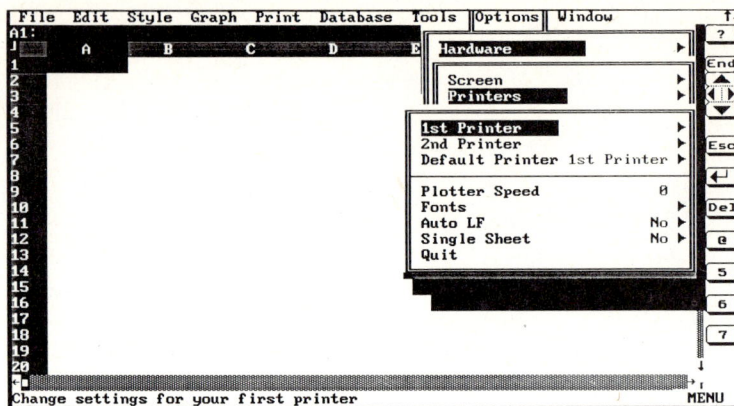

Printer Configuration Data

With the first three options on the Printers menu, you can record configuration data for one or two printers. If you only own one printer, this printer must be the default printer. If you own two printers, you can configure both, and toggle between them with the Default Printer command.

Follow these steps to configure a second printer:

1. Select /**Options** **Hardware** **Printers** **2**nd Printer.

2. Select **Type** of printer. Quattro Pro displays a scrollable list of printer manufacturers.

3. Select the correct printer manufacturer from the list. Quattro Pro displays a scrollable list of printer models.

4. Select the appropriate printer model from the list. Quattro Pro displays a list of possible print resolution settings.

5. Select a resolution setting. Quattro Pro returns to the 2nd Printer menu.

The next two steps are necessary only when you own a serial printer or when you do not have a standard parallel printer connected to port LPT1, the default printer port for most PCs.

6. Select Device and specify the port to which the printer is connected.

7. If you own a serial printer, enter the appropriate data for **B**aud Rate, **P**arity, and **S**top Bits.

The 2nd Printer menu should now reflect the new printer settings next to the Make, Model, and Mode headings (see fig. 6.6).

```
 File  Edit  Style  Graph  Print  Database  Tools  Options  Window       ↑↓
A1:                                                                      ?
J         A        B        C        D      E  Hardware          ▶
1                                                                       End
2                                            Screen              ▶      ▲
3                                            Printers            ▶     ◀▯▶
4                                                                       ▼
5                                        1st Printer      ▶
6                                        2nd Printer      ▶             Esc
7
8                                  Type of printer              ▶        ↵
9                                  Make───────────────────Panasonic──
10                                 Model──────────────────KX-P1595──   Del
11                                 Mode─────────240 x 216 dpi High (wide)─
12                                 Device               1 Parallel-1 ▶    8
13                                 Baud rate              Leave as is ▶
14                                 Parity                 Leave as is ▶    5
15                                 Stop bits              Leave as is ▶
16                                 Quit                                   6
17
18                                                                        7
19
20
◀▮                                                                    ↓►r
Define the type of printer                                           MENU
```

Fig. 6.6
Quattro Pro updates the 2nd Printer menu.

To choose the new printer as the default printer, follow these steps:

1. Press Esc to return to the Printers submenu.

2. Select **D**efault Printer.

3. Select the number of the printer you want to be the default printer (that is, the one Quattro Pro will print to unless otherwise instructed).

Plotter Speed

The Plotter Speed option enables you to specify the print speed for a color plotter. The fastest speed is 9, and the slowest is 1. The default setting, 0, tells Quattro Pro to run at the plotter's fastest speed.

Experiment with the Plotter Speed setting, because you may want to intentionally slow down the plotter speed when using older pens. Slowing down a plotter that uses old pens helps improve the quality of your plotter's printouts.

Fonts

You can install special printer fonts by using the Fonts command. The first choice on this menu, LaserJet Fonts, is used to install font cartridges for a Hewlett-Packard LaserJet printer. When you choose this command, you need to tell Quattro Pro which fonts you have and in which of the ports, or cartridge slots, on the printer (right or left) they are installed (see fig. 6.7).

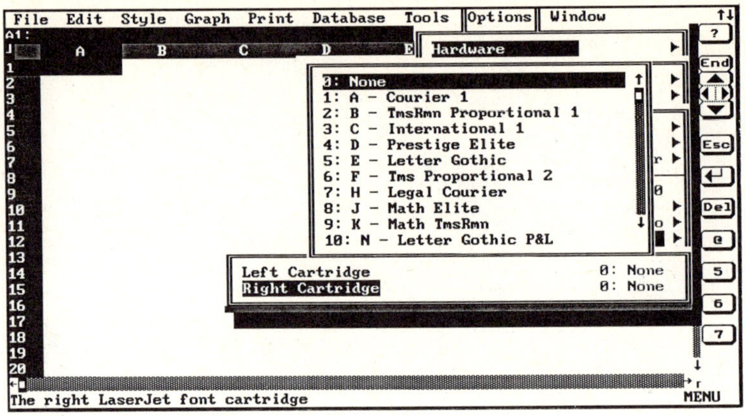

Fig. 6.7
Selecting the
Fonts
command.

The second option, Autoscale Fonts, enables you to decide how Quattro Pro scales fonts when printing graphs. Normally, the way Quattro Pro scales fonts depends on the size of the area in which you choose to display a graph. The less space Quattro Pro has to work in, the smaller the actual font sizes. If you prefer that Quattro Pro not scale your fonts in this manner, choose Autoscale Fonts and select No.

Auto LF

Using the Auto LF option tells Quattro Pro whether to issue a line-feed character after each carriage return. The default setting is No. If your printouts are double spaced, try selecting the Yes option. If the printer crams several lines of text onto one line, try selecting No.

Single Sheet

Quattro Pro assumes that you will be using continuous-feed (tractor-fed) paper to print your spreadsheets. When you choose /Options Printers Single Sheet, the setting is No. This is the normal setting for dot-matrix printers that use tractor feeding. If you want to feed paper into your printer one sheet at a time (for example, when your second printer is a letter-quality printer), set the Single Sheet option to Yes.

Reviewing Normal Memory, EMS, and Coprocessor Data

The Hardware menu gives you access to some of Quattro Pro's knowledge of your computer system. The bottom three entries on this menu indicate the amount of memory available to Quattro Pro (in bytes), the amount of expanded memory available (in bytes), and whether a math coprocessor is installed. All three values are detected by Quattro Pro and displayed here for your convenience.

The following section shows you how to customize the color combinations used to display Quattro Pro.

Using Quattro Pro's Coloring Palette

You can change the colors for each part of Quattro Pro's on-screen display by using the Options Colors command. When you choose this command, you see a submenu listing areas of the program that you may color. Table 6.3 describes the choices that appear on this submenu.

Table 6.3
Changing Color Options

Command	Description
Menu	Changes colors on the pull-down menus
Desktop	Changes colors located behind a spreadsheet
Spreadsheet	Changes colors on a spreadsheet
Conditional	Sets colors for special numbers and formulas
Help	Changes colors on the help windows
File Manager	Sets colors for the File Manager
Palettes	Resets all default Quattro Pro colors

With the Colors command, you can select the colors for Quattro Pro to use in all parts of its program display. Feel free to experiment with new combinations, because the original scheme can be reinstated by using the Palettes command.

When you select a Colors menu command, Quattro Pro displays a special coloring tool called the *coloring palette* (see fig. 6.8). Look closely and notice the tiny bar positioned on one of the color pairs in this box. This bar indicates the current color combination setting for the Quattro Pro screen area selected. For example, figure 6.8 shows this palette's setting when you select /**O**ptions Colors **M**enu **K**ey Letter. Each time you want to alter one of Quattro Pro's display colors, this coloring tool appears. Use the arrow keys or click your mouse to select a different color combination.

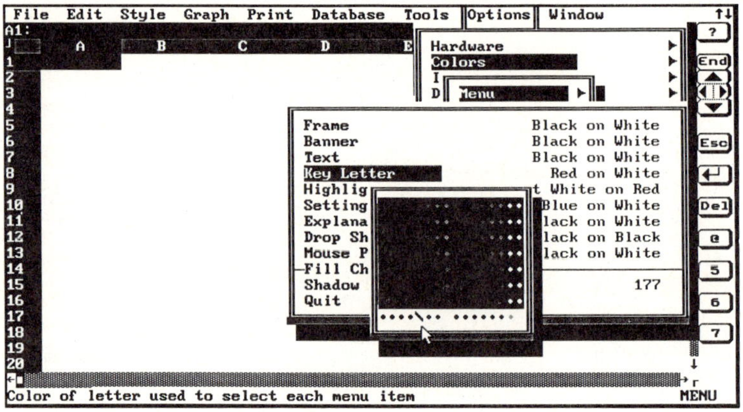

Fig. 6.8
Changing
Quattro Pro's
colors.

Note that a few of the screen elements require that you enter ASCII charac-ter codes (for example, the **M**enu **S**hadow option). Consult the ASCII table in Appendix E for sensible values in these instances.

Choosing Menu Colors

The Menu command enables you to choose new color combinations for Quattro Pro's pull-down menus (see fig. 6.9). When you select **C**olors **M**enu, Quattro Pro displays a list of the parts of a menu that may be colored. Select a part to color and Quattro Pro displays the coloring palette with the rotat-ing bar. Choose a new color and Quattro Pro immediately refreshes the screen display so that it reflects the new color combination.

Choosing Desktop Colors

By using the Desktop command, you can choose new color combinations for Quattro Pro's desktop. The desktop is the part of the display not filled with a

```
 File  Edit  Style  Graph  Print  Database  Tools ‖Options‖ Window            ↑↓
A1:                                                                          [ ? ]
┃┃    A         B         C         D         E   Hardware              ▶
1                                                 Colors                ▶     [End]
2                                                 I                           ◀▮▶
3                                                 D  Menu          ▶ ▮         ▼
4                                            ┌───────────────────────────────┐
5                                            │ Frame                Black on White │ [Esc]
6                                            │ Banner               Black on White │
7                                            │ Text                 Black on White │
8                                            │ Key Letter             Red on White │ [ ↵ ]
9                                            │ Highlight       Bright White on Red  │
10                                           │ Settings              Blue on White  │ [Del]
11                                           │ Explanation          Black on White  │
12                                           │ Drop Shadow   Bright Black on Black  │ [ @ ]
13                                           │ Mouse Palette        Black on White  │
14                                           ├─Fill Characters───────────────┤     [ 5 ]
15                                           │ Shadow                     177  │
16                                           │ Quit                            │     [ 6 ]
17                                           └───────────────────────────────┘
18                                                                                [ 7 ]
19
20
┃▮                                                                        →  ┌↓
Color of menu frames                                                     MENU
```

**Fig. 6.9
The Menu
Submenu
commands.**

spreadsheet window. Here, you also may specify ASCII characters for Quattro Pro to use as background shading.

When you select /**Options** **Hardware Colors Desktop**, Quattro Pro displays a list of the parts of the desktop that may be colored. Select a part to color and Quattro Pro displays the coloring palette with the rotating bar. Choose a new color and Quattro Pro immediately refreshes the screen display so that it reflects the new color combination.

Choosing Spreadsheet Colors

The Spreadsheet command enables you to color various portions of a spreadsheet window. When you select /**Options** **Hardware Colors Spreadsheet**, Quattro Pro displays a list of the parts of the spreadsheet window that may be colored. Select a part to color and Quattro Pro displays the coloring palette with the rotating bar. Choose a new color and Quattro Pro immediately refreshes the screen display so that it reflects the new color combination.

Choosing Conditional Colors

The /**Options** **Colors Conditional** command displays the submenu pictured in figure 6.10. With the Conditional menu options you can specify the color your data will have when certain conditions are met.

The most common use for this option is to specify an acceptable range for a set of data, and require Quattro Pro to show values outside that range in a

Fig. 6.10
Reviewing the
Conditional
submenu
commands.

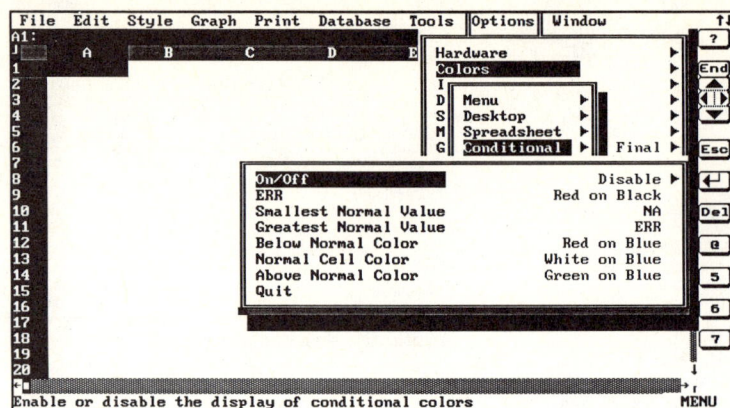

different color. The On/Off command tells Quattro Pro whether to actually display conditional colors. This enables the conditional coloring that you set up with the following commands on this menu.

ERR enables you to specify the color to use when ERR and NA values appear on a spreadsheet. Smallest Normal Value and Greatest Normal Value define the range of values that are considered "normal." The next three command options enable you to define colors to be used when spreadsheet values are Below Normal, Normal (within), and Above Normal.

Remember that, in addition to specifying the normal range and colors, you must enable the conditional color option by choosing the **On**/Off command.

Another good use for the conditional command is to set negative numbers apart from positive numbers. For example, in financial applications, you may need to know whether a business is operating in the red or the black. By assigning the color red to negative numbers on a spreadsheet, you provide conclusive evidence to this question.

Choosing Help Colors

With the Help command, you can choose different color combinations for Quattro Pro's help windows. When you select /**Options** Hardware Colors **Help**, Quattro Pro displays a list of the parts of the help window that may be colored. Select a part to color and Quattro Pro displays the coloring palette with the rotating bar. Choose a new color and Quattro Pro immediately refreshes the screen display so that it reflects the new color combination. Because Quattro Pro does not show help windows as part of its normal display, press F1 to make sure that your color selection is acceptable.

Choosing File Manager Colors

The File Manager command lets you change the color display of Quattro Pro's File Manager. When you select /Options Hardware Colors File Manager, Quattro Pro displays a list of the parts of the screen that may be colored. Select a part to color and Quattro Pro displays the coloring palette with the rotating bar. Choose a new color and Quattro Pro immediately refreshes the screen display so that it reflects the new color combination.

Because Quattro Pro does not show the File Manager as part of its normal display, press /FUF from the active spreadsheet to load the File Manager and make sure that your color selection is acceptable.

Choosing Palettes Colors

The Palettes command enables you to recall Quattro Pro's original color scheme, even if you previously saved custom color combinations with the Update command. To recall Quattro Pro's default color settings, do the following:

1. Select /Options Colors Palettes.

2. Specify your screen type.

3. Select /Options Update to save the change.

Now take a look at how to internationalize your copy of Quattro Pro by using the International options.

Setting International Options

Quattro Pro (Version 1.01) offers excellent foreign-language compatibility.

If you are using a non-English copy of the program, you can enter @function commands in your native language or in English. All other commands, including the menu-equivalent commands listed in Appendix D, must be entered in your local language.

When you retrieve Lotus 1-2-3 spreadsheets (or any other compatible spreadsheet) into Quattro Pro, the program translates the @function commands into your language.

Quattro Pro now supports the LaserJet III printer and some printers that are more common in Europe. If you want to print text using Hershey or Bitstream characters from the international character set, Borland recommends that you contact the company directly to obtain a special set of fonts containing additional international characters.

By default, Quattro Pro uses the United States convention for the currency symbol, numerical punctuation, and dates, and times. To change the default to international standards for displaying currency symbols, punctuation, dates, and times, select /**Options International**, or to change the Quattro Pro sort rules, turn Lotus International Character Set conversion on and print accent symbols above international letters. The international settings that you create with this command are accessed with the /**Style Numeric Format** command. For example, if you enter a new currency symbol, Quattro Pro attaches that symbol to monetary values on your spreadsheet when you format the values with the /**Style Numeric Format Currency** command. The same holds true for international punctuation, dates, and times. Table 6.4 lists the commands on the International submenu.

Businesses with an international clientele will find this command particularly helpful. For example, you can create a contract bid containing the date format, punctuation style, and currency symbol of your client's country. You also can create an import-export company that can format a currency translation spreadsheet to display the client's currency symbol.

Table 6.4
The International Menu Commands

Command	Description
Currency	Assigns location and style of the currency symbol
Punctuation	Assigns type of punctuation used in numbers
Date	Sets Long and Short international date formats
Time	Sets Long and Short international time formats
Use Sort Table	Specifies a set of sort rules to use
LICS Conversion characters	Converts LICS characters into uppercase ASCII
Overstrike Print	Allows for printing of accented characters

The International commands enable you to specify the format in which values are displayed, as well as where in a cell they are placed when you enter them. Figure 6.11 shows the current command settings in the right margin of the menu.

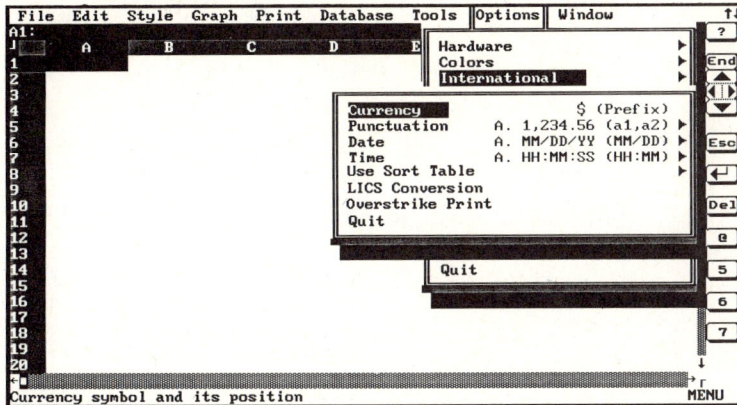

**Fig. 6.11
Reviewing the
International
default settings.**

Choosing a Currency Symbol

With the Currency command, you can choose the symbol that Quattro Pro attaches to monetary values on a spreadsheet. This symbol is the character that displays when you choose the /**S**tyle **N**umeric Format **C**urrency command. By default, Quattro Pro shows the dollar sign ($) symbol as a prefix to a number.

To choose a different currency and symbol setting, do the following:

1. Select /**O**ptions **I**nternational **C**urrency.

2. Press the Backspace key until the current currency symbol is erased.

3. Enter the ASCII characters that correspond to the currency symbol and press Enter to store them or Esc to cancel the operation.

4. Choose **S**uffix or **P**refix to set the orientation for the new currency symbol.

Tip | Entering an ASCII code to create a currency symbol is different from entering a code for a shadow on the **C**olors menu. Here, you must press Alt-Code, where Code is the ASCII code equivalent for the currency symbol. For example, to enter the symbol for the Japanese yen, press Alt-157.

Choosing the Punctuation

The Punctuation command enables you to specify how Quattro Pro displays decimal points, separates arguments in @functions, and segregates zeros in numbers larger than 999.

To choose a new punctuation style, do the following:

1. Select /**O**ptions **I**nternational **P**unctuation.

2. Select a punctuation style from the menu shown in figure 6.12.

Fig. 6.12 Selecting an international punctuation setting.

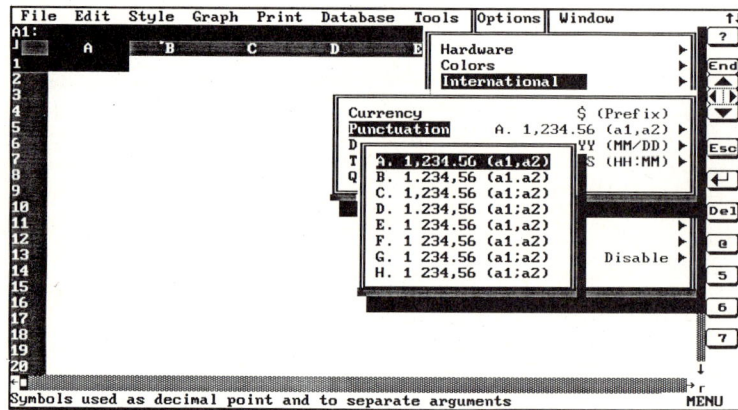

Choosing Date Formats

The Date command can display dates in several popular international formats. The date formats you choose with this command become available as the Long and Short international date formats when you select /Options Formats Numeric Format Date.

1. Select /**O**ptions **F**ormats Numeric Format **D**ate to select the setting that becomes the long international and short international options on the /**O**ptions Format **D**ate menu.

2. When you choose /**O**ptions Format **D**ate, Quattro Pro asks you to specify the date formats that you want to use as the default long international and short international settings on the /**S**tyle Numeric Format **D**ate menu.

To choose a new international date format, do the following:

1. Select /**O**ptions **I**nternational **D**ate.

2. Select a date format from the menu displayed in figure 6.13.

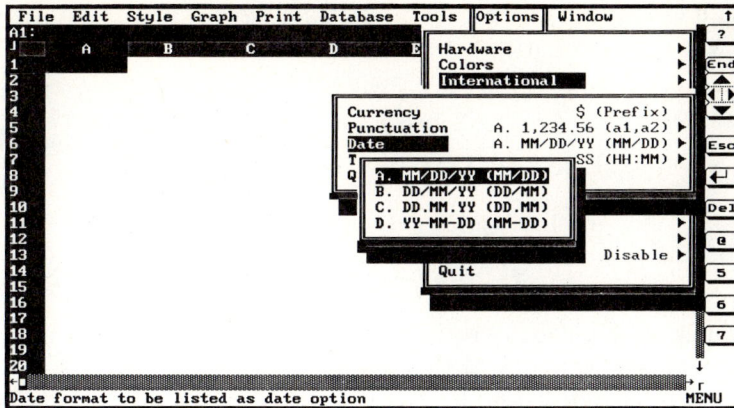

Fig. 6.13
Selecting an
international
date setting.

If you now want to make that setting the default display format for the spreadsheet, select /**O**ptions **F**ormats **N**umeric Format **D**ate.

Choosing Time Formats

The Time command can display times in several popular international formats. The time formats you choose with this command become available as the Long and Short international time formats when you select /**O**ptions **F**ormats **N**umeric Format **T**ime.

To choose a new international time format, do the following:

1. Select /**O**ptions **I**nternational **T**ime.

2. Select a time format from the menu shown in figure 6.14.

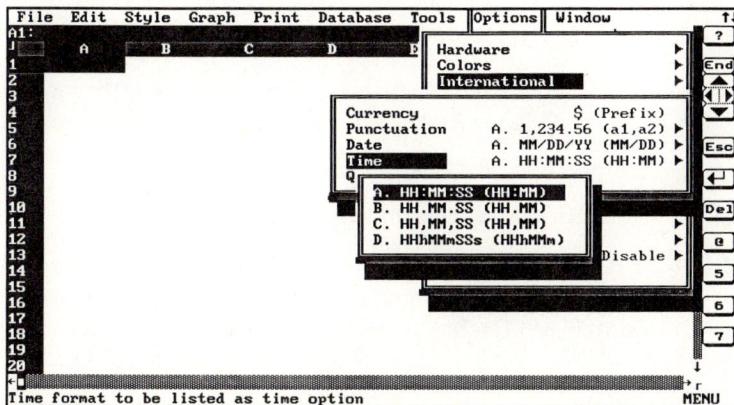

Fig. 6.14
Selecting an
international
time setting.

If you now want to make that setting the default display format for the spreadsheet, select /**O**ptions **F**ormats **N**umeric Format **T**ime.

Choosing New Sort Rules

When you choose /**O**ptions **I**nternational **U**se Sort Table, Quattro Pro displays a menu offering four sort rules: ASCII.SOR, INTL.SOR, NORDAN.SOR, and SWEDFIN.SOR.

The ASCII Sort Rule tells Quattro Pro to sort data so that uppercase letters appear before lowercase and accented letters appear after the lowercase z. See Appendix E for a complete list of ASCII characters.

The International Sort Rule tells Quattro Pro to sort uppercase, lowercase, and accented characters according to the dictionary method (AaBbCc and so on). In this method, the circumflex character (ˆ) appears with C and c; whereas in an ASCII sort, this character appears after the lowercase character grouping.

The Norwegian/Danish and Swedish/Finnish sort rules are like the International Sort Rule, except that Quattro Pro sorts characters unique to these countries to the end of the regular alphabet.

The Use Sort Table command names contain an SOR extension that identifies the name of the file that Quattro Pro uses to manage each type of sort operation. These files are standard Borland files and may be used with Paradox.

Tip | Any file in the default Quattro Pro directory with an SOR extension appears on the Use Sort Table menu.

Choosing LICS Conversion

Lotus 1-2-3 spreadsheets use a proprietary character set called the Lotus International Characters Set (LICS). This character set is the same as the ASCII character set until you reach character 128. The characters in positions 128 through 255 in the LICS table are not the standard IBM international and graphics characters that appear in Appendix E.

When you load a 1-2-3 spreadsheet into Quattro Pro, choose the /**O**ptions **I**nternational LICS Conversion command to convert all LICS characters (128 through 255) to the normal ASCII characters. This procedure ensures that Quattro Pro's sort rules work properly on your 1-2-3 spreadsheets.

When you save a file in a 1-2-3 spreadsheet format, Quattro Pro converts characters to match the LICS character set specifications.

Choosing Overstrike Print

The Overstrike Print command ensures that Quattro Pro places the proper accent symbol over an international character when you own a 7-bit printer.

The Diablo 630, Qume Sprint, Epson FX-80, and Epson LQ-1500 are examples of common 7-bit printers.

Setting Display Mode Options

The Display Mode command enables you to change the overall on-screen appearance of Quattro Pro. Normally, Quattro Pro displays in an 80 × 25 text mode. If you have the right display adapter card, however, you can display Quattro Pro in graphics mode, or in several different condensed modes. Use a graphics mode when you want to display an inserted graph on a spreadsheet.

When you select /Options **D**isplay Mode, Quattro Pro presents you with display mode alternatives (listed in table 6.5). Select the mode you want. After you select a new display mode, Quattro Pro immediately refreshes the screen display to reflect the new mode. Experiment with each of the modes available for your screen type.

Table 6.5
Display Mode Options

Command	Description
A: 80 × 25	Sets display mode to 80 columns by 25 rows
B: Graphics Mode	Switches to a graphics display mode
C: EGA: 80 × 43	Sets display mode to 80 columns by 43 rows
D: VGA: 80 × 50	Sets display mode to 80 columns by 50 rows

The Startup options, covered in the next section, control how Quattro Pro sets itself up when you load it into your system.

Setting Startup Options

When you select /**O**ptions **S**tartup, Quattro Pro displays the submenu shown in figure 6.15. The commands on this menu enable you to specify startup information that Quattro Pro uses each time you load the program into your system, or when you create a new spreadsheet file.

Fig. 6.15
The Startup
menu of
commands.

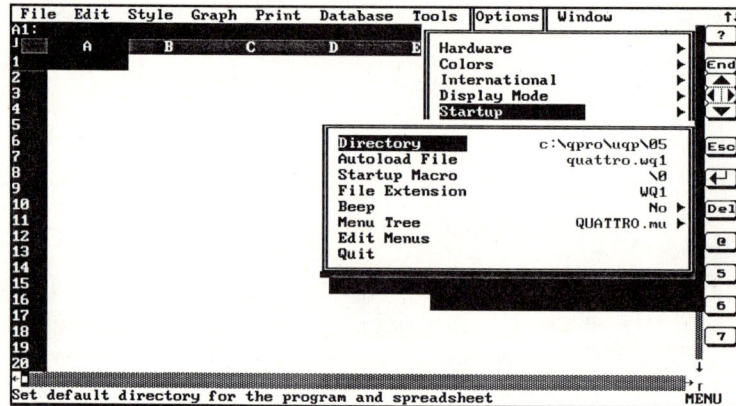

The startup options are system options, so to store them permanently for the next work session you must execute /**O**ptions **U**pdate. The default settings for these commands appear at the right margin of the menu.

Setting the Default Directory

With the **D**irectory command you can select the directory in which Quattro Pro will store spreadsheet files. The **S**ave and **R**etrieve commands on the **F**ile menu enable you to access a file on any drive and directory available to your system, not just the default directory. Even so, setting a default directory is useful when you find that you frequently use the same drive and directory. Although you literally can store your spreadsheet files anywhere on your hard disk drive, you should create a special directory to hold all your Quattro Pro spreadsheets. For example, if you want to store your files in a directory called C:\QPRO\FILES, follow these steps:

1. Select /**O**ptions **S**tartup **D**irectory.

2. Press the Backspace key until the current directory name is erased.

3. Type *c:\qpro\files* (or another valid directory name).

4. Press Enter to record the new name or Esc to cancel the operation.

Tip | The directory name that you enter with the Directory command must already exist on your hard disk drive—Quattro Pro will not create it for you. When you specify a directory name that does not exist, Quattro Pro displays an error message.

You can use another method to configure this default directory, which enables you to load Quattro Pro from any directory on your hard disk drive. This method is called a "wild card" technique, and it makes the correct directory the current one during a work session. To use this technique, enter a blank space in step 3, instead of a directory name.

Using an Autoload File

With the Autoload command you can designate a spreadsheet file for Quattro Pro to open automatically each time you load the program. If the file is not in the directory named with the Directory option, be sure to enter the full path name here.

Initially, the default autoload file name is QUATTRO.WQ1. If you want to autoload a file named QUARTER1, and this file is in a directory named C:\SALES, do the following:

1. Select /**O**ptions **S**tartup **A**utoload.

2. Press the Backspace key until the current file name is erased.

3. Type *QUARTER1.WQ1* (or another valid autoload file).

4. Press Enter to record the new file name or Esc to cancel the operation.

A second method of autoloading a file does not require the use of this command. Type the file name on the DOS command line after Quattro Pro's program file name but before you press Enter to load the program. For example, type *q quarter2* at the DOS prompt and press Enter to load a spreadsheet file named QUARTER2.WQ1. Quattro Pro assumes that this file name's extension is WQ1—if it isn't, type a different extension after the file name and prior to pressing Enter.

You can enter other command-line options as you load the program. The syntax for using these options is

Type Q [filename][macroname][/options]

and press Enter.

These options, shown in table 6.6, tell Quattro Pro how to configure certain parts of itself as it is loading into your system.

**Table 6.6
Command-Line Options**

Option	Description
/D	Tells Quattro Pro to load a specific resource file with an RF extension. If the resource file is not in the current directory, you must also specify the directory and path name.
/I	Tells Quattro Pro to autodetect the screen display and other hardware as it is loading
/IC	Tells Quattro Pro to load with a color palette
/IM	Tells Quattro Pro to load with a monochrome palette
/IB	Tells Quattro Pro to load with a black-and-white palette
/E	Tells Quattro Pro to load with LIM 4.0 Expanded Memory Specification (EMS) disabled and 3.x enabled. Use this option when your EMS board is not fully compatible with LIM 4.0.
/X	Tells Quattro Pro to load with extended-memory code-swapping enabled. This is the recommended setting if you have a 286-based AT computer with 1M of RAM.

Choosing a Startup Macro

The Startup Macro command enables you to run a macro automatically each time you retrieve a new spreadsheet. This command is useful if, for example, you normally use a macro to format your spreadsheets prior to entering data into them (see Chapter 12 for complete coverage of macros).

To execute a macro named \m each time you create a new spreadsheet, do the following:

1. Select /**Options Startup Startup Macro**.

2. Press the Backspace key until the current macro name is erased.

3. Type *m* (or another valid macro file name).

4. Press Enter to record the new name or Esc to cancel the operation.

Selecting a New Default File Extension

The File Extension command tells Quattro Pro the three-letter file name extension that it should put on the end of each spreadsheet file name. By default, Quattro Pro uses the extension WQ1. If you want to change the extension to WQ5, for example, do the following:

1. Select /**O**ptions **S**tartup **F**ile Extension.

2. Press the Backspace key until the current extension is erased.

3. Type *wq5* (or another valid three-character extension).

4. Press Enter to record the new extension or Esc to cancel the operation.

The importance of this process is to enable the user to specify other applications for Quattro Pro to write files to (like Paradox or 1-2-3). If you are in an office in which 1-2-3 and Quattro Pro are used, you probably want to change the extension to WK1.

Specifying Beep Tones

Use the Beep command to turn Quattro Pro's error tone beep on and off. This beep sounds each time you make an illegal entry or incorrectly execute a command. If you prefer not to hear the error tone, select **N**o. The default setting is Yes.

Choosing a Menu Tree

The Menu Tree command enables you to load one of Quattro Pro's three compatible menu trees. When you choose this command, Quattro Pro displays a list of all available menu trees. By default, Quattro Pro shows three menu trees: QUATTRO.MU (the standard Quattro Pro tree), 123.MU (the Lotus 1-2-3 tree), and Q1.MU (compatible with earlier versions of Quattro). When you select a new menu tree, Quattro Pro's menu bar immediately reflects the new menu tree structure.

To switch to the Lotus 1-2-3 menu tree, for example, do the following:

1. Select /**O**ptions **S**tartup **M**enu Tree.

2. Select **1**23.MU.

Quattro Pro immediately displays the 1-2-3 menu tree.

Customizing the Mouse Palette

Note that the mouse palette and the mouse arrow pointer appear on-screen only if you have a mouse attached to your system. Quattro Pro recognizes when a mouse is present.

The mouse palette is the vertical stack of icons appearing on the right side of Quattro Pro's display. With the Mouse Palette option you can redefine the function of macro buttons 1 through 7. The Help icon (?) and the End arrows are not user-assignable.

Reassigning the mouse palette buttons is useful if you find that you frequently execute a keystroke sequence (such as Ctrl-Break to cancel a menu command and return to the active spreadsheet.) If so, you can assign {BREAK} to one of the macro buttons. When you need to press Ctrl-Break, you can click the button assigned that task. Appendix C contains a glossary of macro commands.

To assign a new function to one of the palette buttons, follow these steps:

1. Select /**O**ptions **M**ouse Palette.

2. Select the button you want to customize (**1**st button, **2**nd button, and so on), and Quattro Pro displays an edit menu.

3. Choose **T**ext and enter up to three characters that you want to appear as a label on the button.

4. Choose **M**acro and enter any valid Quattro Pro macro command (for example, {BEEP} is the default used by buttons 5, 6, and 7).

5. Select **Q**uit to leave the menu.

The next section shows you how to modify the graphics quality options to make the best use of your system's memory—and your time.

Setting Graphics Quality Options

The Graphics Quality option enables you to choose the quality of Quattro Pro's on-screen graphics. Specify either Draft or Final quality.

Quattro Pro takes time to build the required font files before it can display or print a font. Each time a new font is chosen, Quattro Pro might pause to build these font files. After Quattro Pro creates a font file, it can access that particular font the next time without making you wait.

You also can elect to have Quattro Pro substitute Hershey fonts for Bitstream fonts to save time. Quattro Pro does not need to stop and build fonts. To do this, choose **D**raft graphics quality. Then, when you want to look in more detail at your file, return to Final quality graphics.

To choose a different Graphics Quality, do the following:

1. Select /**O**ptions **G**raphics Quality.

2. Quattro Pro displays a two-item menu. Select the quality you prefer.

Quattro Pro has several other options that appeal to all users. These options are covered in the next section.

Using Other Options

Selecting the **O**ther command from the **O**ptions menu option displays a submenu of miscellaneous system options (see fig. 6.16). Some of these options, such as the Undo and Macro functions, become invaluable to you as you continue working with Quattro Pro. Notice that the current settings for some of the commands appear at the right margin of this menu.

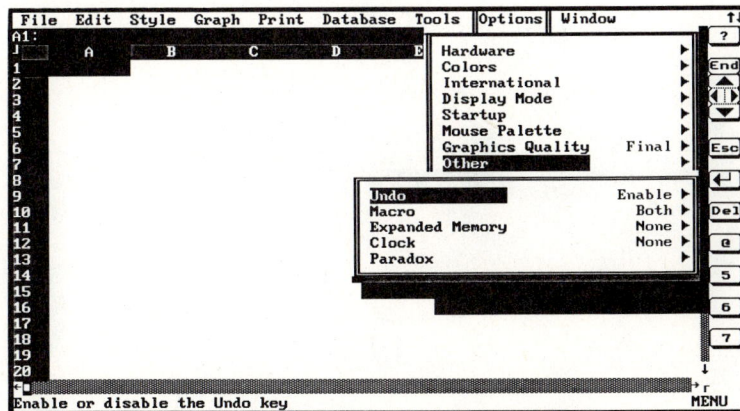

Fig. 6.16
The Options
Other submenu
commands.

Undo

Select **D**isable or **E**nable to control the status of the /**E**dit **U**ndo command. Remember, this command can undo many—but not all— Quattro Pro operations. Disabling this function speeds up Quattro Pro's operation a bit. If you are at all mistake prone (and who isn't?), leave the Undo function enabled. It's well worth the minor loss in operating speed.

Macro Redraw

The Macro Redraw option enables you to specify which parts of the screen to avoid redrawing during macro execution. The default setting, Both, suppresses redrawing of menus and spreadsheet windows until macro execution is completed. This suppression speeds up the execution of macros. You can specify that Quattro Pro suppress redrawing of a spreadsheet Alone, Panel, Window, or turn off redraw suppression altogether (None).

Expanded Memory

If your computer has Expanded Memory Specification (EMS), Quattro Pro detects it and makes use of this memory area to store spreadsheet data. Although this memory enables you to work with more spreadsheets at once, or with larger spreadsheets, using expanded memory exclusively for spreadsheet information slows down performance.

Quattro Pro tries to balance speed and space considerations by storing only some of your spreadsheets in EMS. To influence this balance, you can specify the use of EMS with the expanded memory option (see fig. 6.17).

Fig. 6.17
The Expanded Memory submenu.

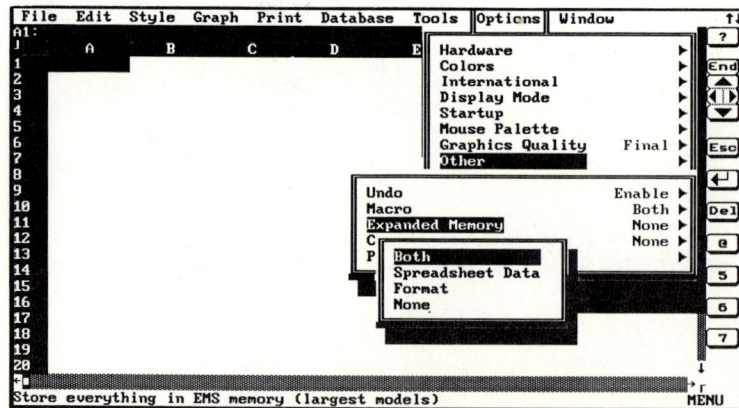

If you are working with large files and need more memory, you may want to have Quattro Pro store spreadsheet and format data in EMS. If you need more speed from Quattro Pro, select Spreadsheet Data or Format. These two commands restrict EMS usage to formulas and labels, or just formats, respectively.

To specify the use of expanded memory, follow these steps:

1. Select /Options Other Expanded Memory.

2. Choose an option from the menu.

Select None to ensure that Quattro Pro operates at the fastest possible speed.

Clock Display

The clock display option enables you to specify whether to display the time on the status line in Standard format, International format, or not at all. The default is None, which does not display the clock. To specify in detail the sort of international format you would like, use the /Options International Time option.

To change the clock display, follow these steps:

1. Select /Options Other Clock.

2. Select one of the three options on the clock menu: Standard, International, or None.

Paradox

The Paradox command option enables you to set options for using Paradox files on a local area network (LAN). If you are working on a LAN, you need to specify further information: the type of area network you have, the directory where you have the PARADOX.NET file, and the time (in seconds) between Quattro Pro's attempts to open a locked file. The Paradox menu provides these options.

Updating the Options

All the options discussed so far in this chapter are system options. If you make changes to your system settings and you do not update Quattro Pro's resource file, when you quit, the new settings are lost. In this case, Quattro

Pro reverts to the old default settings the next time you load the program into your computer. To update new system settings so that they are active the next time you begin a Quattro Pro work session, press /OU.

Specifying Formats

With the Formats option you can change how Quattro Pro displays formatted data on your spreadsheets (see fig. 6.18). Setting the Format option affects the current spreadsheet window. These settings become the global stored settings for that spreadsheet. Notice that the current settings for these commands appear at the right margin on this menu. The following sections discuss each option in detail.

Fig. 6.18
The Formats submenu of commands.

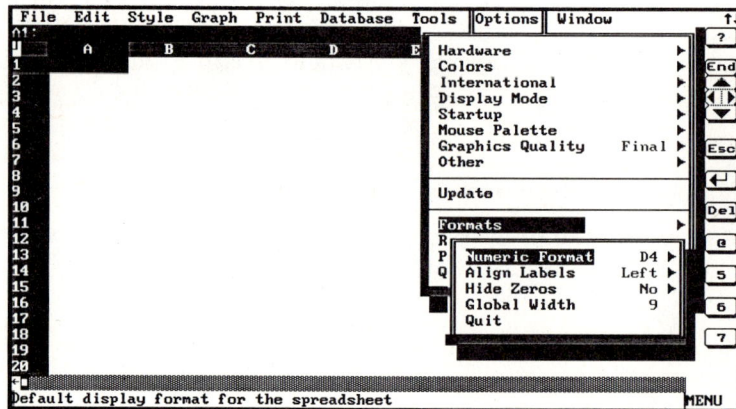

Numeric Format

The Numeric Format option enables you to specify the default format for displaying the values within your spreadsheet. All values are changed to the format you specify except those that have been specified with the /Style Numeric Format command as a block of values. Initially, the default format is General, which right aligns values and dates and aligns labels according to the /Options Formats Align Labels setting.

To change the global numeric format, follow these steps:

1. Select /Options Formats Numeric Format.

2. Select a format from the submenu.

3. If you choose **D**ate or **T**ime, Quattro Pro presents a list of format choices that these may be displayed with.

Align Labels

The Align label option enables you to specify how Quattro Pro aligns labels in a spreadsheet cell. Initially, alignment is set to Left, but you also may select Center or Right alignment. Select /**O**ptions **F**ormats **A**lign Labels to choose one of these three options.

Hide Zeros

With the Hide Zeros option, you can suppress the display of any cell whose value equals zero, whether it was entered directly or returned as the result of a formula calculation. Use this option with caution. When zero suppression is on, it is easy to assume a zero cell is empty and then accidentally write over cells that contain needed formulas.

Global Width

The Column Width option enables you to specify the width of all columns within a spreadsheet at once. The initial default width is nine character spaces. To change the column width, select /**O**ptions **F**ormats **G**lobal Width and type the value you want to be the new default for the current spreadsheet.

Controlling Recalculation

The Recalculation options enable you to specify how Quattro Pro updates formula results when you change cell values that those formulas depend on (see fig. 6.19). The following sections discuss each option in detail.

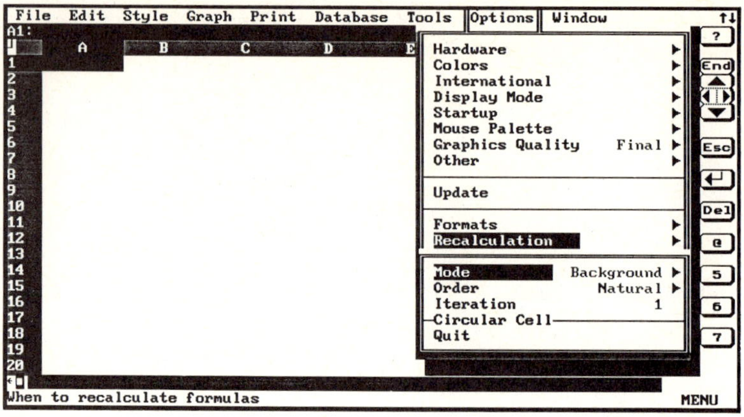

Fig. 6.19
The
Recalculation
submenu.

Mode

The Mode option enables you to specify whether Quattro Pro calculates formulas behind the scenes (Background), while you wait (Automatic), or on request (Manually). Select /Options Recalculation Mode and then select the mode you want.

If you have selected the Manual Mode, your spreadsheet may occasionally need to be recalculated. When a spreadsheet requires formula recalculation, Quattro Pro displays CALC on the status line at the bottom of the spreadsheet window. Press F9 (the Calc key) when you want to recalculate all the formulas on a spreadsheet.

Order of Recalculation

You can use the Order of Recalculation option to specify the order in which the set of formulas are calculated. The order in which formulas update cells can affect the resulting values. The default is Natural order. In Natural order, before a formula is calculated, all the cells it references are first recalculated.

The two other options are Row-wise and Column-wise. In column-wise recalculation, Quattro Pro starts in cell A1 and proceeds down column A. When the formulas in column A are recalculated, Quattro Pro begins at the top of column B. Row-wise calculation also starts at cell A1, but proceeds row by row.

To specify the order of formula recalculation, select /Options Recalculation Order and then select one of the three available orders.

Number of Iterations

Quattro Pro enables the specification of formulas that are circular in nature. A *circular formula* contains a cell or block address reference that includes the location of the formula. Each time you recalculate a circular formula, it adds itself to the resulting value.

The Number of Iterations option enables you to specify the number of cycles of recalculation Quattro Pro should perform each time the spreadsheet is recalculated. Only in the most complex of engineering or financial situations are circular references desirable.

To specify the number of recalculation iterations if there are circular references, follow these steps:

1. Select /**O**ptions **R**ecalculation **I**teration.

2. Enter any number up to 255 iterations.

Circular Cell

Circular Cell is a noninteractive menu field. If your spreadsheet contains a formula with a circular reference, the address of the first cell in that formula is displayed in this cell. When you correct a circular reference, this field redisplays the heading `Circular`.

Next, you will see how easy it is to use Quattro Pro's protection feature to safeguard your valuable spreadsheet data.

Setting Protection Options

The Protection Option is used to enable and disable global spreadsheet protection. When enabled, this feature prevents cells that have not been protected otherwise (with **S**tyle **P**rotection **U**nprotect) from being overwritten.

As you invest time and energy into a spreadsheet, you will want to ensure that a simple error on your part does not result in the loss of valuable data. To avoid data loss, enable global spreadsheet protection.

Questions and Answers

This chapter introduced you to the Options menu commands. If you have questions concerning particular situations that are not addressed in the examples given, look through the Question and Answers section; your question may be answered here.

System Options

Q: Quattro Pro seems to be running slower than it should, yet my spreadsheet applications are not all that big. What's going on?

A: In general, when Quattro Pro slows down, it is because you are running out of system memory. However, if you are running Quattro Pro with the VROOMM utility, running out of hard disk space also can affect Quattro Pro's speed. The VROOMM utility periodically writes part of the program onto your hard disk drive. If you have limited space on your hard disk drive, the VROOMM utility becomes less efficient. See how much memory is available to Quattro Pro on the Hardware menu, and then check to see how much space is free on your hard disk drive. If you have free memory and disk space, consider making the following changes on the Options menu:

Select /**Options D**isplay Mode and choose a text display.

Select /**Options** Colors Conditional **O**n/Off **D**isable.

Select /**Options O**ther Undo and choose **D**isable.

Select /**Options O**ther Expanded Memory and choose **N**one (only if you have expanded memory in your computer.).

Making some or all these changes will improve Quattro Pro's operating speed. You must weigh the loss of each feature, however, against a gain in operating speed for yourself.

Q: I installed a second printer on my computer system. I also have an AB switch box so that I can change quickly from one printer to the other. Do I need to tell Quattro Pro that I have two printers?

A: Using an AB switch box is not a substitute for configuring a second printer. Quattro Pro creates a printer driver file for each printer you configure. Not all printers use the same codes; therefore, using an AB switch box is no guarantee that one printer's driver file will work with a second printer.

To configure the second printer, select /**O**ptions **H**ardware **P**rinters **2**nd Printer and specify the manufacturer, model, printing mode, and port connection. Next, select /**U**pdate to store this information permanently. Finally, select /**O**ptions **H**ardware **P**rinters **D**efault Printer to define this printer as the default printer.

Q: I'm getting garbled printer output. What should I check for?

A: First, make sure that the definition file contains the correct configuration information (select /**O**ptions **H**ardware **P**rinters and **1**st Printer or **2**nd Printer.)

Second, if you are using a serial printer, make sure that the parity, baud rate, and stop bits match those set on your printer's configuration panel. If you don't know these values, check your printer manual.

Third, select /**O**ptions **H**ardware **P**rinters **A**uto LF and choose **N**o—Quattro Pro might be printing the data correctly, but all on the same line.

Q: When I choose /**O**ptions **D**isplay **M**ode and choose **G**raphics Display, why does Quattro Pro "hang-up?" I cannot control the cell selector or input commands.

A: Make sure that you selected the correct screen driver with the /**O**ptions **H**ardware **S**creen **S**creen Type command. When in doubt, set this option to Autodetect and let Quattro Pro take over.

Q: Why does nothing happen when I select **U**pdate?

A: Unfortunately, Quattro Pro gives little indication that the system settings are actually being saved (they no doubt are, however). To make sure that they were saved, exit and reload Quattro Pro. Now, see whether the new system specifications are in effect.

Q: I customized a button on the mouse palette, but why isn't the text I entered appearing on the button.

A: This feature is a bit confusing because, although you don't see your text label, it really is there. Any macro command you entered also is operative. The problem is that Quattro Pro doesn't allow text changes in graphics mode.

Select /**O**ptions **D**isplay **M**ode and change to text mode (80 × 25) to view your label setting.

Default Format Options

Q: When I select /Options Formats Hide Zeros, Quattro Pro does not remove the trailing zeros from a block of values I have marked. Why?

A: This option does not remove trailing zeros, it only enables you to suppress the display of entries whose numeric value equals exactly zero.

To remove trailing zeros from a value, select one of the formats on the /Style Numeric Format menu and reduce the number of displayed decimal places.

Q: Why isn't Quattro Pro recalculating my formulas when I enter new data into a spreadsheet?

A: Check the mode indicator on the status line at the bottom of your spreadsheet. If it says CALC, press F9, and Quattro Pro recalculates your formulas.

If you want Quattro Pro to recalculate formulas as the referenced data changes, select /Options Recalculation Mode Automatic.

Chapter Summary

Chapter 6 has shown you how to change many of the system settings Quattro Pro uses to interact with your computer and screen display. In addition, this chapter discussed how Quattro Pro calculates values and sets global formats for the active spreadsheet.

You now should understand that system settings may be stored permanently by choosing the Update command, and that the global format settings apply only to the active spreadsheet.

After completing this chapter you should understand the following Quattro Pro concepts:

- Reconfiguring installed printers and displays

- Changing Quattro Pro's screen colors

- Defining formats for displaying currency symbols, numerical punctuation, and dates and times

- Changing screen display modes

- Choosing your own "startup rules"

- Setting the miscellaneous system settings

- Renaming and redefining the function of the mouse palette buttons

- Choosing between slower but high quality on-screen fonts, or the faster but low quality on-screen fonts

- Storing the current system settings in Quattro Pro's resource files as the new defaults

- Changing the default global spreadsheet settings

- Specifying a recalculation mode, and enabling global spreadsheet protection

In the next chapter you will learn how to use Quattro Pro's best, newest feature: multiple spreadsheet operations. With these techniques you will learn how to link data on spreadsheets and pass information between applications. Chapter 7 also introduces you to the File Manger—Quattro Pro's built-in file-management utility. With the File Manager, you never again need to exit Quattro Pro to copy, move, or erase files.

Managing Spreadsheet Files and Windows

In this chapter, you learn how to create and use files, workspaces, and windows; oversee file operations with the File Manager; link multiple spreadsheets with special formulas; and combine and extract spreadsheet data. You can perform these operations by using the commands from the File, Window, and Tools menus.

In the first section of this chapter, you learn how to create, preserve, and recover spreadsheet files by selecting commands from the File menu. You also learn the rules for creating a spreadsheet, saving the spreadsheet to a file on your hard disk drive, and then recalling the spreadsheet for use in a future work session. This section continues by demonstrating how to create a workspace file and how to save Quattro Pro spreadsheets in file formats that can be read by other programs.

The second section demonstrates the use of the File Manager. With the File Manager, you can perform DOS-like file-management operations without leaving Quattro Pro. For example, you can copy, move, rename, and erase files from the File Manager, as well as display a directory tree graphic depicting the organization of files on your hard disk drive.

Next, you learn about managing Quattro Pro windows. You learn how to display, move, resize, pick, and split windows. This section also shows you how to create special display effects for windows.

The chapter continues by introducing you to linked spreadsheets. By creating linked formulas, you can pass data back and forth between spreadsheet applications. Linked spreadsheets can improve your productivity and Quattro Pro's speed of execution.

The final section of this chapter introduces advanced file operations. Using commands found on the Tools menu, you learn how to import, combine, and extract data from multiple spreadsheet files.

Reviewing the File Menu Commands

You can use the 12 File menu commands to create, retrieve, and save files and to manage the directories in which your files are stored (see fig. 7.1). After creating your own library of spreadsheet files, you can use the File menu to develop workspace applications that juggle several spreadsheets at the same time.

You can use workspace applications to save nonlinked spreadsheets as one unit, save a file manager window with a group of spreadsheets, and help reserve the screen position and sequential order of a group of spreadsheets.

Fig. 7.1
The File menu commands.

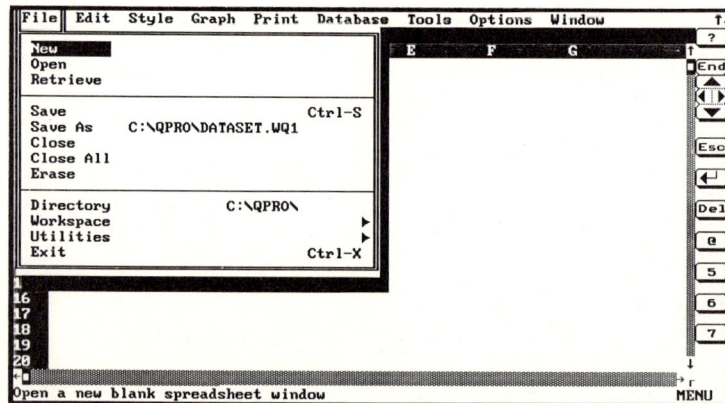

The File menu consists of three types of commands: file-access commands, file-management commands, and miscellaneous file commands. Quattro Pro displays the Ctrl-key shortcuts and current command settings at the right margin of the File menu.

In figure 7.1, the active spreadsheet, DATASET.WQ1, is stored in the current directory named \QPRO. Two commands on the File menu have Ctrl-key shortcuts.

The file-access commands control the flow of file data from your hard disk drive into Quattro Pro's operating environment. With these commands, you can create a spreadsheet file, load a saved file from your hard disk drive into its own window, and retrieve a previously saved file.

The file-management commands move file data from Quattro Pro's operating environment onto your hard disk drive. These commands save, rename, close, and erase spreadsheet files.

The miscellaneous commands perform operations such as setting the current directory, creating a workspace file, exiting to DOS, and accessing file utilities.

Table 7.1 describes the purpose of each File menu command.

Table 7.1
File Menu Commands

Command	Description
New	Loads a new, blank spreadsheet into its own window
Open	Loads a previously saved spreadsheet file into its own window
Retrieve	Loads a previously saved spreadsheet file into the current window, closing the current spreadsheet
Save	Saves the current spreadsheet using a previously entered file name; if a file name has not been specified, Quattro Pro prompts you to supply one.
Save As	Prompts you for a file name and then saves the current spreadsheet using that name
Close	Closes the spreadsheet in the current window
CLose All	Closes all spreadsheets in all open windows
Erase	Erases the current spreadsheet from RAM memory and displays a new, blank spreadsheet
Directory	Designates the directory path name for storing files on the hard disk drive
Workspace	Saves the names of all open spreadsheets to a workspace file name and restores previously saved workspaces

Table 7.1—*continued*

Command	Description
Utilities	Exits to the **DOS** shell, activates the **File Manager** window and sets the SQZ! file compression options
Exit	Terminates a work session by closing all open windows and returns system control to DOS

Learning File Operations

This section reviews the File menu terminology and demonstrates the processes that every user goes through in a Quattro Pro work session.

Reviewing Terminology

Spreadsheet describes the physical area containing rows and columns into which you enter data. When you finish entering data, assign a unique file name to the spreadsheet so that you easily can locate and recall the spreadsheet the next time you want to use that data.

A new feature of Version 1.0 enables you to open and view up to 32 windows at a time. A *window* is the area in which Quattro Pro displays the current spreadsheet. Each time you open a new spreadsheet, Quattro Pro assigns the spreadsheet a window number from 1 to 32 and displays the number within brackets on the status line.

Workspace describes a group of related spreadsheet files that are open in Quattro Pro's memory at the same time. When you restore a workspace file name, Quattro Pro loads each spreadsheet in the workspace into RAM memory.

Creating, Opening, and Retrieving Files

Each time you access Quattro Pro from your PC, the program displays a new, blank spreadsheet named SHEET1.WQ1 in the current window. You can do several things with this spreadsheet: you can enter data; you can ignore the blank spreadsheet and open a saved spreadsheet; or you can close the blank spreadsheet by retrieving a saved spreadsheet.

The top three commands on the File menu give you access to new and saved spreadsheet files. To display another new, blank spreadsheet, select the /File New command. You can load up to 32 new spreadsheets into Quattro Pro's memory with this command.

To load a previously saved spreadsheet into the current window without affecting other spreadsheets that are open in memory, select the /File **O**pen command. When you select this command, Quattro Pro displays the file list box, which shows the names of the spreadsheet files saved in the current directory. While this box is on-screen, you can execute several keystrokes to display more information about your files (see table 7.2).

**Table 7.2
Keys Affecting the File List and File Name Prompt Boxes**

Key	Description
Backspace	Displays a list of all files in the parent directory
Ctrl-backspace	Removes the default prompt and file list
Enter	Accepts the file name highlighted on the list
Esc	Erases data on the line, one directory path name at a time
F2	Enters Search mode so that you can enter the first letter of the file you are searching for
F3	Expands the file list so that the list fills up the screen
+	Displays the file size and the last date altered for the files in the file list
—	Removes the file size and the last date altered from the file list display
Space bar	Edits the existing file name

To load a spreadsheet into Quattro Pro's memory, highlight the file name in the file list box and press Enter. Press + (the plus key) and F3 for a full-screen display of the file list box (see fig. 7.2).

To load a saved spreadsheet into the current window, select /File **R**etrieve. If changes to the spreadsheet in the current window have not been saved recently, Quattro Pro asks whether you want to lose your changes. Select **N**o to return to the spreadsheet (so that you can save the file) or **Y**es to erase the spreadsheet from memory. Like the **O**pen command, this command dis-

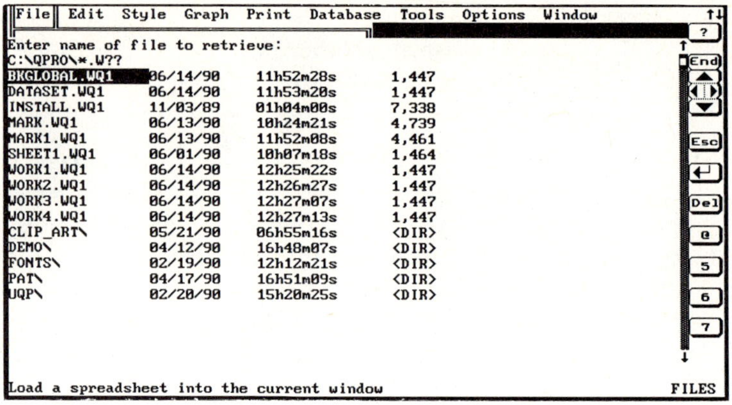

**Fig. 7.2
Displaying the
file list box in
full-screen
format.**

```
 File  Edit  Style  Graph  Print  Database  Tools  Options  Window        ↑↓
                                                                          ?
Enter name of file to retrieve:                                          ↑
C:\QPRO\*.W??                                                           End
BKGLOBAL.WQ1      06/14/90    11h52m28s      1,447                       ▲
DATASET.WQ1       06/14/90    11h53m20s      1,447                      ◄▌▶
INSTALL.WQ1       11/03/89    01h04m00s      7,338                       ▼
MARK.WQ1          06/13/90    10h24m21s      4,739
MARK1.WQ1         06/13/90    11h52m08s      4,461                      Esc
SHEET1.WQ1        06/01/90    10h07m18s      1,464
WORK1.WQ1         06/14/90    12h25m22s      1,447                       ↵
WORK2.WQ1         06/14/90    12h26m27s      1,447
WORK3.WQ1         06/14/90    12h27m07s      1,447                      Del
WORK4.WQ1         06/14/90    12h27m13s      1,447
CLIP_ART\         05/21/90    06h55m16s      <DIR>                       @
DEMO\             04/12/90    16h48m07s      <DIR>
FONTS\            02/19/90    12h12m21s      <DIR>                       5
PAT\              04/17/90    16h51m09s      <DIR>
UQP\              02/20/90    15h20m25s      <DIR>                       6

                                                                        7
                                                                        ↓
Load a spreadsheet into the current window                            FILES
```

plays a filename box. Highlight a file name and press Enter to retrieve that spreadsheet.

The major difference between these two commands is that Quattro Pro closes the current spreadsheet when you retrieve a saved spreadsheet file. When you choose /**F**ile **O**pen, Quattro Pro loads the spreadsheet file on top of all existing open spreadsheets.

You use the **O**pen command most when you link spreadsheets with formulas. The **O**pen command enables you to open and simultaneously work with several Quattro Pro spreadsheets.

Quattro Pro assigns each open spreadsheet a window number according to the order in which the spreadsheet was opened in memory originally. Quattro Pro displays the window number in brackets on the status line.

Saving, Closing, and Erasing Files

The five commands located in the middle of the File menu enable you to save spreadsheet files permanently, close previously saved files without saving changes, and erase the current spreadsheet from Quattro Pro's memory.

When you finish entering data, select the /**F**ile **S**ave command to assign a unique name to the spreadsheet. When you choose this command, Quattro Pro prompts you to enter a name. Press Enter to permanently store the name. When you choose /**F**ile **S**ave, Quattro Pro displays a File Already Exists prompt. The program remembers the spreadsheet's name and asks you to specify whether you want to cancel the operation, replace the stored spreadsheet file with the current spreadsheet, or create a backup of the spreadsheet file. This command also transfers a copy of the file onto your hard disk drive.

Tip | Press Ctrl-S, the Ctrl-key shortcut for the **S**ave command, to save a Quattro Pro spreadsheet file.

After a spreadsheet is saved to a file, you can recall the spreadsheet using the **O**pen or **R**etrieve command.

To give the current spreadsheet a new file name, select the /File Save **As** command. When prompted, type a new file name and press Enter to duplicate the spreadsheet. When executed, Quattro Pro displays the new file name and window number on the status line.

To close a spreadsheet and remove its window from the screen, select the /File Close command. To perform this operation for all open spreadsheet windows, use the /File Close All command.

To quickly close a spreadsheet, click the close box in the upper left portion of a spreadsheet. Quattro Pro treats a spreadsheet closed in this manner like one closed by choosing the /File Close command.

Occasionally, you may want to erase a spreadsheet from Quattro Pro's memory without deleting the file from your hard disk drive. Select /File Erase, and Quattro Pro asks whether you really want to erase the spreadsheet. Press **N** to cancel the operation or **Y** to blank the screen.

Setting the Directory Path Name

The current directory setting determines where Quattro Pro looks for files on your hard disk drive. The current setting appears at the right margin of the File menu next to the **D**irectory command.

Select the /File Directory command to create a current directory setting. When prompted, type a path name and press Enter to record the setting. When you select this command and change the name of the current directory, the new setting remains in effect only for the current work session.

You can change a **D**irectory command setting permanently so that Quattro Pro recognizes the directory as the default directory each time you begin a new work session. Select the /Options Startup **D**irectory command and specify a new directory name. (See Chapter 6 for complete coverage of Quattro Pro's start-up options.)

284 Part I: Using Quattro Pro Spreadsheets

Creating a Workspace File

The **W**orkspace command is a spreadsheet file-organization tool. Whenever you design applications that use more than one open spreadsheet at a time, consider creating a workspace to group the associated spreadsheets under one file name—grouping the spreadsheets makes reloading the files much easier.

For example, to save five spreadsheets currently open in Quattro Pro's memory to a workspace file named SALES.WSP, do the following:

1. Select /**F**ile **W**orkspace **S**ave.

2. When prompted, type *SALES* and press Enter to record the new workspace file name.

Quattro Pro stores the name, the window number, and the position number for all of the open spreadsheets in the workspace file. This command does not save changes made to individual spreadsheets. When you are done with the current work session, you must save and replace each file before exiting Quattro Pro.

To reload the SALES.WSP workspace file, do the following:

1. Select /**F**ile **W**orkspace **R**estore.

2. When prompted, highlight SALES on the displayed list and press Enter.

Quattro Pro loads all five spreadsheets into memory in their original order.

Translating Spreadsheets

Quattro Pro can save spreadsheet files in non-Quattro Pro file formats that can be retrieved by several popular spreadsheet and database programs. Table 7.3 presents a complete list of the file formats that Quattro Pro can write to. These file formats fall into three major categories: spreadsheet files, database files, and compressed files.

Table 7.3
File Formats that Quattro Pro Can Read and Write

File extension	Program name
Spreadsheet file formats	
DIF	Visicalc
SLK	Multiplan, Versions 1 or 2
WKS	Lotus 1-2-3, Version 1A
WK1	Lotus 1-2-3, Version 2.01
WKE	Lotus 1-2-3, Educational Version
WRK	Symphony, Version 1.2
WR1	Symphony, Version 2.0
WKQ	Quattro (earlier versions)
WQ1	Quattro Pro
WKP	Surpass
Database file formats	
DB	Paradox
DB2	dBASE II
DBF	dBASE III, III+, and IV
RXD	Reflex, Version 1
R2D	Reflex, Version 2
Compressed file formats (SQZ)	
WK$	Lotus 1-2-3, Version 1A
WK!	Lotus 1-2-3, Version 2.01
WR$	Symphony, Version 1.2
WR!	Symphony, Version 2.0
WKZ	Quattro (earlier versions)
WQ!	Quattro Pro

To save a Quattro Pro spreadsheet in one of the file formats listed in table 7.3, append the appropriate extension to the file name that you create with the /File Save **As** command.

Tip	This is one of only two Quattro Pro operations that require you to supply a file-name extension (the other is with SQZ!). In all other cases, the program appends the extension specified in the startup menu with WQ1 as the default.

Translating Quattro Pro spreadsheets into dBASE file formats requires a slightly different approach. dBASE II and III use the same file-name extension (DBF), even though their file formats are different. To differentiate between the versions, Quattro Pro assigns a temporary extension (DB2) to spreadsheet files that you translate for use with dBASE II. Before you retrieve a translated file into dBASE II, rename the file so that the extension is DBF.

For example, to save a Quattro Pro spreadsheet named DATA.WQ1 in a dBASE II file format, do the following:

1. Make DATA.WQ1 the active spreadsheet.

2. Select /File Save **As**.

3. When prompted, type *DATA.DB2* and press Enter to create the dBASE II file.

4. At DOS command level, type *REN DATA.DB2 DATA.DBF* and press Enter to rename the file.

5. Load dBASE II and retrieve the file named DATA.DBF.

Setting the SQZ! File Compression Options

Quattro Pro has a built-in file compression utility that helps you to conserve storage space on your hard disk drive. You also can use this facility when copying large spreadsheet files onto a floppy disk and before transmitting files over a telecommunications line.

To compress a file, append the appropriate extension after typing a name at the file-name prompt (see table 7.3). To compress a file named DATELINE.WQ1, do the following:

1. Make DATELINE the active spreadsheet.

2. Select the /File Save **As** command.

3. When prompted, type *DATELINE.WQ!* and press Enter to compress the file.

Tip | If you are using an earlier version of Quattro, you must specify the WKZ file-name extension to squeeze a file.

Figure 7.3 shows the menu options that Quattro Pro displays when you select the /**F**ile Utilities **S**QZ! command. These options control how much data Quattro Pro eliminates from a spreadsheet file prior to squeezing the spreadsheet.

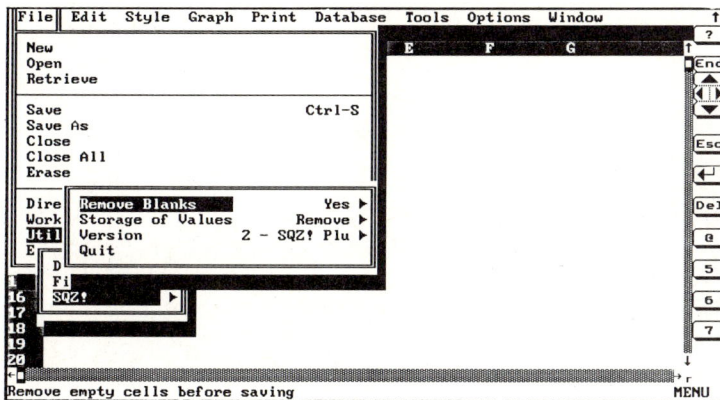

Fig. 7.3.
Reviewing the
SQZ! menu
options.

One way Quattro Pro can conserve space is by removing all of the blank cells from a spreadsheet. To remove the blank cells, select the **R**emove Blank option and choose **Y**es.

Another way to conserve storage space is to let Quattro Pro remove spreadsheet values that result from formula calculations. Quattro Pro retains the formulas themselves but removes the cell results. When you retrieve the file, Quattro Pro recalculates all of the formulas before displaying the spreadsheet. To invoke this setting, select the **S**torage of Values option and choose **R**emove. You also can choose **A**pproximate, and Quattro Pro saves formula values using seven (instead of 15) significant digits.

The third **S**QZ! menu option enables you to choose the SQZ! version to use. If you do not intend to use your compressed files in Symphony, choose the **S**QZ! Plus option.

Quattro Pro expands the compressed file the next time you retrieve it.

Password Protecting Your Files

Quattro Pro offers you the option of password protecting your files to prevent unauthorized viewing of confidential data. Password-protected files can be retrieved only when you have the correct access code.

To password protect a Quattro Pro file named NPV.WQ1, do the following:

1. Make NPV the active spreadsheet.

2. Select /File Save **As**.

3. When prompted, type *NPV P* and press Enter to invoke the password-protection facility.

4. Type a password consisting of up to 15 characters. (Quattro Pro does not display the characters on-screen as you type them.)

5. Press Enter to assign the password to the NPV spreadsheet.

6. When prompted, re-enter the password to verify it (see fig. 7.4).

7. Press Enter to store the password.

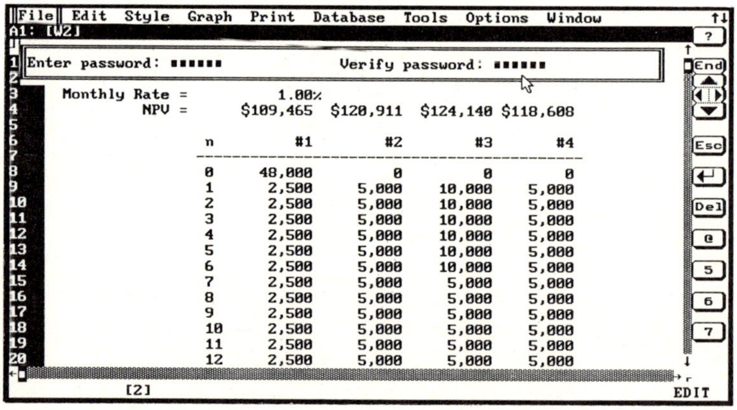

Fig. 7.4
Quattro Pro requires verification before assigning a password to a spreadsheet file.

After you have assigned a password to a file, you cannot access the file except by issuing the correct sequence of characters. Quattro Pro has no facility for recovering a forgotten password; remember, when a password is lost, so is the file!

You can rename or remove a spreadsheet password, but only when the spreadsheet is active. When a password-protected spreadsheet is active, the file prompt box displays Password Protected next to the file name.

To remove password protection from the NPV spreadsheet, do the following:

1. Select the /**File** **R**etrieve command.

2. Type *NPV* and press Enter.

3. When prompted, type the password and press Enter to retrieve the file.

4. Select the /**File** Save **As** command.

5. When Quattro Pro displays the file prompt box, press the Backspace key to delete Password Protected from the line.

6. Press Enter and select **R**eplace to save NPV without a password.

To rename the password assigned to the NPV spreadsheet, do the following:

1. Select the /**File** **R**etrieve command.

2. Type *NPV* and press Enter.

3. When prompted, type the password and press Enter to retrieve the file.

4. Select the /**File** Save **As** command.

5. When Quattro Pro displays the file prompt box, press the Backspace key to delete Password Protected from the line.

6. Type *P* after the file name (be sure to insert a space between the file name and the P) and then press Enter to invoke the password protection facility.

7. Type a new password.

8. Press Enter to assign the new password to the NPV spreadsheet.

9. When prompted, re-enter the password to verify it.

Using the File Manager

The File Manager enables you to link Quattro Pro directly to the DOS command environment. The File Manager can perform many useful file-management activities without requiring you to first exit Quattro Pro.

Use the File Manager to list, move, copy, rename, and delete files using the same wild-card designations that you use in DOS. This tool also can sort files by name, extension, size, DOS order, or stamp the time on files and can display a tree graphic that shows the structure of the directory paths on the current disk.

Learning the File Manager Menus

When the File Manager is in the active window, Quattro Pro displays a slightly different set of menus at the top of the screen. You activate these menus and select the menu commands as if a spreadsheet were in the active window. Table 7.4 reviews the purpose and function of each of these menus.

Table 7.4
File Manager Menus

Menu name	Description of commands
File	Creates, opens, and closes windows; reads existing directories and creates directories; accesses DOS; and exits the File Manager
Edit	Selects files for copy, move, erase, paste, duplicate, and rename operations
Sort	Sorts files using DOS wild cards
Tree	Opens, resizes, and closes the tree pane
Print	Prints a list of files in a directory
Options	Sets File Manager display options and standard spreadsheet options
Window	Resizes, reorganizes, and picks active windows

Maneuvering through the File Manager Window

To display the File Manager in the current window, select the /File Utilities File Manager command (see fig. 7.5). Repeat this command to open a second File Manager window. To close the active File Manager, press /File Close —the same command that closes a spreadsheet.

The File Manager window is divided into three sections: the control pane, the file list pane, and the tree pane. When you load this tool into the active window, Quattro Pro fills only half of the screen, leaving a spreadsheet in view behind the File Manager window.

All of the file-management operations that you perform with this tool are accomplished from inside one of the three panes. Before you can work in a

```
 File  Edit  Sort  Tree  Print  Options  Window                    ↑↓
┌─┬──────────────────────────────────────┬──────────────────────┐
│ │C:\QPRO\                             2│ E      F      G      │ ?
│1│    Drive: C                       ↑ │                      │
│2│Directory: \QPRO\                    │                      │End
│3│   Filter: *.*                       │                      │▲
│4│File Name: █                         │                      │◀▶
│5│                                     │                      │▼
│6│                                     │                      │
│7│..                                   │                      │Esc
│ │123       MU      200,200   5-07-90  │                      │
│8│123       RF        1,448  11-03-89  │                      │↵
│9│BKGLOBAL  WQ1       1,447   6-14-90  │                      │
│10│BSINST   DAT      12,001  11-03-89  │                      │Del
│11│BSINST   EXE     115,053  11-03-89  │                      │
│12│COUR     SFO      26,530  11-03-89  │                      │e
│13│DATASET  WQ1       1,447   6-14-90  │                      │
│14│DTBI     SFO      25,852  11-03-89  │                      │5
│15│DUT      SFO      28,102  11-03-89  │                      │
│16│DUTB     SFO      27,360  11-03-89  │                      │6
│17│DUTI     SFO      26,664  11-03-89  │                      │
│18│EMSTEST  COM      19,664  11-03-89  │                      │7
│19│EURO     CHR       8,439  11-03-89 ↓│                      │
│20│<more>                               │                      │
├─┴──────────────────────────────────────┴──────────────────────┤
│C:        [2]                                          READY    │
└────────────────────────────────────────────────────────────────┘
```

Fig. 7.5
The File Manager window.

pane, however, you must make that pane active. By default, Quattro Pro makes the control pane the active pane each time you load the File Manager. Table 7.5 lists all of the key sequences that you can use to navigate through the File Manager window.

Table 7.5
File Manager Window Keys

Key	Description
Shift-F5	The Pick Window key displays a list of all windows open in memory; also works by pressing Alt-0.
F6	The Pane key activates the next pane in the File Manager window; also works by pressing Tab.
Shift-F6	The Next Window key activates the next open File Manager window. If no window is open, the Next Window key activates a spreadsheet.
Alt-F6	The Zoom Window key enlarges and shrinks the active File Manager window.
Alt #	Press Alt plus a window number, and Quattro Pro makes that window active.

Using the Control Pane

The *control pane* displays the current drive letter, the current directory path name, the filter prompt, and the file-name prompt. While in the control pane, you can change any of these settings to create a different type of directory display.

For example, to display all files with a WQ1 extension in a directory called \FINANCE, do the following:

1. Press ↑ twice to highlight the current directory path name.

2. Press Esc to erase the entry.

3. Type *FINANCE* and press Enter to record the new directory path name. Quattro Pro moves the cursor back to the file-name prompt.

4. Press ↑ to move the cursor to the filter prompt setting.

5. Press the Backspace key to erase the second asterisk.

6. Type *WQ1* and press Enter to store the new filter setting.

Quattro Pro displays all files in the \FINANCE directory that have a WQ1 file-name extension.

To create a negative filter, embed the filter setting inside brackets, and Quattro Pro searches for all files that do not meet the bracketed condition. For example, the filter setting [*.WQ1] searches for all files that do not have a WQ1 file-name extension.

The file-name prompt is blank each time you load the File Manager. You can make any spreadsheet file active by typing a file name in this field. When you type the first letter of a file name, Quattro Pro moves the cursor to the first file in the current directory that begins with that letter. This search and highlight procedure continues as long as you continue to enter additional letters.

Table 7.6 lists all of the keys that affect data displayed in the control pane.

Table 7.6
Control Pane Keys

Key	Description
F2	The Rename key duplicates the action of selecting the /Edit Rename command.
F5	The GoTo key moves the cursor to the file name specified at the file-name prompt.
Esc	Erases the current setting at a control pane prompt
Enter	Opens the file or subdirectory indicated next to the prompt settings

Using the File Pane

The *file pane* shows all of the file names and directory path names that meet the conditions specified on the control pane. The file pane lists the full name, byte size, and the date last altered for each file.

Use the /**O**ptions **F**ile **L**ist command to specify a **F**ull View or a **W**ide View of the data displayed in the file pane.

Table 7.7 lists all of the key sequences that you can use when the file pane is active.

Table 7.7
File Pane Keys

Key	*Description*
F2	The Rename key duplicates the action of selecting the /**E**dit **R**ename command.
Shift-F7	The Select key selects and unselects a highlighted file name.
Alt-F7	The All Select key selects all of the file names in the displayed list.
Shift-F8	The Move key transfers selected files into the paste buffer.
Del	Deletes all highlighted or selected files
F9	The Calc key duplicates the action of selecting the /**F**ile **R**ead Dir command.
Shift-F9	The Copy key copies selected files into the paste buffer.
Shift-F10	The Paste key moves all files from the paste buffer to the current directory, at the location of the cursor.
Esc	Cancels file selections and moves the cursor to the file-name prompt in the control pane
Enter	Opens the file or subdirectory indicated next to the prompt settings

You also can press any of the cursor-movement keys on the numeric keypad to move around the file pane.

Using the Tree Pane

Select the /**Tree O**pen command to display the tree pane in the lower portion of the File Manager window. To display a full-screen tree pane, open a tree pane inside a second File Manager window. For example, figure 7.6 shows a tree pane added to a second File Manager window.

**Fig. 7.6
Displaying a
tree pane in a
second File
Manager
window.**

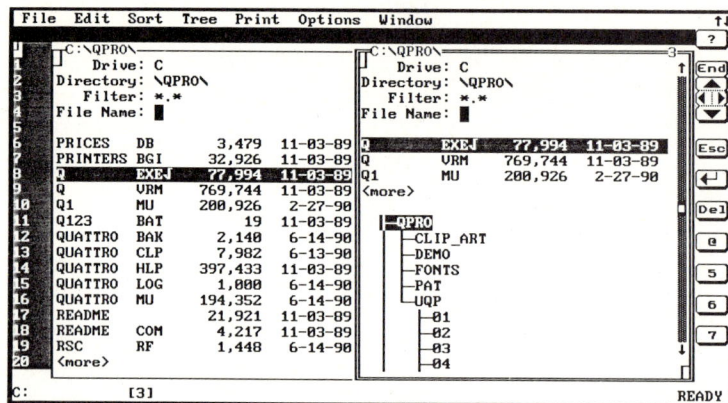

A *tree pane* displays all of the file names existing in each directory path name. In figure 7.6, the current directory specified in each pane is \QPRO, yet one tree pane displays a list of files and the other tree pane shows the relative position of the current directory to other directories.

You can redisplay new files in the File Manager window by changing the current directory in the tree pane, and vice versa.

The tree pane enables you to copy and erase entire directories and to move large blocks of files from one directory into another. To learn how to scroll through a tree pane, review the keys defined in table 7.8.

**Table 7.8
Tree Pane Keys**

Key	Description
Esc	Cancels file selections and moves the cursor to the file-name prompt in the control pane
Del	Deletes all highlighted or selected files
F9	The Calc key duplicates the action of selecting the /**File R**ead Dir command.

To remove a tree pane from the active window, select the /Tree Close command.

Using the File Manager

The best way to learn about the File Manager is to use it. Many of the menu commands are the same commands you use to manipulate data in spreadsheet files. A few other commands also perform operations not available with spreadsheets. These special commands are covered in the next section.

Performing Multiple File Operations

The one characteristic shared by the File menu commands is that each can perform an operation simultaneously on many files. You can copy, move, and erase all of the files in the current directory. You also can rename a group of files simultaneously and then copy the files to another location on the same disk drive.

These maneuvers are possible due to the inclusion of two special menu commands: Select File and All Select. When you select a file, Quattro Pro displays the file name in reverse intensity or in a different color and places a check mark at the end of the cursor so that you can clearly see that the file is selected. Using the /All Select command, you can select all of the files displayed in the file pane (see fig. 7.7).

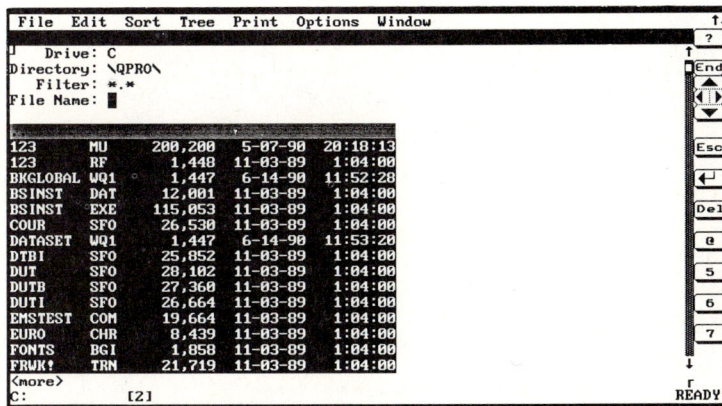

```
File   Edit   Sort   Tree   Print   Options   Window                    ↑↓
                                                                        ?
    Drive: C                                                            ↑
Directory: \QPRO\                                                      End
   Filter: *.*                                                          ▲
File Name: ■                                                           ◀ ▶
                                                                        ▼
123       MU     200,200   5-07-90   20:18:13                          Esc
123       RF       1,448  11-03-89    1:04:00
BKGLOBAL  WQ1      1,447   6-14-90   11:52:28                           ⏎
BSINST    DAT     12,001  11-03-89    1:04:00
BSINST    EXE    115,053  11-03-89    1:04:00                          Del
COUR      SFO     26,530  11-03-89    1:04:00
DATASET   WQ1      1,447   6-14-90   11:53:20                           0
DTBI      SFO     25,852  11-03-89    1:04:00
DUT       SFO     28,102  11-03-89    1:04:00                           5
DUTB      SFO     27,360  11-03-89    1:04:00
DUTI      SFO     26,664  11-03-89    1:04:00                           6
EMSTEST   COM     19,664  11-03-89    1:04:00
EURO      CHR      8,439  11-03-89    1:04:00                           7
FONTS     BGI      1,858  11-03-89    1:04:00
FRWK↑     TRN     21,719  11-03-89    1:04:00
<more>                                                                ┌
C:             [2]                                                    READY
```

Fig. 7.7
Selecting all of the files in the file pane.

After the files are selected, you can perform any of the File Manager commands on that block of files—an operation not available in other electronic spreadsheet programs.

Printing File Manager Data

The Print menu in the File Manager is an abbreviated version of the Print menu accessible when a spreadsheet is active. Using the commands on this menu, you can print lists of files in the displayed directory, a copy of the entire directory tree, or both (see fig. 7.8).

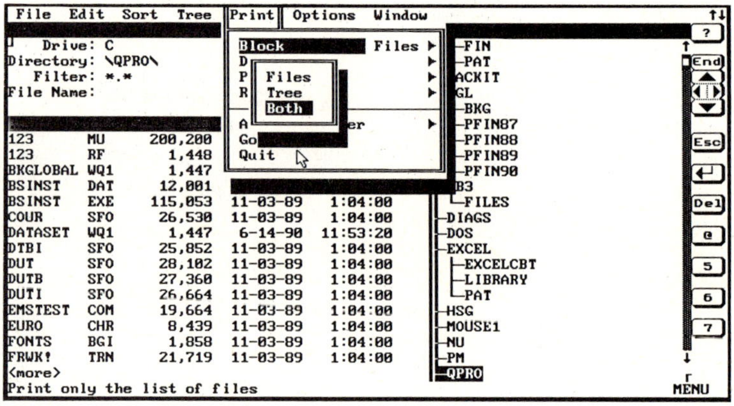

Fig. 7.8
Printing a
report that lists
files and the
directory tree
graphic.

```
 File  Edit  Sort  Tree │Print│ Options  Window                    ↑↓
┌─────────────────────────┐                                        ┌──┐
      Drive: C         │Block          Files ▶│ ─FIN            ↑  │ ?│
  Directory: \QPRO\     │D                    │ ─PAT               └──┘
     Filter: *.*        │P┌─────────┐         │ ─ACKIT          ┌End┐
  File Name:            │R│ Files  ▶│         │ ─GL              ────
                        │ │ Tree   ▶│         │  ─BKG            ◄█►
                        │A│█Both████│      er ▶│ ─PFIN87         ┌───┐
  123      MU    200,200│Go└─────────┘         │ ─PFIN88         │Esc│
  123      RF     1,448 │Quit          ▷       │ ─PFIN89         └───┘
  BKGLOBAL WQ1    1,447 └─────────────────────┘ ─PFIN90          ┌───┐
  BSINST   DAT   12,001                         ─B3              │ ◄┘│
  BSINST   EXE  115,053  11-03-89    1:04:00     └─FILES         └───┘
  COUR     SFO   26,530  11-03-89    1:04:00    ─DIAGS           ┌───┐
  DATASET  WQ1    1,447   6-14-90   11:53:20    ─DOS             │Del│
  DTBI     SFO   25,852  11-03-89    1:04:00    ─EXCEL           └───┘
  DUT      SFO   28,102  11-03-89    1:04:00     ─EXCELCBT       ┌───┐
  DUTB     SFO   27,360  11-03-89    1:04:00     ─LIBRARY        │ @ │
  DUTI     SFO   26,664  11-03-89    1:04:00     └─PAT           └───┘
  EMSTEST  COM   19,664  11-03-89    1:04:00    ─HSG             ┌───┐
  EURO     CHR    8,439  11-03-89    1:04:00    ─MOUSE1          │ 5 │
  FONTS    BGI    1,858  11-03-89    1:04:00    ─NU              └───┘
  FRWK!    TRN   21,719  11-03-89    1:04:00    ─PM              ┌───┐
  <more>                                        ─QPRO       ↓   │ 6 │
  Print only the list of files                                  └───┘
                                                              ┌───┐
                                                              │ 7 │
                                                              └───┘
                                               r
                                             MENU
```

Using the Window Menu Commands

You can have up to 32 windows open in Quattro Pro's memory at one time, but you can work in only one window at a time—the active window.

Even if you never create an application that uses 32 windows, you eventually will need at least two, three, or four windows open at the same time. Therefore, you need to understand how to manage multiple windows.

Using the six Options menu commands, you can enlarge and shrink, tile and stack, and move and size windows that are open in Quattro Pro's memory (see fig. 7.9).

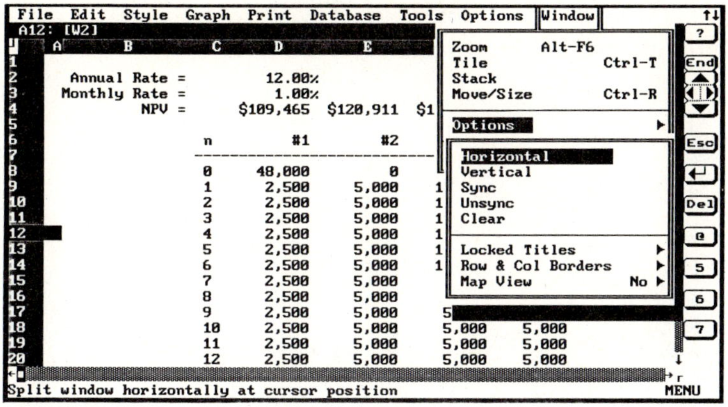

**Fig. 7.9
The Options menu commands.**

The /**W**indow **O**ptions command reveals a menu of window display options that enable you to work with large spreadsheets. For example, you can split the active window into two panes or create a condensed map view of an entire spreadsheet.

Whenever you are unsure about the number of files open in memory, select /**W**indow **P**ick, and Quattro Pro displays a compete list of all open windows and their file names. You also can press Alt-0, the Pick Window key, to produce the same display.

To move from window to window, press Shift-F6, the Next Window key. If you already know the window number of the window you want to move to, press Alt plus the window number, and Quattro Pro makes that window active.

Organizing Windows On-Screen

Quattro Pro offers several alternatives for managing a window or for displaying all open windows. The following three sections teach you how to execute the Window menu commands that organize windows on-screen.

Enlarging and Shrinking Windows

When you want the active window to fill up your screen, select the /**W**indow **Z**oom command or press Alt-F6, the Zoom key. Selecting this command twice in succession causes the active window to return to its original size.

Mouse users can perform this operation quickly by clicking the zoom icon located in the upper-right corner of the screen (the two opposing arrows at the top of the mouse palette).

Tiling and Stacking Windows

Another useful way to display multiple windows involves processes called tiling and stacking (see figs. 2.24 and 7.14 for examples of these two views).

Tiling reduces each window to a size that enables Quattro Pro to display the windows side-by-side on-screen. To tile all of the windows open in memory, select the /Window Tile command or press Ctrl-T, the Ctrl-key shortcut for this command.

Stacking shuffles the open windows into sequential order by window number and displays the windows in layers on-screen. In a stacked window display, the top of each window is revealed so that you can see the file name and window number. To stack all windows open in memory, select the /Window Stack command.

Moving and Sizing Windows

The /Window Move/Size command enables you to fine-tune the size and position of a spreadsheet in the active window. This technique is useful when tiling and stacking do not create the display effect that you want.

To change the size and position of a spreadsheet in a window, select /Window Move/Size or press Ctrl-R, the Ctrl-key shortcut for this command.

Quattro Pro highlights the right and bottom edges of the spreadsheet and displays MOVE in a box at the upper left corner of the spreadsheet. Initially, you cannot move the spreadsheet because it already fills up the entire display. You first must resize the spreadsheet.

To resize the spreadsheet, do the following:

1. Hold down the Shift key and press the cursor-movement keys until the spreadsheet is the correct size (see fig. 7.10).

2. Press Enter to store the new spreadsheet size.

3. Quattro Pro draws the resized spreadsheet in the current window (see fig. 7.11).

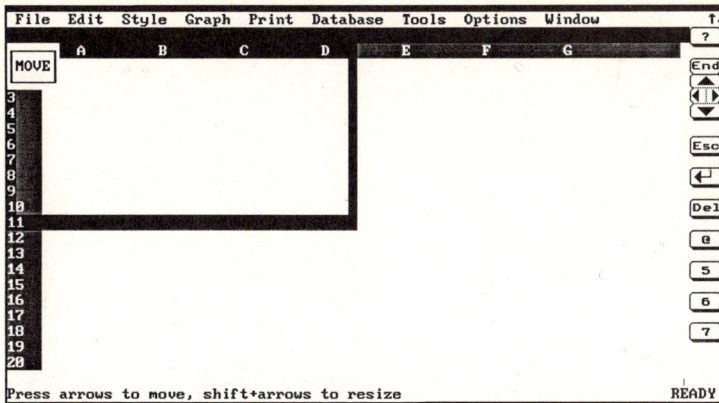

**Fig. 7.10
Resizing a
spreadsheet in
the current
window.**

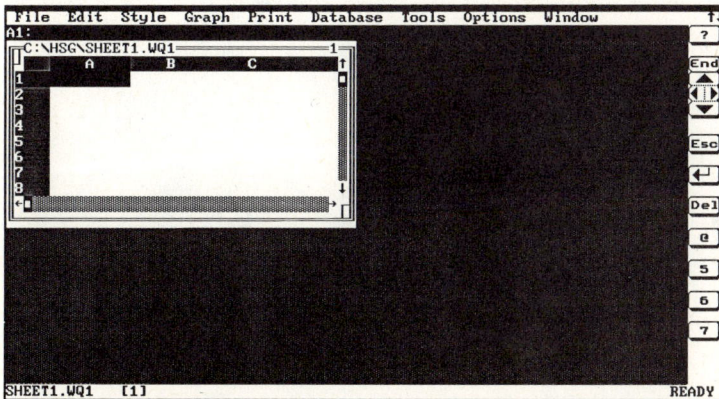

**Fig. 7.11
Quattro Pro
draws the
resized
spreadsheet in
the current
window.**

When a spreadsheet is smaller than the current window, you can move it around the screen display. To move a spreadsheet, do the following:

1. Choose the /Windows Move/Size command. Quattro Pro highlights all four spreadsheet borders.

2. Press the cursor-movement keys to move the spreadsheet to another part of the current window.

3. Press Enter to store the new spreadsheet location.

4. Quattro Pro redraws the spreadsheet at that location.

If you have a mouse, you quickly can move and size a spreadsheet. The next sequence of steps describes the most efficient way to do both:

1. Click and hold down your mouse pointer on the resize box located at the bottom right portion of the spreadsheet. Quattro Pro highlights the right and bottom spreadsheet borders.

2. Drag the mouse pointer to resize the spreadsheet.

3. Release the mouse button to retain a size, and Quattro Pro draws the resized spreadsheet.

4. To move a resized spreadsheet, click and hold down the mouse pointer on any border and drag the entire spreadsheet elsewhere in the current window (see fig. 7.12).

Fig. 7.12 Moving a spreadsheet in the current window.

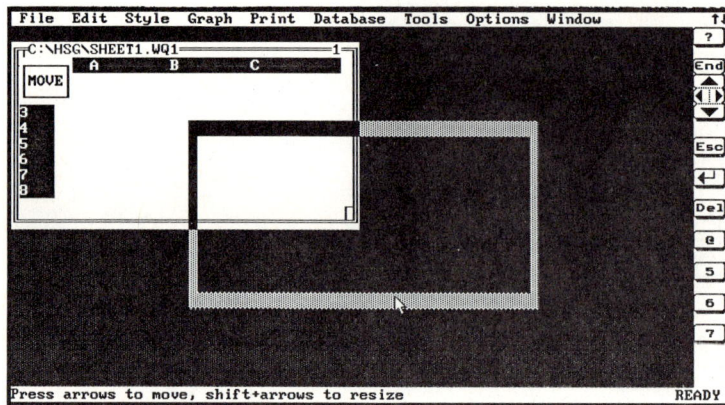

5. Release the mouse button, and Quattro Pro draws the spreadsheet at that location.

Tip | Press Alt-F6 to enlarge or shrink the active spreadsheet in the current window.

Creating Special Display Effects

The /Window Options menu gives you access to commands that can create special window display effects. These effects are by no means strictly cosmetic—each effect can help you locate, organize, and manipulate spreadsheet data.

Splitting Windows into Panes

Select the /**W**indow **O**ptions **H**orizontal command to split a window into two horizontal panes at the position of the cell selector (see fig. 7.13). This effect is useful when a spreadsheet has more row data than column data. The Horizontal command also helps enter cell formulas that reference data in distant parts of the active spreadsheet.

```
 File   Edit   Style   Graph   Print   Database   Tools   Options   Window        ↑↓
A11: [W1]                                                                         [ ? ]
  A              B          C        D          E          F          G        ↑
1                                                                              [End]
2          Annual Rate =           12.00%                                      [ ▲ ]
3          Monthly Rate =           1.00%                                      [◄│►]
4      Net Present Value =       $109,465  $120,911  $124,140  $118,608        [ ▼ ]
5
6                         n         #1        #2        #3        #4            [Esc]
7      -----------------------------------------------------------------
8                         0      48,000         0         0         0          [ ← ]
9                         1       2,500     5,000    10,000     5,000
10                        2       2,500     5,000    10,000     5,000          [Del]
11                        3       2,500     5,000    10,000     5,000
  A              B          C        D          E          F          G        [ 0 ]
28                        20      2,500         0         0         0
29                        21      2,500         0         0         0          [ 5 ]
30                        22      2,500         0         0         0
31                        23      2,500         0         0         0          [ 6 ]
32                        24     14,500         0         0    48,000
33                                                                             [ 7 ]
34     Total Cash Flows:        $120,000  $138,000  $138,000  $138,000         ↓
35                                                                            →▪r
            [2]                                                        READY
```

Fig. 7.13
Splitting a spreadsheet window into two horizontal panes.

Select the /**W**indow **O**ptions **V**ertical command to split a window into two vertical panes at the position of the cell selector. This effect is useful when a spreadsheet has more column data than row data. The **V**ertical command, like its counterpart, helps in the process of entering formulas into a spreadsheet.

To move between panes in a split window, press F6, the Pane key. To reset a split window to one pane, select the /**W**indow **O**ptions **C**lear command.

Unsynchronizing Window Panes

By default, split window panes are synchronized so that any cell selector movement in one pane is duplicated in the second. To scroll window panes independently of each other, you must unsynchronize the panes by selecting the /**W**indow **O**ptions **U**nsync command. When executed, you can scroll around one pane without affecting the other. To return the panes to synchronized scrolling, select the /**W**indow **O**ptions **S**ync command.

Clearing Split Window Pane Settings

Select the /Window Options Clear command to return split windows to a single window display. When you issue this command, Quattro Pro retains the column width, locked title, and hidden column settings for the top or left panes only. Any changes made to the right or lower panes are discarded.

Locking Titles

Title locking is a useful display tool for a spreadsheet that contains numerous rows or columns of data. By anchoring a row (or column) of labels, you can scroll through the data underneath (or to the right) without moving the titles out of the spreadsheet area (see fig. 7.14). Quattro Pro displays locked title data in high-intensity colors so that you can identify clearly where the locking begins.

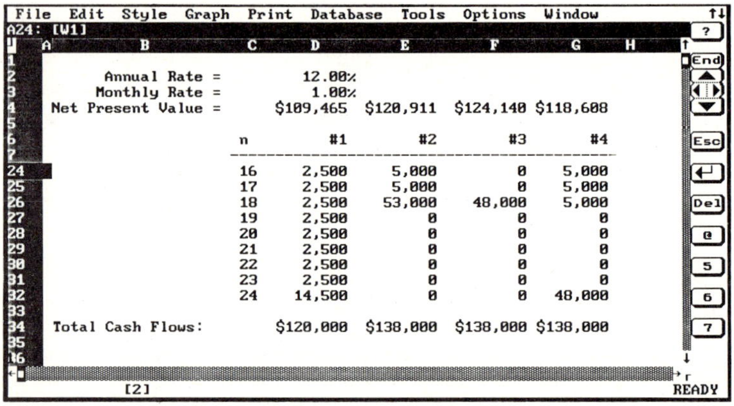

Fig. 7.14 Locking spreadsheet titles to restrict cursor movement to the data-entry area.

To lock spreadsheet titles, place the cell selector in the row below or the column to the right of the titles you want to lock. Then select the /Window Options Locked Titles command, and Quattro Pro displays a menu offering four options: Horizontal, Vertical, Both, and Clear. Quattro Pro locks titles above or to the left of the cell selector—depending on which locked title option you choose.

When locked titles are in effect, Quattro Pro does not enable the cell selector to be moved into the locked title area with the usual cursor-movement techniques. Press F5, the GoTo key, and specify a cell in the title area you want to make active. You can change data in the active cell while in the title area, but you cannot move around the locked title area.

Removing Row and Column Borders

In some spreadsheet applications, removing the row and column borders can make a spreadsheet look more like a report. If you create an application that prompts a user to enter figures into a data-entry form, for example, it is not critical that you display the row and column borders. The borders even may be distracting to someone unfamiliar with the look of a spreadsheet. Also, by eliminating the borders from your screen, you can view more of the spreadsheet area on-screen at one time.

To remove column and row borders from your display, select the /Window Options Row & Col Borders command. When prompted, choose the Hide option, and Quattro Pro immediately redraws the screen without row and column borders (see fig. 7.15).

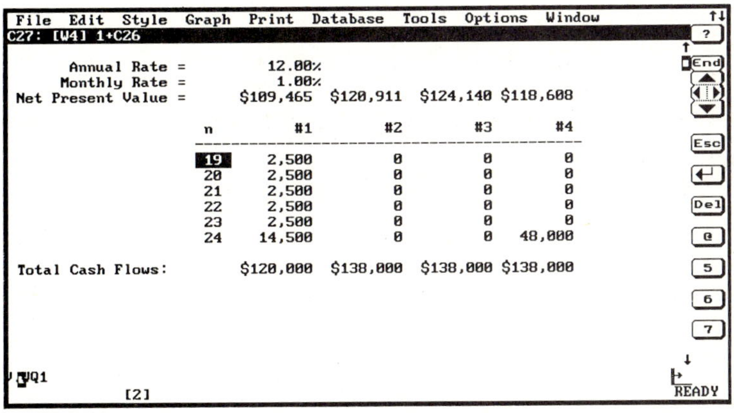

Fig. 7.15
Removing row and column borders makes a document look less like a spreadsheet and more like a report.

To redisplay the row and column borders, reselect the command and choose the Display option.

Note that the row and column border setting is spreadsheet dependent; when you choose /File Save, Quattro Pro saves this display setting with the current spreadsheet only.

Creating a Map View

The /Window Options Map View command creates a unique on-screen effect that can be described as a "bird's-eye view" of a spreadsheet (see fig. 7.16). In this mode, Quattro Pro compresses the column widths to one character space and then assigns and displays one character code that identifies the type of data in each cell (see table 7.9).

Fig. 7.16
Displaying a
bird's-eye view
of a
spreadsheet.

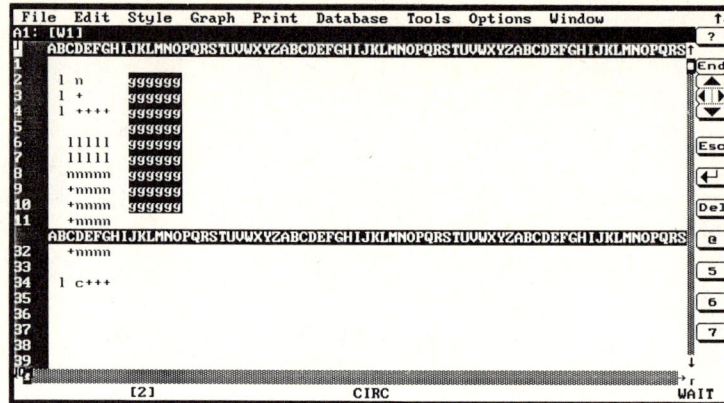

Table 7.9
Map Mode Codes

Code	Type of cell data
l	Label
n	Number
+	Formula
−	Linked formula
c	Circular cell formula
g	Inserted graph

You can use the /Edit Search & Replace command to locate data quickly on a spreadsheet displayed in Map mode. Instead of specifying a label or number to search for, you can use any of the codes listed in table 7.8. For example, the Search & Replace command can be used to locate the presence of a circular formula, such as the one pictured in figure 7.16.

Linking Spreadsheets

This section introduces you to the concept of linked spreadsheets. *Linked spreadsheets* simplify complex relationships, help you design more flexible applications, access information from a database, and enable Quattro Pro to be more memory-efficient.

Like a group of related spreadsheets that you save to a workspace file, linked spreadsheets have something in common: they share data. Specifically, you can pass information back and forth between linked spreadsheets using live formula references.

An ordinary formula references data in cells on the current spreadsheet and displays a result in another cell on the same spreadsheet. A live formula references data in cells on supporting spreadsheets open in Quattro Pro's memory and displays a result in a cell on a primary spreadsheet, also open in memory. When you change data on a supporting spreadsheet, Quattro Pro updates the data displayed on the primary spreadsheet—as long as all of the spreadsheets are open in memory at the same time.

Linked spreadsheets introduce a whole new set of possibilities for creating Quattro Pro applications. For example, you can break down a large database spreadsheet into several smaller ones that are easier to access and update. You also can create a small bookkeeping application that stores ledger transactions on supporting spreadsheets and transfers the end-of-period balances (via live formula references) to a group of primary financial statement spreadsheets.

After you learn how to create the links that tie spreadsheets together, you begin to envision your own uses for this type of application.

Creating Linking Formulas

You can use several techniques to create linking formulas. You can type the formula directly on the input line; you can create three-dimensional consolidation formulas to link spreadsheets with common structures; and if you have a mouse, you can use the familiar point-and-click method to create formulas "as you go."

Before examining the process of building live formulas, review the linked spreadsheet application shown in figure 7.17. The active spreadsheet in figure 7.17, PARENT.WQ1, is the primary document in a linked spreadsheet application. The data that eventually appears on this spreadsheet comes from SUBSID_1.WQ1, SUBSID_2.WQ1, and SUBSID_3.WQ1—income statement spreadsheets for each of the sample company's three subsidiaries.

Figure 7.17 shows that in linked spreadsheet applications, you have to design and create two, three, or more spreadsheets. In the sample application, the structure of each spreadsheet—except for a few label descriptions—is the same.

You can use three procedures to create formulas that link spreadsheets.

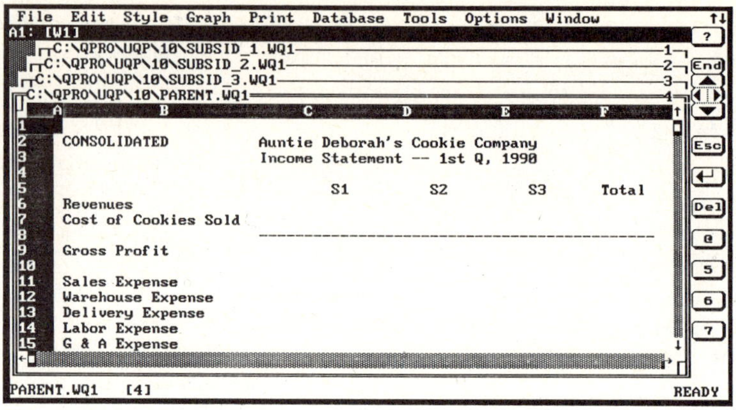

Fig. 7.17
Reviewing a
linking
application that
uses one
primary and
three
supporting
spreadsheets.

Typing a Linking Formula

A *linking formula* is a basic Quattro Pro formula that contains a reference to an external spreadsheet file name. In figure 7.15, the formula appearing in cell C6 on PARENT.WQ1 is created by doing the following:

1. Open all of the spreadsheets to be linked into Quattro Pro's memory.

2. Make cell C6 on PARENT.WQ1 active.

3. Type +*[SUBSID_1]F6* on the input line.

4. Press Enter to record the linking formula.

Quattro Pro evaluates cell F6 on SUBSID_1.WQ1 and displays the value 84,107.96 in the active cell on PARENT.WQ1 (see fig. 7.18).

Fig. 7.18
Creating the
initial linking
formula.

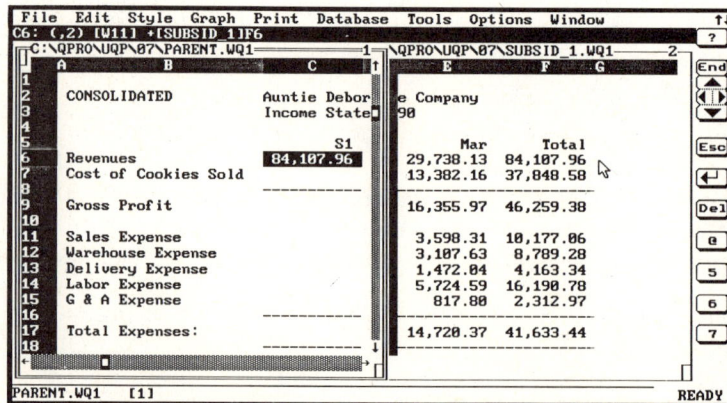

Every linking formula contains three elements: the plus symbol (+), a bracketed file name, and an external cell (or block) reference.

The + tells Quattro Pro that you are entering a formula. If you leave out this important symbol, the program thinks that you are entering a label.

When Quattro Pro encounters a file name in brackets, the program recognizes that it must look at another spreadsheet file open in memory. The description SUBSID_1 tells Quattro Pro the name of a specific supporting spreadsheet.

The third element in this syntax is the cell or block reference. Quattro Pro uses this reference to link to a specific cell address or block address on the spreadsheet file indicated in the brackets. In the example, the cell reference is C6—a cell address on SUBSID_1.

The syntax of this formula indicates that the primary and supporting spreadsheets reside in the same directory on the same disk drive. If the spreadsheets are not in the same directory, the formula might look something like this:

+[A:\REPORT\SUBSID_1.WQ1]F6

This syntax says that the supporting spreadsheet is stored in a directory called \REPORT on a disk in the A drive. Although you may link spreadsheets in different directories on different drives, you always should create and save the spreadsheets in the same directory on the same disk drive. Then, when you create linking formulas, you do not wonder whether you entered the correct drive name and path name, and you do not have to place a disk into a disk drive every time you want to work with the application.

This strategy also keeps the length of your linking formulas to an absolute minimum—an important point when you create longer, more complex formulas.

Creating 3-D Consolidation Formulas

There is a great advantage to creating linking applications that use supporting spreadsheets with exactly the same structure: you have an additional formula-entry alternative at your disposal. This method, *3-D formula consolidation*, uses wild-card designations in a linking formula to create live references to the same location on all of the spreadsheets open in Quattro Pro's memory.

Tip | This method references all spreadsheets open in Quattro Pro's memory. Before you begin, remember to close each and every spreadsheet file that will not be a part of the linking application.

Substituting the familiar wild-card code * (the asterisk) in place of a file name in a linking formula causes Quattro Pro to look at all open spreadsheets. To do more than just look, you must include an @function command that performs a mathematical operation.

Every 3-D consolidation formula contains three elements: an @function command, a bracketed 3-D link code, and an external cell (or block) reference.

The @function command indicates a mathematical operation for Quattro Pro to perform. For example, to average all of the values appearing in the same cell on three supporting spreadsheets, you use the @AVG function.

A properly constructed 3-D link code is critical to the success of this operation. The link code tells Quattro Pro exactly which spreadsheets the program should look at when performing the mathematical operation indicated by the @function command. For example, if you want Quattro Pro to perform a mathematical operation using data on all of the supporting spreadsheets open in memory, use the [*] link code. For example, to look only at those spreadsheets with names that begin with the letter S, enter *[S*]*.

The third element in this syntax is the cell or block reference. Quattro Pro examines the value residing in this cell on each spreadsheet open in memory, according to the 3-D link code specification. For example, to look at block A5..A10 on all open spreadsheets, type *A5.A10* as the reference.

Suppose that you re-enter the linking formula shown in figure 7.18 as @SUM([*]F6). This formula tells Quattro Pro to sum the F6 values from all open supporting spreadsheets and display the total in the active cell on the primary spreadsheet.

What value does this formula produce for the sample application? The formula displays total subsidiary revenues for the first quarter of 1990—a useful figure for this application, but one that does not belong in this particular cell. The viability of a consolidated formula depends mostly on proper placement on a spreadsheet. In this example, the consolidated formula would make more sense appearing in a column that displays data for all subsidiaries.

With a little bit of forethought, you can streamline the process of building a linking application by duplicating your spreadsheet structures and then building formulas using 3-D consolidation. Be careful, however, to consolidate similar information in the correct location on the primary spreadsheet.

Creating Linking Formulas in Point Mode

Look at the formula displayed in cell C6 on PARENT.WQ1 in figure 7.18. The final method for building linking formulas is achieved when your screen looks like the one pictured in this figure.

To enter the same linking formula by pointing and clicking with a mouse, do the following:

1. Move and resize two spreadsheet windows so that the windows appear side-by-side on-screen.

2. Click your mouse on the primary spreadsheet to make that spreadsheet active. Choose a cell as the destination cell and click that cell to make it active.

3. Press the + key to enter VALUE mode.

4. Click your mouse on the supporting spreadsheet to make that spreadsheet active. Locate the cell containing the value you want to use as the external reference.

5. Click to copy that cell reference—complete with the external file name—onto the input line next to the plus symbol.

6. Press Enter to record the linking formula. For example, in the sample application you first make cell C6 active on PARENT.WQ1. Then, you press the + key, point to cell F6 on SUBSID_1.WQ1, and then click twice to copy that cell reference onto the input line. Press Enter to store the formula.

Quattro Pro evaluates cell F6 on SUBSID_1.WQ1 and again displays the value 84,107.96 in the active cell on PARENT.WQ1.

You can use this technique in a way that does not require you to move and resize windows. With the primary spreadsheet displayed in a full-screen format, enter VALUE mode, press Alt-0, select a window from the displayed menu, click the target cell, and then press Enter to record the linking formula. If you already know the number of the window, press Alt plus the window number to directly move there.

Moving and Copying Linking Formulas

Now that you are familiar with each of the methods for creating and entering linking formulas, you can return to the sample application and complete PARENT.WQ1. After you create a linking formula, you can copy the formula to other cells on the primary spreadsheet (see fig. 7.19).

Fig. 7.19
Subsidiary 1's
data now is
linked to the
primary
document.

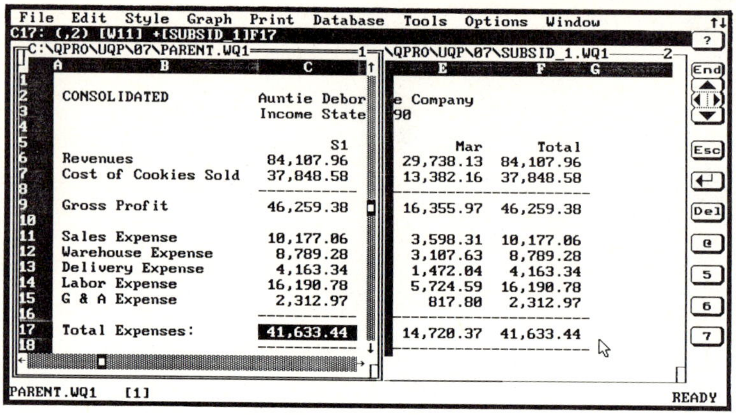

For example, to duplicate the linking formula in cell C6, make that cell active and then do the following:

1. Select /Edit Copy and press Enter to select C6 as the source block.

2. Make cell C7 the active cell and press Enter to select cell C7 as the destination block.

Quattro Pro copies the formula into cell C7. Continue this operation, copying the linking formula into all of the appropriate cells, until you fill in all of the subsidiary data on the primary spreadsheet. When you finish, you have one final task: sum the values in each column to derive the parent company's totals. You can enter @SUM functions that total the subsidiary data or you can use the 3-D consolidation technique to create additional linking formulas.

Review the spreadsheet shown in figure 7.20. The formula displayed on the input line results when the 3-D consolidating formula @SUM([*]F6) is entered into cell F6 on PARENT.WQ1. Quattro Pro converts the consolidating formulas into results so that you can later edit the individual external references.

You can copy this formula into the remaining cells in column F to complete the linking application.

When you apply Copy and Move operations to linking formulas, Quattro Pro treats relative and absolute references the same as with other formulas. If you move a linking formula into the spreadsheet that the formula references, however, Quattro Pro cancels and erases the link from the formula.

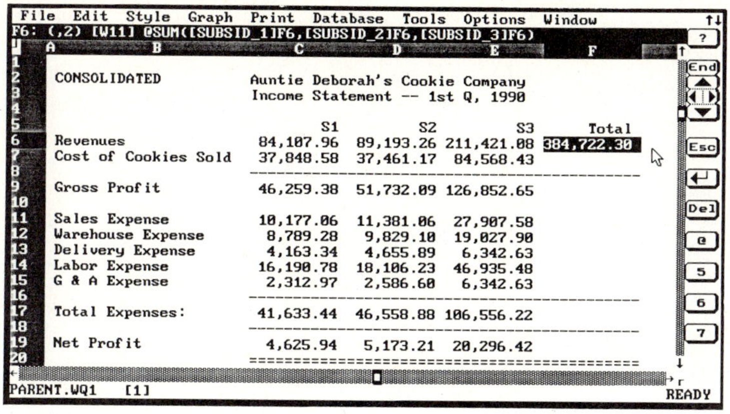

Fig. 7.20 A 3-D consolidation formula that sums values entered on the supporting spreadsheets.

Performing Linked Spreadsheet File Operations

After you finish creating the primary and supporting spreadsheets, save the spreadsheets to disk. Normally, you create a workspace file for multiple spreadsheets, which is helpful when you want to save and later load all of the associated spreadsheets. Loading linked spreadsheet applications, however, requires special handling.

Loading a Linked Spreadsheet Application

If you select the /**File R**etrieve command to load the sample application, you specify PARENT.WQ1 as the spreadsheet to retrieve. When you retrieve a primary file in a linked spreadsheet application, Quattro Pro displays the linking options menu shown in figure 7.21.

To load each of the supporting spreadsheets, select the **L**oad Supporting option. The **U**pdate Refs option causes Quattro Pro to update the linked formula results on the primary spreadsheet using data from the unopened supporting spreadsheets.

If you do not want to update the linking references on the primary spreadsheet, select the **N**one option. This option causes Quattro Pro to display NA (not available) values in each cell on the primary spreadsheet that has a linking reference to an unopened, supporting document (see fig. 7.22).

This display enables you to review the structure of a primary document in a large linking application without first having to load each supporting document.

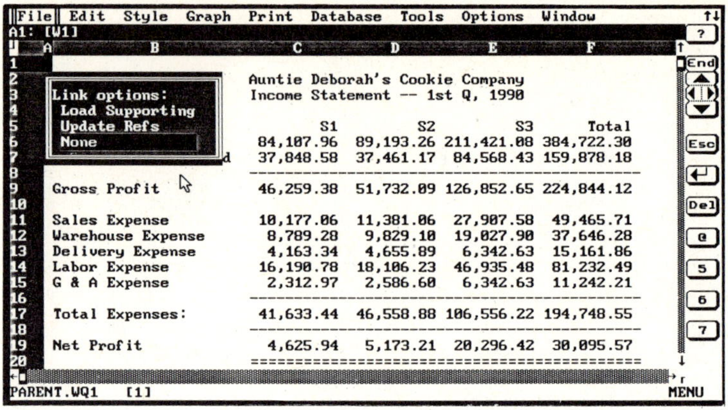

Fig. 7.21
Three options
for retrieving a
linked
spreadsheet
application.

```
||File  Edit  Style  Graph  Print  Database  Tools  Options  Window        ↑↓
A1: [W1]                                                                    ?
|| A          B            C          D          E          F           ↑
1                                                                     End
2                          Auntie Deborah's Cookie Company            ▲
3  Link options:          Income Statement -- 1st Q, 1990             ◄│►
4  Load Supporting                                                    ▼
5  Update Refs                 S1        S2        S3      Total
6  None                   84,107.96  89,193.26 211,421.88 384,722.30  Esc
7                    d     37,848.58  37,461.17  84,568.43 159,878.18
8                                                                     ↵
9  Gross Profit            46,259.38  51,732.09 126,852.65 224,844.12
10                                                                    Del
11 Sales Expense           10,177.06  11,381.06  27,907.58  49,465.71
12 Warehouse Expense        8,789.28   9,829.10  19,027.90  37,646.28  @
13 Delivery Expense         4,163.34   4,655.89   6,342.63  15,161.86
14 Labor Expense           16,190.78  18,106.23  46,935.48  81,232.49  5
15 G & A Expense            2,312.97   2,586.60   6,342.63  11,242.21
16                        -----------------------------------------   6
17 Total Expenses:         41,633.44  46,558.88 106,556.22 194,748.55
18                        -----------------------------------------   7
19 Net Profit              4,625.94   5,173.21  20,296.42  30,095.57
20                        =========================================
PARENT.WQ1   [1]                                              MENU
```

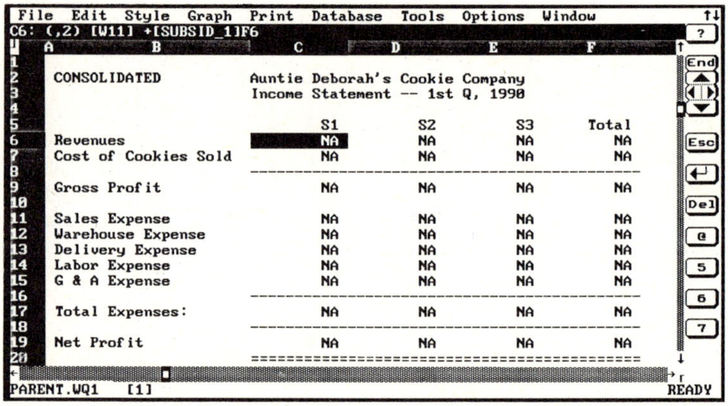

Fig. 7.22
Displaying NA
values on the
primary
spreadsheet.

```
 File  Edit  Style  Graph  Print  Database  Tools  Options  Window         ↑↓
C6: (,2) [W11] +[SUBSID_1]F6                                               ?
|| A          B            C          D          E          F           ↑
1                                                                     End
2  CONSOLIDATED           Auntie Deborah's Cookie Company             ◄│►
3                         Income Statement -- 1st Q, 1990             ▼
4
5                              S1        S2        S3      Total
6  Revenues                    NA        NA        NA        NA        Esc
7  Cost of Cookies Sold        NA        NA        NA        NA
8                                                                     ↵
9  Gross Profit                NA        NA        NA        NA
10                                                                    Del
11 Sales Expense               NA        NA        NA        NA
12 Warehouse Expense           NA        NA        NA        NA        @
13 Delivery Expense            NA        NA        NA        NA
14 Labor Expense               NA        NA        NA        NA        5
15 G & A Expense               NA        NA        NA        NA
16                        -----------------------------------------   6
17 Total Expenses:             NA        NA        NA        NA
18                        -----------------------------------------   7
19 Net Profit                  NA        NA        NA        NA
20                        =========================================
PARENT.WQ1   [1]                                              READY
```

Using the Update Links Menu

Select the /Tools Update Links command to display the Update Links menu. The four options on this menu enable you to control the interaction between primary and supporting documents in a linked spreadsheet application.

Select the Open option to open individual supporting spreadsheets without reloading the entire linked application. When prompted, highlight the names of the spreadsheets you want to open and press Enter to load those spreadsheets (see fig. 7.23).

When no supporting spreadsheets are open in Quattro Pro's memory, select the Refresh option to recalculate results for the linking formulas on a primary spreadsheet. When prompted, highlight the names of the supporting

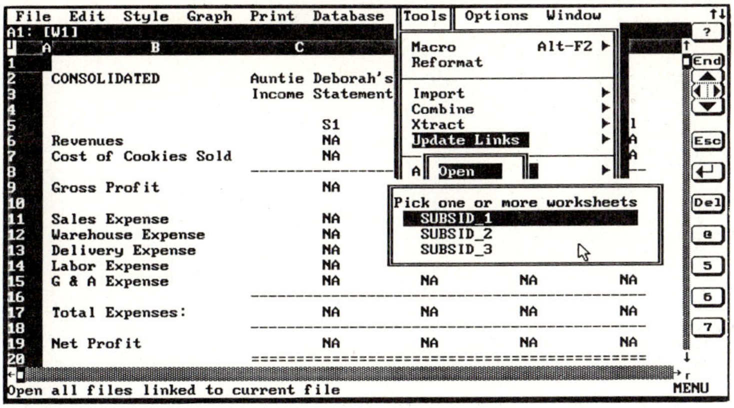

Fig. 7.23
Loading
unopened
supporting
spreadsheets
into Quattro
Pro.

spreadsheets that contain cell values referenced by linking formulas on the primary spreadsheet. Press Enter to refresh the linking formula results on the primary spreadsheet.

Select the **C**hange option to unlink a supporting spreadsheet from the primary spreadsheet and to relink it to a new spreadsheet (see fig. 7.24).

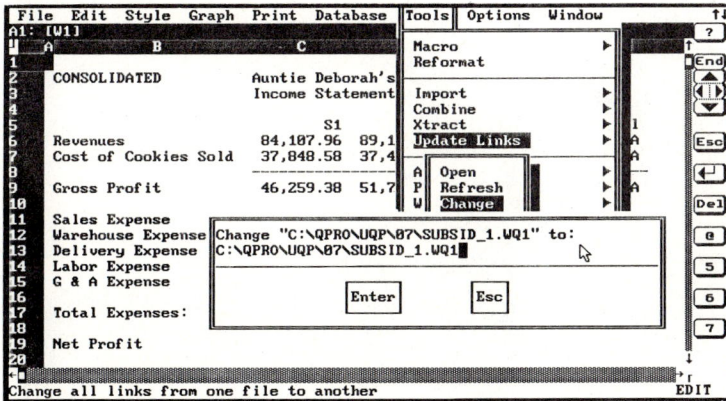

Fig. 7.24
Quattro Pro
prompts you
for the name of
the spreadsheet
you want to
relink to.

Select the **D**elete option to erase links between the primary spreadsheet and one or more supporting spreadsheets.

Using Advanced File Tools

The first three commands located in the middle of the Tools menu provide you with the means to import, combine, and extract spreadsheet data. These commands can operate both on spreadsheet data and data from other programs. By continuing with the sample application, you learn how to use each of the commands to perform special file manipulations.

Importing a File

The **I**mport command enables you to load data from text files into a Quattro Pro spreadsheet. This operation is recommended for users who want to access data stored in file formats that Quattro Pro cannot translate automatically. For example, importing text from a word processing file and financial data stored in a file used by an accounting software program is common.

The **I**mport command can access data stored in three common file formats: ASCII text, comma and quote delimited, and comma delimited. When you import data, Quattro Pro reads the foreign file format and copies the data into one column on the current spreadsheet.

To import text into a Quattro Pro spreadsheet, do the following:

1. Place the cell selector into the cell in which you want Quattro Pro to begin copying the imported data.

2. Select the /**T**ools **I**mport command and choose **A**SCII Text File, **C**omma S " " Delimited File, or **C**ommas Only from the displayed list.

3. When prompted, type the name of the file to import and press Enter to begin importing text from that file.

Review the data after Quattro Pro finishes importing the text. Depending on the source file format, Quattro Pro may have copied the imported data into one column without breaking up long labels. This situation occurs, for example, when you import data from an ASCII text file that does not delineate items on the same row. To break up the long labels, you can use the /**T**ools **P**arse command (see Chapter 11 for comprehensive coverage of this command).

Generally, Quattro Pro copies comma- and quote-delimited files into separate columns on the spreadsheet.

Combining Two Files

The **C**ombine command enables you to copy, add, and subtract data on two spreadsheets. This command is useful for applications that are not formula linked, yet do require a certain level of data association. In most cases, linked formulas are easier to work with and provide you a greater degree of flexibility when designing and building spreadsheet applications.

Return to the sample application introduced in the preceding section. Start by making the assumption that the four spreadsheets are no longer linked by formulas. Additionally, PARENT>WQ1 contains no values. Using the **C**ombine command, you can create the same end result that was achieved with linked formulas.

Tip	Combined files do not update each other automatically like linked files do. To refresh the values in combined files, you must reselect the command and then combine the data again.

Before issuing this command, you must gather data about the two spreadsheets. First, jot down the exact block coordinates of the data from the source spreadsheet. Second, review the destination spreadsheet and select an area that you want to combine data to.

Before executing the command, you should note that Quattro Pro overwrites existing cell data (including protected cells) on the destination spreadsheet, unless you are performing an **A**dd or **S**ubtract combine operation.

Copying Data

To combine data from PARENT.WQ1 and SUBSID_1.WQ1, do the following:

1. Retrieve PARENT.WQ1 and place the cell selector in cell E6.

2. Select /**T**ools **C**ombine **C**opy.

3. When prompted, choose the **B**lock option to copy only a block of data.

4. When prompted, type *F6..F19* and press Enter to record the source block.

5. When Quattro Pro displays the file list box, highlight SUBSID_1.WQ1 and press Enter.

Quattro Pro begins copying the source block to the active spreadsheet, beginning at the location of the cell selector. When you select the **C**opy combine option, Quattro Pro reproduces the data exactly as the data appears in the source block, including cell formatting and presentation-quality display settings (see fig. 7.25).

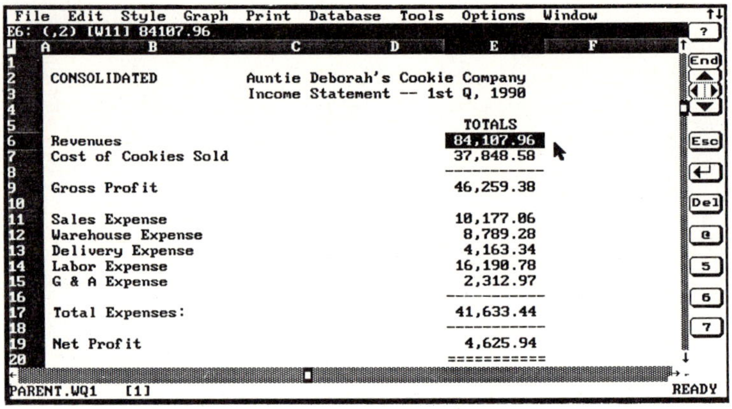

Fig. 7.25 Combining the data by copying the values from the source block onto the destination spreadsheet.

```
File  Edit  Style  Graph  Print  Database  Tools  Options  Window        ↑↓
E6: (,2) [W11] 84107.96                                                    [?]
     A          B              C        D        E        F               ↑
1                                                                        [End]
2     CONSOLIDATED        Auntie Deborah's Cookie Company                 [▲]
3                         Income Statement -- 1st Q, 1990                  [◄▐►]
4                                                                          [▼]
5                                              TOTALS
6     Revenues                             84,107.96    ◄                 [Esc]
7     Cost of Cookies Sold                 37,848.58
8                                          ----------                     [↵]
9     Gross Profit                         46,259.38
10                                                                        [Del]
11    Sales Expense                        10,177.06
12    Warehouse Expense                     8,789.28                      [8]
13    Delivery Expense                      4,163.34
14    Labor Expense                        16,190.78                      [5]
15    G & A Expense                         2,312.97
16                                         ----------                     [6]
17    Total Expenses:                      41,633.44
18                                         ----------                     [7]
19    Net Profit                            4,625.94
20                                         ==========                     ↓
                              □                                         ►▐◄┘
PARENT.WQ1   [1]                                                       READY
```

Adding and Subtracting Data

To add data to PARENT.WQ1, which is located on SUBSID_2.WQ1, do the following:

1. Retrieve PARENT.WQ1 and place the cell selector in cell E6.

2. Select /**T**ools Combine **A**dd.

3. When prompted, choose the **B**lock option to copy only a block of data.

4. When prompted, type *F6..F19* and press Enter to record the source block.

5. When Quattro Pro displays the file list box, highlight SUBSID_2.WQ1 and press Enter.

Quattro Pro adds the values from the source block to the corresponding values on the active spreadsheet, beginning at the location of the cell selector. When you **A**dd data, Quattro Pro does not alter any cell formatting or presentation-quality display settings in the target block (see fig. 7.26).

The **S**ubtract option on the Combine menu works like the **A**dd option, except that the Subtract option subtracts the source block values from the destination block values.

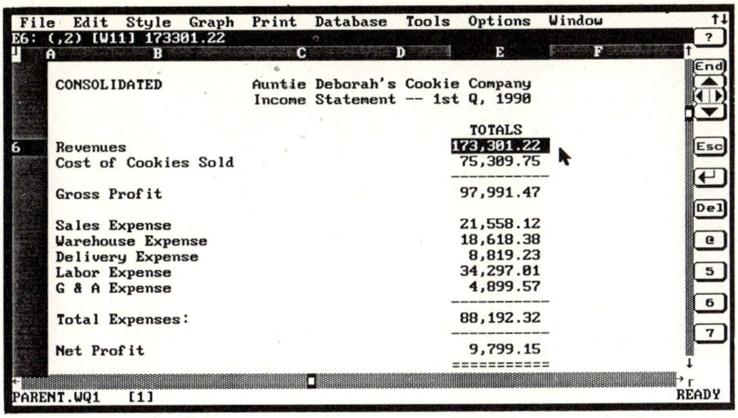

Fig. 7.26
Combining the data by adding the values from the source block onto the destination spreadsheet.

Extracting Part of a File

The /Tools Xtract command copies a portion of a spreadsheet and saves the portion in a new spreadsheet file. This command is useful for breaking large spreadsheet applications into several smaller, more manageable spreadsheets.

When Quattro Pro performs an extraction operation, the program retains all of the block names, graph names, and format settings that applied to the source block prior to extraction. Also, you can extract Formulas or Values from the source spreadsheet. Selecting the Values option is like selecting the /Edit Values command.

To extract data from one spreadsheet and copy the data to another, do the following:

1. Select /Tools Xtract.

2. Choose Formulas or Values.

3. When prompted, type a file name to extract to.

4. When prompted, type the coordinates of the source block and press Enter to extract the data.

Questions & Answers

Q: After I loaded two documents into Quattro Pro, I pressed Alt-0 to reveal the open windows menu, but only one file name was displayed. What happened to my second spreadsheet?

A: You chose /**File R**etrieve to open the second document when you should have used /**File O**pen. The latter command overlays the current spreadsheet window with a saved spreadsheet, but the former command loads a saved spreadsheet into the current window, erasing the current spreadsheet from memory.

Q: Why doesn't Quattro Pro save my **D**irectory command setting for new work sessions?

A: They are saved, but not via the Directory command. Choose /**O**ptions **S**tartup **D**irectory to choose a new default directory setting. Also, choose /**O**ptions **U**pdate to save the new setting. Quattro Pro writes the new directory name on the File menu next to the Directory command.

Q: Why don't my presentation-quality settings appear when I retrieve spreadsheet files saved in non-Quattro Pro file formats?

A: The file formats for many of the programs that Quattro Pro can read and write to do not support features like line drawing, font selections, inserted graphs, and formula links. These features are Quattro Pro-specific and should be added only to spreadsheet files with the WQ1 extension.

Q: I cannot remember the password for a spreadsheet. How can I display a list of the current passwords?

A: You can't. Quattro Pro does not enable you to access a password-protected file without the password. If you have forgotten the password, you have to build the spreadsheet again.

Q: How do I rename a spreadsheet file without returning to DOS?

A: Choose the /**File** Save **A**s command and type a new file name when prompted. This method creates a duplicate of the original spreadsheet. You also can highlight a name in the File Pane of the File Manager window and choose the /**E**dit **R**ename command. Quattro Pro prompts you for a new name. This method does not duplicate the file.

Q: Why is Quattro Pro sometimes unable to split a spreadsheet window into two panes?

A: There are three cases in which Quattro Pro cannot execute the Vertical or Horizontal commands on the Window menu: when the cell selector is in row 1, you cannot split a window into two vertical panes; when the cell selector is in column A you cannot split a window into two horizontal panes; when a spreadsheet window already is split into two panes, you cannot select another split setting. To change the split pane style, choose /**W**indow **O**ptions **C**lear before you select a new split pane setting.

Q: I can't seem to scroll my split window panes together. Am I doing something wrong?

A: Quattro Pro does not synchronize split window scrolling. To do this, choose /**W**indow **O**ptions **S**ync.

Q: When I try to enter a linking formula Quattro Pro beeps and displays an error message that says a drive is not ready. Then the program displays NA in the cell. What is going on?

A: You created and attempted to enter a linking formula containing a drive letter in front of the file-name reference. The drive you specified currently does not have a disk in it. Quattro Pro attempts to read the drive for several seconds and then records the formula anyway; because the file name reference is not valid, however, the program displays the NA value in the cell.

   If you intended to include the drive letter, place the disk in the drive and then re-enter the formula. This time, Quattro Pro finds the value and displays the correct formula result. If you did not intend to use the drive letter, delete the letter from the formula. In both cases the NA value disappears.

Q: Why does Quattro Pro sometimes not display the link options prompt when I load a linking application?

A: Quattro Pro displays the link options prompt whenever you open a spreadsheet containing references to unopened spreadsheets. When you load the primary spreadsheet first, Quattro Pro always displays the link options prompt. When you load supporting document(s) first and then load the primary document, Quattro Pro does not need to display this prompt.

Q: I loaded the primary spreadsheet in a linking application, and Quattro Pro displayed a prompt box asking me to change a linking reference to a different file name. Why?

A: You deleted or renamed a spreadsheet file referenced by a primary spreadsheet in a linking application.

   Press Esc until you cancel this prompt box, and Quattro Pro continues to load the rest of the linking application. When the application is completely loaded, Quattro Pro shows NA values in the cells that reference the unknown document. If you renamed the spreadsheet, change the name back, and Quattro Pro displays the correct values. If you accidentally deleted the spreadsheet, you must edit the linking formulas and remove the references to this file name.

Q: I created a circular formula when I combined data from two spreadsheets in a linking application. What happened?

A: Don't use the /**Tools Combine** command to copy blocks containing formulas. If you use this command, you run the risk of creating circular formulas. Instead, choose /**Tools Xtract Values**, and Quattro Pro copies only the formula results instead of the formulas.

Chapter Summary

Chapter 7 demonstrated some basic file-management skills that you can use when working with spreadsheets and windows. This chapter reviewed the File menu and Window menu commands and introduced you to using the File manager.

You now should know how to link spreadsheets and how to use some advanced file tools. After completing this chapter, you should understand the following Quattro Pro concepts:

- Creating, opening, and retrieving files

- Saving, closing, and erasing files

- Translating spreadsheets

- Password protecting your files

- Using the File Manager to perform multiple file operations

- Enlarging, shrinking, tiling, stacking, moving, and sizing windows

- Splitting windows into panes

- Creating linking formulas in Point mode

- Moving and copying linking formulas

- Importing and combining files

II

Printing and Graphing

Includes

Quick Start: Printing a Spreadsheet and Creating a Graph

Printing

Creating, Managing, and Displaying Graphs

Customizing and Annotating Graphs

Quick Start 2

Printing a Spreadsheet and Creating a Graph

Quattro Pro provides several different ways to format and print your spreadsheet reports. You can create an unformatted snapshot of your screen's display, print a specific block on a spreadsheet, or create the final version of a presentation-quality report.

A Quattro Pro graph offers several advantages over a numerical report. Graphs visually point out differences in magnitude. Graphs summarize data—enabling you to consider several different relationships at the same time. Most importantly, graphs disclose trends and pin point problem areas that otherwise may be lost in the numbers.

Printing with Quattro Pro

This Quick Start begins by reviewing the several ways of creating printed reports from a Quattro Pro spreadsheet. Consider the spreadsheet shown in figure QS2.1. This report displays several rows and columns of data for a sample firm called J. Dunn & Company, an industrial goods manufacturer. The firm purchases three types of raw materials (plastics, metals, and chemicals) from domestic and international vendors.

Fig. QS2.1
The J. Dunn &
Company Total
Value of
Materials
Purchased
report.

```
 File   Edit   Style   Graph   Print   Database   Tools   Options   Window      ↑↓
A1: [W2]                                                                         ?
    A      B         C          D         E              F          G   H ↑
1                                                                            ■End
2                          J. DUNN & COMPANY                                   ▲
3                   TOTAL VALUE OF MATERIALS PURCHASED                        ◄▌▶
4                          Fiscal Year 1990          \                         ▼
5
6    REGION      PLASTICS      METALS   CHEMICALS       TOTALS      (%)       Esc
7    East          37,459      75,575      72,384      185,418    18.9%       ◄┘
8    South         27,755      83,736      33,889      145,379    14.8%
9    Midwest       96,707      68,988      76,888      242,583    24.7%       Del
10   North         27,984       7,115      80,413      115,512    11.8%
11   West          72,193      81,365      18,339      171,897    17.5%        8
12   Int'l.        39,023      32,195      48,903      120,120    12.2%
13                                                                             5
14       TOTALS:  $301,122    $348,973    $330,815    $980,909
15          (%)      30.7%       35.6%       33.7%                             6
16
17                                                                             7
■□
TVMP.WQ1        [1]                                                        ↓→⌐
                                                                         READY
```

Printing an Unformatted Version
of a Spreadsheet

To obtain a draft-quality printout of the sample spreadsheet—without having to change a default print setting—you need only use two commands: /**Print B**lock and /**Print S**preadsheet **P**rint.

To print the unformatted version of the sample spreadsheet, do the following:

1. Press /PB to select the /**Print B**lock command.

2. When prompted, type *A1..H16* as the block coordinates to print.

3. Press Enter to select that print block.

4. Turn your printer on, and position the paper in the printer at the top of a page.

5. Press A to display the Adjust Printer menu, and then press A to execute the **A**lign command.

6. Press S to execute the /**Print S**preadsheet **P**rint command and print the spreadsheet report (see fig. QS2.2).

7. Press AF to execute the **F**orm **F**eed command from the Adjust Printer menu.

8. Press Q to quit the Print menu and return to the active spreadsheet.

Press Ctrl-Break to abort a printing operation and return to the active spreadsheet.

```
                    J. DUNN & COMPANY
              TOTAL VALUE OF MATERIALS PURCHASED
                     Fiscal Year 1990
+-----------------------------------------------------------+
|REGION        PLASTICS    METALS  CHEMICALS     TOTALS    (%) |
+-----------------------------------------------------------+
|East            37,459    75,575    72,384     185,418   18.9%|
|South           27,755    83,736    33,889     145,379   14.8%|
|Midwest         96,707    68,988    76,888     242,583   24.7%|
|North           27,984     7,115    80,413     115,512   11.8%|
|West            72,193    81,365    18,339     171,897   17.5%|
|Int'l.          39,023    32,195    48,903     120,120   12.2%|
|
|     TOTALS:   $301,122  $348,973  $330,815    $980,909
|        (%)       30.7%     35.6%     33.7%
+-----------------------------------------------------------+
```

Fig. QS2.2
The unformatted version of the sample spreadsheet.

Customizing the Layout of a Spreadsheet

You can do several things to enhance the look of the printed report in figure QS2.2. For example, you can add a footer, change the print orientation, and then print the report in graphics printer mode. The following sections lead you through the steps to make these changes.

Adding a Footer

Use headers or footers to clarify data and to add footnotes to a spreadsheet printout. For example, to add a footer note that describes the source of the sample spreadsheet report, do the following:

1. Press /PL to display the Print Layout menu.

2. Press F to select the Footer option.

3. Type *Source: 1989 Annual Report* and press Enter to record the footer.

Quattro Pro prints headers and footers on each page of a spreadsheet printout.

Changing the Orientation

When your spreadsheet has too many columns to fit on the width of a printed page, print the report in landscape (horizontal) orientation. To print the sample spreadsheet horizontally, do the following:

1. Press OL to select the Orientation Landscape command.

When you are finished changing the Layout menu command settings (see fig. QS2.3), you are ready to print out a new version of the sample report.

Fig. QS2.3
The Layout
menu shows
the command
settings at the
right margin of
the menu.

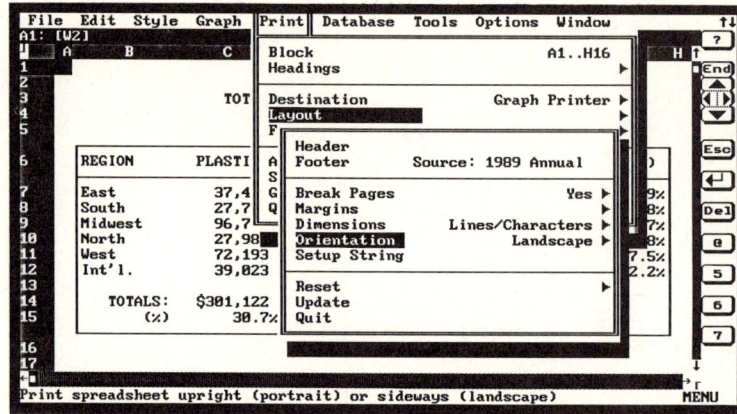

Previewing a Spreadsheet On-Screen before Printing

The Screen Preview command enables you to view your spreadsheet on a screen display in the same form in which the spreadsheet will be printed. To invoke the screen preview tool, do the following:

1. Press /PDS to select the /Print Destination Screen Preview command.

2. Press S to choose Spreadsheet Print.

Press /Q to return to the active spreadsheet from the Screen preview tool.

Printing in Graphics Printer Mode

To obtain a final-quality printout of a spreadsheet report, select the /Print Destination command prior to beginning a printing operation. For example, to print the presentation-quality version of the sample spreadsheet, do the following:

1. Press /PD to select the Printer Destination menu.

2. Press G to select the Graphics Printer option.

3. Press A A to execute the **A**djust Printer **A**lign command.

4. Press S to execute the **S**preadsheet Print command (see fig. QS2.4).

5. Press AF to execute the **A**djust Printer **F**orm Feed command.

6. Press Q to quit the Print menu and return to the active spreadsheet.

Creating a Quattro Pro Graph

You can build ten types of Graphs in Quattro Pro:

- Line
- Bar
- XY
- Stacked-bar
- Pie
- Area
- Rotated bar
- Column
- High-low (open-close)
- Text

If you do not specify a particular style when you create a graph, Quattro Pro automatically builds a stacked-bar graph.

The quickest way to build a graph is by using the **F**ast Graph command from the **G**raph menu. When you choose the **F**ast Graph command, Quattro Pro draws a "bare-bones" graph on your screen. A "bare-bones" graph shows only the basic graph elements: a scaled x-axis, a scaled y-axis, and the graphed data. When the block to be graphed contains labels in the first row and column, the graph also shows a legend and axis labels.

Before you choose this command be sure that the graph data block does not contain any blank rows or columns; if the data block does include blank rows or columns, Quattro Pro shows gaps within the graph.

The spreadsheet shown in figure QS2.2 displays several rows and columns of data for a sample firm called J. Dunn & Company. The firm purchases three types of raw materials (plastics, metals, and chemicals) from domestic and international vendors.

To build a fast graph using the data pictured in this figure, execute the following commands:

1. Press /GF to execute the /**Graph F**ast Graph command (or press Ctrl-G, the Ctrl-key shortcut).

2. When prompted, type *B6..E12* and press Enter to choose the Fast-Graph block.

When you execute the **F**ast Graph command, Quattro Pro evaluates the selected block of data and builds the graph shown in figure QS2.4. To return to the active spreadsheet, press Enter or Esc.

Fig. QS2.4
A "bare-bones"
stacked-bar
graph created
from the data
block.

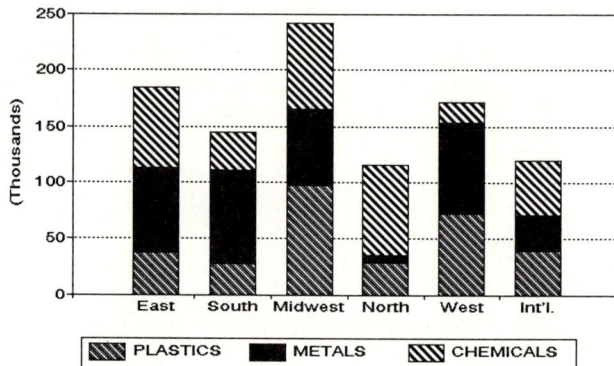

Adding Titles

Report titles add clarity and definition to a graph. You can add report titles to the J. Dunn & Company graph by performing the following steps:

1. Press /GT1 to execute the /**Graph T**ext **1**st Line command.

2. When prompted, type *J. Dunn & Company* and press Enter to record the title description.

3. Press 2 to execute the **2**nd Line command.

4. When prompted, type *Total Value of Materials Purchased* and press Enter to record the title description.

5. Press X to execute the **X**-Title command.

6. When prompted, type *Region* and press Enter to add this description to the x-axis.

To add an additional report title that does not appear on the original spreadsheet, perform the following steps:

7. Press Y to execute the **Y**-Title command.

8. When prompted, type *Purchase Volume* and press Enter to add this description to the y-axis.

9. Press Q to return to the Graph menu.

Displaying Graphs

You can view a graph on-screen in two ways. To display a graph at any time during a graph-building session, return to the Graph menu and press V to execute the **View Graph** command. To display a graph from anywhere on the spreadsheet and at any time during a graph-building session, press F10, the Graph key.

Because fast graphs are so easy to create, they are natural what-if? analysis tools. After you have made a fast graph, choose the **Q**uit command from the Graph menu to return to the active spreadsheet. Now modify any of the values appearing in the graphed block. When you finish editing the data, press F10 to regenerate a new fast graph.

Saving a Graph

Managing graphs files is an important part of every graph-building session. You must assign a unique name to a graph's settings, or you lose the graph if you exit Quattro Pro without saving the active spreadsheet.

Fortunately, every time you save a spreadsheet, Quattro Pro also saves the current graph settings with that spreadsheet. The next time you retrieve the spreadsheet, you can press F10, and Quattro Pro displays the entire graph.

This mechanism only works with one graph per spreadsheet and does not actually name the graph. Eventually, you will want to build more than one graph from a spreadsheet. In this case, you must assign a name for each unique graph setting.

The **Name** command on the Graph menu assigns a unique name to the current graph settings. To name the sample graph, perform the following steps:

1. Press /GNC to execute the /**Graph Name Create** command.

2. When prompted, type *VENDOR* and press Enter to assign that name to the current graph settings (see fig. QS2.5).

Fig. QS2.5
Assigning a
unique name to
a graph.

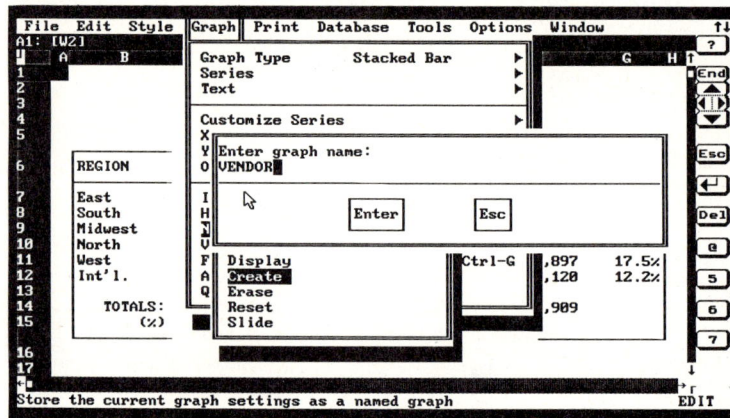

A valid graph name may have up to 14 characters, and each name must be unique, or Quattro Pro overwrites existing graph settings.

Inserting a Graph in a Spreadsheet

Select the /**Graph Insert** command to insert a copy of a graph into a spreadsheet. Doing so enables you to simultaneously view the graph and the data from which the graph was created. To insert and then view a graph, you need to prepare Quattro Pro's display environment.

Switching to Graphics Display Mode

To switch to graphics display mode, do the following:

1. Press /OD to execute the /**Options Display Mode** command.

2. Press B to choose **B**: Graphics Mode.

3. Press Q to quit the Options menu and return to the active spreadsheet.

Changing the Graph Aspect Setting

To insert a graph onto the J. Dunn & Company spreadsheet so that the graph fills up the target insert block, you must reset the 4:3 Aspect command setting. This command setting tells Quattro Pro how to project a graph on your screen. By default, the command setting is **Yes**. By changing the setting to **N**o, Quattro Pro forces a graph to conform to the size of the insert block that you specify.

To reset the aspect setting, do the following:

1. Press /PGL4N to execute the /**Print Graph Print Layout** 4:3 **Aspect** **N**o command.

2. Press Q three times to quit the Print menu.

Inserting the Graph

To insert a graph onto the spreadsheet, do the following:

1. Press /GI to execute the /**Graph Insert** command.

2. When prompted, highlight the name VENDOR on the displayed names list and press Enter to choose that graph.

3. When prompted, type *C13..F21* and press Enter to record the cell block in which you want to insert the graph.

4. Press Q to quit the Graph menu and review the inserted graph (see fig. QS2.6).

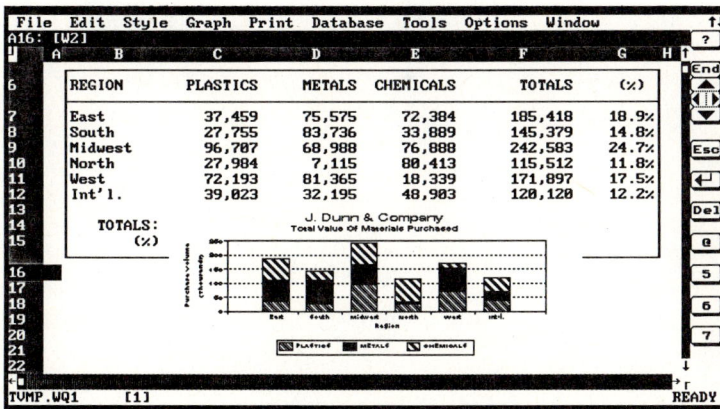

Fig. QS2.6
A Quattro Pro spreadsheet with an inserted graph.

Customizing Graphs

You can customize a graph using the four commands located in the middle of the Graph menu. The graph type typically determines which customizing tools you can use.

For example, you can enhance the appearance of the stacked-bar graph, add a new fill pattern to the stacked bars, shrink the width of the bars, format the numerical display on the y-axis, and then turn the entire graph into a three-dimensional display.

To customize the fill patterns, follow these steps:

1. Press /GCF2 to execute the /**G**raph **C**ustomize Series **F**ill Patterns **2**nd Series command.

2. When Quattro Pro displays the Fill Patterns menu, select the light dots choice (see fig. QS2.7).

Fig. QS2.7 Changing the fill patterns in the stacked bars.

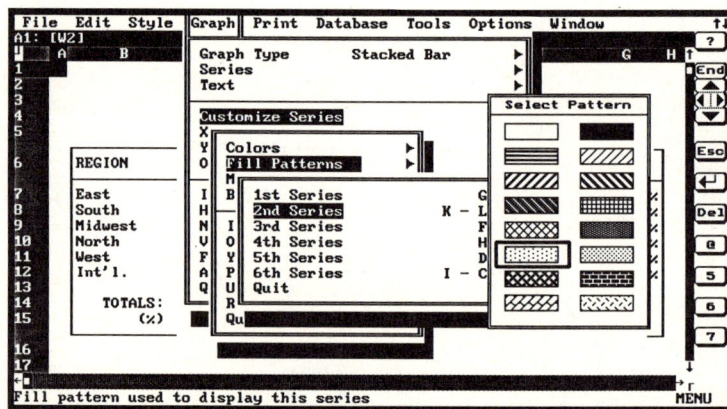

3. Press F10 to view the altered graph.

4. Press Enter to return to the Fill Patterns menu.

5. Press Q to return to the Customize Series menu.

To customize the width of the stacked bars, follow these steps:

1. Press B to execute the **B**ar Width command on the Customize Series menu.

2. Type *50* and press Enter to record the new width.

3. Press F10 to view the altered graph.

4. Press Enter to return to the Customize Series menu.

5. Press Q to return to the Graph menu.

To customize the y-axis numerical format, follow these steps:

1. Press YFC to execute the **Y**-Axis **F**ormat of Ticks **C**urrency command.

2. When prompted, type *0* and press Enter to select 0 displayed decimal places (see fig. QS2.8).

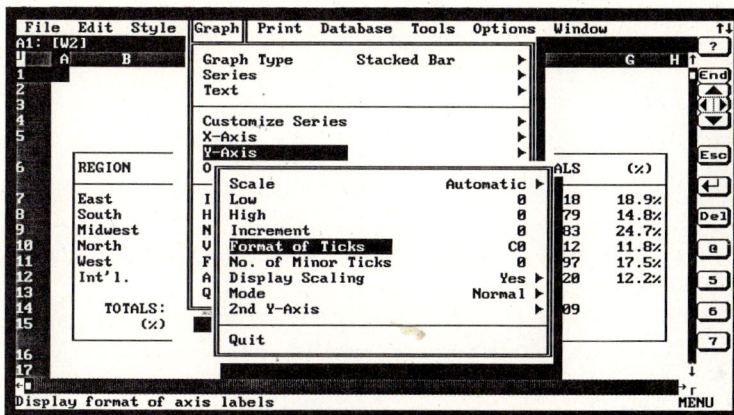

Fig. QS2.8
Formatting the numbers on the y-axis.

3. Press F10 to view the altered graph.

4. Press Enter to return to the Customize Series menu.

5. Press Q to quit to the Graph menu.

To customize the overall appearance of the graph, follow these steps:

1. Press OTY to execute the **O**verall **T**hree-D **Y**es command on the **G**raph menu.

2. Press F10 to view the altered graph (see fig. QS2.9).

3. Press Enter and then press Q to return to the active spreadsheet.

Fig. QS2.9
The customized
version of the
J. Dunn &
Company graph.

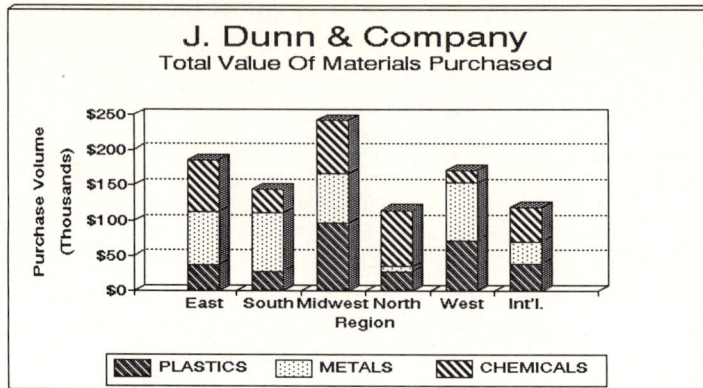

Annotating a Graph

To add the finishing, presentation-quality touches to a graph, use Quattro Pro's Graph Annotator. This built-in graphics editor enables you to add descriptive text, boxes, lines, arrows, and other geometric shapes to your graphs. Although you can operate all of the Graph Annotator commands with a keyboard, you should use a mouse if possible.

You can access this tool in two ways: from the Graph menu or while on a graph. Press /GA to execute the /Graph Annotate command, and Quattro Pro loads the current graph into the tool. You also can press / (the forward slash key) while displaying a graph on-screen, and Quattro Pro loads the current graph into the annotator.

Figure QS2.10 shows the sample graph loaded into the annotator.

Fig. QS2.10
The parts of the
Graph
Annotator
screen.

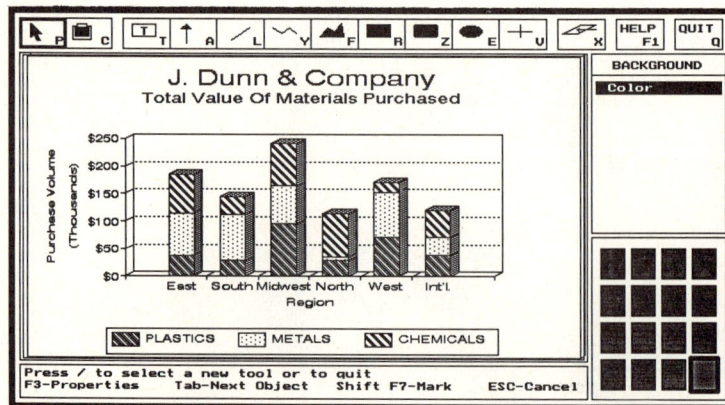

You can use the Graph Annotator to add a descriptive text box and an arrow to the sample graph.

Annotating Boxed Text

To add boxed text to the graph, do the following:

1. Press /GA to execute the /Graph Annotator command.

2. Press /T to select the boxed text icon from the Toolbox.

Quattro Pro displays a cross icon on the graph in the draw area. (If you have a mouse, the familiar arrow symbol is already present.)

3. Using the cursor-movement keys, position the icon directly above the smallest stacked bar (North region).

4. Press Enter and Quattro Pro draws the left portion of the box, waiting for your text input.

5. Type *Metals In Short Supply* and press Enter to store the boxed text.

Annotating an Arrow

To draw an arrow from the boxed text, pointing downward to the North stacked bar, do the following:

1. Press/A to choose the arrow icon from the Toolbox.

2. Using the cursor-movement keys, position the cross icon at the left edge of the boxed text.

3. Press the period key to anchor the top of the arrow.

4. Press ↓ until the arrow line extends downward to the top of the stacked bar.

5. Press Enter to anchor the end of the arrow to that location.

Concluding an Annotation Session

When you finish annotating a graph, do the following:

1. Press Esc to return to the draw area.

2. Press /Q (or click the Quit icon) to exit the Graph Annotator.

3. Press /NC, type *VENDOR*, and press Enter to rename the new graph setting.

4. Press Q to quit the Graph menu.

5. Press F10 to view a full-screen version of the annotated graph (see fig. QS2.11).

**Fig. QS2.11
The annotated
version of the
sample graph.**

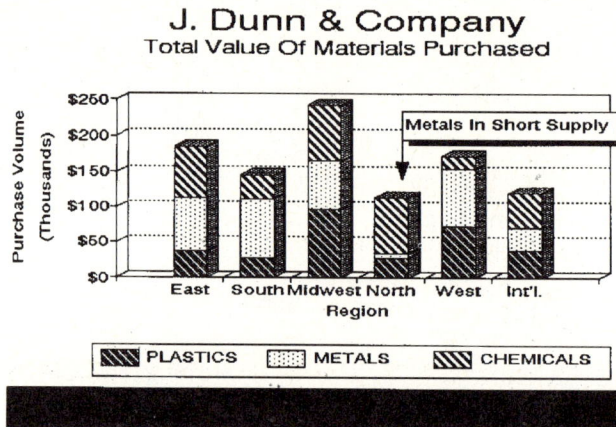

J. Dunn & Company — Total Value Of Materials Purchased

6. Press Enter to return to the active spreadsheet.

7. Press /FSR to save the spreadsheet and the named graph settings.

Printing a Graph

With Quattro Pro, you can preview a copy of a graph on your screen prior to printing the graph. Previewing ensures that the look of the printed graph is acceptable.

To designate a graph to print, select /**Print G**raph Print **N**ame. When executed, this command displays the Name menu that you saw after selecting the /**Graph N**ame command. When you do not supply a graph name, Quattro Pro prints a copy of the current graph settings.

Previewing a Graph

To preview the sample graph, do the following:

1. Press /**PGL4Y** to execute the /**Print G**raph Print **L**ayout 4:3 Aspect **Y**es command.

2. Press Q to Quit the Layout menu.

3. Press DS to execute the **D**estination **S**creen Preview command.

4. Press G to execute the **G**o command, and Quattro Pro displays the sample graph in the Screen Preview environment (see fig. QS2.12).

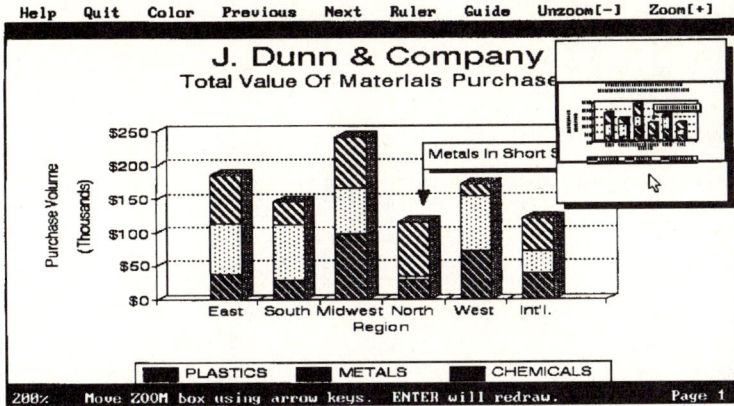

Fig. QS2.12 Previewing a graph prior to printing.

While in this environment, you can execute any of the commands at the top of the screen by pressing / and the first letter in the command name.

5. When you finish previewing the graph, press /Q to return to the Graph menu.

6. Press Q twice to return to the active spreadsheet.

Printing a Graph

To print the sample graph on a graphics printer, do the following:

1. Press /PGDG to execute the /**P**rint **G**raph Print **D**estination **G**raphics Printer command.

2. Press G to execute the **G**o command, and Quattro Pro begins printing the graph.

Summary

After completing this Quick Start, you should be familiar with the following Quattro Pro concepts:

- Printing a spreadsheet in draft mode

- Customizing a printout by adding footers and changing the print orientation

- Previewing a printout on-screen with the Screen Preview tool

- Printing a spreadsheet in graphics mode

- Creating a "bare-bones" fast graph of spreadsheet data

- Adding titles to a graph

- Displaying and saving graphs

- Inserting a "live" graph onto a spreadsheet

- Customizing a graph by selecting new fill patterns, changing bar widths, formatting the display of numbers, and creating a three-dimensional display.

- Annotating boxed text and an arrow to a graph

- Previewing a graph on-screen with the Screen Preview tool

- Printing a graph

Printing

Quattro Pro provides you with the tools to format and print spreadsheet reports and graphs in several different ways. You can print an unformatted snapshot of your screen's display, print a specific block of spreadsheet values, or print a presentation-quality version of a spreadsheet report. In this chapter, you learn the many printing techniques available on Quattro Pro's Print menu.

You are introduced to the Print menu commands that enable you to select data on a spreadsheet, prepare the layout and format of a report, and then print the report.

In the next section, you look at each step in the process of printing a small spreadsheet report. You also learn a technique for generating a rough draft screen preview of your spreadsheet data—a useful prelude to creating the final version of every printed report.

Next, you see how to access, understand, and set all of the options that control the appearance of a printed spreadsheet report. Specifically, you learn how to set layout options (such as footers, margins, and page orientation) that enable you to print larger spreadsheet reports successfully.

The chapter continues by illustrating the two format styles that Quattro Pro can use when printing out a spreadsheet report.

The next section covers methods for preparing for a printing session. You learn about aligning paper, issuing form feeds, and skipping lines to control the movement of paper in your printer.

The material continues by illustrating why and how to choose various destinations for your printed output. For example, you can print to a printer, to a file, or to your screen.

The final section of this chapter reviews the procedures for printing a graph. Like a spreadsheet report, you can reproduce a graph on paper, print a graph to a file, and preview the finished form of a graph on-screen. An additional graph printing option enables you to write a graph to a different file format for additional processing.

Reviewing the Print Menu

You can use the eight Print menu commands to define a print block, define a heading block, create a custom layout, control the movement of paper in a printer, and generate printouts of spreadsheet reports and graphs (see fig. 8.1).

Fig. 8.1
The Print menu
commands.

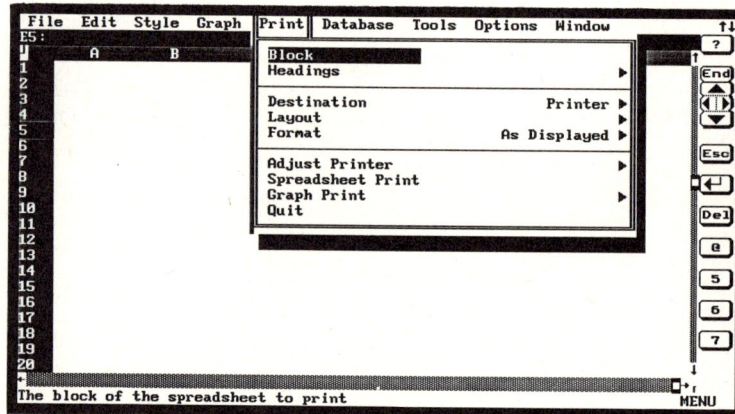

The Print menu consists of three types of commands: block definition commands, report formatting commands, and printer control commands. Quattro Pro displays the current system settings for certain commands at the right margin of the Print menu.

The block definition commands tell Quattro Pro which block to print and which block to use as a heading at the top of each printed page.

The **Destination** command—found in the middle section of the Print menu— enables you to choose where Quattro Pro prints a report: to a printer, to a file, or to the screen. The remaining commands in this section enable you to set print margins, set the page length, insert page breaks, and alter the print orientation of a report. You also can choose to print spreadsheet cell data as the data appears on-screen or in a cell-listing format.

The commands found at the bottom section of the Print menu control the printer. These commands advance the paper in a printer one line or one page at a time and align the printer to top-of-form. The final two commands tell Quattro Pro to print a spreadsheet or a graph.

Printing Small Spreadsheet Reports

Before learning how to use each of the print options, you should review two ways of obtaining a basic printout of a spreadsheet report.

First, you can obtain a draft-quality printout of a spreadsheet by using the **B**lock, **A**djust Printer, and **S**preadsheet **P**rint commands. This method, which does not require you to alter any of Quattro Pro's default print settings, is accomplished by doing the following:

1. Select /**F**ile **R**etrieve and retrieve a spreadsheet report.

2. Select /**P**rint **B**lock.

3. When prompted, type the block coordinates of the area you want to print.

4. Turn the printer on, position the printer paper to the top of a page, and choose the **A**djust Printer **A**lign command to set the paper to top-of-form.

5. Select **S**preadsheet Print, and Quattro Pro begins to print the data on the printer.

6. Select **A**djust Printer **F**orm Feed to advance the last page of the printout to the top of the form, so that the printer is ready for the next printout.

Tip Press Ctrl-Break to abort a print operation and return to the active spreadsheet.

This simple printing method works well for producing a working draft of a spreadsheet that is not more than 80 characters wide.

Second, you can print the portion of a spreadsheet showing on-screen by performing a screen dump operation. A *screen dump* sends an unformatted snapshot of the data displayed on your screen to a printer. This quick-print method is convenient for producing rough draft versions of your printouts. With a rough draft, you can verify the look of the cell formats, the accuracy of data, and the spelling of labels and report headings prior to printing the final draft.

To execute a screen dump operation, Quattro Pro must be in text display mode, or the program prints a page full of unrecognizable graphic symbols. Also, before trying this operation, be sure that your printer is on and is on-line.

Follow these steps to produce a screen dump output:

1. Select /**O**ptions **D**isplay Mode **A**: 80x25.

2. Press Q to quit the Options menu and return to the active spreadsheet.

3. Press Shift-PrtSc. (If you have an extended keyboard, press only the PrtSc key.)

Quattro Pro begins printing text. Even in text mode, the output from a screen dump operation is "rough" in appearance, which is why Quattro Pro offers other ways of producing higher quality versions of your printouts.

Printing out larger spreadsheets and creating higher quality printouts that display fonts, drawn lines, and shaded cells is fairly simple. Quattro Pro's layout options, as well as the procedures for generating higher quality spreadsheet and graph printouts, are covered in the remainder of this chapter.

Printing Large Spreadsheet Reports

The real benefit of using an electronic spreadsheet is that you can create complex reports made up of hundreds of rows and columns of data. When you print large reports, Quattro Pro occasionally wraps the text so that the text fits within the margins specified by the default print settings.

Text wrapping typically occurs when you define a block of data that is much wider than the width of your printer. For example, if you try to print a report that contains 30 columns of data, and each column is 15 characters wide, the printed report needs to be at least 450 characters wide.

When your spreadsheet report is wider than the width of a page, Quattro Pro prints as many columns as fit onto the page and then prints the remaining columns on a new page (see fig. 8.2).

Fortunately, you have several alternatives for printing such a large spreadsheet so that it reproduces in a more readable form.

If you own a wide carriage printer, you can print your report on wider paper; however, your printouts still are restricted to a width of approximately 132 standard characters. You also can use wider paper, change the

```
Business Decisions Consulting, Inc.
6-Month Cash Flow Report
```

	Jan (a)	Feb (a)	Mar (a)	Apr (a)	May (a)	Jun (pf)
INFLOWS						
C.Ed. Software	8,629	846	4,477	3,560	2,998	0
Positive Solutions, Inc.	8,188	8,430	8,597	6,052	541	6,221
S.D. County School District	1,260	8,006	1,915	5,059	7,467	9,731
Miscellaneous Consulting	4,000	8,809	5,380	5,382	6,520	9,903
Total Cash Inflows	22,076	26,091	20,369	20,052	17,525	25,855
Cumulative Inflows	22,076	48,168	68,537	88,588	106,114	131,968
OUTFLOWS						
Rent	2,500	2,500	2,500	2,500	2,500	2,500
Utilities	425	415	395	387	490	425
Supplies	1,745	1,299	366	244	1,443	750
Salaries	10,000	10,000	10,000	10,000	10,000	10,000
Debt Service	2,500	2,500	2,500	2,500	2,500	2,500
Subcontractor Payments	0	0	0	0	0	1,000
Taxes and Legal	0	0	575	0	0	575
Other Expenses	1,273	2,633	1,225	1,274	1,419	1,225
Total Cash Outflows	18,443	19,347	17,561	16,905	18,352	18,975
Cumulative Outflows	18,443	37,790	55,351	72,256	90,608	109,583
NET CASH FLOW	3,633	6,744	2,808	3,147	(827)	6,880
CUMULATIVE CF	3,633	10,378	13,186	16,333	15,506	22,386
Beginning Cash:	1,199	4,832	11,577	14,385	17,532	16,705
Ending Cash:	4,832	11,577	14,385	17,532	16,705	23,585

Fig. 8.2
The Business Decisions Consulting, Inc., spreadsheet report.

default margins, and print in compressed mode, giving you a report width of up to 254 characters.

An alternative way of dealing with text wrapping involves using a header at the top of each printed page. This technique does not control text wrapping, but accepts the situation and helps to make the text more presentable in a printed report.

You can create many different report styles by changing Quattro Pro's default print settings. For example, the /**Print H**eadings command enables you to print column and row headings on each page. When you choose / **Print H**eadings, Quattro Pro displays a menu on which you specify whether to print a **L**eft heading or a **T**op heading. A left heading appears along the left border of each page, and a top heading prints at the top of each page.

To specify a block to be printed as a heading, do the following:

1. Select /**Print H**eadings.

2. Select **L**eft Heading or **T**op Heading.

3. Type the coordinates of a block (on the active spreadsheet) that contains the heading you want to use.

Be sure to exclude the heading block from the print block. If you specify a column or row of labels as a heading and then include the same column or row as part of the print block, Quattro Pro prints the heading twice on every page—once as data and once as a heading.

344 Part II: Printing and Graphing

Choosing Layout Options

Initially, Quattro Pro produces printouts using default print settings. For example, Quattro Pro assumes that you are using standard 8 1/2-by-11-inch printer paper, printing each page using a portrait orientation, and inserting margins around the entire printed document. Default settings can be changed for an individual spreadsheet or for all future spreadsheets.

The Layout menu commands create report headers and footers; print reports without page breaks, footers, or headers; enable you to change the default margins, dimensions, and print orientation; and send special setup strings to your printer.

Quattro Pro stores the Layout menu command settings with the current spreadsheet. If you open a new file or exit Quattro Pro and then return to the Layout menu, each menu command displays its original default setting. To save custom settings as the new defaults, select the /**Print Layout Update** command. To reinstate the preceding set of default settings, select /**Print Layout Reset**.

Adding Headers and Footers

Headers and footers are lines of text (up to 254 characters in length) that may be added to the top or bottom of each page in a spreadsheet printout. A header (/**Print Layout Header**) is different from a heading (/**Print Headings**)—a *header* is text that you type into a dialog box, and a *heading* is a block of labels already existing on the spreadsheet.

Use headers and footers to append text to a printout. The advantage of using headers and footers is that you need to enter them only once for Quattro Pro to reproduce them on every page. If the header or footer data changes, you need to change the header or footer definition only once to update the text for all pages.

Commonly used header types include dates, file names, and titles. Commonly used footers types include comments, file names, and data legends.

For example, to add a footer to the sample spreadsheet report pictured in figure 8.2, do the following:

1. Select /**Print Layout Footer**.

2. When prompted, type the text of the footer with any alignment prefixes. For example, type |*(a)* = *actual; (pf)* = *pro forma* and press Enter to record the footer text (see fig. 8.3). This text header centers the footer on the bottom of each page in the printout.

After you perform step 2, Quattro Pro displays the new setting at the right margin of the Layout menu, next to the footer command.

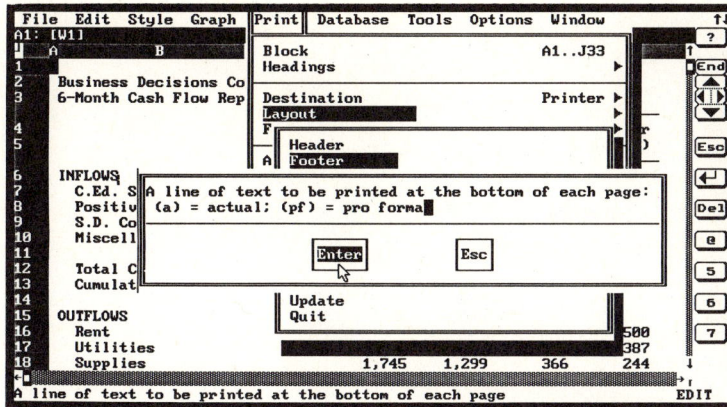

Fig. 8.3
Adding a footer to a spreadsheet report.

To delete a header or footer entry, reselect the command and backspace over the existing text. To change an entry, modify the text.

Three characters can be used to justify headers and footers on a page. When one of these characters is included as part of the text entry, the following actions take place:

Displays the current page number

@ Displays the current date

| Justifies text (right, center, or left)

Actually, the | header and footer symbol is like a Tab key that has three justification settings: left, center, and right. In a Quattro Pro printout, text is leftjustified automatically. When you precede text with a | symbol, Quattro Pro centers the text on the page. When you precede text with two || symbols, Quattro Pro right justifies the text.

Controlling Page Breaks

Quattro Pro observes hard and soft page breaks. Hard page breaks are inserted using the /**Style Insert Break** command or by placing the string || into a spreadsheet cell. Soft page breaks occur automatically between pages.

By default, soft page breaks occur every 56 spreadsheet rows. This row count assumes that your spreadsheet uses the default margin settings covered in the next section. When you change the default margin settings you alter the amount of rows that Quattro Pro prints.

You can suppress the automatic placement of soft page breaks, which results in data being printed in one continuous block. However, Quattro Pro continues to observe hard page breaks.

To suppress soft page breaks, do the following:

1. Select /**P**rint **L**ayout **B**reak Pages.

2. When prompted, select **N**o from the displayed menu.

To undo this command so that Quattro Pro continues inserting soft page breaks, reselect the **B**reak Pages command and choose **Y**es.

Setting Margins

The Margins menu commands enable you to set margins and alter the number of lines that Quattro Pro prints on a page. By default, Quattro Pro places 1/2-inch margins on the top, bottom, left, and right of a document and prints 66 lines per page.

To change any of these settings, select one of the commands described in the following sections.

Page Length

The **P**age Length command determines how many lines are to be printed on each page. The default setting of 66 lines is the standard for most printers. Laser printer owners should try a setting of about 60 lines per page. If your pages do not seem to break well in your printouts, adjust the **P**age Length command until you achieve the effect that you want.

A good rule of thumb to use when calculating a page length is that the length should equal the lines-per-inch value times the number of printable inches per page. Most dot-matrix printers print 6 lines per inch on a standard 8 1/2-by-11-inch page; therefore, page length equals 6 times 11, or 66 lines. The maximum page length setting for Quattro Pro is 100.

Top Margin

The **T**op margin command determines how much space is left between the top edge of the paper and the first row of data. The default setting is 2 rows, or approximately 1/2 inch. To change the default, select **T**op margin and enter a new setting. The maximum setting is 32.

Bottom Margin

The **B**ottom margin command determines the number of blank lines to leave at the bottom of each page. The default setting is 2 rows, or approximately 1/2 inch. To change the default, select **B**ottom margin and enter a new setting. The maximum setting is 32.

Left Margin

The **L**eft margin command determines how much space is left between the left edge of the paper and the first column of data. The default setting is 4 characters, or approximately 1/2 inch. Select **L**eft margin and enter a new setting to change the left margin.

The maximum left margin setting for Quattro Pro is 254. Be careful that you do not choose a left margin that is to the right of the right margin (for example, left margin equal to 80 and right margin equal to 30). In this case, Quattro Pro cannot print your spreadsheet. The program displays an error message requesting that you change the margin settings.

Right Margin

The **R**ight margin command determines the space to leave between the left edge of the paper and the beginning of the right margin. The default setting is 76 characters, leaving approximately 1/2 inch at the right margin. To change the default, select **R**ight margin and enter a new setting. The maximum setting is 254.

To change the right margin of the sample spreadsheet, for example, perform the following steps:

1. Select /**P**rint **L**ayout **M**argins.

2. Choose **R**ight.

3. Type *254* and press Enter to record the new right margin setting (see fig. 8.4).

Quattro Pro displays the new setting at the right margin of the Margins menu, next to the command.

Fig. 8.4
Changing the
right margin of
a spreadsheet
report.

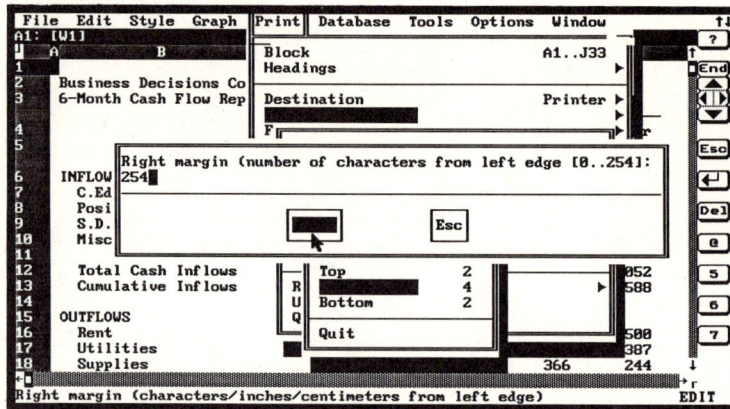

```
 File  Edit  Style  Graph │ Print │ Database  Tools  Options  Window        ↑↓
A1: [W1]                                                                      ?
   A              B          Block                              A1..J33   ↑
1                             Headings                                  ▶   End
2    Business Decisions Co                                                  ▲
3    6-Month Cash Flow Rep    Destination                      Printer ▶  ◀ ▶
4                            F                                         ▶    ▼
5
         │Right margin (number of characters from left edge [0..254]:│   Esc
6   INFLOW│254▮                                                       │
7    C.Ed │                                                           │   ↵
8    Posi │                                                           │   Del
9    S.D. │              ┌────────┐          ┌────┐                   │
10   Misc │              │   ▯    │          │Esc │                   │    @
11        │              └────────┘          └────┘                   │
12    Total Cash Inflows  ┌─┌─────────────┐────┐       ▶    │052       5
13    Cumulative Inflows  │R│ Top       2 │            ▶    │588
14                        │U│ Bottom    4 │                            6
15   OUTFLOWS             │Q│           2 │
16    Rent               │ │ Quit        │              500            7
17    Utilities          └─└─────────────┘────┘        387
18    Supplies                                   366    244          ↓
                                                                      ▶ r
Right margin (characters/inches/centimeters from left edge)        EDIT
```

Defining Dimensions

By default, Quattro Pro specifies the page length and margin settings in terms of characters. The size of a character is 1/10 of an inch horizontally and 1/6 of an inch vertically. Rather than specify the margins and page length in terms of characters, you may want to use inches or centimeters. Select /**P**rint **L**ayout **D**imensions and choose the measurement system you prefer.

Choosing a Print Orientation

By default, Quattro Pro prints a spreadsheet using a portrait (vertical) orientation. By selecting the **O**rientation command, you can print a report using a landscape (horizontal) orientation.

To print a spreadsheet using landscape orientation, do the following:

1. Select **L**ayout **O**rientation.

2. Select **L**andscape.

The **D**estination command must be set to **G**raphics Printer, or Quattro Pro will not print a spreadsheet using landscape orientation.

Using Setup Strings

All printers require codes to create nonstandard printing effects such as underlining, compressed and enhanced printing, and character strikeout. Many manufacturers allow you to select various printing modes directly from your printer's control panel. If you cannot achieve a certain printing effect from your panel, Quattro Pro enables you to send the control codes directly to your printer via the **S**etup String command.

Because each manufacturer uses a different set of printer codes, you have to refer to your printer manual for a list of the available effects and their corresponding codes. When you enter a printer code, you must supply the code in keyboard terms (the ASCII code equivalent) prior to entering the code as a setup string.

For example, to print the sample spreadsheet in compressed mode, do the following:

1. Select /**P**rint **L**ayout **S**etup String.

2. When prompted, type the appropriate setup string and press Enter. For the example, type \015 and press Enter to accept the setup string (see fig. 8.5).

Setup strings are printer dependent. For example, the \015 compressed mode printing string works for most IBM dot-matrix, Epson-compatible, and some Okidata printers. Other printers use different setup strings for compressed mode printing. For example, if you own an Okidata Microline, you must enter \029, or \027\091 for the Toshiba P1350. Check your printer manual for the specific codes when you want to enter setup strings on your spreadsheets.

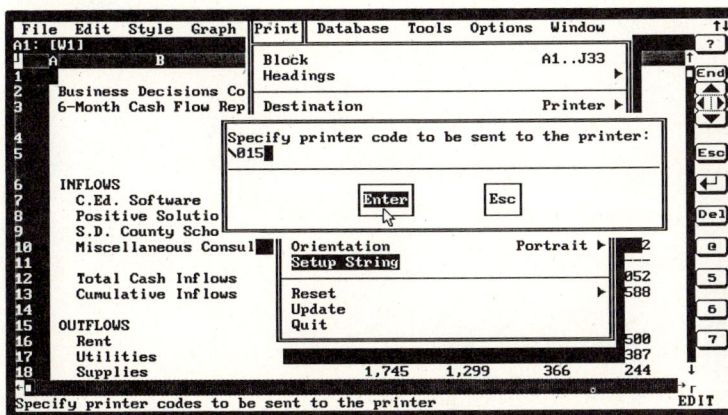

Fig. 8.5
Adding a setup
string to a
spreadsheet
report.

Quattro Pro displays the new setting at the right margin of the Layout menu, next to the command.

You may combine two or more printing effects by typing multiple setup strings, one after another. Valid setup strings may contain up to 39 characters, but may not contain any spaces between multiple strings.

The Setup String command causes Quattro Pro to apply the printer codes to the entire printed spreadsheet. To create two printing effects for different parts of the same spreadsheet, you may embed extra printer codes in a spreadsheet.

To embed a setup string in a spreadsheet, enter the setup string into a blank cell just above the area where you want to create the second printing effect. Be sure to precede the string with two vertical bar characters.

For example, to embed the IBM setup string that cancels compressed mode printing so that Quattro Pro prints out the remaining portion of a document in draft mode, do the following:

1. Select a blank cell directly above where you want to begin printing in draft mode and make that cell active.

2. Type ||\018.

3. Press Enter to embed the setup string.

Cells that follow this code now reflect this print setting.

Updating and Resetting the Layout Options

If you find that you use the same custom print settings for all of your printouts, you can store the values permanently by selecting the /Print Layout Update command (see fig. 8.6).

To restore a spreadsheet to a preceding set of saved defaults, select the /Print Layout Reset command.

Choosing the Display Format

When you select the /Print Format command, Quattro Pro displays the Format menu. The Cell-Formulas format displays the address, the numeric for-

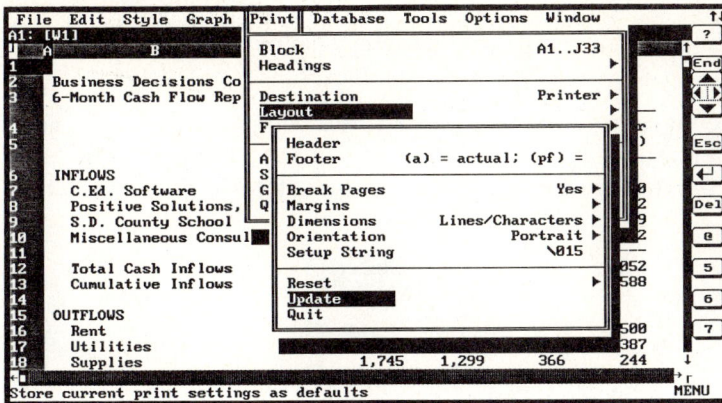

Fig. 8.6
Update saves
the current
print settings.

mat, the column width settings, and the contents of each cell in the print block. This display format provides you with a quick way to check the integrity of data entered into a spreadsheet. Figure 8.7 shows the result of printing block B1..D13 on the sample spreadsheet using this format style.

```
B2:  [W22]  'Business Decisions Consulting, Inc.
B3:  [W22]  '6-Month Cash Flow Report
D4:  "Jan
D5:  "(a)
B6:  [W22]  'INFLOWS
B7:  [W22]  '   C.Ed. Software
D7:  (,0)  8629.1506991256
B8:  [W22]  '   Positive Solutions, Inc.
D8:  (,0)  8187.5160161871
B9:  [W22]  '   S.D. County School District
D9:  (,0)  1259.5506419893
B10: [W22]  '   Miscellaneous Consulting
D10: (,0)  4000.1366811339
D11: (,0)  "-------
B12: [W22]  '   Total Cash Inflows
D12: (,0)  @SUM(D7..D10)
B13: [W22]  '   Cumulative Inflows
D13: (,0)  +D12
```

Fig. 8.7
Printing a
spreadsheet
using the Cell-
Formulas
format.

When you print a spreadsheet in the Cell-Formulas format, Quattro Pro ignores formatting specifications such as page breaks, headers, and margins.

Adjusting the Printer

Before sending data to a printer, make sure that your printer is on and in the on-line mode. Of course, the printer also must have a supply of paper.

The Adjust Printer menu commands help you properly position paper in a printer that uses a tractor pin-feeding system. This menu offers three command choices.

The Skip Line command moves the paper forward one line, and the Form Feed command advances the paper to the top of the next page. The Align command tells Quattro Pro that the paper in your printer is positioned at the top of the page.

You always must align the paper in your printer prior to printing. To do this for the sample spreadsheet report, perform the following steps:

1. Select /Print Adjust Printer.

2. Highlight Align on the menu and press Enter (see fig. 8.8).

Fig. 8.8
The Adjust
Printer menu.

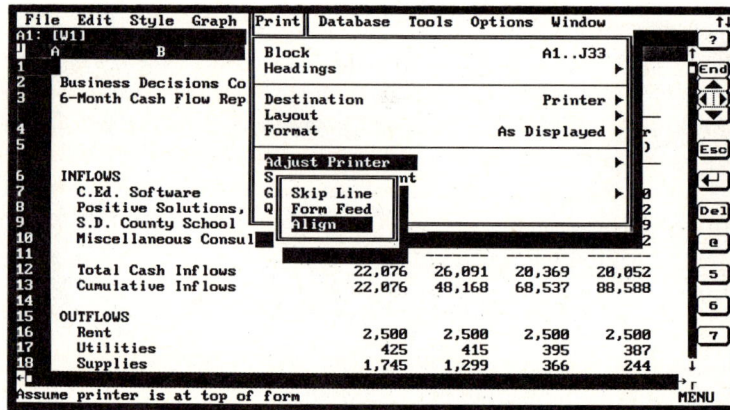

File	Edit	Style	Graph	Print	Database	Tools Options Window

Tip | When you execute the Align command, there is no visible change on your screen. The only way to check whether the command was issued correctly is by viewing a printout. When large blank areas appear on a printout, Quattro Pro is using the wrong top-of-page location. To fix this, reset the paper to the top-of-page and issue the Align command before printing again.

If you own a daisywheel printer, you also can use the commands on the Adjust Printer menu to prepare your printer for printing. Select the Skip Line and Form Feed commands to move your paper so that the printing head is placed at the top of a page. Then use the **Align** command to notify Quattro Pro that the paper is set to the top-of-form in your printer.

Choosing a Print Destination

The commands on the Destination menu enable you to specify where Quattro Pro sends a printout. You have two draft-mode and three final-quality destination choices (see fig. 8.9).

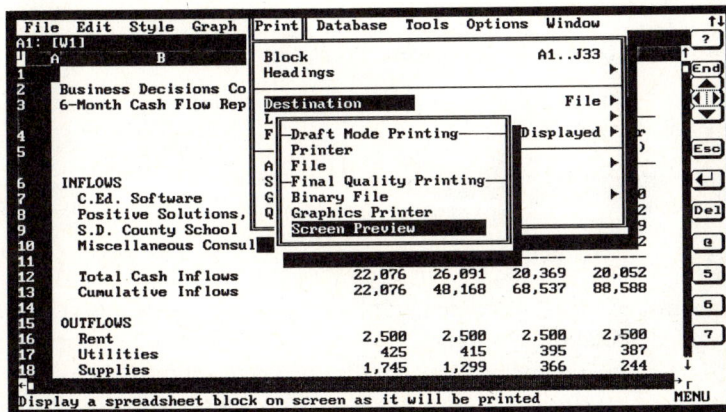

Fig. 8.9
The Destinations menu.

The first, most obvious destination choice is to print a document on a printer. The **Printer** option is the default destination setting. Choosing this command sends an unformatted, basic printout to your default printer. In addition to the default, you can select other options, described in the following sections.

Printing to a Text File

If you want to import Quattro Pro spreadsheet data into other programs for additional processing, you can print a spreadsheet to a text file. A *text file* stores only the spreadsheet data and print format settings—it does not retain presentation-quality options created with the Style menu commands.

You can import a text file into any program that can read DOS-text file formats because this file format contains only ASCII characters. Most word processing programs, spreadsheets, and database programs read ASCII text file formats.

By loading a Quattro Pro text file into a word processor, you can include spreadsheet data in your reports. To tap into the power of a dedicated database program, load a text file into the program and create a database using your spreadsheet data.

To print to a text file, perform the following steps:

1. Select /**Print Destination File**.

2. When prompted, type a file name and press Enter.

3. Return to the Print menu and change the print layout and format settings as you want.

4. Select **Spreadsheet Print**, and Quattro Pro writes the data to the file name you specified.

5. Choose **Q** to quit the Print menu and close the text file.

Quattro Pro does not close the text file until you specify another text file, choose a new print destination, or press Q to exit the Print menu. As long as you continue to execute commands on the Print menu, Quattro Pro continues to append data to the open text file. As soon as you quit the Print menu, Quattro Pro closes the text file and adds a PRN extension to the file name.

Tip | When you create a text file, be sure to use the **Align** command before and the **Form Feed** command after printing the document—just as if you are printing the spreadsheet on paper. Your document then reproduces correctly when you print the text file on a printer.

To print a text file on a printer, do the following:

1. Select /**File Exit** and exit Quattro Pro.

2. At the DOS command prompt, type *COPY filename PRN*.

3. Press Enter to begin printing the data on your printer.

If you remembered to issue a **Form Feed** command when you created the file, your printer is now reset to the top-of-form.

Printing to a Binary File

Unlike the text file, when you print spreadsheet data to a *binary file*, Quattro Pro records all of the presentation-quality settings created using the Style menu commands.

You can load a binary graphics file into any program that can convert the file into its own graphics file format. This conversion usually is accomplished from a conversion facility that comes with the software.

For example, WordPerfect 5.1 enables you to create and embed WPG graphics files in your word processing documents. The program also has a facility that converts a binary graphics file into a WPG graphics file. When you print your document in WordPerfect, the program reproduces the presentation-quality version of your graph in the word processing document.

To print a spreadsheet to a disk file in binary form, do the following:

1. Select /**P**rint **D**estination **B**inary File.

2. When prompted, type a file name and press Enter.

3. Return to the Print menu and change the print layout and format settings.

4. Select **S**preadsheet Print, and Quattro Pro writes the data to the file name you specified.

6. Choose **Q**uit to return to the Print menu and close the text file.

Like a text file, Quattro Pro does not close a binary file until you specify another text file, choose a new print destination, or quit the Print menu. Quattro Pro then closes the file and adds a PRN extension to the file name.

To print a binary file on a printer, do the following:

1. Select /**F**ile **E**xit and exit Quattro Pro.

2. At the DOS command, type *COPY filename /B LPT1*.

3. Press Enter to begin printing the data on your printer.

This command sequence sends the binary file to the LPT1 printer port. If your printer is connected to a different port, type that port address in place of LPT1 in step 2.

Printing to a Graphics Printer

Figure 8.9 lists Graphics Printer as one of three final-version printing options available on the Destination menu. Actually, you can achieve two different results with this command depending upon the current /Options Graphics Quality command setting.

When /Options Graphics Quality is set to Draft, the Graphics Printer command on the Destination menu produces "draft graphics quality" printouts.

This style of printout contains all of the presentation-quality graphics that you expect (drawn lines, shaded cells, and custom font selections). This printout is considered to be draft quality because Quattro Pro encounters a Bitstream font that has not been built and substitutes a Hershey font for the Bitstream font rather than pausing to build it.

When /Options Graphics Quality is set to Final, the Graphics Printer command on the Destination menu produces "final graphics quality" printouts.

Like the draft graphics quality printouts, this style contains presentation-quality graphics. If Quattro Pro encounters a Bitstream font that has not been built, the program pauses to build the font before printing the final graphics version.

Tip | After Quattro Pro builds a Bitstream font, the font can be used in other spreadsheets.

To produce a final draft version of a report that contains presentation-quality settings, select the Graphics Printer option from the Destination menu (see fig. 8.10).

Previewing a Printout On-Screen

Before you print a spreadsheet, you can preview how the spreadsheet looks on a printed page with Quattro Pro's Screen Previewer. Specify Screen Preview on the Destination menu and then select Spreadsheet Print. Quattro Pro displays the spreadsheet on-screen in the form the spreadsheet will take when printed (using Graphics Printer as a destination), including all of the special print settings and presentation-quality options (see fig. 8.10).

The Screen Previewer tool displays a group of commands at the top of the screen (see table 8.1).

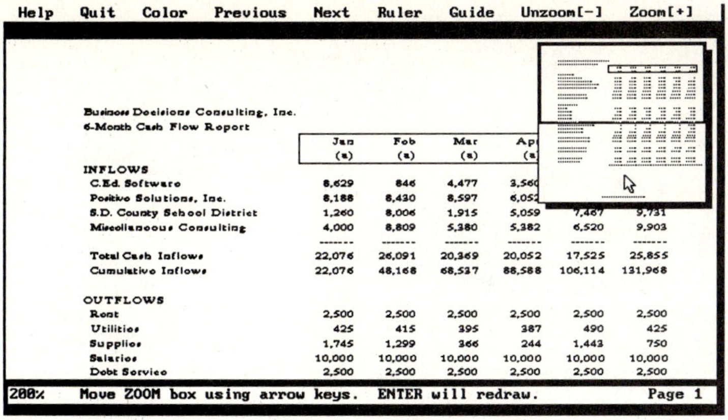

Fig. 8.10
The Screen Preview tool.

Table 8.1
Screen Previewer Command Options

Command	Description
Help	Invokes a context-sensitive help window
Quit	Quits to the active spreadsheet
Color	Toggles between a black-and-white and color screen.
Previous	Displays the preceding page of the print job
Next	Displays the next page of the print job
Ruler	Overlays a one-inch grid on-screen.
Guide	When in a zoomed view, displays a miniature page in the upper-right corner of the screen. Press the cursor-movement keys to move the box around the miniature page. Press Enter once to relocate the screen to that portion of the spreadsheet.
Unzoom	Moves you down one zoom level
Zoom	Enlarges the display by 100%, 200%, and 400%

Use any of the following three methods to choose a command from the
Screen Previewer menu bar:

- Press the boldfaced letter key in a command name

- Click on the command with a mouse

- Press / to activate the menu bar, highlight the desired command,
  and press Enter.

While in the Screen Previewer environment, you may use the keys in table 8.2 to navigate through a spreadsheet report.

Table 8.2
Screen Previewer Movement Keys

Key	Description
Esc	Exits the Screen Previewer
Arrow keys	Scroll the zoomed display in four directions
PgUp	Moves to the preceding page
PgDn	Moves to the next page
Home	Displays the top of a zoomed page
End	Displays the bottom of a zoomed page
Del	Removes the page guide when a page is zoomed

Previewing spreadsheet printouts is important when you use presentation-quality settings like drawn lines, shaded cells, and custom font selections. Occasionally, when you preview a spreadsheet, you do not see the font you expected, or text and drawn lines are missing from the edge of the spreadsheet.

These things happen because Quattro Pro uses graphics characters to display some on-screen presentation-quality settings. For example, Quattro Pro inserts extra spaces between rows and columns when you draw lines on a spreadsheet.

Sometimes, you do not know what effect the presentation-quality settings have until you preview your spreadsheet. For example, when you insert a font with a large point size into a spreadsheet cell, Quattro Pro does not display the font. Instead, the program assigns a font code to the cell; the code tells Quattro Pro which font to use for printing.

You must return to the spreadsheet and increase column widths to accommodate larger fonts and lopped off text or enlarge the print block setting on the Print menu so that all drawn lines appear on the printout.

Printing Graphs

To print a Quattro Pro graph successfully, your printer must support a graphics character set. As a rule, most dot-matrix and all laser and thermal printers can print graphics images. Daisywheel printers cannot print Quattro Pro graphs because they are designed to produce text-only printouts.

When you select the **G**raph Print command, Quattro Pro displays the Graph Print menu shown in figure 8.11. The commands on this menu are similar to those that you use to control the printing of spreadsheet reports—except that these commands control the printing of graphs.

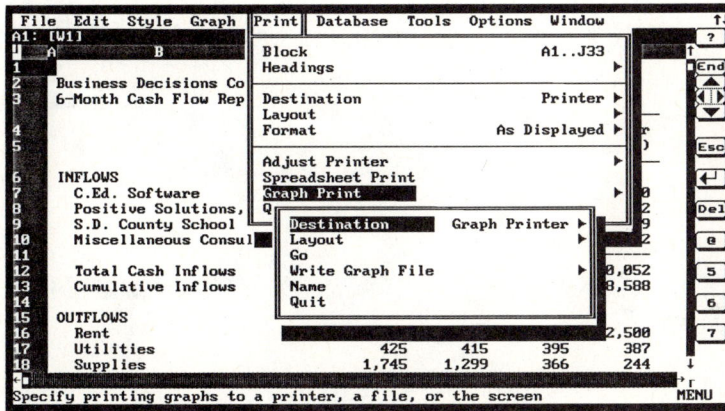

Fig. 8.11
The Graph Print menu.

The basic procedure for printing a graph is as follows:

1. Select /**F**ile **R**etrieve and retrieve a spreadsheet file.

2. Select /**P**rint **G**raph Print **N**ame and select a graph to print.

3. Make changes to the layout options on the **L**ayout menu as desired.

4. Select **A**djust **A**lign to align your printer to the top-of-form.

5. Select **G**raph Print **G**o.

When executed, Quattro Pro begins printing the current graph.

Choosing a Destination

Three **D**estination options are on the Graph Print menu: File, **G**raph Printer, and **S**creen Preview. The default setting is **G**raph Printer.

Choosing **File** causes Quattro Pro to print the graph to a disk file. You print a graph to a file using the same procedure used for saving a spreadsheet in binary file format.

The **Screen Preview** option instructs Quattro Pro to display the graph on-screen so that you can preview the graph's final print form. The preview facility functions exactly the same with a graph as with a spreadsheet (see fig. 8.12).

Fig. 8.12
Previewing a graph on-screen prior to printing.

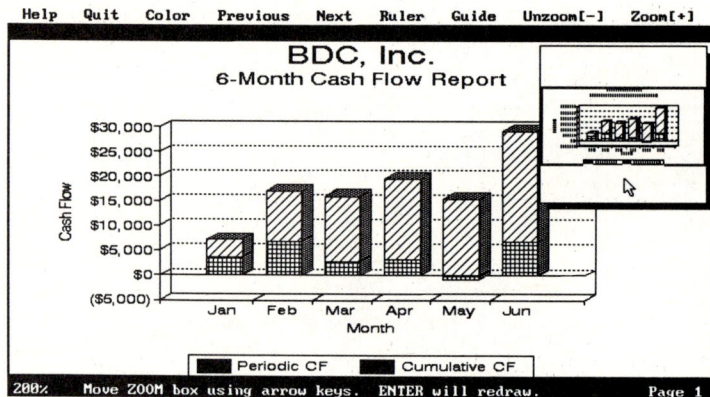

Creating the Layout of the Graph

Select **Layout** to access a menu of commands that enable you to alter the margins, size, page orientation, and aspect ratio of the printed graph. These options are described in the following sections.

Setting the Graph Margins

The **Left Edge** option defines the distance between the left edge of the paper and the location where Quattro Pro prints a graph. The **Top Edge** option defines the distance between the top edge of the paper and the location where Quattro Pro prints a graph. The **Height** and **Width** options determine the height and width of the graph. By altering the margin settings on the Layout menu, you can create virtually any size graph to meet your reporting needs.

The **Dimensions** option specifies whether the edge and size settings are measured in terms of inches or centimeters. The default setting for this command is **Inches**.

Positioning and Shaping the Graph

You can change the orientation of the graph on a printed page using the **Orientation** option. Just like with a spreadsheet, you can print a graph in **Portrait** or **Landscape** orientation.

The **4:3 Aspect** option determines whether Quattro Pro uses the default margin settings or prints a graph using your preferred settings. By default, this option is set to **Yes**. In the default condition, every Quattro Pro graph has a size ratio of four to three. If you want Quattro Pro to print a graph to your own margin specifications, select **No**. In this case, Quattro Pro scales a graph to fit precisely within the area you defined.

Tip | In Chapter 9, you learn how to insert a graph into a spreadsheet. When you want to insert a graph so that the graph entirely fills up any spreadsheet block that you highlight, set the 4:3 Aspect option to No.

Figure 8.13 shows the Layout menu with four custom command settings. The **Left Edge**, **Top Edge**, **Height**, and **Width** commands are set to 1, 2, 3, and 8, respectively. To enable these commands to go into effect for printing, the **4:3 Aspect** command is set to **No**.

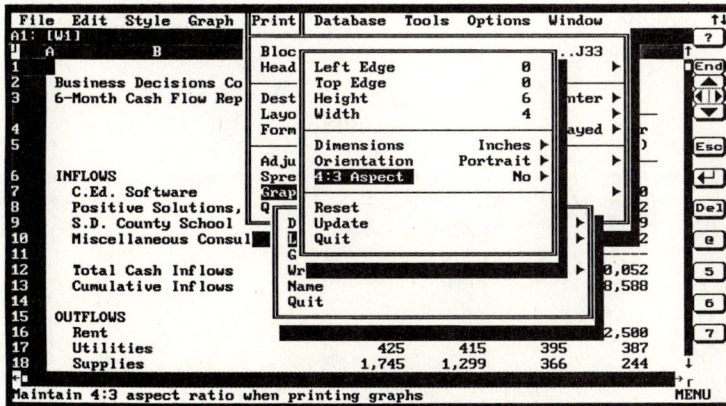

Fig. 8.13
The /Print Graph Print Layout menu.

Sometimes when you alter the shape of a graph, Quattro Pro pauses to build additional fonts. This hesitation occurs whenever the Layout menu command settings are far enough from the default conditions that Quattro Pro requires differently sized fonts.

Updating and Resetting the Layout Options

Choose the Update option to replace the default graph layout settings with new settings that you have created. To restore the last saved set of defaults, select the Reset option. Depending on the speed of your personal computer, Quattro Pro may take a while preparing a graph image for printing. If you need to halt the printing process, press Ctrl-Break, and Quattro Pro returns you to the active spreadsheet.

Creating a Special Graph File

A Quattro Pro graph can be loaded into any graphics image editing program that can read EPS or PIC file formats. You can load EPS files into desktop publishing programs like Ventura and PageMaker, as well as into word processors like Borland's Sprint, WordPerfect 5.1, and Freelance. Some of these programs (like WordPerfect 5.1) have built-in conversion utilities that enable you to covert EPS or PIC files into formats that can be loaded and modified from within the program. Select the Write Graph File command, and Quattro Pro displays the menu shown in figure 8.14.

Fig. 8.14
The Write
Graph File
menu options.

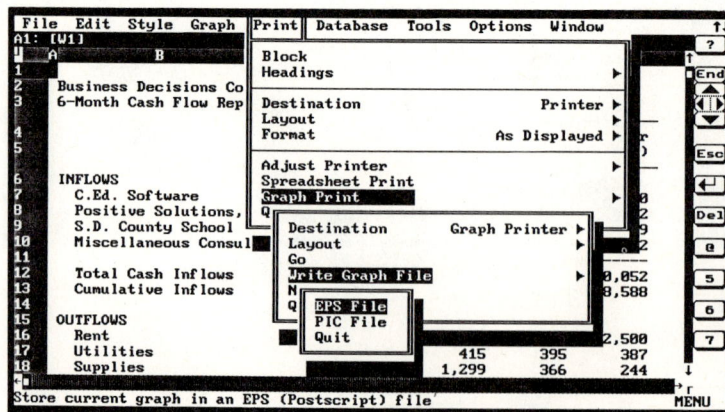

Choose **EPS** to write a graph into an encapsulated PostScript file format. To print an EPS file, you must have a PostScript printer. Choose **PIC** to write a graph into a file format that can be accessed by Lotus 1-2-3 and many of the graphics editors available on the market today.

Questions & Answers

This chapter introduces you to the Print menu commands. If you have questions concerning particular situations that are not addressed in the examples given, look through this question and answers section.

Q: I want to generate a simple printout of a spreadsheet. I specified a print block and selected the **S**preadsheet Print command, but nothing happened. Why?

A: Make sure that your printer is on and in the on-line mode.

Also, Quattro Pro may be unable to write to your printer because your printer may be configured incorrectly. Select /**O**ptions Hardware **P**rinters and reconfigure the **D**efault Printer settings to match your printer's definition.

Q: I am trying to print on legal size paper. Why isn't my **P**age Length definition creating the exact length I need?

A: Use the /**P**rint Layout **D**imensions command to tell Quattro Pro to use **I**nch measurements. Then respecify your page length as 14 inches.

Q: Why are the drawn lines on my spreadsheet appearing as dots and dashes instead of solid lines?

A: Before you can create a printout that reflects all of the presentation-quality options defined on a spreadsheet, specify the **G**raphics Printer options on the **D**estination menu.

Q: Quattro Pro is placing blank gaps in the middle of my printouts that do not exist on the spreadsheet I am printing. Why?

A: You forgot to issue the **A**lign command prior to printing. When the paper in your printer is not aligned properly, Quattro Pro cannot recognize where the top of the form is, and the program prints gaps in the printout.

Q: When I tried to print a binary file on my printer, why didn't the printer reproduce the presentation-quality settings I saved with the file?

A: Several things are possible. First, be sure that you saved the file using the **Binary File** command from the Destination menu, and not the **File** command. In both cases, Quattro Pro appends a PRN extension to a print file. The only way to tell the difference between a text file and a binary file created from the same spreadsheet is that the binary file's size is much larger than the text file.

Second, when you print a binary file, you must use the following syntax: COPY filename /B LPT1. Don't forget to add the PRN extension to the file-name argument. For example, to print a binary file named DATA.PRN, type: *COPY DATA.PRN /B LPT1*. To print a text file with the same name, type: *COPY DATA.PRN PRN*.

Q: Why isn't Quattro Pro printing the fonts that I specified on my spreadsheet?

A: Make sure that the /**Options Graphics Quality** command is set to **Final**. If this command is set to **Draft**, Quattro Pro does not print any Bitstream fonts that are not already built.

Q: I am trying to print a graph. When I specify **Graph Printer** and then **Spreadsheet Print**, my printer hangs up. Why?

A: This is not the procedure for printing a graph. You must use the **Graph Print** command to print graphs and the **Spreadsheet Print** command to print spreadsheets.

Q: I printed a graph using landscape orientation. Why are my margin alignments completely wrong?

A: When you print a graph horizontally, the orientation of the margin commands changes. For example, **Height** becomes **Width** and **Width** becomes **Height**. Return to the **Graph Print Layout** menu and switch the definition for the margin settings.

Q: Why did Quattro Pro cut off the left and right portion of the graph's title text when I printed my graph?

A: Be very careful about choosing new margin, height, and width settings. When you enter a large left margin (say 6) and choose a large **Width** setting, Quattro Pro may not have enough space to print an entire report title. In this case, you can alter the margin and aspect settings, shorten the title by selecting the /**Graph Text** command, or do a combination of both.

Chapter Summary

This chapter discussed many different methods for printing spreadsheets and graphs in rough draft and final draft form. After completing this chapter, you should be able to do the following:

- Print a screen dump of spreadsheet data

- Generate draft form, cell-listing form, and final form printouts of a spreadsheet

- Add headings, headers, and footers to a printout

- Adjust the margins and page length of a printout

- Print in a portrait and landscape orientation

- Add special printing effects using setup strings

- Properly control the movement of paper in your printer

- Print a spreadsheet to text and binary file formats

- Use the Screen Previewer to examine spreadsheets and graphs prior to printing them

- Print a graph on a printer or to a file

- Adjust the margins and aspect settings to alter the shape of a printed graph

- Write a graph to PIC and EPS file formats

Creating, Managing, and Displaying Graphs

In previous chapters, you learned how to enter, edit, view, and print spreadsheet data. You also learned how to improve the style of your spreadsheets and manage multiple documents. Creating versatile, stylish-looking reports is important, yet sometimes it is difficult to get an overall picture of the data just by looking at numbers on a spreadsheet. In this chapter, you learn how to create, manage, and display Quattro Pro graphs.

A Quattro Pro graph offers several advantages over a numerical report. Graphs visually point out variations in data. Graphs summarize data, enabling you to consider several different relationships at the same time. Most importantly, graphs disclose trends and pinpoint problem areas that otherwise may go unnoticed on a spreadsheet.

The first section of this chapter reviews the Graph menu commands and the system hardware that you need to display Quattro Pro graphs. The next section defines the utility and anatomy of a graph. You learn Quattro Pro's graph terminology, survey each of the elements that make up a graph, and study the 10 different graph styles that Quattro Pro can display. The sample graphs shown in this section use real-world applications. After reviewing these sample graphs, you will better understand how to match your data with the most appropriate graph style.

The chapter continues by demonstrating two ways to create a basic Quattro Pro graph: from the ground up and by using the Fast Graph command. This command enables you to preview your spreadsheet data as a plain, unformatted graph—an important feature when you have 10 distinct styles to choose from.

Next, you learn how to enhance the appearance of the basic graph by adding titles, legends, and customized fonts.

The final section in this chapter shows you how to manage graph files. When you save graph settings with a spreadsheet, a change on the spreadsheet is reflected on the graph. Finally, you learn two techniques for displaying your graphs: in a slide show and inserted as a "live graph" onto the spreadsheet from which the graph was created.

The rules and techniques for printing Quattro Pro graphs appear in the last half of Chapter 8.

Reviewing the Graph Menu

The Graph menu consists of three types of commands: graph building commands, graph customizing commands, and graph management commands. This chapter covers all of the graph building commands, except for Annotate, and all of the graph management commands. Chapter 10 offers complete coverage of the graph customizing commands and Quattro Pro's graph annotation tool.

Reviewing the Commands

The graph building commands, found at the top of the Graph menu, are used to select a graph style, to record the location of the data to be graphed, and to add text to the basic graph (see fig. 9.1).

**Fig. 9.1
The Graph
menu
commands.**

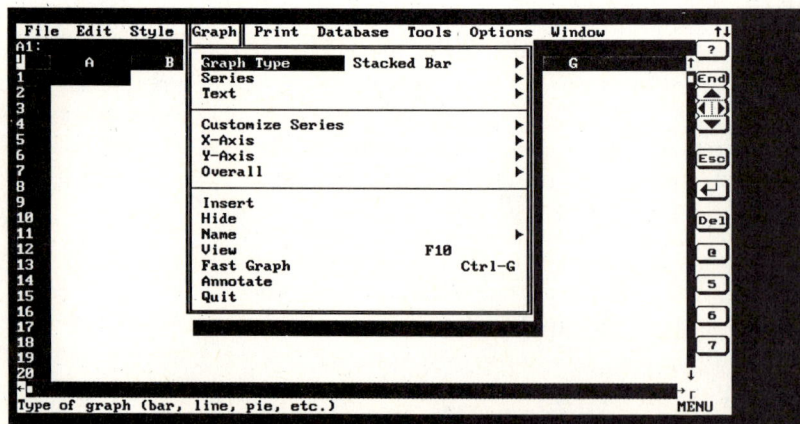

The graph customizing commands, found in the middle of the Graph menu, are used to customize an individual data series, to change the x- and y-axis scaling, and to format the background of the whole graph (graph customizing commands are covered in Chapter 10).

The graph management commands, located at the bottom of the Graph menu, perform operations on a graph after the graph is created. With graph management commands, you can insert a graph onto a spreadsheet, assign a graph name to a particular spreadsheet, or view a graph on your screen. The final menu command, **Annotate**, calls up a Quattro Pro editing tool that you can use to add finishing touches to your graphs (the **Annotate** command is covered in Chapter 10).

Table 9.1 explains the functions of the Graph menu commands. Like most other Quattro Pro commands, Graph menu commands are intuitive. For example, to use a particular type of graph select **Graph Type**. To add text to a graph, select **Text**, and to insert a graph onto a spreadsheet, select **Insert**.

Table 9.1
Graph Menu Commands

Command	*Description*
Graph Type	Selects one of the 10 graph types
Series	Specifies a spreadsheet cell block to graph
Text	Adds titles and a legend to a graph
Customize Series	Customizes the display of a data series
X-Axis	Adjusts the display and scaling of the x-axis
Y-Axis	Adjusts the display and scaling of the y-axis
Overall	Adds lines, patterns, and colors to a graph
Insert	Inserts a copy of a graph onto a spreadsheet
Hide	Removes a copy of a graph from a spreadsheet
Name	Creates, uses, and deletes named graphs
View	Displays a graph using the current graph settings
Fast Graph	Produces a rudimentary graph using a cell block
Annotate	Adds text, lines, arrows, and shapes to a graph

Tip | After you create the basic graph, press F10 to display the graph on-screen. As you add extra features to a graph, you can re-examine the new graph settings by pressing F10 or selecting /Graph View.

Reviewing Hardware Requirements for Creating Graphs

Quattro Pro enables anyone to create a graph, but to view a graph, your system must have the correct display hardware. Your screen and the display adapter card must be able to display graphics. If your system does not have a graphics display adapter, you cannot view a created graph on-screen.

If you are using an older PC or XT system, you may not have a graphics display adapter. Although you cannot view graphs on-screen, you still can print them.

Fortunately, most of today's PCs come equipped with at least a monochrome graphics display adapter (see Appendix A for a complete list of the display adapters that Quattro Pro supports). To view Quattro Pro graphs, you must have one of the following types of display adapter systems or compatible:

    Hercules monochrome graphics card
    Color Graphics Adapter (CGA)
    Enhanced Graphics Adapter (EGA)
    Video Graphics Adapter (VGA)

A monochrome graphics card shows Quattro Pro graphs in black and white, and the CGA, EGA, and VGA cards can show graphs in color. EGA and VGA adapter systems display graphics with a much sharper resolution than the monochrome or CGA systems.

Tip | Select /**O**ptions **H**ardware **S**creen **R**esolution and pick the highest resolution that your display adapter supports. See Chapter 6 for complete coverage of the **O**ptions menu commands that affect the display of graphs.

If your PC does not have any of the preceding graphics systems, you may view your graphs if you have the right printer or plotter. To view a graph, print the graph to the printer specified by the /**O**ptions **H**ardware **P**rinters **D**efault Printer command. If you own a dot-matrix or laser printer, your graph printouts contain various shades of gray.

Understanding Graphs

Graphs can provide a clearer medium for analyzing your spreadsheet data. In this section, the benefits of using graphs are covered; then you learn about the anatomy of a graph—the parts of a graph. Finally, you are introduced to the types of graphs that Quattro Pro offers.

Utility of Graphs

Graphs help you arrive at conclusions about spreadsheet data. Moreover, graphs point out problem areas with a clarity often not available with even the most comprehensive spreadsheet reports (see fig. 9.2).

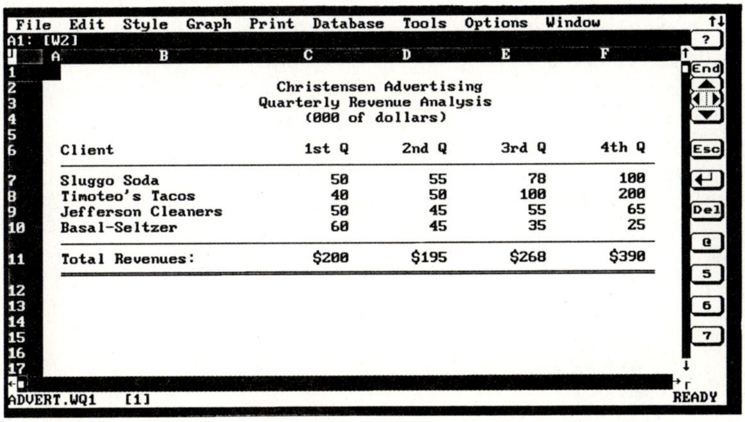

Fig. 9.2
The Christensen
Advertising
spreadsheet
report.

The spreadsheet in figure 9.2 shows that Christensen's revenues nearly doubled over the course of the year (from $200,000 to $390,000). The report also shows that the firm's growth in revenues dipped between the first and second quarters (from $200,000 to $195,000).

Now look at the same report displayed in the form of a stacked-bar graph (see fig. 9.3). Graphs sometimes display data trends that you didn't anticipate. For example, take another look at figure 9.3 and see whether you can spot a third, less obvious trend.

Notice that during the first and second quarters, revenues were divided evenly among all four clients. In the third and fourth quarters, however, Basal-Seltzer revenues declined, and Timoteo's Tacos revenues skyrocketed.

**Fig. 9.3
A stacked-bar
graph created
from
Christensen's
spreadsheet
report.**

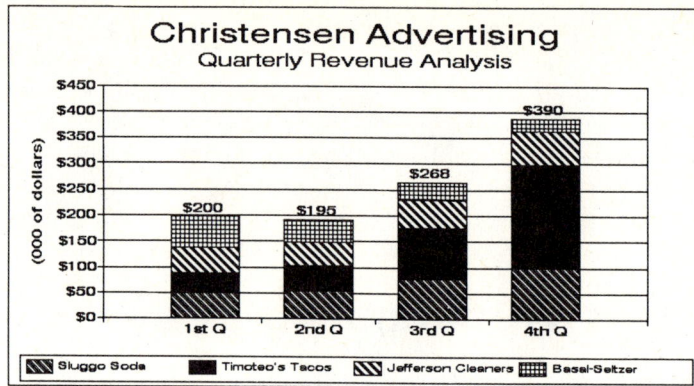

The stacked-bar graph indicates that something is awry with the Basal-Seltzer account. Did Basal-Seltzer spend less with Christensen and more with other advertisers? Is Basal-Seltzer suffering fiscal difficulties? Should management now pay special attention to the Timoteo's Tacos account? These are the types of questions that an analyst would consider when reviewing this graph.

Graphs are an important form of expression because they convey in a picture what sometimes is hard to articulate. Imagine the difficulty of evaluating revenue growth trends on a spreadsheet report if Christensen had 100 clients instead of only four.

Anatomy of Graphs

Just as a medical student learns about the parts of the human anatomy, so must a Quattro Pro user learn about the elements that make up a graph. This section teaches you about the purpose and function of each part of a Quattro Pro graph and introduces the terminology that defines each part.

Line graphs illustrate how data changes over time. In this type of graph, the *x-axis* (horizontal axis) represents time, and the *y-axis* (vertical axis) represents a data category. When you locate an intersection between the two axes, you have a *data point*.

Most graphs have several data points, each one representing a different intersection between the x-axis and y-axis. A collection of x-axis data points forms a *data series*, as does a collection of y-axis data points. On a spreadsheet, a data series appears in a cell block. *Cell blocks* can be vertical (as in block D5..D10) or horizontal (as in block D5..H5). You tell Quattro Pro which data to display on a graph by specifying the cell block.

Quattro Pro also can use spreadsheet *labels* when displaying a graph. For example, a block of spreadsheet labels can appear on a graph to signify a time period (January, February, March, and so on), to identify the parts of a group (Client A, Client B, or Client C), or to display as a title.

Together, the x- and y-axis data points form a *scale*.

Graphs also are used to show the relationship between two or more categories of data; one category is expressed as a function of another. *Function* implies that one of the categories is a dependent variable and the other is an independent variable. This means that the value of one category depends on the value of the second.

For example, business owners express profit as a function of revenue. When revenue increases, profit also is expected to increase. Profit is the dependent variable, and revenue is the independent variable.

Research psychologists graph intelligence as a function of age, because it generally is accepted that people get smarter as they grow older. In this case, the dependent variable, intelligence, depends on the independent variable, age.

Family physicians plot approximate weight as a function of height to monitor a child's growth. Again, it is expected that as children get taller (independent variable), they gain weight (dependent variable).

How do you know when a data category is an independent or a dependent variable? Common sense dictates this relationship much of the time. Consider the family physician example. Children do not get taller just because they gain some weight.

Now consider the graph pictured in figure 9.4. This graph expresses the height-weight relationship. The range of height values appears on the x-axis

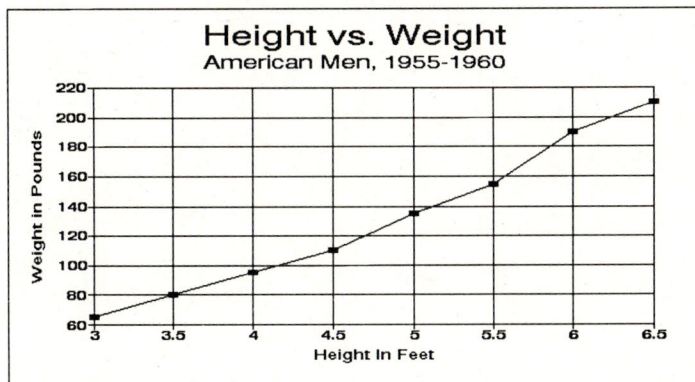

Fig. 9.4
A graph showing the relationship between height and weight for American males.

and the range of weight values on the y-axis. Together, the x-axis data points form a data series, as do all of the y-axis data points.

The hyphens that cross the axes beside each weight and height are called *tick marks* and are used to mark off regular intervals in the scale of that axis. Notice that the x-axis is scaled at intervals of 1/2 foot, and the y-axis scale is marked off in intervals of 20 pounds.

Each pair of values on a spreadsheet report corresponds to exactly one data point on a graph. In this example, therefore, each height on the x-axis corresponds to a weight on the y-axis, and together these paired values can be found on the original spreadsheet report.

Quattro Pro can express data relationships using 10 different styles of graphs. Many of these graphs share the same anatomy as the examples just described.

Basic Graphs

The first step in the process of creating a basic graph is selecting a graph style for your data. When you select /Graph Type, Quattro Pro displays a style options box (see fig. 9.5). Often, you can use two or three graph styles to display the same data. For example, data on a bar graph also can be shown on a rotated bar graph or on a line graph. To change the graph type after a graph has been created, re-select the /Graph Type command and pick a new style.

Fig. 9.5 Choosing a graph style from the Type menu.

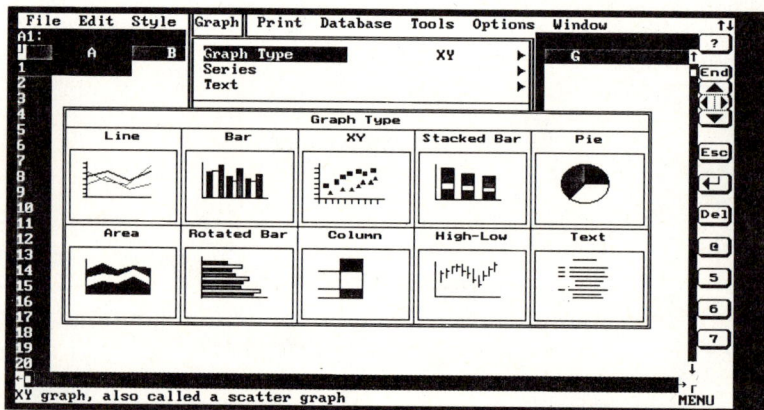

At other times, the data is so specific that it makes sense only when viewed using a particular graph style. For example, the high-low (open-close) graph plots a range of prices for a firm's stock. This data makes little sense displayed on a pie or column graph.

Take a look at all 10 graph styles. As you examine each style, pay close attention to the types of data that work well with each graph type.

Line Graphs

The line graph is one of the most recognized graph types. Professionals in the business and scientific communities use line graphs to show a progression of values over a period of time.

A line graph, for example, is good for summarizing monthly sales data from an annual report or plotting the results of an IQ test taken over an 80-year period. In either case, because time is the independent variable, time is plotted on the x-axis (see fig. 9.6).

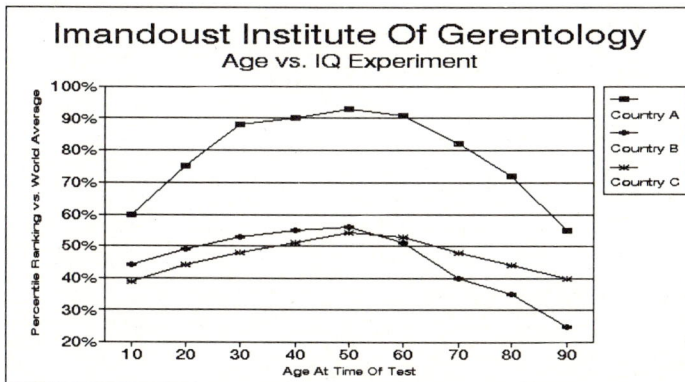

Fig. 9.6
A line graph showing the IQ test results for three countries over an 80-year period.

This graph shows that citizens from country A have higher tested IQ's than citizens from countries B and C. This result can occur, for example, if B and C are underdeveloped countries and A is a developed nation. An interesting trend, however, is that regardless of a country's percentile ranking versus the world, the tested IQ's for all three countries decline as their citizens grow older.

A line graph provides a useful way to track trends over time and to predict future irregularities using current data.

Bar Graphs

The bar graph is useful for comparing the values of different items at set periods in time. The primary advantage of a bar graph is that it clearly illustrates differences in the magnitude of the data: the higher the bar, the bigger or larger the value.

In figure 9.7, the bar graph is used to summarize the results of a six-month crop production report for two products: dates and nuts.

**Fig. 9.7
A bar graph showing a six-month crop production report.**

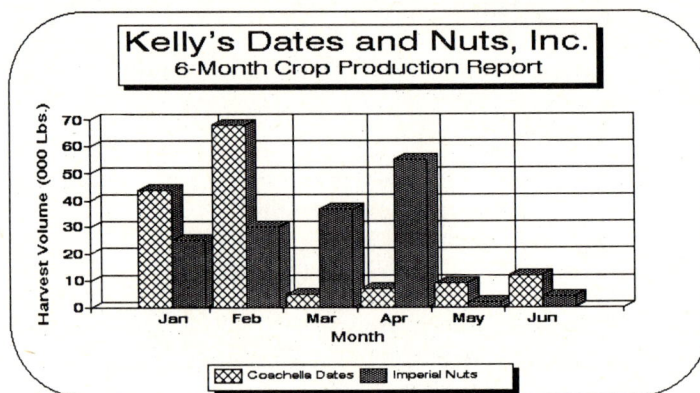

On the bar graph spotting the peak seasons for dates and nuts is easy to do by examining the different bar heights. According to this report, date production peaks in February, and nut production peaks in April. Because those months are the peak for harvesting, the months immediately following the peak months have the lowest production.

XY Graphs

The XY graph (also called scatter graph) is uniquely different from the graphs discussed so far. This graph type is used commonly in social science research to relate the value of one economic variable to another.

At first glance, an XY graph resembles a line graph. The x-axis and y-axis, however, are each scaled with numeric data. In most of the graphs you have seen so far, the x-axis has represented a point in time, for example, a month or a quarter. Generally, XY graphs directly relate one set of data to one or more other sets of data—without regard to time.

An XY graph, for example, is useful for showing the relationship between production volume, revenues, and costs for a manufacturing firm (see fig. 9.8).

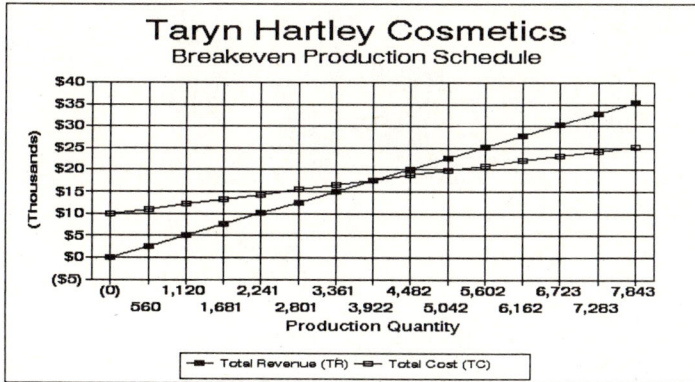

Fig. 9.8
An XY graph showing total revenues, total costs, and production quantity for a manufacturing firm.

The XY graph shown in figure 9.8 plots a range of production volumes on the x-axis. The x-axis measurement is not time; this measurement is production quantity. The associated costs and revenues at each production level appear on the y-axis.

Stacked-Bar Graphs

The stacked-bar graph is a combination of the bar graph and the area graph. To create this type of graph, Quattro Pro first sums the value of each item in a data set. The program then plots the total value at a specific period in time, showing the contribution that each item makes to the total.

The stacked-bar graph pictured in figure 9.9 shows total sales per quarter. This graph also breaks down sales by territory for each quarter.

The stacked-bar graph is useful for looking at broader performance statistics (total sales) and for evaluating individual performance statistics (territory sales).

Pie Graphs

The pie graph shows the contribution of individual values to a whole. The individual values are called *slices*, and the whole value is called the *pie*. Fig-

Fig. 9.9
A stacked-bar graph showing total quarterly sales by territory.

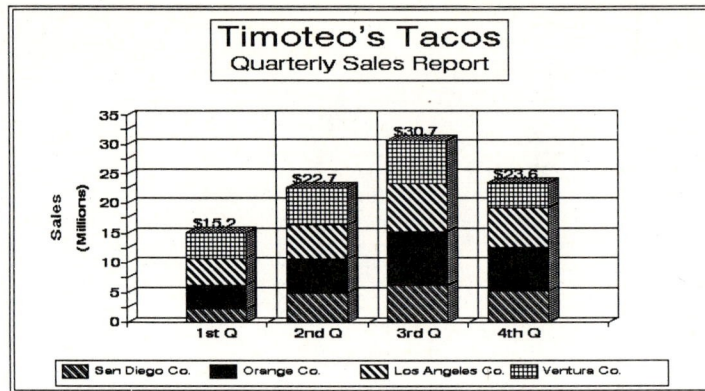

Fig. 9.10
A pie graph showing allocated expenses in a household budget.

ure 9.10 shows the percentage of total expenses allocated to each category in a sample household budget.

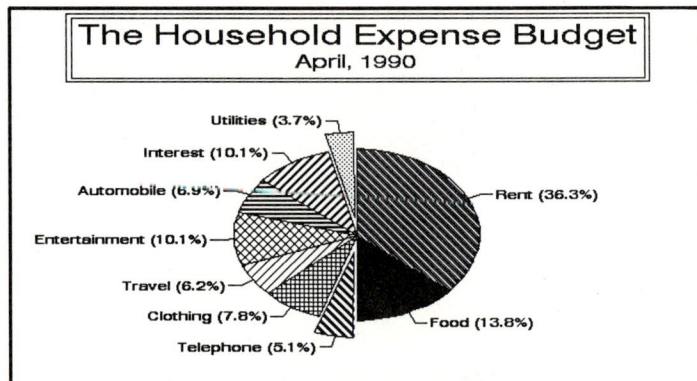

The two smallest pieces of this pie are shown set slightly out of the pie. This technique, called *exploding*, draws attention to key figures in the graph.

Like the column graph, the individual parts of the pie graph may be formatted to display values instead of percentages.

Area Graphs

The area graph is a combination of the line graph and bar graph. This graph type emphasizes changes in magnitude (like a bar graph) at a point in time and reveals trends over time (like a line graph). When plotting two or more data series, Quattro Pro stacks each data series on top of the other to convey a sense of "total area" for the graph. For example, figure 9.11 is a graphic representation of Kelly's 12-month production report, part of which is shown in figure 9.7.

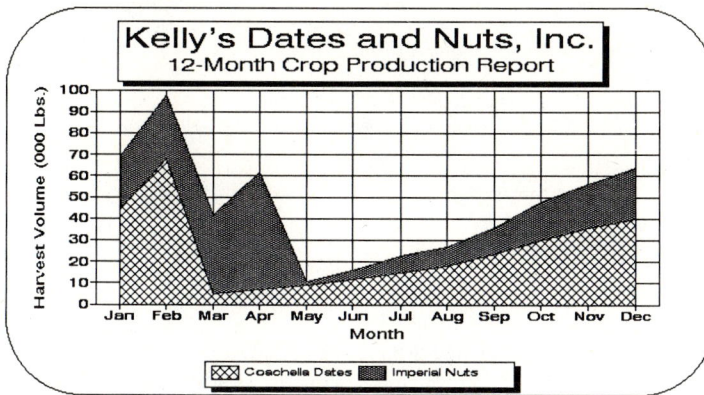

Fig. 9.11
An area graph showing a 12-month crop production report.

This report shows Kelly's total harvest volume for each month and the contribution made individually by dates and nuts. By looking at the entire graph, you also see how Kelly's total date and nut production volume fluctuates during the year.

Rotated Bar Graphs

The rotated bar graph is strikingly similar to the bar graph; this graph style is simply a bar graph turned on its side. Here, the x-axis and y-axis are reversed so that the graph bars extend horizontally.

The decision to use a rotated bar graph instead of a bar graph (or vice versa) is one of aesthetics. If you prefer the way a bar graph displays certain data, use the bar graph. Typically, rotated bar graphs are used to illustrate the results of a competitive event. A sales competition, a leg race, or a typing test are examples of such events. Often, this graph type is used to express data already displayed on a bar graph. Figure 9.12 shows the rotated bar graph form of the data displayed in figure 9.9.

Fig. 9.12
A rotated bar graph showing quarterly sales totals by territory.

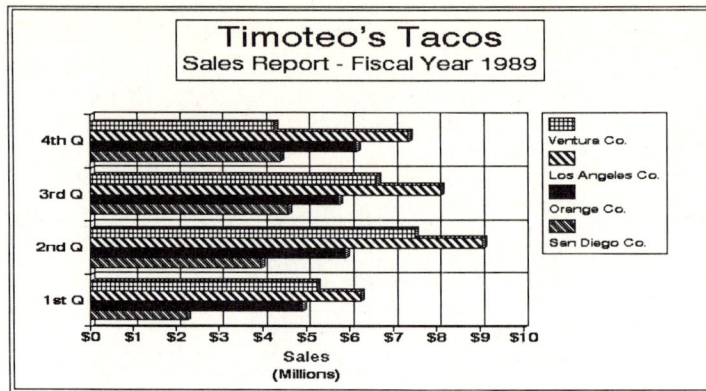

Timoteo's Tacos
Sales Report - Fiscal Year 1989

4th Q
3rd Q
2nd Q
1st Q

$0 $1 $2 $3 $4 $5 $6 $7 $8 $9 $10

Sales
(Millions)

Ventura Co.
Los Angeles Co.
Orange Co.
San Diego Co.

Column Graphs

The column graph, like the pie graph, shows the contribution of individual values to a whole. The individual values in a column graph also are called *slices*. Quattro Pro stacks the slices vertically, one on top of each other, to form the column. The column graph allows you plenty of room to create label descriptions for Quattro Pro to display next to each slice.

The column graph shown in figure 9.13 displays a typical college student's expense budget. The height of the bar is the expected annual expense, and the sections within the bar indicate the portion of the annual expense allocated to tuition, books, rent, and so on.

Fig. 9.13
A column graph showing allocated expenses in a student budget.

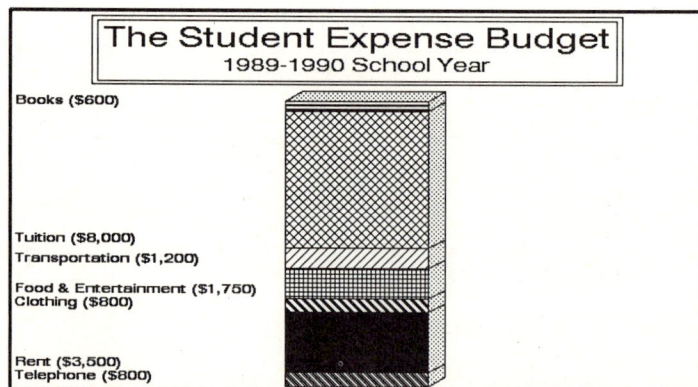

The Student Expense Budget
1989-1990 School Year

Books ($600)

Tuition ($8,000)
Transportation ($1,200)

Food & Entertainment ($1,750)
Clothing ($800)

Rent ($3,500)
Telephone ($800)

Like a pie graph, the individual parts of the column graph may be formatted to display percentages instead of values.

High-Low (Open-Close) Graphs

The high-low (open-close) graph is a data-specific graph. To use this graph properly, you need the high and low price of a stock at some point in time. You also may include the opening and closing prices to provide a complete assessment of a stock's performance (see fig. 9.14).

Although generally used to plot stock performance data, you can use a high-low graph to plot high, low, open, and close prices for other commodities (gold, silver, pork bellies). You also can plot any item where you may want want to track high and low numbers only (temperatures, prices of homes, or interest rates).

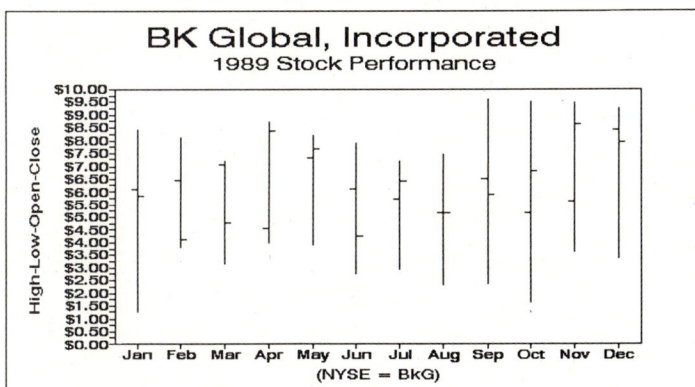

Fig. 9.14
A high-low (open-close) graph showing the one-year performance for BK Global, Incorporated stock.

The top of the vertical bar on this graph represents the high price, and the bottom of the bar represents the low price of the stock at the end of each month. The small, vertical bar facing right indicates the opening price, and the bar facing left shows the closing price.

Text Graphs

A text graph is radically different from any graph covered so far. This type of graph has no x-axis, no y-axis, and no data series. Instead, a text graph consists of only text and special graphics available with the **A**nnotator tool (covered in Chapter 10).

A popular use for the text graph is to draw an organizational chart illustrating the hierarchy of management in a firm. Another use for a text graph is to display two or three simple, enlarged words on the screen. Then, using Quattro Pro's "slide-show" capability, you can flash text graphs that say "Sales Up!" or "Increased Profits!" during a presentation.

Creating a Basic Graph

With Quattro Pro, you can create a basic graph in two ways: from the ground up or using the **Fast Graph** command. Although both methods achieve roughly the same result, the **Fast Graph** command is much easier to use.

When you execute the **Fast Graph** command, Quattro Pro evaluates a selected block of data on the active spreadsheet and builds a graph from that block.

Preselecting a Block

Building Quattro Pro graphs with the **Fast Graph** command is easy when you know how to preselect a block to graph. This *preselecting* technique is discussed in Chapter 3.

You can preselect a cell block in two ways:

1. Place the cell selector in the uppermost left cell in the target block, press Shift-F7, press the cursor-movement keys to highlight the target block, and then choose the command you want to execute.

2. Point the mouse arrow at the uppermost left cell in the target block, and press and hold down the left mouse button. Drag the mouse arrow to the last cell in the target cell block and release the button. Execute the command.

The following set of rules describe how Quattro Pro evaluates a preselected block when the block has more rows than columns:

- Each column is considered a single series.

- Labels appearing in the first column are designated as the x-axis labels.

- Labels appearing in the first row are designated as the graph legend labels.

- When the preselected block does not contain labels in the first column or row, Quattro Pro creates a graph without labels or legends.

The following set of rules describe how Quattro Pro evaluates a preselected block when the block has more columns than rows:

- Each row is considered a single series.

- Labels appearing in the first row are designated as the x-axis labels.

- Labels appearing in the first column are designated as the graph legend labels.

- When the preselected block does not contain labels in the first column or row, Quattro Pro creates a graph without labels or legends.

Creating a Fast Graph

When you preselect a block of data on the active spreadsheet and then choose **Fast Graph** from the **Graph** menu, Quattro Pro draws a "bare-bones" graph on-screen. A "bare-bones" graph shows only the basic graph elements: a scaled x-axis, a scaled y-axis, and the graphed data. When the preselected block contains labels in the first row and column, the graph also shows a legend and axes labels.

By default, Quattro Pro creates a stacked bar graph when you choose **Fast Graph**.

Before you choose the **Fast Graph** command, be sure that the preselected block does not contain any blank rows or columns, because Quattro Pro will show the rows or columns as gaps within the graph.

Tip	To remove blank areas from a graph, return to the active spreadsheet and delete all blank rows and columns from the selected data block. Next, reselect the data block, choose Fast Graph, and Quattro Pro redisplays the same graph without the gaps.

The preselected data block shown in figure 9.15 (B5..E9) is ready to be fast graphed. To create a "bare-bones" stacked-bar graph (the default graph type), do the following:

1. Highlight cell block B5..E9 on the active spreadsheet.

2. Choose **Fast Graph** from the Graph menu (or press Ctrl-G, the Ctrl-key shortcut for this command).

Tip	If you choose Fast Graph prior to preselecting a block, Quattro Pro returns you to the spreadsheet and asks you to enter the block address containing the data you want to fast graph.

**Fig. 9.15
A preselected
cell block on a
spreadsheet.**

```
 File  Edit  Style  Graph  Print  Database  Tools  Options  Window      ↑↓
E9: (,0) [W14] 25000                                                     ?
 U  A   B          C           D              E              F           End
 1                                                                       ▲
 2                     California Design Partnership                    ◄||►
 3                     Labor Expense Analysis: 1989                      ▼
 4
 5              Management    Sales Staff    Accounting        Y-T-D
 6     1st Q       45,000       25,000         15,000          85,000     Esc
 7     2nd Q       50,000       27,000         15,000          92,000
 8     3rd Q       55,000       29,000         15,000          99,000     ↵
 9     4th Q       75,000       35,000         25,000         135,000
10     Total:     225,000      116,000         70,000         411,000     Del
11
12                                                                        @
13
14                                                                        5
15
16                                                                        6
17
18                                                                        7
19
20                                                                        ↓
                                                                        →r
LABOR.WQ1    [1]                                                       READY
```

After choosing the **Fast Graph** command, Quattro Pro builds a graph on-
screen (see fig. 9.16). To return to the active spreadsheet, press Enter once.

**Fig. 9.16
A "bare-bones"
stacked-bar
graph created
from the
preselected data
block.**

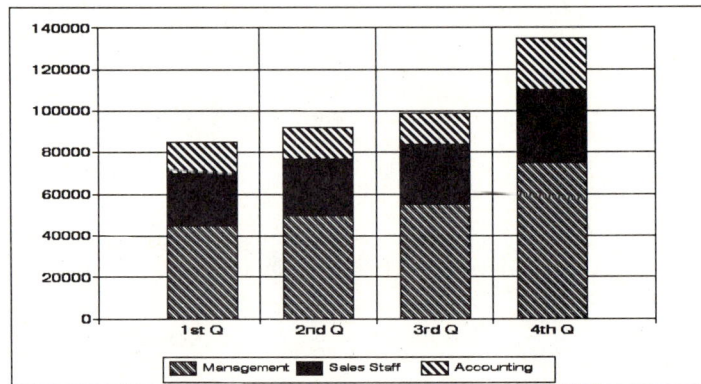

A review of the four-step process that Quattro Pro used to create the fast
graph follows. If you follow this same logic, your own fast graphs will make
sense.

1. The selected block has more rows than columns—follow the first set
    of rules outlined above.

2. Create x-axis labels using the labels appearing in the first column of
    the block (B6..B9).

3. Create a legend using the labels appearing in the first row of the
    block (C5..E5).

4. Use the remaining row data (C6..E9) to create four unique series.

Because fast graphs are so easy to create, they are natural "what if?" analysis tools. After you make a fast graph, choose **Q**uit from the **G**raph menu to return to the active spreadsheet. Now modify any of the values in your graph block. When the data is edited to your satisfaction, press F10 (or Ctrl-G) to regenerate a new fast graph.

This approach to building graphs requires minimal effort on your part. The major drawback of using this method is that the **F**ast Graph command interprets only one block of data. When evaluating that block, Quattro Pro builds a graph based on one of only two possible conditions: # of columns > # of rows or # of rows > # of columns.

But what if the number of rows equals the number of columns? Or what if you want to use data from different locations on the same spreadsheet?

The **F**ast Graph command cannot meet all possible graph building needs. In fact, this command does not offer the flexibility that custom graph building provides.

Building a Customized Graph

The Series menu commands enable you to choose up to six data series to graph. The primary advantage of using Series menu commands instead of the **F**ast Graph command is that you can select the data series that appears on the graph.

In Quattro Pro, a valid series can be numbers in adjacent rows or columns or numbers from different parts of the same active spreadsheet.

When you choose /**G**raph **S**eries, Quattro Pro displays the Series menu. The commands found on this menu appear in table 9.2.

Table 9.2
Series Menu Commands

Command	Description
1st-6th Series	Defines up to six data series for Quattro Pro to graph
X-Axis Series	Defines a block containing labels to be used for the x-axis labels
Group	Defines a block of data to be graphed

Tip On an XY graph, the **X-Axis Series** command defines a data series rather than a block containing labels (as with all other graph types). With XY graphs, the x-axis must contain data.

When you choose the **Group** command, Quattro Pro asks you to specify how to create a series from the block of data: by **Columns** or by **Rows**. If you choose the **Columns** option, Quattro Pro assigns each column of values to a series; choosing the **Rows** option assigns each row of values to a series. The benefit of using the **Group** command is that you can avoid specifying each individual series.

Now use the data from the spreadsheet pictured in figure 9.15 to create a basic graph by specifying the data series, one at a time.

Specifying Individual Series

You can specify individual data series, one at a time, and achieve the same result as with the **Fast Graph** command. The benefit of building a graph in this manner is that you can select data series from anywhere on the active spreadsheet. You even can link a graph to data in other spreadsheets open in Quattro Pro's memory or stored on disk. Also, the **Series Menu** command is invaluable when you want to go back and append additional data series to an existing graph.

To build a graph by specifying each individual data series, do the following:

1. Choose **1**st Series from the Series menu.

2. Type the range containing the first series—*C6..C9*, for example—and press Enter to record the first series.

3. Repeat step 2 for the second and third series.

4. Choose **X-**Axis Series from the Series menu.

5. Type the range containing the labels—for example, *B6..B9*—and press Enter to record the x-axis labels.

6. Choose **Q**uit to return to the Graph menu.

7. Choose **V**iew to examine the graph.

At this point, your displayed graph should look like figure 9.16.

Specifying a Group Series

The **G**roup command works like the **F**ast Graph command, except that you can choose how the data series are retrieved from the spreadsheet: by **C**olumn or **R**ow. The **F**ast Graph command does not give you this option, because it retrieves the data series according to the dimensions of the pre-selected data block.

To build a graph by specifying a group data series, do the following:

1. Choose **G**roup from the Series menu.

2. Choose **C**olumns from the Group menu.

3. Type the range containing the data series—*C5..E9*, for example—and press Enter to record the data series.

4. Choose **X**-Axis Series from the Series menu.

5. Type the range containing the labels—*B6..B9*, for example—and press Enter to record the x-axis labels.

6. Choose **Q**uit to return to the Graph menu.

7. Choose View to examine the graph.

At this point, your displayed graph should look like figure 9.16.

The next section introduces techniques for enhancing a basic Quattro Pro graph by adding titles, a legend, and custom fonts.

Enhancing the Appearance of a Basic Graph

So far, you have learned how to build a basic, unadorned graph. Although some of the graphs you create with **F**ast Graph show axes labels or a legend, they often lack a finished quality common to most professional reports. In this section, you learn how to use the **T**ext command to turn a basic graph into a presentation-quality visual report.

The Text menu commands add titles to a graph, append descriptive labels to the x-axis and y-axis, insert a legend, and control all of the fonts appearing on the graph. When you select the **T**ext menu command, the Text menu appears. The Text menu commands are listed in table 9.3.

Table 9.3
Text Menu Commands

Command	Description
1st Line	Adds a main title to a graph
2nd Line	Adds a secondary title to a graph
X-Title	Adds a descriptive label below the x-axis
Y-Title	Adds a vertical label to the left of the y-axis
Secondary Y-Axis	Adds a vertical label to the right of the y-axis
Legends	Inserts and positions a graph legend
Font	Controls the typeface, point size, color, and style of the fonts appearing on the graph

Adding Titles

Use the first five commands on the Text menu to add titles to a basic graph. Titles add definition and lend clarity. For example, the main title generally defines the name of a company or a report. The secondary title clarifies the main title by specifying a relevant time period (Fiscal Year 1989), the name of a department (Sales & Marketing Division), or the abbreviation style used for numbers appearing in the graph (All Values in 000's of Dollars).

You can create other titles to describe specific parts of the graph, such as the x-axis and y-axis data. *Legends* are a type of title—they describe the data series appearing on a graph.

For example, you can create the graph shown in figure 9.17 by using these five commands.

To add a main title to the top of a graph, do the following:

1. Choose **1st Line** from the Text menu.

2. Type the title when prompted.

3. Press Enter to record the title.

4. Press F10 or choose **View** from the Graph menu to review the new graph title.

You can perform this same operation for the remaining four title commands—they work the same. To remove a title from the graph, reselect the

Fig. 9.17
Adding titles to the basic graph.

command, press Esc, and then press Enter to record a blank space in place of the old title.

Figure 9.18 shows the Text menu after all of the titles shown in figure 9.17 are entered.

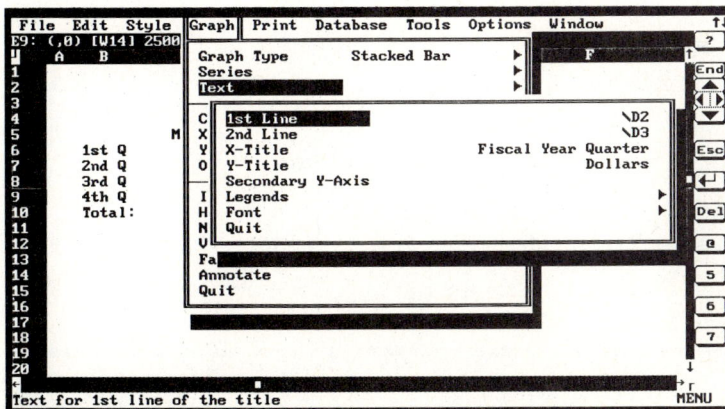

Fig. 9.18
Reviewing the title entries on the Text menu.

Figure 9.18 demonstrates the two ways in which Quattro Pro can recognize title data. When you enter a graph title via the Text menu, Quattro Pro reproduces your keyboard entry at the right margin of the menu. For example, the **X**-Title and **Y**-Title entries reflect the text titles "Fiscal Year Quarter" and "Dollars."

Look at the title entries recorded with the **1st** Line and **2nd** Line commands. These entries are a combination of a backslash and a cell address. To use a label appearing on the active spreadsheet as a graph title, enter the label's cell address preceded by a backslash, or type the text to appear for that title.

Tip	You also may enter bullet characters as part of a graph title by preceding the title text with a backslash character followed by the bullet code. See Chapter 4 for a review of the valid bullet codes.

The graph shown in figure 9.18 conveys more information to the viewer than does the original fast graph shown in figure 9.16.

Adding Legends

The **Legends** command adds a legend to a graph. A legend is a coding system that defines the individual parts that make up a data series on a graph. The legend shown in figure 9.18 shows which section of each stacked bar is representative of management, staff, and accounting labor expense.

To add and position a legend on a graph, do the following:

1. Choose **Legends** from the Text menu.

2. Select **1**st Series, type the text, and press Enter to record the first legend series.

3. Repeat step 2 for each remaining legend series.

4. Choose **Position** and select a legend position from the Position menu. Quattro Pro displays three choices: **B**ottom, **R**ight, and **N**one.

Figure 9.19 shows the Series menu for the **Legends** command.

Fig. 9.19 Reviewing the entries that define each series in the legend.

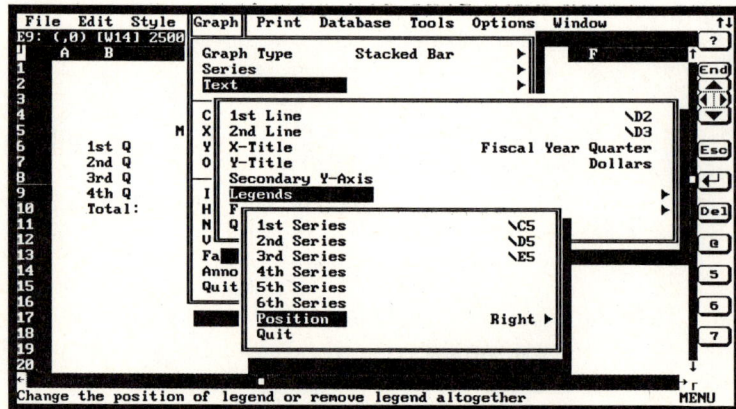

Like the title entries, the legend series entries are a combination of a back-slash and a cell address. To use a label appearing on the active spreadsheet as legend text, enter the label's cell address preceded by a backslash, or you can type the text to appear in the legend box.

Changing the Font

The Font command enables you to change the typeface, point size, style, and color of each text element on a graph. This command is powerful because Font gives you the ability to alter the appearance of text on a graph like a typesetter can manipulate the appearance of a résumé or a restaurant menu.

For example, to change the font used to display a legend's text, select /Graph Text Font Legends and then alter each of the available font characteristics. When you select /Graph Text Font, the Font menu appears. The commands found on this menu are listed in table 9.4.

Table 9.4
Font Menu Commands

Command	Description
1st Line	Changes the font display of the main title
2nd Line	Changes the font display of the secondary title
X-Title	Changes the font display of the x-axis title
Y-Title	Changes the font display of the y-axis title
Legends	Changes the font display of the legend text
Data & Tick Labels	Changes the font display of the tick labels and scaling data

Changing the Typeface

Quattro Pro's default typeface is Bitstream Swiss. To change the typeface used to display the main title on a graph, for example, do the following:

1. Select /Graph Text Font 1st Line.

2. Choose Typeface.

3. Select a new typeface from the menu (see fig. 9.20).

4. Press F10 to review the new typeface on the graph.

**Fig. 9.20
Reviewing the
Typeface menu
selections.**

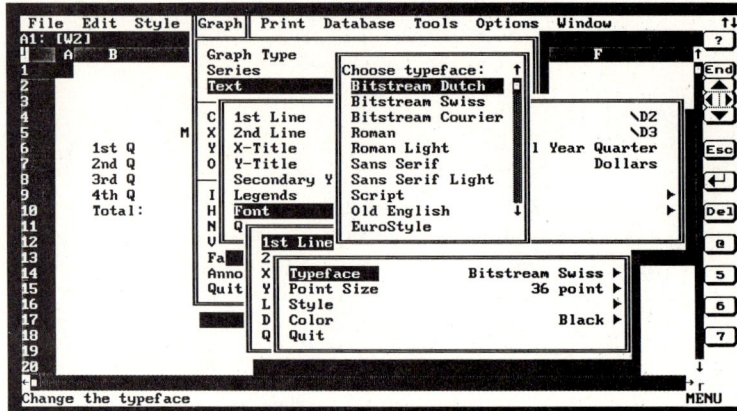

If you select a typeface that has not been built by Quattro Pro, the program displays a `Now building` font message. After a font is built, Quattro Pro does not need to build the font again. (See Appendix B for information about building custom Bitstream fonts).

Changing the Point Size

Quattro Pro has different default point sizes for each text element on a graph. For example, the **1st Line** title appears in 36-point type; the **2nd Line** title appears in 24-point type; and all other text appears in 18-point type.

To change the point size used to display the secondary title on a graph, for example, do the following:

1. Select **/Graph Text Font 2nd Line**.

2. Choose **Point Size**.

3. Select a new point size from the menu (see fig. 9.21).

4. Press F10 to review the new point size on the graph.

Tip | Because LaserJet typefaces have fixed point sizes, you cannot change point size using the **Font** menu commands.

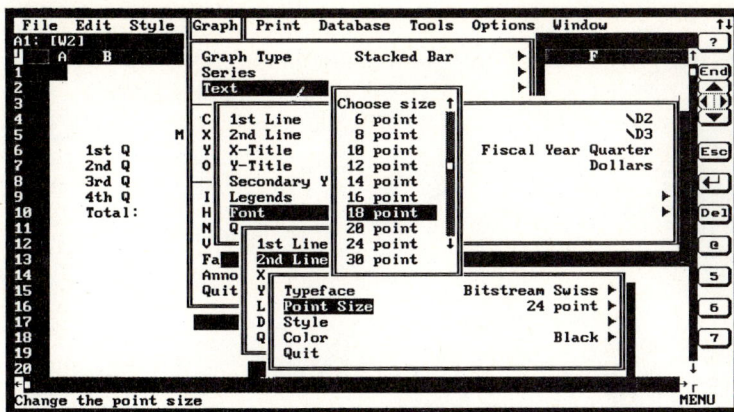

Fig. 9.21
Reviewing the Point Size menu selections.

Changing the Style

Quattro Pro has four different font styles: regular (default), bold, italic, and underlined. To change the font style used to display the text in a legend, for example, do the following:

1. Select /**Graph T**ext **F**ont **L**egends.

2. Choose **Style**.

3. Select a new font style from the menu (see fig. 9.22).

4. Press F10 to view the new font style on the graph.

Fig. 9.22
Viewing the Style menu selections.

Tip | Because LaserJet typefaces have fixed styles, you cannot change style using the **Font** menu commands. Also, not all typefaces support all of the listed styles. If a style is unavailable, Quattro Pro uses the default (regular) style.

To return a text element to its original font style display, select **R**eset from the Style menu.

Changing the Colors

Quattro Pro enables you to change the colors used to display text on a graph with the **Font Colors** command. If you do not own a color monitor, this command still can be used to control the color coding scheme transmitted to color printers and plotters.

To change the colors used to display the data and tick labels, for example, do the following:

1. Select /**G**raph **T**ext **F**ont **D**ata & Tick Labels.

2. Choose **C**olor.

3. Select a new color from the color palette (see fig. 9.23).

4. Press F10 to view the new font color on the graph.

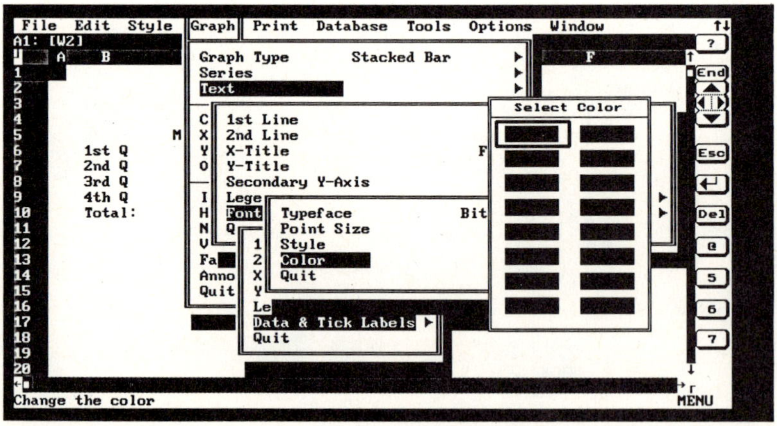

Fig. 9.23
Viewing the
Color menu
selections.

Tip | Use the cursor-movement keys to move around the color palette. If you have a mouse, point and click a color to select it.

The final section of Chapter 9 shows you how to manage your spreadsheet graphs so that you can recall, edit, update, and save them for future work sessions.

Managing Graph Files

Managing graph files is an important part of every graph building work session. When you are building a graph, you must store that graph's settings with the active spreadsheet or the graph is lost if you leave the current spreadsheet without saving the current changes.

A graph's settings include the data series definitions, the title text, the legend, the font definitions, and so on—everything that makes the graph more than just a blank screen.

Fortunately, every time you save a spreadsheet, Quattro Pro also saves the current graph settings with the spreadsheet. The next time you retrieve the spreadsheet, you can press F10, and Quattro Pro will display the graph. This mechanism, however, works with only one graph per spreadsheet and does not actually name the graph.

Eventually, you will want to build more than one graph from a spreadsheet. Then, you need to use the Name menu commands to help manage your graph files. The Name menu commands are defined in table 9.5.

Table 9.5
Name Menu Commands

Command	Description
Display	Displays a new graph using a saved name
Create	Names a graph and saves it to a spreadsheet
Erase	Erases a saved graph name from a spreadsheet
Reset	Erases all saved graph names from the current spreadsheet
Slide	Displays a named graph for a user-specified number of seconds or when any key is pressed.

Naming a Graph

You must name a graph only when you want to create a second graph from the same spreadsheet. You should save every graph under a unique name to ensure that you do not accidentally overwrite one graph's settings with another.

Saving Current Graph Settings

To name a graph and assign that graph's settings to the active spreadsheet, do the following:

1. Select /Graph Name Create. Quattro Pro displays a list of graph names, if any exist.

2. If you are creating a graph, enter a name for the graph when prompted (no extension is necessary). If you are saving an existing graph, highlight the name on the list.

3. Press Enter to assign the graph name to the current spreadsheet.

Displaying a Saved Graph

When you create two or more graphs from the same spreadsheet data, you need a way to choose which group of settings display when you press F10.

To display a graph assigned to the active spreadsheet, do the following:

1. Select /Graph Name Display. Quattro Pro displays a list of graph names, if any exist.

2. Highlight a graph name on the list.

3. Press Enter to retrieve the graph settings assigned to that name.

Tip Before you execute this command, be sure that you have saved the current graph settings, because Quattro Pro replaces the current settings with those of the graph you specified in step 3.

When you execute Graph Name Display, Quattro Pro displays the graph. Press Enter to return to the active spreadsheet.

Erasing a Saved Graph

To erase a graph name from the active spreadsheet, do the following:

1. Select /**G**raph **N**ame **E**rase. Quattro Pro displays a list of graph names, if any exist.

2. Highlight a graph name on the list.

3. Press Enter to erase the graph settings assigned to that name.

Resetting the Current Graph Settings

Finding a particular graph when you have 10 or 20 names to choose from can become tedious. Deleting the entire list of names and then re-saving the current settings under a new name often is easier.

To erase all of the saved graph names assigned to the active spreadsheet, do the following:

1. Select /**G**raph **N**ame **R**eset. Quattro Pro displays a dialog box asking whether you want to Delete all named graphs?

2. Choose **Y**es to erase all graph names or **N**o to cancel the operation.

Displaying a Graph

You already have learned two methods for displaying a graph on-screen: pressing F10 or choosing /**G**raph **V**iew. Two other techniques for viewing graphs go beyond displaying them on-screen.

Creating a Slide Show

This chapter has shown you techniques to create presentation-quality graphics for use in important business meetings or at sales presentations. Quattro Pro's **S**lide command can help you prepare for these meetings by creating a slide show of named graphs.

To use the slide show tool, you first must create a data table on the active spreadsheet that lists the name of the graph and the length of time you want to display the graph on your screen (see fig. 9.24).

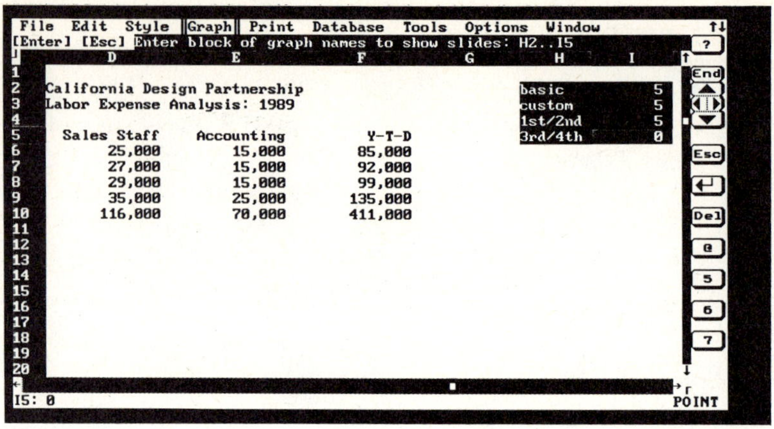

**Fig. 9.24
Entering slide
show
instructions
onto a
spreadsheet.**

The two columns of data shown in figure 9.24 tell Quattro Pro to display four named graphs in a slide show. Notice that each graph name is followed by an integer—this number tells Quattro Pro the number of seconds to pause between each slide. To continue displaying a slide until you press a key, enter *0* next to the graph name.

To create this slide show, do the following:

1. Enter the data table (see fig. 9.24).

2. Preselect the range containing the data table.

3. Choose /**Graph Name Slide.**

Tip | If you omit the column of data containing the slide display intervals, Quattro Pro assumes a value of 0 for each slide. To scroll forward through the slide show, you have to press a key after Quattro Pro shows each slide. Press the Backspace key to scroll backwards through the slide show.

When you execute **Graph Name Slide,** Quattro Pro begins the slide show. If a graph name does not exist, Quattro Pro skips that slide and moves down the list.

Inserting a Graph onto a Spreadsheet

The **Insert** command offers another unique way to view a graph. Using this command, you can insert a graph onto a spreadsheet so that you can view simultaneously the graph and the data that created the graph (see fig. 9.25).

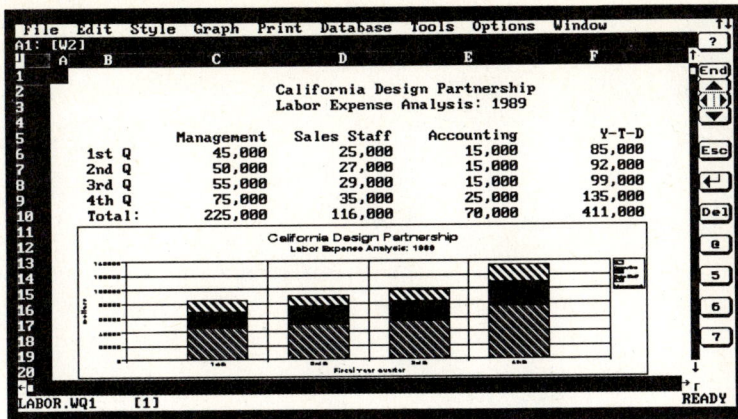

Fig. 9.25
A spreadsheet containing an inserted graph.

For the **Insert** command to work, you must have an EGA or VGA graphics adapter system, and you must invoke Quattro Pro's graphics display mode. You can print a spreadsheet containing an inserted graph as long as you include the graph in the print range and select /**Print Destination Graphics Printer**.

To insert this graph onto the spreadsheet, do the following:

1. Choose /**Options Display Mode B**:Graphics.

2. Preselect the target insert range—for example, C10..E20.

3. Choose /**Graph Insert**.

4. Highlight a graph name from the displayed names list.

5. Press Enter to insert the graph onto the spreadsheet.

When you insert a graph onto a spreadsheet, Quattro Pro floats the graph image in the target block that you specify. If this block is a cell, the inserted image is unreadable. In this situation, you have two choices.

First, you can place the cell selector in the target block and press F10 so that the graph fills your entire screen. This method is only a temporary fix because when you press Enter and return to the active spreadsheet, the inserted graph still appears in the cell. A second, better method for solving this problem is to reselect a larger target block and then select /**Graph Insert** again.

To remove the inserted graph from the spreadsheet, do the following:

1. Preselect the range—for example, B11..F20.

2. Choose /**Graph Hide**.

3. Highlight the graph's name on the displayed names list.

4. Press Enter to remove the inserted graph.

Questions & Answers

This chapter introduces you to the Graph menu commands. If you have questions concerning situations not addressed in the examples given, look through this question and answers section.

Creating a Graph

Q: When I press F10, why don't my graphs appear on my screen?

A: Remember, to display Quattro Pro graphs you must have a graphics adapter system, and to display a graph inserted on a spreadsheet, the /Options Display Mode command must be set to **B**:Graphics.

If you don't have at least a monographics display adapter system, you still can create and print graphs—you just cannot view them.

Q: Why can't I show a fast graph on my screen?

A: Assuming that you have the correct display adapter system, be sure that you have selected a valid block of data to fast graph—Quattro Pro does not do this for you.

The easiest way to create a fast graph is to preselect (highlight) a block of data on the active spreadsheet and press Ctrl-G.

Enhancing the Appearance of a Basic Graph

Q: I created special fonts for a graph, but why aren't they showing when I press F10 to display the graph?

A: Remember, certain Bitstream font typefaces do not support bold and italic styles. Try selecting a different font typeface/style combination.

Q: How do I stop Quattro Pro from building so many fonts when I want to preview a graph?

A: Select /**O**ptions **G**raphics **Q**uality **D**raft to turn font-building off. Quattro Pro substitutes Hershey fonts for every Bitstream font that is not already built. While the on-screen difference between these two font styles is not dramatic, the differences on a graph printout are.

If you want to use Bitstream fonts for printing graphs, select /**O**ptions **G**raphics **Q**uality **F**inal before printing a graph, and Quattro Pro builds the necessary fonts for the printout.

Displaying Graphs

Q: Why do my pie graphs look like pancakes?

A: Don't flip, Jack—it's an easy problem to fix. Select /**O**ptions **H**ardware **S**creen **A**spect Ratio and press the cursor-movement keys until the object on-screen becomes a perfect circle.

Q: I have a color graphics display system; why does Quattro Pro show my graphs in black and white?

A: When your system has a color graphics display, Quattro Pro can display graphs in black and white to give you an idea of how the graphs will appear in printed form. To do this, select /**G**raph **O**verall **C**olor **B&W**.

If you have a color graphics adapter card and a monochrome display, Quattro Pro can display graphs only in black and white.

Q: Why does the slide show I created display only some of the graphs I entered into the data table?

A: Remember, the slide show works only for graph names assigned to the active spreadsheet. If you included the names of graphs from other spreadsheets, Quattro Pro ignores them and continues reading down the column.

Be sure that the graph names match those created for the active spreadsheet. To check, select /**G**raph **N**ame **D**isplay, and Quattro Pro shows a list of the valid graph names for the active spreadsheet.

You may have accidentally deleted all of the named graphs from the active spreadsheet by using the /**G**raph **N**ame **R**eset command. You have to re-create and save each graph again.

Q: Why is the graph I inserted onto a spreadsheet too small to see?

A: To increase the size of the inserted graph, reselect a larger target block and choose /**Graph Insert** again.

Q: Why doesn't the graph I inserted onto a spreadsheet fill the target block that I preselected before executing the **Insert** command?

A: Select /**Print Graph Print Layout** 4:3 **Aspect** and choose **No**. This command forces an inserted graph to fill up the entire target cell block on the spreadsheet.

Chapter Summary

In this chapter, you learned how to build and enhance the basic Quattro Pro graph and how to manage graph files. You also learned techniques for displaying a graph on-screen and inserting the graph onto a spreadsheet.

After completing this chapter, you should understand the following Quattro Pro concepts:

- The anatomy and utility of a basic graph
- Selecting appropriate graph types for different data
- Creating a fast graph from a preselected block of data
- Creating a basic graph from the ground up
- Choosing individual or group series from which to create graphs
- Adding titles, legends, and customized fonts to a graph
- Creating, displaying, and erasing graph names
- Producing a slide show using graph names assigned to the active spreadsheet
- Inserting a graph onto a spreadsheet
- Removing an inserted graph from a spreadsheet

Chapter 10 continues the discussion of building Quattro Pro graphs. In Chapter 10, you learn how to use the graph customizing commands located in the middle of the Graph menu and how to use Quattro Pro's graph editing tool to produce finished-quality, presentation-ready graphs.

10

Customizing and Annotating Graphs

In Chapter 9, you learn how to create and enhance the basic Quattro Pro graph. A basic graph is suitable for applications in which the viewer can draw his or her own conclusions about the graph data. Basic graphs convey general ideas and feelings about spreadsheet data.

To leave a viewer with more than just a general feeling, use the four commands located in the middle of the Graph menu to add impact to the graph. Using the Customize Series command, for example, you can customize the fill pattern in a bar graph, select unique marker symbols for a line graph, create unique color schemes for a pie graph, and turn basic graphs into three-dimensional displays.

You also can customize each element connected to the graph axes. If you don't like the default axis scale, design one that meets your own specifications. If you are having trouble choosing between two graph types for a data set, you also can create a combination graph that uses both.

In this chapter's first section, you learn how to customize individual data series by changing colors, adding patterns, thickening lines, and using marker symbols. You also learn how to impact your data by changing bar widths and appending labels to each point in a data series.

The next section covers the process of creating combination graphs and teaches you how to plot a second y-axis. You also learn the differences in customizing pie and column graphs and the other Quattro Pro graph types.

The chapter continues with a presentation of the rules for customizing a graph's x-axis and y-axis. You learn how to scale an axis manually, format the values associated with tick marks, and switch between a normal and logarithmic display mode.

In the next section, you learn how to customize the overall appearance of a graph by displaying grid lines, designing special foreground and background color combinations, adding boxes around titles and legends, and displaying a graph in three dimensions.

This chapter concludes with an overview of the rules and procedures for using Quattro Pro's built-in Graph Annotator tool.

Reviewing the Customize Series Menu Commands

The 11 commands found on the /Graph Customize Series menu enable you to fine-tune the appearance of a basic graph by customizing its individual parts (see fig. 10.1). Each command works on a specific part of a graph. To change the colors used to display a particular series, for example, select the Colors command. To change the design of the patterns that fill the bars on a bar graph, use the Fill Patterns command.

Fig. 10.1
The Customize Series menu commands.

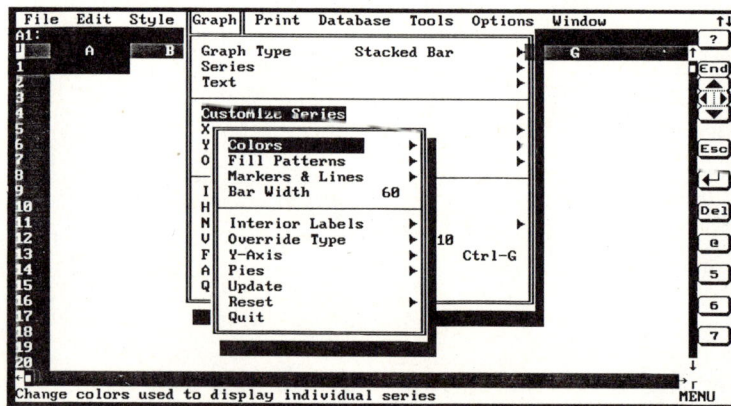

Certain commands on the Customize Series menu require that you select colors, fill patterns, line styles, and marker symbols. When you are operating in text mode, Quattro Pro displays a menu of word choices. For example, the Colors menu contains the names of each available color (see fig. 10.2). To make a selection, just press the boldfaced letter key appearing in the option name, use the cursor-movement keys to move to a selection and press Enter, or click the name with a mouse.

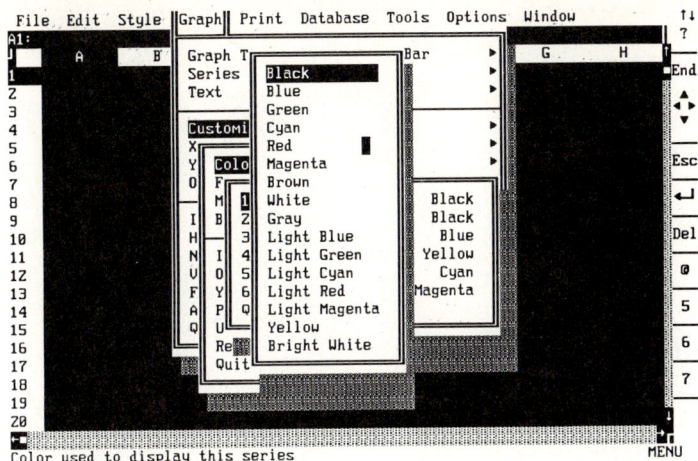

Fig. 10.2 Making a selection from the Colors menu.

If you have a graphics screen display system, and you are operating in graphics mode, Quattro Pro displays "graphic" menus, such as a palette or a gallery. The Colors command displays a coloring palette in graphics mode (see fig. 10.3). To make a selection, highlight the option and press Enter (or click the option with a mouse) to record the new setting.

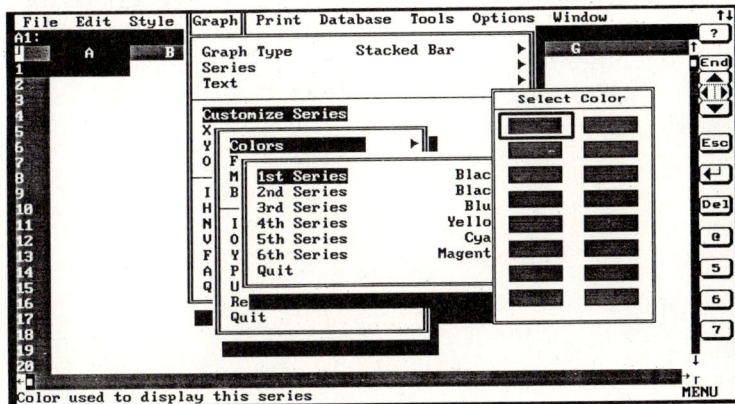

Fig. 10.3 Making a selection from the coloring palette.

All figures and instructions in this chapter assume that you are operating in graphics display mode. To see whether your system can support graphics display mode, select /Options Display Mode. If the selection B: Graphics Mode appears, select that option.

If you are using a monochrome screen display, Quattro Pro displays all data series in black. When you choose any other color on the palette, Quattro Pro displays that data series in white.

Press +, the Expand key, to display the current settings for any **Customize Series** command if the current settings do not display on-screen when you select a particular command.

If you are using the same customizing commands repeatedly, consider selecting **Update** to store those settings as the new default settings for use in other spreadsheets.

Customizing a Graph Data Series

When the default settings that Quattro Pro uses to display a basic graph do not enhance your work, you can use any or all of the following commands to give your graphs "something extra."

Changing Colors

The **Colors** command stores the color settings for each data series on a graph. By default, Quattro Pro assigns a different color to each series so that you can distinguish one from the other. For example, on a line graph where the data series often parallel and intersect each other, colored lines can help you follow the progression of a particular series.

To change the color assignment of a data series, do the following:

1. Select **/Graph Customize Series Colors**. Quattro Pro displays a menu listing six data series and their current color assignments.

2. Choose the number of the series you want to change. Quattro Pro displays the coloring palette.

3. Highlight a color on the palette and press Enter to record the new color assignment for that series.

    Quattro Pro returns you to the Colors menu, where you can select a new series to change.

4. Press Q to return to the Customize Series menu.

Changing Fill Patterns

The **F**ill Patterns command stores the pattern settings for each data series on a bar graph. Fill patterns help to distinguish one data series from the next. Without fill patterns, a viewer has to match the height of each bar to a value on the spreadsheet to distinguish between each data series.

To change the fill pattern assignment for a data series, do the following:

1. Select /**G**raph **C**ustomize Series **F**ill Patterns. Quattro Pro displays a menu listing six data series and their current fill pattern assignments.

2. Choose the number of the series you want to change. Quattro Pro displays the fill patterns gallery (see fig. 10.4).

3. Highlight a pattern in the gallery and press Enter to record the new fill pattern assignment for that series.

    Quattro Pro returns you to the **F**ill Patterns menu, where you can select a new series to change.

4. Press Q to return to the Customize Series menu.

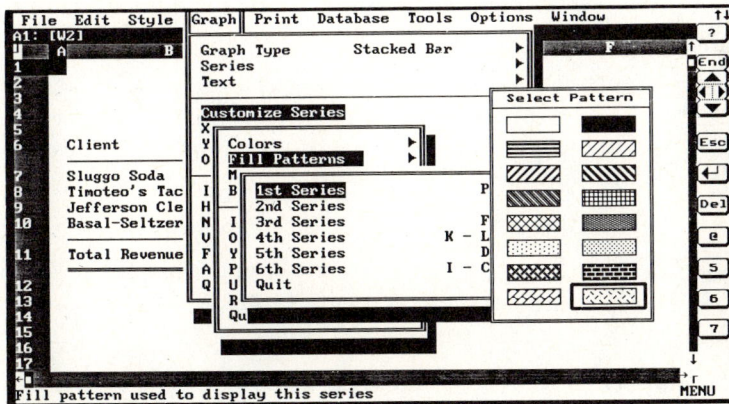

Fig. 10.4
Selecting a fill pattern from the gallery.

The **F**ill Pattern command affects only bar and area graphs. Altering the fill pattern assignments for data series that appear on a pie graph, area graph, line graph, or XY graph has no visible effect on the display of that graph.

If you select /**G**raph **G**raph Type and change a line graph to a bar graph, however, Quattro Pro reflects the new fill pattern assignments. For example, figure 10.5 shows a graph that has custom fill patterns.

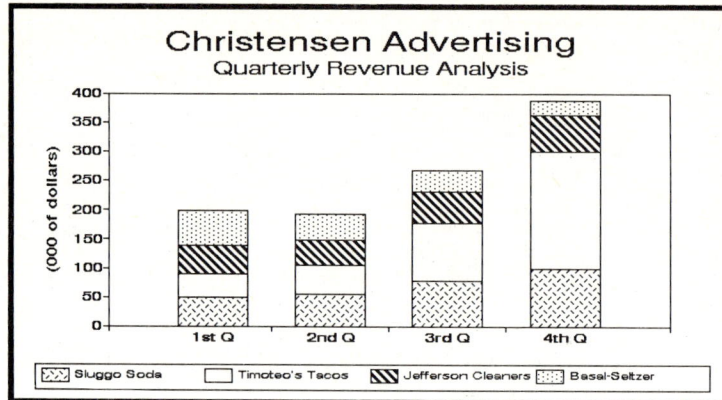

**Fig. 10.5
Creating a
custom look
with fill
patterns.**

Changing Markers and Lines

The **Markers & Lines** command stores the marker symbol and line style settings for each data series on a line and XY graph. This command also enables you to create your own display combinations for markers and lines.

Marker symbols indicate the location of each data point in a series. Without markers, line graphs lose much of their impact because they can describe only an overall trend, rather than a series of intermediate trends. In cases in which showing an overall trend is the objective of the graph, you can control the display of markers and lines.

To change the line style setting for a data series, do the following:

1. Select **/Graph Customize Series Markers & Lines Line Styles.** Quattro Pro displays a menu listing six data series and their current line style assignments.

2. Choose the number of the series you want to change. Quattro Pro displays the line styles gallery (see fig. 10.6).

3. Highlight a line style and press Enter to record the new line style assignment for that series.

   Quattro Pro returns you to the Line Styles menu, where you can select a new series to change.

4. Press Q to return to the Markers & Lines menu.

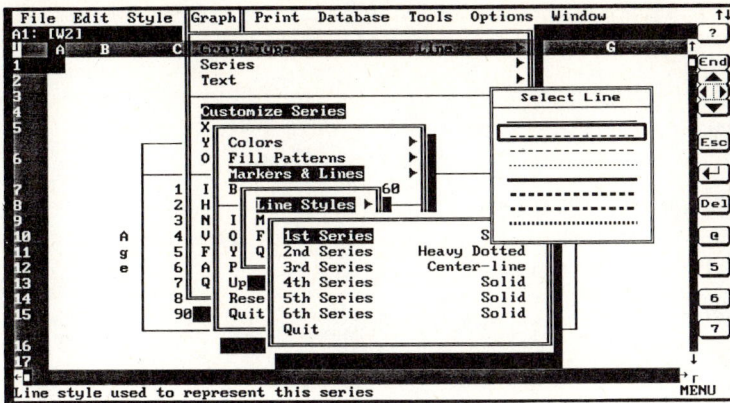

Fig. 10.6
Selecting a new line style from the gallery.

To change the marker symbol setting for a data series, do the following:

1. Select /**Graph Customize Series Markers & Lines Markers**. Quattro Pro displays a menu listing six data series and their current symbol assignments.

2. Choose the number of the series you want to change. Quattro Pro displays the marker symbol gallery (see fig. 10.7).

3. Highlight a symbol in the gallery and press Enter to record the new symbol assignment for that data series.

   Quattro Pro returns you to the Markers menu, where you can select a new series to change.

4. Press Q to return to the Markers & Lines menu.

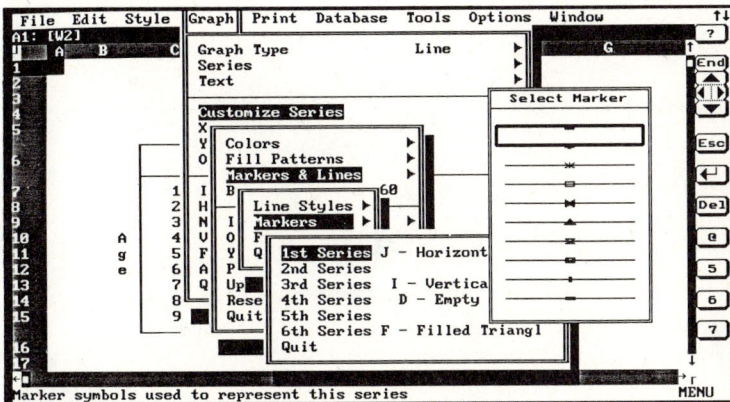

Fig. 10.7
Selecting a new marker symbol from the gallery.

When you want to create a custom display format for markers and lines, do the following:

1. Select /**Graph Customize Series Markers & Lines Formats**. Quattro Pro displays a menu listing six individual data series command choices and one for the entire graph called **Graph**.

2. Choose the number of the series you want to change, or press G to change all six data series. Quattro Pro displays a second menu listing four choices: **Lines**, **Symbols**, **Both**, and **Neither**.

3. Press a letter to select a display combination.

   Quattro Pro returns you to the Formats menu, where you can select a new series to change.

4. Press Q to return to the Markers & Lines menu.

5. Press Q again to return to the Customize Series menu.

Figure 10.8 shows a line graph that has customized line styles and marker symbols.

Fig. 10.8
Enhancing the
appearance of a
line graph with
customized line
styles and
marker
symbols.

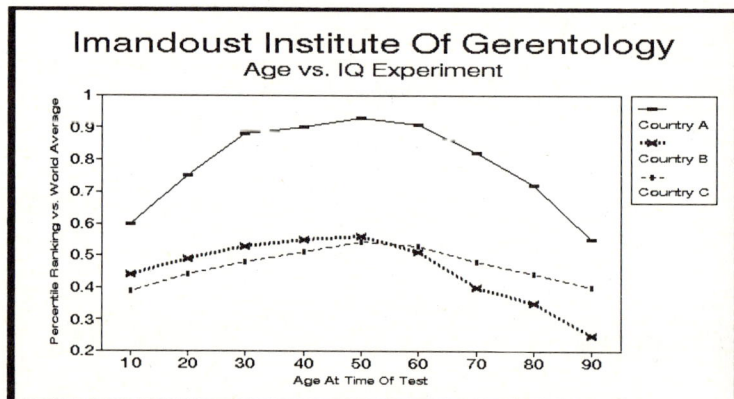

Changing the Width of Bars

The **Bar Width** command stores a value that Quattro Pro uses to determine the width of bars on a bar graph. By default, Quattro Pro creates bar widths that occupy 60 percent of the x-axis (bar) or y-axis (rotated bar) area. You can change this setting to any value in the range between 20 and 90 percent. The lower the value, the thinner the bar; the higher the value, the thicker the bar.

To change the width value that Quattro Pro uses to build bars, do the following:

1. Select /**G**raph **C**ustomize Series **B**ar Width. Quattro Pro displays a dialog box listing the default width setting of 60 percent.

2. Type a number between 20 and 90 and press Enter to record that value.

When you execute this command, Quattro Pro stores the new bar width setting at the right margin of the Customize Series menu, next to the **B**ar Width command.

Press F10 to view the new bar width on the current graph.

Adding Interior Labels

The **I**nterior Labels command places a value or a label from the active spreadsheet directly onto a particular data series on a graph. This command is useful for pointing out the exact magnitude of a data series when the axis scaling is too vague to permit accurate visual inspection. Interior labels also can be labels that, when added to a data series, function as an interior legend.

The **I**nterior Labels command has display restrictions dependent on the type of graph. For example, this command has no effect on area, pie, and column graphs. Interior labels always appear above a data series on a bar graph and to the right of a data series on a rotated bar graph. On a stacked-bar graph, Quattro Pro can display interior labels for only the last, or top, data series.

To add interior labels to a data series, do the following:

1. Select /**G**raph **C**ustomize Series **I**nterior Labels. Quattro Pro displays a menu listing the six data series.

2. Choose the number of the series to which you want to add a label.

3. Quattro Pro returns you to the active spreadsheet. Enter the cell address of a value or label to use.

4. Press Enter to record the address. Quattro Pro displays a second menu listing six placement choices.

5. Select a placement choice from the menu. Quattro Pro returns you to the Interior Labels menu, where you may select a new series to change.

6. Press Q to return to the Customize Series menu.

Figure 10.9 shows a graph that has been customized by thickening the width of the bars and adding interior labels.

Fig. 10.9
The appearance of a basic bar graph enhanced by altering the bar width and adding interior labels.

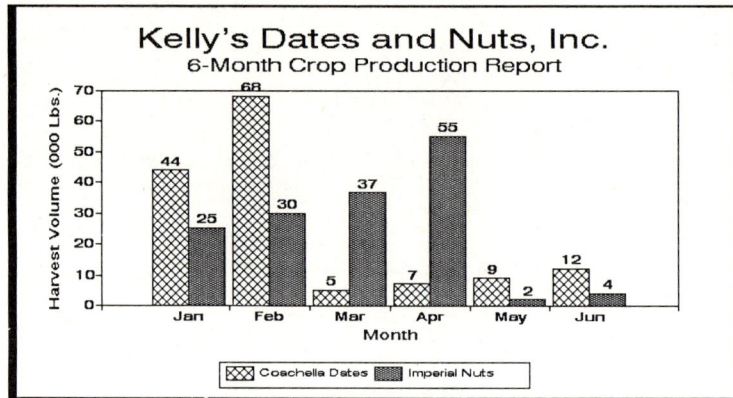

Creating Combination Graphs

If you have difficulty deciding which graph type to use for a particular set of data, consider the following novel approach to graph-building in Quattro Pro: the combination graph. This type of graph displays two graph types simultaneously on one graph.

To create this effect, use the Override Type command on the Customize Series menu. Figure 10.10 shows a combination line and bar graph. This graph plots key financial data used in a firm's employee profit-sharing program. The firm's profits are plotted as a line graph, and the revenue dollars are plotted on a bar graph.

To create a combination graph using the current graph, do the following:

1. Select /Graph Customize Series Override Type. Quattro Pro displays a menu listing six data series.

2. Choose the number of the series you want to change.

3. When prompted, choose Default, Bar, or Line. Quattro Pro returns you to the Override Type menu.

4. Press Q to return to the Customize Series menu.

Press F10 to review the combined graph on-screen.

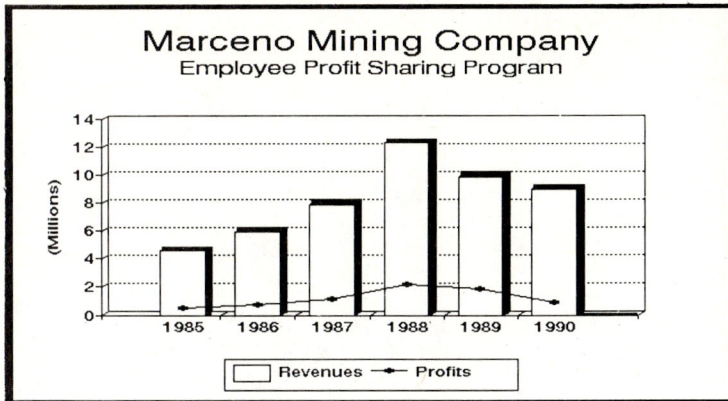

Fig. 10.10 Creating a combination line and bar graph.

If you choose not to override all of the data series, Quattro Pro continues to use the default settings prescribed by the original **G**raph Type command selection.

To return the current graph to its original look, select **D**efault for each altered series on the Override Type menu.

Plotting a Second Y-Axis

The **Y**-Axis command creates a second y-axis on the current graph. This technique is useful particularly for displaying data set values that have dramatically different magnitudes or use completely different systems of measurement.

For example, you have been instructed by your manager to create a bar graph depicting a subsidiary firm's total yearly postage expense versus the parent company's total revenues. Because the difference in the magnitudes of these two data sets is very dramatic, consider creating the dual y-axis bar graph shown in figure 10.11.

To create a graph with a second y-axis, do the following:

1. Select /**G**raph **C**ustomize Series **Y**-Axis. Quattro Pro displays a menu listing six data series.

2. Choose the number of the series you want to plot on the second y-axis.

3. When prompted, choose **S**econdary Y-Axis. Quattro Pro returns you to the Y-Axis menu.

4. Press Q to return to the Customize Series menu.

Press F10 to review the graph with two y-axes.

Fig. 10.11
A bar graph
with two y-axes.

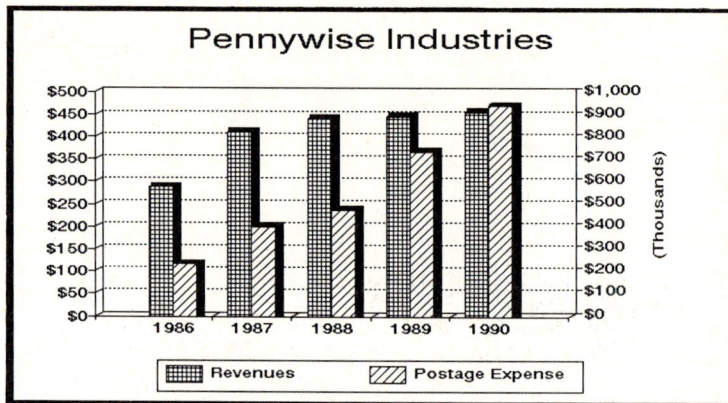

You can move a data series to another axis by selecting that data series and then choosing **Primary Y-Axis** or **Secondary Y-Axis**. You can continue adding data series to the secondary y-axis. Every time you add data series, Quattro Pro rescales the secondary y-axis to reflect the absolute-upper and absolute-lower range of values contained in both data series.

Now consider the graph shown in figure 10.12. This graph is a derivative of the graph shown in figure 10.10. In figure 10.10, the profits and revenues data series are measured in terms of dollars. The profit-sharing data series in figure 10.12 is expressed as a percentage of total revenues.

Fig. 10.12
A graph that
uses data series
with different
systems of
measurement.

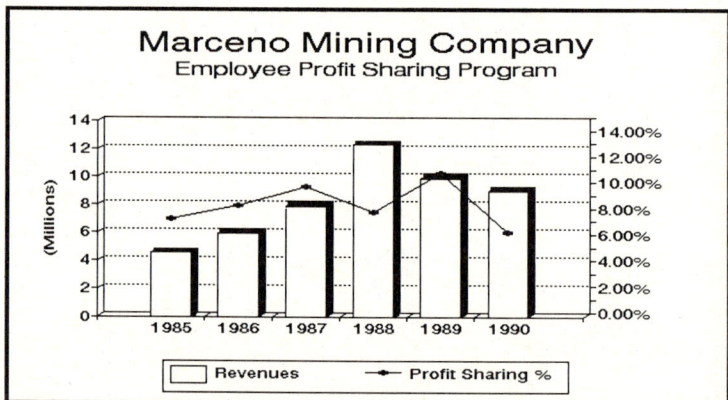

Customizing Pie Graphs and Column Graphs

Pie graphs and column graphs are so different from other Quattro Pro graph types that these graphs merit their own menu of customizing commands. To access this menu, select /**G**raph **C**ustomize **S**eries **P**ies. Quattro Pro displays the menu shown in figure 10.13.

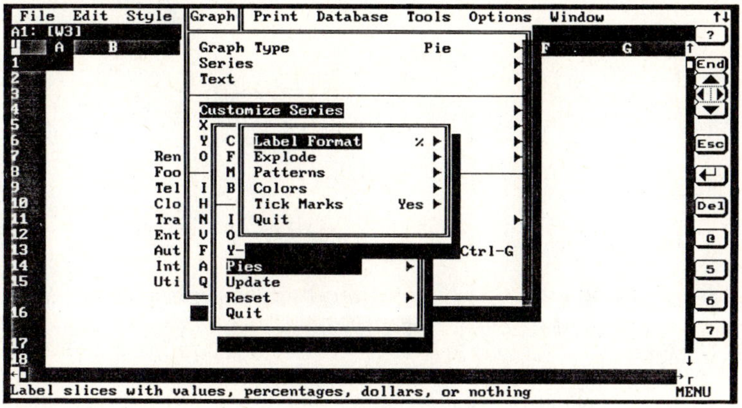

Fig. 10.13
The Pies menu commands.

Changing the Label Format

Quattro Pro has four format options for labeling the slices of a pie graph and column graph: Value, % (percent), $ (dollar), and None. Initially, Quattro Pro displays these two graph types using percent labels.

To change the label format, do the following:

1. Select /**G**raph **C**ustomize **S**eries **P**ies **L**abel Format.

2. When prompted, choose a label option from the displayed menu. Quattro Pro returns you to the Label Format menu, where you can select a new series to change.

3. Press Q to return to the Pies menu.

Press F10 to review the graph with the new label format.

The **L**abel Format command affects only the six data series elements on the Series menu—the command does not affect any data selected with the **X**-Axis Series command.

Exploding a Piece of the Pie

What pie graph is complete without at least one piece appearing exploded from the rest of the pie? Because this display option is one of the most recurrent features in data graphing programs, Quattro Pro has given you this capability.

To explode an element in a pie graph, do the following:

1. Select /Graph Customize Series **P**ies **E**xplode. Quattro Pro displays nine data series.

2. Choose the series that you want to explode.

3. When prompted, choose Explode. Quattro Pro returns you to the Explode menu, where you can select a new pie slice to explode.

4. Press Q to return to the Pies menu.

Press F10 to view the pie graph with an exploded slice.

Figure 10.14 shows a pie graph of the household budget report. The Entertainment category is exploded from the pie and the percent symbol is added to the labels for effect.

Fig. 10.14
Exploding a pie slice from the pie draws attention to a data series.

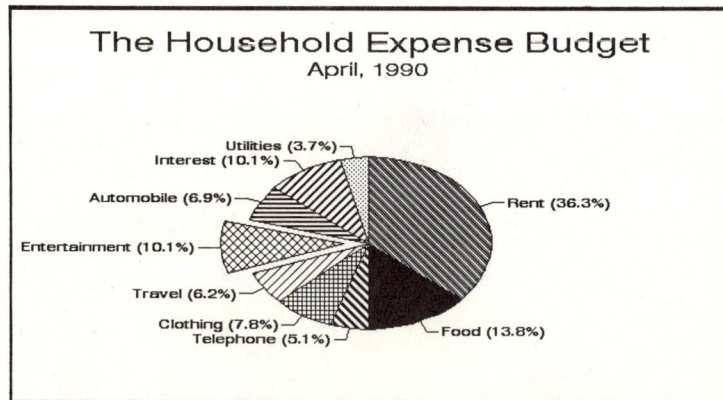

The Household Expense Budget
April, 1990

Utilities (3.7%)
Interest (10.1%)
Automobile (6.9%)
Entertainment (10.1%)
Travel (6.2%)
Clothing (7.8%)
Telephone (5.1%)
Rent (36.3%)
Food (13.8%)

If you want to unexplode a piece of the pie, select the data series and then select the **D**on't Explode option.

Changing Fill Patterns

The **P**atterns command on the Pies menu stores the pattern settings for up to nine slices of pie. Although 16 patterns are available on the fill patterns gallery, you can use only nine at a time. When your data set exceeds nine data series, Quattro Pro repeats the fill patterns beginning with slice 10.

Fill patterns help to distinguish one pie slice from another. Without fill patterns or labels, a viewer has difficulty distinguishing between the data series values.

To change the fill pattern assignment for a data series, do the following:

1. Select /**G**raph **C**ustomize Series **P**ies **P**atterns. Quattro Pro displays nine pie slice series and their current fill pattern assignments.

2. Choose the series you want to change. Quattro Pro displays the fill pattern gallery.

3. Highlight a pattern in the gallery and press Enter to record the new fill pattern assignment for the selected series.

    Quattro Pro returns you to the Patterns menu, where you can select a new series to change.

4. Press Q to return to the Pies menu.

Press F10 to view the new fill patterns in the graph.

Changing Colors

The **C**olors command stores the color settings for each pie slice or column section on a graph. By default, Quattro Pro assigns a different color to each series, so that you can distinguish one from the other. When your data set exceeds nine data series, Quattro Pro repeats the colors again, starting with slice 10.

To change the color assignment of a data series, do the following:

1. Select **C**olors from the Pies menu. Quattro Pro displays nine pie slice series and their current color assignments.

2. Choose the series you want to change. Quattro Pro displays the coloring palette.

3. Highlight a color on the palette and press Enter to record the new color assignment for the selected pie slice series.

Quattro Pro returns you to the Colors menu, where you can select a new pie slice series to change.

4. Press Q to return to the Pies menu.

Press F10 to view the new color selections on the graph.

Removing Tick Marks

A tick mark is the little line drawn from a data series label to the slice of the pie. Each time you create a column graph or pie graph, Quattro Pro draws tick marks.

To remove the tick marks from a graph, do the following:

1. Select **Tick Marks** from the Pies menu. Quattro Pro displays an options menu.

2. Select **No** to remove the tick marks or select **Yes** to return the tick marks to the graph.

Updating and Resetting Default Settings

If you use many of the same custom graph settings for all of your graphs, consider storing the values permanently by selecting the /Graph Customize Series **Update** command.

To erase the current graph settings and begin building a new set, select /Graph Customize Series **Reset Graph**. To reset an individual series, select the series name instead of **Graph**.

Customizing the X-Axis and Y-Axis

Another way you can enhance the basic graph is by altering the scale and format of a graph axis. Quattro Pro scales a graph when you create it by looking at the range of values in each data series, recording the highest and lowest values, and then creating an axis value range that encompasses these values.

A Quattro Pro graph can have up to three axes: an x-axis, a y-axis, and a secondary y-axis. The commands for adjusting the scales and formats of these axes are nearly identical, so that you can see how to make adjustments to any axis by reviewing the commands found on the Y-Axis menu.

When necessary, differences in the procedures or commands for adjusting an axis are pointed out in this chapter.

Adjusting the Scale of an Axis

Quattro Pro develops the scale of an axis using the highest and lowest values in the selected data series. By changing the scale of an axis, you can blow-up a graph so that Quattro Pro compresses each data series to fit within a specified percentage of the graph area. You also can zoom-in on a graph. Quattro Pro expands each data series, so that portions of each data series may not appear on the graph.

Use the Scale, Low, High, and Increment commands to change the scale of the y- or x-axis on an XY graph. For example, you can adjust the scale of the y-axis for the graph shown in figure 10.15.

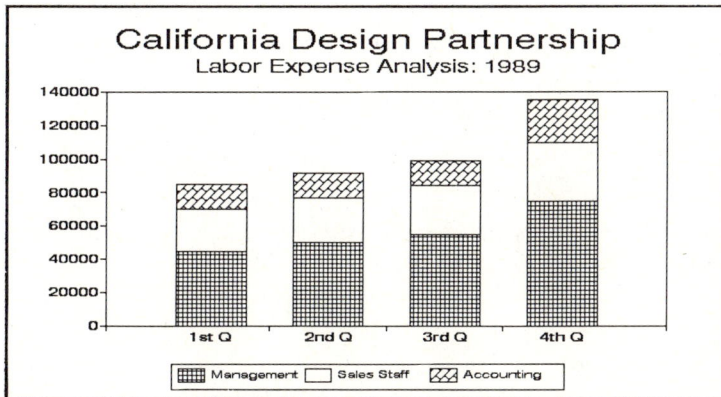

Fig. 10.15
A graph scaled automatically.

Manually Scaling an Axis

The default setting for axis scaling is Automatic. When you create a graph, Quattro Pro uses values from the data series to determine the scale.

To adjust the scale of the y-axis on a graph, do the following:

1. Select /Graph **Y**-Axis **Scale**. Quattro Pro displays two **Scale** menu options.

2. Choose **Manual**. Quattro Pro returns you to the Y-Axis menu.

When the Scale command is set to **Manual**, Quattro Pro uses the values stored on the Low and High menus to determine how to scale an axis.

To enter high and low scaling values, do the following:

1. Select **Low** from the Y-Axis menu. Quattro Pro displays the Low menu dialog box.

2. Type a number that you want to represent the smallest value on the y-axis. This number should be equal to or less than the smallest number in the data series.

3. Press Enter to record that number. Quattro Pro returns you to the Y-Axis menu.

4. Select **High** from the Y-Axis menu. Quattro Pro displays the High menu dialog box.

5. Type a number that you want to represent the largest value on the y-axis. This number should be equal to or greater than the largest number in the data series. To zoom in, select a number less than the largest number in the data series.

6. Press Enter to record that number. Quattro Pro returns you to the Y-Axis menu.

Choosing a Scale Increment

Quattro Pro increments numbers on an axis using the **Increment** command setting's value. For example, to scale an axis in increments of one thousand, enter *1000*.

To set an increment value, do the following:

1. Select **Increment** on the Y-Axis menu. Quattro Pro displays the Increment dialog box.

2. Type the number you want to use as the incremental axis scaling value.

3. Press Enter. Quattro Pro returns you to the Y-Axis menu.

You may press F10 to view the newly scaled graph on-screen. If the scaling is unacceptable, press Enter to return to the Y-Axis menu and adjust each value accordingly.

Adjusting Axis Ticks

Axis ticks help you match an axis label to its data point on a graph. Ticks also delineate regular scale intervals on an axis. In Quattro Pro, you can adjust the format and display of ticks on an axis.

Formatting Ticks

The Format of Ticks command enables you to choose a numeric display format for each value that corresponds to a tick on a graph axis. The numeric format menu that Quattro Pro displays when you select this command is the same as the menu displayed when you select /Style Numeric Format.

To format the ticks on the y-axis, do the following:

1. Select /Graph Y-Axis Format of Ticks.

2. When Quattro Pro displays the Format menu, highlight a format and press Enter to record the new format for the selected series.

3. Enter the number of decimal places and select the style, if required.

4. Press Enter. Quattro Pro returns you to the Y-Axis menu.

Tip | To format the ticks on the x-axis of an XY graph, select /Graph X-Axis Format of Ticks.

Adding Minor Ticks

When you add labels to a graph axis, Quattro Pro sometimes displays labels that overlap each other, because the width (or height) of the graph is not sufficient to accommodate the total combined width (or height) of the labels.

The No. of Minor Ticks command can correct the problem of overlapping labels by replacing every other label with a tick mark. This command works on all graph types, except for pie and column graphs.

To skip labels on the y-axis, do the following:

1. Select /Graph **Y**-Axis **N**o. of Minor Ticks.

2. When prompted, type a number of minor ticks to appear between each labeled tick.

3. Press Enter. Quattro Pro returns you to the Y-Axis menu.

The default value for this command, which displays all graph labels, is 0.

Alternating the Display of Ticks

Setting the number of minor ticks is one way to correct the problem of over-lapping labels. Another way to solve this problem is to use the **Alternate Ticks** command.

When you select this x-axis-specific command, Quattro Pro reproduces every other tick label slightly below the x-axis labels, so that long labels display in full.

To alternate labels on the x-axis, do the following:

1. Select /Graph **X**-Axis **A**lternate Labels.

2. When prompted, choose **Y**es to alternate the labels. Quattro Pro returns you to the X-Axis menu.

Tip | If your labels continue to overlap after trying both tick mark commands, shorten the label descriptions on the spreadsheet from which the graph was created.

The default setting for this command, which displays all graph labels next to each other on the x-axis, is **No**. Figure 10.16 shows the Y-Axis menu after all of the customizing values are entered.

You must set the **Scale** command to **Manual**, or Quattro Pro does not put the entered values into effect. Figure 10.17 shows the new form of this graph after Quattro Pro has redrawn the graph using the new axis scaling settings.

Altering the Display of an Axis Scale

One final technique for adjusting the display of graph scales involves two commands. The **Display Scaling** command determines whether Quattro Pro truncates long values on an axis and then appends a scale label. The **Mode** command enables you to toggle the display of your graph between normal and logarithmic modes.

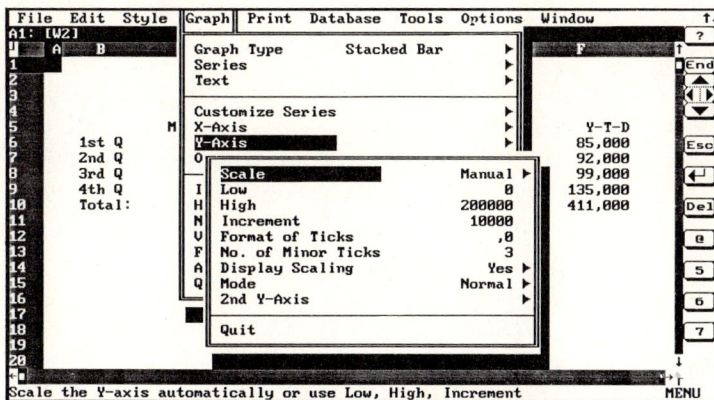

Fig. 10.16
The new scale settings stored at the right margin of the Y-Axis menu.

Fig. 10.17
Manually setting the scaling values creates an alternative display for the sample graph.

Adding and Removing Scaling Labels

When Quattro Pro encounters a data series that contains large numbers, the program reduces the numbers by a factor of 1,000 or 10,000 to save space on the graph area. Quattro Pro then appends a label by the axis, indicating that the numbers have been reduced.

By reducing the number 10,000,000 to 1,000, for example, Quattro Pro frees up space equal to five character widths—space that can be used to display the graph.

If you do not want Quattro Pro to scale large numerical data, do the following:

1. Select /Graph **Y**-Axis **D**isplay Scaling.

2. When prompted, choose **N**o. Quattro Pro returns you to the Y-Axis menu.

Press F10 to view the new form of your graph on-screen. If you decide that your graph looks better with scaled data, reselect this command and choose **Yes** on the Display Scaling menu.

Displaying Data on a Logarithmic Scale

A logarithmically scaled graph is different from the graphs discussed so far. In normal scale mode, each data series value corresponds to a value on the graph.

On a logarithmically scaled graph, each major axis division represents 10 times the value of the preceding division. This scaling mode is useful when the values in your data series have substantially different magnitudes.

It is impossible to graph zeros and negative numbers on a logarithmic scale. If you attempt to do so, Quattro Pro beeps and displays an error message. The following description includes an extra step that the other scale customizing commands do not use.

To scale a graph in logarithmic mode, do the following:

1. If the lowest value on the axis to be scaled is zero or negative, rescale the axis using the **L**ow command and reset the value to 1.

2. Select /Graph **Y**-Axis **M**ode. Quattro Pro displays the Mode menu.

3. Choose **L**og. Quattro Pro returns you to the Y-Axis menu.

Press F10 to view the newly scaled graph. To return to a normal scale mode, reselect the command and choose **N**ormal from the Mode menu.

Customizing the Overall Graph

Consider the graph shown in figure 10.18. After you alter the individual parts of the graph, you can evaluate the overall look of the graph. Is the coloring okay? Have other customizing operations caused the graph titles and legend to loose their impact?

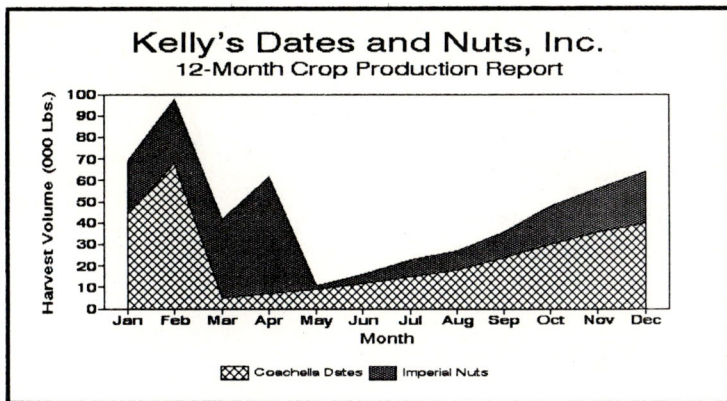

Fig. 10.18 Reviewing a properly scaled graph that is ready for the finishing customizing touches.

Using the Overall menu commands, you can enhance each part of this graph's overall display. For example, you can add grid lines, draw outlines around the report titles, lighten the background colors, and even change the graph to a three-dimensional display.

Using Grid Lines on a Graph

Quattro Pro enables you to draw grid lines behind the data appearing in the graph area. Grid lines are like an on-screen ruler, making it easy to match data series points to corresponding axis values.

Adding Grid Lines

To add grid lines to a graph, do the following:

1. Select **/Graph Overall Grid**. Quattro Pro displays the Grid menu of commands.

2. Choose **H**orizontal, **V**ertical, or **B**oth on the Grid menu.

Press F10 to view the grid lines on the current graph. To remove grid lines from a graph, select **C**lear on the Grid menu.

Changing the Grid Color

The **G**rid Color command determines the color used to display the lines surrounding the following items: the main title, the legend, bars on a bar graph, pie and column slices, areas, and the overall graph.

To change the color of the grid lines, do the following:

1. Select /**G**raph **O**verall **G**rid **G**rid Color. Quattro Pro displays the familiar coloring palette.

2. Highlight a color on the palette and press Enter to record the new color assignment for the selected series.

Changing the Line Style

Like on a line graph, you can change the line style used to display grid lines.

To alter the line style, do the following:

1. Select /**G**raph **O**verall **G**rid **L**ine **S**tyle. Quattro Pro displays a menu of line styles.

2. Pick a new line style. Quattro Pro returns you to the Overall menu.

Changing the Fill Color

You also can determine the color that Quattro Pro uses to display the graph area (the area behind the grid lines). When you change the colors used to display grid lines, you also probably need to change the graph area color setting.

To change the default color selection, do the following:

1. Select /**G**raph **O**verall **G**rid **F**ill Color. Quattro Pro displays the coloring palette.

2. Choose a new color from the palette. Quattro Pro returns you to the Grid menu.

Adjusting Outlines

When you create a graph, Quattro Pro draws a box around the legend, but does not draw a box for any other part of the graph. To draw a box around other parts of the graph, use the **Outlines** command.

To draw boxes on a graph, do the following:

1. Select **/Graph Overall Outlines**. Quattro Pro displays the Outlines menu.

2. Choose **Titles**, **Legend**, or **Graph**. Quattro Pro displays a menu of outline types.

3. Select an outline from the menu. Quattro Pro immediately returns you to the Outlines menu.

Quattro Pro offers seven outline styles, including **None**, which removes a drawn box from the graph for the selected item.

Changing the Background Color

You can change the portion of your screen outside the graph area (the area not affected by the **/Graph Grid Fill Color** command). Like other color commands, when you begin to change one or more colors, you usually end up changing all of the colors to maintain proper consistency.

To color outside the graph area, do the following:

1. Select **/Graph Overall Background Color**. Quattro Pro displays the coloring palette.

2. Highlight a new color on the palette and press Enter to record the new color setting.

Press F10 to view the new custom color setting.

Displaying a Graph in 3D

Quattro Pro's capability to turn a flat graph into a three-dimensional display is one of the most impressive customizing tools on the Overall menu. Quattro Pro displays most graphs in this mode.

To turn a three-dimensional graph into a two-dimensional display, do the following:

1. Select /Graph **O**verall **T**hree-D.

2. When prompted, choose **N**o.

Press F10 to view the new dimensional display setting. To revert to the original three-dimensional display, reselect the command and choose **Y**es.

Toggling On-Screen Color Display

The final command on the Overall menu toggles your screen between color and black and white. To use this command, select /**G**raph **O**verall **C**olor/B&W.

Figure 10.19 illustrates one example of a fully customized graph. Only a few of the available customizing tools were used to create this graph. You are not obligated to use every customizing command on your graphs. The best way to learn which commands go well together is to experiment with your graphs.

Fig. 10.19
The finished form of a customized graph.

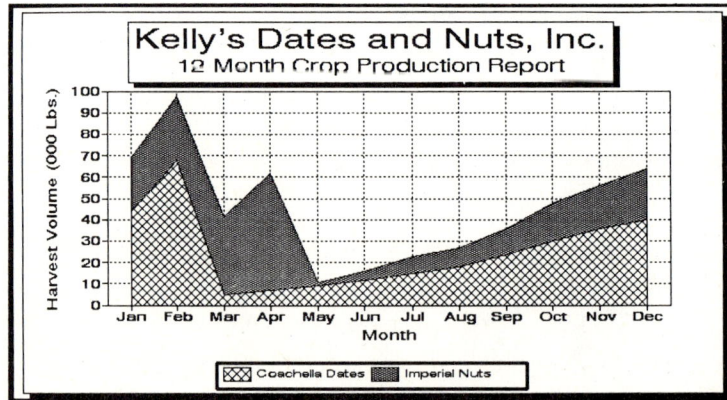

Annotating Graphs

Using the Customize Series menu commands, you easily can turn a basic graph into a finished product. When your graph is missing that extra something, use Quattro Pro's Graph Annotator tool to finish the job.

The Graph Annotator is the final link in the graph-building process. This built-in graphics editor enables you to add descriptive text, boxes, lines, arrows, and other geometric shapes to your graphs.

To access this tool, select /Graph Annotate, and Quattro Pro loads the current graph into the annotator environment. To load a different graph, select /Graph Name Display, highlight the name of the graph you want to load, and then press Enter to display the graph on-screen. After the graph is displayed on-screen, press /, and Quattro Pro loads the graph into the annotator environment.

To use the Graph Annotator, your graphics display system must meet the specifications outlined in Chapter 9.

Reviewing the Annotator Screen

A quick look at the Annotator screen reveals that this tool has many of the same features as stand-alone graphics editor programs (see fig. 10.20). In fact, finding a tool of this caliber in an electronic spreadsheet program is surprising.

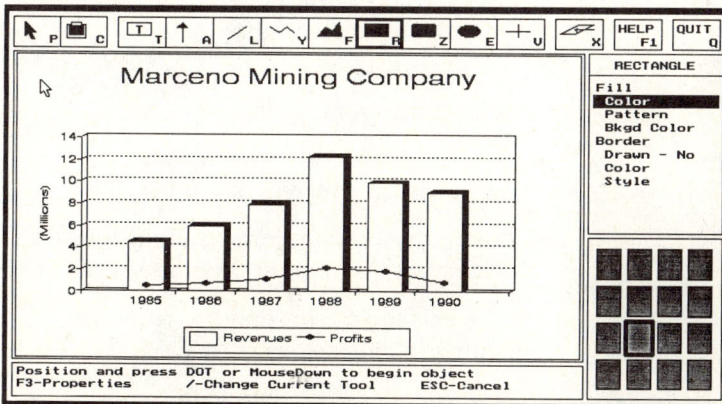

Fig. 10.20 A graph loaded into the Graph Annotator environment.

A graphics editor is essentially a mouse-driven tool, although you can execute all of the Graph Annotator commands directly from your keyboard.

The Annotator screen contains various icons, boxed areas, letters, and a few commands that should be familiar to you.

Draw Area

Quattro Pro displays a graph in the draw area. In the draw area, you position, move, resize, delete, draw geometric elements, and paste clip art into the current graph.

Toolbox

The toolbox is the long, rectangular row of symbols at the top of the screen. These icons describe actions that you can perform on a graph. For example, you can add text boxes, draw arrows and lines, add geometric elements, link data series, invoke a Help window, and Quit the annotator from this facility. Table 10.1

Table 10.1
Graphics Design Elements in the Toolbox

Design element	Description
Boxed T (/T)	The text icon adds boxed text.
Arrow (/A)	The arrow icon draws a line with an arrowhead at the end.
Line (/L)	The line icon draws a straight line anchored in one place.
Polyline (/Y)	The polyline icon draws a line anchored in two places.
Polygon (/F)	The polygon icon draws a multisided figure with up to 1,000 points.
Rectangle (/R)	The rectangle icon draws a rectangle with any dimensions.
Rounded Rectangle (/Z)	The rounded rectangle icon draws a rounded rectangle with any dimensions.
Ellipse (/E)	The ellipse icon draws a circle using dimensions that you specify.
Vertical/Horizontal Line (/L)	This line icon draws vertical and horizontal lines.

Press / to activate the toolbox and then press the capitalized letter beneath the icon. If you have a mouse, click any icon to activate that tool. You then can scroll through the toolbox by pressing the ← and → keys.

Property Sheet

The property sheet lists the command options available with each toolbox element. For example, when you select the rectangle tool, the property sheet lists six command options: **Color**, **Pattern**, **Bkgd Color**, **Drawn - Yes**, Color, and **Style** (see fig. 10.20).

To activate the property sheet from elsewhere in the Annotator, press F3. Quattro Pro displays the command options for the active element.

Gallery

Quattro Pro displays special tools in the gallery. These tools are used with commands from the property sheet. For example, when the rectangle tool is activated, select Color, and Quattro Pro displays the coloring palette in this area.

Status Box

The status box displays instructions, points out keyboard shortcuts, and describes menu commands when the commands are activated.

Learning Annotator-Specific Keyboard Assignments

Table 10.2 lists the Annotator-specific keys that you use to operate the tool.

Additionally, you may use the mouse and cursor-movement keys to move and resize a selected element or group of elements.

Table 10.2
Graph Annotator Keys

Key	Description
F2	Enters Edit mode when a text element is activated
F3	Activates the property sheet
F7	Resizes a group of selected elements
Shift-F7	Selects multiple elements in the draw area when used with the Tab key
F10	Redraws the Annotator screen in full
Tab	Selects the next element in the draw area
Shift-Tab	Selects the preceding element in the Draw Area
Shift	Selects multiple elements in the draw area when used with a mouse
Del	Erases a selected element from a group of selected elements
Period (.)	Anchors the selected element so that you can resize it
Ctrl-Enter	Creates a line when you are in Text or Edit mode
Backspace	Deletes one character at a time to the left when you are in Edit mode
/ Key	Activates the toolbox
Esc	Exits a menu selection and cancels an operation from the draw area
Enter	Accepts the results of an Annotation operation
Alt	When used with a mouse, selects multiple elements while in Proportional Resizing mode

Annotating a Graph

When you understand how to operate the Graph Annotator, this tool is quite
fun to use. To use the Graph Annotator, do the following:

1. Load a graph into the Graph Annotator.

2. Highlight an icon in the toolbox.

3. Position the pointer at the part of the graph that you want to annotate.

4. Press Enter to move the pointer into the draw area.

5. Annotate symbols and text to the graph.

6. Press /Q to display the full-screen version of the graph.

7. Press Enter to return to the active spreadsheet.

8. Save the newly annotated graph with the /Graph Name Create command.

Figure 10.21 illustrates the results of annotating boxed text to a graph using these steps.

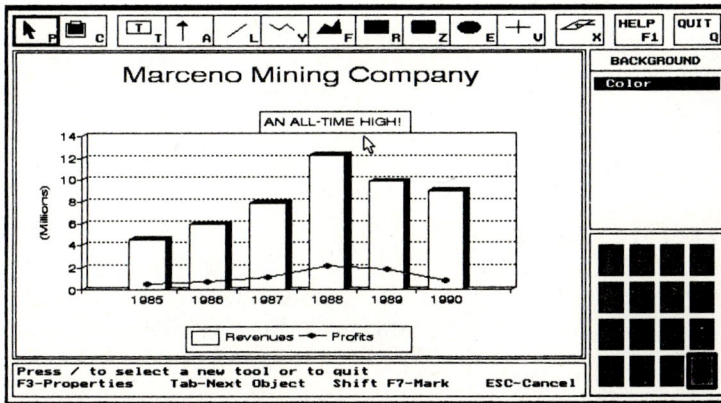

Fig. 10.21
Adding boxed text to a graph.

Selecting a Design Element

Selecting a design element is similar to selecting a cell on a spreadsheet. When a spreadsheet cell is active, the cell is highlighted; when a design element is selected, Quattro Pro places a ring of small boxes around the element (see fig. 10.22).

Before you can perform operations on a design element, you must select that element. To select a design element using the keyboard, do the following:

1. Press Esc and move to the draw area.

2. Press /P to activate the arrow pointer.

3. Press Tab and Shift-Tab to relocate the arrow pointer to the target design element.

4. Press Shift-F7 to retain the current design element selection and continue selecting additional elements.

With a mouse, the process of selecting design elements is more direct. Point at the design element and click the mouse. To select multiple elements, hold down the Shift key and click each element you want to select.

Fig. 10.22 Reviewing a selected design element on a graph.

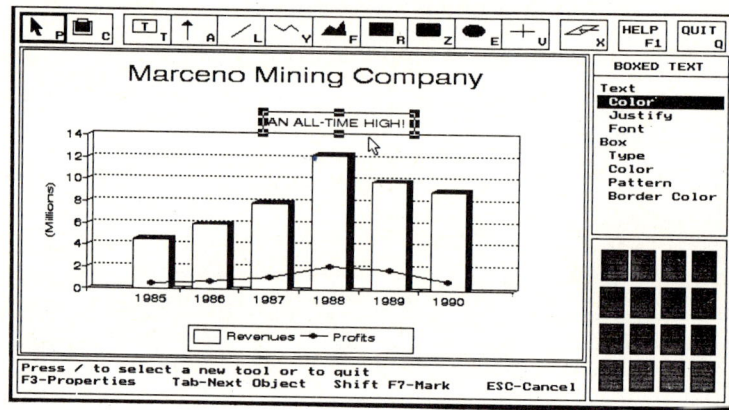

Moving a Design Element

Moving a design element is like moving data from one cell into another. In the Annotator, you move a design element to reposition it on the graph.

To move a design element using the keyboard, do the following:

1. Press Esc and move to the draw area.

2. Select the design element(s) that you want to move.

3. Press the cursor-movement keys to relocate the element elsewhere on the graph.

4. Press Enter to affix the design element to the new location.

5. Press Esc to unselect the design element.

To move a design element with a mouse, first select the design element. Click the element box, drag the box to a new location on the graph, and release the button when you want to affix the element. In figure 10.23, for example, the boxed text is moved from the top to the bottom of the graph using this procedure.

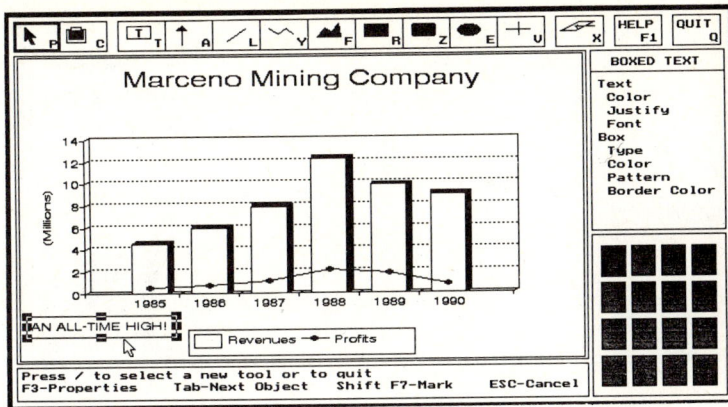

Fig. 10.23
Moving a design element elsewhere on the graph.

Resizing a Design Element

Quattro Pro enables you to resize any element created in the Annotator environment. This capability gives you complete flexibility when you annotate a Quattro Pro graph. If you can change the typeface of a spreadsheet font, why not the size of a graph element?

To resize an element using the keyboard, do the following:

1. Press Esc and move to the draw area.

2. Select the design element(s) that you want to resize.

3. Press the period key (.) to enter Resize mode.

4. Continue pressing the period key until you highlight the corner of the element that you want to resize (see fig. 10.24).

5. Press the cursor-movement keys to resize the element.

6. Press Enter to retain the new size.

7. Press Esc to unselect the element.

To resize an element using a mouse, begin by selecting the element. Click any of the boxes appearing on the outline of the selected element and drag until the desire size is attained. Release the mouse to retain the new size.

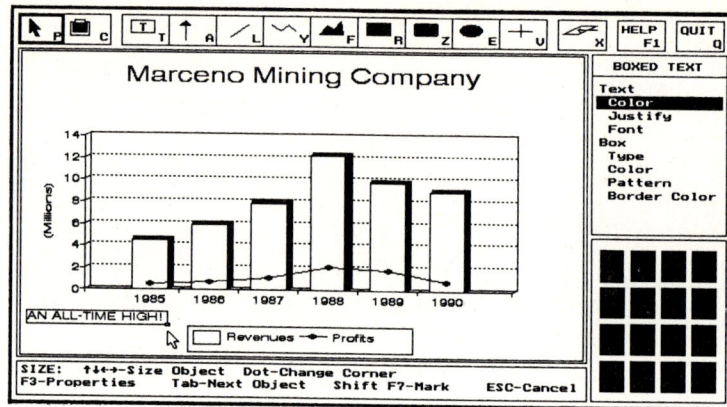

Fig. 10.24
A small box
displayed in the
corner of the
element you
are resizing.

Editing a Text Design Element

To edit any text design element that originated in the Annotator environment, do the following:

1. Press Esc and move to the draw area.

2. Select a text design element to edit.

3. Press F2 to enter Edit mode.

4. Edit a design element's text using the same keys and procedures that you use for editing spreadsheet cells.

5. When you finish editing the text, press Enter to reaffix the modified design element to the graph.

You also can perform Clipboard menu operations on a selected design element. To delete a group of selected elements, position the arrow pointer over the element and press Del.

Setting Design Element Properties

Each design element has a unique set of cosmetic properties that determines how Quattro Pro displays the element on-screen. If you annotate boxed text to a graph, for example, you can return later and change its color, justification, box style, text font, border color, and fill pattern. You also can set all of the design element properties beforehand; later, when you annotate that element to a graph, the preset properties are in effect.

To preset the properties for a design element, do the following:

1. Select a design element icon from the toolbox.

2. Press F3 to display that element's property commands in the property sheet.

3. Press the boldfaced letter key in the command name to select the command.

4. Choose the desired property from the options displayed in the gallery area, and Quattro Pro returns you to the property sheet.

5. Continue editing properties as desired.

6. Press Esc to return to the draw area.

The new properties now are in effect for the next time you select that element. In figure 10.25, for example, in addition to the text being edited, several of the boxed text properties are altered.

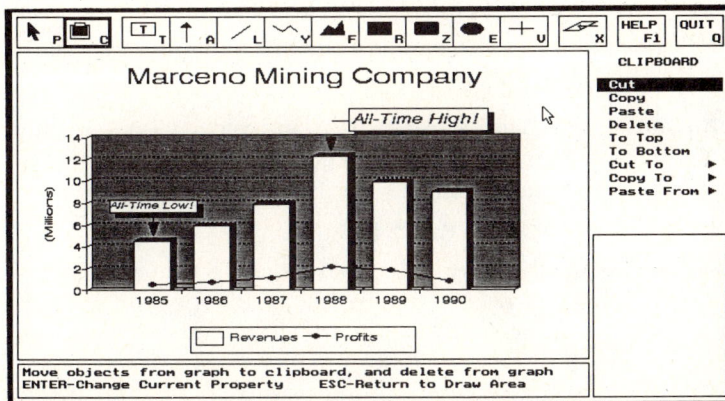

Fig. 10.25 Altering design element properties to add clarity and impact to a graph.

The new font is smaller (to de-emphasize the "all-time low" data point), the text displays in an italic typeface, and the box now appears with a shaded background. Finally, an arrow is added to connect the boxed text to a data series on the graph.

Using the Clipboard

Use the Clipboard icon commands to manage your annotation elements. When you activate this icon, Quattro Pro displays a menu containing nine commands (see fig. 10.25).

These commands enable you to cut, copy, paste, and delete selected elements in the draw area. You also can create and paste clip art to and from other graphs using these commands. In fact, Quattro Pro comes with its own library of clip art that you may import into the Annotator for use with your graph files.

To copy a piece of clip art into the current graph, do the following:

1. Select an element in the draw area.

2. Activate the Clipboard icon by pressing /C.

3. Select Copy to copy an element (for example).

4. Press /Q to quit the toolbox. Quattro Pro returns you to the current graph (or to the active spreadsheet if no graph is displayed).

5. Select /Graph Name Display to display a different graph.

6. Press / to load the displayed graph into the Annotator.

7. Activate the Clipboard icon by pressing /C.

8. Select Paste From to copy the element from the Clipboard into the draw area.

Use this sample operation as a guideline for choosing and executing other Clipboard menu operations. In most cases, the sequence of steps is the same. Fortunately, the Clipboard menu commands are intuitive enough that their operational peculiarities can be learned quickly.

The final three commands on this menu are used to move elements in and out of clip art files for use with other Quattro Pro graphs or with applications that can read the CLP file format.

Linking an Element to a Graph Data Series

The Graph Annotator redraws itself periodically as you move in and out of the draw area. When this happens, Quattro Pro retains the integrity of the selected elements that you are working with.

If later you recall an annotated graph into the Annotator, the graph looks the same, as long as you have not modified any of the original graph settings. One way to guard against the possibility of ruining your annotation work (if you do choose to alter a graph's settings) is to link an annotation element to a graph data series.

This technique maintains the original organization of the annotated graph as long as the original data series definition stays intact. When you do change graph settings, Quattro Pro moves the linked annotation element with the data series.

To link an annotation element to a data series on the current graph, do the following:

1. Select the element (or elements) in the draw area.

2. Press /X to select the **Link** command.

3. When prompted, select the number of the data series you want to link.

4. When prompted, type in the link index number (the relative position of the data series point to the whole data series).

5. Press Enter to create the link.

The link between the data series and the selected element remains intact until you reset a data series by selecting the /**Graph** Customize Series **Reset** command.

Questions & Answers

This chapter introduces you to Quattro Pro's graph customizing commands. If you have questions concerning particular situations that are not addressed in the examples given, look through this question and answers section.

Customizing Graphs

Q: When I press F10, why don't my graphs appear on-screen?

A: Remember, to display Quattro Pro graphs, you must have a graphics adapter system, and to display a graph inserted on a spreadsheet, the /**Options D**isplay Mode command must be set to **B**:Graphics.

Q: Why do most of my color selections for the data series appear white?

A: You must have a monochrome display system. With this type of system, you should change color selections with care. Remember that any color selection other than black always appears white when you display the graph on-screen.

Q: Why is it that when I save a Quattro Pro spreadsheet in a Lotus 1-2-3-compatible format that spreadsheet's graphs do not display in color?

A: Quattro Pro does not store graph color information when you create 1-2-3-compatible spreadsheets from your Quattro Pro spreadsheets. If you retrieve the 1-2-3-compatible spreadsheet into Quattro Pro, however, the graph colors return to their default settings.

Q: Why doesn't Quattro Pro show the fill pattern selections I make for my pie graphs and column graphs?

A: You used the /Graph Customize Series Fill Patterns command to select the new fill pattern. Instead, choose the /Graph Customize Series Pies Patterns command.

Q: Why is Quattro Pro showing the same marker symbol for all of the text appearing in a legend box?

A: You selected the same marker symbol for every data series via the /Graph Customize Series Markers & Lines Markers command. Re-select this command and specify a different marker symbol for each data series. Quattro Pro updates the displayed symbol in the legend box.

Q: I can't see any marker symbol assignments on the Markers menu—where are they?

A: Press the Expand key (+) on your numeric keypad to display a full view of the Markers menu marker assignments.

Q: Quattro Pro keeps displaying a line graph when I want to display an area graph. How can this happen?

A: If you began by creating a combination graph, you must reset any overridden data series before selecting a new graph type. Choose /Graph Customize Series Override Type Default and reset all applicable data series.

Q: Is there a quick way to erase a graph and begin all over again?

A: Yes. Select /Graph Customize Series Reset Graph, and Quattro Pro erases the current graph and returns the last save settings.

Q: I can't seem to adjust the x-axis scale on a line graph. What's going on?

A: Quattro Pro enables x-axis scale adjustments only to XY graphs. To get around this restriction, you can add extra data series on your spreadsheet that define the upper and lower limits of the scale you want to create. Be sure to re-select the /Graph Series command and define the new series so that Quattro Pro shows the series on a graph.

Q: I can't seem to alter the numeric format of the x-axis values on an area graph by using the /Graph X-Axis Format of Ticks command. What's going on?

A: Quattro Pro enables x-axis numeric format adjustments only to XY graphs. To get around this restriction, return to the active spreadsheet, select /Style Numeric Format and format the cell data you want to alter. When you redisplay the graph, it reflects the new numeric formats.

Q: I thought that Quattro Pro displays most graphs in three-dimensional form. Why aren't any of my graphs displaying in 3D?

A: The graphs you create may make it impossible for Quattro Pro to use three-dimensional display. For example, when a bar graph has numerous bars or when a pie graph has a great number of slices, the program may be unable to display in three dimensions. To correct this situation, you can reduce the number of displayed data series until the graph does display in 3D.

If you saved a set of graph defaults that included no 3D display, Quattro Pro does not display graphs this way. To change this, select /Graph Overall Three-D Yes and then select /Graph Customize Series Update.

Q: Why does Quattro Pro superimpose a text graph on my current graph?

A: Anything you do in the Graph Annotator environment affects the current graph. To create a text graph by itself, save the current graph setting with the /Graph Name Create command and then reset the current graph settings. Choose /Graph Customize Series Reset Graph.

Chapter Summary

In this chapter, you learned how to turn a finished graph into a presentation-quality visual aid, using the commands found in the middle section of Quattro Pro's Graph menu. You also learned how to use the Graph Annotator tool, Quattro Pro's special built-in graphics editor facility.

After completing this chapter, you should understand the following Quattro Pro concepts:

- Changing colors, fill patterns, markers and lines, and bar widths for individual data series

- Appending labels to individual points in a data series

- Creating combination bar and line graphs

- Plotting two y-axes on one graph

- Plotting two or more data series that use different systems of measurement

- Changing label formats, colors, fill patterns, and tick marks on pie and column graphs

- Updating and resetting the default Customize Series menu command settings for use with other spreadsheets

- Manually adjusting the default axis scale

- Adjusting, formatting, adding, and deleting axis tick marks

- Displaying a graph on a logarithmic scale

- Using grid lines, outlines, background colors, and special display settings to enhance the overall appearance of a graph

- Using the Graph Annotator to append boxed text, arrows, lines, and geometric figures to a graph

- Pasting clip art to and from the Annotator tool for use on graphs

III

Advanced Spreadsheet Applications

Includes

Quick Start: Creating a Database and Database Macro

Managing Your Data

Creating Macro Programs

Quick Start 3

Creating a Database and Database Macro

Besides being an electronic spreadsheet program, Quattro Pro is a relational database manager and a macro programming tool.

This quick start begins by focusing on how you can transform a spreadsheet into a database. You learn how to create a phone list manager that stores the names and phone numbers of your friends. Then you sort this information and discover how easily you can create different reports using the same database.

The second part of this quick start demonstrates how to auto-record a macro to pre-format new, blank spreadsheets each time you load a spreadsheet into Quattro Pro. Next you name and paste the macro to a spreadsheet. Finally, you learn how to create a macro library, manually edit a macro, and include documentation so that others can understand and use your macro.

Turning a Spreadsheet into a Database

The primary advantage of a database is that it enables you to segregate information on a spreadsheet into sets of related data and then reorganize the information to create different reports. Oftentimes, the structure of an individual database is portable to other applications. For example, if you create a database to catalog the addresses of your friends and family, you can use the same database structure to catalog the information for your business associates.

Designing the Database Shell

A database, like a spreadsheet report, has a title and label headings that describe the type of information stored in a column or row. Each row in a database is a record, and each column is a field. The database area is the part of the spreadsheet in which you store your records.

You easily can turn a spreadsheet into a database. Figure QS3.1 shows the shell of a database used to store the last name, first name, title, and phone number data for 10 of your friends.

Fig. QS3.1
Building the shell of a database.

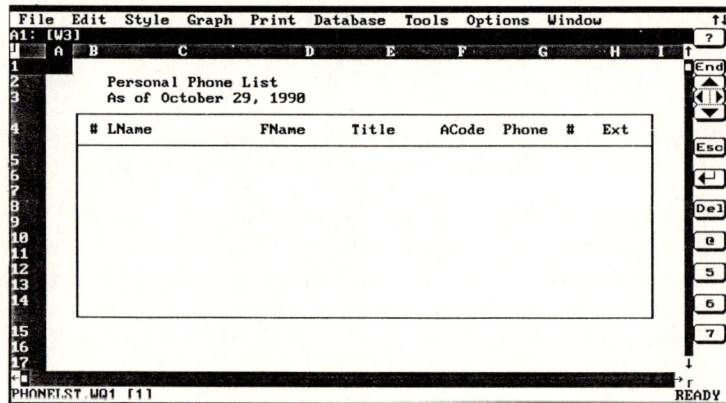

The database phone list contains seven columns of data. The field names row contains the label descriptions for all seven fields: #, LName, FName, Title, ACode, Phone #, and Ext. These fields identify the type of data that you enter into the database.

To create the database shell shown in figure QS3.1, you perform four distinct Quattro Pro operations:

- Open and name a new spreadsheet

- Type the report title and the field name labels

- Draw lines around the database shell

- Assign a unique name to the database area

These four operations are accomplished by performing the following steps:

1. Open a new, blank spreadsheet into Quattro Pro.

2. Press /FS to select the /**F**ile **S**ave command.

3. Type *PHONELST* and press Enter to name the spreadsheet.

4. Make cell C1 the active cell. Type *Personal Phone List* and press Enter to record the primary database title.

5. Press the ↓ key to move to C2. Type *as of October 29, 1990* and press Enter to record the secondary database title.

6. Make cell B4 the active cell. Type *'#* and press Enter to record the first field name.

7. Press the → key to move to cell C4. Type *LName* and press Enter to record the second field name.

8. Press the → key to move to cell D4. Type *FName* and press Enter to record the third field name.

9. Press the → key to move to cell E4. Type *Title* and press Enter to record the fourth field name.

10. Press the → key to move to cell F4. Type *ACode* and press Enter to record the fifth field name.

11. Press the → key to move to cell G4. Type *Phone #* and press Enter to record the sixth field name.

12. Press the → key to move to cell H4. Type *Ext* and press Enter to record the seventh, and final, field name.

13. Press /SL to select the /Style Line Drawing command and draw a line around the database shell and the field names row.

14. Press /ENC to select the /Edit Names Create command.

15. When prompted, type *DATABASE* and press Enter.

16. When prompted, type *B5..H14* and press Enter.

Figure QS3.1 illustrates the common way of creating the shell of a database. As you begin to design your own database applications, try to design a database shell that looks like the document or report from which the shell is created.

Entering Data into the Database

Apply the techniques you use for entering data into a spreadsheet to enter into a database. Like a spreadsheet, a database may contain three types of data: labels, numbers, and formulas.

For example, cell G5 in figure QS3.2 demonstrates that you must enter a phone number as a label because the number includes the minus symbol.

Normally, Quattro Pro treats this value as a subtraction operation—placing a label prefix before the number ensures that Quattro Pro treats the value as a label.

Fig. QS3.2
The first record in the phone list database.

To enter the first record in this database, do the following:

1. Place the cell selector in cell B5.

2. Type *1* and press → to move to cell C5.

3. Type *Jones* and press → to move to cell D5.

4. Type *Morgan* and press → to move to cell E5.

5. Type *Mr.* and press → to move to cell F5.

6. Type *619* and press → to move to cell G5.

7. Type *^555-3493* and press → to move to cell H5.

8. Type *22* and press Enter to record the last field entry in this record.

9. Press F5, the GoTo key; type *B6*; and press Enter to move to the first field in the second record.

Figure QS3.3 shows the completed phone list database. Enter the same data into your database shell, or you can enter data of your own instead of the sample data.

```
 File  Edit  Style  Graph  Print  Database  Tools  Options  Window      ↑↓
A1: [W3]                                                                  ?
U   A   B        C         D          E       F        G       H    I ↑  ┌──┐
1                                                                    │  │End│
2          Personal Phone List                                      ▲
3          As of October 29, 1990                                   │◄│▶│
4        ┌──┬──────────┬───────────┬─────────┬───────┬─────────┬──────┐ ▼
         │ #│ LName    │ FName     │ Title   │ ACode │ Phone # │ Ext  │ ┌───┐
5        │ 1│ Jones    │ Morgan    │ Mr.     │ 619   │ 555-3493│ 22   │ │Esc│
6        │ 2│ Gonzales │ Danielle  │ Ms.     │ 619   │ 555-9033│      │ └───┘
7        │ 3│ Bernstein│ Roger     │ Mr.     │ 619   │ 555-4445│      │ ┌───┐
8        │ 4│ Fraticelli│ Daryl    │ Mrs.    │ 619   │ 555-9313│      │ │ ↵ │
9        │ 5│ Thomas   │ Mark      │ Mr.     │ 619   │ 555-0389│ 3322 │ └───┘
10       │ 6│ Cohn     │ Gary      │ Dr.     │ 714   │ 555-9167│      │ ┌───┐
11       │ 7│ Imandoust│ John      │ General │ 202   │ 555-4009│      │ │Del│
12       │ 8│ Frump    │ Donald    │ Sir     │ 212   │ 555-2110│      │ └───┘
13       │ 9│ Roberts  │ Deborah   │ Miss    │ 415   │ 555-5117│ 22   │ ┌───┐
14       │10│ Donnelly │ Ted       │ Mr.     │ 216   │ 555-2122│ A4   │ │ @ │
         └──┴──────────┴───────────┴─────────┴───────┴─────────┴──────┘ └───┘
15                                                                    │ ┌───┐
16                                                                    │ │ 5 │
17                                                                    ↓ └───┘
                                                                        ┌───┐
PHONELST.WQ1 [1]                                              READY     │ 6 │
                                                                        └───┘
                                                                        ┌───┐
                                                                        │ 7 │
                                                                        └───┘
```

Fig. QS3.3
The phone list database with data entries.

Sorting the Database

Select the /**D**ata **S**ort command to produce different combinations of the same data set without changing the value of any record in the database. You tell Quattro Pro how to sort your database by specifying sort criteria. You can sort a database alphabetically or numerically, in ascending or descending order.

The fields used to sort the records are *sort field keys*. You can specify up to five sort keys per operation. Quattro Pro sorts a database according to each sort key's priority: the **1**st Key has first priority; the **2**nd Key has second priority; and so on.

Sorting a database is a three-step process:

1. Define the block to sort.

2. Specify the sort key criteria.

3. Select /**D**atabase **S**ort **G**o to begin the sort operation.

Using One Sort Key

When you define the database area to sort be sure to omit the field names row from the block definition. Otherwise, Quattro Pro sorts the row of labels into your database.

To sort the phone list database, perform the following steps:

1. Press /**DS** to display the /**D**ata **S**ort menu.

2. Press B to select the **B**lock command, type *DATABASE*, and press Enter to choose the block to sort.

3. Press 1 to select the **1**st Key, type *C4*, and press Enter to choose the LName field as the sort key.

4. When prompted, press A to sort the data in **A**scending order.

Your Sort menu should look like the one in figure QS3.4. If not, press R to select the **R**eset command and reset the block definition and sort criteria. Make the necessary changes so that your sort menu matches the one in figure QS3.4.

Fig. QS3.4
Reviewing the block and criteria definitions on the Sort menu.

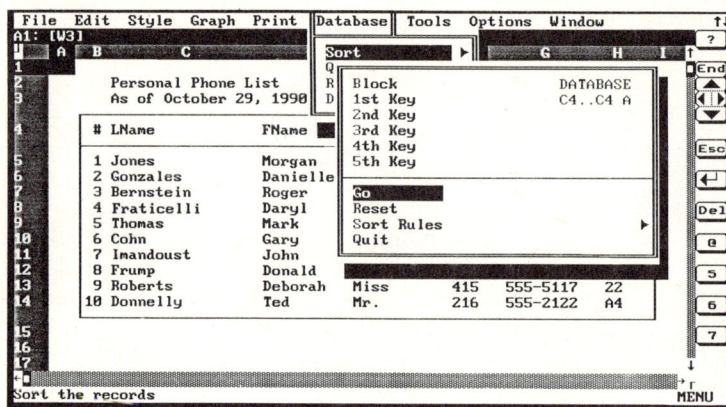

5. Press G to begin the sort operation.

When Quattro Pro finishes the sort operation, your database looks like figure QS3.5.

Fig. QS3.5
The phone list database sorted in ascending order by last name.

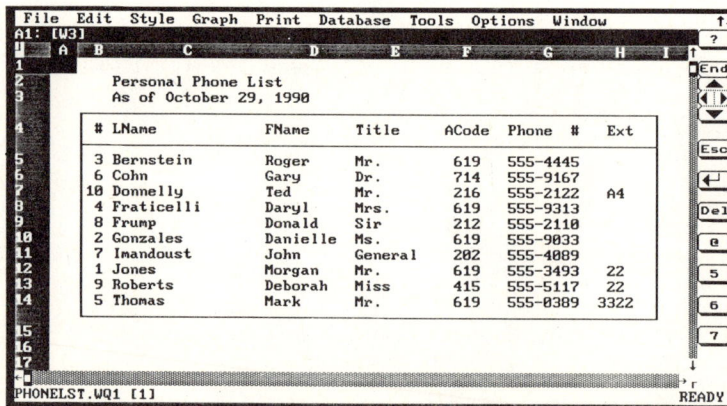

6. Press R to select the **Reset** command and reset the block definition and sort criteria in preparation for the next sort operation.

Tip | Press Alt-F5 to undo a sort operation.

Using Multiple Sort Keys

In this section, you learn how to sort the phone list database by using three sort keys instead of one. Organize the database in ascending order by ACode, in descending order by Title, and in ascending order by LName. You always can substitute block names for cell addresses when you define sort criteria—a useful shortcut for Data menu operations.

For example, you already named the database area DATABASE. Now, name the field names row by performing the following steps:

1. Press /ENC to select the /**E**dit **N**ames **C**reate Command.

2. When prompted, type # and press Enter.

3. When prompted, type *B5..B14* and press Enter.

4. Repeat steps one through three for the remaining field names. Their names and cell blocks are *LName* (C5..C14), *FName* (D5..D14), *Title* (E5..E14), *ACode* (F5..F14), *Phone #* (G5..G14), and *Ext* (H5..H14).

To define the criteria for a multiple-key sort operation, do the following:

1. Press /DS to display the /**D**ata **S**ort menu.

2. Press B to select the **B**lock command, type *DATABASE*, and press Enter to choose the sort block.

3. Press 1 to select the **1**st Key, type *ACODE*, and press Enter to choose this field as the first sort key.

4. When prompted, press A to sort the data in **A**scending order.

5. Press 2 to select the **2**nd Key, type *TITLE*, and press Enter to choose this field as the second sort key.

6. When prompted, press D to sort the data in **D**escending order.

7. Press 3 to select the **3**rd Key, type *LNAME*, and press Enter to choose this field as the third sort key.

8. When prompted, press A to sort the data in **A**scending order.

Your Sort menu now should look like figure QS3.6. If not, press R to select the **Reset** command and reset the block definition and sort criteria. Make the necessary changes so that your Sort menu matches the one in figure QS3.6.

Fig. QS3.6
Reviewing the block and criteria definitions on the Sort menu.

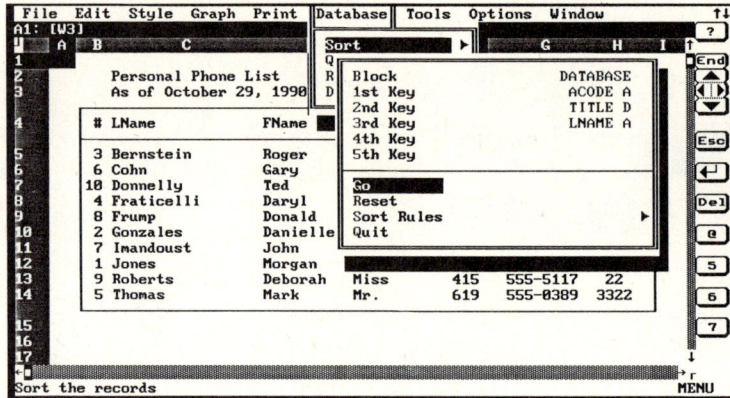

9. Press G to begin the sort operation.

After Quattro Pro finishes the sort operation, your database looks like figure QS3.7.

Fig. QS3.7
The phone list database sorted on three keys.

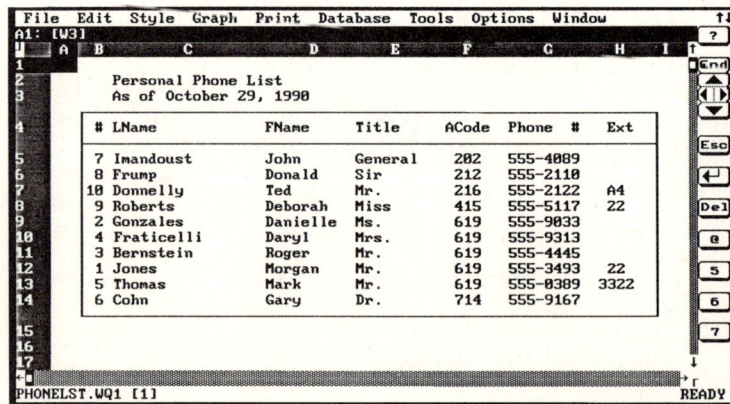

10. Press R to select the **Reset** command and reset the block definition and sort criteria in preparation for the next sort operation.

You can experiment with this same procedure by altering each sort key definition until you achieve the report style you seek.

Returning the Database to its Original Order

Sometimes after sorting a database several different ways, you may want to return the database to its original order. Fortunately, you are prepared for this contingency because the # field is included in the phone list database.

To return the database to its original order, perform the following steps:

1. Press /DS to display the /**D**ata **S**ort menu.

2. Press B to select the **B**lock command, type *DATABASE*, and press Enter to choose the sort block.

3. Press 1 to select the **1**st Key, type #, and press Enter to choose this field as the first sort key.

4. When prompted, press A to sort the data in **A**scending order.

5. Press G to begin the sort operation.

Quattro Pro sorts your database into its original entry order.

6. Press R to select the **R**eset command and reset the block definition and sort criteria in preparation for future sort operations.

Creating a Database Macro

A macro is a productivity tool that enables you to store common keystrokes and menu command selections as instructions in a file for future use. When you invoke a macro, Quattro Pro performs each instruction on the active spreadsheet—without requiring you to do a thing.

To create a macro, you enter each instruction, or command, into a column of cells on the active spreadsheet. You can use three kinds of commands: keystroke commands, menu-equivalent commands, and special macro commands.

When you press PgDn or Enter, you are issuing a keystroke command. These commands are essential because they tell the macro how to move around the spreadsheet and when to accept data into a cell.

A menu-equivalent command is formed when you select a menu and then choose a command on that menu. In a macro, these commands can open files, align data in cells, adjust column widths, draw lines, and so on.

Macro commands are programming commands which perform special functions that cannot be accomplished by keystroke or menu-equivalent commands. These special commands are used in advanced macro program applications. See Appendix C for a glossary of these commands.

Quattro Pro's macro programming facility is accessed by selecting the /**Tools Macro** command.

Auto-Recording a Macro

The /**Tools Macro Recorder** command makes creating macros extremely simple. Creating a basic macro program is a four-step process:

1. Envision an application.

2. Record the macro.

3. Paste and name the macro.

4. Execute the macro.

For example, you can create a macro that can preformat a new, blank spreadsheet to look like the database shell from the preceding section. Each time you need to use the database for another application, you can execute the macro, and the database shell appears on-screen.

The simplest way to accomplish this goal is to open PHONELST.WQ1 into Quattro Pro, turn the recorder on, and reselect each menu command that originally created the phone list database shell.

To auto-record a macro in this manner, do the following:

1. Press /FN to open a new, blank spreadsheet into memory.

2. Press /FA to select the /**File Save As** command, type *MACRO*, and press Enter to name the new spreadsheet.

3. Press /FO to select the /**File Open** command, type *PHONELST*, and press Enter to open this file into a new Quattro Pro window, overlaying the blank spreadsheet.

4. Press /TMR to select the /**Tools Macro Record** command and to turn Quattro Pro's recorder on.

When executed, Quattro Pro displays the REC mode indicator on the status line at the bottom of your screen.

Tip | Press Alt-F2-R to quickly execute the **Record** command.

5. Reissue the /**Style Column-Width** command and set the width of columns A through I. (Retype the number—don't just press Enter when Quattro Pro displays the current width number.)

6. Retype all of the data appearing in the PHONELST spreadsheet directly on top of the existing data.

7. Reissue the /Style **Alignment** command and realign the labels in the field names row.

8. Reissue the /Style **Line Drawing** command and redraw the lines around the database shell.

9. Press /TMR again to turn off the macro recorder.

Pasting the Recorded Macro to a Spreadsheet

When you record a macro, Quattro Pro retains the instructions in memory until you paste the macro or select **Record** and record a new macro. To save a macro so that you can recall and execute it at a later time, select the **Paste** option from the **Macro** menu. This command does two things: it names and pastes the last recorded macro into a block on the active spreadsheet you specify.

You can assign two types of names to a macro. The first kind is a descriptive name like the ones assigned to the database area and field names in the preceding example.

The second kind of name is a macro-specific name that enables you to create an instant macro. This name is created with only two characters: the \ (backslash) and any letter. To execute an instant macro, press Alt plus the letter.

To paste the recorded macro onto the active spreadsheet and assign a unique name to the macro, do the following:

1. Press /TMP to select the /**Tools Macro Paste** command.

Tip | Press Alt-F2-P to quickly execute the **Paste** command.

2. When prompted, type *D*, a macro-specified name which reminds you that it creates a database, and press Enter to create an instant macro (see fig. QS3.8).

3. When Quattro Pro prompts you to enter a macro block to paste, press Alt-0, the Pick Windows key.

4. Highlight the name MACRO and press Enter to load the macro into the active window.

Fig. QS3.8
Creating an
instant macro
name for the
phone list
database macro.

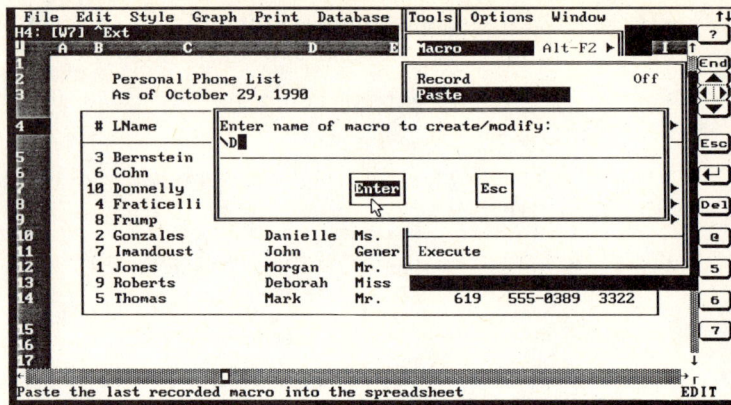

5. Press Enter to paste the macro into cell A1 on MACRO (see fig. QS3.9).

Fig. QS3.9
Pasting a
recorded macro
into a block on
the MACRO
active
spreadsheet.

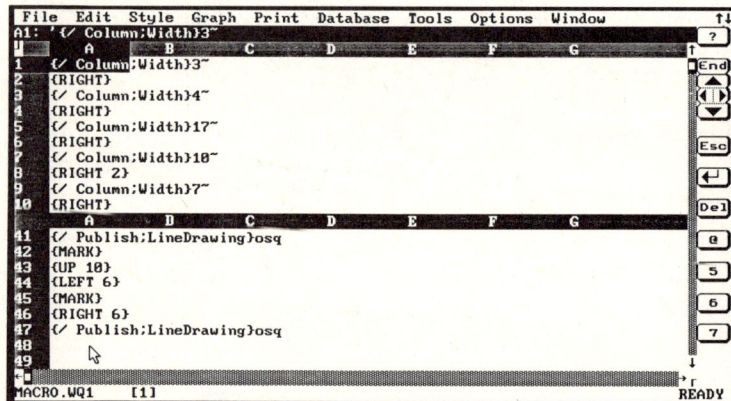

6. Press /FSR to save and replace the MACRO spreadsheet.

Creating a Macro Library

In this section, you classify the MACRO spreadsheet as a macro library. A macro library is a spreadsheet that stores all of your macros on one document. You conserve spreadsheet file sizes by not having to copy macros over and over again onto new spreadsheets. A macro library is a permanent reference source; whereas spreadsheets often outlive their usefulness.

The commands in a macro executed from a macro library affect the active spreadsheet only, unless you specify otherwise. When Quattro Pro cannot locate a macro that you want to execute on the active spreadsheet, the program searches through all of the macro libraries loaded in memory.

To classify MACRO.WQ1 as a macro library, do the following:

1. Press /TML to select the /**T**ools **M**acro **L**ibrary command.

2. Press Y to choose the **Y**es option.

3. Press /FSR to save and replace MACRO.WQ1.

Quattro Pro enables you to create as many macro libraries as you want. For example, you can create separate macro libraries for business and personal spreadsheet applications.

Manually Appending to the Macro

You can take several approaches to create a macro:

1. Use the macro recorder exclusively.

2. Create the macro by typing each command into a column of cells on the active spreadsheet.

3. Use the macro recorder first and then append additional macro commands into the macro.

As you experiment more with macros, you will find that the most efficient approach is to use the macro recorder for some tasks and to manually enter macro commands for other tasks. This approach gives you the best of both worlds.

Entering a macro manually is no different than entering other data manually. With a macro, however, be extra careful about the accuracy of your data because one missing brace, disoriented bracket, or misspelled command can cause the macro to crash.

When a macro crashes, it terminates before executing all of its commands. This event can have minor and serious consequences.

If the macro that crashes performs spreadsheet operations like copying data, aligning labels, and formatting numbers, the consequences of a crash are minor. At worst, Quattro Pro abandons the operation, leaving an unfinished or unformatted spreadsheet on-screen.

If your macro contains commands that perform external file operations like opening a file on disk, writing data to the file, and saving the file, a macro crash may cause irreparable damage to the file.

When a macro crashes, Quattro Pro displays an error message that indicates the cell address at which the execution error occurred. Press Esc and return to the active spreadsheet.

In figure QS3.9, each cell in column A contains a macro command. You can streamline the macro by joining each line containing a menu command with the following line that contains a keyboard command. Streamlining the macro makes it easier to trace the action that the macro performs and provides you with added incentive to document the macro in the next section.

The intent of this exercise is to demonstrate that the editing and creation processes are the same when you are working with macros manually.

Figure QS3.10 shows how to combine the commands in the first two cells into cell A1.

Fig. QS3.10
Combining cell commands to streamline the macro.

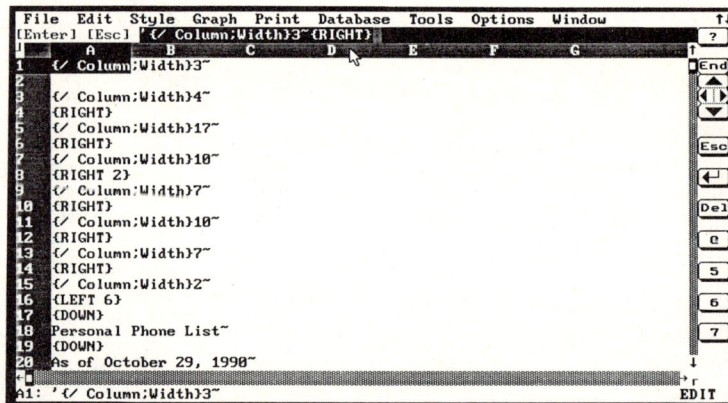

```
 File  Edit  Style  Graph  Print  Database  Tools  Options  Window      ↑↓
[Enter] [Esc] '{/ Column;Width}3~{RIGHT}                                  ?
        A         B         C        D       E       F       G          ↑End
1   {/ Column;Width}3~                                                   ▲
2                                                                        ◄ ►
3   {/ Column;Width}4~                                                    ▼
4   {RIGHT}
5   {/ Column;Width}17~
6   {RIGHT}                                                             Esc
7   {/ Column;Width}10~
8   {RIGHT 2}                                                            ↵
9   {/ Column;Width}7~
10  {RIGHT}                                                             Del
11  {/ Column;Width}10~
12  {RIGHT}                                                              c
13  {/ Column;Width}7~
14  {RIGHT}                                                              5
15  {/ Column;Width}2~
16  {LEFT 6}                                                             6
17  {DOWN}
18  Personal Phone List~                                                 7
19  {DOWN}
20  As of October 29, 1990~                                              ↓
                                                                        ► r
A1:  '{/ Column;Width}3~                                               EDIT
```

Follow these steps:

1. Place the cell selector in cell A1 and press F2 to enter Edit mode.

2. Type {*RIGHT*} and press Enter to append this command to the end of the one appearing in cell A1.

3. Place the cell selector in cell A2.

4. Press /EDR and press Enter to delete row 2 and move the remainder of the macro below cell A1.

5. Repeat steps 1 through 3 for the remaining lines in the macro program.

As you perform this operation, keep the following items in mind:

- You always can press Alt-F5 to undo an Edit mode operation.

- To re-enter an entire command line, be sure to type ' (the apostrophe label-prefix character) before you type the macro command.

Documenting Macros

You should document your macro programs to help others understand what you are trying to accomplish. Also, when you return to a macro that you created long ago, you can review the documentation to refresh your memory.

Macro documentation serves two specific needs: it displays the macro name and auto-execute name if one exists and briefly describes the purpose of each instruction.

To document the MACRO spreadsheet, do the following:

1. Place the cell selector in cell A1.

2. Press /EIR and the ↓ key to highlight cell block A1..A2. Press Enter to insert two rows.

3. Press /EIC and Enter to insert one column.

4. Move to cell A1, type *Name*, and press Enter to record the macro name column title.

5. Press the → key to move to cell B1. Type *Macro Command* and press Enter to record the macro command column title.

6. Press the → key to move to cell C1. Type *Action Performed* and press Enter to record the action performed column title.

7. Move to cell A3. Type '\D and press Enter to document the instant macro name.

8. Move to cell C3.

Type descriptions of the actions performed by each macro command (or series of commands) in column B. Remember that you are documenting the macro so that others can understand its purpose and function. Be brief, but be exact.

For example, in cell C3 you may enter the label '*Set column width A = 3* to document that the macro command in cell B3 changes the width of column A to 3.

Figure QS3.11 shows the streamlined version of the MACRO macro library spreadsheet complete with documentation.

Fig. QS3.11
Documenting a
macro program
that appears in
a library.

\D {/ Column;Width}3 ~ {RIGHT}	Set column width A = 3
{/ Column;Width}4 ~ {RIGHT}	Set column width B = 4
{/ Column;Width}17 ~ {RIGHT}	Set column width C = 17
{/ Column;Width}10 ~ {RIGHT 2}	Set column width D = 10
{/ Column;Width}7 ~ {RIGHT}	Set column width F = 7
{/ Column;Width}10 ~ {RIGHT}	Set column width G = 10
{/ Column;Width}7 ~ {RIGHT}	Set column width H = 7
{/ Column;Width}2 ~ {LEFT 6}{DOWN}	Set column width A = 3
Personal Phone List ~ {DOWN}	Enter title label 1
As of October 29, 1990 ~ {DOWN}{LEFT}	Enter title label 2
'# ~ {RIGHT}	Enter field name label 1
LName{RIGHT}	Enter field name label 2
FName{RIGHT}	Enter field name label 3
Title{RIGHT}	Enter field name label 4
ACode{RIGHT}	Enter field name label 5
Phone #{RIGHT}	Enter field name label 6
Ext{LEFT 6}	Enter field name label7
{/ Publish;AlignCenter} ~ {RIGHT 4}	Align field name label 1
{/ Publish;AlignCenter}{RIGHT 2} ~	Align field name labels 5, 6, 7
{LEFT 4}{MARK}{RIGHT 6}{DOWN 10}	Select database shell
{/ Publish;LineDrawing}osq{MARK}	Draw single outside line
{UP 10}{LEFT 6}{MARK}{RIGHT 6}	Select field names row
{/ Publish;LineDrawing}osq	Draw single outside line
{HOME}	Terminate macro program

Placing the documentation comments in the column immediately to the right of the macro accomplishes two things. First, this placement ensures that the comment labels are not accidentally assigned as names. Second, the placement prevents Quattro Pro from trying to execute the labels as macro instructions.

Notice that the final command has been omitted at the bottom of the \D macro shown in figure QS3.11. The {QUIT} command signifies the end of a macro program. Be sure to add this command to the bottom of all of your macros when you create a macro library. This command causes Quattro Pro to stop reading cells and returns control of the keyboard to the user.

Executing a Macro

To execute this macro, do the following:

1. Press /FR, type *MACRO*, and press Enter to load the macro library into memory.

2. Press /FN to open a new, blank spreadsheet that overlays the MACRO spreadsheet.

3. Press Alt-D to execute the database macro.

4. Press /FS to select the /File Save command. Type a name and press Enter to save the spreadsheet using that name.

Quattro Pro creates the shell of the phone list database on the new, blank spreadsheet. To halt the execution of a macro before it executes, press Ctrl-Break and then press Esc to return to Ready mode.

Summary

After completing this quick start, you should be familiar with the following concepts:

- Creating a database shell on a spreadsheet

- Entering data into a database

- Assigning names to the database and to the data in each field to make the process of selecting sort criteria easier

- Sorting a database using one sort key

- Sorting a database using multiple sort keys

- Returning a database to its original order of entry

- Auto-recording a macro

- Pasting a macro into a spreadsheet

- Assigning a unique name to a macro

- Creating a macro library spreadsheet

- Manually editing a macro

- Documenting a macro

- Executing a macro program

11

Managing Your Data

In addition to being an electronic spreadsheet program, Quattro Pro can function as a relational database manager. This chapter focuses on this process and shows you how to use the commands on the Data menu to sort, extract, and delete records—operations basic to every good database software product.

This chapter begins by showing you how to turn a spreadsheet into a database. This material defines each of the parts of a typical database, reviews the data management commands, and illustrates how to prepare your data for processing into reports and documents.

The next section discusses the different techniques you can use to sort database records, guidelines for maintaining the integrity of your database records, and instructions for returning an altered database to its original order. This section concludes with a brief review of how to modify Quattro Pro's default sort rules to meet special needs.

The chapter continues by discussing how to search a database and locate records that meet user-specified criteria. You learn how to locate, extract, and delete records—one of the most useful database operations.

The next section describes how to use a spreadsheet as a data-entry form and demonstrates how to control record accuracy by restricting the types of permissible entries.

Even the most complete and meticulously kept database can be ineffective if it does not yield simple and interpretable answers to specific questions. Quattro Pro's mathematical tools provide methods that enable you to identify relationships within large sets of data. You also learn to perform advanced mathematical analysis on a data set. This section demonstrates how to use the four analytical tools available at the bottom of the Tools menu and presents rules and procedures for regression analysis, optimization modeling, matrix operations, what-if analysis, and frequency distribution analysis.

463

Turning a Spreadsheet into a Database

The Quattro Pro database is a powerful information management and report creation tool. With this tool, you can manipulate large amounts of information and present the information in many different ways. Like a spreadsheet, a database helps you organize names and numbers that appear on reports.

A database enables you to segregate information on a spreadsheet into sets of related data and then reorganize the data instantly to create different reports. To reorganize a spreadsheet report, you have to execute several involved Copy and Move operations.

You can use a database to store all kinds of information. For example, a phone book is a database that stores a set of related information: a name, an address, and a phone number. The uses for a database are literally endless and limited by only your imagination. You can build a database to catalog your favorite video tapes, to devise a business check register, or to create a statistical report for major league baseball players.

Often, the structure of an individual database is portable to other applications. If you create a database to catalog your video tapes, for example, you can use the same database structure to catalog your cassettes, CDs, and albums.

You can easily turn a spreadsheet into a database. Figure 11.1 shows the shell of a database that will be used to store performance statistics for the top 10 National League batters.

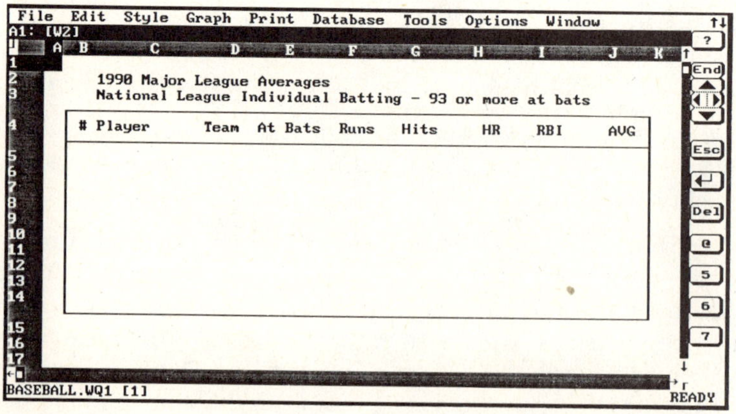

**Fig. 11.1
Building the
shell of a
database.**

Follow these six steps to create the database shell shown in figure 11.1:

1. Envision the database application. Do you want to manage employee names, business phone numbers, contact lists, baseball statistics? Enter a report title at the top of a new, blank spreadsheet that describes the envisioned application.

2. Create field names. Because each field name corresponds to an element in a database record (for example, a phone number), they should be descriptive of the field data. Create short, single-word names because many of the database operations enable you to use cell block names.

3. Enter the field names on the row below the database title.

4. Set the widths of the columns in the database with the /Style Column Width command.

5. Estimate the maximum number of records likely to appear in the database. Count down that number of rows from the field names row—that row is the bottom of the database shell.

6. Draw lines around the database shell. This technique helps when you build criteria tables and output blocks below the database shell.

A database, like a spreadsheet report, uses label headings to define the type of information stored in a column or row. Each row in a database is a record, and each column is a field. The database area is the part of the spreadsheet in which you store your records.

The baseball database has nine field names that appear on row 4: #, Player, Team, At Bats, Runs, Hits, HR (home runs), RBI (runs batted in), and AVG (batting average). These fields identify the individual performance statistics collected for a group of baseball players.

The shell pictured in figure 11.1 illustrates the commonly accepted way of creating the shell of a database. Like all good spreadsheet reports, you should create a database that looks like the document or report from which the database was created. For example, to create a database using the names, addresses, and phone numbers of business associates, design one that looks like a page out of your phone book.

When you build a database, follow these guidelines:

1. The database area must be rectangular. Quattro Pro does not perform Data menu operations on unconnected blocks of data.

2. Each column should contain only one type of data: numerical, alphabetic, or date and time serial numbers. (Don't mix dates with labels or labels with numbers.)

3. Do not place an empty row (or column) between the field name row and the first record in the database.

4. A Quattro Pro database can contain a maximum of 8,191 entries (8,192 total rows less one for the row containing field names).

Reviewing the Data Menu

Use the four Data menu commands to sort, search through, control movement, and enter data into a database (see table 11.1).

Table 11.1
Data Menu Commands

Command	Description
Sort	Changes the order of database records
Query	Searches through a database
Restrict Input	Restricts movement of the cell selector to unprotected cells
Data Entry	Specifies the data type permitted in a block of cells

Except for the **R**estrict Input command, selecting a Data menu command displays a second menu. The following sections illustrate how to use each of these commands to build your own database applications.

Entering Data

To enter data into a database, apply the same techniques you use when you enter data into a spreadsheet. Like a spreadsheet, a database can contain several types of data: labels, numbers, and even formulas. For example, cell J5 in figure 11.2 contains a formula that computes batting average by dividing the number of hits by the number of at bats.

As you enter data into a database, remember the following three simple rules:

1. Each category of data should have its own field. If you design a phone book database, for example, create one field for a person's first name and one for the last name. Entering the first and last

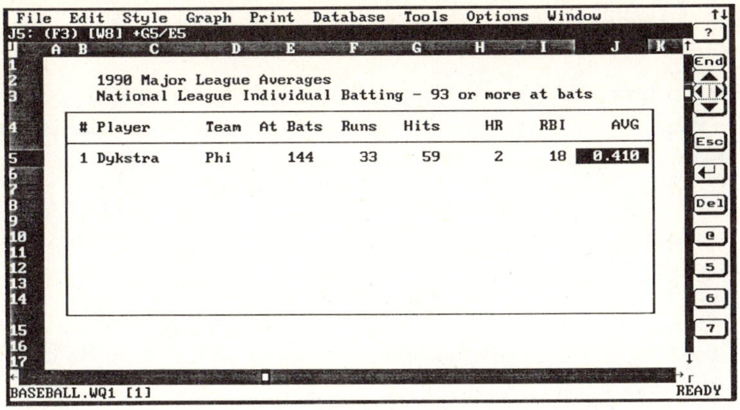

**Fig. 11.2
Entering the
first record into
the baseball
database.**

names into one field offers you no flexibility when creating reports
from sorted data.

When you have two or more people with the same last name, you
need to distinguish between them. You can place their first name,
their middle initial, or title into a field of its own.

2. Do not enter different types of data into the same field. For example,
   if you create a field for dates, enter only dates into that field. When
   you enter a mixture of dates, labels, and numbers into a field, sorting
   and analyzing database reports becomes more difficult.

3. Be careful about entering formulas into the database area. As long as
   the formulas are record-dependent, you can sort the formulas safely
   without generating bad data. A record-dependent formula solely
   references values existing on that record's row (see cell J5 in figure
   11.2).

   In a sort operation, the order of the records is shifted around. If you
   create field-dependent formulas that rely on the location of one
   record in relation to another, shifting records can cause formulas to
   return different data, depending upon the order of the record in the
   database.

Sorting a Database

The Sort command is a powerful Data menu tool, because this command
enables you to produce different combinations of the same data set without
changing the value of any record in the database. You always should main-

tain the integrity of a database—it is integral to creating meaningful reports from one data set.

If you sort two fields out of sequence—for example, a first name field and a last name field—you destroy the integrity of a database. How useful is a database if a person's first name doesn't match the last?

After you finish entering data into a database, you are ready to manipulate the data to use in a report. Figure 11.3, for example, shows several different ways of reorganizing the baseball database.

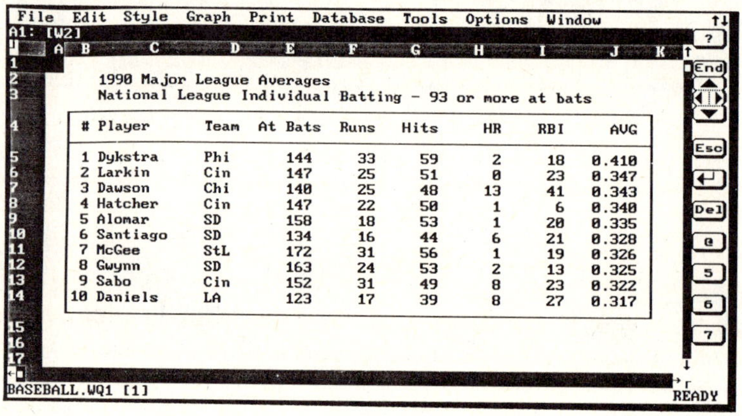

Fig. 11.3
The baseball database complete with 10 records.

```
 File   Edit   Style   Graph   Print   Database   Tools   Options   Window          ↑↓
A1: [W2]                                                                            ?
   A B      C          D      E      F      G       H       I        J      K       End
1
2        1990 Major League Averages
3        National League Individual Batting - 93 or more at bats
4        # Player      Team   At Bats  Runs   Hits    HR      RBI      AVG          Esc
5        1 Dykstra     Phi    144      33     59      2       18       0.410
6        2 Larkin      Cin    147      25     51      0       23       0.347        ↵
7        3 Dawson      Chi    140      25     48      13      41       0.343
8        4 Hatcher     Cin    147      22     50      1       6        0.340        Del
9        5 Alomar      SD     158      18     53      1       20       0.335
10       6 Santiago    SD     134      16     44      6       21       0.328        @
11       7 McGee       StL    172      31     56      1       19       0.326
12       8 Gwynn       SD     163      24     53      2       13       0.325        5
13       9 Sabo        Cin    152      31     49      8       23       0.322
14      10 Daniels     LA     123      17     39      8       27       0.317        6
15
16                                                                                 7
17
BASEBALL.WQ1 [1]                                                                 READY
```

With nine available sort fields, you can create many different reports. You can create a report that lists the players sorted by team. For example, because the triple crown honor is awarded to a player who finishes the season with the highest batting average, the greatest number of RBI, and the most home runs, you also can sort the database three times to locate the best candidates for that honor.

You tell Quattro Pro exactly how to sort your database by specifying sort criteria. You can sort a database alphabetically or numerically, in ascending and descending order.

The fields used to sort the records are called sort field keys, or *sort keys*. You can specify up to five sort keys per operation. Quattro Pro sorts a database according to each sort key's priority: the 1st Key has first priority; the 2nd Key has second priority; and so on.

Sort key priorities enable Quattro Pro to perform mini-sort operations. For example, if there are five records with the same field value specified by the 1st key, Quattro Pro re-sorts those records according to the 2nd key. If two records remain with the same field value specified by the 2nd key, Quattro Pro re-sorts the two records according to the 3rd key.

Sorting a database is typically a three-step process: you define the block to be sorted, specify the sort key criteria, and then select /Database Sort Go to begin the sort operation. To reset the sort criteria in preparation for a new operation, choose **Reset**.

Using One Sort Key

Suppose that you want to sort the baseball database alphabetically and in ascending order by each player's name. Specify the Player field as the first sort key and follow these steps:

1. Highlight the block you want to sort—for example, B5..J14.

2. Select /**D**atabase **S**ort to display the Sort menu.

3. Select **B**lock. (Quattro Pro records the highlighted block as the sort block.)

Tip | Omit the field names row from the database block definition, or Quattro Pro sorts that row of labels into your database. If you do not omit the field names and Quattro Pro performs the sort, press Alt-F5 to undo the sort operation.

4. Select **1**st Key, type the column you want to use as the key—C5—and press Enter.

Tip | You can enter any cell address or block that exists in the sort key column. For example, the addresses C1, C5..C14, and C392 all designate column C as the sort key column.

5. When prompted, choose **A**scending (or **D**escending) and press Enter.

6. Choose **G**o, and Quattro Pro rearranges the records according to your sort criteria (see fig. 11.4).

Figure 11.4 displays the result of this sort operation. Notice that Quattro Pro displays each sort criteria definition used at the right margin of the Sort menu, next to each command.

Using Multiple Sort Keys

You also can sort databases using two sort keys instead of one. For example, you may want to organize the database alphabetically by Team in ascending

Fig. 11.4
The results of sorting the baseball database alphabetically by Player.

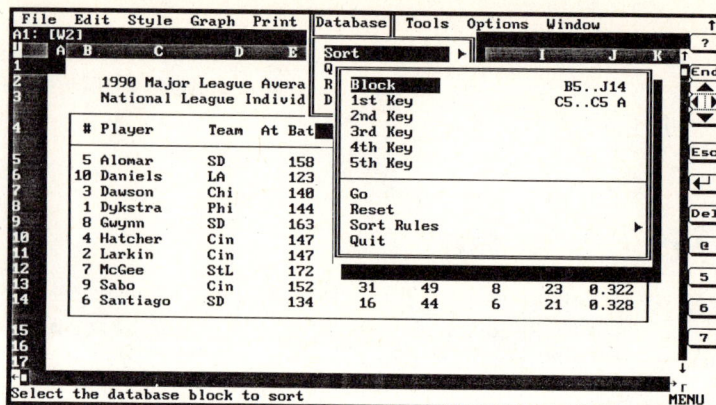

order; you also may want to sort members of the same team by the number of At Bats, in order from highest to lowest. You must specify the Team field as the **1**st Key and the At Bats field as the **2**nd Key.

You always can substitute block names in place of cell addresses—a particularly useful technique for Data menu operations.

By naming the database area DATABASE, for example, you can type that name in place of the block address B5..J14. Likewise, when you name the fields (using the names on row 4), you can enter each name in place of a cell address when defining the sort keys. (See Chapter 3 for more information about naming a cell block.)

To define the criteria for this sort operation, do the following:

1. Select /**D**atabase **S**ort to display the Sort menu.

2. Select **B**lock, type the block name or coordinates— DATABASE, for example—and press Enter.

Tip	After you enter a Block or sort key address, Quattro Pro keeps the definition active as long as you are working with the same spreadsheet. When you later create names for your database, Quattro Pro replaces cell blocks and sort key addresses with their new names.

3. Select **1**st Key, type the key coordinates or name—TEAM, for example—and press Enter.

4. When prompted, choose the sort order—**A**scending, for example—and press Enter.

5. Select **2**nd Key, type the second key coordinates or name— AT BATS, for example—and press Enter.

6. When prompted, choose the sort order and press Enter. (For the example, choose **D**escending and press Enter.)

7. Choose **G**o, and Quattro Pro rearranges the records according to your sort criteria (see fig. 11.5).

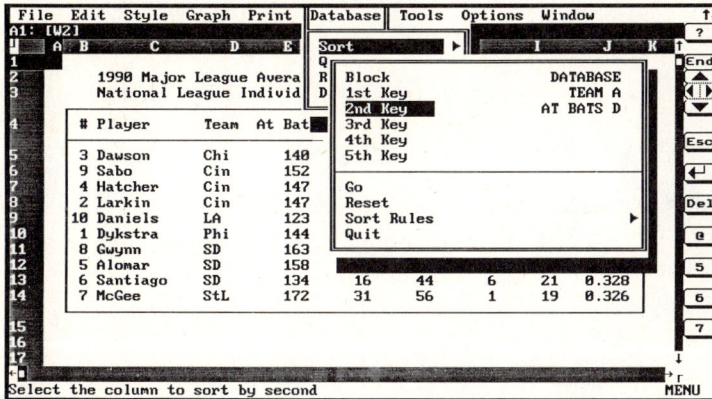

Fig. 11.5
The results of sorting the baseball database alphabetically by Team **and numerically by the number of** At bats.

Figure 11.5 displays the result of this sort operation. Notice that Quattro Pro now displays each sort criterion definition at the right margin of the Sort menu, next to each command.

Experiment with this same procedure by altering each sort key definition until you achieve the report style you want.

Returning the Database to Its Original Order

After you sort a database using several different sort keys, you sometimes need to return the database to its original order. Before you encounter this situation, consider the following three strategies for managing your database operations:

1. Make a backup copy of the database file. When you need to recover the original database, select /**F**ile **R**etrieve, type the name of the backup file, and press Enter to recover the original database.

2. Copy the database records (the database area) to another part of the active spreadsheet. To guarantee the integrity of this data, do not perform any Data menu operations on the copied data.

3. The most direct method is best understood by looking at the baseball database. Notice that the first field, #, identifies the numerical order of entry for each record. This technique, when used with all of your databases, ensures that you always can return a sorted database to its original order. Select # as the 1st Key and sort the database in Ascending order.

Fine-Tuning a Sort Operation

The final two commands on the Sort menu help to fine-tune a sort operation. By default, Quattro Pro sorts data in the following order when **A**scending is chosen on a sort key menu:

1st   Blank cells

2nd   Labels starting with numbers (sorted in numerical order)

3rd   Labels beginning with letters and special characters sorted in ASCII order)

4th   Values (sorted in numerical order)

When **D**escending order is chosen on a key menu, Quattro Pro sorts data in the opposite order (from 4th to 1st).

Figure 11.6 shows the two Sort Rules menu options: **N**umbers before Labels and **L**abel Order. The default settings appear at the right margin of the menu, next to each command.

Fig. 11.6
Reviewing the
options on the
Sort Rules
menu.

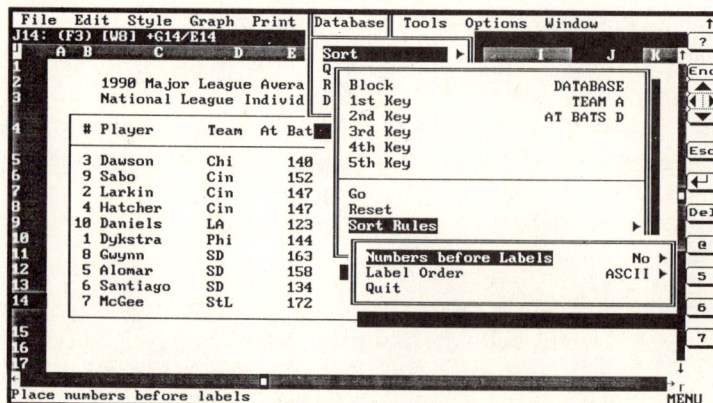

To change the default sorting order, select /**D**atabase **S**ort **S**ort Rules **N**umbers before Labels. When prompted, choose **Yes** to sort numbers before labels.

To change how Quattro Pro sorts labels, select /**D**atabase **S**ort **S**ort Rules **L**abel Order, and choose **ASCII** (the default) or **D**ictionary. The dictionary method disregards case in sorting labels so that player appears before Plenty

The ASCII sort method considers case in sorting labels so that uppercase labels appear before lowercase labels (*Plenty* before *player*). Labels beginning with special characters appear at the end.

Tip | After you change the sort rules, select /**O**ptions **U**pdate to record those settings for future sort operations.

Searching a Database

You use the commands found on the Query menu to search a database, locate records that meet specific conditions, and then copy the records elsewhere on the same spreadsheet.

The records appearing in the baseball database, for example, came from a larger database containing statistics for all National League baseball players. To create the example database, you searched for the 10 players with the highest batting averages. You could have extracted the 10 lowest battings averages, the 10 highest averages with at least 120 hits, or all players whose last name begins with the letter Z.

Figure 11.7 shows a database containing inventory data for a sports car rental agency. In figure 11.7, the database shell is block B4..H10, and the database area is block B5..H10. Notice that the database area is a subset of the database shell.

Remember, the database shell is the framework of the database: the field names row, the drawn lines (if any), and the database area where the records reside.

Defining the Search Block

The first step in every search operation is to define the search block. In most cases, the search block includes an entire database. Other valid search blocks include a portion of a database or even a database that resides on another

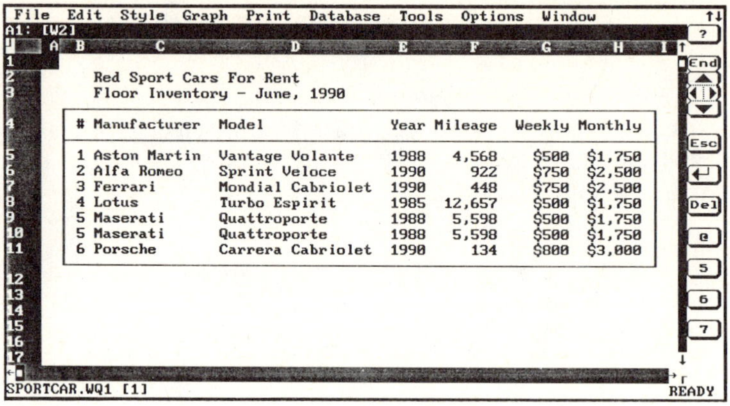

**Fig. 11.7
The Red Sports
Car rental
agency
database.**

```
 File   Edit   Style   Graph   Print   Database   Tools   Options   Window        ↑↓
A1: [W2]                                                                           ?
    A  B        C              D            E      F         G        H    I  ↑
1                                                                            ▓End
2          Red Sport Cars For Rent                                           ▲
3          Floor Inventory - June, 1990                                      ◀█▶
                                                                            ▼
4          # Manufacturer   Model            Year Mileage  Weekly Monthly
5          1 Aston Martin   Vantage Volante  1988   4,568   $500  $1,750   Esc
6          2 Alfa Romeo     Sprint Veloce    1990     922   $750  $2,500
7          3 Ferrari        Mondial Cabriolet 1990    448   $750  $2,500   ↵
8          4 Lotus          Turbo Espirit    1985  12,657   $500  $1,750
9          5 Maserati       Quattroporte     1988   5,598   $500  $1,750   Del
10         5 Maserati       Quattroporte     1988   5,598   $500  $1,750
11         6 Porsche        Carrera Cabriolet 1990    134   $800  $3,000    e
12                                                                          5
13
14                                                                          6
15
16                                                                          7
17                                                                          ↓
                                                                          →r
SPORTCAR.WQ1 [1]                                                          READY
```

spreadsheet in Quattro Pro's memory. Quattro Pro even can search databases not in memory, yet are stored on disk. Just supply the familiar linking syntax described in Chapter 7.

You must follow one rule when you define a search block: the block must include the database field names that you want to search. Except for a few special cases, however, the search block and the database shell have the same coordinates.

This rule is the opposite of the rule applying to sort operations. In sort operations, you omit the field names when naming the database area. This action prevents Quattro Pro from sorting the field names into your database.

In a search operation, Quattro Pro does not shift the order of the records—the program only looks at the records. When you define the search criteria, you must specify which field names the criteria apply to. After Quattro Pro knows what to search for, you need to indicate where in the search block to begin searching.

Tip | Select /**E**dit **N**ames **C**reate and assign a unique name to the database shell. In this example, the name SHELL is assigned to block B4..H10.

To specify the search block, do the following:

1. Select /**D**atabase **Q**uery **B**lock.

2. Type the name of the search block (SHELL, for the example) or type the block coordinates and press Enter.

Whether you choose to name your database shell or to supply block coordinates, be sure to include the field names row in the search block. If you don't, Quattro Pro does not search through your database correctly.

Assigning Names to the Field Names Row

To assign names to the field names, select \Database Query Assign Names. When you execute this command, Quattro Pro names the first entry in the first row below each field, using its field name label. In figure 11.7, for example, the name # is assigned to cell B5, Manufacturer to cell C5, Model to cell D5, and so on. This procedure enables Quattro Pro to begin the search operation at record #1 in the baseball database.

Assigning names to the field names row is optional but makes the process of creating and entering search criteria much easier—a name is easier to remember than a cell address.

Quattro Pro assigns the labels in the field names row to each field in the first record of the database. Quattro Pro knows which is the field names row and which is the first record in the database because when you specified the search block, you included the field names row as part of that block.

Tip | Quattro Pro requires that your field names be 15 characters or less in length to execute a Query menu operation properly.

Defining the Search Criteria

The next step in the search process is to define the search criteria. You first must select an area of the spreadsheet in which you can place the search conditions. In figure 11.8, a criteria table is entered into block B12..H13.

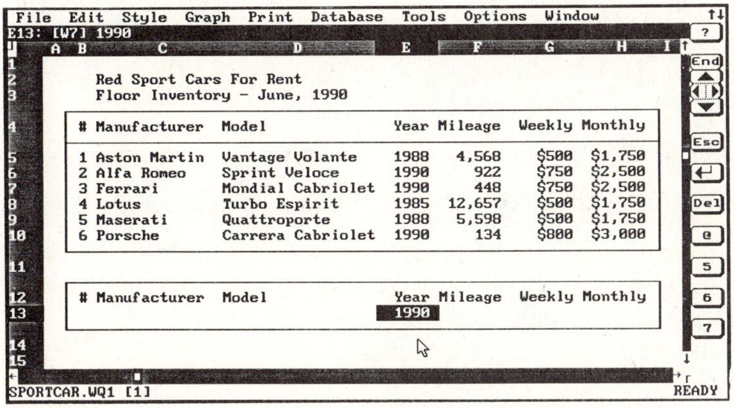

Fig. 11.8
Adding a criteria table to the sports car database.

A *criteria table* contains field names and the criteria definitions that specify what to look for in a search block. A valid criteria table must include the name of at least one field and beneath that a condition (or conditions) to be met.

The first line of the criteria table in figure 11.8 is a duplicate of row 4 from the database shell. Although you need to include only one field name, this criteria table format enables you to define criteria selectively for one, some, or all of the field names so that you can create an array of search conditions.

Although the Year field in this criteria table contains only one definition, you easily can define additional criteria for the Year field. Enter the extra criteria definitions in the cells beneath the first one (for example, in cells E14, E15, and so on).

The following rules explain how Quattro Pro evaluates the search conditions appearing in a criteria table:

1. When you enter more than one criterion definition on a row, Quattro Pro searches for records that satisfy all of the search conditions. This operation is an *AND* search.

2. When fields have multiple criteria definitions, Quattro Pro searches for records that satisfy either of the conditions. This operation is an *OR* search.

The single criterion in figure 11.8 tells Quattro Pro to search for all records whose Year field contains the value 1990.

You can decide where on the spreadsheet to put the criteria table, although choosing an area just outside the database shell is usually most convenient.

To set up the criteria table, do the following:

1. Highlight block B4..H4.

2. Select /**E**dit **C**opy.

3. Make cell B12 the active cell.

4. Press Enter to copy the field name labels to the criteria table.

5. Make cell E13 the active cell. Type *1990* and press Enter to record the criterion definition.

Tip | Select /**E**dit **N**ames **C**reate and assign a unique name to the criteria table. In this example, the name CRITERIA is assigned to block B12..H13.

To define the criteria table, do the following:

1. Select /**D**atabase **Q**uery **C**riteria **T**able.

2. Type *CRITERIA* and press Enter to record the coordinates of the criteria table.

In Step 2, you also can enter the block coordinates of the criterion definition, E12..E13. Both approaches return the same result. Also, when a field in a criteria table has no definition, Quattro Pro ignores that field during a search operation.

Creating Search Formulas

The criterion definition in figure 11.8 is rather simple. To create more complex definitions, include formulas in your search criteria. For example, you can search the rental car database for all cars whose model year is greater than or equal to 1988 (+YEAR>=1988) or locate those cars whose monthly rental rate is less than four times the value of the weekly rate (MONTHLY<+WEEKLY*4).

Criteria formulas must contain a cell reference, an operator, and a value. If you previously executed the **A**ssign **N**ames command, use those names instead of cell addresses in your criteria formulas. You can use any of the following mathematical and logical operators in a search formula:

=	Equal
<	Less than
<=	Less than or equal to
>	Greater than
>=	Greater than or equal to
<>	Not equal
#AND#	AND logical operator
#NOT#	NOT logical operator
#OR#	OR logical operator

When you enter a formula as a search criterion, Quattro Pro displays a 1 or a 0 in the cell. A 0 value indicates that the first cell searched returned a FALSE value, and a 1 indicates a TRUE condition. These displayed values do not affect the search in any way. If you prefer to display a particular cell formula in text form, make that cell active, press Ctrl-F, and select **T**ext.

Using Wild Cards

You also can use wild cards in your criteria table to delineate the conditions of a label search. Quattro Pro uses three different wild cards:

? A question mark replaces one character in a search label. When the search label is p?t, for example, Quattro Pro locates the labels pat, pet, pit, pot, and put.

* An asterisk replaces any number of characters in a label. When the search label is tre*, for example, Quattro Pro could locate the labels tree, tread, and treaty.

~ The tilde searches for all labels except those matching the label designation. For example, when the search label is ~T*, Quattro Pro finds all labels that do not begin with "T."

Tip If you leave the criteria definitions blank in the criteria block, Quattro Pro locates every record in the database.

Searching a Database

After you define the search block and the criteria table, Quattro Pro stores these definitions at the right margin of the Query menu, next to each command (see fig. 11.9). You now are ready to perform a search operation.

Fig. 11.9
The output block and criteria table definitions recorded on the Query menu.

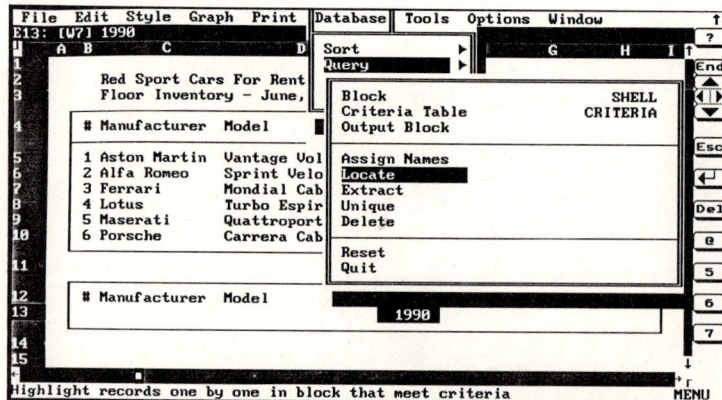

```
File  Edit  Style  Graph  Print  Database  Tools  Options  Window        ↑↓
E13: [W7] 1990                                                            ?
U  A  B      C            D    Sort          ▶         G      H    I ↑
1                              Query         ▶                        End
2            Red Sport Cars For Rent                                  ◀▮▶
3            Floor Inventory - June,  Block              SHELL        ▼
4                              Criteria Table    CRITERIA
   # Manufacturer  Model   ▮ Output Block                            Esc
5  1 Aston Martin  Vantage Vol  Assign Names
6  2 Alfa Romeo    Sprint Velo  Locate                               ↵
7  3 Ferrari       Mondial Cab  Extract
8  4 Lotus         Turbo Espir  Unique                               Del
9  5 Maserati      Quattroport  Delete
10 6 Porsche       Carrera Cab                                       ●
11                             Reset                                  5
12  # Manufacturer  Model   Quit                                     6
13                               1990                                 7
14                                                              ↓
15
      ■                                                          +r
Highlight records one by one in block that meet criteria          MENU
```

Locating Records

To begin a search-and-locate operation, select /**D**atabase **Q**uery **L**ocate. Figure 11.10 illustrates how Quattro Pro highlights the first record in the search block whose Year field contains the value 1990.

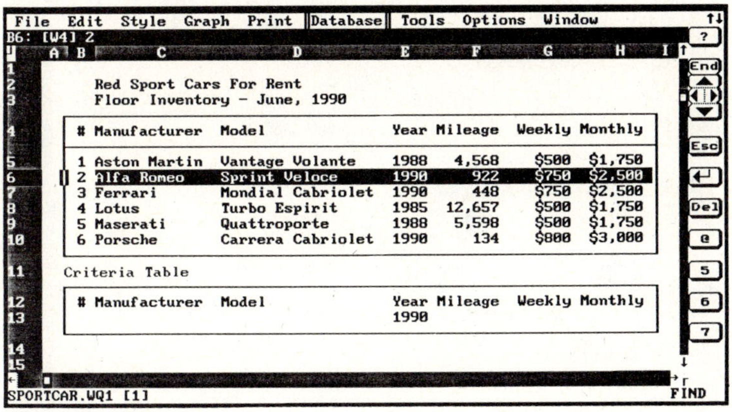

Fig. 11.10
Quattro Pro locates the first record in the database meeting the search criterion definition.

In the sports car database, the first match that Quattro Pro locates is record #2. To move to the next matching record, record #3, press ↓; to move to previous matches, press ↑. Press Home to move to the first matching record in the list and press End to move to the last matching record.

Occasionally, you may want to edit the contents of a highlighted record. Press the → or ← keys until the cell selector is in the field you want to edit. Then press F2 to enter EDIT mode. Make your changes on the input line and press Enter to accept the new field data.

Figure 11.11 illustrates how to use a formula to narrow a search operation. The criterion formula in cell F13, +MILEAGE<400, adds an additional restriction that tells Quattro Pro to locate the records for all cars (built in 1990) whose mileage is under 400 miles. Only one record, #6, meets this condition (see fig. 11.12).

Deleting Records

When you select /**D**atabase **Q**uery **D**elete, Quattro Pro removes from the database all records that satisfy the defined criteria. Before deleting these records, Quattro Pro asks you to confirm your selection. Select **D**elete to delete the records or **C**ancel to abort the operation.

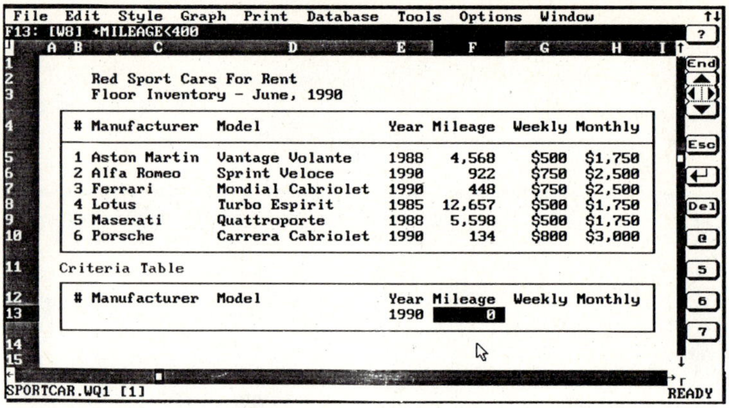

Fig. 11.11 Using a formula to narrow the search operation.

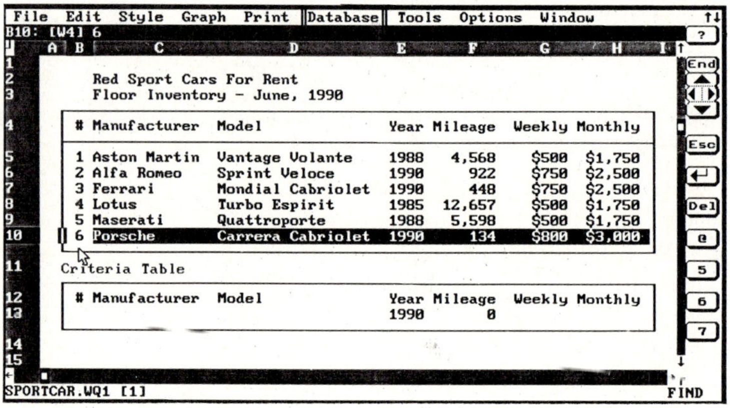

```
 File  Edit  Style  Graph  Print  Database  Tools  Options  Window        ↑↓
 F13: [W8] +MILEAGE<400                                                     ?
    A B     C           D              E      F       G       H    I     End
 1                                                                         ◄□►
 2          Red Sport Cars For Rent                                        ▼
 3          Floor Inventory - June, 1990
 4          # Manufacturer   Model          Year Mileage  Weekly Monthly   Esc
 5          1 Aston Martin   Vantage Volante 1988   4,568   $500  $1,750   ↵
 6          2 Alfa Romeo     Sprint Veloce   1990     922   $750  $2,500
 7          3 Ferrari        Mondial Cabriolet 1990   448   $750  $2,500   Del
 8          4 Lotus          Turbo Espirit   1985  12,657   $500  $1,750
 9          5 Maserati       Quattroporte    1988   5,598   $500  $1,750   @
10          6 Porsche        Carrera Cabriolet 1990  134    $800  $3,000
11          Criteria Table                                                 5
12          # Manufacturer   Model          Year Mileage  Weekly Monthly   6
13                                          1990      0
14                                                                         7
15
 SPORTCAR.WQ1 [1]                                                     READY
```

Fig. 11.12 Record #6, the only match in the sports car database, is highlighted.

```
 File  Edit  Style  Graph  Print [Database] Tools  Options  Window        ↑↓
 B10: [W4] 6                                                                ?
    A B     C           D              E      F       G       H    I     End
 1                                                                         ◄□►
 2          Red Sport Cars For Rent                                        ▼
 3          Floor Inventory - June, 1990
 4          # Manufacturer   Model          Year Mileage  Weekly Monthly   Esc
 5          1 Aston Martin   Vantage Volante 1988   4,568   $500  $1,750   ↵
 6          2 Alfa Romeo     Sprint Veloce   1990     922   $750  $2,500
 7          3 Ferrari        Mondial Cabriolet 1990   448   $750  $2,500   Del
 8          4 Lotus          Turbo Espirit   1985  12,657   $500  $1,750
 9          5 Maserati       Quattroporte    1988   5,598   $500  $1,750   @
10          6 Porsche        Carrera Cabriolet 1990  134    $800  $3,000
11          Criteria Table                                                 5
12          # Manufacturer   Model          Year Mileage  Weekly Monthly   6
13                                          1990      0
14                                                                         7
15
 SPORTCAR.WQ1 [1]                                                      FIND
```

When Quattro Pro deletes all matching records from a database, all other records move up to fill the vacated spaces. If you accidentally delete records that you want to keep, press Ctrl-F5 to bring the records back.

Setting Up an Output Block

The **Extract** and **Unique** search commands find records that satisfy the criteria and then move the records to a different part of the spreadsheet for further processing. Before you use either of these search commands, you must define an output block so that Quattro Pro knows where to store the extracted data.

These two commands are useful for extracting data from databases in several locations: spreadsheets open in memory, spreadsheets on disk, and other databases.

In figure 11.13, an output block appears in block B20..H20. When Quattro Pro locates records meeting the conditions specified in the criteria table, Quattro Pro copies the records to the output block beginning at the first line below the field names row.

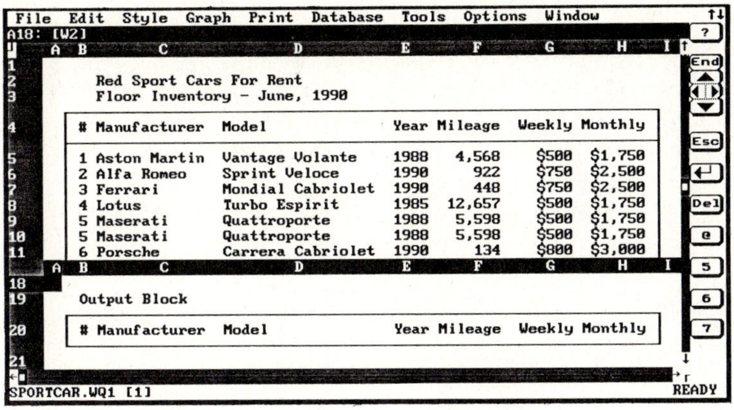

Fig. 11.13 Creating an output block below the database and the criteria table.

To create this output block, do the following:

1. Highlight block B4..H4.

2. Select /**E**dit **C**opy.

3. Make cell B20 the active cell.

4. Press Enter to copy the field name labels to the output block.

To define the output block, perform the following steps:

1. Highlight block B20..H20.

2. Select /**E**dit **N**ames **C**reate.

3. Type *OUTPUT* and press Enter to record this name.

4. Select /**D**atabase **Q**uery **O**utput **B**lock.

5. Type *OUTPUT* and press Enter to record the name of the output block.

An output block, like a criteria table, does not need to contain every field name from the database—only the ones that currently are being searched. However, you should create an output block in the same manner that you create a criteria table. This procedure ensures the greatest flexibility when you perform search operations.

Extracting Records

When you select /**Database Query Extract**, Quattro Pro copies all of the matching records into the output block. Only those fields whose names appear on the first line of the output block are included in the copied records.

If you specify only the field names row when defining the output block, Quattro Pro uses as much space as necessary to copy the matching records. If you specify a limited number of rows below the field names row, Quattro Pro uses that space until it is filled. When Quattro Pro runs out of space to copy to, the program displays a warning message explaining that all records cannot be extracted into the existing output block.

This problem is fairly easy to correct. First, erase all of the records in the output block. Next, redefine the size of the output block. Finally, restart the search operation.

Using the same criteria as before, figure 11.14 illustrates the result of an extract operation. Instead of highlighting a matched record, Quattro Pro extracts a copy of the record and places the copy in the first row underneath the field names row in the output block.

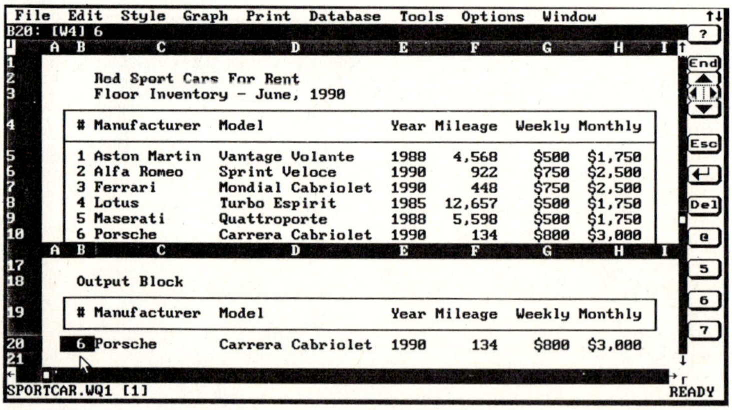

Fig. 11.14
Quattro Pro
extracts a
matching
record and
copies that
record to the
output block.

Identifying Unique Records

When you select /**Database Query Unique**, Quattro Pro copies all unique records that meet the specified criteria into the output block. Unique works like **Extract**, except that **Unique** does not copy duplicate records into the output block.

Consider the revised sports car database shown in figure 11.15. Notice that record #5 appears twice in this version of the database. The larger the database, the greater the chances that you will encounter duplicated records.

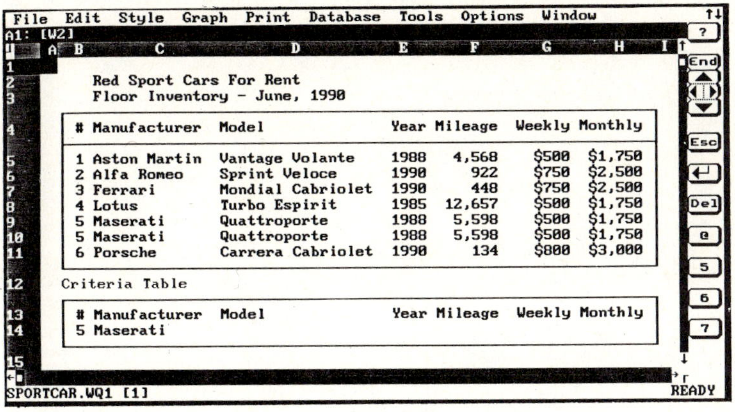

Fig. 11.15
Entering criteria to extract a list of unique records from the database.

The criteria table specifies all records whose # field equals 5 and whose Manufacturer field contains the label Maserati. In this situation, the Unique command copies the unique records that meet these conditions (see fig. 11.16).

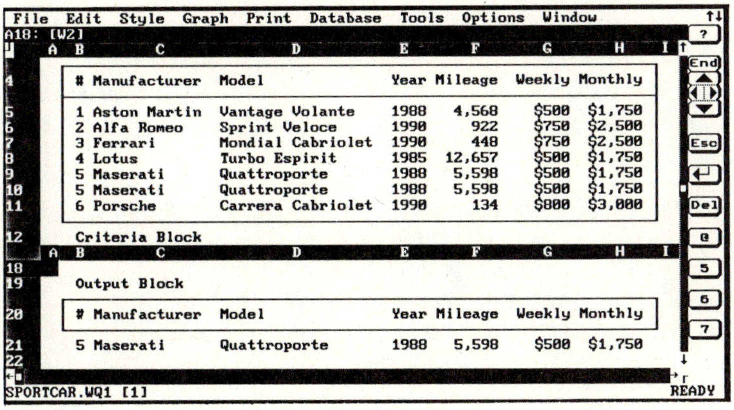

Fig. 11.16
All unique records are copied from the database into the output block.

Notice that the output block in this figure contains only one record. Because only two records met the search conditions in the criteria table, and these records are duplicates, Quattro Pro copies only one record into the output block.

Now look at the split window shown in figure 11.17. The results displayed in this output table were achieved by not specifying any criteria in the criteria table.

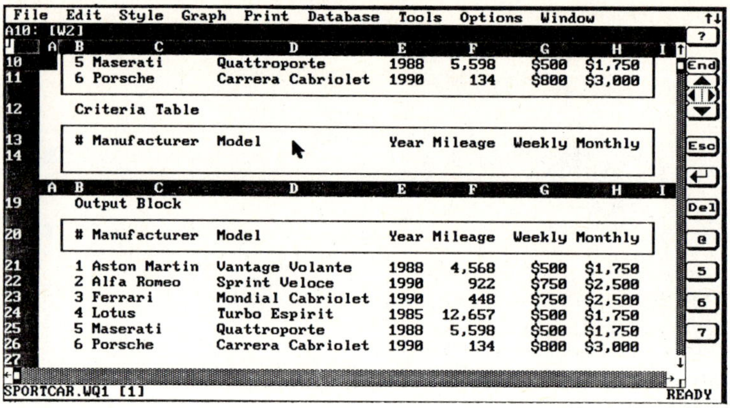

Fig. 11.17
Results of not specifying criteria.

Not specifying any criteria forces Quattro Pro to copy all unique records from the database into the output table (a clever way of updating a database when you suspect duplicate records exist).

Using a Database as a Data-Entry Form

The /**D**atabase **R**estrict Input command enables you to set up your spreadsheet as a data-entry form. After executing this command, Quattro Pro limits movement of the cell selector to unprotected cells only.

To set up the sports car database for data entry, do the following:

1. Select /**S**tyle **P**rotection **U**nprotect.

2. When prompted for a block to unprotect, type the block name (DATABASE, for the example) and press Enter.

3. Select /**D**atabase **R**estrict Input.

4. Type the block to restrict—*DATABASE*—and press Enter.

Quattro Pro immediately restricts movement of the cell selector to the database area for the sports car database.

When you execute this command, Quattro Pro reframes the database in the window by positioning the first unprotected field in the database at the upper left portion of your screen.

To prevent Quattro Pro from reframing your database, perform the following steps prior to selecting /**D**ata **R**estrict Entry:

1. Place the cell selector in the first unprotected field in the database.

2. Select /**W**indows **L**ocked Titles.

3. When prompted, select **B**oth.

When you perform these steps, you cannot move your cell selector to any location above, or to the left of, the active cell. When you execute the **R**estrict Entry command, Quattro Pro does not move your database.

While in restricted entry mode, use the cursor-movement keys to move about the database. To disable the restricted access, press Enter or Esc.

Controlling the Types of Data Entered into a Database

The /**D**atabase **D**ata Entry command controls the type of data that Quattro Pro accepts into a cell or a block. Use this command to increase the accuracy of data-entry activities.

For example, suppose that a field (column) of data in a database is designated for dates only. By restricting the cells in this column to date-only entries, you can prevent data-entry errors.

To restrict the type of data acceptable in an entry, do the following:

1. Select /**D**atabase **D**ata Entry.

2. When prompted, select **L**abels Only to restrict all input to labels or select **D**ates Only to restrict input to dates.

Select /**D**atabase **D**ata Entry **G**eneral to enable a cell to accept any type of data.

Analyzing Data

The remaining part of this chapter is devoted to demonstrating how to use the four commands found on the bottom of the **T**ools menu (see table 11.2). These advanced analytical tools use information from a database to perform a regression analysis, parse labels from an imported data set, execute what-if sensitivity analysis, and create frequency distributions.

Table 11.2
Tool Menu Commands

Command	Description
Advanced Mathematics	Performs regression analysis, matrix operations, and optimization testing
Parse	Breaks apart long labels and places the individual parts into separate cells
What-If	Performs 1-way and 2-way sensitivity analysis
Frequency	Creates a frequency distribution from a data set

The examples in the remaining sections offer sufficient coverage of each command to enable you to use most or all of the features available for each tool. You can consult a statistics text for more comprehensive presentations of the mathematical proofs and axioms on which these tools are based.

Using Advanced Math Tools

The /Tools Advanced Math menu offers four powerful statistical tools that you can use to analyze different types of data. The Advanced Math menu commands are listed in table 11.3.

Table 11.3
Advanced Math Menu Commands

Command	Description
Regression	Performs single- and multi-variable data set regressions
Invert	Creates an inverted matrix from a matrix
Multiply	Multiplies one matrix by a second matrix
Optimization	Calculates the best solution to complex what-if? questions

Regression Analysis

Regression analysis attempts to devise an equation in which an independent variable predicts the value of a dependent variable.

A regression can be performed using more than one independent variable. Regression analysis, in fact, is one of the most effective methods for determining a linear relationship between a set of independent variables and a single dependent variable.

Suppose that you want to determine the relationship between the average yearly price of gasoline and the quantity that you purchase. The hypothesis is that your consumption (Cy) depends on the price (Px) of gasoline. Because there is only one independent variable, (Px), this problem is a single-variable regression analysis.

The table in figure 11.18 contains data about average gasoline prices and consumption in gallons for a 10-year period. Also notice that the Regression menu displays the definitions for each variable, the output block, and a y-axis intercept. You must enter these definitions before executing the **Regression** command.

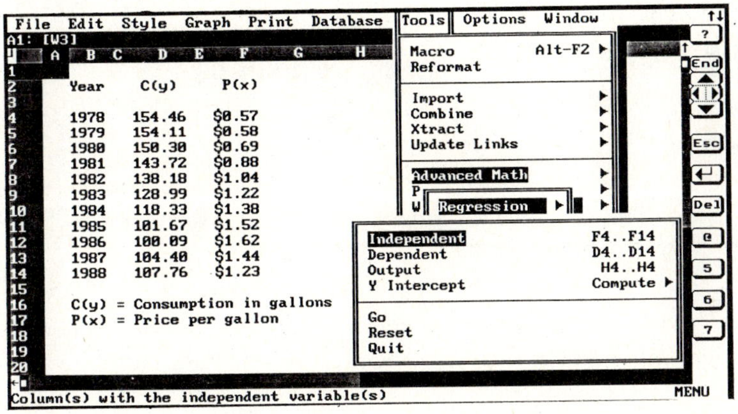

Fig. 11.18
A data table containing yearly gasoline consumption and average yearly price per gallon.

To do a regression analysis using this data, perform the following steps:

1. Select /**Tools** Advanced Math **Regression**.

2. Select **Independent**, type *F4..F14*, and press Enter.

3. Select **Dependent**, type *D4..D14*, and press Enter.

Tip | To include other independent variables, enter additional data into the columns to the right of the first independent variable. Then include these columns in the block you enter in step 2.

4. Select **Output**, type *H4*, and press Enter.

Tip | Use the **Compute** setting for most basic regression problems. To force the y-intercept value to 0, choose **Y Intercept Zero**.

5. Select **Go** to calculate the regression.

The Regression tool appraises each pair of points supplied in your data table and then derives an equation that minimizes each pair's distance from a "best fit" line. Quattro Pro calculates a formula constant and the coefficients for each independent value and then displays the results in a regression table (see fig. 11.19). With this equation, you can predict a new dependent value based on a new independent value.

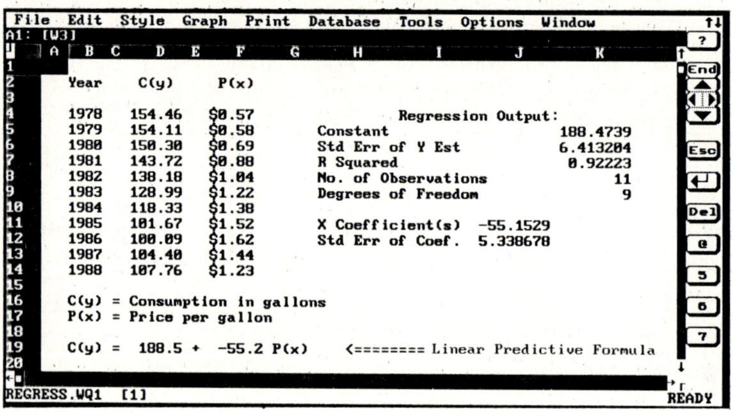

Fig. 11.19
A regression
analysis table
copied into the
Output Block.

The constant and the X coefficient(s) are the key components of the equation. Each independent variable that you specify in your data table always has one constant and one coefficient. Use the following syntax to build a linear predictive formula from the data in this table:

Dependent Variable = Constant +

    (1st independent variable * 1st X coefficient) +
    (2nd independent variable * 2nd X coefficient) +
... + (nth independent variable * nth X coefficient)

Because the consumption versus price example contains only one independent variable, only one X coefficient exists.

The linear predictive formula appears at the bottom of figure 11.19. To create this formula, the value +K5 was placed in cell D19, and the value +J11 was placed in cell F19. This formula updates itself each time you re-run the regression with new data—as long as you do not change the location of the output table. If you add independent variables to your data table, you must create additional cell references in the formula appearing on row 19 to accommodate the new X coefficients.

Using Matrix Operations: Invert and Multiply

Using matrices, you can solve multivariable linear equations simultaneously. A *matrix* is a rectangular array of numbers that describe the coefficients for variables in a group of linear equations. If you have to solve linear equations using matrices, use Quattro Pro's **Invert** and **Multiply** commands to calculate the answers quickly.

Consider the matrices shown in figure 11.20. Each time you create an inverted matrix, you must go through the four-step process outlined in this figure. The values that you are required to supply are highlighted.

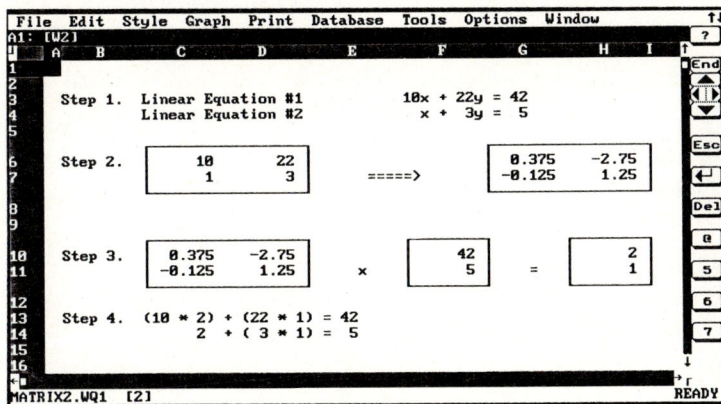

Fig. 11.20 Creating an invert matrix to solve two linear equations simultaneously.

Suppose that you want to solve simultaneously the two linear equations pictured on rows 3 and 4. You can solve the equations using the **Invert** and **Multiply** commands.

To invert a matrix, perform the following steps:

1. Create an input matrix using the coefficients from each equation and enter the matrix onto a spreadsheet. The sample input matrix appears in cells C6..D7.

2. Select /**Tools Advanced Math Invert**.

3. Type *C6..D7* and press Enter to specify the input matrix.

4. Type *G6* and press Enter to specify the upper left cell of the block in which you want to place the invert matrix.

The invert matrix from G6..H7 is copied to block C10..D11 in preparation for the next steps.

To multiply matrices, perform the following steps:

1. Create a matrix using the constants from the original equations and enter the matrix onto the same spreadsheet. The sample constant matrix appears in cells F10..F11.

2. Select /Tools Advanced Math Multiply.

3. Type *C10..D11* and press Enter to specify the first matrix to multiply.

4. Type *F10..F11* and press Enter to specify the second matrix to multiply.

5. Type *H10* and press Enter to specify the upper left cell of the block in which you want to place the solution matrix.

The solution matrix provides the two values that solve both linear equations. To prove that these values are correct, review Step 4 in figure 11.20.

When you multiply two matrices, the number of columns in the first matrix must equal the number of rows in the second matrix, or Quattro Pro does not perform this operation.

In figure 11.21, matrix #1 contains the number of units produced for three products: X, Y, and Z. matrix #2 contains the units of material (M) and labor (L) required to build a unit of X, Y, and Z. To produce one unit of X, for example, you need 4 units of material and 1 unit of labor.

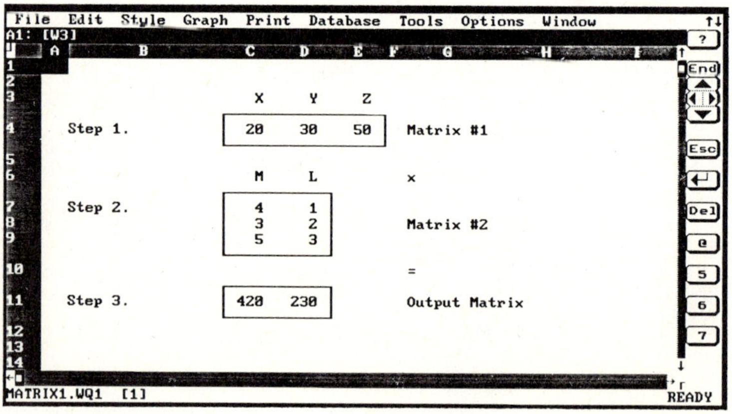

**Fig. 11.21
Using matrix multiplication to determine the input requirements for a production run.**

To determine the total number of units of material and labor required to produce 20 units of X, 30 units of Y, and 50 units of Z, multiply matrix #1 by matrix #2. As you can see from the bottom of figure 11.21, you need 420 units of material and 230 units of labor.

Using Optimization Modeling

Optimization modeling enables you to find the optimal solution to a problem given a set of constraints. If you have an objective function that you want to maximize, minimize, or keep within certain bounds, optimization modeling finds the "best fit" values to the function.

The preceding example demonstrates how to use matrices to calculate the total number of units of material and labor required to produce certain amounts of products X, Y, and Z. Suppose that you want to determine the optimal production level for each product, given a set of bounds and constraints.

The following data is known about products X, Y, and Z:

- Each unit of X requires 4 units of material and 1 unit of labor and provides $10 per unit profit.

- Each unit of Y requires 3 units of material and 2 units of labor and provides $12.50 per unit profit.

- Each unit of Z requires 5 units of material and 3 units of labor and provides $15 per unit profit.

Consider the following constraints on the production of X, Y, and Z:

- The maximum number of units of material available each month is 32,500 (4X + 3Y + 5Z <= 32,500).

- The maximum number of units of labor available each month is 20,000 (.5X + 2Y + 3Z <= 20,000).

- Total production output cannot exceed 8,500 units (X + Y + Z <= 8,500).

Management has set the following production bounds for itself:

- Produce a minimum of 1,000 units each of X, Y, and Z each month to accommodate pre-orders from long-standing clients

- Each month, produce no more than 5,000 units of any one product (X, Y, or Z)

You do not have to solve all of the possible solutions to this problem using matrices, because a much better tool is at your disposal: the **O**ptimization command.

Optimization analysis is linear programming, a tool commonly used in business management and social science research, although optimization analysis may be used in any discipline to juggle multiple considerations (for example, pollution versus jobs versus health versus profits).

For complete details about optimization modeling and linear programming, consult a statistics text. To gather ideas about how you can use optimization in your own field, review the journal studies and papers published by professionals in that discipline. In this discussion, you learn how to prepare an optimization model using known data about products X, Y, and Z.

Optimization modeling involves the following four steps:

1. Entering the input values

2. Specifying a location for the output values

3. Executing the model

4. Reviewing the results of a model run

Linear Constraint Coefficients are the coefficients from a matrix describing the constraints placed on the variables in the system. In the example, the variables are Material, Labor, and Capacity. The coefficients come from the three linear equations that appear below each statement of constraint. You can combine these coefficients into the following three-by-three matrix:

	X	Y	Z
Material	4	3	5
Labor	5	2	3
Capacity	1	1	1

Quattro Pro does not accept nonlinear equations as valid constraint coefficients.

Inequality/Equality Relations are the symbols that describe the relationship between the linear constraint coefficients and the constant constraint terms. In the example, all of the relations are of the less-than-or-equal-to type.

When you do not specify an inequality or equality relation, Quattro Pro defaults to equality relations.

Constant Constraint Terms describe upper or lower limits. You must enter one constraint term for each row in the linear constraint coefficient matrix. In the example, these three values are 32,500 for material, 20,000 for labor, and 8,500 for capacity.

The **B**ounds For Variables command defines the upper and lower bounds for the variables, if and when they exist. In the example, **B**ounds For Variables defines management's established minimum and maximum production levels.

You can create a two-by-three matrix that describes these bounds:

	X	Y	Z
Pre-orders	1,000	1,000	1,000
Desired Production Maximum	5,000	5,000	5,000

If you do not specify upper and lower bounds for your variables, Quattro Pro restricts all variables to non-negative real numbers.

Formula Constraints are the formulas that you want treated as constraints. In the example, you choose the Profit/unit, Pre-orders, and Desired Production Maximum as the formula constraints.

By specifying formula constraints, Quattro Pro must locate values for each variable, so that when each variable is entered into the formula, a nonnegative value is returned.

Objective Function enables Quattro Pro to determine the optimal solution to the problem by plugging a range of variables into one allowable objective function. The intent of this model is to maximize (or minimize) the objective function.

In the example, the objective function that you want to maximize is total profit earned: 10X + 12.5Y + 15Z; the objective function row contains the values 10, 12.5, and 15.

Extremum enables you to specify whether Quattro Pro should maximize or minimize the objective function. To maximize, choose **L**argest; to minimize, choose **S**mallest. By default, Quattro Pro minimizes the objective function. In the example, you maximize the objective function.

Figure 11.22 shows one way to record each of the input values onto a spreadsheet.

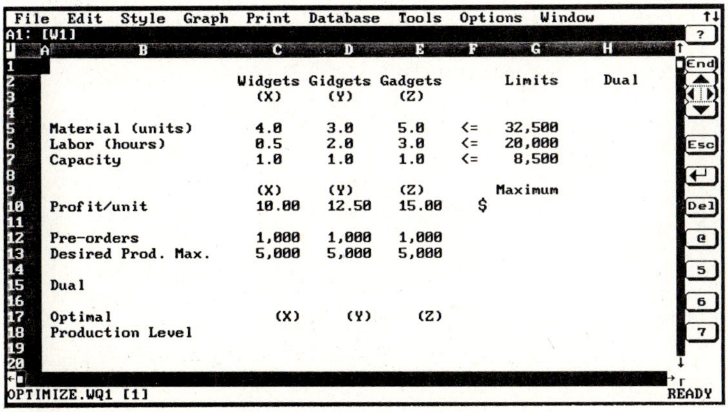

Fig. 11.22 Creating the format of the model and entering the input values.

Variables are the optimal values attained after executing the model. Quattro Pro returns one value for each variable in your system in a location on the spreadsheet that you specify.

Because the example has three variables, Quattro Pro outputs three optimal values. By plugging these values into the objective function, you can derive an optimal value for the entire function.

Solution is the optimal value that Quattro Pro calculates when plugging the optimal values into the objective function. Quattro Pro returns only one solution per model, in a location on the spreadsheet that you specify.

Dual values and **Additional dual values** offer additional information about the relationship between the optimal value and the bounds and constraints that you have set for your system.

A dual value tells you how much the optimal value increases (or decreases) if you lower or raise a constant constraint term or bound by one unit. In the example, the first dual value tells you how much profits increase or decrease when you alter the constant constraint terms. The second dual value tells how much profits increase or decrease when you alter the bounds of production (set by management) by one unit.

The dual values are optional values. If you do not enter dual values in your model, Quattro Pro ignores these values when executing the model.

Before executing the model, you must specify the location of each piece of input and output data for your model. Figure 11.23 illustrates the Optimization menu after each of these values is defined.

Fig. 11.23 Defining the locations of the input and output values for the model.

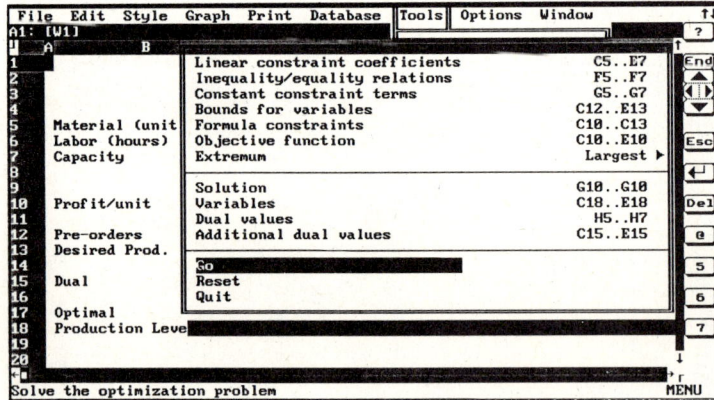

To execute the model, choose **G**o from the Optimization menu.

After executing the optimization model, your spreadsheet looks like figure 11.24. Quattro Pro has filled in four sets of values: dual values for the linear constraint coefficients, the maximum profit value, dual values for the production bounds, and the optimal production values for X, Y, and Z.

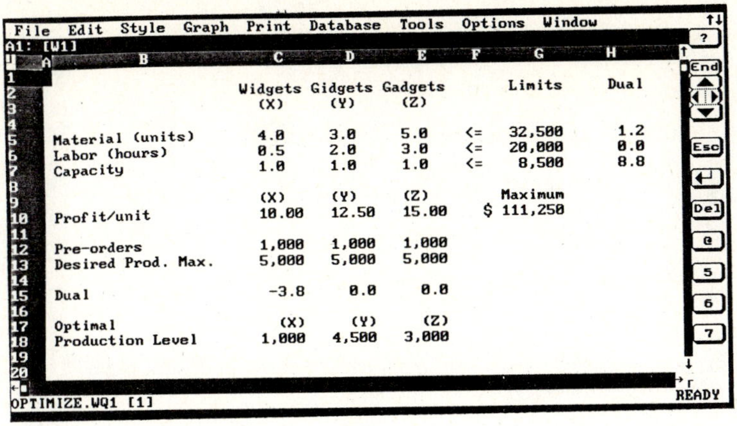

Fig. 11.24 Reviewing the results on the spreadsheet.

The spreadsheet results indicate that, given the availability of material and labor and the desired minimum and maximum production bounds, you can achieve a maximum monthly profit of $111,250 when you produce 1,000 units of X, 4,500 units of Y, and 3,000 units of Z.

The dual values for the linear constraints coefficients indicate that although labor constraints are not affecting profitability, you can increase profits if you raise the constraints on material and production capacity. In other words, you can increase maximum profits if you locate additional material suppliers, increase your production capacity, or both.

The dual values for the production bounds indicate that the dual values are having no adverse affect on your profitability.

Using the Parse Command

The Parse command is used to break long labels into two or more smaller labels. Although this may not sound like a very interesting or useful proposition, consider the Parse command in the more familiar context of database management.

In Chapter 7, you learn how to import outside data files into the Quattro Pro spreadsheet environment. When Quattro Pro imports a file, the program often places all of the data into one column. This placement really isn't a problem—although the imported file loses its original formatting, the imported file usually retains its general organization (see fig. 11.25).

This database appears to have three individual fields: NAME, SS#, and RATE/HR. In fact, each record is contained in a cell within column B. Look at the input line at the top of the spreadsheet and review record #1.

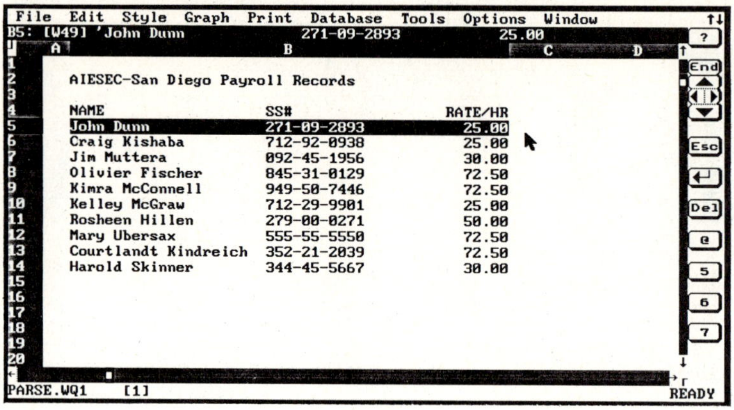

Fig. 11.25
An imported database in which each record appears in a cell in column B.

With the **P**arse command, you can re-create this database's original field structure without having to re-enter any records.

Executing a Parse Operation

A parse operation involves the following four steps:

1. Creating a format line

2. Defining the input block

3. Defining the output block

4. Selecting **G**o to parse the data

You can use the **P**arse command to reformat the database shown in figure 11.25 by following these steps:

1. Place the cell selector in cell B4.

2. Select **C**reate, and Quattro Pro designs a new field format line in the row directly above the field names row (see fig. 11.26).

3. Select **I**nput, type *B4..B15*, and press Enter to record the input block. The input block always must include the field format line.

4. Select **O**utput, type *B18*, and press Enter to record the output block (see fig. 11.27).

5. Select **G**o to parse the database.

If you defined the input and output blocks correctly, the results of the operation looks like figure 11.28. Quattro Pro creates three columns of data, one for each field name that the program recognized.

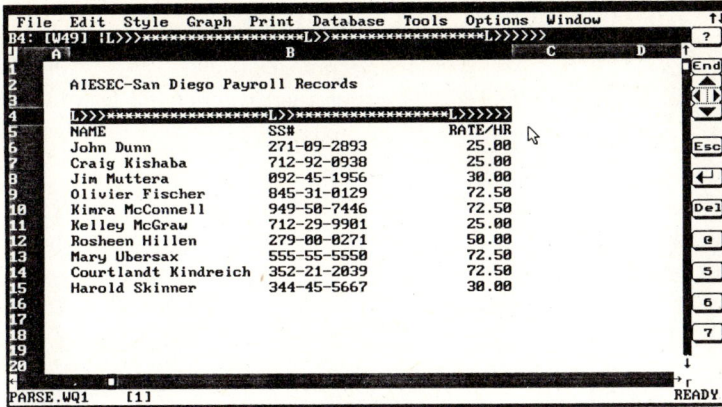

Fig. 11.26
A field format line created for the database.

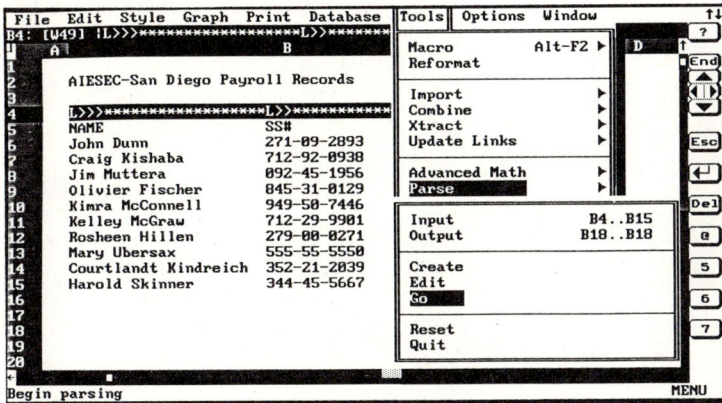

Fig. 11.27
Quattro Pro stores each definition at the right of the Parse menu, next to each command.

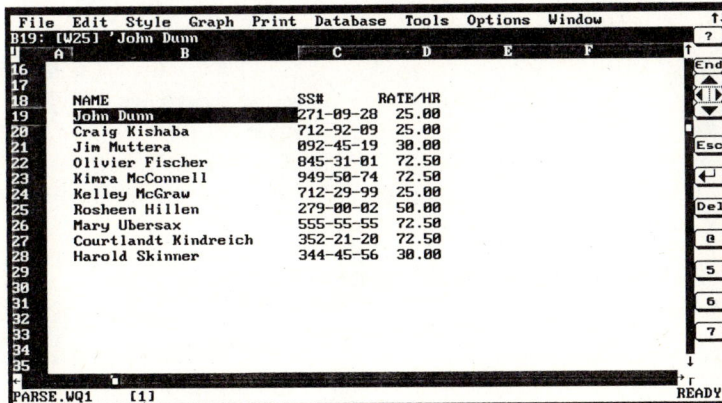

Fig. 11.28
The database regains its original field name organization.

Performing Multiple Parse Operations

Quattro Pro has no rule restricting how many times you can parse a set of data. You should parse data as long as it is easier than re-entering all of the records into a database.

Fortunately, you seldom need to parse a set of data more than a few times, because the **Edit** command (on the Parse menu) enables you to create custom format lines. When the format line that Quattro Pro creates is not adequate, select **Edit** and create a custom format using any of the characters shown in table 11.4.

Table 11.4
Format Line Symbols

Symbol	Description
|	Denotes the beginning of a format line
V	Precedes a value cell entry
L	Precedes a label cell entry
T	Precedes a time value entry
D	Precedes a date value entry
>	Indicates a continuing entry
*	Points out blank spaces that Quattro Pro can fill in with longer entries
S	Tells Quattro Pro to skip the character in this position

Performing Advanced Parse Operations

Earlier in this chapter, you are advised to create a unique field for each category of information in a database. The logic of creating separate fields for the two parts of a name—one field for the first name and one for the last—is discussed. When this logic is not followed (such as in the NAME field of the sample database), the **Parse** command is limited.

Although the **Parse** command can create a format line and reorganize long labels into individual columns, the **Parse** command generally cannot break apart two labels contained within one field.

You first must understand how the **Parse** command functions. On the format line in figure 11.27, each L symbol tells Quattro Pro exactly where one field ends and another field begins. The data in each field is left-justified and far enough from the data in neighboring fields so that Quattro Pro has no problem distinguishing between the fields.

Now take another look at the two elements in the NAME field. The last names are not left-justified, because the first names have different lengths. Quattro Pro does not know where to place the L symbols to distinguish between the two names.

The **P**arse command can be used to break apart multiple labels within a field——but only when each label is left-justified and far enough from other labels in that field so that Quattro Pro can distinguish between the labels.

With a little imagination and experimentation, however, you can sidestep these constraints by combining the capabilities of the **P**arse command with those of the Edit menu's **S**earch & Replace command (see Chapter 4 for complete coverage of this command).

You should place enough distance between the first and last names in the NAME field so that Quattro Pro can distinguish between the names. Because the longest first name in the NAME field is 10 characters long (Courtland), you must left-justify all of the last names somewhere past column 11. Remember, column 11 must be blank so that Quattro Pro can distinguish between the two categories of data.

To allow enough space between first and last names, perform the following steps:

1. Highlight block B18..B28.

2. Select /**E**dit Copy, type *B38*, and press Enter to copy the NAME field data to block B38..B48.

3. Select /**E**dit Search & Replace.

4. Select **B**lock, type *B39..B48*, and press Enter to record the location of the object block.

5. Select Search String, press the space bar once to enter a blank space, and press Enter.

6. Select **R**eplace String, press the space bar 10 times to enter 10 blank spaces, and press Enter.

7. Select **N**ext to begin the search operation.

After you complete step 7, Quattro Pro displays the menu shown in figure 11.29.

The first blank space that Quattro Pro locates is between "John" and "Dunn" in the first record. To check this result, look at the input line at the top of the spreadsheet.

```
File ‖Edit‖ Style  Graph  Print  Database  Tools  Options  Window        ↑↓
[Enter] [Esc] 'John Dunn                                                   ?
    A               B              C         D       E       F
36                                                                      End
37
38  NAME                                                                 ▲
39  John Dunn                                                            ▼
40  Craig Kishab
41  Jim Muttera  Replace this string:                                   Esc
42  Olivier Fisc  Yes
43  Kimra McConn  No                                                     ↵
44  Kelley McGra  All
45  Rosheen Hill  Edit                                                   Del
46  Mary Ubersax  Quit
47  Courtlandt K                                                          @
48  Harold Skinner
49                                                                        5
50
51                                                                        6
52
53                                                                        7
54
55
B39: [W25] 'John Dunn                                               MENU
```

Fig. 11.29
Quattro Pro displays the Replace This String menu when a match to the search condition is located.

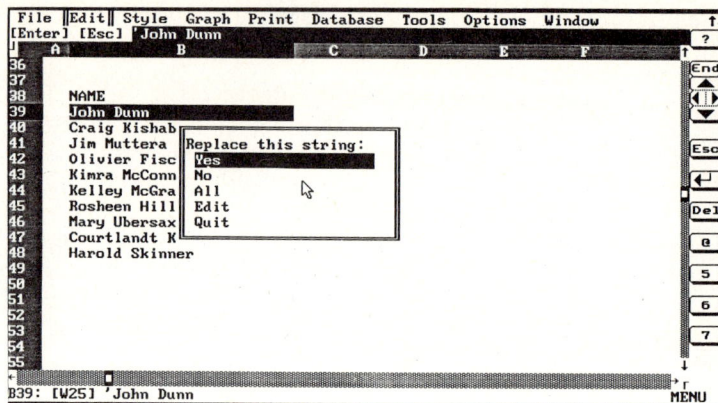

8. Select the **All** option to search and replace each record in the database.

Next, parse the data appearing in block B38..B49 and store the results beginning in cell B39. To do this operation properly, use the **Create** command to create a format line. Then use the **Edit** command to create and edit the format line so that the format line looks like figure 11.30.

```
File  Edit  Style  Graph  Print  Database  Tools  Options  Window       ↑↓
B38: [W25] |L>>>>>>>>>>>L>>>>>>>>>>>>>>                                   ?
    A               B              C         D       E       F
36                                                                      End
37
38  L>>>>>>>>>>>L>>>>>>>>>>>>>>>>                                         ▲
39  NAME                                                                 ▼
40  John          Dunn
41  Craig         Kishaba                                               Esc
42  Jim           Muttera
43  Olivier       Fischer                                                ↵
44  Kimra         McConnell
45  Kelley        McGraw                                                Del
46  Rosheen       Hillen
47  Mary          Ubersax                                                @
48  Courtlandt    Kindreich
49  Harold        Skinner                                                5
50
51                                                                        6
52
53                                                                        7
54
55
PARSE.WQ1   [1]                                                   READY
```

Fig. 11.30
The last names are now far enough from the first names for Quattro Pro to distinguish between the fields.

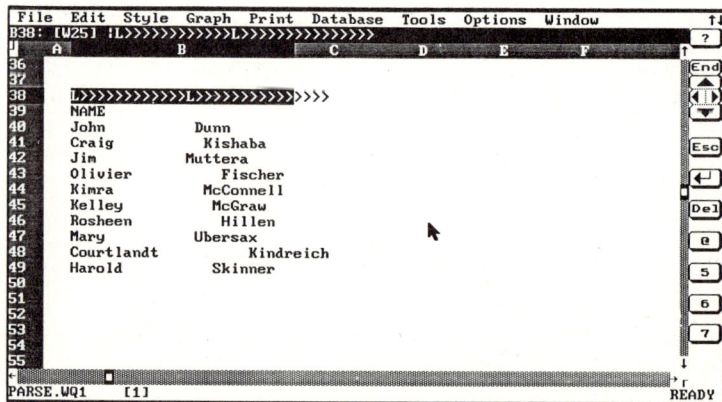

To use the **Search & Replace** command to left-justify the last name labels in column C, perform the following steps:

1. Select /**Edit Search & Replace Options Reset** to reset the search and replace conditions.

2. Select **Block**, type *C40..C49*, and press Enter to record the location of the object block.

3. Select **S**earch String, press the space bar once to enter a blank space, and press Enter.

4. Select **N**ext to begin the search operation.

You did not enter a replacement string this time. By entering *nothing* as the **R**eplace String condition, you tell Quattro Pro to search for blank spaces and replace the spaces with *nothing*. After completing step 4, Quattro Pro displays the menu shown in figure 11.31.

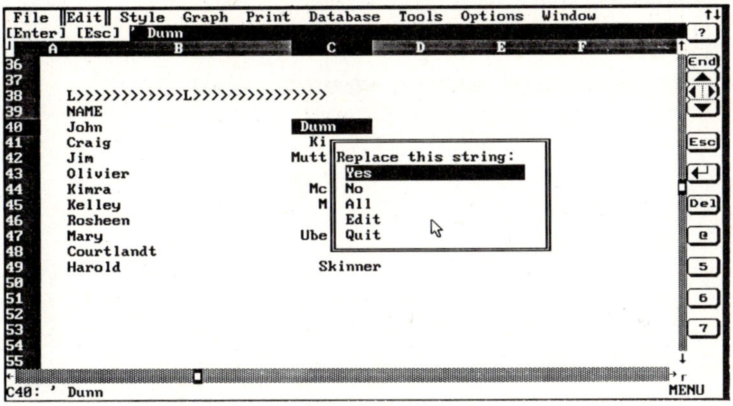

Fig. 11.31 The Replace This String menu is displayed when Quattro Pro locates a match to the search condition.

The first blank space that Quattro Pro locates is before "Dunn" in the first record. To check this result, look at the input line at the top of the spreadsheet.

5. Select the **A**ll option to search and replace each record in the database.

When step 5 is completed, Quattro Pro displays the results shown in figure 11.32.

To complete this exercise, enter the label LAST above the last name data on the field names row (into cell C40) and delete the format line from Cell B38.

Using the What-If Function

The **W**hat-if command enables you to create one-way and two-way sensitivity tables. A *sensitivity table* contains a range of column values and row formulas that define the parameters of a problem. When executed, the **W**hat-if command returns one answer for each row and column intersection.

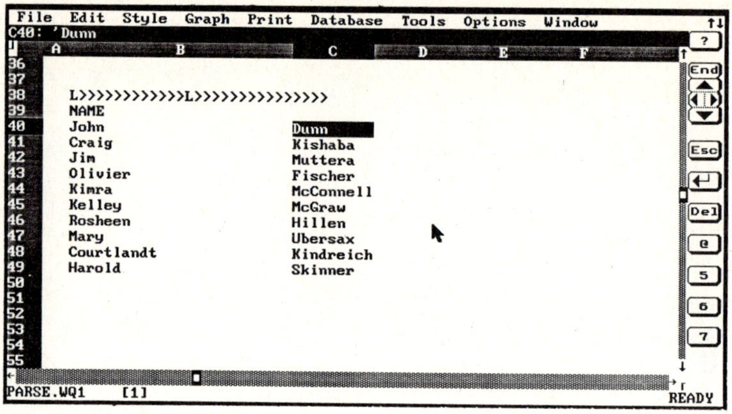

Fig. 11.32
The last names now are left-justified.

By using sensitivity analysis, you can review in one table a wide range of solutions for virtually any what-if questions that you may encounter.

One-Way Sensitivity Analysis

A one-way sensitivity analysis table substitutes values into a variable appearing in one or more formulas. You set up a column of substitution values and then create a formula in which to substitute the values.

Suppose that you want to analyze how varying sales and costs affect the gross profits for a business. In this business, sales range from $10,000 to $24,000 per month, and costs fluctuate between 55 and 75 percent of sales. The following formula relates sales to costs to gross profit:

Gross Profit = Sales − Cost Of Goods Sold

In this example, you want to create a sensitivity table that describes all possible gross profit values that can occur within a given range of sales values and cost percentages.

The first step is to enter the range of sales values into a column. The next step is to enter the formulas that calculate the gross profit values into a row. You enter five formulas, one for each likely cost percentage. You may want to change the format of this row to **Text** to see the actual formulas (see fig. 11.33).

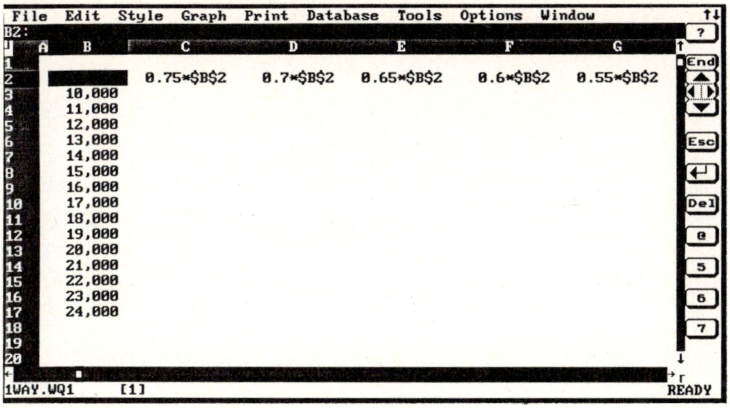

Fig. 11.33
Creating a one-way sensitivity table.

After you enter all of the appropriate values and formulas, you are ready to create the one-way sensitivity table:

1. Select /**T**ools **W**hat-if **1** Variable.

2. When prompted to specify the data table block, type *B2..G17* and press Enter.

3. When prompted to specify the input cell, type *B2* and press Enter.

Quattro Pro substitutes each sales value into cell B2, multiplies the substituted value by each formula on row 2, and then places an answer in each intersection cell (see fig. 11.34).

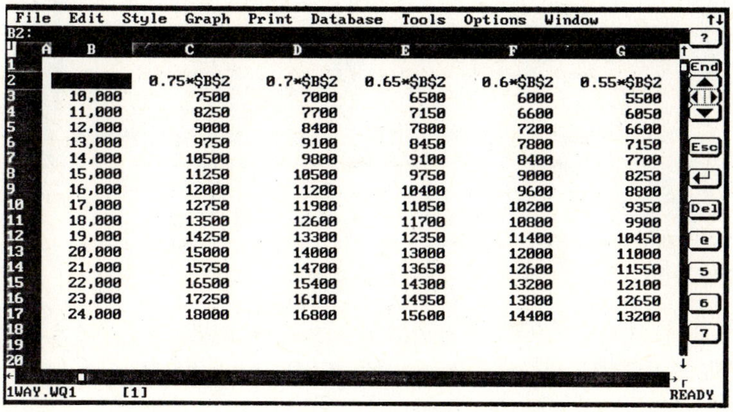

Fig. 11.34
The one-way sensitivity table after calculation.

Two-Way Sensitivity Analysis

Two-way sensitivity analysis uses a data table in a slightly different manner; you substitute two sets of values into a formula.

Consider a retail business that sells a particular product for $28 to $38, depending upon the cost charged by their wholesale supplier. The following formula relates retail price to wholesale cost, and the percent of profit on a sale:

Percent Profit = (Retail Price − Wholesale Cost) / Retail Price

To determine the percent of profit that the business is earning, you can construct a two-way sensitivity table that analyzes various price-cost combinations and computes the corresponding profit percentage.

The first step is to enter the range of retail prices and wholesale prices into a row and column (see fig. 11.35). The next step is to enter a formula that calculates the percent of profit. The formula, (A6-A5/A6), references two input cells that fall outside the sensitivity table, such as cells A5 and A6.

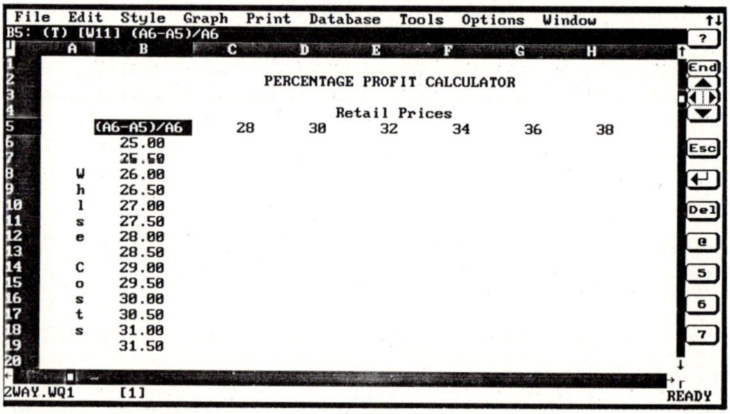

**Fig. 11.35
Creating a two-way sensitivity table.**

After you enter all of the appropriate values and formulas, you are ready to create the two-way sensitivity table:

1. Select /Tools **W**hat-if **2** Variable.

2. When prompted to specify the data table block, type *B5..H19* and press Enter.

Tip | Make sure that the data table block definition includes only the area bounded by the column and row—do not include the addresses for the blank input cells (A5 and A6).

3. When prompted to specify the input cell for the column of values, type *A5* and press Enter.

4. When prompted to specify the input cell for the row of values, type *A6* and press Enter.

Quattro Pro substitutes each pair of retail and wholesale prices into the input cells, performs the operation indicated by the formula in cell B5, and then places an answer in each intersection cell (see fig. 11.36).

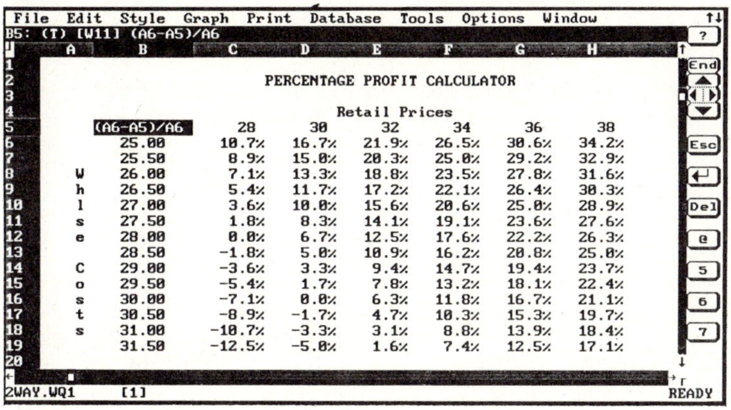
File Edit Style Graph Print Database Tools Options Window

B5: (T) [W11] (A6-A5)/A6

PERCENTAGE PROFIT CALCULATOR

Retail Prices

	A	B	C	D	E	F	G	H
5		(A6-A5)/A6	28	30	32	34	36	38
6		25.00	10.7%	16.7%	21.9%	26.5%	30.6%	34.2%
7		25.50	8.9%	15.0%	20.3%	25.0%	29.2%	32.9%
8	W	26.00	7.1%	13.3%	18.8%	23.5%	27.8%	31.6%
9	h	26.50	5.4%	11.7%	17.2%	22.1%	26.4%	30.3%
10	l	27.00	3.6%	10.0%	15.6%	20.6%	25.0%	28.9%
11	s	27.50	1.8%	8.3%	14.1%	19.1%	23.6%	27.6%
12	e	28.00	0.0%	6.7%	12.5%	17.6%	22.2%	26.3%
13		28.50	-1.8%	5.0%	10.9%	16.2%	20.8%	25.0%
14	C	29.00	-3.6%	3.3%	9.4%	14.7%	19.4%	23.7%
15	o	29.50	-5.4%	1.7%	7.8%	13.2%	18.1%	22.4%
16	s	30.00	-7.1%	0.0%	6.3%	11.8%	16.7%	21.1%
17	t	30.50	-8.9%	-1.7%	4.7%	10.3%	15.3%	19.7%
18	s	31.00	-10.7%	-3.3%	3.1%	8.8%	13.9%	18.4%
19		31.50	-12.5%	-5.0%	1.6%	7.4%	12.5%	17.1%
20								

2WAY.WQ1 [1] READY

Fig. 11.36 The two-way sensitivity table after calculation.

In figure 11.36, the calculated values are formatted to display the percent format with one decimal place.

Creating Frequency Distributions

The **Frequency** command counts the number of values that fall within specified ranges, groups the values into bins, and then produces a frequency distribution table using the bin data. Frequency distribution tables provide a summary grouping of large data sets, enabling you to get a better picture of their distribution. After a table has been created, those values can be displayed effectively in an XY graph.

Consider a commissioned study that analyzes the distribution of population among cities on Prince Edward Island (see fig. 11.37).

The name of each city appears in one column, the population in another, and the bin block definition in a third. To count the number of cities whose population falls into each bin block, follow these steps:

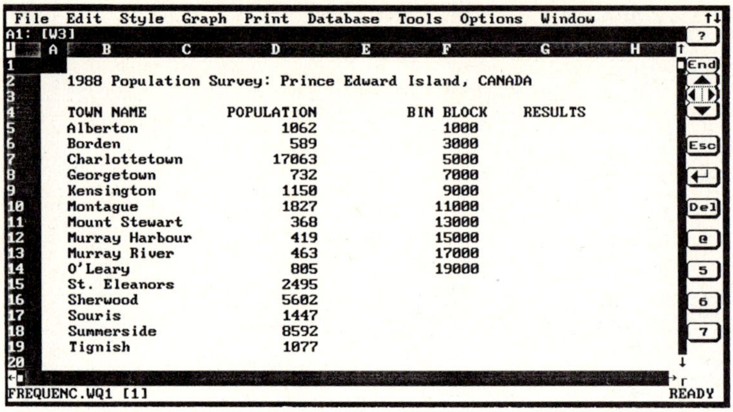

Fig. 11.37
Organizing data to be used in frequency distribution analysis.

```
 File  Edit  Style  Graph  Print  Database  Tools  Options  Window      ↑↓
A1: [W3]                                                                  ?
    A    B        C        D        E        F        G        H    ↑
1                                                                   ►End
2        1988 Population Survey: Prince Edward Island, CANADA        ▲
3                                                                   ◄□►
4        TOWN NAME      POPULATION          BIN BLOCK    RESULTS     ▼
5        Alberton          1862              1000                   Esc
6        Borden             589              3000                   ↵
7        Charlottetown    17063              5000
8        Georgetown         732              7000                   Del
9        Kensington        1150              9000
10       Montague          1827             11000                    @
11       Mount Stewart      368             13000
12       Murray Harbour     419             15000                    5
13       Murray River       463             17000
14       O'Leary            805             19000                    6
15       St. Eleanors      2495
16       Sherwood          5602                                      7
17       Souris            1447
18       Summerside        8592                                    ↓
19       Tignish           1077                                    ►r
20                                                                 READY
FREQUENC.WQ1 [1]
```

1. Enter the names of each city into column B and enter each city's population into column C.

2. Define a bin block grouping that specifies the bounds of the bins into which you want values to be placed.

Tip | Bin block numbers must appear in ascending order on the spreadsheet, but do not necessarily require the same interval size.

3. Select /Tools Frequency.

4. When prompted, type *D5..D19* and press Enter to define the values to include in the frequency analysis.

5. When prompted, type *F5..F14* to define the bin block.

6. When prompted, type *G5* to define the location where Quattro Pro is to copy the results.

After executing step 6, Quattro Pro copies the results of the frequency analysis into a block beginning at cell G5 (see fig. 11.38). Quattro Pro included an extra result in cell G15 at the bottom of the results column. This result is 0 as long as Quattro Pro does not locate a value in the frequency table that is greater than the largest defined bin number.

Frequency distribution analyses lend themselves to XY graphing. Figure 11.39 shows a graph constructed with the values appearing in the BIN BLOCK and RESULTS columns.

This graph was created by defining the BIN BLOCK column data as the X-axis and the RESULTS data as the Y-axis. Because the final value in the RESULTS column is 0, this cell is not included in the X-axis series definition.

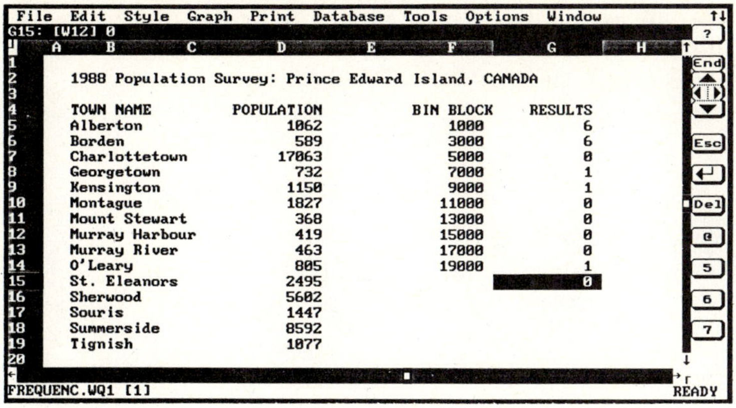

Fig. 11.38
A completed frequency distribution analysis.

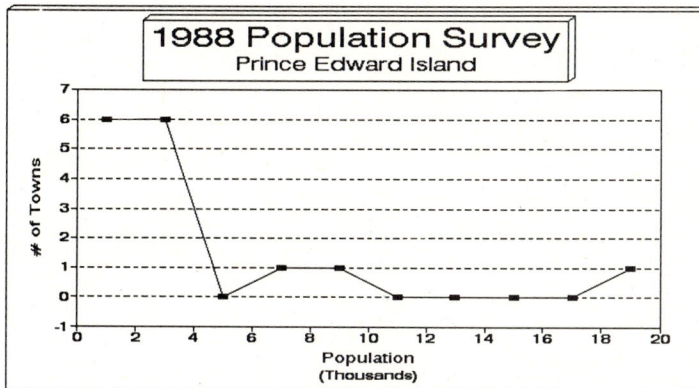

Fig. 11.39
An XY graph showing the distribution of the population on Prince Edward Island.

Questions & Answers

This chapter introduces you to the Data menu commands and to the analytical tools found on the Tools menu. If you have questions concerning particular situations that are not addressed in the examples given, look through this question and answers section.

Sort Operations

Q: I want to sort my database so that all clients from Oklahoma (having OK in the STATE field) are at the top of my database. Am I confined to ascending and descending orders?

A: Yes, sort is confined to a few sorting orders. What you need to do is a search. If you really want to place all OK records on the top rows of your database, use /Database **Query Extract**, then use /Database **Query Delete**, and finally copy the extracted records to the top lines of your database.

Q: Can I specify Sort Key 1 as an ascending sort, with Sort Key 2 as a descending sort?

A: Yes, Quattro Pro prompts you for sort direction after each key. However, the specified sort rules apply equally to all sort keys and operations.

Search Operations

Q: When I enter a formula in my criteria table I get the warning message Invalid cell or block address. What's wrong?

A: Quattro Pro doesn't recognize the field name you have used. First, make sure that the spelling matches that defined in the search block. Second, make sure that you have used the Assigned Names command following any changes you made to the Field names. Third, supply the cell address in the formula.

Q: Is it possible to search for (and extract) all records in which any one field is zero?

A: Certainly. Set up a criteria table specifying that records in which field1 = 0, field2 = 0 and so on, are selected.

Data Analysis

Q: I want to perform a two-way sensitivity analysis (using what-if). I made my column and row of values, entered my formula, and calculated the table. Unfortunately, each cell in the table was filled with a copy of my formula. Why?

A: You most likely changed the formula cell to display as text so that you can observe the formula. When you actually create the table, however, Quattro Pro must be able to decipher the formula in the cell. Change the cell format back to a general display format by selecting the /Style **Numeric Format** command.

Chapter Summary

In this chapter, you learned how to manipulate and analyze your data using the commands found on the Data and Tools menus. The commands on these two menus enable you to turn a Quattro Pro spreadsheet into an efficient environment for storing, accessing, and analyzing database information.

After completing this chapter's material, you should understand the following concepts:

- Creating a database shell on a spreadsheet

- Entering data into a database

- Sorting records using field names as sort keys

- Searching a database for records that meet specific criteria definitions

- Using a spreadsheet as a data-entry form

- Performing regression analysis using one or more independent variables

- Multiplying and inverting matrices

- Building and executing a linear programming (optimization) model

- Parsing long labels into smaller parts and placing each part into a separate column

- Using the **P**arse and **S**earch & Replace commands together to meet special parsing needs

- Creating one-way and two-way sensitivity tables

- Producing a frequency distribution and graphing the results

12

Creating Macro Programs

Quattro Pro's macro programming facility is accessed from the Tools menu. A macro is a productivity tool that enables users to store commonly used keystrokes and command selections in a file for future use. When a macro is executed, Quattro Pro reproduces each keystroke action and menu command exactly.

You can accomplish a wide variety of tasks with macros. Macros can automate tedious and repetitive actions that you perform during your work sessions. Macros also can be self-running mini-programs that solicit data input from a user and then manipulate and display the data on a report. You can even create macros to generate printouts and graphs from your spreadsheet data.

In the first section of this chapter, you learn about creating a basic macro program. The commands on the Macro menu are defined, and then you review a step-by-step process for envisioning, planning, and writing a Quattro Pro macro.

The next section shows you how to auto-create a macro using the macro recorder. You learn how to paste a recorded macro into a spreadsheet, audit the macro commands, and then replay the macro on-screen.

The chapter continues by showing you how to assign a name to a macro and how to create an autoload macro that executes each time you load a new, blank spreadsheet into Quattro Pro.

Managing spreadsheet macros is the topic of the next section. You learn how to document and create a macro library. This section concludes with a presentation of guidelines for editing and executing a macro and deleting an out-of-date macro.

The balance of this chapter is devoted to advanced macro topics. You learn how to enter macro commands manually into an auto-recorded macro. You are introduced to Quattro Pro's powerful macro debugger—a tool that enables you to locate and correct problems that cause macro execution errors.

This chapter concludes with an overview of the Transcript facility. Using this tool, you can reproduce a command history of your work session efforts and monitor and protect these same efforts from power outages and system crashes.

Learning about Macros

A macro program (macro for short) is a collection of special instructions that Quattro Pro can execute. To create a macro, you enter each instruction into a column of cells on the active spreadsheet. When you execute a macro program—much like you execute any other program—Quattro Pro evaluates each cell and then performs the specific action called for by each instruction.

The actions performed by a macro depend entirely on you, because a macro can be made to duplicate any command action possible on a Quattro Pro menu. For example, you can write a simple macro that alters the width of a column. You also can write a more involved macro that completely formats a new, blank spreadsheet and then prompts a user to enter data.

A Quattro Pro macro also contains instructions that mimic keystrokes, cursor movements, and other keyboard actions that you press as you select menu commands. For example, many Quattro Pro commands require you to supply block coordinates, type values, or press other keys as part of that command's execution. In a macro program, you store all of these keystrokes so that Quattro Pro performs each cell instruction exactly.

Quattro Pro macros also can include macro commands. Macro commands perform functions that cannot be accomplished by menu commands. For example, you can use a macro command to request input from a user during the execution of a macro, much as Quattro Pro requires you to supply data before executing a menu command. Other macro commands meet specific programming objectives such as looping, branching, and passing program control to macro subroutines.

Reviewing the Macro Menu

You can use the ten commands found on the /**T**ools **M**acro menu to create, execute, debug, and delete macros. This Quattro Pro feature has been assigned an Alt-key sequence that displays the Macro menu from anywhere on the active spreadsheet. To display the Macro menu, press Alt-F2 (see fig. 12.1).

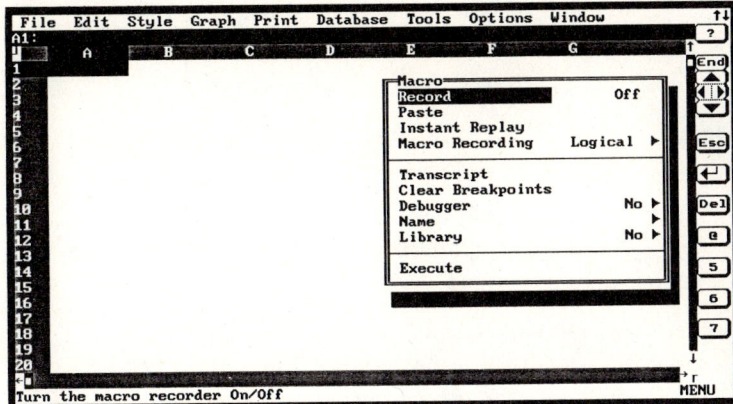

Fig. 12.1
The Macro menu of commands.

The commands in the top third of this menu are macro creation commands. Using these commands, you can record and store keystrokes in Quattro Pro's memory, paste a stored macro into a block on a spreadsheet, replay a macro that is stored in memory, and toggle the setting that controls how Quattro Pro interprets your keystrokes.

The commands in the middle third of the macro menu are macro debugging commands. Using these commands, you can display a command history of recent Quattro Pro work sessions, debug your macro programs, and name and create libraries of macro programs for use in future works sessions.

The bottom menu division contains a single command: **E**xecute.

Table 12.1 briefly defines each command on the Macro menu.

Creating a Basic Macro Program

The process of creating a basic macro program involves at least three steps:

1. Programming the macro.

2. Pasting and name the macro (optional).

Table 12.1
Macro Menu Commands

Command	Description
Record	Turns Quattro Pro's macro recorder on and off
Paste	Copies the last recorded macro into a spreadsheet block that you specify
Instant Replay	Replays the last recorded macro
Macro Recording	Toggles between **Keystroke** and **Logical** macro recording modes
Transcript	Displays a command history of all recently executed keystrokes and menu command selections
Clear Breakpoints	Removes debugging breakpoints from a macro
Debugger	Turns the Macro Debugger on and off
Name	Assigns a name to a macro so that you can execute it
Library	Designates a spreadsheet as a macro library
Execute	Executes a macro specified by name

3. Executing the macro.

4. Debugging the macro (optional).

5. Executing the macro.

First, you create the macro program. You must have a clear idea of which tasks you want the program to perform. Even though some people have the uncanny knack of being able to program as they go, for the rest of us proper planning and development are essential to achieving success.

Naming a macro is no more complicated than, and very similar to, naming a spreadsheet block. You can create a library of commonly used macros that you can execute quickly on every spreadsheet in a new application.

Once programmed, the macro is ready to be executed. If for some reason the macro fails to perform correctly, or if Quattro Pro encounters a macro program error, you need to debug the macro.

Debugging is the process of testing, editing, and re-testing the integrity of your macro program. To help you locate and correct errors, Quattro Pro offers myriad debugging tools. These tools help you transform even the most bug-infested program into a fully functional, streamlined and efficient macro tool.

Using the Macro Recorder

The most frightening prospect about programming is the idea that you have to learn a new, cryptic way of expressing yourself. With this concern in mind, Quattro Pro offers you the capability to auto-record macro programs so that you do not have to become a multilingual programming genius.

Suppose that you want to create a macro that enters and aligns label headings into a new, blank spreadsheet. The spreadsheet is used to record high and low automobile repair quotes at an insurance company (see fig. 12.2).

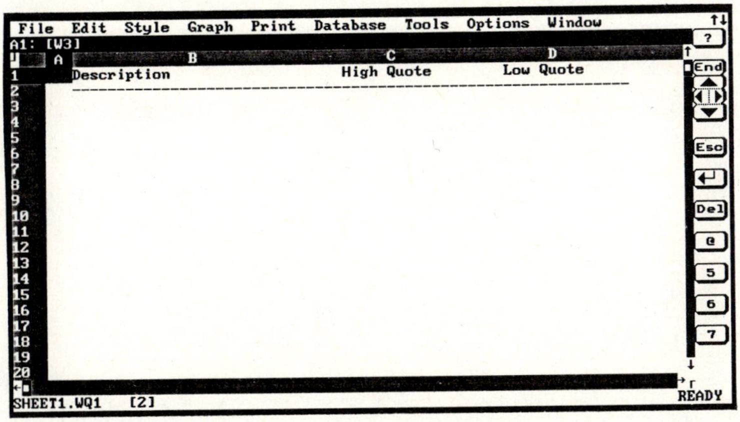

Fig. 12.2
Report headings
for an
automobile
repair quote
spreadsheet.

To record a macro that reproduces this report, do the following:

1. Select the /**Tools** **M**acro **R**ecord command. Quattro Pro displays the REC mode indicator on the status line.

Tip | Press Alt-F2 R to execute the **R**ecord command.

2. Type the headings on row 1, enter the repeating lines on row 2, center-align the labels in columns C and D, and alter the column widths as desired.

3. Reselect the /Tools **Macro Record** command to turn the recorder off and return to the active spreadsheet.

Once recorded, you can paste this macro into a block on a spreadsheet to store the instructions permanently. In future work sessions, retrieve the spreadsheet, execute the macro, and Quattro Pro reproduces the headings for this report.

Pasting the Recorded Macro to a Spreadsheet

When you record a macro, Quattro Pro retains the instructions in its memory until you either paste the macro or select **Record** and record a new macro. To save a macro so that you can recall and execute the macro at a later time, select the **Paste** option on the Macro menu. This command names and pastes the last recorded macro into a block on the active spreadsheet that you specify.

To paste the recorded macro onto the active spreadsheet and assign a unique name to the macro, do the following:

1. Select the /Tools **Macro Paste** command. Quattro Pro prompts you for a macro name to create/modify (see fig. 12.3).

Tip | Press Alt-F2 P to execute the **Paste** command.

2. Type the name of the macro—*HEADING1* for the example—and press Enter to assign that name to the recorded macro.

3. When prompted, type *B4* and press Enter to paste the macro.

Fig. 12.3
Pasting a recorded macro into a block on the active spreadsheet.

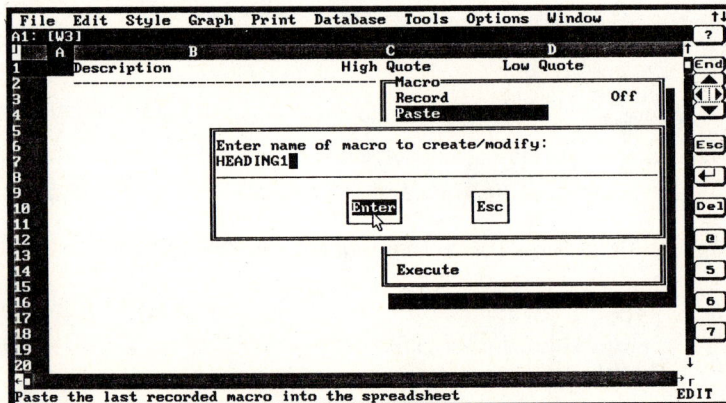

Quattro Pro can paste a recorded macro into a block on the active spreadsheet or on another spreadsheet open in memory. To paste a recorded macro to another spreadsheet, supply the appropriate linking syntax (covered in Chapter 7). By typing *[PROGRAM]A1*, for example, you can paste the macro onto a spreadsheet named PROGRAM.WQ1 beginning in cell A1. In this syntax, PROGRAM is the name of a spreadsheet (the .WQ1 is assumed). The brackets tell Quattro Pro that you are performing an operation on a spreadsheet other than the active one, and A1 signifies the cell in PROGRAM.WQ1 in which Quattro Pro should begin the operation.

You also can specify a block address to paste to, instead of a single cell address. Specifying a block address prevents Quattro Pro from overwriting data on the spreadsheet. Quattro Pro truncates a macro when the macro is longer than the destination paste block. By specifying a block address, you confine the target paste area to an area bounded by the block coordinates.

When you specify a single cell address, Quattro Pro pastes the macro beginning in that cell and continues pasting down the column until the entire macro is copied. Quattro Pro overwrites any data that is inside the paste destination.

Interpreting the Macro

Quattro Pro records macro instructions in one of two formats: as keystroke-equivalent commands or as menu-equivalent commands (see fig. 12.4).

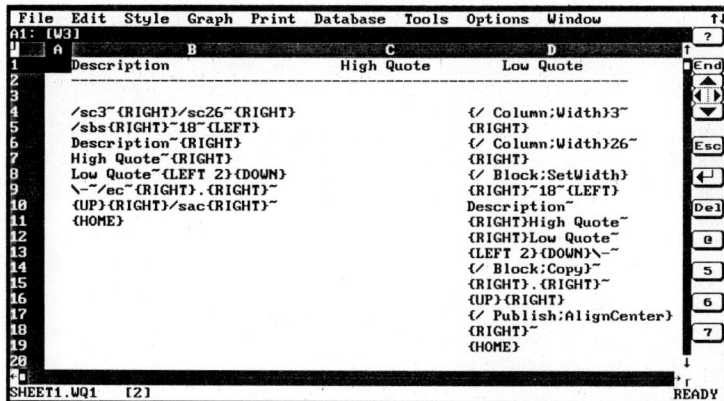

Fig. 12.4
Two recorded macros—one created using logical recording and the other created using keystroke recording.

The two macros shown in figure 12.4 perform the exact same operation. The macro on the left, however, contains keystroke-equivalent commands, and the macro on the right contains menu-equivalent commands.

A *keystroke-equivalent command* contains the forward slash key, followed by each boldfaced letter key that you press to execute a menu command. Keystroke-equivalent commands conclude with a ~ (the tilde) to signify that Enter was pressed.

For example, the first row in the macro shown in the left portion of figure 12.4 contains two commands. The first of these commands is /sc3~, which indicates that the /Style Column-Width command was selected, the number 3 was typed, and Enter was pressed to store the command. A keystroke-equivalent macro records each action that you make in a keystroke-by-keystroke fashion.

A *menu-equivalent command* looks different from a keystroke-equivalent command. A menu-equivalent command is embedded inside a pair of braces and is composed of the forward slash key, two special commands separated by a semicolon, and also concludes with the tilde character.

For example, the first command in the macro shown in the right portion of figure 12.3 is {/ Column;Width}3~, which more clearly shows that the /Style Column-Width command was selected, the number 3 was typed, and Enter was pressed. Menu-equivalent commands are easier to read than keystroke-equivalent commands because, instead of single letters, they contain whole word descriptions.

Another advantage to using menu-equivalent commands is that they are fully compatible with other menu trees; whereas the keystroke-equivalents are not.

You can select a menu command in three distinct ways: clicking a mouse; pressing the boldfaced letter key; and highlighting the command and pressing Enter. Regardless of which method you use, Quattro Pro records the same macro command.

When the Caps Lock key is on, Quattro Pro records keystroke-equivalent macros in uppercase instead of lowercase. This does not affect the performance of the macro.

See Appendix D for a complete list of the menu-equivalent commands.

Switching the Macro Recording Mode

By default, the Macro Recording command is set to Logical, which instructs Quattro Pro to record macro instructions as menu-equivalent commands. This default setting ensures that Quattro Pro macros work with all compatible menu trees.

To create a Quattro Pro macro under the 1-2-3-compatible menu tree and then execute the macro in Lotus 1-2-3, you must set this command to **Keystroke**.

Quattro Pro macros that contain keystroke-equivalent commands do not work with every compatible menu tree. Each tree has its own menu names and command names and therefore has different boldfaced letter keys.

In the Quattro Pro menu tree, for example, you select the /Edit Copy command by typing */EC*. In the 1-2-3-compatible menu tree, you type */C* to select the **Copy** command.

Tip | To ensure complete compatibility between your Quattro Pro macros and the various menu trees, set **Macro Recording** to **Logical**.

To change the default recording setting, do the following:

1. Select the /**Tools** Macro Recording command.

2. When prompted, choose **Keystroke**.

Viewing an Instant Replay

Use the **Instant Replay** command to execute the last recorded macro in Quattro Pro's memory. This command is useful for testing a macro prior to pasting the macro into a block on a spreadsheet.

To show an instant replay of the last macro you recorded, select the /**Tools** Macro Instant Replay command.

Tip | Press Alt-F2 I to execute the **Instant Replay** command.

Quattro Pro preserves the last recorded macro in memory so long as you are on the same active spreadsheet and have not recorded another macro. You can select the **Instant Replay** command several times in succession as long as these two conditions hold.

Naming a Macro

To save a macro program for future use, you must paste the macro to the active spreadsheet and then save that spreadsheet in a file. When you use the **Paste** command, Quattro Pro requires you to name the macro.

To name a macro that you type into a spreadsheet, or to assign a new name to a previously named macro, you must use the **Name** command.

Using the Name Command

Naming a macro is like creating a block name. You can select the **/E**dit **Names Create** command to name a macro when you are not on the Macro menu. Be sure that you do not assign an existing block name to a macro or vice versa. If this happens, the block or the macro loses its name definition.

You can create auto-execute names that turn macros into instant macros. An instant macro has a special name that is comprised of the backslash key (\ ) and a single letter, for example \A. The backslash key represents the action of pressing the Alt key on your keyboard.

You can execute an instant macro directly from your keyboard without having to select **Instant Replay** or **Execute**. Press Alt plus the letter name, and Quattro Pro invokes that macro.

For example, to assign the name \H to the sample macro program, do the following:

1. Select the **/T**ools **Macro Name** command.

2. When prompted, type \H and press Enter to assign that name to the current macro (see fig. 12.5).

Fig. 12.5
Assigning a
name to an
instant macro.

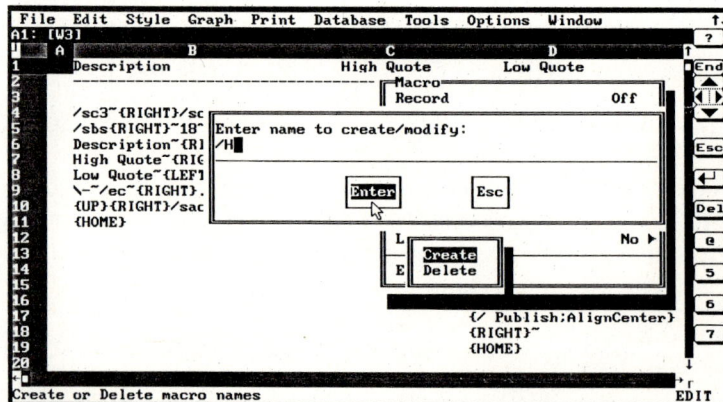

You can assign more than one unique name to a macro. For example, the first name can be descriptive of the macro's purpose (HEADING2), and the second name can be an auto-execute name that enables the name to be an instant macro (\H).

| Tip | Press F3 from the input line to display the block names choice list. This list shows all block and macro name assignments for the active spreadsheet. |

Creating an Autoload Macro

In Chapter 6, you learn how to specify an autoload macro name by selecting the /**Options Startup Startup Macro** command. By default, the setting for this command is \0.

Each time you load a spreadsheet, Quattro Pro checks for a macro named \0 (unless you press /OSS and type in a new name). If the macro exists, Quattro Pro executes it. The autoload macro feature is useful if you consistently perform the same formatting commands before entering data into a new spreadsheet.

Always begin a \0 macro with the {ESC} command (press Esc if you are recording the macro, or type the command in the first cell.) This ensures that your autoload macros work with linked spreadsheets. Remember, when you initially load a linked spreadsheet, Quattro Pro displays the Linking Options menu. Pressing Esc cancels this menu and permits Quattro Pro to continue executing the autoload macro.

When you use linked spreadsheets and define an autoload macro in this manner, be sure to update links when the macro finishes executing. Select /**Tools Update Links** and choose **Open** or **Refresh**. Remember, the **Open** option loads all linked spreadsheets into Quattro Pro's memory; the **Refresh** option only updates linked references appearing in the active spreadsheet.

| Tip | You also can create and delete autoload macro names by selecting the /**Tools Macro Name** command and choosing **Create** or **Delete**. |

Managing Quattro Pro Macros

You can store macros on the active spreadsheet or create a special spreadsheet called a macro library to hold the macros. A macro library enables you to select and execute a macro from another spreadsheet that is open in Quattro Pro's memory. The only condition is that the macro library also must be open in memory.

Another aspect of macro management concerns documentation. A properly documented macro can be a blessing in disguise. By including the name and adding brief comments to a macro, you guarantee that the user can understand what you are trying to accomplish with the code.

Storing Macros on a Spreadsheet

The execution of a macro is not affected by its location on the active spreadsheet. A macro stored in column IV executes just as quickly as a macro stored in column A. You should consider a few points prior to storing your macros. Depending on the instructions contained within a macro, its location on a spreadsheet relative to the spreadsheet data is significant. As a rule, you should store macros close to your spreadsheet data, but not so close that the macro accidentally overwrites itself.

A close proximity (but not too close) enables you to move quickly to the macro when you need to review its instructions.

Documenting Macros

You should document your macro programs. Documentation helps others understand what you are trying to accomplish and helps you evaluate your program logic during the debugging phase (described in a later section). When you return to a macro that you created long ago, you can review the documentation to refresh your own memory. You may forget the purpose and logic behind a macro after you create twenty or thirty macros.

Macro documentation serves two specific needs: documentation displays the macro name and auto-execute name if one exists; and documentation briefly describes the purpose of each instruction.

Figure 12.6 shows a typical macro library. The macro pictured here is the menu-equivalent version of the macro created in the preceding section.

When Quattro Pro executes a macro, the program starts in the first cell and moves down the column until the program encounters the last command. By placing macro names in their own column, you can take advantage of Quattro Pro's quick-naming facility.

Tip | Select the /**Edit** **Names** **Labels** **Right** command to quickly assign all names appearing in column B to the macros appearing in column C.

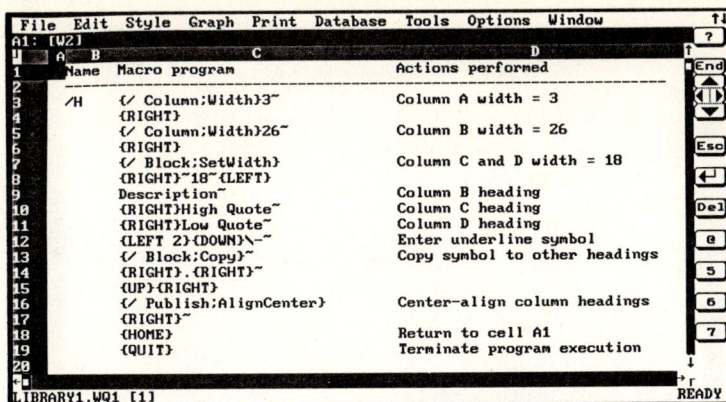

Fig. 12.6
Documenting a macro program that appears in a library.

Placing the documentation comments in the column immediately to the right of the macro accomplishes two things. First, this placement ensures that the comment labels are not assigned accidentally as names. Second, this placement prevents Quattro Pro from trying to execute the labels as macro instructions.

A final command has been added to the bottom of the \H macro shown in figure 12.6. The {QUIT} command signifies the end of a macro program. Be sure to add this command to the bottom of all of your macros when you create a macro library. This command causes Quattro Pro to stop reading cells and returns control of the keyboard to the user.

Creating Macro Libraries

When creating a macro library, be sure that you follow the instructions outlined for documenting and terminating a macro. Also, so that Quattro Pro does not execute a string of macros in the library, be sure to leave a blank cell between macros and enter {QUIT} as the last macro command (see fig. 12.7).

The advantages of storing macros in a macro library far outweigh those of storing macros on individual spreadsheets.

- When Quattro Pro cannot locate a macro that you want to execute on the active spreadsheet, the program searches through the macro libraries loaded in memory.

- You can eliminate any possibility of a macro overwriting itself on the active spreadsheet.

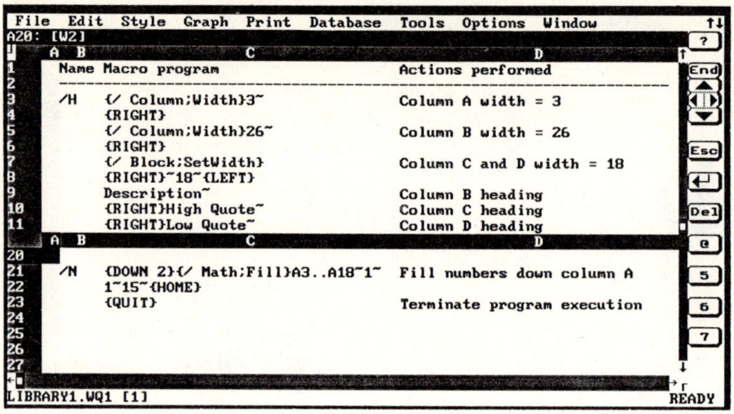

Fig. 12.7
A split-screen view of the first two macros stored on the LIBRARY1.WQ1 spreadsheet.

```
File   Edit   Style   Graph   Print   Database   Tools   Options   Window      ↑↓
A20: [W2]                                                                      ?
   A  B                    C                              D               ↑
1      Name Macro program                        Actions performed           End
2      -----------------------                   -----------------------
3      /H     {/ Column;Width}3~                  Column A width = 3          ◄│►
4             {RIGHT}                                                         ▼
5             {/ Column;Width}26~                 Column B width = 26
6             {RIGHT}                                                        Esc
7             {/ Block;SetWidth}                  Column C and D width = 18
8             {RIGHT}~18~{LEFT}                                              ↵
9             Description~                         Column B heading
10            {RIGHT}High Quote~                   Column C heading           Del
11            {RIGHT}Low Quote~                    Column D heading
   A  B                    C                              D                  @
20
21     /N     {DOWN 2}{/ Math;Fill}A3..A18~1~    Fill numbers down column A  5
22            1~15~{HOME}
23            {QUIT}                               Terminate program execution 6
24
25                                                                           7
26
27
LIBRARY1.WQ1 [1]                                                        READY
```

- You conserve spreadsheet file sizes by not having to copy macros over and over again onto new spreadsheets.

- A macro library is a permanent reference source, whereas spreadsheets often outlive their usefulness.

To create the macro library pictured in figure 12.7, do the following:

1. Select the /**File New** command to open a new spreadsheet into memory.

2. Copy any existing macros into the macro library or type macros directly onto the new spreadsheet.

3. Choose the /**Tools Macro Library** command.

4. When prompted, choose the **Yes** option.

5. Select /**File Save**, type *LIBRARY1*, and press Enter to save the macro library.

Quattro Pro enables you to create as many macro libraries as you want. For example, you can create separate macro libraries for both business and personal spreadsheet applications.

The rules that apply to one macro library apply to all. You may create as many unique macro names as you want, but you are limited to 26 Alt-key macro names per library. Be careful about opening two or more macro libraries at the same time. If macro libraries contain duplicate macro names, you cannot predict which macro will execute, if at all.

The commands in a macro executed from a macro library affect the active spreadsheet only, unless you specify otherwise. For example, a command that instructs Quattro Pro to select /**Style Line** and draw a Single line around block A20..E25 does so on the active spreadsheet—not on the macro library spreadsheet.

Tip | Be careful not to execute library macros when the macro library spreadsheet is active. If you do, Quattro Pro executes the macro on the library spreadsheet. When the executed macro calls for Quattro Pro to delete rows and columns or write labels and values into cells, the macro overwrites itself.

You should create commands that directly affect a macro stored in a macro library for several reasons. For example, consider a macro that issues the same /**Style** Line **Drawing** **Single** command after a looping subroutine is executed five times. Storing the loop execution value in a cell may seem useful. Because this value pertains specifically to the operation of the macro, however, the value should be recorded in the library near the macro so that the subroutine can refer to it. In this case, the macro actually executes a command on itself prior to executing a command on the active spreadsheet.

Executing a Macro

To execute a macro that does not have an Alt-key name, do the following:

1. Select the /**Tools** **Macro** **Execute** command.

Tip | Press Alt-F2 E to execute the /**Tools** **Macro** **Execute** command.

2. When prompted, type the name of the macro you want to execute.

Quattro Pro executes the macro program. During execution, Quattro Pro displays the Macro mode indicator at the bottom of the spreadsheet on the status line.

If you do not know the name of the macro you want to execute, press F3, and Quattro Pro displays the block names list. Highlight the name on the list and press Enter to execute the macro.

To execute the insurance macro after you load Quattro Pro into your PC, type *Q CLAIMS \H* and press Enter at the DOS command prompt.

Quattro Pro loads into your PC, retrieves the file named CLAIMS.WQ1, and then executes the \H macro. If the macro contains an error, Quattro Pro beeps and displays an error message. If the macro does not exist, Quattro Pro ignores the command.

To halt the execution of a macro, press Ctrl-Break and then press Esc to return to Ready mode. You can use the {BREAKOFF} macro command to disable the effect of pressing Ctrl-Break to disrupt macro execution. When {BREAKOFF} is included in a macro you are trying to terminate, Quattro Pro ignores the action of pressing Ctrl-Break. This technique is useful for preventing macro users from accessing and altering your macro commands.

Editing a Macro

You have two options for editing a macro—manually or with the Macro Debugger. To edit a macro manually, simply apply the same editing tools that you use to edit spreadsheet cells.

Tables 12.2 through 12.4 list each of the key-equivalent commands that you can use when writing or editing macros. Refer to Appendix C for a comprehensive list of Quattro Pro's macro command language and Appendix D for a complete list of menu-equivalent commands.

Press Shift-F3, the Macros key, to display a list of the seven macro categories. Highlight a category name and press Enter, and Quattro Pro displays a list of all commands in that category. To enter a command onto the input line, highlight the command and press Enter.

Deleting Macros and Macro Names

Deleting macros and macro names is another aspect of macro program management. By deleting out-of-date macros and macro names, you accomplish three things. First, you conserve spreadsheet space. Second, you reduce the number of names displayed on the block names list. Third, by eliminating instant macros, you free up a letter of the alphabet that can be used to create another, more useful instant macro.

Tip Deleting a macro and deleting a macro name are two different procedures. If you delete a name but not the macro, you still can use the macro by renaming it. If you delete a macro but not the name, Quattro Pro does what it always does when encountering a blank cell—the program terminates the execution.

Quattro Pro has two commands that meet this macro management objective. Select either the /Edit Names Delete command or the /Tools Macro Name

Delete command to display the block names list. Choose a macro name from the list (or type a name) and press Enter to delete the macro name.

This command deletes the macro name only. To delete the macro from the spreadsheet, select the /Edit Erase Block command and type in the block coordinates for the macro.

Using Advanced Macro Techniques

You now know how to record, paste, name, execute, and delete a basic macro. The remaining material in this chapter is devoted to reviewing macro programming techniques that assist you in managing longer, more sophisticated macros.

In the next few sections you learn how to type macros directly into a spreadsheet, link macros, debug macros, and enter macro commands directly onto the input line for inclusion in your programs.

Entering a Macro Manually

Consider the following approaches to creating a macro:

- Use the macro recorder exclusively.

- Create the macro from scratch by typing each command manually into a column of cells on the active spreadsheet.

- Use the macro recorder first, then append additional macro commands into the macro.

As an advanced macro user, you use the macro recorder for some tasks and enter macro commands manually to do other tasks. This approach gives you the best of both worlds. First, you can rely on the macro recorder to duplicate commonly used menu commands. Second, you have the option of applying advanced programming logic to create loops, branches, and subroutines.

Entering a macro manually is no different than entering any other data manually. With a macro, though, you must be careful about the accuracy of your data entry—a single missing brace, disoriented bracket, or misspelled command can cause the macro to crash.

When a macro crashes, it terminates before executing all of its commands. This event can have minor and serious consequences.

If the macro that crashes performs spreadsheet operations like copying data, aligning labels, and formatting numbers, the consequences of a crash are minor. At worst, Quattro Pro abandons the operation, leaving an unfinished or unformatted spreadsheet on-screen.

If your macro contains commands that perform external file operations like opening a file on disk, writing data to the file, and saving the file, a macro crash may cause irreparable damage to the file.

When a macro crashes, Quattro Pro displays an error message that indicates the cell address at which the execution error occurred. You have only one option: press Esc and return to the active spreadsheet.

To enter commands manually into a macro after using the macro recorder, do the following:

1. Envision the macro application. This planning stage helps you to divide tasks into two command groups: tasks that can be accomplished with the recorder and tasks that must be entered manually.

2. Sketch out the structure of the macro on paper. For more complex applications, you may want to use the /Graph Annotate command to create a flow chart.

3. Select /**Tools** Macro **R**ecord and create the part of the macro that will contain menu command selections.

4. **P**aste the macro to a new, blank spreadsheet.

5. Move the cell selector to a blank area on the macro in which you want to enter commands manually.

6. Type ' (the apostrophe label-prefix character) to enter Label mode, type in a macro command, and press Enter to record that command.

7. Continue entering commands until you finish. Then follow normal procedures for naming and executing the macro.

Macros must be entered into cells as labels, particularly if you are writing a keystroke-equivalent macro. Try to enter the label /FS into a cell without using a label-prefix character—it is impossible! When you type the forward slash character (/), Quattro Pro enters Menu mode.

To include keyboard key-equivalents in your macros, use the special key-equivalent commands shown in table 12.2. You can enter these commands either in uppercase or lowercase letters. Asterisks denote Quattro Pro-specific commands that are not included in other spreadsheet products.

Table 12.2
Keyboard Key-Equivalent Commands

Keyboard key	Key-equivalent command
←	{LEFT} or {L}
→	{RIGHT} or {R}
↑	{UP} or {U}
↓	{DOWN} or {D}
Backspace	{BACKSPACE} {BS}
Ctrl-←	{BIGLEFT}
Ctrl-→	{BIGRIGHT}
Ctrl-Backspace	{CLEAR} *
Ctrl-Break	{BREAK} *
Ctrl-D	{DATE} *
Ctrl-L	{DELEOL} *
Del	{DEL} {DELETE}
End	{END}
Enter	{CR} or ~
Esc	{ESC} {ESCAPE}
Home	{HOME}
PgUp	{PGUP}
PgDn	{PGDN}
Shift-Tab	{BACKTAB}
Tab	{TAB}

To include function key actions in your macros, use the special key-equivalent commands shown in table 12.3. You can enter these commands either in uppercase or lowercase letters. Asterisks denote Quattro Pro-specific commands that are not included in other spreadsheet products.

Table 12.3
Function Key-Equivalent Commands

Function key	Key-equivalent command
F2	{EDIT}
Shift-F2	{STEP} *
F3	{NAME} *
Shift-F3	{MACROS} *
Alt-F3	{FUNCTIONS} *
F4	{ABS}
F5	{GOTO}
Shift-F5	{CHOOSE} *
Alt-F5	{UNDO} *
F6	{WINDOW}
Shift-F6	{NEXTWIN} *
Alt-F6	{ZOOM} *
F7	{QUERY}
Shift-F7	{MARK} *
Alt-F7	{MARKALL} *
F8	{TABLE}
Shift-F8	{MOVE} *
F9	{CALC}
F9 (in a File Manager window)	{READDIR}
Shift-F9	{COPY} *
F10	{GRAPH}
Shift-F10	{PASTE} *

To toggle status keys in your macros, use the special key-equivalent commands shown in table 12.4. You can enter these commands either in uppercase or lowercase letters. Asterisks denote Quattro Pro-specific commands that are not included in other spreadsheet products.

Table 12.4
Status Key-Equivalent Commands

Status key	Key-equivalent command
Caps Lock off	{CAPOFF} *
Caps Lock on	{CAPON} *
Toggles Ins on or off	{INS} {INSERT} *
Ins off	{INSOFF} *
Forward slash (/)	{INSON} *
Num Lock off	{NUMOFF} *
Num Lock on	{NUMON} *
Scroll Lock off	{SCROLLOFF} *
Scroll Lock on	{SCROLLON} *

You also can repeat the action of pressing most of these keys by specifying a repeat number with the code. For example, to move the cell selector down five pages from its current position, type {*PGDN 5*}, or type {*PGDN B10*} if cell B10 contains the value 5.

Entering Menu-Equivalent Commands

The easiest and most accurate way to enter a menu-equivalent command into a macro is by pressing Shift-F3, the Macros key. When you press this key, Quattro Pro displays a menu of seven command categories.

Consider the macro shown in figure 12.8. This macro writes three expense values onto the spreadsheet and then sums their values. The menu-equivalent command appearing in cell G12, for example, is entered by selecting commands from the menu displayed in the figure.

The first six items on the menu are special categories. The last item, / Commands, enables you to enter menu-equivalent commands.

To enter the menu-equivalent of /**Style** Numeric Format into cell G12, do the following:

1. Make cell G12 the active cell.

2. Press Shift-F3 to display the Macros menu.

3. Press / to select the / Commands option.

Fig. 12.8
Entering menu-equivalent commands directly from the Macro menu.

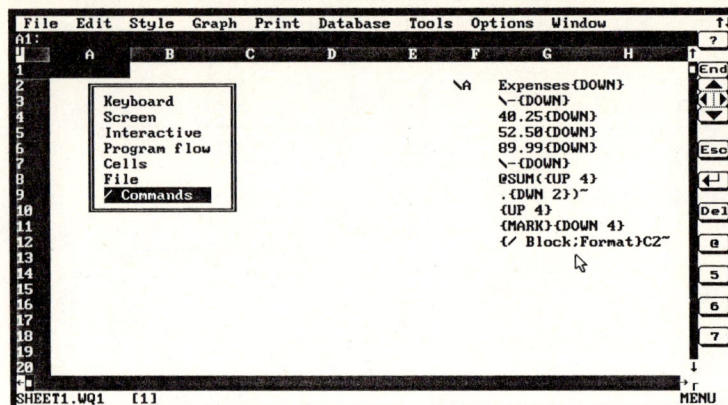

4. Highlight Block, the general-action category, and press Enter.

5. Highlight Format, the specific action category, and press Enter.

Quattro Pro writes the menu-equivalent command that you selected onto the input line and places you in Edit mode.

6. Type *C2~* to select Currency with 2 decimal places, and press Enter to place the command in cell G12.

See Appendix D for a complete listing of the menu-equivalent commands.

Using Linking in Macros

Linking enables you to execute a macro in a different spreadsheet, use data from another file, or pass data back and forth between spreadsheet applications. The linking syntax in macro programs is exactly the same as for spreadsheets (see Chapter 7).

For example, to link a macro to cell F15 on a spreadsheet named SALES that is stored in a directory named \ACCOUNTING on a disk in drive B, type

    [B:\ACCOUNTING\SALES]F15

In this syntax, *B:* is the drive name; *\ACCOUNTING* is the path name; and *SALES* is the file name (Quattro Pro assumes that the extension is WQ1).

The *[ ]* (brackets) surrounding the formula tell Quattro Pro that you are linking to another spreadsheet, and *F15* indicates the cell in SALES.WQ1 to which Quattro Pro will link.

If you want to branch directly from a macro library to a cell on the active spreadsheet (in which, for example, another macro exists), use the standard linking syntax.

For example, to branch a macro to cell B10 on the active spreadsheet, type

{BRANCH []B10}

The closed brackets [] in this syntax tell Quattro Pro to branch to the active spreadsheet. If the brackets are left out, Quattro Pro branches to cell B10 on the macro library spreadsheet.

Debugging a Macro

Quattro Pro's Macro Debugger helps you isolate problems that cause macro execution errors. To use this tool, you execute a macro while Quattro Pro is in Debug mode. In Debug mode, Quattro Pro executes each macro command one step at a time, pausing until you press a key to tell the program to continue.

You also can insert breakpoints and trace cells into a macro. Quattro Pro suspends execution when the program reaches a *breakpoint* (a cell that you define). Quattro Pro also suspends execution when a program *trace cell* (a cell containing a logical formula) returns a TRUE value. You also can edit the contents of a macro command while Quattro Pro is in Debug mode.

To enter Debug mode and then execute a macro, do the following:

1. Press Shift-F2 to place Quattro Pro in Debug mode.

2. Select the /Tools Macro Execute command to invoke the macro you want to debug, or press Alt plus the instant macro letter.

Once executed, Quattro Pro displays the Debug window in the bottom half of your screen and positions the first cell of the macro program in the middle of the Debug window (see fig. 12.9).

The active cell in this figure is B12, in which Quattro Pro begins executing the macro. Quattro Pro highlights the first letter in the first word in the first macro command appearing in the Debug window. When you press the space bar, Quattro Pro does two things. First, the program highlights the next character in the command displayed in the Debug window. Second, Quattro Pro types the character on the input line at the top of the screen.

Tip | Press Shift-F2 to place Quattro Pro in Debug mode and Alt-F2 E to execute the macro.

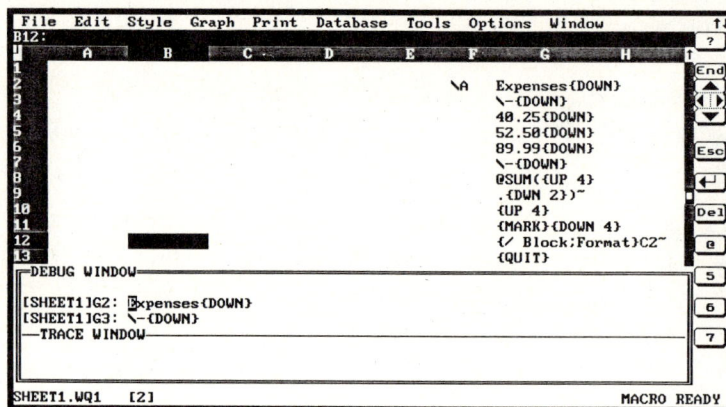

Fig. 12.9
The Debug window displayed when you execute a macro in Debug mode.

While in Debug mode, Quattro Pro stops when the program encounters an execution error. Macro errors can be traced to many things: a missing tilde character, an illegal block name, or even an incorrectly spelled macro command.

Figure 12.10 illustrates how Quattro Pro reacts to locating a macro error. The displayed error message gives a specific reference to the spreadsheet name and the cell address in which the error was encountered. A review of the macro in this figure indicates that the cursor-movement command in cell G9 is misspelled.

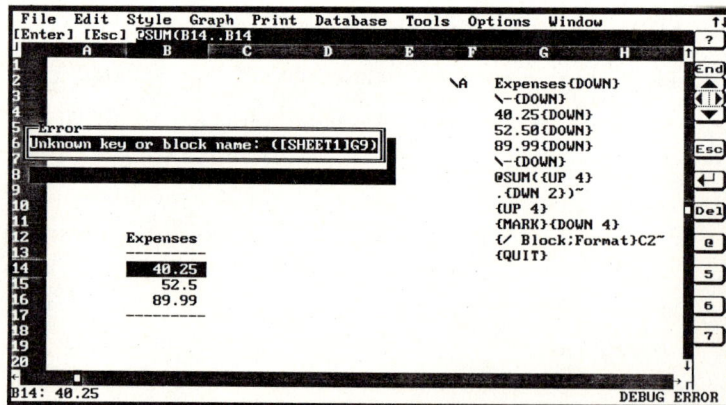

Fig. 12.10
An error encountered during the execution of a macro in Debug mode.

To display the Macro Debugger Commands menu, press the forward slash key (/) while the Debug window is active. Quattro Pro displays the Macro Debugger Commands window. From this window, you can fine-tine a Debug operation by specifying several conditions. You can insert and reset standard and conditional breakpoints, select trace cells to monitor, and abort Debug mode. You also can edit individual cells in the macro (see table 12.5).

Table 12.5
Macro Debugger Commands Menu

Command	Description
Breakpoints	Specifies macro execution breakpoints
Conditional	Specifies logical conditions for evaluating breakpoints
Trace Cells	Tracks values in up to four cells during Debug
Abort	Halts macro execution and exits Debug mode
Edit a Cell	Enters Edit mode from within Debug mode
Reset	Removes all breakpoint definitions
Quit	Exits Debug mode and executes the macro at full speed

Defining Standard Breakpoints

Executing a long macro in Debug mode can be time-consuming. By inserting breakpoints in a macro, you can specify which parts of the macro to debug step-by-step and which parts to execute at full speed.

When Quattro Pro encounters a breakpoint, the program pauses execution. Press the space bar to continue in Debug mode, or press Enter to resume macro execution until Quattro Pro encounters the next breakpoint. You can define up to four standard breakpoints per spreadsheet.

To see how breakpoints work, insert two into the sample Expenses macro. Do the following:

1. Press / (the slash key) from within the Debug window. Quattro Pro displays the Macro Debugger Commands menu (see fig. 12.11).

2. Choose the **B**reakpoints option.

3. When prompted, press 1 to insert the **1**st Breakpoint.

4. When prompted, choose **B**lock, type *G9*, and press Enter to record the first breakpoint.

5. Now press 2 to insert the **2**nd Breakpoint.

6. When prompted, choose **Block**, type *G12*, and press Enter to record the second breakpoint.

7. Choose **Quit** to return to the Debug window.

Fig. 12.11
Select the Breakpoints option on the Macro Debugger Commands menu to define macro breakpoints.

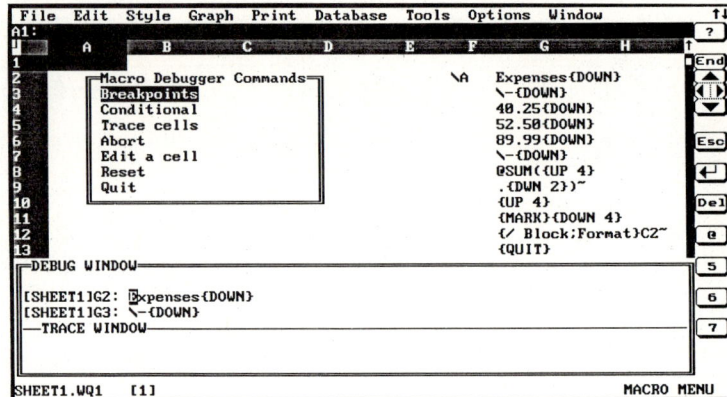

Select the **Reset** option on the Macro Debugger Commands menu to clear all standard breakpoints, conditional breakpoints, and trace cells. Or, select the **Clear Breakpoints** option on the /Tools **Macro** menu.

Defining Conditional Breakpoints

You also may define up to four conditional breakpoints. This type of break-point causes Quattro Pro to pause the execution of a macro when the value TRUE is returned by a cell condition that you define.

To define a conditional breakpoint, do the following:

1. Press / (the slash key) from within the Debug window.

2. Choose the **Conditional** option.

3. When prompted, choose the number of the conditional breakpoint you want to define.

4. When prompted, type in the address of the cell containing the condition.

5. Set additional conditional breakpoints if you want.

6. Choose **Quit** to return to the Debug window.

Conditional breakpoints are different from standard breakpoints. When you define a cell as a conditional breakpoint, you also must place some type of logical expression in the cell—for example, B25>=500. This logical expression forces Quattro Pro to wait until the value in B25 becomes greater than or equal to 500 before the program pauses the execution of the macro.

Defining Trace Cells

Advanced macro programs often use counter cells to keep track of values that the macro uses during execution. For example, a counter cell can store the number of passes that a macro makes in a looping operation. Advanced macro programs also store results from macro-generated calculations in results cells.

In either case, in a Debug operation, you can monitor the values stored in these cells to determine whether the execution error is somehow related. You may specify up to four trace cells per spreadsheet to monitor the values. During a Debug operation, Quattro Pro displays the contents of the trace cells in the Trace window pane at the bottom of the Debug window.

A trace cell can be a useful addition to the sample macro. Remember, this macro sums up three expense amounts and places the value in a results cell. By defining the results cell as the trace cell, you can monitor whether the macro program is performing this operation correctly.

To define a trace cell, do the following:

1. Press / (the slash key) from within the Debug window.

2. Choose the **Trace Cells** option.

3. When prompted, press 1 to insert the **1st Trace Cell**.

4. When prompted, type *A7* and press Enter to define the trace cell.

5. Choose **Quit** to return to the Debug window.

Editing a Cell in Debug mode

When you have located the problem with a macro, use the **Edit a Cell** command to edit the command in the problem cell. To review the use of this command, correct the spelling error uncovered in cell G9 during the previous Debug operation.

Do the following:

1. Press / (the slash key) from within the Debug window.

2. Choose the **E**dit a Cell option.

3. When prompted, type *G9* and press Enter to enter Edit mode so that you can edit the command.

4. Quattro Pro displays the contents of cell G9 on the input line. Correct the misspelling and press Enter to record the correct spelling.

Figure 12.12 shows the newly edited version of the Expenses macro. In this version of the Debug operation, Quattro Pro executes the macro commands on the cell selector location, which was in cell A1 initially.

Fig. 12.12
Editing a macro
command while
in Debug mode.

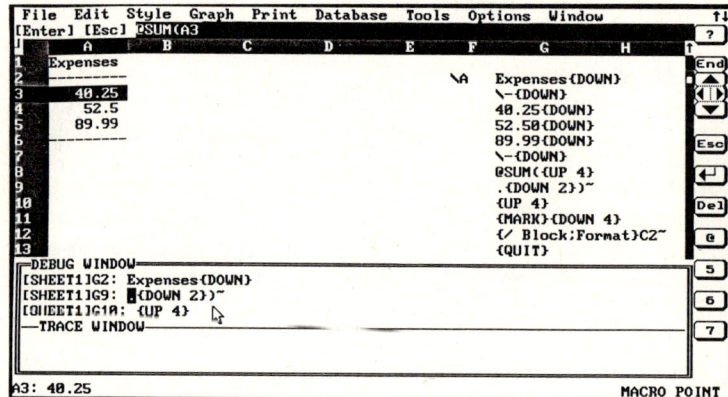

The edited command from cell G9 now appears in the Debug window when Quattro Pro encounters the first breakpoint. Press Enter to continue executing the macro.

Quattro Pro halts again when the program reaches cell G12, the next breakpoint. Because this breakpoint occurs after the macro has already summed the three expense values, Quattro Pro displays the trace cell result in the Trace pane on the Debug window (see fig. 12.13).

Resetting Breakpoints and Trace Cells

Select the **R**eset option on the Macro Debugger Commands menu to remove all breakpoints and trace cells set for the spreadsheet.

```
  File  Edit  Style  Graph  Print  Database  Tools  Options  Window        ↑↓
  A7: @SUM(A3..A5)                                                          ?
  U      A         B        C        D        E      F       G       H  ↑
  1   Expenses                                                            End
  2                                                                        ▲
  3        40.25                                  \A    Expenses{DOWN}    ◀▐▶
  4        52.5                                        40.25{DOWN}         ▼
  5        89.99                                       52.50{DOWN}
  6                                                    89.99{DOWN}        Esc
  7       182.74                                       \~{DOWN}
  8                                                    @SUM({UP 4}        ↵
  9                                                    .{DOWN 2})~
 10                                                    {UP 4}             Del
 11                                                    {MARK}{DOWN 4}
 12                                                    {/ Block;Format}C2~ @
 13                                                    {QUIT}
 ┌─DEBUG WINDOW───────────────────────────────────────────────────────┐   5
 │[SHEET1]G9:  .{DOWN 2}}~                                             │
 │[SHEET1]G12: {/ Block;Format}C2~                                    │   6
 │[SHEET1]G13: {QUIT}                                                 │
 │─TRACE WINDOW───────────────────────────────────────────────────────│   7
 │[SHEET1]A7: 182.74                                                  │
 │              ▷                                                      │
 └─────────────────────────────────────────────────────────────────────┘
  SHEET1.WQ1    [1]                                EXT       MACRO READY
```

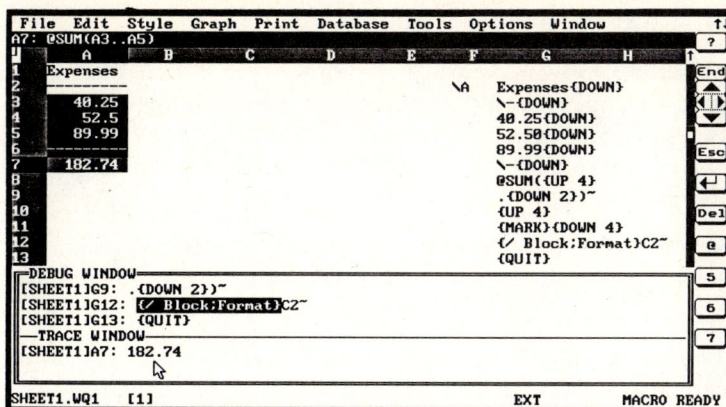

Fig. 12.13
A value
displayed in the
Trace pane on
the Debug
window.

To reset all breakpoints and trace cells from within the spreadsheet instead of from the Debug window, select the /**T**ools **M**acro **C**lear Breakpoints command.

Exiting Debug Mode

When a macro is finished executing in Debug mode, Quattro Pro removes the Debug window from your screen and removes the Debug mode indicator from the status line at the bottom of the screen.

If, however, the macro terminates prematurely (due to an error or Ctrl-Break being pressed), Quattro Pro does not exit Debug mode.

You can exit Debug mode in three ways:

- Select the /**T**ools **M**acro **D**ebugger **N**o command.

- Press Shift-F2, the Debug key, and then choose **N**o. (The Debug key toggles the Debug mode from **Y**es to **N**o and back to **Y**es.)

- Press Alt-F2 DN.

To terminate the execution of a macro before Quattro Pro is finished debugging it, press the forward slash key (/) and choose the **A**bort option displayed on the Macro Debugger Commands menu.

Tip | When the Debug window is active, press Esc to return to the active spreadsheet so that you can view the current effects of the macro. Press Esc again to redisplay the Debug window.

Using the Transcript Facility

Quattro Pro's Transcript facility is truly a "behind-the-scenes" tool. Each time you access Quattro Pro, the Transcript facility records each keystroke you make and every menu command you select. Transcript recording is virtually undetectable; you cannot tell that the Transcript is working during your Quattro Pro work sessions.

The Transcript enables you to undo spreadsheet mistakes, protect valuable work against power failure and system crashes, audit the changes you make to a spreadsheet, and even create working macros out of pasted transcripts.

This utility stores keystrokes and menu command selections in a transcript. Quattro Pro writes the transcript data periodically to a file called QUAT-TRO.LOG, which resides in the directory into which Quattro Pro was originally installed. Even during this updating operation, you barely can detect that the Transcript is working behind the scenes.

To restore lost work or to reverse mistakes made on the active spreadsheet, simply play back the transcript. To print a copy of your transcript, copy the transcript to a spreadsheet and use the **Print** menu commands.

Reviewing a Command History

To review the current entries in the Transcript log, select the /Tools Macro **Transcript** command and Quattro Pro displays the Transcript window.

Tip | Press Alt-F2 T to execute the /Tools Macro Transcript command.

The Transcript window reveals each keystroke and command selection that you have taken during recent work sessions. The last command that you execute prior to invoking the Transcript window appears highlighted at the bottom of the Transcript window (see fig. 12.14).

Notice the thin, vertical line drawn at the left margin of the Transcript window. The commands appearing to the right of this line have not been written into the QUATTRO.LOG file but still reside in Quattro Pro's memory. These commands represent all of the keystroke and command selections that you have made since the last Transcript *checkpoint*.

Quattro Pro creates a checkpoint each time you select / **File Save**, / **File Retrieve**, or / **File Erase** and saves the transcript to the log file. This action creates a new vertical line checkpoint in the Transcript that indicates where Quattro Pro will record new keyboard actions until the next log update.

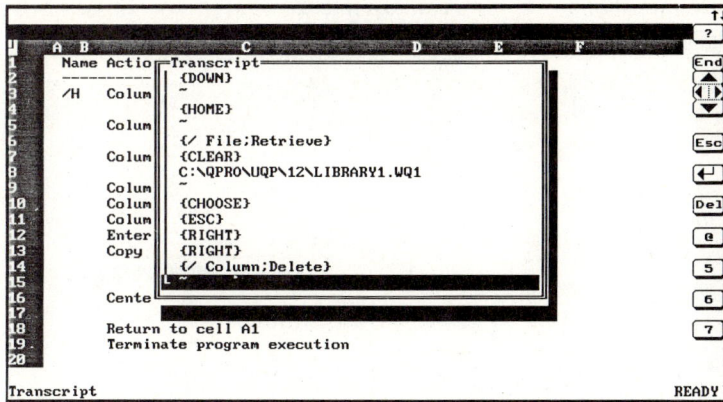

Fig. 12.14 The menu-equivalent form of your keystrokes and command selections displayed on the Transcript window.

The commands in the transcript resemble the commands appearing in macros because they are one and the same. To paste commands from the Transcript to the active spreadsheet, you can execute the commands just as you execute a macro. And like a macro, the commands in the Transcript can appear as menu-equivalent or keystroke-equivalent commands. Use the /Tools Macro Recording options to create the display format that you prefer (remember that all of the pros and cons of choosing between these two formats still hold).

Use the cursor-movement keys to scroll through the command lines in the Transcript. If any command appears to extend beyond the width of the Transcript window, highlight the command, and Quattro Pro displays the entire command on the input line at the top of your screen.

Manipulating a Command History

The Transcript menu contains the commands that enable you to manipulate the data stored in the transcript. To access this menu, do the following:

1. Select the /Tools Macro Transcript command to activate the Transcript window.

2. Press / (the forward slash) to display the Transcript menu (see fig. 12.15).

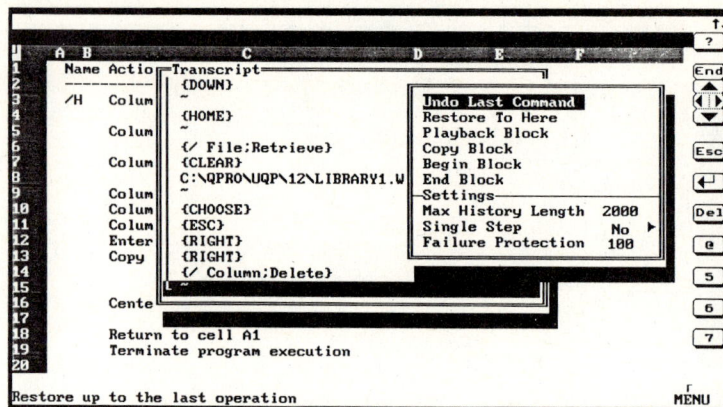

Fig. 12.15
Reviewing the
commands on
the Transcript
menu.

Table 12.6 defines each of the commands found on the Transcript Window.

Table 12.6
Transcript Window Commands

Command	Description
Undo Last Command	Restores the last recorded command
Restore to Here	Restores the command history from the last checkpoint to the end of the line highlighted in the Transcript window
Playback Block	Plays back a marked block of commands
Copy Block	Pastes a block of commands into a block on the active spreadsheet
Begin Block	Marks the beginning of a transcript block
End Block	Marks the end of a transcript block
Max History Length	Sets the maximum number of Transcript characters
Single	Replays commands one keystroke at a time
Failure Protection	Sets the maximum number of keystrokes before Quattro Pro writes the Transcript to disk

Undoing the Last Command

Suppose that you select the /Edit Delete Column command and delete column B on the active spreadsheet. Suddenly, you realize that you deleted the wrong column. If the Undo command is enabled (on the Options menu), you can select the /Edit Undo command and Quattro Pro brings back column B.

What if you opted against enabling the Undo feature to conserve RAM memory? Selecting the /Edit Undo command has no effect on the deleted column.

In this event, select the Undo Last Command on the Transcript menu to reverse the last operation you made. The Undo Last Command does not actually reverse the last operation like /Edit Undo does. Instead, Quattro Pro plays back all of the commands in your Transcript, beginning at the last checkpoint and through the command preceding the one you want to undo ({/ Column;Delete} in figure 12.15).

When executed, Quattro Pro takes control of your spreadsheet, replaying all of the keystrokes and command selections until your spreadsheet appears just as it did prior to issuing the /Edit Delete Column command.

To use this command properly, you must enter the Transcript menu immediately and select Undo Last Command. If you issue other keystrokes prior to doing so, you create a new "last command" in the Transcript. To abort an Undo Last Command operation, press Ctrl-Break and Quattro Pro terminates the playback as soon as the current command finishes.

Restoring Parts of the Transcript

The Restore to Here command plays back portions of a Transcript. In this operation, Quattro Pro replays your command history beginning at the last checkpoint and concludes with the command that is highlighted in the Transcript window.

Tip | The Restore to Here command replays your Transcript for the active spreadsheet only. If you have multiple windows open in Quattro Pro's memory, this command does not replay simultaneously the Transcripts for the other spreadsheets.

The Restore to Here command provides the security and flexibility not available with the Undo Last Command option. Now suppose that you make the same delete column error described previously. But this time, instead of selecting Undo Last Command immediately, you continue to work with the active spreadsheet. Later, you realize your mistake.

To replay a portion of your transcript and undelete the column, do the following:

1. Highlight the Transcript line containing the command immediately preceding the /**E**dit **D**elete **C**olumn command.

2. Select the Transcript menu and choose **R**estore to Here.

Quattro Pro replays your Transcript history up to the point prior to the delete operation.

Another valuable benefit of the **R**estore to Here command is that this command can protect your spreadsheet data in the event you experience a system crash or power failure. Although the **R**estore to Here command cannot restore commands appearing prior to the last checkpoint, this command is extremely useful.

In either of these events, do the following:

1. Highlight the last command line in your Transcript.

2. Select the transcript menu and chose **R**estore to Here.

Quattro Pro replays your transcript history from the last checkpoint to the point of failure. To abort this command, press Ctrl-Break. Quattro Pro terminates the replay operation at the end of the current command.

Playing Back a Transcript Block

The **P**layback Block command, like the **R**estore to Here command, plays back portions of a Transcript. This command replays all commands appearing inside a block in the Transcript that you specify.

To use this command, do the following:

1. Press / while in the Transcript window to activate the Transcript menu.

2. Highlight the first command you want to play back, then choose /**B**egin Block.

3. Highlight the last command line you want to play back, then choose /**E**nd Block (see fig. 12.16).

4. Choose **P**layback Block. Quattro Pro replays the commands marked in the block.

When you choose **P**layback Block, Quattro Pro plays back the marked command block and displays the RESTORE indicator on the status line at the bot-

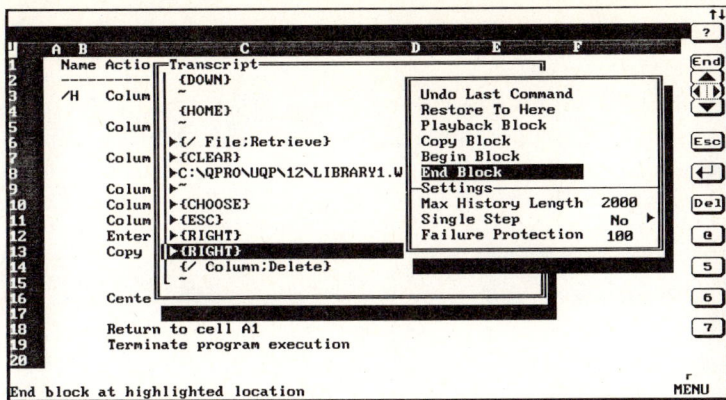

Fig. 12.16
Quattro Pro marks the block by placing arrowheads next to each command line appearing in the block.

tom right corner of your screen. To abort this operation, press Ctrl-Break. Quattro Pro terminates the playback at the end of the current command.

Copying a Transcript Block

The commands appearing in the Transcript are exactly the same as the commands that appear in a macro. By copying commands from the Transcript into a spreadsheet, you can turn the commands into a macro.

A Copy Block operation is similar to a Playback Block operation—you specify the beginning and end blocks in the Transcript on which to perform an operation. For example, to copy the block defined in the preceding section to a spreadsheet, do the following:

1. Select Copy Block. Quattro Pro prompts you to create/modify a macro name.

2. Type a name and press Enter to record the macro name.

3. When prompted, type the cell address in which you want to copy the Transcript commands.

4. Press Enter to copy the Transcript commands into the active spreadsheet.

To copy the block to another spreadsheet open in memory, you can use one of following two methods.

First, when Quattro Pro prompts you for a destination block, press Alt-0, the Pick Key, to display a list of open spreadsheets. Highlight a spreadsheet name and press Enter to load the spreadsheet into the active window. Position the cell selector on the spreadsheet and press Enter to copy the block to that location.

A second, more direct method is possible by typing the standard link syntax when prompted for a destination block. For example, figure 12.17 illustrates the syntax that was used to copy the block from the Transcript onto SHEET.WQ1 beginning at cell A5.

Fig. 12.17 Copying a transcript command block onto another spreadsheet that is open in Quattro Pro's memory.

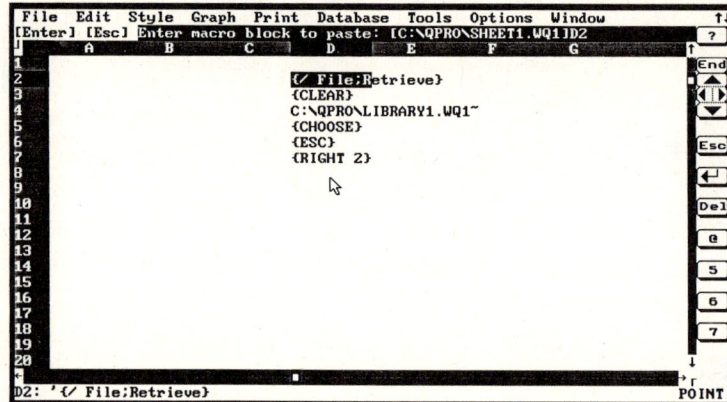

You can select the /**T**ools **M**acro **N**ame command to assign a macro name to the block and select the /**T**ools **M**acro **P**aste command to copy the block into SHEET.WQ1.

Defining the Maximum History Length

Transcript records your keystrokes and command selections in a file called QUATTRO.LOG. When you load Quattro Pro into your PC, the program opens this file and begins appending to it.

Quattro Pro enables you to establish the number of keystrokes the program stores in the QUATTRO.LOG file. By default, this setting is 2000 keystrokes. When the QUATTRO.LOG file reaches this maximum, Quattro Pro renames the file QUATTRO.BAK and opens a new, empty QUATTRO.LOG file. When Quattro Pro updates QUATTRO.LOG, the program overwrites the QUATTRO.BAK file.

You can change the **M**aximum History Length setting, for example, to 7,500 keystrokes. Do the following:

1. Choose **M**aximum History Length from the Transcript menu.

2. When prompted, type *7500* (see fig. 12.18).

3. Press Enter to record the new setting.

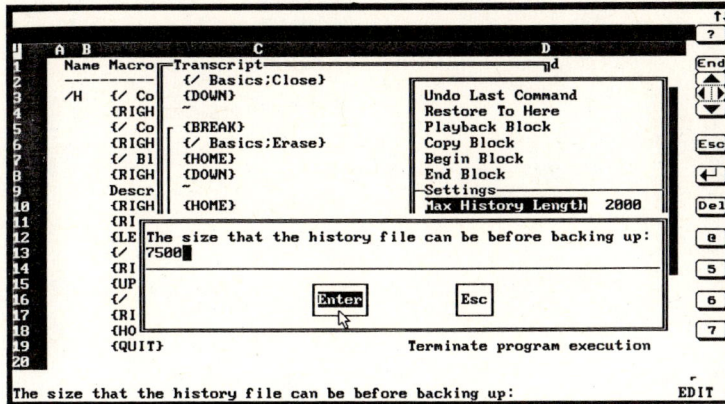

Fig. 12.18 Increasing the size of the Transcript log file by choosing a higher maximum history length setting.

The maximum value permitted for this setting is 25,000 keystrokes. Be careful of the value you enter here; if you type *0* as the setting, Quattro Pro disables the Transcript facility altogether.

Defining the Playback Mode

Select the **Single** command to determine the speed with which Quattro Pro replays a Transcript command history when prompted.

By default, this command is set to **No**. A **Yes** setting causes Quattro Pro to display the Transcript command history in Debug mode.

The **Timed** setting pauses the replay operation momentarily between each Transcript command line; the **Yes** setting pauses the replay until you press a key on the keyboard.

To replay a block of commands in Timed mode, do the following:

1. Select **Single** from the Transcript menu.

2. Choose the **Timed** option (see fig. 12.19).

Now choose a replay operation. When executed, Quattro Pro replays the Transcript one command line at a time, pausing for a moment between commands.

Press Ctrl-Break during a replay operation to terminate the operation.

Fig. 12.19
Pausing the
steps in a replay
operation
enables you to
watch the
process.

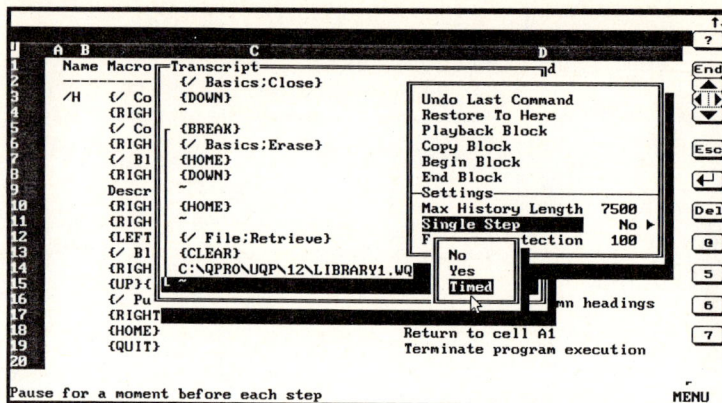

Defining Failure Protection

By default, Quattro Pro writes the Transcript to disk after every 100 key-strokes. The Failure Protection facility ensures that you can recover most or all of your work in the event of a power failure.

When you lower this setting, Quattro Pro writes to disk more often and increases the likelihood that the Transcript will slow down your work sessions. If you are comfortable with increasing the risk of data loss, choose the Failure Protection command and enter a higher setting.

To set this command to 500 keystrokes, for example, do the following:

1. Select Failure Protection from the Transcript menu.

2. When prompted, type *500* (see fig. 12.20).

3. Press Enter to record the new setting.

Fig. 12.20
Increasing the
number of
keystrokes that
Quattro Pro
stores prior to
writing the
keystrokes to
disk.

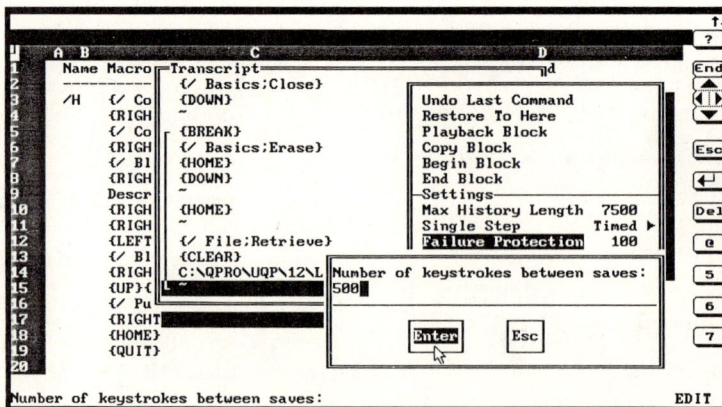

At higher settings, Quattro Pro stores your keystrokes and command selections in a memory buffer and writes the keystrokes to disk at less frequent intervals.

Exiting Transcript

Press Esc to leave the Transcript menu and return to the Transcript window. To return to the active spreadsheet, press Esc again.

Tip | To disable the Transcript facility altogether and free RAM memory up for use in other areas of Quattro Pro, set the Maximum History Length setting to 0.

Questions & Answers

This chapter introduces you to the /Tools Macro menu of commands. If you have questions concerning particular situations that are not addressed in the examples given, look through the questions and answers section.

Q: I pressed Alt-F2-R to begin recording a macro but nothing happened. Did I do something wrong?

A: When Quattro Pro is recording a macro, the program displays REC on the status line at the bottom of your screen. If this mode indicator does not appear, select /**Tools Macro Recording Yes** and try again. Note that Quattro Pro does not do anything spectacular to indicate that it is recording a macro.

Q: Why doesn't Quattro Pro give me an instant replay of a macro I just recorded?

A: You may not have turned the Macro Recorder on, and Quattro Pro hasn't recorded anything. Make sure that the REC mode indicator is showing on the status line while you are recording. You also may have exited the active spreadsheet before choosing the Instant Replay command, and Quattro Pro erased the recorded macro from memory.

   To properly replay a macro, be sure to select /**Tools Macro Instant Replay** when you finish recording.

Q: Why doesn't Quattro Pro execute my instant macro?

A: Remember, Quattro Pro accepts only letters as valid instant macro names. If you named your macro Alt-5, for example, select /**Tools Macro Name** and rename the macro with a letter.

Q: Why doesn't Quattro Pro execute the instant macro I named /A?

A: When you name an instant macro, you must include the backslash key (\ ) and not the forward slash key (/). If your macro name contains the forward slash key, Quattro Pro does nothing when you press Alt-A. Select /**Tools Macro Name** and rename the macro.

Q: Why doesn't my autoload macro work when I load a linked spreadsheet application?

A: Look at your macro. Is the first command in the macro {ESC}? If not, type {*ESC*} above the first command—this command is necessary to back Quattro Pro out of the linking options prompt. Select /**Tools Macro Name** and rename the macro, defining the cell that {ESC} is in as the first cell in the macro block.

Q: I don't want my autoload macro to affect every spreadsheet that I load. What should I do?

A: Select /**Options Startup Startup Macro**, press Backspace until you delete the autoload name, and press Enter to record no autoload name. Select /**Options Update** to save the new setting.

You must rename the macro if you originally named it \0 to correspond to the default setting for the Startup Macro command.

Q: When I execute a macro, Quattro Pro modifies the spreadsheet that the macro is on and not the spreadsheet that I want modified. What's happening?

A: You did not define the first spreadsheet as a macro library. Select /**Tools Macro Library Yes**. Press Alt-0 and activate the target spreadsheet. Execute the macro again.

Q: Why doesn't Quattro Pro execute a macro that I created from the 1-2-3-compatible menu tree?

A: You can use such a macro only when the 1-2-3-compatible menu tree is active. If you switched menu trees since creating the macro, switch back by selecting /**Options Startup Menu Tree** 123.MU.

Q: Why can't I execute a recorded macro in the 1-2-3-compatible menu tree?

A: Before you record macros from the Quattro Pro menu tree, you must select /Tools **Macro Macro Recording Logical**. In this setting, Quattro Pro records menu-equivalent commands that are compatible across menu trees.

In the **Keystroke** setting, Quattro Pro records keystroke commands that vary from menu tree to menu tree.

Q: Why is the Transcript window empty when there should be plenty of command history?

A: Quattro Pro disables the Transcript facility when the /Tools **Macro Transcript Max History Length** setting is 0. Enter a larger number if you want Quattro Pro to maintain a Transcript history of your work sessions.

Chapter Summary

This chapter showed you how to create, debug, edit, and execute macro programs. In addition, you were introduced to the Transcript facility, a tool that helps you maintain the integrity of your Quattro Pro work sessions.

After completing this chapter you should understand the following Quattro Pro concepts:

- Recording, pasting, naming, editing, and executing basic macro programs

- Using the Macro Debugger to ferret out commands in macros that cause execution errors

- Applying the commands on the Transcript menu to view your command history, replay Transcript blocks, and undo spreadsheet mistakes

- Copying a Transcript block to a spreadsheet, naming the block as a macro, and then replaying the block on-screen

- Defining parameters that determine the size of the Transcript, how often the Transcript is updated, and the transcript's replay mode

The remainder of *Using Quattro Pro* is devoted to topics crucial to advancing your user skills. If you have not glanced through the appendixes, do so now.

Appendix A addresses installation and advanced user issues that help you create the most efficient operating environment for Quattro Pro.

Appendix B contains instructions for creating a macro program to install Bitstream fonts. If during the installation you opted against installing the entire font library, this macro enables you to install the font library now.

Appendix C is a glossary of macro command terms. The glossary includes descriptions and definitions of each command's syntax so that you know how to use the commands in your own macro programs.

Appendix D is a glossary of menu-equivalent commands. These commands are used in macros to duplicate selections command on any of Quattro Pro's menus.

Appendix E is an ASCII table. This appendix contains instructions for using ASCII characters and decimal equivalent codes with three commands on the Options menu. Appendix E also discusses how to convert printer codes into setup strings using the ASCII table.

Installing Quattro Pro

Creating an ideal hardware and operating system environment is critical to installing and using Quattro Pro. Many possible hardware and operating system combinations exist for Quattro Pro because the program can run on an IBM PC, an 80386 system, and everything in between.

Appendix A begins by discussing how to create the ideal operating environment. Issues covered include obtaining peak performance from your computer's microprocessor, managing random access memory (RAM), managing your disk effectively, selecting an appropriate video display and printer, and using peripherals.

Throughout the discussion, you can take stock of your computer equipment. You may uncover the need for additional hardware. Because Quattro Pro can push your equipment to the limit, however, you may find that your computer system is sufficient to install Quattro Pro.

The next section offers step-by-step instructions for installing your copy of Quattro Pro.

After Quattro Pro is installed, you can reconfigure many of the hardware settings from the Options menu. The commands on this menu enable you to fine-tune your copy of Quattro Pro until you attain the most productive operating environment.

This appendix concludes with a look at some common questions and answers about installing the program. Scan through this section if you need a quick resolution to questions concerning system configuration or program installation issues.

Setting Up the Ideal System Configuration

The ideal system configuration depends on your computer equipment. Unless you can afford to purchase a fully loaded AT-80286 or 80386 system with lots of RAM, a math coprocessor chip, a VGA display, and so on, you are in the same boat as most Quattro Pro users. Most users need to know several good tricks for getting the best performance from their computers—given whatever equipment they have.

What You Need To Run Quattro Pro

To operate Quattro Pro, you must have at least the following hardware and operating system software available:

Hardware

- IBM XT or AT compatible

- 512K (kilobytes) of RAM

- 3M (megabytes) of free space on your hard disk drive

- A monochrome graphics display system

Operating system

- DOS 2.0 or later

The following configuration is an example of an ideal operating environment for using Quattro Pro.

Hardware

- 80386-based computer

- 2M of RAM

- 4M of free space on your hard disk drive

- VGA graphics display system

Operating system

- Microsoft- or Logitech-compatible mouse

- DOS 4.0

The performance of Quattro Pro improves noticeably when you can improve the recommended minimum hardware configuration. Not all users have access to an 80386-based computer, and you have to make the best of what you have. Fortunately, even with the minimum recommended configuration, Quattro Pro performs well.

Microprocessor Clock Speed and Math Coprocessor Chip

Your computer's microprocessor clock speed determines how fast Quattro Pro processes commands. The original IBM PC and XT systems use the 8086 or 8088 chip, running at 4.77 MHz (megahertz). A *hertz* is a unit of frequency equal to one cycle per second. A *megahertz* is equal to one million cycles per second.

The AT systems use an 80286 chip with clock speeds ranging from 8 to 25 MHz. The new 80386 chips process data from 16 to 35 MHz. The processing speed difference between the first PC and today's powerful 80386 ATs is truly remarkable. In some instances, the processing speed of a 80386 is 30 times faster than the original IBM PC.

Unless you want to upgrade your microprocessor chip, which may mean purchasing a new computer system, only two methods exist for speeding up Quattro Pro execution via the microprocessor. First, if your current chip has an adjustable clock speed, make sure that the clock speed is on the highest setting.

Second, you can purchase a math coprocessor chip. These add-on chips decrease your microprocessor's workload by assuming many of the number-crunching responsibilities. Best of all, math chips are relatively inexpensive. Quattro Pro detects the presence of a math coprocessor chip—no special installation is necessary.

Random Access Memory Management

To use Quattro Pro, your personal computer must have a minimum of 512K of random access memory (RAM). Quattro Pro can operate more efficiently with more RAM. Gains in efficiency come in two forms: the ability to create bigger spreadsheets with more complex formulas and increased program execution speed.

Most AT-80286 and 80386 systems come with a minimum of 640K of RAM. This RAM is *conventional* memory and is used by DOS to store program code and other data while your computer is on. When your computer has 640K of RAM, DOS uses 512K to store Quattro Pro program code—the rest is available for building and temporarily storing spreadsheets.

When you have other software programs running on your system, they also require some of the 640K. For example, terminate-and-stay-resident (TSR) programs like Microsoft Windows, DESQview, and mouse drivers load into your system's RAM and remain there during Quattro Pro work sessions. The RAM that your computer allocates to these program means decreases the memory available to Quattro Pro for building spreadsheets.

You can add two types of memory beyond the 640K of RAM: *extended memory* and *expanded memory*. The first extra 384K of RAM that you add to the basic 640K is *high* memory. This memory primarily is used to store CPU instructions and video display data. Neither DOS nor Quattro Pro can use this memory to store program code or spreadsheet data.

Memory beyond 1M is *extended* memory. Extended memory is used by ram disks, printer spoolers, and window applications. DOS and Quattro Pro cannot access and use extended memory. Fortunately, however, memory drivers enable you to configure extended memory as expanded memory.

Expanded memory can be used by Quattro Pro to store spreadsheet data. This memory usually comes on a card that you plug into an expansion slot inside your computer. Expanded memory cards are sold with software driver programs that enable you to install the cards for use with your computer (the names of four cards that Quattro Pro supports appear in the next section). You add the driver name to your CONFIG.SYS file.

Regardless of how your memory is configured, recognize that all RAM has the same purpose—to store data while your computer is on. What differentiates one type from the other is that DOS can recognize and use only the first 640K of RAM. Although Quattro Pro recognizes and uses expanded memory, the program cannot use extended memory. Remember the following rule of thumb: if your computer has more than 640K of RAM, configure the added memory as expanded memory so that Quattro Pro can use it.

One of the new Quattro Pro features is the *Virtual Real-Time Object-Oriented Memory Manager (VROOMM)*. Borland created this RAM management utility to enable Quattro Pro to work on a wide range of personal computers. VROOMM technology takes into account the different memory allocation schemes used by different systems. VROOMM helps you manage your memory by allocating as much RAM as possible to spreadsheet operations. VROOMM accomplishes this allocation by loading small portions of program code at a time, on an as-needed basis.

VROOMM works no matter what memory configuration your computer has. If your computer system has less than 1M of RAM, and all memory above 640K is configured as extended memory, you can invoke a special startup parameter to tell Quattro Pro to set up a cache for VROOMM objects in extended memory.

To use VROOMM in this way, type *Q /X* and press Enter to load Quattro Pro. If you have a Windows application manager such as Microsoft Windows, enter */X* as the loading parameter. Similarly, you can enter *Q /X* as the final line in the AUTOEXEC.BAT file. Each time you boot your system, Quattro Pro loads VROOMM.

This startup parameter is not recommended for systems with more than 1M of RAM. Remember, always configure memory above 1M as expanded memory. Quattro Pro operates with any LIM 3.2 or 4.0 card and supports the following expanded memory cards:

- Intel Above Board

- AST RAMpage!

- Quadram Liberty

- STB Memory Champion

The amount of RAM available to Quattro Pro is affected by external activities like operating systems, memory-resident utilities, and application drivers. You can maximize the memory available to Quattro Pro by removing unused peripheral driver programs and terminate-and-stay-resident (TSR) applications from your system's memory. These programs consume RAM that Quattro Pro can otherwise use for storing spreadsheet data. To free up RAM used by a TSR application or set aside for peripheral driver programs, remove the program name from the CONFIG.SYS or AUTOEXEC.BAT file and reboot your system.

Entering data into a spreadsheet, building a graph, and opening multiple spreadsheets are examples of internal activities that consume your computer's RAM. You can maximize the memory available to Quattro Pro by building efficient spreadsheets. Quattro Pro activities such as cell formatting, the Undo feature, and open multiple spreadsheets gobble system memory. To prevent this memory loss, follow these rules:

- Quattro Pro uses system memory in blocks. The larger the active area of a spreadsheet, the more memory Quattro Pro needs. When you erase areas of your spreadsheet, memory remains allocated but unused. You can regain unused memory blocks. First save your spreadsheet. Then erase the spreadsheet from memory and recall the spreadsheet. Quattro Pro recalls the spreadsheet into a smaller memory block.

- Review the number of open spreadsheet files. Keep open only those spreadsheet files that need to be open for the Quattro Pro session at hand. Close unneeded documents to recover system memory.

- Quattro Pro uses memory to retain the data and cell formats for the current spreadsheet(s). You can recover memory by erasing unneeded data and cell formats from the current spreadsheet.

- Build streamlined spreadsheets. Instead of creating huge spreadsheets to assimilate large volumes of data, try using several smaller linked spreadsheets. You can recall and update several smaller spreadsheets faster—and with less memory used—than struggling with large spreadsheets. On the other hand, if you are using several spreadsheets, each containing a small amount of data, combine them into one larger spreadsheet. The idea is to find the happy medium between using one large, memory-intensive spreadsheet and several small spreadsheets, which, when loaded into memory at the same time, can be equally memory-intensive.

Hard Disk Drive Management

Borland recommends that you have a minimum of 3M of free space on your hard disk drive for Quattro Pro. In reality, you need at least 4M to install the program and the entire Bitstream font library. This figure is based on the total disk storage space necessary for the program files, the font files, and several spreadsheet and graph files.

Although Quattro Pro can run without the entire font library, installing all the fonts at one time is convenient. (See Appendix B for complete coverage of adding custom Bitstream fonts.)

Video Displays and Printers

Quattro Pro supports all the video display types available in today's market and the following graphics cards:

- IBM Color/Graphics Adapter

- Hercules Graphics Card (monochrome)

- IBM Enhanced Graphics Adapter (monochrome and color)

- IBM Video Graphics Array (monochrome or color)

- IBM 3270/PC and 3270/AT with APA

- AT&T 6300 640 x 640

- MCGA (IBM Model 30)

- IBM 8514 Graphics Adapter

Quattro Pro also supports most dot-matrix, daisywheel, laser, and PostScript printers.

The super-VGA graphics display system is the current state-of-the-art in video displays. This display type offers superior color graphics and unsurpassed resolution. If you can afford one, a super-VGA display system is the ideal way to display Quattro Pro graphs on-screen.

Fortunately, Quattro Pro enables you to build and annotate graphs with just a graphics card and a monochrome display capable of high-resolution graphics. If you do not have a graphics card, you can build and print graphs, but you cannot see them on-screen. You also can display Quattro Pro in text or graphics display modes. You can toggle between the two modes from the Quattro Pro Options menu.

Mice

If you have never used a mouse, you are missing out on a great productivity tool. Building Quattro Pro spreadsheets is easier and more efficient when you use a mouse and a keyboard together. Quattro Pro supports all mice compatible with the Microsoft Mouse interface, including the Microsoft serial and bus mice, the Mouse Systems Mouse (with the MSMOUSE driver), and the Logitech Mouse.

Installing the Program

Quattro Pro's installation utility is self-explanatory and mostly self-running. Before you begin installing Quattro Pro, review the following checklist to ensure that you have the correct system configuration for using Quattro Pro:

- IBM-XT, IBM-AT, or PS/2-compatible computer with at least 512K of RAM

- PC DOS or MS-DOS Version 2.0 or later

- Hard disk drive with at least 4M of available storage space

- RAM exceeding 1M defined as expanded memory

Tip | The Quattro Pro installation utility changes your CONFIG.SYS and AUTOEXEC.BAT files if you allow the program to do so. The installation utility is the easiest way to change those files. To change them yourself—for example, to later add an expanded memory card—use a word processing program in nondocument or DOS text file mode.

The CONFIG.SYS file must contain the following statements:

    BUFFERS=20

    FILES=20

The AUTOEXEC.BAT file should contain QPRO, the name of the directory in which Quattro Pro resides.

Copying Files

During the first part of the installation process, Quattro Pro copies program files to the default directory. To start the installation, place installation disk 1 of 8 into the A drive. Type *A:INSTALL* and press Enter. After a moment or two, the screen shown in figure A.1 appears.

Fig. A.1
The initial
installation
screen.

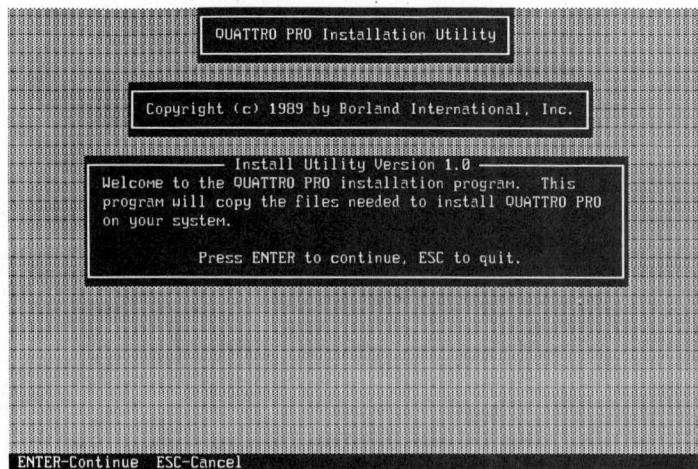

Press Enter to begin the installation or Esc to quit. If you need help during the installation process, press F1 and a context-sensitive help screen appears.

Quattro Pro can install itself from any drive you specify. Generally, drive A is the source drive from which you copy the Quattro Pro files (see fig. A.2). If you copy the Quattro Pro files onto your hard disk drive prior to installing the program, enter *C:* as the source drive. If your A drive is a 3 1/2-inch drive, you can specify B as the source drive if you have only 5 1/4-inch disks.

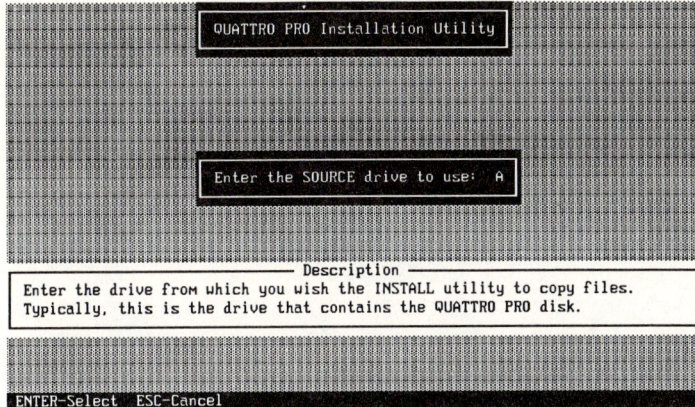

Fig. A.2
Selecting the source drive from which to install.

The installation utility ensures that you have enough free storage space on your computer's hard disk drive and displays the directory to which files are copied (see fig. A.3).

If you do not have at least 4M of free storage space, Quattro Pro displays an error message telling you so. If you see this error message, exit the installation program and delete files from your hard disk drive until you free up at least 4M of storage space.

The installation utility copies the Quattro Pro files to the default path, \QPRO. During this process, Quattro Pro prompts you to change disks and press a key until the files are copied from all disks (see fig. A.4).

You see the progress of the installation on-screen as the installation utility reads and writes files.

Fig. A.3
Checking the
Quattro Pro
directory name.

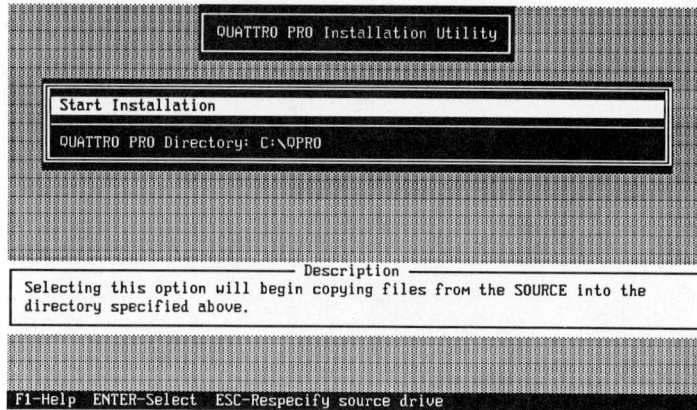

```
                    QUATTRO PRO Installation Utility

   ┌──────────────────────────────────────────────────────────────┐
   │ Start Installation                                             │
   │                                                                │
   │ QUATTRO PRO Directory: C:\QPRO                                 │
   └──────────────────────────────────────────────────────────────┘

   ───────────────────────── Description ─────────────────────────
   Selecting this option will begin copying files from the SOURCE into the
   directory specified above.



   F1-Help  ENTER-Select  ESC-Respecify source drive
```

Fig. A.4
Copying
Quattro Pro
files.

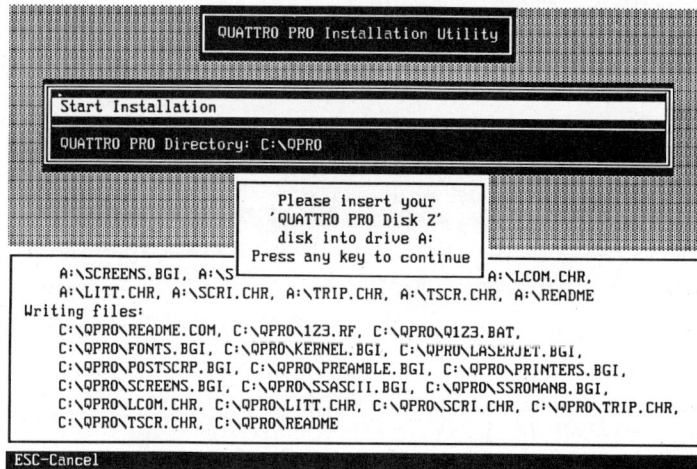

```
                    QUATTRO PRO Installation Utility

   ┌──────────────────────────────────────────────────────────────┐
   │ Start Installation                                             │
   │                                                                │
   │ QUATTRO PRO Directory: C:\QPRO                                 │
   └──────────────────────────────────────────────────────────────┘
                              ┌──────────────────────┐
                              │   Please insert your │
                              │  'QUATTRO PRO Disk 2' │
                              │   disk into drive A: │
                              │ Press any key to continue │
                              └──────────────────────┘
     A:\SCREENS.BGI, A:\S                              A:\LCOM.CHR,
     A:\LITT.CHR, A:\SCRI.CHR, A:\TRIP.CHR, A:\TSCR.CHR, A:\README
   Writing files:
     C:\QPRO\README.COM, C:\QPRO\1Z3.RF, C:\QPRO\Q1Z3.BAT,
     C:\QPRO\FONTS.BGI, C:\QPRO\KERNEL.BGI, C:\QPRO\LASERJET.BGI,
     C:\QPRO\POSTSCRP.BGI, C:\QPRO\PREAMBLE.BGI, C:\QPRO\PRINTERS.BGI,
     C:\QPRO\SCREENS.BGI, C:\QPRO\SSASCII.BGI, C:\QPRO\SSROMAN8.BGI,
     C:\QPRO\LCOM.CHR, C:\QPRO\LITT.CHR, C:\QPRO\SCRI.CHR, C:\QPRO\TRIP.CHR,
     C:\QPRO\TSCR.CHR, C:\QPRO\README

   ESC-Cancel
```

When all the files are transferred, Quattro Pro displays the message shown in figure A.5.

Selecting Your Equipment

You must tell Quattro Pro about your equipment. In the second part of the installation process, you select a monitor type, choose which menu tree interface to use, and define how you want Quattro Pro to display printouts and graphs. You also choose whether to install the Bitstream font software that displays Quattro Pro graphs.

```
┌──────────────────────────────────────────────┐
│          QUATTRO PRO Installation Utility      │
└──────────────────────────────────────────────┘

        ┌─────────────────────────────────────────────┐
        │ The QUATTRO PRO files have now been installed on │
        │ your hard disk.  In order to complete the     │
        │ installation of QUATTRO PRO, please answer the │
        │ questions that follow as best you can.        │
        │                                               │
        │        PRESS ANY KEY TO CONTINUE              │
   C:\QPRO\                                           │
Reading file└───────────────────────────────────────┘
   C:\QPRO\Q.CA3
Writing files:
   C:\QPRO\Q.VRM
Reading files:
   C:\QPRO\QUATTRO.CA1, C:\QPRO\QUATTRO.CAZ
Writing files:
   C:\QPRO\Q.VRM, C:\QPRO\QUATTRO.HLP, C:\QPRO\QUATTRO.HLP

Any Key-Continue
```

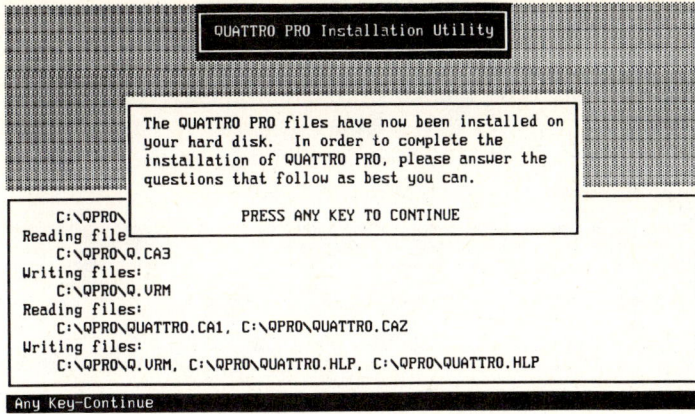

Fig. A.5
A successful file transfer.

Selecting Monitor Type

The installation utility detects whether you have a color graphics display card installed in your computer. You must, however, tell Quattro Pro whether your monitor is color or monochrome (see fig. A.6).

To change the default selection, press F2, use the cursor-movement keys to move to your selection, and press Enter. When finished, press Enter to continue or press Ctrl-X to quit.

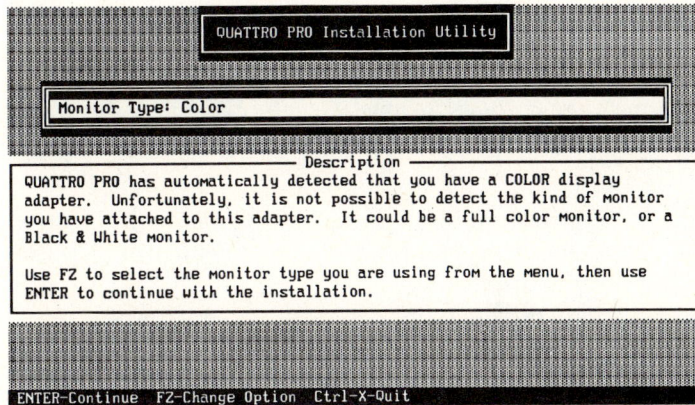

```
┌──────────────────────────────────────────────┐
│          QUATTRO PRO Installation Utility      │
└──────────────────────────────────────────────┘

┌──────────────────────────────────────────────┐
│ Monitor Type: Color                            │
└──────────────────────────────────────────────┘

──────────────────── Description ────────────────────
QUATTRO PRO has automatically detected that you have a COLOR display
adapter.  Unfortunately, it is not possible to detect the kind of monitor
you have attached to this adapter.  It could be a full color monitor, or a
Black & White monitor.

Use FZ to select the monitor type you are using from the menu, then use
ENTER to continue with the installation.

ENTER-Continue  FZ-Change Option  Ctrl-X-Quit
```

Fig. A.6
Specifying a color or monochrome monitor.

Selecting the Menu Tree Interface

The user interface enables you to choose how you operate Quattro Pro (see fig. A.7). The default is QUATTRO. To accept this menu tree, press Enter. To change to a different menu tree, press F2, use the cursor-movement keys to highlight your selection, and press Enter twice.

If you are accustomed to Lotus 1-2-3's menu structure, you may want to configure Quattro Pro to emulate 1-2-3. If you prefer Quattro Pro's old menu structure, select the Q1 interface. The best interface for most people, however, is the default Quattro Pro menu tree interface.

Fig. A.7
Choosing the
menu tree.

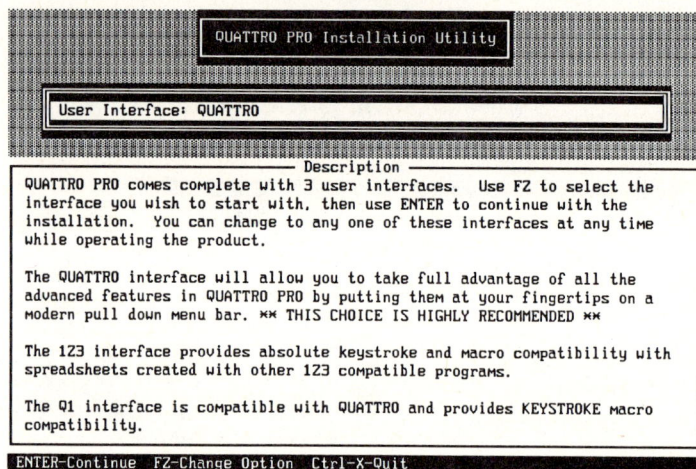

Selecting a Printer

Select a printer manufacturer and model from the Printer Manufacturer screen (see fig. A.8). Press F2, use the cursor-movement keys to highlight the appropriate manufacturer, and then press Enter. If your printer manufacturer is not on this screen, check your printer manual for information on the types of printers your printer can emulate. Many printers emulate Epson and IBM printers.

After you select a printer manufacturer, Quattro Pro displays the Printer Model screen (see fig. A.9). To choose a printer model, highlight the appropriate name on the list and press Enter.

After you select a printer model, Quattro Pro asks you to choose an initial mode and resolution at which to print spreadsheets and graphs. Figure A.10 displays a low-resolution mode in which the dots per inch (dpi) is 120×72.

You can select a medium or high mode by pressing F2 and selecting a different option. The actual dpi ratings available on this menu depend on the individual printer. If you select an Epson LQ-2500 printer, for example, the dpi rating in high mode is 360 x 180.

Fig. A.8
Selecting
Panasonic as a
printer
manufacturer.

Fig. A.9
Selecting
KX-1595 as a
printer model.

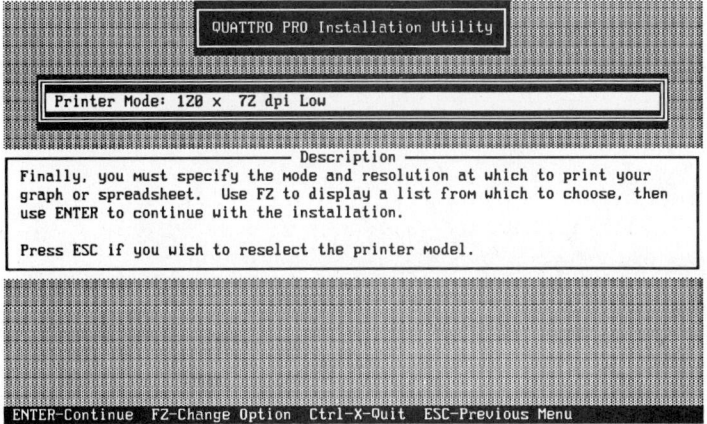

Fig. A.10
Selecting a
default printer
mode and
resolution.

Selecting Graph Quality

To conclude the installation of Quattro Pro, you must specify how you want the program to build graphs. If you select Draft (see fig. A.11), Quattro Pro installs only the basic fonts.

Fig. A.11
Specifying the
size of your
font library.

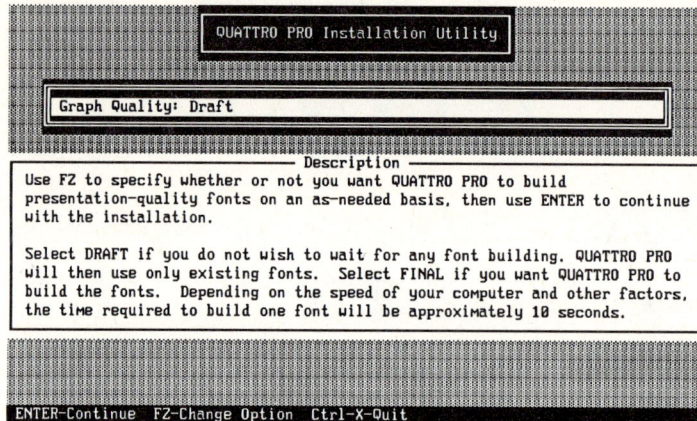

```
┌─────────────────────────────────────────────────────────┐
│            QUATTRO PRO Installation Utility               │
└─────────────────────────────────────────────────────────┘

┌─────────────────────────────────────────────────────────┐
│ Graph Quality: Draft                                      │
└─────────────────────────────────────────────────────────┘

───────────────────────── Description ─────────────────────
Use F2 to specify whether or not you want QUATTRO PRO to build
presentation-quality fonts on an as-needed basis, then use ENTER to continue
with the installation.

Select DRAFT if you do not wish to wait for any font building.  QUATTRO PRO
will then use only existing fonts.  Select FINAL if you want QUATTRO PRO to
build the fonts.  Depending on the speed of your computer and other factors,
the time required to build one font will be approximately 10 seconds.


ENTER-Continue  F2-Change Option  Ctrl-X-Quit
```

If you select Final, Quattro Pro enables you to choose how many fonts to install. Quattro Pro has 150 graphic fonts and takes anywhere from 20 seconds to 1 minute to build a font. If you choose to install the entire set of fonts, Quattro Pro may need over two hours to install the entire set (depending on the speed of your computer).

When installed, each font file takes up from 2K to 6K of storage space on your hard disk drive. Larger font files require more space, from 6K to 12K. To install all 150 fonts, Quattro Pro requires 600K.

You should invest the time to install the entire font library. If you choose to install a partial set of fonts, however, be aware that Quattro Pro needs to build fonts during certain operations. During these times, you must wait as Quattro Pro builds (installs) the needed font.

Completing the Installation

When the installation utility successfully installs Quattro Pro, the screen shown in figure A.12 is displayed.

If Quattro Pro fails to successfully transfer all configuration files, you must begin the process again. Installation can fail for a number of reasons. The most common reason for failure is because the hard disk drive is full. Make sure that you have 4M on your hard disk before attempting to install Quattro Pro.

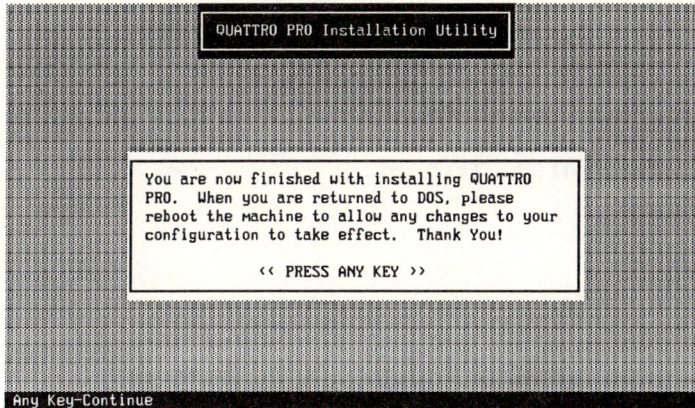

Fig. A.12
The
Installation
Successful
screen.

Loading and Quitting Quattro Pro

To load Quattro Pro, press Q and then press Enter. To quit the program, select **File Exit** (press */FE*), and Quattro PRO returns you to the operating system.

Reconfiguring and Enhancing Quattro Pro

You should never have to install Quattro Pro again. Many software companies require you to reinstall their program when you want to alter the way your computer equipment interacts with the software.

You easily can reconfigure your copy of Quattro Pro. You can add new printers, customize the mouse palette functions (when you display Quattro Pro in graphics mode), and switch menu trees directly from Quattro Pro's Options menu (see Chapter 6). If you need to add Bitstream fonts to enhance the presentation of your spreadsheet graphs, or if you must delete unimportant font files to regain storage space on your hard disk drive, you can create and execute a simple macro to auto-build new fonts for you (see Appendix B).

Questions & Answers

This section deals with commonly asked questions and start-up problems. This section solves glitches encountered when creating the ideal system configuration and installing Quattro Pro.

Ideal System Configuration

Q: Why does Quattro Pro operate slowly on my system?

A: If you have expanded memory, make sure that the EMS driver is included in the CONFIG.SYS file.

If your system has 1M or less of RAM, load Quattro Pro by using the Q /X option. The /X option enables Borland's VROOMM memory manager to use extended memory for object caching.

Q: Why doesn't my mouse work properly when I use Quattro Pro's graphics display mode.

A: Older mouse drivers support only 80 x 24 screen displays. Quattro Pro supports EGA 80 x 43, VGA 80 x 50 and EGA/VGA graphics modes. To display Quattro Pro in a mode other than 80 x 24, your mouse driver version must conform to the following specifications:

Microsoft Mouse   6.0 or higher
Mouse Systems   6.01 or higher
Logitech   4.0 or higher
PC Mouse   6.01 or higher

Installation Utility

Q: The text of the installation utility is difficult to read. What can I do?

A: Exit INSTALL. Then type *A:INSTALL /B* and press Enter to force Quattro Pro to display in a black-and-white mode.

Q: The computer displays the message Not enough disk space to install Quattro when I try to install the program. What can I do?

A: Exit the installation utility. Erase nonessential files from your hard disk drive until you have at least 4M of free storage space on your hard disk drive.

Q: The computer displays the message `Not enough memory to run Quattro` when I try to load the program. What can I do?

A: Erase all TSR programs from your CONFIG.SYS and AUTOEXEC.BAT files. Reboot your system and try again.

If your computer has expanded memory, the memory card may not be Quattro Pro-compatible. Try loading Quattro Pro without loading the EMS driver via the CONFIG.SYS file.

Load CONFIG.SYS into a word processing program as a DOS text file. Delete the name of the driver program, resave the file, and then re-boot your computer so that the new CONFIG.SYS settings take effect.

B

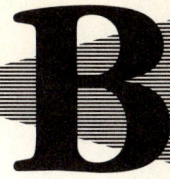

Customizing Your Font Library

Bitstream fonts do not come pre-built when you purchase Quattro Pro. To use a font, Quattro Pro must create a bitmap file for that font. A bitmap file stores data about a font's typeface, style, and point size for your screen or printer.

A bitmap font file can be built in three ways: during program installation, during a work session, and via a font-building macro that you create and execute.

Building Bitstream Fonts during Program Installation

Appendix B contains information about customizing your screen font library. When you install the program, Quattro Pro offers four choices for creating Bitstream fonts:

Choice	Fonts installed	Storage required
Limited	6 Swiss fonts	24K
Swiss	30 Swiss fonts	120K
Swiss & Dutch	30 Swiss and 30 Dutch fonts	240K
Swiss, Dutch, Courier, Swiss and Dutch Italics	30 Swiss, 30 Dutch, 30 Courier fonts 30 Swiss Italic and 30 Dutch Italic fonts	600K

571

During installation, the decision you make about building the initial Bitstream font library has an impact on your Quattro Pro work sessions. Quattro Pro can display and print only fonts that have been built.

If you select the Limited option, Quattro Pro installs only six Swiss fonts. The Limited option installs the smallest amount of fonts, making it extremely likely that you will need to build others.

If you choose the fourth option, however, Quattro Pro builds bitmap files for 150 fonts.

Building Bitstream Fonts during a Work Session

You cannot view or print a spreadsheet containing a font for which you have no bitmap file. Quattro Pro first must build a bitmap file for that font.

To have Quattro Pro create bitmap files for unbuilt fonts on an "as-needed" basis, choose /**O**ptions **G**raphics Quality **F**inal. Under this setting, Quattro Pro pauses program execution every time the program encounters a font without a bitmap file. Quattro Pro then builds the bitmap file—a process that can take from 15 to 45 seconds depending on your computer's speed. After a bitmap file is created for a font, Quattro Pro does not pause program execution the next time it encounters that font.

If you do not want Quattro Pro to pause every time the program encounters an un-built font (and this can happen often if you select the Limited option), choose /**O**ptions **G**raphics Quality **D**raft. In this condition, Quattro Pro substitutes unbuilt Bitstream fonts with lower quality Hershey fonts.

Building Bitstream Fonts with a Macro

Quattro Pro can create a maximum of 150 screen fonts during installation. To install the complete screen font library, you need to build a macro program. The macro can install one, several, or the entire font library onto your hard disk drive.

The typeface styles and their abbreviated macro names appear in table B.1. You need this information to add screen fonts to your library.

Table B.1
Quattro Pro's Screen Font Library

Typeface	Macro name
Swiss	SWS
Swiss, bold	SWSB
Swiss, Italic	SWI
Swiss, bold, Italic	SWBI
Dutch	DUT
Dutch, bold	DUTB
Dutch, Italic	DUTI
Dutch, bold, Italic	DTBI
Courier	COUR

Creating the Macro Program

Figure B.1 shows a split window view of a macro created to install the entire Swiss bold font library.

You can use the same macro to install any combination of Bitstream fonts. For example, if you initially installed the Limited font library (an assortment of six commonly used Bitstream Swiss fonts), you can use this macro to install the remaining Swiss fonts.

The first line of the macro program in cell C2 is the critical one. The command {/ Hardware;PreRender} tells Quattro Pro to initiate the font-building operation using abbreviated macro names defined by you.

The font table is stored in block C4..C33. This table tells Quattro Pro which fonts to build. The active cell in this figure is C33. Notice that the data in this cell is a label. This label is the abbreviated name of one of the fonts from the Swiss bold font library. The final cell in the macro is a {QUIT} command, indicating where Quattro Pro should terminate the macro's execution.

The abbreviated macro names also contain numbers, ranging from 7 to 36. These sequential file numbers identify each font in a particular library. These

Fig. B.1
A font-building
macro.

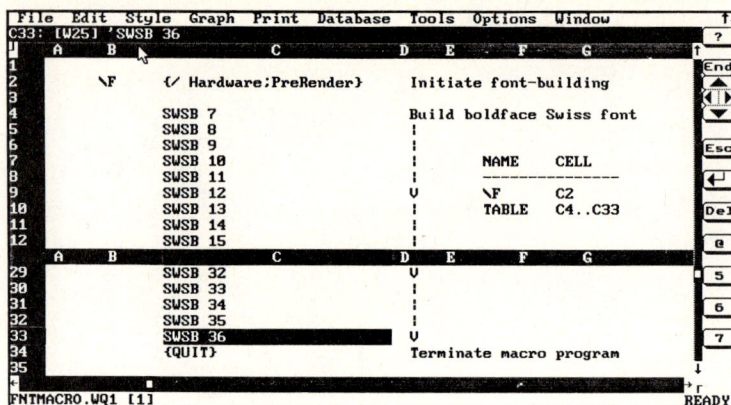

numbers, however, do not correspond to a font's point size. For example, SWSB 7 is not a 7-point file.

Each Quattro Pro screen font uses the same numbering system to categorize individual fonts in the library. For example, to install all of the Courier fonts, enter 30 labels, beginning with 'COUR 7 and ending with 'COUR 36.

The data appearing in block F7..G10 is a Names Table created by selecting the /**Edit N**ames **M**ake Table command. This macro has two names; an instant macro name (\F) and a name that describes the location of the table in which the abbreviated font names are stored (TABLE). You don't have to create names to operate this macro, but creating names enables you to easily understand what is going on.

Executing the Macro Program

To execute this macro and install the entire Swiss bold font library, do the following:

1. Press Alt-F, and Quattro Pro prompts you for the name of the font table (see fig. B.2).

2. Type *TABLE* and press Enter to install the fonts. Quattro Pro pauses to display a screen message prior to installing the fonts (see fig. B.3).

After Quattro Pro has read all of the data in the font table, the program displays a status message at the top of your screen. This message describes information about the current font-building operation (see fig. B.4).

When Quattro Pro finishes installing the fonts, the program returns you to the active spreadsheet.

```
 File  Edit  Style  Graph  Print  Database  Tools  Options  Window      ↑↓
[Enter] [Esc] Enter font table: TABLE                                    ?
   A      B            C              D    E      F      G              ▓End
 1                                                                       ▲
 2        \F      {/ Hardware;PreRender}      Initiate font-building     ◄┼►
 3                                                                       ▼
 4               SWSB 7                   Build boldface Swiss font
 5               SWSB 8                   ¦                              Esc
 6               SWSB 9                   ¦
 7               SWSB 10                  ¦       NAME     CELL           ↵
 8               SWSB 11                  ¦      ─────────────────
 9               SWSB 12                  ∪       \F       C2           Del
10               SWSB 13                  ¦      TABLE    C4..C33
11               SWSB 14                  ¦                              @
12               SWSB 15                  ¦
13               SWSB 16                  ¦                              5
14               SWSB 17                  ∪
15               SWSB 18                  ¦                              6
16               SWSB 19                  ¦
17               SWSB 20                  ¦                              7
18               SWSB 21                  ¦
19               SWSB 22                  ∪
20               SWSB 23                  ¦                              ↓
←▓                                                                    ►ᵣ
A1: [W2]                                                              EDIT
```

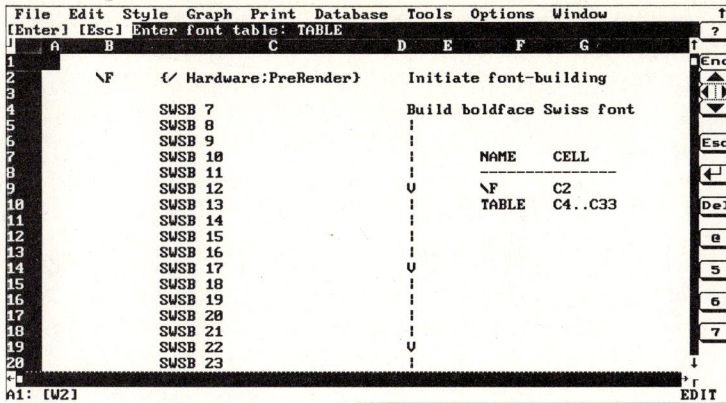

Fig. B.2
Quattro Pro prompts you for the location of the font table in which the abbreviated font names are stored.

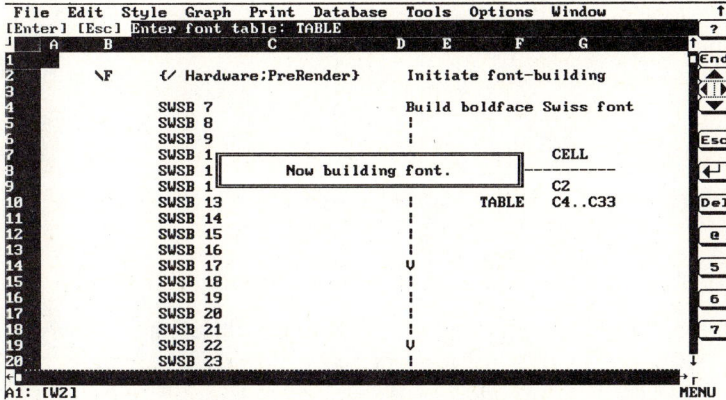

```
 File  Edit  Style  Graph  Print  Database  Tools  Options  Window      ↑↓
[Enter] [Esc] Enter font table: TABLE                                    ?
   A      B            C              D    E      F      G              ↑End
 1                                                                       ▲
 2        \F      {/ Hardware;PreRender}      Initiate font-building     ◄┼►
 3                                                                       ▼
 4               SWSB 7                   Build boldface Swiss font
 5               SWSB 8                   ¦
 6               SWSB 9                   ¦                              Esc
 7               SWSB 1                                      CELL
 8               SWSB 1  │   Now building font.   │          ──────      ↵
 9               SWSB 1                                      C2
10               SWSB 13                  ¦      TABLE    C4..C33        Del
11               SWSB 14                  ¦
12               SWSB 15                  ¦                              @
13               SWSB 16                  ¦
14               SWSB 17                  ∪                              5
15               SWSB 18                  ¦
16               SWSB 19                  ¦                              6
17               SWSB 20                  ¦
18               SWSB 21                  ¦                              7
19               SWSB 22                  ∪
20               SWSB 23                  ¦                              ↓
←▓                                                                    ►ᵣ
A1: [W2]                                                              MENU
```

Fig. B.3
Quattro Pro displays a message prior to installing the fonts on your hard disk drive.

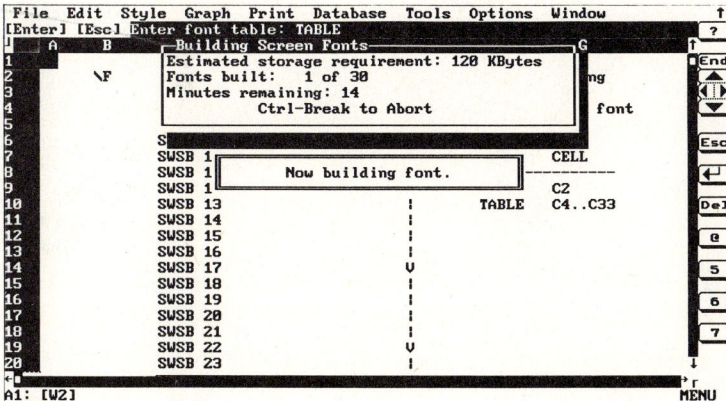

```
 File  Edit  Style  Graph  Print  Database  Tools  Options  Window      ↑↓
[Enter] [Esc] Enter font table: TABLE                                    ?
   A      B        ┌─Building Screen Fonts────────┐   G                ↑End
 1                 │ Estimated storage requirement: 120 KBytes │        ▲
 2        \F       │ Fonts built:    1 of 30       │        ng          ◄┼►
 3                 │ Minutes remaining: 14         │                    ▼
 4                 │      Ctrl-Break to Abort      │        font
 5                 └──────────────────────────────┘
 6        S                                                             Esc
 7        SWSB 1                                        CELL
 8        SWSB 1   │    Now building font.    │         ──────          ↵
 9        SWSB 1                                        C2
10        SWSB 13                  ¦      TABLE    C4..C33              Del
11        SWSB 14                  ¦
12        SWSB 15                  ¦                                    @
13        SWSB 16                  ¦
14        SWSB 17                  ∪                                    5
15        SWSB 18                  ¦
16        SWSB 19                  ¦                                    6
17        SWSB 20                  ¦
18        SWSB 21                  ¦                                    7
19        SWSB 22                  ∪
20        SWSB 23                  ¦                                    ↓
←▓                                                                    ►ᵣ
A1: [W2]                                                              MENU
```

Fig. B.4
The font-building status screen tells how much time and disk space is needed to install the fonts you specified.

To cancel a font-building operation, press Ctrl-Break. Quattro Pro finishes building a draft version of the font currently being installed and returns you to the active spreadsheet.

Installing the Entire Font Library

The most powerful application of this macro is using it to install the entire Bitstream font library. For example, if you initially installed the Limited font library and are tired of Quattro Pro pausing program execution to build fonts, use this macro to install all Bitstream fonts.

Before you try to install the entire screen font library, delete all of the existing fonts from your hard disk drive. Borland recommends that you follow this procedure to ensure congruence between the INDEX.FON file and the fonts that Quattro Pro builds. The INDEX.FON file is an organizer that tells Quattro Pro about the fonts that you have built. For example, if your fonts are stored in the FONTS subdirectory, do the following:

1. Press /FX to return to the DOS command prompt.

2. Type *CD\QPRO\FONTS* and press Enter to log onto your fonts directory.

3. Type *DEL *.FON* and press Enter to delete all existing font files.

4. Return to Quattro Pro and retrieve your font-building macro. Enter the abbreviated macro names for all of the fonts listed in table B.1. Be sure to specify all 30 sequential file numbers (from 7 to 36) for each font.

5. Press Alt-F to execute the font-building macro.

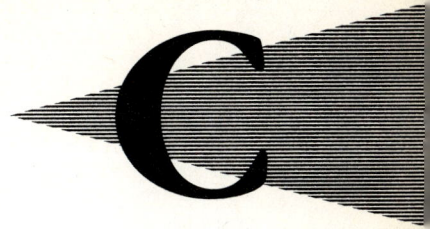

Macro Commands

Appendix C is a guide to Quattro Pro's macro commands. The discussion begins with general guidelines for using macro commands within macro programs. The second half of Appendix C is a glossary of Quattro Pro's macro commands. The glossary is organized alphabetically so that you can reference each command quickly and easily.

Using Macro Commands in a Macro Program

Quattro Pro offers an extensive set of commands that you use in macro programs to accomplish specific tasks and perform unique functions.

Macro commands enable you to access functions and accomplish tasks that generally cannot be accomplished by pressing keys. For example, the {BEEP} macro command causes your computer to emit a beep tone. The {GETLABEL} macro command prompts the macro user to type a label on the input line. Additionally, macro commands like {BRANCH} and {DISPATCH} help you to control the execution flow of a macro program—like with other programming languages.

Quattro Pro's macro commands may be used with menu-equivalent commands to create advanced macros. For example, the macro shown in figure C.1 uses the {GETNUMBER} and {GETLABEL} commands to prompt a user for an account name and three account values. Quattro Pro stores each response in a specific cell, creates an @function command that sums the three values, and then executes the menu-equivalent command that displays the numbers in currency format with no decimal places.

Fig. C.1
Use macro
commands with
menu-
equivalent and
keystroke
commands to
build advanced
macros.

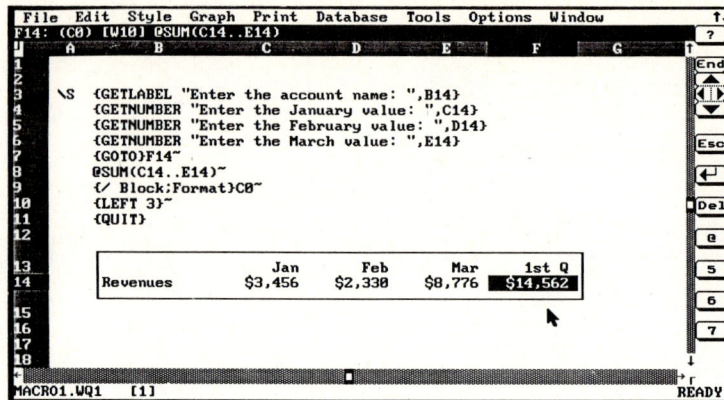

```
 File  Edit  Style  Graph  Print  Database  Tools  Options  Window      ↑↓
F14: (C0) [W10] @SUM(C14..E14)                                          ?
      A           B           C          D          E          F       G    ↑
1                                                                         End
2
3    \S  {GETLABEL "Enter the account name: ",B14}                        ▲
4        {GETNUMBER "Enter the January value: ",C14}                      ◄▮►
5        {GETNUMBER "Enter the February value: ",D14}                     ▼
6        {GETNUMBER "Enter the March value: ",E14}
7        {GOTO}F14~                                                       Esc
8        @SUM(C14..E14)~
9        {/ Block;Format}C0~                                              ⏎
10       {LEFT 3}~
11       {QUIT}                                                           Del
12
                                                                          @
13                        Jan       Feb       Mar      1st Q
14       Revenues      $3,456    $2,330    $8,776    $14,562              5
15                                                                        6
16                                              ▶
17                                                                        7
18
←                              ■                                      →
MACRO1.WQ1    [1]                                                    READY
```

As you build advanced macro programs notice that each command has its own distinctive syntax. The general syntax for Quattro Pro macro commands is as follows:

```
{MACRO_COMMAND_NAME Argument1,Argument2,Argument3...}
```

MACRO_COMMAND_NAME is the exact name of the command.

Argument$_n$, where n denotes the argument's order of appearance in the macro command, is additional data needed by the macro command. Typically, an argument specifies the data or cell address that the macro operates on.

The four types of arguments are as follows:

1. A valid Number argument can be an actual number (a number not enclosed in quotes), a formula that returns a number, or the address of a cell containing a number.

2. A valid String argument can be a text string, or the address of a cell that references another cell containing a text string.

3. A valid Location string can be a cell address that contains a reference to a cell or cell block. The reference can be a block name or the cell coordinates for a block containing one or more cells.

4. A valid Condition argument must be a logical expression: an expression that contains a cell reference, a number, a string, or a string-valued formula that Quattro Pro can evaluate as TRUE or FALSE.

When you use string values in a macro, you don't always need to enclose the string in quotes. If a string value contains a comma or a semicolon, however, you must enclose strings and block names in quotes.

A formula that appears as a label must be enclosed in quotes. Any string value identical to a block name also must be enclosed in quotes.

In macro programs, Quattro Pro does not update block references when you change the block coordinates. For example, if you move a cell or insert or delete a row or column, the macro no longer references the correct block.

You should create block names whenever possible. If you move a named block referenced in a macro program, Quattro Pro updates the cell addresses associated with the block, and the macro program continues to reference the correct block.

When you use macro commands in your macro programs, use the following rules to create the correct syntax:

1. Always begin and end a macro command with braces { }.

2. Place a space between the command name and the argument(s).

3. Separate multiple arguments with commas.

4. Always enter the type of argument specified by the macro command definition. If an argument requires a string, enter a string; if the argument requires a number, enter only a number.

5. Do not enter extra spaces or punctuation, except within quoted strings.

   For example, {GETLABEL "Enter the account name",A4} is allowed, but {GETLABEL 'Enter the account name; A4} is not.

6. Enter each expression into one cell.

7. Macro commands can appear in uppercase and lowercase letters.

8. When you enter more than one command per line, type each command before typing the next one.

Note that some macro commands—such as {QUIT}—do not require arguments.

Using Subroutines in a Macro Program

As you develop more advanced programming skills, you will find yourself recreating certain sequences of macro commands again and again in your applications. For example, you may develop your own techniques for controlling the input and output of data. All of your macro programs also may use the same print routine (for example, the same margin settings, setup strings, graphics quality, and so on). You also may have retyped a sequence of commands over and over again in the same macro program.

You can reduce the effort and time required to recreate these commands by designing mini-macros, or subroutines. A subroutine assumes responsibility for repetitive operations in a macro program. Then, by referencing the subroutine many times, you can execute the operation over and over without having to retype the commands.

When you reference a subroutine, you can instruct Quattro Pro to "pass along" arguments to the subroutine. These arguments are stored in cells referenced by the subroutine.

For example, the subroutine {DATA1 D5,D6} sends control of the macro to a subroutine named DATA1 and passes two arguments (D5 and D6) along. Using the {DEFINE} command, you instruct the subroutine to perform an operation on the passed arguments. The {DEFINE} command tells Quattro Pro where to store the arguments and whether they are values or labels.

Warning | Do not assign macro command names to your subroutines. Doing so invalidates the macro command for the active spreadsheet until you delete the name or assign a new name.

Using /x Commands

Quattro Pro also uses /x commands in macro programs. The /x commands are abbreviated versions for eight commonly used macro commands (see table C.2). The advantage of using /x commands is that you can enter them from your keyboard while recording a macro. You also can enter a /x commands from the Macro menu that Quattro Pro displays when you press Shift-F3.

When you use a /x command in a macro, place the argument directly after the command—just as with its macro command equivalent. For example, to pass control of a macro program to a subroutine named SUB5, enter the following:

   /xcSUB5~

Suppose that you write a macro that solicits a sales value from a user and then enters the value into cell E5 on the active spreadsheet. The /x command syntax might look like the following:

   /xnSales?~E5~

Table C.2
/X Commands

/x command	Macro command equivalent
/xc	{Subroutine}
/xl	{GETLABEL}
/xn	{GETNUMBER}
/xg	{BRANCH}
/xi	{IF}
/xm	{MENUBRANCH}
/xq	{QUIT}
/xr	{RETURN} and {RET}

When Quattro Pro reaches the line containing this syntax, the program displays Sales? as a prompt at the top of the screen. When you enter a value and press Enter, Quattro Pro copies the value into cell E5.

You must place a ~ (tilde) after each argument used in an /x command. The /xl and /xn commands do not require a location paramenter as do their macro command equivalents. When you do not specify a location argument, Quattro Pro uses the active cell.

Appendix D offers a menu tree list of Quattro Pro's menu-equivalent macro commands. For examples of how to use the macro commands defined in this appendix, see Chapter 12.

Macro Command Glossary

Quattro Pro macro commands fall into seven categories. In this appendix, each category name follows the command name, making it easy to cross-reference the commands. The seven macro categories are listed in table C.1.

Table C.1
Macro Command Categories

Command category	Command function
Keyboard	Reproduces the action of the keyboard keys
Screen	Affects the display of items on a screen

Table C.2—_continued_

Command category	_Command function_
Interactive	Pauses a macro's execution and prompts a user to enter data from the keyboard
Program Flow	Controls the flow of data in a macro program
Cell	Affects the contents of cells
File	Manipulates data stored in non-spreadsheet files
Miscellaneous	Performs miscellaneous actions on a macro program

{ }

Command category: Miscellaneous

The { } command inserts a blank line in a macro. This command does not affect the execution of a macro because Quattro Pro skips over the command and executes the next macro command in the program.

The { } command is useful for segregating blocks of commands in a macro program that perform different functions.

{;String}

Command category: Miscellaneous

The {;} macro command enters side remarks into a macro program without affecting the execution of the program. In this syntax, _String_ can be any combination of alphanumeric characters that does not exceed a length of 237.

The {;} command is useful for documenting a macro program. For example, {;SUm all sales values} can be placed above the first command in a group of commands that sum sales values.

{?}

Command category: Interactive

The {?} macro command pauses the execution of a macro program so that a user can enter data from the keyboard. Press Enter to continue the program execution.

{ABS}

Command category: Keyboard

The {ABS} macro command is equivalent to pressing F4, the Abs key.

{BACKSPACE} and {BS}

Command category: Keyboard

These macro commands are equivalent to pressing the Backspace key.

{BACKTAB}

Command category: Keyboard

The {BACKTAB} macro command is equivalent to pressing Ctrl← or Shift-Tab. This command functions like the {BIGLEFT} macro command.

{BEEP<Number>}

Command category: Screen

The {BEEP} macro command sounds a beeping tone from the computer's built-in speaker. The argument *Number* determines the frequency of the tone. If *Number* is omitted, Quattro Pro defaults to the low tone.

In this syntax, *Number* can be any number from 1 to 4, where:

    {BEEP1}   Sounds a low tone
    {BEEP2}   Sounds a standard tone
    {BEEP3}   Sounds a medium tone
    {BEEP4}   Sounds a high tone

The {BEEP} command can be used to call attention to a screen prompt, to indicate that the user did not enter the correct type of data, and to signify the end of a macro program.

{BIGLEFT}

Command category: Keyboard

The {BIGLEFT} macro command is equivalent to pressing Ctrl← or Shift-Tab. This command functions like the {BACKTAB} macro command.

{BIGRIGHT}

Command category: Keyboard

The {BIGRIGHT} macro command is equivalent to pressing Ctrl→ or Tab. This command functions like the {TAB} macro command.

{BLANK Location}

Command category: Cell

The {BLANK} macro command is equivalent to selecting /**Edit Erase Block**. Because this macro command does not access Quattro Pro's Edit menu directly, you can execute the command while another menu is on your screen.

In this syntax, *Location* designates a cell or block to erase.

{BRANCH Location}

Command category: Program flow

The {BRANCH} macro command exits the current macro and branches to another macro.

In this syntax, *Location* is the location or name of another macro.

For example, think of a macro named SALES that prompts a user to input 10 sales values. When all 10 values are entered, the user types Q to quit. The macro shown below tests the value entered into a cell named INPUT. If this value is not Q, the macro branches to a macro called SALES; if the value is Q, the macro branches to RATIOS.

```
{IF INPUT‹›/"Q"} {BRANCH SALES} {BRANCH RATIOS}
```

{BREAK}

Command category: Keyboard

The {BREAK} macro command is equivalent to pressing Ctrl-Break.

{BREAKOFF}

Command category: Interactive

The {BREAKOFF} macro command prevents a user from stopping the execution of a macro program by pressing Ctrl-Break.

{BREAKON}

Command category: Interactive

The {BREAKON} macro command cancels the {BREAKOFF} command, enabling a user to stop the execution of a macro program by pressing Ctrl-Break.

{CALC}

Command category: Keyboard

The {CALC} macro command is equivalent to pressing F9, the Calc key.

{CAPOFF} and {CAPON}

Command category: Keyboard

These macro commands are equivalent to pressing Caps Lock, which toggles between capital and lowercase letters.

{CHOOSE}

Command category: Keyboard

The {CHOOSE} macro command is equivalent to pressing Shift-F5, the Pick Window key.

{CLEAR}

Command category: Keyboard

The {CLEAR} macro command is equivalent to pressing Ctrl-Backspace. This command erases any preceding entry on a prompt line.

{CLOSE}

Command category: File

The {CLOSE} macro command saves and closes an open file. Quattro Pro enables only one file to be open at a time.

{CONTENTS Dest,Source, <Width>,<Format>}

Command category: Cell

The {CONTENTS} macro command copies data from one cell into another. Optional arguments enable the user to choose a column width and format for the copied data.

In this syntax, *Dest* is a cell that you want to write data to, and *Source* is a cell containing the data to be copied. The *Width* and *Format* arguments, which specify a column width and format code, are optional. Valid *Width* arguments range from 1 to 72. Valid *Format* arguments appear below in table C.3.

Table C.3	
Valid Format Arguments	
Argument	*Format description*
0-15	Fixed, displaying from 0 to 15 decimals
16-31	Scientific, displaying from 0 to 15 decimals

Argument	Format description
32-47	Currency, displaying from 0 to 15 decimals
48-63	Percent (%), displaying from 0 to 15 decimals
64-79	Comma (,), displaying from 0 to 15 decimals
112	+/− bar graph
113	General
114	Date format 1
115	Date format 2
116	Date format 3
117	Text
118	Hidden
119	Time format 1
120	Time format 2
121	Date format 4
122	Date format 5
123	Time format 3
124	Time format 4
127	Default (specified by selecting /**Options Formats Numeric Format**)

{COPY}

Command category: Keyboard

The {COPY} macro command is equivalent to pressing Shift-F9, the Copy key.

{CR} and ~ (tilde)

Command category: Keyboard

These macro commands are equivalent to pressing Enter.

{DEFINE Location1:Type1, Location2:Type2,...}

Command category: Program Flow

The {DEFINE} macro command passes sequentially ordered arguments for use in a subroutine.

In this syntax, *Location* is the cell in which you want to store a passed argument. The optional argument *Type* defines the type of argument being passed to *Location*.

Type can be string or value, as shown in the following macro:

```
{DEFINE K1:string,K2:value}
```

{DATE}

Command category: Keyboard

The {DATE} macro command is equivalent to pressing Ctrl-D, the Date-entry key.

{DEL}, {DELEOL}, and {DELETE}

Command category: Keyboard

The {DEL} and {DELETE} macro commands are equivalent to pressing Del, the Delete key. The {DELEOL} macro command is equivalent to pressing Ctrl-\, which deletes every character from the cursor to the end of a line.

{DISPATCH Location}

Command category: Program Flow

The {DISPATCH} macro command continues the execution of a macro at a different location in the program.

In this syntax, *Location* defines a cell containing a block name or address of another macro.

Like the {BRANCH} command, {DISPATCH} branches to other locations in the same macro program. The main difference between the two is that the

Location argument in {DISPATCH} can specify a cell containing the address or name of a macro to branch to. If the macro program can place different addresses or names in Location depending upon a set of conditions specified in the macro, {DISPATCH} re-routes the macro execution.

{DOWN} and {D}

Command category: Keyboard

These macro commands are equivalent to pressing ↓, the down-arrow key.

{EDIT}

Command category: Keyboard

The {EDIT} macro command is equivalent to pressing F2, the Edit key.

{END}

Command category: Keyboard

The {END} macro command is equivalent to pressing End on the numeric keypad.

{ESC} and {ESCAPE}

Command category: Keyboard

These macro commands are equivalent to pressing Esc on the keyboard.

{FILESIZE Location}

Command category: File

The {FILESIZE} macro command calculates the size of an open file and copies the result (in bytes) to *Location*.

In this syntax, *Location* indicates a cell address or block name.

{FOR CounterLoc,Start#,Stop#, Step#,StartLoc}

Command category: Program Flow

The {FOR} macro command repeatedly executes a macro subroutine, creating a macro loop.

In this syntax, *CounterLoc* is a cell that keeps track of the number of macro iterations, and *Start#* is the first value placed in cell *CounterLoc*. The *Stop#* argument indicates the maximum value that can appear in cell *CounterLoc*. The value of *Step#* is added to the value in cell *CounterLoc* after each iteration. The *StartLoc* argument indicates a cell containing the subroutine to be executed.

{FORBREAK}

Command category: Program Flow

The {FORBREAK} macro command cancels the execution of a subroutine and stops the processing of the {FOR} macro command.

{FUNCTIONS}

Command category: Keyboard

The {FUNCTIONS} macro command is equivalent to pressing Alt-F3, the Functions key.

{GET Location}

Command category: Interactive

The {GET} macro command pauses the execution of a macro, accepts a keystroke from the user, and stores that keystroke in the form of a left-aligned label in cell *Location*.

In this syntax, *Location* is a cell in which Quattro Pro stores all keystrokes entered by the user.

{GETLABEL Prompt,Location}

Command category: Interactive

The {GETLABEL} macro command pauses the execution of a macro, displays *Prompt*, and accepts a keystroke entered by the user. Press Enter to resume macro execution.

In this syntax, *Prompt* is a string that displays as a prompt, and *Location* is a cell in which Quattro Pro stores the user's response to *Prompt*.

{GETNUMBER Prompt,Location}

Command category: Interactive

The {GETNUMBER} macro command pauses the execution of a macro, displays *Prompt*, and accepts a number entered by the user. Press Enter to resume macro execution. The {GETNUMBER} command accepts only numbers as valid entries.

In this syntax, *Prompt* is a string that displays as a prompt, and *Location* is a cell in which Quattro Pro stores the user's response to *Prompt*.

{GETPOS Location}

Command category: Interactive

The {GETPOS} macro command evaluates an open file and enters the value-equivalent position of the file pointer into *Location*.

In this syntax, *Location* is a cell in which Quattro Pro stores a retrieved value.

{GOTO}

Command category: Keyboard

The {GOTO} macro command is equivalent to pressing F5, the GoTo key.

{GRAPH}

Command category: Keyboard

The {GRAPH} macro command is equivalent to pressing F10, the Graph key.

{GRAPHCHAR Location}

Command category: Interactive

The {GRAPHCHAR} macro command stores in *Location* the character pressed to exit a displayed graph or to remove a message box.

The stored character can be used to branch to other parts of the macro. For example, when an input prompt asks you to type *Y* for yes or *N* for no, {GRAPHCHAR} can store and use the response to branch to other parts of the macro.

In this syntax, *Location* is a cell address or block name in which Quattro Pro stores a returned character.

{HOME}

Command category: Kcyboard

The {HOME} macro command is equivalent to pressing Home.

{IF Condition}

Command category: Program Flow

The {IF} macro command is an "@IF function" for macros. {IF} evaluates *Condition* and returns the value TRUE or FALSE.

When Quattro Pro returns the value TRUE, the macro continues to execute in the same row; when the program returns False, the macro skips to the next row and continues to execute in the first cell.

In this syntax, *Condition* is a logical expression or a cell address containing a label, a value, or another logical expression.

{IFKEY String}

Command category: Interactive

The {IFKEY} macro command returns TRUE when the macro name of a valid key is encountered.

In this syntax, *String* is a valid macro name for a key, such as HOME or PgUp and is not surrounded by braces. *String* also can be a string that returns a key macro name without braces.

{INDICATE String}

Command category: Screen

The {INDICATE} macro command displays *String* as a mode indicator on the status line at the bottom of a spreadsheet.

In this syntax, *String* is a character string.

{INS},{INSERT},{INSOFF}, and {INSON}

Command category: Keyboard

The macro commands {INS} and {INSERT} are equivalent to pressing Ins to turn INSERT mode on and off. The {INSOFF} macro turns the INSERT mode off, and {INSON} turns INSERT mode on.

{LEFT} and {L}

Command category: Keyboard

These macro commands are equivalent to pressing ←, the left- arrow key.

{LET Location,Value:Type}

Command category: Cell

The {LET} macro command enters a value into a cell while a macro is running, without first moving the cell selector to that cell.

In this syntax, Quattro Pro stores *Value* in *Location*. Use the *Type* argument to specify whether *Value* should be stored as a string or as a value.

{LOOK Location}

Command category: Interactive

The {LOOK} macro command ensures that any keystrokes stored in Quattro Pro's typeahead buffer are executed after the current macro program execution stops.

A *typeahead buffer* is an internal storage facility where Quattro Pro records the keys you press after a macro begins executing.

In this syntax, Quattro Pro stores a typed character in cell *Location*.

{MACROS}

Command category: Keyboard

The {MACROS} macro command is equivalent to pressing Shift-F3, the Macros key.

{MARK}

Command category: Keyboard

The {MARK} macro command is equivalent to pressing Shift-F7, the Select key.

{MARKALL}

Command category: Keyboard

The {MARKALL} macro command is equivalent to pressing Alt-F7, the Select All key.

{MENU}

Command category: Keyboard

The {MENU} macro command is equivalent to pressing the slash key (/).

{MENUBRANCH Location}

Command category: Interactive

The {MENUBRANCH} macro command displays a custom menu. When the user selects a choice from the custom menu, Quattro Pro continues executing the macro directly below the description of that choice in the macro program.

In this syntax, *Location* is a cell containing the definition for a custom Quattro Pro menu.

{MENUCALL Location}

Command category: Interactive

The {MENUCALL} macro command displays a custom menu. When the user selects a choice from the custom menu, Quattro Pro continues executing the macro directly below the cell containing the {MENUCALL} macro command.

In this syntax, *Location* is a cell containing the definition for a custom Quattro Pro menu.

{MESSAGE Block,Left,Top,Time}

Command category: Interactive

The {MESSAGE} macro command displays a message box during the execution of a macro program.

In this syntax, *Block* is a block name or cell address containing message text. The *Left* and *Top* arguments indicate the screen column number and line number, respectively, where the top left corner of the message box should display. The *Time* argument is an @ function expression that tells Quattro Pro how long to display the message. Enter *0* as the *Time* argument to keep the message box on-screen until the user presses a key.

{MOVE}

Command category: Keyboard

The {MOVE} macro command is equivalent to pressing Shift-F8, the Move key.

{NAME}

Command category: Keyboard

The {NAME} macro command is equivalent to pressing F3, the Choices key.

{NEXTWIN}

Command category: Keyboard

The {NEXTWIN} macro command is equivalent to pressing Shift-F6, the Next Window key.

{NUMOFF} and {NUMON}

Command category: Keyboard

These macro commands are equivalent to pressing Num Lock to toggle between numbers and other key functions on the numeric keypad.

{ONERROR BranchLocation, <MessageLocation>, <ErrorLocation>}

Command category: Program Flow

The {ONERROR} macro command prevents Quattro Pro from stopping a macro program when encountering an error. Use this command to trap errors that occur when the user enters commands from the keyboard.

In this syntax, *BranchLocation* is the first cell of the macro that Quattro Pro should execute when an error is encountered. *MessageLocation* tells Quattro Pro the cell in which the error message is stored, and *ErrorLocation* identifies the address of the cell containing the error.

{OPEN Filename,AccessMode}

Command category: File

The {OPEN} macro command opens a file so that Quattro Pro can use other file-access macro commands with the file.

In this syntax, *Filename* is the name of an open file. You can use four valid *AccessMode* arguments: R (read-only), M (modify), W (write), and A (append).

{PANELOFF}

Command category: Screen

The {PANELOFF} macro command disables the normal display of menus and prompts during the execution of a macro. Use this macro command to speed up the execution of macro programs that rely on keystrokes to select commands from Quattro Pro's menus.

{PANELON}

Command category: Screen

The {PANELON} macro command enables Quattro Pro to display all of the menus and prompts that previously were disabled with the {PANELOFF} command.

{PASTE}

Command category: Keyboard

The {PASTE} macro command is equivalent to pressing Shift-F10, the Paste key.

{PGDN} and {PGUP}

Command category: Keyboard

These macro commands are equivalent to pressing PgDn and PgUp on the keyboard.

{PUT Location,Column#,Row#, Value:Type}

Command category: Cell

The {PUT} macro command copies a value into a cell. The copied value is offset a user-specified number of columns and rows.

In this syntax, Quattro Pro stores *Value* in the block specified by *Location*. The optional *Type* argument specifies whether Value should be stored as a string or as a label. The *Column#* and *Row#* arguments indicate how many columns and rows into the specified block Quattro Pro should offset before storing *Value*.

This command is similar to the {LET} macro command.

{QUERY}

Command category: Keyboard

The {QUERY} macro command is equivalent to pressing F7, the Query key.

{QUIT}

Command category: Program Flow

The {QUIT} macro command stops the execution of a macro and returns Quattro Pro to READY mode.

{READ #Bytes,Location}

Command category: File

The {READ} macro command reads a certain number of bytes worth of characters from an open file and stores these characters in a cell on the spreadsheet.

In this syntax, *#Bytes* is the number of bytes of characters to read, and *Location* is the cell in which Quattro Pro stores the characters.

{READDIR}

Command category: Keyboard

The {READDIR} macro command is equivalent to pressing F9 when Quattro Pro's File Manager is open.

{READLN Location}

Command category: File

The {READLN} macro command is similar to the {READ} command. The only difference is that {READLN} automatically reads forward from the current file pointer location, up to and including the carriage-return (or linefeed) command at the end of the line.

A *file pointer* is a number that defines the location in a file where new data is written.

In this syntax, *Location* is the cell in which Quattro Pro stores the characters.

{RECALC Location,<Condition>, <Iteration#>}

Command category: Cell

The {RECALC} macro command forces Quattro Pro to recalculate a specific part of the active spreadsheet in row-by-row order.

In this syntax, *Location* indicates the cell block to recalculate. The optional argument *Condition* must be met before Quattro Pro halts the recalculation. The optional argument *Iteration#* sets the maximum number of recalculations that Quattro Pro should execute.

{RECALCCOL Location,<Condition>, <Iteration#>}

Command category: Cell

The {RECALCCOL} macro command forces Quattro Pro to recalculate a specific part of the active spreadsheet in column-by-column order.

In this syntax, *Location* indicates the cell block to recalculate. The optional argument *Condition* must be met before Quattro Pro halts the recalculation. The optional argument *Iteration#* sets the maximum number of recalculations that Quattro Pro should execute.

{RESTART}

Command category: Program Flow

The {RESTART} macro command changes the current subroutine to the starting routine. Quattro Pro accomplishes this change by removing all preceding FOR loops and subroutine calls.

{RETURN}

Command category: Program Flow

The {RETURN} macro command halts execution of the current subroutine and passes control back to the original macro.

{RIGHT} or {R}

Command category: Keyboard

These macro commands are equivalent to pressing →, the right- arrow key.

{SCROLLOFF} and {SCROLLON}

Command category: Keyboard

These macro commands are equivalent to pressing Scroll Lock to toggle between locking the scrolling feature on and off.

{SETPOS FilePosition}

Command category: File

The {SETPOS} macro command moves the file pointer for an open file to the value *FilePosition*.

In this syntax, *FilePosition* indicates the number of bytes that Quattro Pro should set the file pointer to.

{STEP}

Command category: Keyboard

The {STEP} macro command is equivalent to pressing Shift-F2, the Debug key.

{STEPOFF}

Command category: Interactive

The {STEPOFF} macro command exits Quattro Pro's Debug mode, returning macro execution to normal operation.

{STEPON}

The {STEPON} macro command enters Quattro Pro's Debug mode, causing the macro to execute one step at a time.

{SUBROUTINE Subroutine, ArgumentList}

Command category: Program Flow

The {SUBROUTINE} macro command passes arguments to a called subroutine.

In this syntax, *Subroutine* is the name of the subroutine being called, and *ArgumentList* is a list containing one or more arguments to be passed to the subroutine.

{TAB}

Command category: Keyboard

The {TAB} macro command is equivalent to pressing Ctrl→ or Tab.

{TABLE}

Command category: Keyboard

The {TABLE} macro command is equivalent to pressing F8, the Table key.

{UNDO}

Command category: Keyboard

The {UNDO} macro command is equivalent to pressing Alt-F5, the Undo key.

{UP} and {U}

Command category: Keyboard

These macro commands are equivalent to pressing ↑, the up-arrow key.

{WAIT DateTimeNumber}

Command category: Interactive

The {WAIT} macro command pauses the execution of a macro until a user-specified time.

In this syntax, *DateTimeNumber* indicates the date and time when Quattro Pro resumes macro execution.

{WINDOW}

Command category: Keyboard

The {WINDOW} macro command is equivalent to pressing F6, the Pane key.

{WINDOWSOFF}

Command category: Screen

The {WINDOWSOFF} macro command prevents Quattro Pro from displaying any screen changes that normally would occur during the execution of a macro program.

{WINDOWSON}

Command category: Screen

The {WINDOWSON} macro command cancels a {WINDOWSOFF} command, enabling Quattro Pro to display any screen changes that normally would occur during the execution of a macro program.

{WRITE String}

Command category: File

The {WRITE} macro command copies a string of characters into an open file, beginning at the location of the file pointer. (A *file pointer* is a number that defines the location in a file where new data is written.)

In this syntax, *String* is a string of characters that Quattro Pro writes into the open file.

{WRITELN String}

Command category: File

The {WRITELN} macro command copies a string of characters into an open file, starting at the location of the file pointer. The command adds a carriage return and linefeed command to the end of the written string.

In this syntax, *String* is a string of characters that Quattro Pro writes as a line into the open file.

{ZOOM}

Command category: Keyboard

The {ZOOM} macro command is equivalent to pressing Alt-F6, the Zoom Window key.

D

Menu-Equivalent Commands

Appendix D is a comprehensive reference source of Quattro Pro's menu-equivalent commands.

Quattro Pro uses menu-equivalent commands in macro programs to represent keystroke actions. When you record a logical macro (instead of a keystroke macro), Quattro Pro converts each of your keystrokes into a menu-equivalent command.

See Appendix C for a comprehensive glossary of Quattro Pro's macro commands. See Chapter 12 for more information about creating macro programs.

To understand how Quattro Pro uses menu-equivalent commands in a macro program, suppose that you want to create a macro that opens a file called SALES.WQ1, moves the cell selector down five rows, inserts a line, and then saves the edited file. To create this program using Quattro Pro's recorder, perform the following steps:

1. Select /**Tools Macro Recording Logical** so that Quattro Pro stores your keystrokes as macro-equivalent commands.

2. Select /**Tools Macro Record** to turn on the recorder.

3. Select /**File Retrieve**, type *SALES*, and press Enter.

4. Press the ↓ key five times.

5. Select /**Edit Insert Rows** and press Enter.

6. Select /**File Save Replace**.

Quattro Pro converts these keystrokes into the following macro program:

{/ File;Retrieve}	(menu-equivalent command)
{CLEAR}	(keyboard command)
C:\QPRO\SALES.WQ1~	
{DOWN 5}	
{/ Row;Insert}~	(menu-equivalent command)
{/ File;SaveNow}r	(menu-equivalent command)

Use menu-equivalent commands in your macro programs to instruct Quattro Pro to perform operations such as saving a file, erasing a block, switching display modes, and so on.

The following tables show each Quattro Pro menu and menu-equivalent commands.

Table D.1
File Menu Commands

Command	Menu-equivalent command
New	{/ View;NewWindow}
Open	{/ View;OpenWindow}
Retrieve	{/ File;Retrieve}
Save	{/ File;SaveNow}
Save As	{/ File;Save}
Close	{/ Basics;Close}
Close All	{/ System;TidyUp}
Erase	{/ Basics;Erase}
Directory	{/ File;Directory}
Workspace	
Save	{/ System;SaveWorkspace}
Restore	{/ System;RestoreWorkspace}
Utilities	
DOS Shell	{/ Basics;OS}
File Manager	{/ View;NewFileMgr}
SQZ!	
Remove Blanks	{/ SQZ;Blanks}
Storage of Values	{/ SQZ;Values}
Version	{/ SQZ;Version}
Exit	{/ System;Exit}

Table D.2
Edit Menu Commands

Command	Menu-equivalent command
Copy	{/ Block;Copy}
Move	{/ Block;Move}
Erase Block	{/ Block;Erase}
Undo	{/ Basics;Undo}
Insert	
Rows	{/ Row;Insert}
Columns	{/ Column;Insert}
Delete	
Rows	{/ Row;Delete}
Columns	{/ Column;Delete}
Names	
Create	{/ Name;Create}
Delete	{/ Name;Delete}
Labels	
Right	{/ Name;RightCreate}
Down	{/ Name;UnderCreate}
Left	{/ Name;LeftCreate}
Up	{/ Name;AboveCreate}
Reset	{/ Name;Reset}
Make Table	{/ Name;Table}
Fill	{/ Math;Fill}
Values	{/ Block;Values}
Transpose	{/ Block;Transpose}
Search & Replace	
Block	{/ Audit;ReplaceRange}
Search String	{/ Audit;SearchString}
Replace String	{/ Audit;ReplaceString}
Options	
Look-In	{/ Audit;SearchLookIn}
Formula	{/ Audit;SearchFormula}
Value	{/ Audit;SearchValue}
Condition	{/ Audit;SearchCondition}
Direction	{/ Audit;SearchDirection}

Table D.2—*continued*

Command	Menu-equivalent command
Row	{/ Audit;SearchByRow}
Column	{/ Audit;SearchByCol}
Match	{/ Audit;SearchMatch}
Part	{/ Audit;SearchForPart}
Whole	{/ Audit;SearchForWhole}
Case Sensitive	{/ Audit;SearchCase}
Any Case	{/ Audit;SearchAnyCase}
Exact Case	{/ Audit;SearchExactCase}
Options Reset	{/ Audit;SearchReset}
Next	{/ Audit;Replace}
Previous	{/ Audit;SearchPrev}

Table D.3
Style Menu Commands

Command	Menu-equivalent command
Alignment	
General	{/ Publish;AlignDefault}
Left	{/ Publish;AlignLeft}
Right	{/ Publish;AlignRight}
Center	{/ Publish;AlignCenter}
Numeric Format	{/ Block;Format}
Protection	
Protect	{/ Block;Protect}
Unprotect	{/ Block;Unprotect}
Column Width	{/ Column;Width}
Reset Width	{/ Column;Reset}
Hide Column	
Hide	{/ Column;Hide}
Expose	{/ Column;Display}
Block Widths	
Set Width	{/ Block;SetWidth}
Reset Width	{/ Block;ResetWidth}
Auto Width	{/ Block;AdjustWidth}
Line Drawing	{/ Publish;LineDrawing}

Command	Menu-equivalent command
Shading	
None	{/ Publish;ShadingNone}
Grey	{/ Publish;ShadingGrey}
Black	{/ Publish;ShadingBlack}
Font	{/ Publish;Font}
Insert Break	{/ Print;CreatePageBreak}

Table D.4
Graph Menu Commands

Command	Menu-equivalent command
Graph Type	{/ Graph;Type}
Series	
1st Series	{/ 1Series;Block}
2nd Series	{/ 2Series;Block}
3rd Series	{/ 3Series;Block}
4th Series	{/ 4Series;Block}
5th Series	{/ 5Series;Block}
6th Series	{/ 6Series;Block}
X-Axis Series	{/ XAxis;Labels}
Group	
Columns	{/ Graph;ColumnSeries}
Rows	{/ Graph;RowSeries}
Text	
1st Line	{/ Graph;MainTitle}
2nd Line	{/ Graph;SubTitle}
X-Title	{/ XAxis;Title}
Y-Title	{/ YAxis;Title}
Secondary Y-Axis	{/ Y2Axis;Title}
Legends	
1st Series	{/ 1Series;Legend}
2nd Series	{/ 2Series;Legend}
3rd Series	{/ 3Series;Legend}
4th Series	{/ 4Series;Legend}
5th Series	{/ 5Series;Legend}
6th Series	{/ 6Series;Legend}
Position	{/ Graph;LegendPos}
Font	{/ GraphPrint;Fonts}

Table D.4—*continued*

Command	Menu-equivalent command
Customize Series	
Colors	
1st Series	{/ 1Series;Color}
2nd Series	{/ 2Series;Color}
3rd Series	{/ 3Series;Color}
4th Series	{/ 4Series;Color}
5th Series	{/ 5Series;Color}
6th Series	{/ 6Series;Color}
Fill Patterns	
1st Series	{/ 1Series;Pattern}
2nd Series	{/ 2Series;Pattern}
3rd Series	{/ 3Series;Pattern}
4th Series	{/ 4Series;Pattern}
5th Series	{/ 5Series;Pattern}
6th Series	{/ 6Series;Pattern}
Markers & Lines	
Line Styles	
1st Series	{/ 1Series;LineStyle}
2nd Series	{/ 2Series;LineStyle}
3rd Series	{/ 3Series;LineStyle}
4th Series	{/ 4Series;LineStyle}
5th Series	{/ 5Scries;LineStyle}
6th Series	{/ 6Series;LineStyle}
Markers	
1st Series	{/ 1Series;Markers}
2nd Series	{/ 2Series;Markers}
3rd Series	{/ 3Series;Markers}
4th Series	{/ 4Series;Markers}
5th Series	{/ 5Series;Markers}
6th Series	{/ 6Series;Markers}
Formats	
1st Series	{/ CompGraph;AFormat}
2nd Series	{/ CompGraph;BFormat}
3rd Series	{/ CompGraph;CFormat}
4th Series	{/ CompGraph;DFormat}
5th Series	{/ CompGraph;EFormat}
6th Series	{/ CompGraph;FFormat}
Graph	{/ CompGraph;GraphFormat}
Bar Width	{/ Graph;BarWidth}

Command	Menu-equivalent command
Interior Labels	
1st Series	{/ CompGraph;ALabels}
2nd Series	{/ CompGraph;BLabels}
3rd Series	{/ CompGraph;CLabels}
4th Series	{/ CompGraph;DLabels}
5th Series	{/ CompGraph;ELables}
6th Series	{/ CompGraph;FLabels}
Override Type	
1st Series	{/ 1Series;Type}
2nd Series	{/ 2Series;Type}
3rd Series	{/ 3Series;Type}
4th Series	{/ 4Series;Type}
5th Series	{/ 5Series;Type}
6th Series	{/ 6Series;Type}
Y-Axis	
1st Series	{/ 1Series;YAxis}
2nd Series	{/ 2Series;YAxis}
3rd Series	{/ 3Series;YAxis}
4th Series	{/ 4Series;YAxis}
5th Series	{/ 5Series;YAxis}
6th Series	{/ 6Series;YAxis}
Pies	
Label Format	{/ Pie;ValueFormat}
Explode	
1st Slice	{/ PieExploded;1}
2nd Slice	{/ PieExploded;2}
3rd Slice	{/ PieExploded;3}
4th Slice	{/ PieExploded;4}
5th Slice	{/ PieExploded;5}
6th Slice	{/ PieExploded;6}
7th Slice	{/ PieExploded;7}
8th Slice	{/ PieExploded;8}
9th Slice	{/ PieExploded;9}
Patterns	
1st Slice	{/ PiePattern;1}
2nd Slice	{/ PiePattern;2}
3rd Slice	{/ PiePattern;3}
4th Slice	{/ PiePattern;4}
5th Slice	{/ PiePattern;5}
6th Slice	{/ PiePattern;6}
7th Slice	{/ PiePattern;7}

Table D.4—*continued*

Command	Menu-equivalent command
8th Slice	{/ PiePattern;8}
9th Slice	{/ PiePattern;9}
Colors	
1st Slice	{/ PieColor;1}
2nd Slice	{/ PieColor;2}
3rd Slice	{/ PieColor;3}
4th Slice	{/ PieColor;4}
5th Slice	{/ PieColor;5}
6th Slice	{/ PieColor;6}
7th Slice	{/ PieColor;7}
8th Slice	{/ PieColor;8}
9th Slice	{/ PieColor;9}
Tick Marks	{/ Pie;TickMarks}
Update	{/ Graph;UpdateGraph}
Reset	
1st Series	{/ Graph;Reset1}
2nd Series	{/ Graph;Reset2}
3rd Series	{/ Graph;Reset3}
4th Series	{/ Graph;Reset4}
5th Series	{/ Graph;Reset5}
6th Series	{/ Graph;Reset6}
Graph	{/ Graph;ResetAll}
X-Axis	
Scale	{/ XAxis;ScaleMode}
Low	{/ XAxis;Min}
High	{/ XAxis;Max}
Increment	{/ XAxis;Step}
Format of Ticks	{/ XAxis;Format}
No. of Minor Ticks	{/ XAxis;Skip}
Alternate Ticks	{/ XAxis;Alternate}
Display Scaling	{/ XAxis;ShowScale}
Mode	{/ XAxis;ScaleType}
Y-Axis	
Scale	{/ YAxis;ScaleMode}
Low	{/ YAxis;Min}
High	{/ YAxis;Max}
Increment	{/ YAxis;Step}
Format of Ticks	{/ YAxis;Format}
No. of Minor Ticks	{/ YAxis;Skip}
Display Scaling	{/ YAxis;ShowScale}

Command	Menu-equivalent command
Mode	{/ YAxis;ScaleType}
2nd Y-Axis	
Scale	{/ Y2Axis;ScaleMode}
Low	{/ Y2Axis;Min}
High	{/ Y2Axis;Max}
Increment	{/ Y2Axis;Step}
Format of Ticks	{/ Y2Axis;Format}
No. of Minor Ticks	{/ Y2Axis;Skip}
Display Scaling	{/ Y2Axis;ShowScale}
Mode	{/ Y2Axis;ScaleType}
Overall	
Grid	{/ Graph;GridStatus}
Horizontal	{/ CompGraph;GridHoriz}
Vertical	{/ CompGraph;GridVert}
Both	{/ CompGraph;GridBoth}
Clear	{/ CompGraph;GridClear}
Grid Color	{/ Graph;GridColor}
Line Style	{/ Graph;GridLines}
Fill Color	{/ Graph;GridFill}
Outlines	
Titles	{/ Graph;TitleOtl}
Legend	{/ Graph;LegendOtl}
Graph	{/ Graph;GraphOtl}
Background Color	{/ Graph;BackColor}
Three-D	{/ Graph;3D}
Color/B&W	
Color	{/ Graph;Color}
B&W	{/ Graph;BW}
Insert	{/ Graph;NameInsert}
Hide	{/ Graph;NameHide}
Name	
Display	{/ Graph;NameUse}
Create	{/ Graph;NameCreate}
Erase	{/ Graph;NameDelete}
Reset	{/ Graph;NameReset}
Slide	{/ Graph;NameSlide}
View	{/ Graph;View}
Fast Graph	{/ Graph;FastGraph}
Annotate	{/ Graph;Annotate}

Table D.5
Print Menu Commands

Command	*Menu-equivalent command*
Block	{/ Print;Block}
Headings	
Left Heading	{/ Print;LeftBorder}
Top Heading	{/ Print;TopBorder}
Destination	{/ Print;Destination}
Draft-Mode Printing	
Printer	{/ Print;OutputPrinter}
File	{/ Print;OutputFile}
Final-Quality Printing	
Binary File	{/ Print;OutputHQFile}
Graphics Printer	{/ Print;OutputHQ}
Screen Preview	{/ Print;OutputPreview}
Layout	
Header	{/ Print;Header}
Footer	{/ Print;Footer}
Break Pages	{/ Print;Breaks}
Margins	
Page Length	{/ Print;PageLength}
Left	{/ Print;LeftMargin}
Top	{/ Print;TopMargin}
Right	{/ Print;RightMargin}
Bottom	{/ Print;BottomMargin}
Dimensions	{/ Print;Dimensions}
Orientation	{/ Print;Rotated}
Setup String	{/ Print;Setup}
Reset	
All	{/ Print;ResetAll}
Print Block	{/ Print;ResetBlock}
Headings	{/ Print;ResetBorders}
Layout	{/ Print;ResetDefaults}
Update	{/ Print;Update}
Format	{/ Print;Format}
Adjust Printer	
Skip Line	{/ Print;SkipLine}
Form Feed	{/ Print;FormFeed}
Align	{/ Print;Align}

Command	Menu-equivalent command
Spreadsheet Print	{/ Print;Go}
Graph Print	{/ GraphPrint;Destination}
Destination	
File	{/ GraphPrint;DestIsFile}
Graphics Printer	{/ GraphPrint;DestIsPtr}
Screen Preview	{/ GraphPrint;DestIsPreview}
Layout	
Left Edge	{/ GraphPrint;Left}
Top Edge	{/ GraphPrint;Top}
Height	{/ GraphPrint;Height}
Width	{/ GraphPrint;Width}
Break Pages	{/ GraphPrint;FFMode}
Dimensions	{/ GraphPrint;Dimensions}
Orientation	{/ GraphPrint;Rotated}
4:3 Aspect	{/ Hardware;Aspect43}
Reset	{/ Print;ResetAll}
Update	{/ Print;Update}
Go	{/ GraphPrint;Print}
Write Graph File	
EPS File	{/ GraphFile;PostScript}
PIC File	{/ GraphFile;PIC}
Name	{/ GraphPrint;Use}

Table D.6
Database Menu Commands

Command	Menu-equivalent command
Sort	
Block	{/ Sort;Block}
1st Key	{/ Sort;Key1}
2nd Key	{/ Sort;Key2}
3rd Key	{/ Sort;Key3}
4th Key	{/ Sort;Key4}
5th Key	{/ Sort;Key5}
Go	{/ Sort;Go}
Reset	{/ Sort;Reset}
Sort Rules	
Numbers before	{/ Startup;CellOrder}
Labels	
Label Order	{/ Startup;LabelOrder}

Table D.6—*continued*

Command	Menu-equivalent command
Query	
Block	{/ Query;Block}
Criteria Table	{/ Query;CriteriaBlock}
Output Block	{/ Query;Output}
Assign Names	{/ Query;AssignNames}
Locate	{/ Query;Locate}
Extract	{/ Query;Extract}
Unique	{/ Query;Unique}
Delete	{/ Query;Delete}
Reset	{/ Query;Reset}
Restrict Input	{/ Block;Input}
Data Entry	
General	{/ Publish;DataEntryFormula}
Labels Only	{/ Publish;DataEntryLabel}
Dates Only	{/ Publish;DataEntryDate}

Table D.7
Tools Menu Commands

Command	Menu-equivalent command
Macro	{/ Macro;Menu}
Record	{/ Macro;Record}
Paste	{/ Macro;Paste}
Instant Replay	{/ Macro;Menu}I
Macro Recording	{/ Startup;Record}
Transcript	{/ Macro;Menu}T
Clear Breakpoints	{/ Name;BkptReset}
Debugger	{/ Macro;Debug}
Name	
Create	{/ Name;Create}
Delete	{/ Name;Delete}
Library	{/ Macro;Library}
Execute	{/ Name;Execute}
Reformat	{/ Block;Justify}

Command	Menu-equivalent command
Import	
ASCII Text File	{/ File;ImportText}
Comma & "" Delimited File	{/ File;ImportNumbers}
Only Commas	{/ File;ImportComma}
Combine	
Copy	
File	{/ File;CopyFile}
Block	{/ File;CopyRange}
Add	
File	{/ File;AddFile}
Block	{/ File;AddRange}
Subtract	
File	{/ File;SubtractFile}
Block	{/ File;SubtractRange}
Xtract	
Formulas	{/ File;ExtractFormulas}
Values	{/ File;ExtractValues}
Update Links	
Open	{/ HotLink;Open}
Refresh	{/ HotLink;Update}
Change	{/ HotLink;Change}
Delete	{/ HotLink;Delete}
Advanced Math	
Regression	
Independent	{/ Regression;Independent}
Dependent	{/ Regression;Dependent}
Output	{/ Regression;Output}
Y Intercept	{/ Regression;Intercept}
Go	{/ Regression;Go}
Reset	{/ Regression;Reset}
Invert	{/ Math;InvertMatrix}
Multiply	{/ Math;MultiplyMatrix}
Optimization	
Linear Constraint Coefficients	{/ Optimization;Coefficients}
Inequality/Equality Relations	{/ Optimization;Relations}
Constant Constraint Terms	{/ Optimization;Constants}
Bounds for Variables	{/ Optimization;Bounds}
Formula Constants	{/ Optimization;Formulas}
Objective Function	{/ Optimization;Objective}
Extremum	{/ Optimization;Extremum}
Solution	{/ Optimization;Solution}

Table D.7—*continued*

Command	Menu-equivalent command
Variables	{/ Optimization;Variables}
Dual Values	{/ Optimization;Dual}
Additional Dual Values	{/ Optimization;Additional}
Go	{/ Optimization;Go}
Reset	{/ Optimization;Reset}
Parse	
Input	{/ Parse;Input}
Output	{/ Parse;Output}
Create	{/ Parse;CreateLine}
Edit	{/ Parse;EditLine}
Go	{/ Parse;Go}
Reset	{/ Parse;Reset}
What-If	
1 Variable	{/ Math;1CellWhat-If}
2 Variables	{/ Math;2CellWhat-If}
Reset	{/ Math;ResetWhat-If}
Frequency	{/ Math;Distribution}

Table D.8
Options Menu Commands

Command	Menu-equivalent command
Hardware	
Screen	
Screen Type	{/ ScreenHardware;GraphScreenType}
Resolution	{/ Graph;ScreenMode}
Aspect Ratio	{/ ScreenHardware;AspectRatio}
CGA Snow	{/ ScreenHardware;Retrace}
Suppression	
Printers	
1st Printer	
Type of printer	{/ GPrinter1;Type}
Make	{/ GPrinter1;ShowMake}
Model	{/ GPrinter1;ShowModel}
Mode	{/ GPrinter1;ShowMode}
Device	{/ GPrinter1;Device}
Baud Rate	{/ GPrinter1;Baud}

Command	Menu-equivalent command
Parity	{/ GPrinter1;Parity}
Stop Bits	{/ GPrinter1;Stop}
2nd Printer	
Type of printer	{/ GPrinter2;Type}
Make	{/ GPrinter2;ShowMake}
Model	{/ GPrinter2;ShowModel}
Mode	{/ GPrinter2;ShowMode}
Device	{/ GPrinter2;Device}
Baud Rate	{/ GPrinter2;Baud}
Parity	{/ GPrinter2;Parity}
Stop Bits	{/ GPrinter2;Stop}
Default Printer	{/ Defaults;PrinterName}
Plotter Speed	{/ GraphPrint;PlotSpeed}
Fonts	
LaserJet Fonts	
Left Cartridge	{/ Hardware;LJetLeft}
Right Cartridge	{/ Hardware;LJetRight}
Autoscale Fonts	{/ Hardware;AutoFonts}
Auto LF	{/ Hardware;AutoLF}
Single Sheet	{/ Hardware;SingleSheet}
Normal Memory	{/ Basics;ShowMem}
EMS	{/ Basics;ShowEMS}
Coprocessor	{/ Basics;ShowCoProc}
Colors	
Menu	
Frame	{/ MenuColors;Frame}
Banner	{/ MenuColors;Banner}
Text	{/ MenuColors;Text}
Key Letter	{/ MenuColors;FirstLetter}
Highlight	{/ MenuColors;MenuBar}
Settings	{/ MenuColors;Settings}
Explanation	{/ MenuColors;Explanation}
Drop Shadow	{/ Startup;Shadow}
Mouse Palette	{/ Startup;PaletteCo}
Fill Characters	
Shadow	{/ Startup;ShadowChar}
Desktop	
Status	{/ Color;Status}
Highlight (Status)	{/ Color;Indicators}
Errors	{/ ErrorColor;SetErrorColor}
Background	{/ Startup;DesktopColor}

Table D.8—*continued*

Command	Menu-equivalent command
Fill Characters	
Desktop	{/ Startup;DesktopChar}
Spreadsheet	
Frame	{/ Color;Frame}
Banner	{/ Color;Banner}
Cells	{/ Color;Cells}
Borders	{/ Color;Border}
Titles	{/ Color;Titles}
Highlight	{/ Color;Cursor}
Graph Frames	{/ Color;GraphFrame}
Input Line	{/ Color;Edit}
Unprotected	{/ Color;Unprotect}
Labels	{/ ValueColors;Labels}
Shading	{/ Color;Shading}
Drawn Lines	{/ Color;LineDrawing}
Conditional	
On/Off	{/ ValueColors;Enable}
ERR	{/ ValueColors;Err}
Smallest Normal Value	{/ ValueColors;Min}
Greatest Normal Value	{/ ValueColors;Max}
Below Normal Color	{/ ValueColors;Low}
Normal Cell Color	{/ ValueColors;Normal}
Above Normal Color	{/ ValucColors;High}
Help	
Frame	{/ HelpColors;Frame}
Banner	{/ HelpColors;Banner}
Text	{/ HelpColors;Text}
Keywords	{/ HelpColors;Keyword}
Highlight	{/ HelpColors;Highlight}
File Manager	
Frame	{/ FileMgrColors;Frame}
Banner	{/ FileMgrColors;Banner}
Text	{/ FileMgrColors;Text}
Active Cursor	{/ FileMgrColors;ActiveCursor}
Inactive Cursor	{/ FileMgrColors;InactiveCursor}
Marked	{/ FileMgrColors;Marked}
Move	{/ FileMgrColors;Cut}
Copy	{/ FileMgrColors;Copy}

Command	Menu-equivalent command
Palettes	
Color	{/ Color;ColorPalette}
Monochrome	{/ Color;BWPalette}
Black & White	{/ Color;BWCGAPalette}
International	
Currency	{/ Intnl;Currency}
Punctuation	{/ Intnl;Punctuation}
Date	{/ FormatChanges;IntlDate}
Time	{/ FormatChanges;IntlTime}
Display Mode	{/ ScreenHardware;TextScreenMode}
Startup	
Directory	{/ Defaults;Directory}
Autoload File	{/ Startup;File}
Startup Macro	{/ Startup;Macro}
File Extension	{/ Startup;Extension}
Beep	{/ Startup;Beep}
Menu Tree	{/ Startup;Menus}
Mouse Palette	
1st Button	{/ Defaults;Button1}
2nd Button	{/ Defaults;Button2}
3rd Button	{/ Defaults;Button3}
4th Button	{/ Defaults;Button4}
5th Button	{/ Defaults;Button5}
6th Button	{/ Defaults;Button6}
7th Button	{/ Defaults;Button7}
Graphics Quality	{/ Defaults;GraphicsQuality}
Other	
Undo	{/ Defaults;Undo}
Macro	{/ Defaults;Suppress}
Expanded Memory	{/ Defaults;ExpMem}
Clock	{/ Defaults;ClockFormat}
Paradox	
Network Type	{/ Paradox;NetType}
Directory	{/ Paradox;Directory}
Retries	{/ Paradox;Retries}
Update	{/ Defaults;Update}

Table D.8—*continued*

Command	Menu-equivalent command
Formats	
Numeric Format	{/ Defaults;Format}
Align Labels	{/ Defaults;Alignment}
Hide Zeros	{/ Defaults;Zero}
Global Width	{/ Defaults;ColWidth}
Recalculation	
Mode	{/ Defaults;RecalcMode}
Automatic	{/ CompCalc;Automatic}
Manual	{/ CompCalc;Manual}
Background	{/ CompCalc;Background}
Order	{/ Defaults;RecalcOrder}
Natural	{/ CompCalc;Natural}
Columnwise	{/ CompCalc;ColWise}
Rowwise	{/ CompCalc;RowWise}
Iteration	{/ Defaults;RecalcIteration}
Protection	{/ Protection;Status}
Enable	{/ Protection;Enable}
Disable	{/ Protection;Disable}

Table D.9
Windows Menu Commands

Command	Menu-equivalent command
Zoom	{/ View;Zoom}
Tile	{/ View;Arrange}
Stack	{/ View;Cascade}
Move/Size	{/ View;Size}
Options	
Horizontal	{/ Windows;Horizontal}
Vertical	{/ Windows;Vertical}
Sync	{/ Windows;Synch}
Unsync	{/ Windows;Unsynch}
Clear	{/ Windows;Clear}
Locked Titles	
Horizontal	{/ Titles;Horizontal}
Vertical	{/ Titles;Vertical}

Command	Menu-equivalent command
Both	{/ Titles;Both}
Clear	{/ Titles;Clear}
Row & Col Borders	
Display	{/ Windows;RowColDisplay}
Hide	{/ Windows;RowColHide}
Map View	{/ Windows;MapView}
Pick	{/ View;Choose}

Table D.10
File Manager File Menu Commands

Command	Menu-equivalent command
New	{/ View;NewWindow}
Open	{/ View;OpenWindow}
Close	{/ Basics;Close}
Close All	{/ System;TidyUp}
Read Dir	{/ FileMgr;ReadDir}
Make Dir	{/ FileMgr;MakeDir}
Workspace	
Save	{/ System;SaveWorkspace}
Restore	{/ System;RestoreWorkspace}
Utilities	
OS	{/ Basics;OS}
File Manager	{/ New;NewFileMgr}
SQZ!	
Remove Blanks	{/ SQZ;Blanks}
Storage of Values	{/ SQZ;Values}
Version	{/ SQZ;Version}
Exit	{/ System;Exit}

Table D.11
File Manager Edit Menu Commands

Command	Menu-equivalent command
Select File	{/ FileMgr;Mark}
All Select	{/ FileMgr;AllMark}
Copy	{/ FileMgr;Copy}
Move	{/ FileMgr;Cut}
Erase	{/ FileMgr;Erase}
Paste	{/ FileMgr;Paste}
Duplicate	{/ FileMgr;Duplicate}
Rename	{/ FileMgr;Rename}

Table D.12
File Manager Sort Menu Commands

Command	Menu-equivalent command
Name	{/ FileMgr;SortName}
Timestamp	{/ FileMgr;SortDate}
Extension	{/ FileMgr;SortExt}
Size	{/ FileMgr;SortSize}
DOS Order	{/ FileMgr;SortNone}

Table D.13
File Manager Tree Menu Commands

Command	Menu-equivalent command
Open	{/ FileMgr;TreeShow}
Resize	{/ FileMgr;TreeSize}
Close	{/ FileMgr;TreeClear}

Table D.14
File Manager Print Menu Commands

Command	Menu-equivalent command
Block	{/ FileMgrPrint;Block}
Destination	
Printer	{/ FileMgrPrint;OutputPrinter}
File	{/ FileMgrPrint;OutputFile}
Page Layout	
Header	{/ FileMgrPrint;Header}
Footer	{/ FileMgrPrint;Footer}
Break Pages	{/ FileMgrPrint;Breaks}
Margins & Length	
Page Length	{/ FileMgrPrint;PageLength}
Left	{/ FileMgrPrint;LeftMargin}
Top	{/ FileMgrPrint;TopMargin}
Right	{/ FileMgrPrint;RightMargin}
Bottom	{/ FileMgrPrint;BottomMargin}
Setup String	{/ FileMgrPrint;Setup}
Reset	
All	{/ FileMgrPrint;ResetAll}
Print Block	{/ FileMgrPrint;ResetBlock}
Layout	{/ FileMgrPrint;ResetDefaults}
Adjust Printer	
Skip Line	{/ FileMgrPrint;SkipLine}
Form Feed	{/ FileMgrPrint;FormFeed}
Align	{/ FileMgrPrint;Align}
Go	{/ FileMgrPrint;Go}

Table D.15
File Manager Options Menu Commands

Command	Menu-equivalent command
Hardware	
Screen	
Screen Type	{/ ScreenHardware;GraphScreenType}
Resolution	{/ Graph;ScreenMode}
Aspect Ratio	{/ ScreenHardware;AspectRatio}
CGA Snow	{/ ScreenHardware;Retrace}

Table D.15—*continued*

Command	Menu-equivalent command
Suppression	
Printers	
1st Printer	
Type of printer	{/ GPrinter1;Type}
Make	{/ GPrinter1;ShowMake}
Model	{/ GPrinter1;ShowModel}
Mode	{/ GPrinter1;ShowMode}
Device	{/ GPrinter1;Device}
Baud Rate	{/ GPrinter1;Baud}
Parity	{/ GPrinter1;Parity}
Stop Bits	{/ GPrinter1;Stop}
2nd Printer	
Type of printer	{/ GPrinter2;Type}
Make	{/ GPrinter2;ShowMake}
Model	{/ GPrinter2;ShowModel}
Mode	{/ GPrinter2;ShowMode}
Device	{/ GPrinter2;Device}
Baud Rate	{/ GPrinter2;Baud}
Parity	{/ GPrinter2;Parity}
Stop Bits	{/ GPrinter2;Stop}
Default Printer	{/ Defaults;PrinterName}
Plotter Speed	{/ GraphPrint;PlotSpeed}
Fonts	
LaserJet Fonts	
Left Cartridge	{/ Hardware;LJetLeft}
Right Cartridge	{/ Hardware;LJetRight}
Autoscale Fonts	{/ Hardware;AutoFonts}
Auto LF	{/ Hardware;AutoLF}
Single Sheet	{/ Hardware;SingleSheet}
Normal Memory	{/ Basics;ShowMem}
EMS	{/ Basics;ShowEMS}
Coprocessor	{/ Basics;ShowCoProc}
Colors	
Menu	
Frame	{/ MenuColors;Frame}
Banner	{/ MenuColors;Banner}
Text	{/ MenuColors;Text}

Command	Menu-equivalent command
Key Letter	{/ MenuColors;FirstLetter}
Highlight	{/ MenuColors;MenuBar}
Settings	{/ MenuColors;Settings}
Explanation	{/ MenuColors;Explanation}
Drop Shadow	{/ Startup;Shadow}
Mouse Palette	{/ Startup;PaletteCo}
Fill Characters	
Shadow	{/ Startup;ShadowChar}
Desktop	
Colors	
Status	{/ Color;Status}
Highlight (Status)	{/ Color;Indicators}
Errors	{/ ErrorColor;SetErrorColor}
Background	{/ Startup;DesktopColor}
Fill Characters	
Desktop	{/ Startup;DesktopChar}
Spreadsheet	
Frame	{/ Color;Frame}
Banner	{/ Color;Banner}
Cells	{/ Color;Cells}
Borders	{/ Color;Border}
Titles	{/ Color;Titles}
Highlight	{/ Color;Cursor}
Graph Frames	{/ Color;GraphFrame}
Input Line	{/ Color;Edit}
Unprotected	{/ Color;Unprotect}
Labels	{/ ValueColors;Labels}
Shading	{/ Color;Shading}
Drawn Lines	{/ Color;LineDrawing}
Conditional	
On/Off	{/ ValueColors;Enable}
ERR	{/ ValueColors;Err}
Smallest Normal Value	{/ ValueColors;Min}
Greatest Normal Value	{/ ValueColors;Max}
Below Normal Color	{/ ValueColors;Low}
Normal Cell Color	{/ ValueColors;Normal}
Above Normal Color	{/ ValueColors;High}

Table D.15—*continued*

Command	Menu-equivalent command
Help	
Frame	{/ HelpColors;Frame}
Banner	{/ HelpColors;Banner}
Text	{/ HelpColors;Text}
Keywords	{/ HelpColors;Keyword}
Highlight	{/ HelpColors;Highlight}
File Manager	
Frame	{/ FileMgrColors;Frame}
Banner	{/ FileMgrColors;Banner}
Text	{/ FileMgrColors;Text}
Active Cursor	{/ FileMgrColors;ActiveCursor}
Inactive Cursor	{/ FileMgrColors;InactiveCursor}
Marked	{/ FileMgrColors;Marked}
Move	{/ FileMgrColors;Cut}
Copy	{/ FileMgrColors;Copy}
Palettes	
Color	{/ Color;ColorPalette}
Monochrome	{/ Color;BWPalette}
Black & White	{/ Color;BWCGAPalette}
Beep	{/ Startup;Beep}
Startup	
Menu Tree	{/ Startup;Menus}
Directory	
Previous	{/ FileMgr;SameDir}
Current	{/ FileMgr;CurrDir}
File List	
Wide View	{/ FileMgr;Wide}
Full View	{/ FileMgr;Narrow}
Display Mode	{/ ScreenHardware;TextScreenMode}
Update	{/ Defaults;Update}

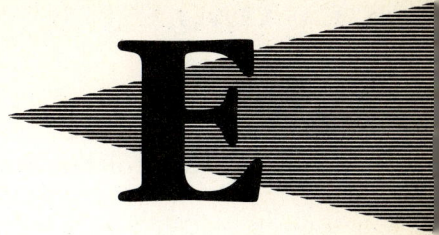

Using ASCII Characters

Table E.1 lists the American Standard Code for Information Interchange (ASCII) character table. The table lists a total of 255 characters and their decimal and hexadecimal equivalents.

Table E.1
ASCII Codes

Decimal	Hex	Graphic Character	Decimal	Hex	Graphic Character
0	0		24	18	↑
1	1	☺	25	19	↓
2	2	●	26	1A	→
3	3	♥	27	1B	←
4	4	♦	28	1C	∟
5	5	♣	29	1D	↔
6	6	♠	30	1E	▲
7	7	·	31	1F	▼
8	8	■	32	20	
9	9	○	33	21	!
10	A	◉	34	22	"
11	B	σ	35	23	#
12	C	♀	36	24	$
13	D	♪	37	25	%
14	E	♫	38	26	&
15	F	☼	39	27	'
16	10	►	40	28	(
17	11	◄	41	29	)
18	12	↕	42	2A	*
19	13	‼	43	2B	+
20	14	¶	44	2C	,
21	15	§	45	2D	–
22	16	▬	46	2E	.
23	17	↨	47	2F	/

Table E.1—*continued*

Decimal	Hex	Graphic Character	Decimal	Hex	Graphic Character
48	30	0	96	60	`
49	31	1	97	61	a
50	32	2	98	62	b
51	33	3	99	63	c
52	34	4	100	64	d
53	35	5	101	65	e
54	36	6	102	66	f
55	37	7	103	67	g
56	38	8	104	68	h
57	39	9	105	69	i
58	3A	:	106	6A	j
59	3B	;	107	6B	k
60	3C	<	108	6C	l
61	3D	=	109	6D	m
62	3E	>	110	6E	n
63	3F	?	111	6F	o
64	40	@	112	70	p
65	41	A	113	71	q
66	42	B	114	72	r
67	43	C	115	73	s
68	44	D	116	74	t
69	45	E	117	75	u
70	46	F	118	76	v
71	47	G	119	77	w
72	48	H	120	78	x
73	49	I	121	79	y
74	4A	J	122	7A	z
75	4B	K	123	7B	{
76	4C	L	124	7C		
77	4D	M	125	7D	}
78	4E	N	126	7E	~
79	4F	O	127	7F	Δ
80	50	P	128	80	Ç
81	51	Q	129	81	ü
82	52	R	130	82	é
83	53	S	131	83	â
84	54	T	132	84	ä
85	55	U	133	85	à
86	56	V	134	86	å
87	57	W	135	87	ç
88	58	X	136	88	ê
89	59	Y	137	89	ë
90	5A	Z	138	8A	è
91	5B	[	139	8B	ï
92	5C	\	140	8C	î
93	5D	]	141	8D	ì
94	5E	^	142	8E	Ä
95	5F	_	143	8F	Å

Decimal	Hex	Graphic Character	Decimal	Hex	Graphic Character
144	90	É	192	C0	└
145	91	æ	193	C1	┴
146	92	Æ	194	C2	┬
147	93	ô	195	C3	├
148	94	ö	196	C4	─
149	95	ò	197	C5	┼
150	96	û	198	C6	╞
151	97	ù	199	C7	╟
152	98	ÿ	200	C8	╚
153	99	Ö	201	C9	╔
154	9A	Ü	202	CA	╩
155	9B	¢	203	CB	╦
156	9C	£	204	CC	╠
157	9D	¥	205	CD	═
158	9E	₧	206	CE	╬
159	9F	ƒ	207	CF	╧
160	A0	á	208	D0	╨
161	A1	í	209	D1	╤
162	A2	ó	210	D2	╥
163	A3	ú	211	D3	╙
164	A4	ñ	212	D4	╘
165	A5	Ñ	213	D5	╒
166	A6	ª	214	D6	╓
167	A7	º	215	D7	╫
168	A8	¿	216	D8	╪
169	A9	⌐	217	D9	┘
170	AA	¬	218	DA	┌
171	AB	½	219	DB	█
172	AC	¼	220	DC	▄
173	AD	¡	221	DD	▌
174	AE	«	222	DE	▐
175	AF	»	223	DF	▀
176	B0	░	224	E0	α
177	B1	▒	225	E1	β
178	B2	▓	226	E2	Γ
179	B3	│	227	E3	π
180	B4	┤	228	E4	Σ
181	B5	╡	229	E5	σ
182	B6	╢	230	E6	µ
183	B7	╖	231	E7	τ
184	B8	╕	232	E8	Φ
185	B9	╣	233	E9	Θ
186	BA	║	234	EA	Ω
187	BB	╗	235	EB	δ
188	BC	╝	236	EC	∞
189	BD	╜	237	ED	φ
190	BE	╛	238	EE	∈
191	BF	┐	239	EF	∩

Table E.1—*continued*

Decimal	Hex	Graphic Character		Decimal	Hex	Graphic Character
240	F0	≡		248	F8	°
241	F1	±		249	F9	·
242	F2	≥		250	FA	·
243	F3	≤		251	FB	√
244	F4	⌠		252	FC	ⁿ
245	F5	⌡		253	FD	²
246	F6	÷		254	FE	∎
247	F7	≈		255	FF	

Entering ASCII Characters in Spreadsheet Cells

Quattro Pro accepts all ASCII characters in spreadsheets cells. When you create a graph from a spreadsheet containing ASCII characters, some of the characters display as text in the graph.

The ASCII characters of particular importance are the international characters (for example, é, £, and ~), mathematical characters (for example, ½ and ~), and border characters.

To enter an ASCII character into a spreadsheet cell, press and hold down the Alt key as you type the decimal code equivalent on your numeric keypad.

For example, to enter the mathematical symbol for a square root into a spreadsheet cell, do the following:

1. Press and hold down the Alt key.

2. Type the decimal code 251.

3. Release the Alt key, and Quattro Pro reproduces the square root symbol on the input line at the top of your screen.

4. Press Enter to store the symbol in the cell.

Entering ASCII Characters in Dialog Boxes

You also enter ASCII characters into Quattro Pro dialog boxes. When you select /**O**ptions **I**nternational **C**urrency, Quattro Pro displays a dialog box and prompts you to enter a new currency symbol. To enter the British pound currency symbol, do the following:

1. Press the Backspace key to delete the dollar sign (the default currency symbol).

2. Press and hold down the Alt key.

3. Type the decimal code *156*.

4. Release the Alt key, and Quattro Pro reproduces the pound symbol in the input box.

5. Press Enter to store the pound symbol setting.

When you select /**S**tyle **N**umeric Format **C**urrency and format a value, the pound symbol appears instead of the dollar sign. To keep the pound symbol as the global default, select /**O**ptions **U**pdate.

Tip | Some terminate-and-stay-resident (TSR) programs like Super-Key assign special operations to the Alt key. Pressing Alt plus a decimal code does not display the ASCII character. Instead, press Shift-Alt and then type the decimal code.

Other special characters can be used with Quattro Pro. For example, the /**O**ptions **C**olors **M**enu **S**hadow command prompts you to enter the decimal code equivalent for the ASCII character that Quattro Pro uses to create menu shadows. ASCII decimal code 2 displays smiling faces in the menu shadows.

The /**O**ptions **C**olors **D**esktop command prompts you to enter the decimal code equivalent for the ASCII character that Quattro Pro uses to create fill characters when no windows are displayed. ASCII decimal code 14 displays musical note symbols in the background area.

Notice that these two commands require you to enter the decimal code equivalents for the ASCII character. Do not enter the actual symbols by pressing Alt plus the decimal code. If you do, Quattro Pro does not interpret the command settings correctly.

Converting ASCII Codes
into Printer Setup Strings

Another use for the ASCII table is to create printer setup strings that you supply at the /Printer Layout Setup String command prompt.

As discussed in Chapter 8, the control panel on a printer enables you to invoke various print modes like draft printing, bold printing, and compressed printing. Often, other print modes that your printer supports do not appear as hardware options on the control panel (italics mode is a good example).

You can create and issue software commands that invoke special print modes. You first must review your printer manual. In the manual, you find a table of software commands. These software commands look like *CTRL + F* or *ESC + 4*.

Generally, printing modes are set through the use of control codes, which consist of one or more ASCII characters. These control codes—which vary from printer to printer—fall into two categories: *control sequences* and *escape sequences*.

In a control sequence, each code begins with the control key and is followed by a hexadecimal character. For example, CTRL + F invokes the compressed printing mode for a Panasonic printer. To use this software command, convert the command to a code that your printer understands. The printer code that signifies a CTRL sequence is \0. The decimal equivalent for the hexadecimal F is 15.

To invoke compressed mode, do the following:

1. Select /**Printer** Layout Setup String.

2. When prompted, type \015 and press Enter.

The next time you print a spreadsheet, the text prints in compressed type.

In an escape sequence, each code begins with the ASCII code for the ESCAPE character (ESC). Do not confuse this character with the Escape (Esc) key on your keyboard—they are not the same thing. For example, ESC + 4 invokes the italic printing mode for a standard IBM printer. To use this software command, convert the command to a code that your printer understands. The code that signifies an ESC sequence is \027.

To invoke the italics printing mode, do the following:

1. Select /**Printer** Layout Setup String.

2. When prompted, type \0274 and press Enter.

The next time you print a spreadsheet, the text appears in italics.

After Quattro Pro sends a setup string to your printer, that printing mode remains the default until you issue a setup string that cancels it.

You also can turn off and then turn your printer back on to clear the setup string settings from your printer's memory. If you use this technique, you must delete the setup string entered at the /**P**rinter **L**ayout **S**etup **S**tring prompt before you print another spreadsheet.

Index

A

Alt-F2 (Macro Menu) key, 46, 513

Alt-F3 (Functions) key, 46, 85

Alt-F5 (Undo) key, 20, 46, 95, 112, 139-140, 451

Alt-F6 (Zoom) key, 47, 297-298

Alt-F7 (All Select) key, 47

anchoring cell references, 87-88

AND searches, 476

annotating graphs, 334-336, 428-438

    Annotator draw area, 430

    Annotator gallery, 431

    Annotator property sheet, 431

    Annotator status box, 431

    Annotator tool box, 430-431

    arrows, 335

    boxed text, 335

    clipboard, 437-438

    editing text design elements, 436

    moving design elements, 434-435

    resizing design elements, 435-436

    selecting design elements, 433-434

    setting design element properties, 436-438

area graphs, 378-379, 407

arguments in macro commands, 577-578

arithmetic @functions, 176

    @ABS, 177-178

    @ExP, 178

    @INT, 178

    @LN, 178

    @LOG, 178

    @MOD, 179

    @RAND, 179

    @ROUND, 179

    @SQRT, 180

arithmetic formulas, 80

arithmetic operators, 80

    * (multiplication), 80

    + (addition), 80

    − (subtraction), 80

    / (division), 80

    ^ (exponential notation), 80

arrows, annotating graphs, 335

ascending sort order, 469-473

ASCII sort order, 473

@ASIN trignometric @function, 181

aspect ratio, 245

aspect settings, 331

assigning names to field names row, 475

@ATAN trignometric @function, 181

@ATAN2 trignometric @function, 182

attribute elements, 196-199

autoload files, 261

autoload macros, 521

automatic line feed (printers), 248

automatic recalculation, 270

averaging numbers, 184

@AVG statistical @function, 184

B

background recalculation, 96, 270

{BACKSPACE} macro command, 583

Backspace (Graph Annotator) key, 432

Backspace key, 42, 94

{BACKTAB} macro command, 583

bar graphs, 376

    fill patterns, 407

    interior labels, 411-412

    width of bars, 410-411

{BEEP<number>} macro command, 583

beep tones, 263

{BIGLEFT} macro command, 584

{BIGRIGHT} macro command, 584

binary files, printing spreadsheets to, 355

Bitstream fonts, 571-576

    building during work sessions, 572

    building with macros, 572-576

    installing, 571-572

    installing entire font library, 576

{BLANK} macro command, 584

blocks of cells, 90-92, 115-117

    address, 65

    copying, 116

    deleting names, 120-121

    erasing, 117

    erasing data, 112

    label names, 121-122

    moving, 116-117

    naming, 117-119

    preselecting, 382-383

    selecting, 382-383

    tables of names, 122-124

    using names in formulas, 124

    viewing tables of names, 123-124

D

E

G

H

I

M

macros, 455-456, 519-521
natural logarithms, 178
negative numbers, 145
negative values, 76-77
nested parentheses in formulas, 93
{NEXTWIN} macro command, 596
@NOW date/time @function, 83-84, 230-231
@NPER financial @function, 220
@NPV financial @function, 221
Num Lock, 43
number of iterations, 271
number values, 75-77
numbers
   entering sequential, 125
   formatting, 23-24
numeric formats, 144-145, 147
   commas, 145
   Currency, 145
   Date, 145, 149-150
   Fixed, 145
   General, 145
   negative numbers, 145
   Percent, 145
   positive numbers, 145
   Scientific, 145, 147
   setting default, 268-269
   Text, 145
   Time, 150-151
numeric keypad, 42-43
{NUMOFF} macro command, 596
{NUMON} macro command, 596
@NUMTOHEX string @function, 193

O

{ONERROR} macro command, 596
one-way sensitivity analysis, 502-503
{OPEN} macro command, 597
opening files, 280-282
operators
   &, 81-82
   arithmetic, 80
     * (multiplication), 80
     + (addition), 80
     − (subtraction), 80
     / (division), 80
     ^ (exponential notation), 80

database search, 477-478
   logical, 82-83
   precedence, 92-93
optimization modeling, 491-495
Options Colors command, 241, 249-253
Options Colors Spreadsheet Shading command, 164
Options Display Mode command, 98-99, 241, 259, 330, 405
Options File Manager menu, 290-291
Options Formats command, 140-141, 241, 268-269
Options Formats Align Labels command, 269
Options Formats Global Width command, 269
Options Formats Hide Zeros command, 269
Options Formats Numeric Format command, 268-269
Options Graphics Quality command, 241, 264-265, 356
Options Hardware command, 241-245
Options International command, 241, 253-259
Options International Date command, 148-150
Options International Time command, 150-151
Options Mouse Palette command, 241, 264
Options Other Clock, 267
Options Other command, 241, 265
Options Other Expanded Memory commands, 266-267
Options Other Macro Redraw command, 266
Options Other Paradox command, 267
Options Other Undo command, 20, 95, 265-266
Options Printers command, 245-248
Options Protection command, 152-153, 241, 271
Options Recalculation command, 241, 269-270
Options Recalculation Mode command, 96
Options Startup command, 241, 260-263
Options Startup Directory command, 283
Options Startup Startup Macro commands, 521
Options Update command, 20, 95, 241, 267-268
Options What-If command, 35
OR searches, 476
order of operator precedence, 92-93
order of recalculation, 270
orientation, 325-326, 348

T

File

New
Open
Retrieve
Save (Ctrl-S)
Save **A**s
Close
Close All
Erase
Directory
Workspace——————— **S**ave
                    Restore
Utilities
E**x**it (Ctrl-X)

DOS Shell
File Manager
SQZ!

Remove Blanks

No
Yes

Storage of Values

Version

Exact
Approximate
Remove

Quit

1 - SQZ!
2 - SQZ! Plus

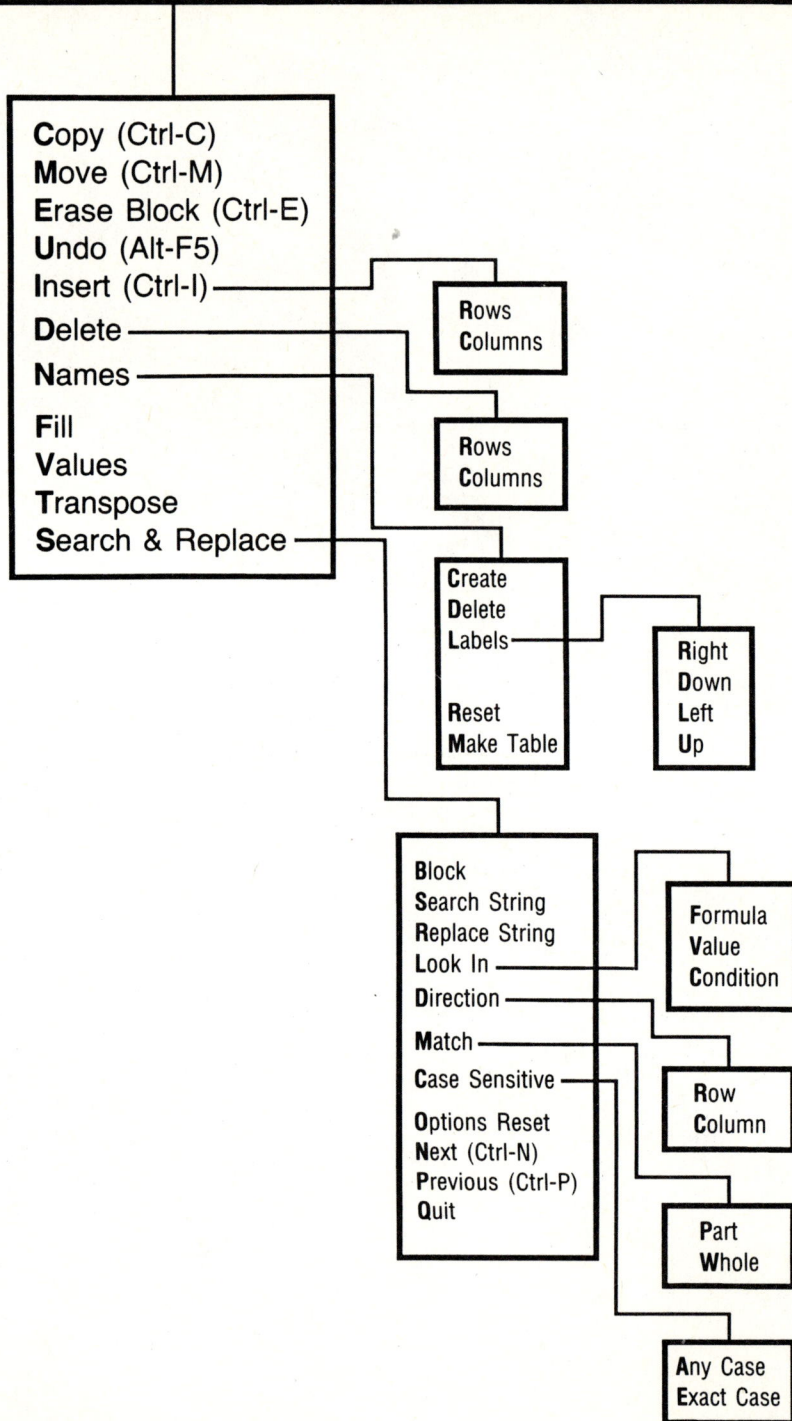

Edit

Copy (Ctrl-C)
Move (Ctrl-M)
Erase Block (Ctrl-E)
Undo (Alt-F5)
Insert (Ctrl-I) ————

Delete ————

Names ————

Fill
Values
Transpose
Search & Replace ————

Rows
Columns

Rows
Columns

Create
Delete
Labels ————

Reset
Make Table

Right
Down
Left
Up

Block
Search String
Replace String
Look In ————
Direction ————
Match ————
Case Sensitive ————

Options Reset
Next (Ctrl-N)
Previous (Ctrl-P)
Quit

Formula
Value
Condition

Row
Column

Part
Whole

Any Case
Exact Case

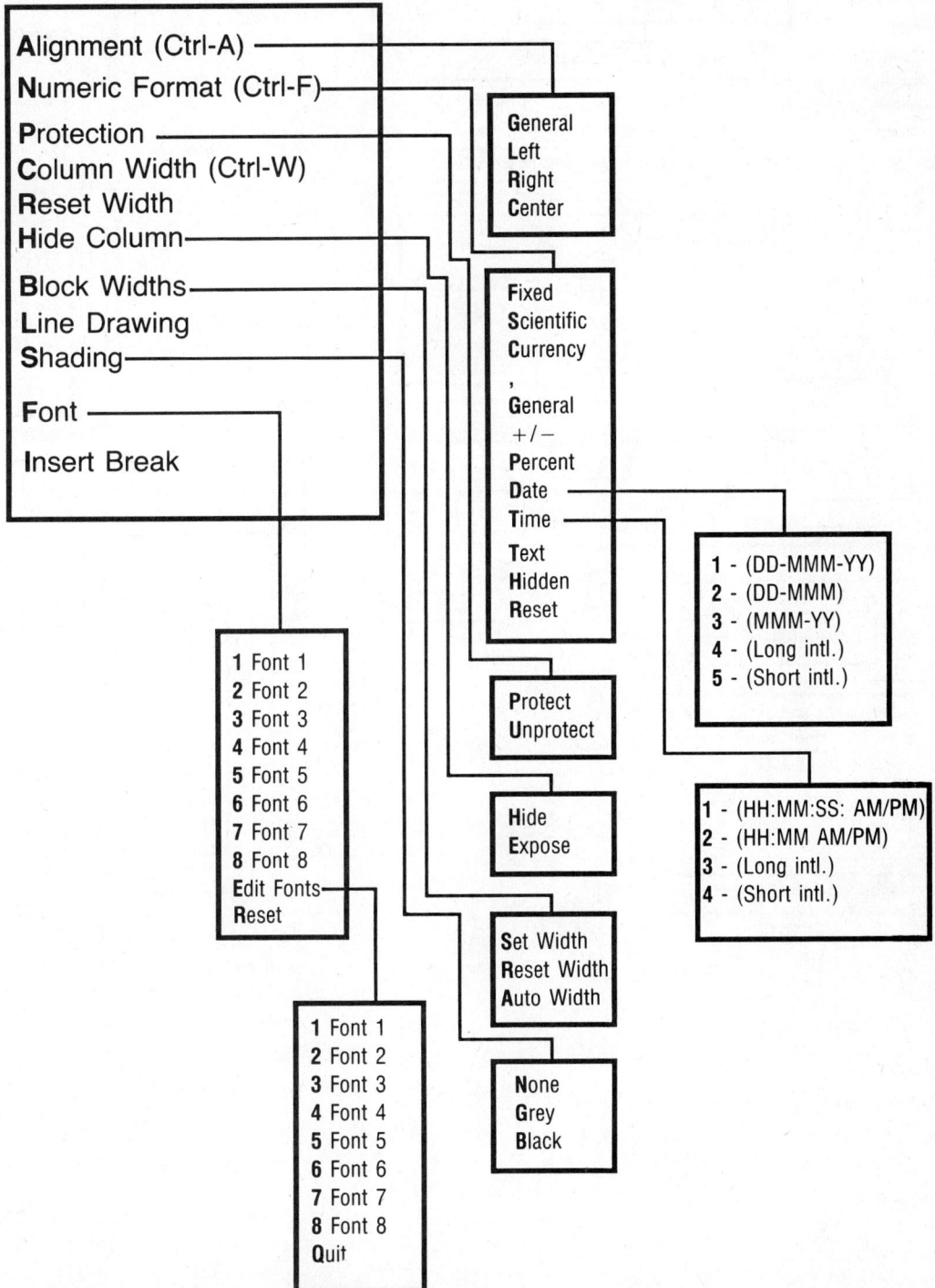

Style

Alignment (Ctrl-A)
Numeric Format (Ctrl-F)
Protection
Column Width (Ctrl-W)
Reset Width
Hide Column
Block Widths
Line Drawing
Shading
Font
Insert Break

General
Left
Right
Center

Fixed
Scientific
Currency
,
General
+ / −
Percent
Date
Time
Text
Hidden
Reset

1 - (DD-MMM-YY)
2 - (DD-MMM)
3 - (MMM-YY)
4 - (Long intl.)
5 - (Short intl.)

Protect
Unprotect

Hide
Expose

1 - (HH:MM:SS: AM/PM)
2 - (HH:MM AM/PM)
3 - (Long intl.)
4 - (Short intl.)

1 Font 1
2 Font 2
3 Font 3
4 Font 4
5 Font 5
6 Font 6
7 Font 7
8 Font 8
Edit Fonts
Reset

Set Width
Reset Width
Auto Width

1 Font 1
2 Font 2
3 Font 3
4 Font 4
5 Font 5
6 Font 6
7 Font 7
8 Font 8
Quit

None
Grey
Black

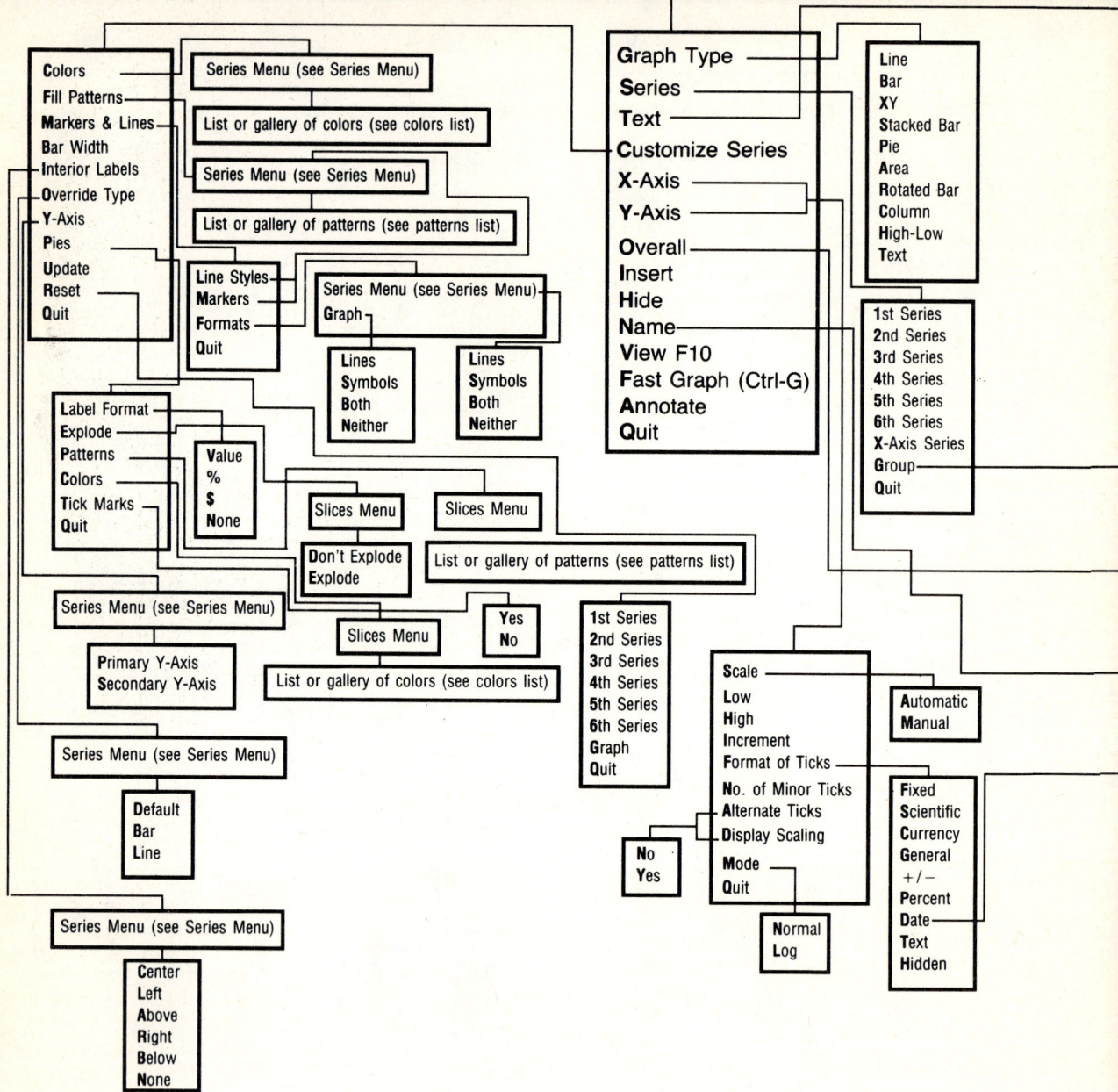

Graph

Graph Type ———
Series ———
Text ———
Customize Series
X-Axis ———
Y-Axis ———
Overall ———
Insert
Hide
Name ———
View F10
Fast Graph (Ctrl-G)
Annotate
Quit

Line
Bar
XY
Stacked Bar
Pie
Area
Rotated Bar
Column
High-Low
Text

1st Series
2nd Series
3rd Series
4th Series
5th Series
6th Series
X-Axis Series
Group ———
Quit

Colors ———
Fill Patterns ———
Markers & Lines ———
Bar Width
Interior Labels ———
Override Type
Y-Axis
Pies ———
Update
Reset ———
Quit

Series Menu (see Series Menu)

List or gallery of colors (see colors list)

Series Menu (see Series Menu)

List or gallery of patterns (see patterns list)

Line Styles ———
Markers ———
Formats ———
Quit

Series Menu (see Series Menu)
Graph ———

Lines
Symbols
Both
Neither

Lines
Symbols
Both
Neither

Label Format ———
Explode ———
Patterns ———
Colors ———
Tick Marks ———
Quit

Value
%
$
None

Slices Menu

Slices Menu

Don't Explode
Explode

List or gallery of patterns (see patterns list)

Series Menu (see Series Menu)

Primary Y-Axis
Secondary Y-Axis

Slices Menu

List or gallery of colors (see colors list)

Yes
No

1st Series
2nd Series
3rd Series
4th Series
5th Series
6th Series
Graph
Quit

Series Menu (see Series Menu)

Default
Bar
Line

Scale ———
Low
High
Increment
Format of Ticks ———
No. of Minor Ticks
Alternate Ticks ———
Display Scaling ———
Mode ———
Quit

Automatic
Manual

Series Menu (see Series Menu)

Center
Left
Above
Right
Below
None

No
Yes

Normal
Log

Fixed
Scientific
Currency
General
+ / −
Percent
Date ———
Text
Hidden

Graph

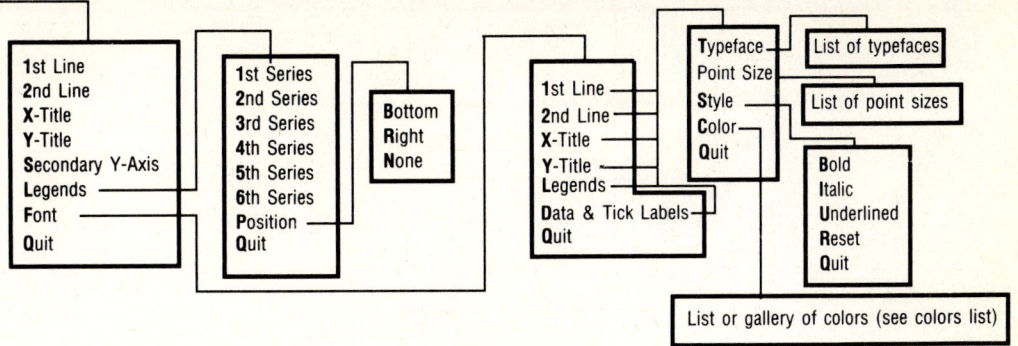

```
1st Line              1st Series                              1st Line      Typeface ──── List of typefaces
2nd Line              2nd Series         Bottom               2nd Line      Point Size ── List of point sizes
X-Title               3rd Series         Right                X-Title       Style
Y-Title               4th Series         None                 Y-Title       Color
Secondary Y-Axis      5th Series                              Legends       Quit         Bold
Legends               6th Series                              Data & Tick Labels          Italic
Font                  Position                                Quit                        Underlined
Quit                  Quit                                                                Reset
                                                                                          Quit

                                                                    List or gallery of colors (see colors list)
```

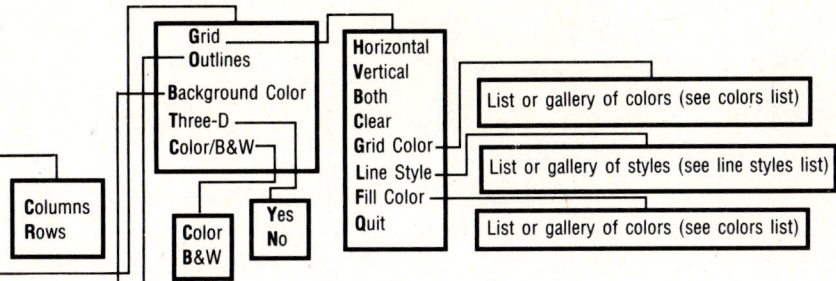

```
                 Grid          Horizontal
                 Outlines      Vertical
                 Background Color   Both              List or gallery of colors (see colors list)
                 Three-D       Clear
        Columns  Color/B&W     Grid Color ──── List or gallery of styles (see line styles list)
        Rows                   Line Style
                               Fill Color ──── List or gallery of colors (see colors list)
                 Color   Yes   Quit
                 B&W     No
```

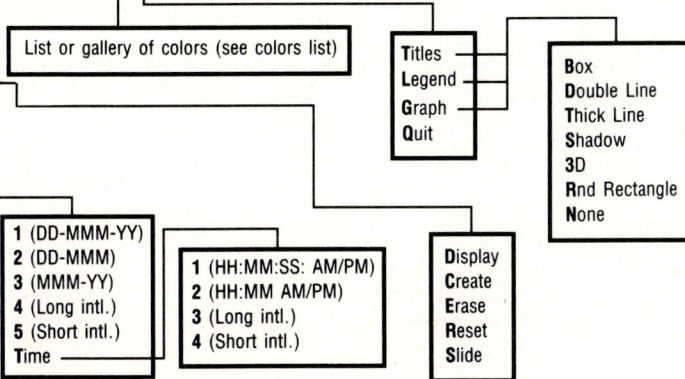

```
List or gallery of colors (see colors list)      Titles     Box
                                                 Legend     Double Line
                                                 Graph      Thick Line
                                                 Quit       Shadow
                                                            3D
                                                            Rnd Rectangle
                                                            None

1 (DD-MMM-YY)     1 (HH:MM:SS: AM/PM)    Display
2 (DD-MMM)        2 (HH:MM AM/PM)        Create
3 (MMM-YY)        3 (Long intl.)         Erase
4 (Long intl.)    4 (Short intl.)        Reset
5 (Short intl.)                          Slide
Time
```

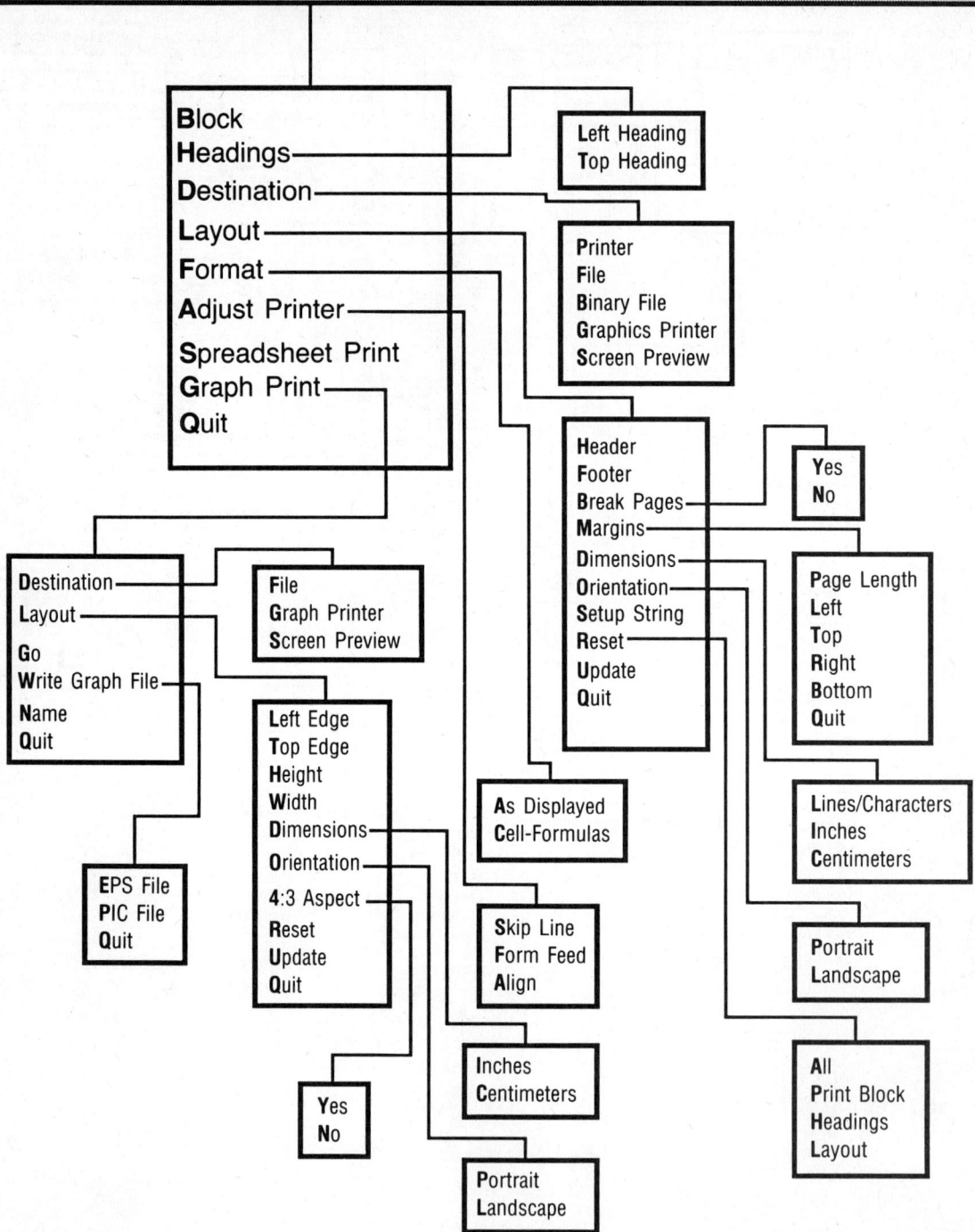

Print

Block
Headings ——————— **L**eft Heading
Destination ——————— **T**op Heading
Layout
Format
Adjust Printer
Spreadsheet Print
Graph Print
Quit

Printer
File
Binary File
Graphics Printer
Screen Preview

Header
Footer
Break Pages ——————— **Y**es
Margins   **N**o
Dimensions
Orientation
Setup String
Reset
Update
Quit

Destination ———————
Layout
Go
Write Graph File
Name
Quit

File
Graph Printer
Screen Preview

Page Length
Left
Top
Right
Bottom
Quit

Left Edge
Top Edge
Height
Width
Dimensions
Orientation
4:3 Aspect
Reset
Update
Quit

As Displayed
Cell-Formulas

Lines/Characters
Inches
Centimeters

EPS File
PIC File
Quit

Skip Line
Form Feed
Align

Portrait
Landscape

Yes
No

Inches
Centimeters

All
Print Block
Headings
Layout

Portrait
Landscape

Database

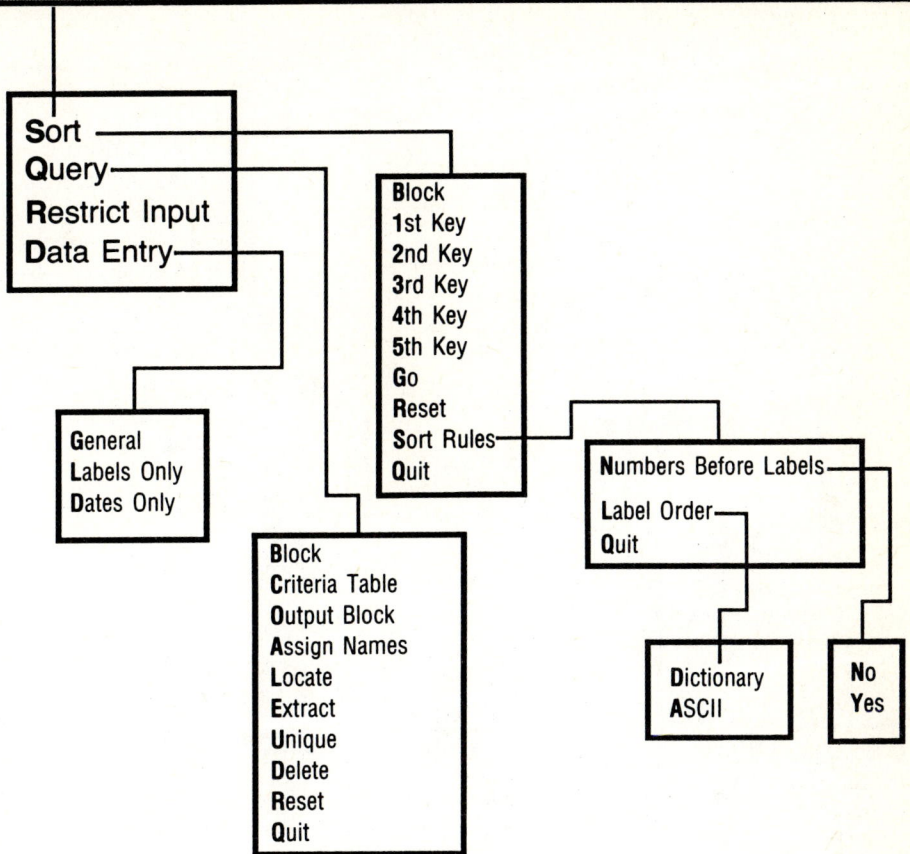

Sort
Query
Restrict Input
Data Entry

General
Labels Only
Dates Only

Block
1st Key
2nd Key
3rd Key
4th Key
5th Key
Go
Reset
Sort Rules
Quit

Block
Criteria Table
Output Block
Assign Names
Locate
Extract
Unique
Delete
Reset
Quit

Numbers Before Labels
Label Order
Quit

Dictionary
ASCII

No
Yes

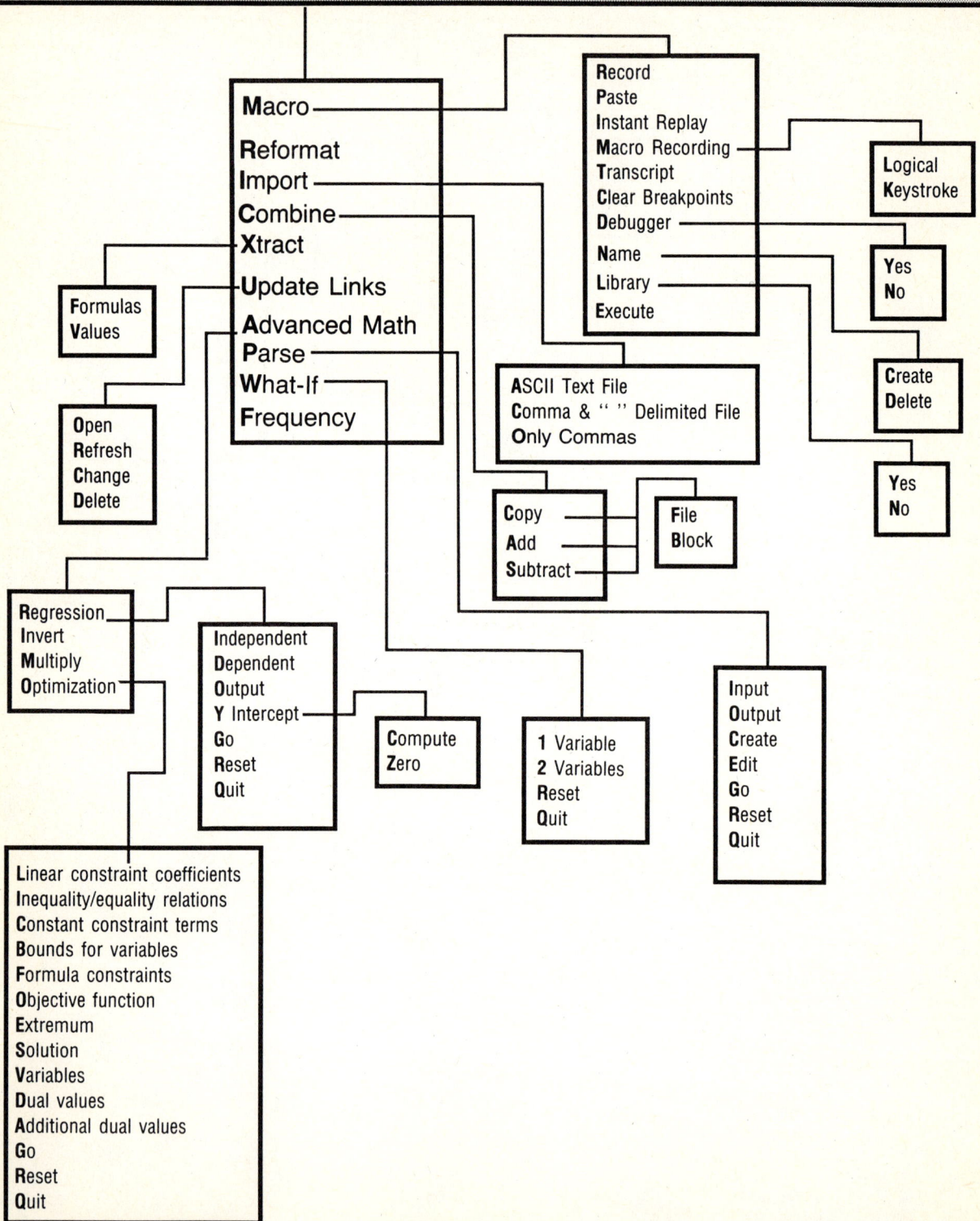

Tools

Macro

Reformat

Import

Combine

Xtract

Update Links

Advanced Math

Parse

What-If

Frequency

Record
Paste
Instant Replay
Macro Recording
Transcript
Clear Breakpoints
Debugger
Name
Library
Execute

Logical
Keystroke

Yes
No

Create
Delete

Yes
No

Formulas
Values

ASCII Text File
Comma & " " Delimited File
Only Commas

Open
Refresh
Change
Delete

Copy
Add
Subtract

File
Block

Regression
Invert
Multiply
Optimization

Independent
Dependent
Output
Y Intercept
Go
Reset
Quit

Compute
Zero

1 Variable
2 Variables
Reset
Quit

Input
Output
Create
Edit
Go
Reset
Quit

Linear constraint coefficients
Inequality/equality relations
Constant constraint terms
Bounds for variables
Formula constraints
Objective function
Extremum
Solution
Variables
Dual values
Additional dual values
Go
Reset
Quit

Series Menu
1st Series
2nd Series
3rd Series
4th Series
5th Series
6th Series
Quit

Colors
Black
Blue
Green
Cyan
Red
Magenta
Brown
White
Gray
Light Blue
Light Green
Light Cyan
Light Red
Light Magenta
Yellow
Bright White

Fill Patterns
Empty
Filled
- - - - -
Lt ///
Heavy //
Lt \\\
Heavy \\
+ + + + + + +
Crosshatch
Hatch
Light Dots
Heavy Dots
Basketweave
Bricks
Cobblestones
Stitch

Markers
Filled Square
Plus
Asterisk
Empty Square
X
Filled Triangle
Hourglass
Square with X
Vertical Line
Horizontal Line

Line Styles
Solid
Dotted
Centered
Dashed
Heavy Solid
Heavy Dotted
Heavy Centered
Heavy Dashed

Options

Screen
Printers

Screen Type
Resolution
Aspect Ratio
CGA Snow Suppression
Quit

List of available settings

No
Yes

Menu
Desktop
Spreadsheet
Conditional
Help
File Manager
Palettes
Quit

Frame
Banner
Text
Key Letter
Highlight
Settings
Explanation
Drop Shadow
Mouse Palette
Shadow
Quit

Status
Highlight-Status
Errors
Background
Desktop
Quit

Color
Monochrome
Black & White
Quit

Frame
Banner
Cells
Borders
Titles
Highlight
Graph Frames
Input Line
Unprotected
Labels
Shading
Drawn Lines
Quit

1st Printer
2nd Printer
Default Printer
Plotter Speed
Fonts
Auto LF
Single Sheet
Quit

Type of Printer
Device
Baud Rate
Parity
Stop Bits
Quit

List of available printers

List of available settings

Frame
Banner
Text
Active cursor
Inactive cursor
Marked
Cut
Copy
Quit

On/Off
ERR
Smallest Normal Value
Greatest Normal Value
Below Normal Color
Normal Cell Color
Above Normal Color
Quit

No
Yes

1st Printer
2nd Printer

Frame
Banner
Text
Keywords
Highlight
Quit

LaserJet Fonts
Autoscale Fonts

Left Cartridge
Right Cartridge

Undo
Macro
Expanded Memory
Clock
Paradox

Enable
Disable

Yes
No

Both
Spreadsheet Data
Format
None

Both
Panel
Window
None

Standard
International
None

Network Type
Directory
Retries
Quit

List of available network types

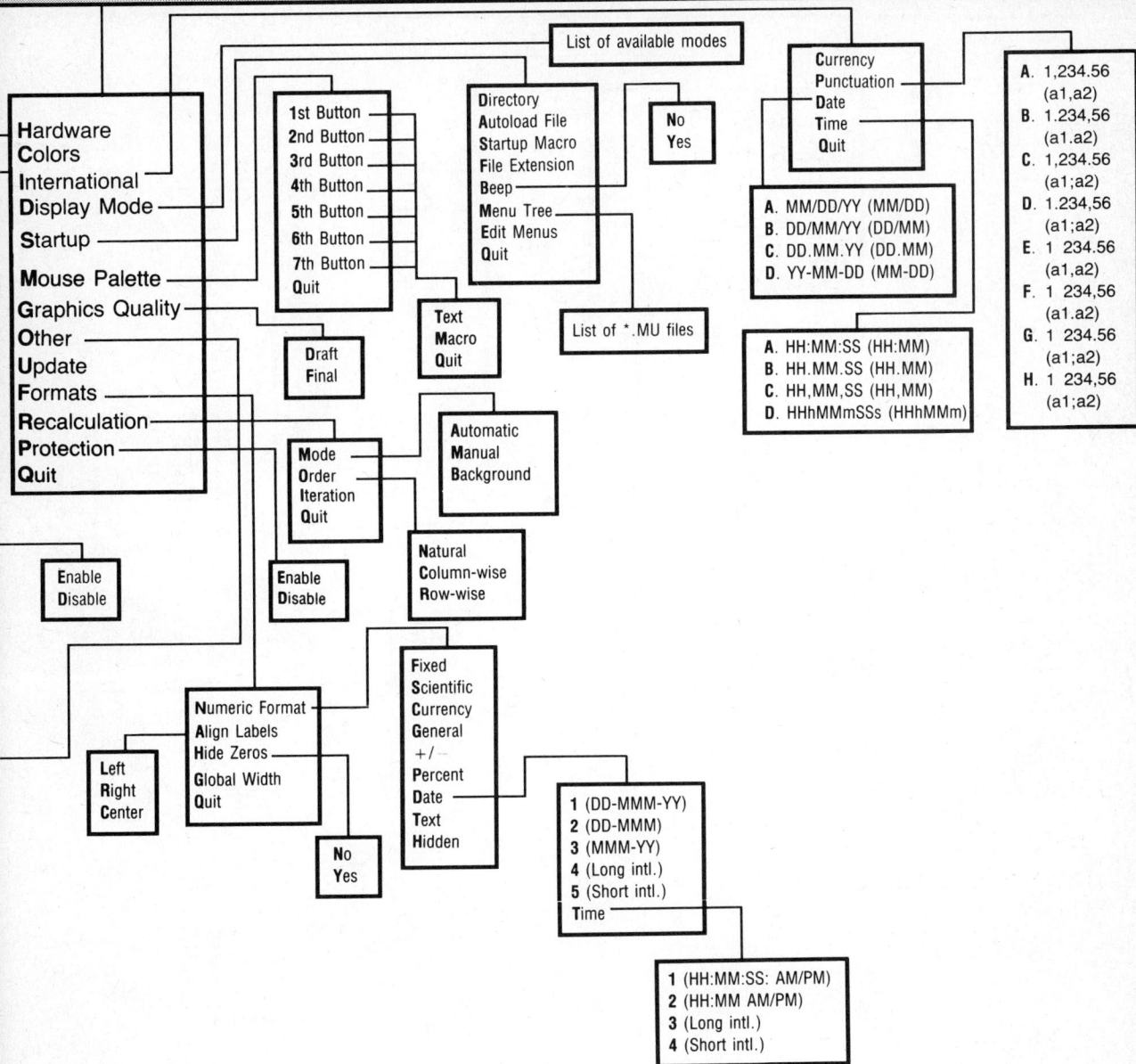

Options

List of available modes

Hardware	1st Button	Directory	No	Currency
Colors	2nd Button	Autoload File	Yes	Punctuation
International	3rd Button	Startup Macro		Date
Display Mode	4th Button	File Extension		Time
Startup	5th Button	Beep		Quit
Mouse Palette	6th Button	Menu Tree		
Graphics Quality	7th Button	Edit Menus		
Other	Quit	Quit		
Update				
Formats				
Recalculation				
Protection				
Quit				

A. 1,234.56 (a1,a2)
B. 1.234,56 (a1.a2)
C. 1,234.56 (a1;a2)
D. 1.234,56 (a1;a2)
E. 1 234.56 (a1,a2)
F. 1 234,56 (a1.a2)
G. 1 234.56 (a1;a2)
H. 1 234,56 (a1;a2)

A. MM/DD/YY (MM/DD)
B. DD/MM/YY (DD/MM)
C. DD.MM.YY (DD.MM)
D. YY-MM-DD (MM-DD)

Text
Macro
Quit

List of *.MU files

A. HH:MM:SS (HH:MM)
B. HH.MM.SS (HH.MM)
C. HH,MM,SS (HH,MM)
D. HHhMMmSSs (HHhMMm)

Draft
Final

Automatic
Manual
Background

Mode
Order
Iteration
Quit

Enable
Disable

Enable
Disable

Natural
Column-wise
Row-wise

Fixed
Scientific
Currency
General
+/−
Percent
Date
Text
Hidden

Numeric Format
Align Labels
Hide Zeros
Global Width
Quit

Left
Right
Center

No
Yes

1 (DD-MMM-YY)
2 (DD-MMM)
3 (MMM-YY)
4 (Long intl.)
5 (Short intl.)
Time

1 (HH:MM:SS: AM/PM)
2 (HH:MM AM/PM)
3 (Long intl.)
4 (Short intl.)

Window

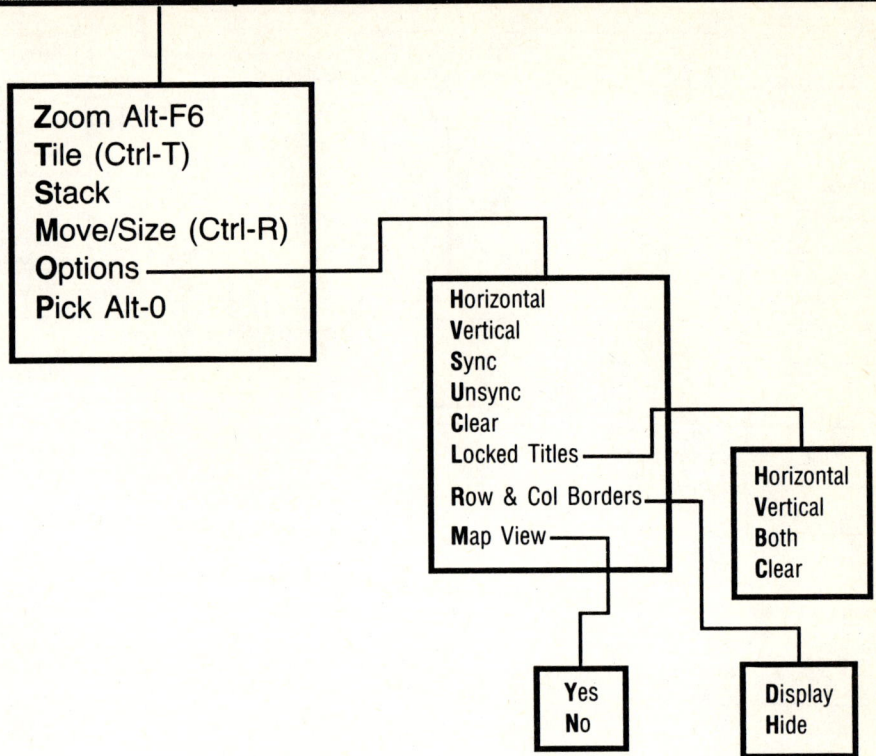

Zoom Alt-F6
Tile (Ctrl-T)
Stack
Move/Size (Ctrl-R)
Options
Pick Alt-0

Horizontal
Vertical
Sync
Unsync
Clear
Locked Titles
Row & Col Borders
Map View

Horizontal
Vertical
Both
Clear

Yes
No

Display
Hide

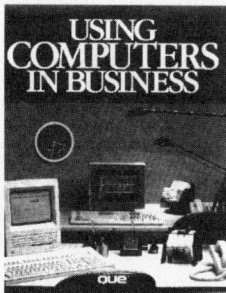

Using Computers in Business

by Joel Shore

This text covers all aspects of business computerization, including a thorough analysis of benefits, costs, alternatives, and common problems. Also discusses how to budget for computerization, how to shop for the right hardware and software, and how to allow for expansions and upgrades.

Order #1020
$22.95 USA
0-88022-470-3, 450 pp.

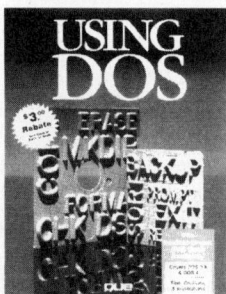

Using DOS

Developed by Que Corporation

The most helpful DOS book available! Que's *Using DOS* teaches the essential commands and functions of DOS Versions 3 and 4 —in an easy-to-understand format that helps users manage and organize their files effectively. Includes a handy **Command Reference**.

Order #1035
$22.95 USA
0-88022-497-5, 550 pp.

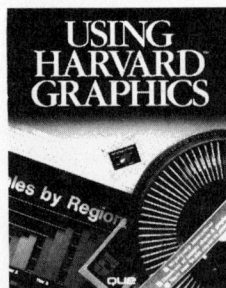

Using Harvard Graphics

by Steve Sagman and Jane Graver Sandlar

An excellent introduction to presentation graphics! This well-written text presents both program basics and presentation fundamentals to create bar, pie, line, and other types of informative graphs. Includes hundreds of samples!

$24.95 USA
Order #941
0-88022-407-X, 550 pp.

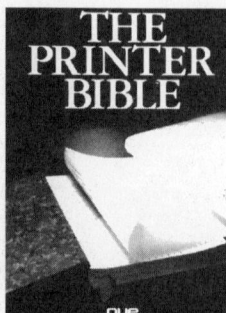

The Printer Bible

by Scott Foerster

From basic printer concepts and purchasing analysis to networking, maintenance, and troubleshooting, *The Printer Bible* is the ultimate printer information resource! Covers all kinds of printers —including laser-jet and dot matrix—and provides troubleshooting tips and a glossary of printer terms. A definite best-seller!

Order #1056
$24.95 USA
0-88022-512-2, 550 pp.

Computer Books From Que Mean PC Performance!

Spreadsheets

1-2-3 Database Techniques	$24.95
1-2-3 Graphics Techniques	$24.95
1-2-3 Macro Library, 3rd Edition	$39.95
1-2-3 Release 2.2 Business Applications	$39.95
1-2-3 Release 2.2 Quick Reference	$ 7.95
1-2-3 Release 2.2 QuickStart	$19.95
1-2-3 Release 2.2 Workbook and Disk	$29.95
1-2-3 Release 3 Business Applications	$39.95
1-2-3 Release 3 Quick Reference	$ 7.95
1-2-3 Release 3 QuickStart	$19.95
1-2-3 Release 3 Workbook and Disk	$29.95
1-2-3 Tips, Tricks, and Traps, 3rd Edition	$22.95
Excel Business Applications: IBM Version	$39.95
Excel Quick Reference	$ 7.95
Excel QuickStart	$19.95
Excel Tips, Tricks, and Traps	$22.95
Using 1-2-3, Special Edition	$26.95
Using 1-2-3 Release 2.2, Special Edition	$26.95
Using 1-2-3 Release 3	$27.95
Using Excel: IBM Version	$24.95
Using Lotus Spreadsheet for DeskMate	$19.95
Using Quattro Pro	$24.95
Using SuperCalc5, 2nd Edition	$24.95

Databases

dBASE III Plus Handbook, 2nd Edition	$24.95
dBASE III Plus Tips, Tricks, and Traps	$22.95
dBASE III Plus Workbook and Disk	$29.95
dBASE IV Applications Library, 2nd Edition	$39.95
dBASE IV Handbook, 3rd Edition	$23.95
dBASE IV Programming Techniques	$24.95
dBASE IV QueCards	$21.95
dBASE IV Quick Reference	$ 7.95
dBASE IV QuickStart	$19.95
dBASE IV Tips, Tricks,and Traps, 2nd Edition	$21.95
dBASE IV Workbook and Disk	$29.95
R:BASE User's Guide, 3rd Edition	$22.95
Using Clipper	$24.95
Using DataEase	$22.95
Using dBASE IV	$24.95
Using FoxPro	$26.95
Using Paradox 3	$24.95
Using Reflex, 2nd Edition	$22.95
Using SQL	$24.95

Business Applications

Introduction to Business Software	$14.95
Introduction to Personal Computers	$19.95
Lotus Add-in Toolkit Guide	$22.95
Norton Utilities Quick Reference	$ 7.95
PC Tools Quick Reference, 2nd Edition	$ 7.95
Q&A Quick Reference	$ 7.95
Que's Computer User's Dictionary	$9.95
Que's Wizard Book	$ 9.95
Smart Tips, Tricks, and Traps	$24.95
Using Computers in Business	$22.95
Using DacEasy, 2nd Edition	$22.95
Using Dollars and Sense: IBM Version, 2nd Edition	$19.95
Using Enable/OA	$24.95
Using Harvard Project Manager	$24.95
Using Lotus Magellan	$21.95
Using Managing Your Money, 2nd Edition	$19.95

Using Microsoft Works: IBM Version	$22.95
Using Norton Utilities	$24.95
Using PC Tools Deluxe	$24.95
Using Peachtree	$22.95
Using PFS: First Choice	$22.95
Using PROCOMM PLUS	$19.95
Using Q&A, 2nd Edition	$23.95
Using Quicken	$19.95
Using Smart	$22.95
Using SmartWare II	$24.95
Using Symphony, Special Edition	$29.95

CAD

AutoCAD Advanced Techniques	$34.95
AutoCAD Quick Reference	$ 7.95
AutoCAD Sourcebook	$24.95
Using AutoCAD, 2nd Edition	$24.95
Using Generic CADD	$24.95

Word Processing

DisplayWrite QuickStart	$19.95
Microsoft Word 5 Quick Reference	$ 7.95
Microsoft Word 5 Tips, Tricks, and Traps: IBM Version	$22.95
Using DisplayWrite 4, 2nd Edition	$22.95
Using Microsoft Word 5: IBM Version	$22.95
Using MultiMate	$22.95
Using Professional Write	$19.95
Using Word for Windows	$22.95
Using WordPerfect, 3rd Edition	$21.95
Using WordPerfect 5	$24.95
Using WordPerfect 5.1, Special Edition	$24.95
Using WordStar, 2nd Edition	$21.95
WordPerfect QueCards	$21.95
WordPerfect Quick Reference	$ 7.95
WordPerfect QuickStart	$21.95
WordPerfect Tips, Tricks, and Traps, 2nd Edition	$22.95
WordPerfect 5 Workbook and Disk	$29.95
WordPerfect 5.1 Quick Reference	$ 7.95
WordPerfect 5.1 QuickStart	$19.95
WordPerfect 5.1 Tips, Tricks, and Traps	$22.95
WordPerfect 5.1 Workbook and Disk	$29.95

Hardware/Systems

DOS Power Techniques	$29.95
DOS Tips, Tricks, and Traps	$22.95
DOS Workbook and Disk, 2nd Edition	$29.95
Hard Disk Quick Reference	$ 7.95
MS-DOS Quick Reference	$ 7.95
MS-DOS QuickStart	$21.95
MS-DOS User's Guide, Special Edition	$29.95
Networking Personal Computers, 3rd Edition	$22.95
The Printer Bible	$24.95
Que's Guide to Data Recovery	$24.95
Understanding UNIX, 2nd Edition	$21.95
Upgrading and Repairing PCs	$27.95
Using DOS	$22.95
Using Microsoft Windows 3, 2nd Edition	$22.95
Using Novell NetWare	$24.95
Using OS/2	$24.95
Using PC DOS, 3rd Edition	$24.95
Using UNIX	$24.95
Using Your Hard Disk	$29.95
Windows 3 Quick Reference	$ 7.95

Desktop Publishing/Graphics

Harvard Graphics Quick Reference	$ 7.95
Using Animator	$24.95
Using Harvard Graphics	$24.95.
Using Freelance Plus	$24.95
Using PageMaker: IBM Version, 2nd Edition	$24.95
Using PFS: First Publisher	$22.95
Using Ventura Publisher, 2nd Edition	$24.95
Ventura Publisher Tips, Tricks, and Traps,	$24.95

Macintosh/Apple II

AppleWorks QuickStart	$19.95
The Big Mac Book	$27.95
Excel QuickStart	$19.95
Excel Tips, Tricks, and Traps	$22.95
Que's Macintosh Multimedia Handbook	$22.95
Using AppleWorks, 3rd Edition	$21.95
Using AppleWorks GS	$21.95
Using Dollars and Sense: Macintosh Version	$19.95
Using Excel: Macintosh Version	$24.95
Using FileMaker	$24.95
Using MacroMind Director	$29.95
Using MacWrite	$22.95
Using Microsoft Word 4: Macintosh Version	$22.95
Using Microsoft Works: Macintosh Version, 2nd Edition	$22.95
Using PageMaker: Macintosh Version	$24.95

Programming/Technical

Assembly Language Quick Reference	$ 7.95
C Programmer's Toolkit	$39.95
C Programming Guide, 3rd Edition	$24.95
C Quick Reference	$ 7.95
DOS and BIOS Functions Quick Reference	$ 7.95
DOS Programmer's Reference, 2nd Edition	$27.95
Oracle Programmer's Guide	$24.95
Power Graphics Programming	$24.95
QuickBASIC Advanced Techniques	$22.95
QuickBASIC Programmer's Toolkit	$39.95
QuickBASIC Quick Reference	$ 7.95
QuickPascal Programming	$22.95
SQL Programmer's Guide	$29.95
Turbo C Programming	$22.95
Turbo Pascal Advanced Techniques	$22.95
Turbo Pascal Programmer's Toolkit	$39.95
Turbo Pascal Quick Reference	$ 7.95
UNIX Programmer's Quick Reference	$ 7.95
Using Assembly Language, 2nd Edition	$26.95
Using BASIC	$19.95
Using C	$27.95
Using QuickBASIC 4	$22.95
Using Turbo Pascal	$22.95

For More Information, Call Toll Free!
1-800-428-5331

All prices and titles subject to change without notice. Non-U.S. prices may be higher. Printed in the U.S.A.

Free Catalog!

Mail us this registration form today, and we'll send you a free catalog featuring Que's complete line of best-selling books.

Name of Book _____

Name _____

Title _____

Phone ( ) _____

Company _____

Address _____

City _____

State _____ ZIP _____

Please check the appropriate answers:

1. Where did you buy your Que book?
   - ☐ Bookstore (name: _____)
   - ☐ Computer store (name: _____)
   - ☐ Catalog (name: _____)
   - ☐ Direct from Que
   - ☐ Other: _____

2. How many computer books do you buy a year?
   - ☐ 1 or less
   - ☐ 2-5
   - ☐ 6-10
   - ☐ More than 10

3. How many Que books do you own?
   - ☐ 1
   - ☐ 2-5
   - ☐ 6-10
   - ☐ More than 10

4. How long have you been using this software?
   - ☐ Less than 6 months
   - ☐ 6 months to 1 year
   - ☐ 1-3 years
   - ☐ More than 3 years

5. What influenced your purchase of this Que book?
   - ☐ Personal recommendation
   - ☐ Advertisement
   - ☐ In-store display
   - ☐ Price
   - ☐ Que catalog
   - ☐ Que mailing
   - ☐ Que's reputation
   - ☐ Other: _____

6. How would you rate the overall content of the book?
   - ☐ Very good
   - ☐ Good
   - ☐ Satisfactory
   - ☐ Poor

7. What do you like *best* about this Que book?

   _____

   _____

8. What do you like *least* about this Que book?

   _____

   _____

9. Did you buy this book with your personal funds?
   - ☐ Yes   ☐ No

10. Please feel free to list any other comments you may have about this Que book.

    _____

    _____

    _____

— QUE —

Order Your Que Books Today!

Name _____

Title _____

Company _____

City _____

State _____ ZIP _____

Phone No. ( ) _____

Method of Payment:

Check ☐ (Please enclose in envelope.)

Charge My: VISA ☐   MasterCard ☐

American Express ☐

Charge # _____

Expiration Date _____

Order No.	Title	Qty.	Price	Total

You can **FAX** your order to **1-317-573-2583**. Or call **1-800-428-5331, ext. ORDR** to order direct.
Please add $2.50 per title for shipping and handling.

Subtotal _____

Shipping & Handling _____

Total _____

— QUE —

BUSINESS REPLY MAIL
First Class Permit No. 9918   Indianapolis, IN

Postage will be paid by addressee

que®

11711 N. College
Carmel, IN 46032

NO POSTAGE
NECESSARY
IF MAILED
IN THE
UNITED STATES

BUSINESS REPLY MAIL
First Class Permit No. 9918   Indianapolis, IN

Postage will be paid by addressee

que®

11711 N. College
Carmel, IN 46032